The Cued Speech Resource Book For Parents of Deaf Children

R. Orin Cornett, Ph.D.
Mary Elsie Daisey, M.Ed.

National Cued Speech Association
Raleigh, North Carolina

The National Cued Speech Association, Inc.
P.O. Box 31345
Raleigh, North Carolina 27622

Library of Congress Catalog Card Number 92-60758
ISBN 0-9633164-0-0

419
C 816 c

Table of Contents

1. Facing the Realities of Deafness. 1
   Effects of Inadequate Communication, 4; The Implications of Methods, 5;
   What Parents Typically Go Through, 9;
   Typical Performance of Deaf Children, 13

2. What is Cued Speech?. 16
   The Deaf Child's Major Problems, 17; The Methods Debate, 19;
   Requirements for a Suitable Method, 20;
   Analytical Description of Cued Speech, 21

3. Life with Leah 25
   Discipline, Manners, Family Relationships, 26; Language and School, 28;
   Speechreading, Hearing, Speech, 28;
   The Best of Both Worlds-1985, 31;
        Schooling, 31; Benefits and Adulthood, 32;
   Dreams Do Come True-1992, 33;
        The Real World of Work, 34; "Happily Ever After," 35;
        Communication Flexibility, 36; "I can do anything," 37

4. You and your Deaf Child .39
   Communication, Discipline, Sense of Family, 40;
   Affective Development of the Child, 41; Mother and Child, 43;
   Family Bonding, 44; The Two-Job Family, 45; Father and Child, 45;
   Mental Development of Your Child, 49.

5. Getting Started 51
   Methods of Learning Cued Speech, 52; Begin With Your Child Right
   Away, 55; Slow is Beautiful!, 56; Think Sounds, 57; Auditory Conceptual-
   ization, 59; Progress to Phrases and Sentences, 61

6. Initiating Communication 65
   Start With What the Child Knows, 65; The Child Who Looks Away, 68;
   The Situation Must Convey the Meaning, 69;
   Use Appropriate Games, 70; The Most Important Ideas, 76

7. What to Expect 77
   Slow Down and Show, 77; Everything Has a Name, 78;
   Expect Progress to be Uneven, 79; How to Handle Incorrect Cueing by the
   Child, 81; Benefits of Expressive Cueing, 82; Language Aberrations and
   "Gaps," 83; What to Expect in Speech Development, 84

8. Advancing in Language 91
   Teaching New Concepts, 93;
   Directions, Questions, and "Danger" Words, 94; Testing, 94;
   Language Awareness in Parents, 95; Advancement in Language
   Complexity, 96; Preschool, 98; The Importance of a Diary, 100;
   Interjections, Exclamations, and Expressions, 101; How Long? 104

9. Higher Levels of Understanding. 109
   Scrapbooks, 111; "Experience" Books, 113; Puppets, 117;
   Telling Stories, 118; The Miracle of Reading to Children, 119;
   "Upside Down" Reading, 120; An Alternative to Upside-Down Reading,
   121; A Hospital Stay for Tiffany, 123

10. Advanced Activities 127
    Nursery Rhymes, 128; Poems, 131; Songs, 131; Finger-Play Songs, 133;
    Board Games, 135; Group Games, 137; "Pretend" Games, 141;
    Auditory Games, 142

11. Language Development. 143
The Power of Language, 143; How Hearing Children Learn Language, 145;
Spoken Language/Written Language, 146; Cued Speech and Language, 147;
Language Evaluation in Deaf Children, 151;
The Clarity of CS is the Key, 152;
The Learning of Abstract Language, 154; Idioms, 155;
Twelve Ways CS Changes the Teaching of Language at Home, 156;
The Parents' Role in Language Development, 157;
Research on Language Development, 159

12. Speech Production 163
Phonemes, 163; Articulation, 165; Voice Quality, 169;
Speech Correction, 170; Intonation, 171;
The Parents' Role in Speech Development, 173

13. Speechreading 177
Speechreading Defined and Described, 177; Factors In Speechreading, 182;
Effects of Cued Speech Upon Speechreading, 190

14. Auditory Training, Cochlear Implants. 193
Auditory Training and Cued Speech, 195;
Advantages of Cued Speech for Auditory Training, 196;
Guidelines for Early Auditory Training, 198;
The Perception of Difference in Paired Items, 199;
Coordinating Auditory Training and Cued Speech, 201;
Description of the Auditory/Visual Model, 204

Cochlear Implants. 209
Impressions from Several Families, 211;
Seven Implant Case Histories, 215

15. Reading. 245
How a Hearing Child Learns to Read, 246; The Function Words, 247;
How Deaf Children Learn to Read, 247; Effects of Lack of Readiness for
Reading, 251; How to Develop Reading Readiness, 251;
Reading to Children, 252; Higher-Level Reading Skills, 253;
The Importance and Limitations of Context, 255;
How to Develop Advanced Reading Skills, 255;
How the Cued Speech Child Reads, 256;
The Role of Parents in Reading Development, 258

16. Roles of Hearing Siblings and Peers. 263
The Sibling Who Feels Left Out, 265;
Issues That Bother Siblings Most, 267; The Value of Cueing-Sibling
Support, 269; Deaf Children with Exemplary Sibling Support, 271;
Observations from 15 Siblings, 272; The Role of Hearing Peers, 289;
Statements from Three Hearing Peers, 292

17. Starting with an Older Child. 297
Begin at the Right Level, 298; Teaching the System Analytically, 299;
Older Students with Very Little Written Language, 301;
Experiences of Parents Starting with 10 Older Deaf Children, 304

18. Starting with a Very Young Child. 329
Cued Speech and Children Under Three, 329;
Four Cueing Activities for Children Under Three, 331;
Four Two-Minute Quickies, 333;
Helping Young Children Adjust to Hearing Aids, 336;
There's More to Cued Speech Than Cueing, 339;
Three Infants with Whom CS Was Used Early, 346;
Four Case Histories, 347

19. Seventy Most Frequently Asked Questions About CS . . 367

20. Mainstreaming **385**
Requirements for Successful Mainstreaming, 386; Needed Services, 389; Mainstreaming with a CS Transliterator, 392; Two Students' Views, 395; Mainstreaming of Aural/Oral Children, 398; Mainstreaming of Signing Children, 398; Mainstreaming with the Rochester Method, 400; Mainstreaming of Cued Speech Children, 400; Qualifications of Transliterators, 401; Experiences of the First CS Mainstreaming Classroom Teacher, 407; Six Mainstreaming Case Histories, 309

21. The Greatest Problem—Time 431
Why is Time Such A Problem? 431; Ideas for Saving and Managing Time, 435; Expanding the Cueing Environment, 438; Twenty More Time-Saving Ideas, 439; Experiences of Six Fathers with Cued Speech, 441; Extended-Family Cuers, 448

22. Going It Alone **453**
"The hard part when yours is the only child...." 453; Your Child's Success May be Used Against You, 455; Seven Case Histories, 458

23. What About Sign Language? 491
Statement of the National Cued Speech Association, 491; Definition of American Sign Language, 492; The Rationale for ASL/English Bilingualism, 493; Principles for Achieving ASL/English Bilingualism, 494; Application of Principles to A Theoretical Model, 495; A Practical Bilingual Model for TC Programs,   500; The Role of Hearing Parents in the TC Model, 501; Implementation of the TC Model, 502; When and If to Go All the Way to ASL, 504; A Theoretical Bilingual Model for CS Programs, 505; Preschool Level, 506; When to Introduce ASL, 506; The Elementary Grades, 507; Examples of Multilingualism in Deaf Children, 508; Six Case Histories, 509

24. The Child With More Than One Disability 537
Specific Overlying Conditions, 538; Minor or Usually Correctable Overlying Conditions, 539; Cerebral Palsy, 539; Memory Problems, 540; Aphasia, 541; Apraxia, 541; Dyslexia, 543; Usher's Syndrome/Retinitis Pigmentosa, 545; Deaf-Blindness, 545; Non-Specific Learning Disability, 546; Six Case Histories, 547

25. Observations of Deaf Young People 563
These 47 selections, written by deaf youngsters whose ages range from 4 years 10 months to 27 years, express their feelings and opinions about growing up deaf, about family, friends, school, life in general, and the future.

26. Odyssey, One Family's Story 639
This entertaining journal records experiences of a family with two hearing-impaired girls, from the time the older was diagnosed at 2 until she reached 4. It provides humorous but penetrating insight into subjects ranging from English/sign bilingualism to child psychology.

27. Observations from Professionals 657
Articles by teachers, speech/language professionals, and transliterators.

28. Research Parents and Teachers Need to Know About, and How to Present Cued Speech 693
Annotations of Nine Significant Research Projects, 693;
How to Present Cued Speech, 703;
    To New Parents, 703; To Signing Parents, 706;
    To Oral Parents, 707; To Signing Teachers, 708;
    To Oral Teachers, 709; To Speech Therapists, 709;
    To Administrators, 710; To Deaf Individuals, 711;
    To the General Public, 712

29. The Fine Points of Cueing. 713
Sound and Pronunciation Guide, 714; Listening Suggestions, 717;
Running Words Together, 718;
The Timing Movements of Cued Speech, 718;
"ŭh hŭh," 722; "Wahdur," 723;
Cueing of Consecutive Identical Consonants, 723;
Cueing of Consonant Clusters, 727;
Cueing Spanish Words When English is Primary, 729;
Cueing of French Words, 730 Dance vs Pants, 730

30. Potpourri 731
The Rights of Deaf Children and Their Parents, 731;
    The Most Relevant Federal Laws, 734;
      Public Law 94-142, 736;
        The Individualized Educational Program, 737;
        The Principle of Least Restrictive Environment, 738;
        What if the Parents Do Not Agree? 738;
        What if the Parents Lose the Due Process Hearing?, 740;
    Post Secondary Educational Opportunities, 741;
Origins of Cued Speech, 743;
Helpful Devices and Techniques, 748

Appendix, Part I 751
Agencies Providing CS Information and Assistance, 751;
Organizations not connected with Cued Speech, but capable of furnishing
information and materials valuable to parents, 753;
Materials for orientation and guidance of parents, 754;
Materials for use by parents with their deaf children, 757

Appendix, Part II, Learning to Cue Accurately and Well . 766
Self-Instruction Materials, 766;
The need for spelling according to pronunciation, 767;
Funetik Speling, 768;
Cuescript Cueing Guidelines and 500-Word Basic Vocabulary, 776;
Practice Primer—488 sentences for use with children, 806

References 811

Author Index 815

Subject Index 819

Foreword

Parents...experience the double trauma of having a child with a severe disability and being confused about how to meet the child's need to learn and to relate to the family and society at large.

When parents discover that their child is deaf, either at birth or during the next few months or years, they are justifiably concerned. The more the parents learn about the impact of deafness on human development—especially speech, language, and intellectual development—the more their concern escalates into fear and worry. As they turn to authorities in the fields of audiology, language, education, or deafness, they discover another unsettling fact: authorities may not agree on major approaches to assisting the deaf child to cope with this disability and to progress in traditional educational subject matter. The parents are left to analyze the claims and counter-claims of people who should be able to provide an unbiased picture of their options and help them choose the best course for their child.

Parents, therefore, experience the double trauma of having a child with a severe disability and being confused about how to meet the child's need to learn and to relate to the family and society at large. I have the utmost respect for parents in this situation. For this reason, I am pleased to introduce to them this book, *The Cued Speech Resource Book for Parents of Deaf Children*. It does not argue with the oral system. It does not oppose the use of the combined method of signs and English—or, for that matter, the use of American Sign Language with deaf friends and associates. It offers a plan for using hand cues with speech that permits the deaf child to learn the English language—the key to education and social development.

When I was a senior administrator at Gallaudet, I took the broad mission of the institution seriously. The college was not only to provide the most meaningful college-level instruction possible, but it was to identify and to solve problems influencing the lives of deaf people: educational, communications, social, occupational, economic, and even psychological problems. For this reason I supported the Cued Speech project. Each year it persisted. Each year new positive data were produced. Twenty years later, Cued Speech has substantial data showing that it enables deaf children to attain competency in English at the level of hearing students grade by grade. I know of no other system that enables this to happen—not oral, not combined, not ASL (although the argument here will be that it has not been tried consistently).

I am aware that some deaf people, including a few deaf leaders, ridicule Cued Speech. This is probably because Cued Speech is heavily oral as it is a means of communication in English, even though the user is free to use ASL or combined systems with other deaf persons. I do not predict often, but in this case I predict that the success of this system will present a "moment of truth" for the deaf community. As more and more young deaf people achieve academically because of this system, deaf leaders will need to re-examine their options.

The Cued Speech Resource Book for Parents of Deaf Children is a fact book about the reality of deafness and how to deal with it. With this book parents will be in a position to support their child's growth, watch him or her develop independence, and see him or her function in the larger society which includes the rich culture of the deaf community but is not limited to it.

Edward C. Merrill, Jr., Ph.D.[1]
President Emeritus
Gallaudet University
September 29, 1992

---

[1]Dr. Merrill was the fourth president of Gallaudet College (now Gallaudet University), 1969-83. Portions of the above statement appeared in his article in the monograph of the National Association of the Deaf, *Perspectives on Deafness*, published in 1991, and edited by Dr. Mervin D. Garretson.

Preface

The Cued Speech Resource Book for Parents of Deaf Children is intended for parents who have decided to use Cued Speech with a hearing-impaired child, or are considering the advisability of doing so. Its purpose is to provide the information and guidance they need in order to 1) assess accurately the problems they face, 2) overcome the trauma they have experienced in learning of their child's problem, 3) acquire the skills and understanding they need in order to meet the needs of their child with Cued Speech, 4) make the choices they need to make regarding the education of their child, and 5) proceed with their parenting role effectively and confidently. When work started on this volume it was intended to be a new edition of the *Cued Speech Handbook for Parents*, published in 1971. As materials and ideas were collected and the text was drafted, it soon became apparent that the book was taking a different direction and a greater scope, with more than 300,000 words, scores of case histories, expansion of the original chapters in the process of updating, and the addition of 13 new chapters strongly oriented toward the problems and needs of parents of deaf children.

In the *Handbook* the chapters on language development, speechreading, auditory training, reading, roles of hearing siblings, and beginning with an older deaf child were very brief. The reason was simple. Experience with Cued Speech was very limited. At that time Cued Speech had been used with the first child for only 4½ years. Ms. Daisey, then Henegar, pioneered in developing methods of using Cued Speech with her deaf child, and took the lead in drafting the chapters related to that experience. Other chapters, such as those on reading, speechreading, and starting with an older child had to be written solely on the theoretical base underlying the creation of Cued Speech. The miracle is that not one of the assertions and predictions made has had to be corrected. Twenty-six years of use of Cued Speech and dozens of research reports have confirmed essentially everything claimed or predicted in the *Handbook*.

In order to make sure that the orientation of the *Resource Book* would be attuned to the problems and interests of parents of deaf children, substantial help was obtained from 14 sets of parents experienced at raising a deaf child with Cued Speech. These parents agreed to read the early drafts of all the chapters and provide reactions and suggestions, and most did so. Some of these parent reviewers, and many other parents as well, wrote case histories for inclusion in the chapters most relevant to their experiences. Additional parents were asked to review drafts of one or more chapters related to their special situations and problems. Deaf youngsters from the United States, Canada, France, Belgium, Spain, and England were invited to write about how they feel about growing up deaf, about their families, schools, friends, and their hopes for the future. Statements from hearing siblings are included to illustrate the possible problems and rewards in the sibling relationships.

The division of work between the authors fell naturally into place as a result of the heavy administrative and professional responsibilities of Ms. Daisey, which limited the amount of time she could devote to the project in its early stages. Her counsel was sought regularly during the gathering of material and the production of the first drafts of the chapters. After the interactions with the parent reviewers resulted in a second draft of the manuscript, she contributed to significant changes in content through her careful review of the successive drafts of the chapters. The final text thus has the full benefit of her expertise and experience.

To emphasize the parent orientation of the book and the invaluable contributions of parents to it, the most important suggestions of the parent reviewers and other parent advisers are attributed to them personally in the body of the text. They also contributed hundreds of additional suggestions regarding wording, clarity, simplification, and emphasis that are not attributed. The parent reviewers and contributors of case histories have indicated their willingness to reply to correspondence in connection with any of their ideas or experiences. Because a list of their names and addresses would soon become out-of-date, the Cued Speech National Center will maintain a list of current addresses. Readers are invited to request further information from any of the parent reviewers, or from other parents who contributed case histories or significant ideas, or from the authors, by addressing them in care of the Cued Speech National Center, P.O. Box 31345, Raleigh, NC 27622, with the marking Please Forward.

Some important references and explanations are cited or given more than once. This is judged appropriate in a resource book, since a reader may not be disposed to actually look up a specific reference in one instance, and yet may want to do so at another point.

The authors hope that parents will find in this book much to help them enable their deaf children to grow up happily and successfully.

R. Orin Cornett, Ph.D.   Mary Elsie Daisey, M.Ed.
Laurel, Maryland   Sept., 1992   Raleigh, North Carolina

Acknowledgments

The authors wish to express gratitude to all those who have contributed to the production of this book. Deserving special recognition are the parent reviewers, the additional parent advisers who replied to specific questions, or were asked to review selected chapters, the parents who furnished or updated their case histories, the deaf youngsters who wrote of their experiences, thoughts, and feelings, the brothers and sisters who responded to our request for their observations on the experience of growing up with a deaf sibling, and the professionals who responded to our requests for their ideas on how parents and specific types of professionals can best work together. We owe a special expression of gratitude to the Cued Speech team at Gallaudet University for allowing us to use material freely from the *Cued Speech News,* including case histories and other articles, and to the Cued Speech Center for use of material from *Cued Speech Center Lines.*

In addition, we wish to express appreciation to Pamela H. Beck, president of NCSA, for wise counsel, good ideas and ready cooperation; to Barbara Caldwell, for advice and sharing in substantive editorial decisions; to Beth Dowling, for substantial assistance with chapters 14 and 18, and especially to Laura-Jean Gilbert, director of publications, Gallaudet University, for lending her exceptional skills to checking and improving the late drafts. We are also indebted to Judith Weiss for designing the prepublication flyer and the dust jacket, and to Cathy Quenin for finding a way to produce on her computer the Cuescript version of the 500-word basic vocabulary in the Appendix. To all the many others who provided ideas and suggestions we convey our heartfelt thanks.

Those who contributed case histories, and the young people who wrote of their own experiences, are listed in the Index of Authors.

The Parent Reviewers

Janie Abell, Linda and Andy Balderson, Osmond and Debbi Crosby, Bob and Joan Gonsoulin, Robert and Kathy Goodall, Mike and Janeane Maslin, Frank and Minta McNally, Mary and Clifford Nemeth, Isabelle and Phil Payonk, Teri and Jerry Poore, William and Diane Robers, Sarina Roffé, and Sheila Scher.

The above and dozens of other parents furnished valuable suggestions and reactions to drafts of selected chapters. The assistance of all of them is deeply appreciated.

Acknowledgments

Chapter 1
Facing The Realities Of Deafness

When your dreams shatter, there is no sound, just the slow-motion vision of icebergs sliding off a glacier, making huge soundless waves and looking so calm—unless you happen to be swimming under the iceberg. That's the way it was when we learned that our beautiful two year old had a hearing problem. (Osmond Crosby, page 639)

Introduction

This book is addressed to parents who have learned that they have a hearing-impaired child. The authors feel that such parents should begin by taking a careful look at what typically happens to parents of a deaf[1] (profoundly hearing-impaired) child, and what typically happens to the child. At the same time they should remember that *it doesn't have to be this way*.

Throughout the following chapters you will also learn what has happened to the children of parents who found an alternative to traditional methods used to educate deaf children and how they learned and used this new approach. We don't say it is easy, and we don't say there won't be both ups and downs, but we do say that it can be done. You can enable your child to avoid the typical fate of deaf children.

We recruited 14 sets of experienced parents of deaf children to review all the chapters in draft and offer suggestions. Our purpose was to make sure that the text is relevant to the interests and concerns of parents. We also had some concern as to whether parents should be confronted, at the outset, with the tragic truth about what happens to typical deaf children. On the one hand, parents need to face the truth in order to recognize the implications of the choices they must make and the effort they must expend if their deaf child is to succeed. On the other hand, we do not want them to be so discouraged by the facts that they will give up hope.

Bob Goodall, one of the parent reviewers, answered this second concern in no uncertain terms:

> *As a parent I would want the simplest, plain English explanation of the probable consequences of deafness in my child, as defined by what happens to most deaf children:*

---

[1]In this book the term "deaf" will be used to denote a pure-tone average threshold of at least 90 dB in the better ear.

1) He won't be able to understand me.
2) I won't be able to understand him.
3) I can't assume that he will be able to understand people by lipreading because so many sounds look alike on the lips. It is a nearly hopeless task for him to distinguish them by sight alone even if he already knows the language, which he doesn't if deaf at birth or before learning language.
4) We and his teachers will have to teach him almost every word he learns, whereas hearing children "pick up" 90% or more of their language.
5) He will lag far behind hearing children in language and reading, and will not like to read.

The five realities listed by this parent have far-reaching implications as regards their impact upon parents. Take a look at that impact as we describe it. If you have just discovered that your child has a serious hearing deficit, look ahead with us. If you have had some time to experience the impact of deafness, perhaps what follows here will help you understand yourself, the problems you have faced, and those to come. Keep in mind that this chapter summarizes the typical effects of deafness upon children and families that do not have the benefits of Cued Speech.

Some Things To Remember

Hearing impairment is an invisible handicap. Not only is the physical problem itself unseen—its most important liability is also unseen. This is one reason why deafness is so poorly understood by the general public.

The root of the problem of a deaf child is the difficulty of acquiring a knowledge of verbal language. Hearing children begin to learn their native language within a few months after birth, and have mastered most of its basic elements before entering first grade. They continue to learn more language—new words, slang, new meanings of old words—in school, after school, on weekends, and during the summer. They learn all this easily, effortlessly, as they interact and communicate within the context of daily activities.

Deaf children are *taught* most of the language they learn. Slowly, artificially, painfully, they are forever taught, corrected, taught and corrected, since they cannot correct themselves by hearing others. They "pick up" very little from incidental communication and lack the ability to eavesdrop. They learn language through repetition and explanation.

In the end, most deaf people tend to learn the English language primarily through the written form. This delays the learning of verbal language until they are old enough to learn to read, and reduces their chances of ever reading well. It also increases the probability that they will never be really "at home" in verbal communication. Without the opportunity to pick up new language from radio, TV, or incidental conversation, they tend to learn new language only during the time they spend in formal education unless the home becomes a schoolroom.

Even though they have to become oriented toward the written language, most deaf people find reading a slow, difficult, and frustrating process. Very few really enjoy reading. This is tragic, because they need to read avidly, broadly, and consistently. Reading is the only means of unlimited access to knowledge for the deaf person. Why? Because reading is the only avenue to learning that is completely under the control of the learner. Only through reading can deaf people hope to manage their own destiny and learn for themselves, on their own terms, about whatever they choose. The knowledge of the world is all there for the deaf person—in books, in magazines, and in newspapers—but only if he or she can read well.

The bright deaf child who has enough ability to do moderately well in spite of his or her hearing impairment is no more overcoming his/her handicap than the child of lower ability who accomplishes much less. Both are performing tragically far below their potentials. It is easy to underestimate the potential of a bright deaf child, and thus to be satisfied with too little development. Think about the experiences hearing children have that your deaf child misses. Parents cannot be content with communicating only about life's necessities: eating, sleeping, bathroom, dressing, etc. You need to provide full environmental information and enrichment. Such a background is essential to full understanding of situations that contribute to language growth and awareness of relationships. Ideally, the deaf child should be exposed to everything the hearing child experiences.

Parents must try to provide full environmental information and enrichment. For example, if the phone rings and Daddy indicates he is starting home, explaining this to your deaf child will help him or her acquire a sense of being "in on everything." Further, it will help your child learn and distinguish the concepts of present and future. Such experiences contribute to full understanding of situations and relationships. They also contribute to language growth. Ideally, the deaf child should be exposed to everything the hearing child experiences. Would that there were enough time!

It is essential that parents avoid the tendency that afflicts many teachers of deaf children, especially in self-contained classes. The primary symptom is a gradual shift toward generally low expectations for deaf children, so that a child is judged to be "doing very well" if he or she performs at the level generally achieved by deaf children. Parents of a deaf child should be very much aware of what a hearing child of the same age understands, learns, does, says, and writes. If you have hearing children, this will help you maintain the needed awareness. If not, be sure that you have adequate opportunities to observe. Above all, you must have faith in your deaf child, faith in yourself, and faith in the value of perseverance.

A full environmental language experience is impossible without an adequate medium for *clear* communication with the deaf child. Some form of visual communication or support is necessary for most severe to profoundly deaf children. Available are signs, fingerspelling, speechreading, written language, and Cued Speech. For informed parents of a hearing-impaired child, the choice is often a difficult one. Specifically, the problem is whether to choose an oral method, a manual method, or some combination of manual and oral elements. Unfortunately, the choice may tend to be dictated or strongly influenced by professionals who are biased or inadequately informed. The deciding factor is often what specific method or methods happen to be most conveniently available in the area where the family lives. Parents need to become well-informed about the alternatives available to them and the implications of the choices they make.

Effects of Inadequate Communication

Inadequate communication during the primary language-learning years of 1 to 5 is a major reason for a low level of language development in so many deaf children. Language is best developed through communication about the everyday, normal activities of the home, such as eating, bathing, dressing, preparing for bed, play activities, pets, family members, and friends. Only a method of clear communication enables these activities to have their normal effects upon learning, language development, and the sense of "belonging." In addition to inhibiting a deaf child's development, limited communication between child and family can result in great frustration, often creating crippling emotional problems for the child and the family.

Parents of a deaf child are faced with a terrible dilemma. For their child they want rapid mental development, speech, speechreading, language development, ability to read—all these, and emotional health. Alexander Graham Bell (1892, p. 27) pointed out that each of the three principal methods of instructing deaf children (oral, manual, sign) addresses a different one of the "three misfortunes" that result from deafness: "...lack of speech, lack of knowledge of written language, and lack of mental development which comes from intercourse with other minds."

Bell indicated that the oral teacher feels that speech is the major problem, that the manual (by which he meant using writing and fingerspelling) teacher makes written language the primary objective, and the teacher who puts the major emphasis on getting through to the child's mind uses sign language. He affirmed (op.cit.): "The language of signs...is the quickest method of reaching the mind of a deaf child." But, he said also: "If you want a child to learn written language, there is no method like using written language...." Finally, he stated: "Then in the case of speech, there is nothing that will develop speech like using the mouth." But, he warned, using the example of a billiard ball that one tries to send in three directions simultaneously, one cannot combine three different approaches (oral, manual, and written) and get the sum of the results each alone will achieve. This is the dilemma.[2]

The Implications of Methods

Many of today's parents are led to believe that they must choose between the oral and Total Communication approaches, each of which (for a majority of children) tends to sacrifice or neglect some of the things parents want for their child. Or, they may know about the new push for American Sign Language as the first language, followed by English taught through the written form, beginning near age 6 years.

A tragic thing about the situation is that most parents of young deaf children do not have an opportunity to know the implications of the choices available to them. The advocates of early manual communication point out that the majority of parents of hearing-impaired children in oral programs "give up" on the oral approach sometime between the ages of 6 and 15 years. They say this is after the unsuccessful attempt to be only oral has damaged the child irreparably by robbing him or her of the potentially best years of linguistic, intellectual, and social development, through an unsuccessful gamble that he/she

---

[2]Alexander Graham Bell, best known as the inventor of the telephone, was the source of a tremendous amount of wisdom regarding the problems and needs of deaf people. Parents of a deaf child may do well to read "The Century-Old Wisdom of Alexander Graham Bell," by R. Orin Cornett. It appeared in the April, 1990, issue of *Volta Review, 92,* 3, pp. 145-153. In it Bell practically wrote a prescription for Cued Speech.

can succeed orally. Many deaf adults oppose an oral approach because of the frustration they experienced with it when young.

The advocates of oralism respond that if the oral approach is not attempted first, the deaf child may develop very little oral communication ability, even if that would have been possible with early aural/oral training. Advocates of manual communication insist that the early use of manual communication promotes early communication and personal development without excessively endangering the potential of the child for oral communication. Many parents and educators of deaf children are not convinced of either assertion.

Parents who learn about the options available often find a choice difficult to make. Or, the option they prefer may not be easily available. These problems are complicated by the fact that they feel under pressure to make a choice quickly, since every day that passes is another day without development of communication and language.

Unfortunately, there is no reliable way to predict accurately whether a given child will succeed in a traditional oral program. Some children seem to progress reasonably well for a few years, only to level off. Others seem not to do well with oral methods for some years, and then improve spectacularly. Parents are in a very difficult position, having to choose between gambling on the hope that their child will be one of the "lucky" ones who can eventually succeed with traditional oral methods, or settling for the typical possibilities of Total Communication. Most parents have tended, at least initially, to follow the advice recommended by the majority of contemporary educators of the deaf, or by local educators, regarding which approach to use during their child's early years. Some parents, through careful study and/or a determined search for what is best for their child, choose a method not immediately available in their area. It is very difficult for parents to adopt and use a method under these conditions. A very helpful procedure for parents to follow is to write down a careful summary of what they will be expected to do with each approach they are considering. This will help them understand what is practical for them.

During this century, until about 1970, educators committed to oralism were in the majority. Even in many schools using signs and/or fingerspelling, preschool instruction was oral. The results were very disheartening to parents. The landmark report, *Education of the Deaf— Report to the Secretary of Health, Education and Welfare*, which is the report of the Advisory Commission on the Education of the Deaf (1965), chaired by Homer D. Babbidge, forced educators of the deaf to recognize the drastic inadequacy of the educational opportunities furnished deaf children. The concern expressed in this report was at least partially responsible for a shift of the majority of educators toward use of manual communication in the form of Total Communication (TC), which uses some combination of signs in the word order of English with grammatical markers to complete an approximation of English syntax. That this did not remedy the situation was attested, 23 years later, by the even more critical report of the Commission on Education of the Deaf, appointed to report to the President and the Congress of the United States (1988). The report is entitled *Toward Equality, Education of the Deaf.* Here are a few of its observations:

1) The present status of education for persons who are deaf in the United States is unsatisfactory. Unacceptably so. This is the primary and inescapable conclusion of the Commission on Education of the Deaf.

2) Most children who are prelingually deaf experience serious difficulties and delays in acquiring English language skills.

3) A child without a strong language and communication base faces barriers that often lead to further educational difficulties.

4) ...learning a language requires interpersonal interaction and ample communication opportunities.

5) Since reading ability is highly correlated with prior English language knowledge, many students who are deaf also have difficulty becoming proficient readers.

6) The ability to express or comprehend language in written form is closely allied with the ability to express and comprehend language through face-to-face spoken communication.

7) The educational system has not been successful in assisting the majority of students who are deaf to achieve reading skills commensurate with those of their hearing peers.

In the method called "Total Communication," the manual presentation of signs in the word order of English is accompanied by and approximately synchronized with simultaneous speech. A very similar method was used at the American School for the Deaf, Hartford, Conn., in 1818, and discarded about 1835 (Keep, 1871). The use of speech in combination with the manual representation is intended to contribute also to development of speechreading and learning of spoken English. There is little or no evidence of this. One probable reason is that making the entire message essentially clear on the hands, as TC does, fails to require any dependence on or support of use of the information visible on the lips.

The move of the majority of educators toward Total Communication in the 1970s and 1980s, in the aftermath of the Babbidge report, received impetus from the rubella epidemic of 1964-65, which greatly increased the number of multiply handicapped children. Many educators thought manual communication would be more feasible for the multiply handicapped children than aural/oral communication.

In the last few years many manualists, particularly deaf adults themselves, have developed a strong push for American Sign Language (ASL) as the basic and first language to be learned by deaf children. This movement is still in its infancy. Its advantages and disadvantages are discussed in Chapter 23, "What About Sign Language?"

In 1965 and 1966 Cornett (1967) devised a new approach called Cued Speech, one that makes the elements of spoken language clear through vision alone. Through it hearing parents can provide their deaf child the opportunity to acquire spoken language through communication in the natural environment of the home.

Cued Speech is designed to give maximum support to the development of speech and speechreading while achieving the clarity and ease of communication required for natural language development. It uses a limited set of eight hand shapes and four hand locations, supplementing what is seen on the mouth during speech, to eliminate ambiguity and guesswork in the perception of spoken language by a deaf person. It relieves parents of making a choice based on the hope that the child is one of the "lucky ones" who can learn easily to communicate orally. Cued Speech advocates claim that it will produce better results in development of oral communication skills and language and reading skills than either "pure oral" or manual methods, or any combination of these, for the majority of profoundly deaf children.

Since 1978 more than a dozen significant experimental studies, one in Australia, three in the United States, and the rest in Belgium, have substantiated practically all of the important claims of advocates of Cued Speech. The studies 1) evaluate the accuracy with which Cued Speech can be understood by profoundly deaf children, 2) compare the reading comprehension levels of Cued Speech children with those of hearing children and hearing-impaired children with whom traditional oral methods or Total Communication have been used, 3) identify and verify the role of Cued Speech in establishing a base for reading, 4) compare the performances of Cued Speech students with those of other hearing-impaired students on language tests, 5) compare the respective values of use of Cued Speech at home and at school, 6) evaluate the effect of Cued Speech upon the mastery of certain aspects of grammar not ordinarily mastered by deaf children, and (7) compare the short-term effects of minimal training in Cued Speech on lipreading ability. These studies are specifically described and their conclusions quoted in the chapters to which they relate most directly, and summarized in Chapter 28, "Research Parents And Teachers Need To Know About."

Hearing parents should remember that, no matter which option they choose for their own communication with their deaf child and for his or her education, most (though not all) deaf children will eventually need and want some interaction with signing deaf persons. At the appropriate time the child should have an opportunity to learn to communicate in the language of signs. There are hazards in starting this too late, and problems associated with starting it too early.

What Parents Typically Go Through

Most parents of a deaf child go through three emotional stages after the child's deafness is confirmed. First is an initial stage of shock, confusion, grief, and depression. They often feel painfully alone. When parents discover that their child will never have normal hearing, they are usually frightened, upset, and desperate. For many parents this is the most traumatic experience of their lives.

The second stage is typically one of hope and optimism after parents read about the success of some deaf children and encounter the assurances of well-meaning professionals. Finally, most parents enter a long period of disappointment, discouragement, and difficulty in adjusting to results below their hopes and expectations.

The First Phase

Our society has not fully outgrown the idea that bad things happen to us as punishment for our own misdeeds. To have a defective child usually causes feelings of guilt. If a child's hearing impairment is due to genetic problems, there may be speculation as to which side of the family it came from (when the truth is that genetic deafness is usually due to a combination of recessive genes from both sides). Self-pity and anger are common in the first stage. But, the greatest source of pain is the shattering of the dreams the parents have shared about their new-born, precious, and presumably perfect child. Usually, this pain is accepted better by the mother than by the father, possibly because the mother's initial relationship with the child enables her to put it aside. Time heals, but the first stage is not over when the first sharp pain begins to lessen. Then come bewilderment, confusion, and a sense of hopelessness. These arise from the fact that the parents don't know which way to turn. Parents begin to feel better when they actually embark on finding out what can be done. Then they find that the professionals disagree sharply among themselves on what should be done for hearing-impaired children. They begin to realize that the weight of all decisions falls ultimately on them. They must decide which professionals they think are right, if any. They typically feel crushed by the realization that they actually need to know more than the professionals know, despite their usually complete lack of initial knowledge about the problems of hearing impairment.

If the parents are hearing (about 95% who have deaf children are) they may have had no contact with deaf people other than those who have lost hearing late in life. Thus, they may have very inaccurate ideas about the deaf segment of our population. They will likely hope that operations or hearing aids can provide a complete remedy, that surely modern medical science has something to overcome this disability. They may cling to that hope for years, but in most cases will have to concentrate on doing what they can to cope with the effects of their child's continuing hearing deficit through special education.

Realizing that immediate access to special education is necessary may only add to the confusion at this stage. Parents are subjected to all kinds of conflicting information about various communication modes and special education programs. Parents often get the feeling that everyone they talk to tells them they should do something different.

The Second Phase

As parents talk further with professionals and read what they can find on the subject, most of them reach a decision as to which way to go and soon enter the second emotional phase—that of high hopes and over-optimism. The proponents of each of the available alternatives can furnish glowing descriptions of successful deaf children. The assurance of well-meaning audiologists, speech pathologists, and oral teachers of the deaf that "...your child *can* learn to speak and read lips" is enough to make many parents begin to minimize the implications of the handicap. The literature presenting the case for Total Communication (which employs signs and fingerspelling as the basic communication mode) often leads parents to believe that with signs their child can learn to communicate well with them (not usually the case) and with deaf people generally (which is usually the case), and make good academic progress (some do; most do not). The use of speech with signs, supplemented with speech therapy, is expected to enable many children to learn spoken language and become able to communicate orally. No matter which way the parents decide to go, they are likely to become over-optimistic at this stage, expecting things to be much easier than they actually will be. The parents usually begin to listen more carefully to the arguments presented by one camp or the other. They may gradually form expectations based on the statements of its proponents. In some cases the parents encounter only the proponents of one method. This makes it easier for them to go along without inner conflict and turmoil until, a few years later, they may begin to suspect that they made the wrong choice.

One way parents can guard against overoptimism at this point is to visit several school programs for the hearing impaired for each of the alternative methodologies they are considering. It is very important to visit elementary, junior high, and high school programs as well as preschool programs, if possible. The reason is that the educational gap between deaf children and hearing children increases as they become older. Observing only preschool programs is likely to engender an unrealistic idea of what a program can be expected to accomplish. Parents can gain the most accurate evaluation of a program or an educational alternative by looking at its products—students at junior-high and high-school levels, or at college level. Visiting preschool and early-elementary programs is also helpful, since it shows what their child may soon encounter. An equally valuable method of evaluation is to visit with families, in their homes, who have been using the alternative you are considering for three years or more. Each family's communication with its deaf child, the degree to which family members include him/her in the conversation, the extent to which what they say to you and to each other is clear to their child—such things should contribute to the evaluation.

The Third Phase

The third emotional phase parents usually enter is one of gradually increasing discouragement and frustration. This is encountered when it becomes apparent that the child is failing to develop in accord with their high expectations. Most parents of young deaf children using traditional aural/oral methods (described later) cling for a long time to the hope that their child will eventually lipread and speak well enough to understand and be understood easily by most people. Some do. But most profoundly deaf children never achieve this goal, and most of their parents undergo a long, painful, slow adjustment to reality as they become older. There is typically the added pain of gradual realization that language development, academic progress, and social acceptance are going to be far slower than was hoped.

Parents who choose one of the signing approaches are also likely to become disappointed and frustrated as it becomes apparent that the child is not learning spoken language at a reasonable rate, and that social interaction with hearing peers is limited. Hearing parents who use signs usually come to realize that their communication with their child will tend to be more and more limited by their own inadequate competence with signs, as the child learns many more signs and signed phrases than they do. Also, with time, they usually find that the child's reading skills are far from adequate. For most parents this can be a long period of disappointment, discouragement, and difficulty in readjusting to results below their hopes and expectations.

Problems of Postlingual Hearing Loss

Parents of a child who suddenly loses most of his or her hearing after already having learned an appreciable amount of language will have some additional problems, despite the child's obvious advantage of having already begun to understand and to use speech. The cause of the hearing loss may contribute to additional problems. For example, if the cause is meningitis the parents may experience the pain of trying to help the child recover physically, relearn how to walk, etc., while at the same time being unable to communicate with him or her effectively. The child will not understand the sudden lack of communication, and may even think his/her parents are punishing him or her by no longer talking or reading to him/her. (These ideas are from an actual case history.) All this may happen while the child is experiencing physical pain and frustration at being unable to walk, run, and play. Serious emotional problems may be associated with the loss of hearing, and the child may require a good many months to adjust fully.

A child who gets a start on language in the normal way, before loss of hearing, has advantages in direct proportion to the length of time he/she has had normal hearing. It is very important that the parents of such a child learn and use Cued Speech (see p.17 for description) as soon as possible to reestablish communication and conserve the spoken language already learned, while it is still implanted in the brain. Parents must realize also that, even though the child already knows some language, he or she cannot pick up *new* language through lipreading. Thus, the danger is that the child's language level will fall rapidly behind that of hearing peers.

Typical Performance of Deaf Children

No one has summarized the typical effects of deafness more succinctly than Daniel Ling (1985, p. 2):

> *Its primary effect is the restriction it can impose on the acquisition and use of language in communication. Its secondary effects are more widespread and can include impoverished communication that restricts experience, hinders personal and social development, and prevents optimal educational attainment. The third level of adverse effects is found when the child is due to leave school. Poor educational attainments will restrict employment options, limit income, and circumscribe leisure activities. These restraints can, in turn, substantially reduce the quality of a person's life in myriad ways.*

Hearing parents are always concerned about speech. They should be. A well-known specialist in the psychology of deafness, McCay Vernon (1970) said: "Few persons prelingually deafened, and this comprises 95% of the (deaf) school population, develop speech that can be understood in most social situations."

In a six-year study of 48 children aged 7 to 17, who were of average intelligence and apparently normal apart from their deafness, Dr. Bernard Tervoort (1970) found that, on average, 65% of their speech was not acceptable for the hearing environment.

Speechreading (lipreading) is a difficult art—so difficult that few deaf children or adults excel at it. Practically all the sounds of spoken English resemble other sounds on the mouth. In speechreading studies done by the John Tracy Clinic (Lowell, 1959), deaf people from elementary to college levels achieved an average lipreading score of 35% of the words in simple sentences. Lowell also reports the following scores: for deaf elementary-school children, 38%; for deaf high-school youngsters, 25.8%, and for Gallaudet College students (a more select group), 44.9%. This low performance in typical deaf youngsters is probably due primarily to an inadequate knowledge of the spoken language on the part of most deaf people. This probability is supported by a statement of Berger (1972): "Although it may not seem 'fair,' persons with normal or nearly normal hearing can with minimum instruction speechread with equal or greater precision than persons with a substantial hearing loss."

It is widely recognized that communication is an early and

continuing problem for most deaf people. However, parents are often slow in becoming aware of the educational retardation that sets in as their deaf child fails to keep up with the academic pace of hearing children his/her age. Limited communication in the preschool years is a major contributor to this lag in educational progress. However, the dominant factor is the failure of the typical deaf child to become able to read well enough to learn efficiently through reading. Like inadequacy in speechreading, the deficient reading skills of an average deaf child are usually due to an insufficient knowledge of verbal language.

The level of reading of deaf people has changed little in more than 75 years. Pintner and Patterson (1916) reported, on the basis of several national studies, that "...the median scores of deaf students at any age on reading measures never reached the median for hearing children 8 years old." Studies made 60 years later (Trybus & Karchmer, 1977) showed "...essentially the same level of performance." The results are consistent over the years. According to a study by Wrightstone, Aronow, and Moskowitz (1962), a study that included 54% of all deaf children in the country in the age range of 10 to 16, the average reading achievement of 16-year-old deaf students was grade level 3.4. Allen (1986) reported the average reading comprehension level of 15- and 16-year-old deaf students in programs in the United States, in 1983, at grade 3.1, and those of 17- and 18-year old students as lower (2.9). The Center for Assessment and Demographic Studies, Gallaudet University Research Institute (1991) *Stanford Achievement Test, 8th Edition, Form J.: Hearing Impaired Norms Booklet* reveals the following median reading comprehension levels for youngsters with severe-profound losses: 15-year-olds, grade 3.0; 16-year-olds, grade 3.2; 17-year-olds, grade 4.0; and 18-year-olds, grade 3.2. These data must be interpreted with realization that the reading ability of hearing youngsters has declined since 1983, making the grade levels for deaf youngsters look better. R. Conrad (1979) reported that in England the reading comprehension level of 16-year-old deaf children was about equal to that of a hearing child 7 years old. This may reflect in part the higher reading levels of 7-year-old hearing children in England.

We know of no evidence that the typical reading levels of deaf children 15 to 18 years old are better anywhere in the world than the range indicated above, that of hearing youngsters 7 to 9 years old.

About 95% of individuals born profoundly deaf never read well enough to look up a word in the dictionary and learn its meaning, or well enough to infer the meaning of a word through context. This means that most never learn a word by themselves. They typically have to be taught every word they ever learn. That this condition is avoidable is shown by Wandel (1989) in a study of reading comprehension levels of 120 hearing and hearing-impaired children. That study will be discussed in the chapter on reading.

Geers, Moog, and Schick (1984) evaluated English language structures of 327 children from oral/aural (OA) and Total Communication (TC) programs. They reported that both OA and TC children, ranging from 5 to 9 years in age, scored far behind normally hearing 4-year-old children. They also reported: "The data clearly indicate that profoundly deaf children do not acquire language at a rate comparable to their normally hearing peers. This is true for those educated in aural/oral programs as well as those in total communication programs."

The Second-Language Problem

Gallaudet University renders a tremendous service to deaf people. It is a place for deaf students of exceptional ability who reach the level required for entry as preps or freshmen at Gallaudet. Reading levels of seventh or eighth grade are required. The tragedy is that most of these students, although they are typically of high mental ability, have studied English for many years, and know a lot *about* English, are simply not competent in English.

During the second week of my (*Cornett's*) tenure at Gallaudet as vice president for long-range planning, President Elstad gave me a copy of a letter he had just received. He said: "Our problem is that this letter is typical of about 80% of our students." The letter read:

Dr. Leonard Elstad   *August 26, 1965*
Gallaudet College
Washington, D.C. 20002

Dear President:

    As soon as you had lend me $15, I felt I must write you to let you know how relievable I am in your aid.
    I have felt that, in spite of the great difficulties I have face in managing my own financial problem, the outstanding ability I recognized in you could help me out. This aid is certainly an excellent relief with my financial problem; I think your aid should be appreciated.
    Thank you for giving me a pleasant relief.
          Gratefully yours,

Over the years I have taken occasion to show the above letter to scores of persons, usually fellow passengers on an airplane, without previously giving them any idea of my connection with Gallaudet or with the deaf. I have in each case asked: "What kind of person do you think wrote this letter?" Not one individual answered "a deaf person," "an illiterate person," "an uneducated person," or "a stupid person." Every answer was the same: "A *foreigner*." Tragically, that was the correct answer. Despite many years of study of English, in signing programs, oral programs, or both, these students still have a foreigner's knowledge of English. This fact is not a reflection on Gallaudet University, but on the education these students receive before they get to Gallaudet. There are students at Gallaudet who are competent in English. They tend to be the ones who qualify to enter as college freshmen by testing at tenth-grade or higher language levels.

Most of those who enter Gallaudet as preps, after five additional years of study of English at Gallaudet, show little evidence of added competence *in* English, though they know more *about* English. This is not the fault of Gallaudet University. These students are hampered by having learned and habituated too much English that is wrong, through unclear and/or distorted input. They know too much English wrong! It is extremely difficult to replace incorrect language patterns with correct ones in such a way that the replacement will be permanent. They do not encounter this problem in learning foreign languages through written presentation.

Chapter Summary

Parents of a deaf child usually go through three stages: a period of shock, grief, and confusion, a period of high hopes and over-optimism, and one of extended discouragement and adjustment to lower and lower expectations.

A majority of parents who use traditional oral methods, as well as those following Total Communication, have to adjust to lowered expectations in the areas of academic progress, reading, speech, speechreading, and social acceptance. Most hearing parents using signing soon find their communication with their deaf child limited by their own inadequate signing skills.

The literature amply documents the fact that most hearing-impaired children have speech and speechreading skills inadequate for effective communication with the general public, and that they fall (and remain) far behind their hearing peers in language, reading, and other academic areas. Cued Speech offers a solution to these problems.

Chapter 2
What Is Cued Speech?

Cued Speech is a visual communication system designed for use with and among hearing-impaired people. In English it utilizes eight handshapes, placed in four different locations near the face, to supplement what is seen on the mouth in such a way as to make the spoken language clear through vision alone.

Cued Speech is designed to overcome the following problems encountered by most children with severe or profound hearing impairment who have hearing parents.

1. The problem of *limited communication* with family in the early years, resulting in delayed personal and social development.

2. The problem of *delayed development of verbal language*. Rapid early verbal language growth rarely occurs in the prelingually deaf child through traditional methods, with which every word must be specifically taught. Cued Speech children can "pick up" language in essentially the same way hearing children do.

3. The failure of most prelingually profoundly deaf children to acquire an *accurate mental model* of the spoken language, including its sounds, its words and phrases, and its grammar. Without such a model stored in the brain a child cannot use speech effectively to speak to others, can speechread very little, and has little chance of becoming a good reader.

4. The lack of a *convenient and easy-to-learn method of communication* for use in the home, the classroom, and elsewhere—for instruction, for clearing up confusion, for instant reminder of the correct pronunciation, and above all for personal and enjoyable interaction with other people.

A Deaf Child's Major Problems

A hearing-impaired child's first problem, of course, is communication. Signing methods can solve this problem, but not the other major problems that are also typical: limited ability to read, very low ability to speechread, and limited ability to use speech for expressive communication.

The ultimate purpose of Cued Speech, and the reason it was developed in the first place, is to enable hearing-impaired children to become good readers. The failure of the education of the deaf to produce good readers is an unnecessary tragedy. Reading is the only way of learning, for deaf children, that is under their complete control. Through it they can learn anything they want to learn, if they can read.

The hearing-impaired child's lack of a clear, internalized model of the spoken language, primarily responsible for his/her difficulties in reading, is also responsible for typically very poor ability to speech-read, often inferior to that of even an untrained hearing person.

Though limited hearing makes it difficult for a child to learn to make speech sounds accurately, this is not the major speech problem. Even if taught to make the individual sounds of speech with reasonable accuracy, a deaf child is not automatically familiar with the pronunciations of the words, their meanings, and the way they must be put together in phrases and sentences in using speech. Hearing children can easily be taught to imitate words and even sentences in Spanish, but this does not make them able to communicate in Spanish. Likewise, deaf children cannot understand or use English just because they can pronounce some sounds and words. They need the internalized model of the spoken language developed through Cued Speech to guide their pronunciation.

The Methods Debate

Those who advocate an exclusively aural/oral education for hearing-impaired children and those who support use of manual communication have debated for more than 140 years. The advocates of each approach find the others lacking in some respects.

Traditional aural/oral approaches attempt to train children to make maximum use of their residual (remaining) hearing, with the aid of amplification, and also to make maximum use of the incomplete information visible on the mouth. Speech and speechreading are intended to be the primary means of communicating. Manual communication is generally forbidden, though supporting natural gestures are used by most teachers, and are typically used extensively among the children. But the low rate of language acquisition attained by a majority of deaf children typically causes a shift to written language as the primary means of teaching language unless the children make exceptionally good progress.

Oralists seek to provide deaf people with skills essential for integration into general society. Their critics say that limiting deaf children to inaccurate oral communication and slow, written communication is frustrating and intellectually restrictive. Specifically, they say this approach fails to produce rapid, natural development of understanding and communication for a majority of deaf children.

The various manual approaches strive for early development of communication and early emergence of personality through the use of a clear visual mode of communication. Most of these are used in combination with speech and within the philosophy of Total Communication. Manually-coded English, of which there are several forms, uses signs as symbols for specific words and adds signed markers to indicate some grammatical details, such as the different forms of a specific verb. Sign languages, such as the American Sign Language (ASL), have their own grammar and idioms and are thus languages in their own right, distinct from verbal languages. The use of signs can enable a deaf child to learn to communicate before learning to speak, or even if he/she never learns to speak effectively. It also prepares the child for social access to the deaf community.

Signs are visual symbols for concepts, just as words are spoken or written symbols for concepts. Because signs have no *code* relationship to words, as Cued Speech and fingerspelling do, learning the meaning of a sign does not cause a child to be able to identify, understand, or produce the corresponding word in either spoken or written form. Thus, all the words have to be specifically *taught* to the child until and unless he/she becomes able to read well enough to learn new words through reading.

The limitations of methods utilizing signs, according to those who argue against them, are that they do not of themselves cause the learning of spoken or written words, do not force dependence upon (and therefore do not develop) speech and speechreading, and do not provide an adequate foundation in verbal language. Proponents of signing argue that deaf children have a right to learn and use the language of deaf people, that signing is "natural" to a deaf child, and that verbal language, speech, and speechreading can be taught later to a signing child.

Many people, including Alexander Graham Bell, Edmund Lyons, G. Dewey Coats (1930), and Z.F. Westervelt, recommended and sought the development of a means of making spoken language visible to deaf people. But the phonetic (based on sounds) methods that were developed were too complex and/or did not consider the possibility of only supplementing the information available visually from the lips. Among these were the Danish (Mouth-Hand) System, developed by Georg Forchhammer in 1923, and Baghcheban's Speech Aid, developed in 1928. All used specific hand configurations and/or motions for specific consonant sounds, making it unnecessary to rely on the lips in the identification of the sounds. It is noteworthy that Coats (1930), deaf himself, expressed the opinion that the ideal system of communication for deaf people would be one based on syllables (as Cued Speech is), but he indicated that to develop such a system would be very difficult because there are so many syllables. He was overlooking the possibility that a system could represent syllables as combinations of smaller units (phonemes, or individual speech sounds) thus requiring fewer individual components. Cued Speech requires only 12 *cues*.

Requirements for a Suitable Method

The following requirements for an adequate and practical system were drawn up by Cornett in advance of his development of Cued Speech (Cornett, 1967, p. 5):

1) It must be clear, making all the essential details of the spoken language visibly evident.

If all the sounds of a spoken language were distinctly different from each other on the lips of the speaker, a hearing-impaired person would easily pick up the language and become able to speechread precisely. He or she would accomplish through vision exactly what the hearing child accomplishes through hearing. But many words look alike. Look in a mirror as you say *met, bet, pet, mid, bid, pid, pit, mean, bin.* There are at least 60 other words or syllables that look essentially the same as these on the mouth. The task is to provide a way for deaf children to see differences among all the words.

To make every speech sound and each syllable look different from all the others, Cued Speech uses eight hand shapes in four hand locations, executed in synchronization with speech. The combination of these "cues" *with what is seen on the mouth* results in different visual patterns for all the syllables and sounds of speech. Syllables that look the same on the mouth look different on the hand. Syllables that look the same on the hand look different on the mouth. There is a visual difference between all syllables or words that *sound* different.

2) It must be oral, so that there is consistent use of and dependence on the information visible on the mouth.

The "cues" (handshapes and locations) *alone* do not identify individual sounds or syllables. The visible mouth-teeth-tongue movements and formations are essential in receiving Cued Speech. Every sound is read from the mouth—with the aid of what is seen on the hand. The hand serves to identify groups of sounds and syllables that are different from each other on the mouth. No individual sound or syllable can be read from the hand alone. The entire system is shown on pages 774 and 775, in the Appendix. You may wish to refer to those pages in connection with parts of the analysis that follows. However, the charts should not be used for learning Cued Speech, but only for learning about it.

3) Any information added to what is available from seeing the mouth must be compatible (in timing, significance, etc.) with what is being said.

4) The system must be learnable by a very young deaf child through the process of consistent exposure to it in the home.

5) It must be learnable by hearing parents of average ability who are willing to make a reasonable effort to help their child.

6) It must be usable at near-normal speaking rates, at distances of up to 20 feet.

To fit the requirements above, it was necessary to develop a system that makes each syllable and each speech sound visually distinct from all others. That is, each syllable and each sound must look different from all others *either* on the hand *or* on the mouth. Many syllables and sounds look the same on the mouth. Many look the same on the hand. But, none look the same on both the hand and the mouth, so the deaf child *can always see a difference*, just as the hearing child can hear a difference between different sounds and spoken syllables.

In English, Cued Speech uses eight hand shapes and four hand locations in synchronization with speech to make all the sounds and syllables of speech look different from each other, either on the hand or on the mouth. In some languages (German, French) five locations are required; in others (Spanish, Japanese) only three are needed.

Analytical Description of Cued Speech

The following description is not intended to teach you Cued Speech. You should already be receiving instruction and/or using self-instructional materials. The purpose here is to help you understand more completely the nature of the system and its advantages. Reading and understanding the following material is not essential to either learning or using Cued Speech. Therefore, if it seems complicated, or if you are anxious to get on to how to use Cued Speech and what it is designed to do, skip to the summary at the end of the chapter. A parent reviewer made this suggestion: *Stress that it's much simpler than it sounds, and that it becomes automatic quickly with use, like typing.*

Four different locations of the hand (all within a few inches of the mouth) are used to distinguish among different *vowel* sounds that look alike on the mouth, such as *uh* in the word <u>but</u>, *i* as in <u>bit</u>, *e* as in <u>bet</u>, and *ee* as in <u>beet</u>. These sounds are cued by different hand locations.

For each location of the hand there are two or three vowel sounds. For example, when the tips of the fingers are at the tip of the chin the vowel sound is *ue* as in <u>blue</u>, short *e* as in <u>bed</u>, or *aw* as in <u>jaw</u>. Notice that these three vowel sounds look clearly different from each other on the mouth. You can verify this by looking in a mirror as you say only the vowel sounds. Cueing is done entirely according to the pronunciation, not the spelling.

When the tips of the fingers are placed at the corner of the mouth the vowel sound is *ee* as in <u>feet</u> or *ur* as in <u>fur</u> (or <u>her</u> or <u>sir</u>). If the tips of the fingers are placed on the throat (near the larynx), the vowel sound may be *a* as in <u>cat</u>, *oo* as in <u>foot</u>, or *i* as in <u>bit</u>. If the hand is in the side location (about four inches from the tip of the chin and approximately on its level, the vowel sound may be *ah*, as in <u>father</u>, *uh* as in <u>but</u>, or *oe* as in <u>note</u>.

At the same time, the location of the hand identifies a group of vowel sounds from which the "listener"/receiver chooses according to the lips; the shape of the hand identifies one of eight different groups of consonants from which one chooses according to what he sees on the mouth. Without the handshapes, each of these consonant sounds would be either invisible or easily confused with at least one other sound.

Since hand configurations and hand locations are executed simultaneously, they can be synchronized with normal speech, which occurs in syllables. Consider the following example: The full hand shape (all four fingers and the thumb extended) is used for the sounds of *m, f,* and *t.* It is also used for the special case in which a vowel is sounded without a consonant before it. Thus, with the tips of the fingers touching the chin, the following syllables are possible: *maw, faw, taw, meh* (as in <u>met</u>), *feh* (as in <u>fellow</u>), *teh* (as in <u>test</u>), and *mue* (<u>mood</u>), fue (<u>food</u>), and *tue* (<u>too</u>). In addition, the same cue is used for the same vowels when they occur alone: *aw, eh,* and *ue.* Each of the 12 syllables used with this one combination of handshape and hand location is clearly different on the mouth from all the others. Thus, each of them can be read from the mouth, without guessing. Cued Speech eliminates the guesswork of speechreading.

With the mouth covered, there is only one chance in 12 of using the above cue combination (full hand at the chin) to guess which syllable is being produced. But, without the cues, there is the same problem in trying to read the lips. For example, if the word *met* is spoken without cues, there are 71 other words (or word-like combinations of sounds) that look the same as it on the mouth. Some of them are: *met, bet, pet, mit, bit, pit, mutt, but, putt, meet, beet, peet, med, mid, ped, ment, meant, mint, mend,* etc. With two cues, one at the chin and the other three or four inches to the side of the face, plus what is seen on the mouth, all 72 combinations of sounds can be clearly differentiated through vision alone.

In order to learn the complete system, one has to learn which of the four locations of the hand is used with each of the 11 vowel sounds used in American English, and which of the eight handshapes is used with each of the 25 consonant sounds. Then, the combinations used for the four diphthongs must be learned. Finally, one must learn the special little motions of the hand used in the side location with the vowel sounds made there. All this requires, for most hearing adults, 12 to 20 hours. Speed and fluency come with use of the system, usually requiring several months to develop. The important thing is that, once one knows the system, he or she can use it with any word or combination in the language. And, with use it becomes automatic.

It should be kept in mind that the young deaf child is not taught the system as such. With Cued Speech the deaf child learns language the same way the hearing child does, without concentrating on or being specifically taught the code. Before long, however, the child knows the code and is able to break it down into its parts, recognizing individual sounds and syllables, and becoming able to cue expressively.

The principle of using two incomplete sources of information (one of which is designed to supplement and complete the other) to fuse into a whole is unique among methods of communication with and among deaf people. This unique characteristic of Cued Speech offers new possibilities for the education and life of deaf children.

Chapter Summary

Cued Speech is a system of communication which uses eight handshapes in four locations near the mouth, in combination with the information visible on the mouth, to make the spoken language clear through vision alone.

Cued Speech is designed to eliminate or reduce the problems of 1) inadequate communication in the home and elsewhere, 2) delayed development of verbal language, 3) failure to acquire a mental model of the *spoken* language, which is essential for good reading and speechreading skills, and for effective use of speech skills, and 4) the lack of a convenient and efficient means of communication for use in the classroom and elsewhere for academic instruction, for clearing up confusion, for correcting pronunciation, and for personal interaction.

When either traditional oral methods or Total Communication is used, almost all *verbal* language has to be specifically *taught* to most deaf children, whereas hearing children (and Cued Speech children) typically learn much more language than they are taught. Oral and TC programs tend to fall back on almost exclusive use of the written language in teaching verbal language when the children lag in language acquisition. Since learning the language through its written form is time-consuming and tedious, the rate of acquisition of verbal language is inadequate.

The specifications drawn up for Cued Speech by its developer included these: 1) It must make spoken language clear through vision alone; 2) The information visible on the mouth must be essential; that is, the information added must be only supplementary; 3) The information added to what is visible on the mouth must be compatible with it, and with the speech message, in timing, duration, rhythm, etc.; 4) It must be capable of being learned by a very young deaf child through communication; 5) It must be learnable by hearing parents who are willing to devote a reasonable amount of time and effort; 6) It must be usable at near-normal rates of speech and at distances up to 20 feet.

Each of the eight handshapes of Cued Speech identifies a group of three or four consonant sounds that are clearly different from each other on the mouth. Thus, they differentiate consonants that look alike on the mouth. Each of the four hand locations identifies a group of two or three vowel sounds that are clearly different from each other on the mouth. Thus, they differentiate those vowel sounds that look alike on the mouth.

Handshapes and hand locations are executed simultaneously, in synchronization with speech. Each combination of a handshape and a location is associated with a group of six to 16 syllables, each of which looks different from the others on the mouth. This syllabic characteristic makes it possible for Cued Speech to fit the rhythm and stress patterns of speech and thus to generate an accurate internalized phonological model. It also makes it possible to execute it at a normal speech rate.

Chapter 3
Life With Leah
by Mary Elsie Daisey

Leah Marie Henegar, the first child exposed to Cued Speech, was 6 years and 8 months old at the time the first part of this chapter was written by her mother for the Cued Speech Handbook for Parents, published in 1971. Leah was born in 1964 with a profound hearing-impairment. Her audiogram at 6 years of age reflected a 107 dB better-ear PTA threshold. She was exposed to CS consistently at home from the age of 24 months.

With a large family and an acute shortage of time, I have always been interested in any labor-saving device that is available. The greatest one I've found so far is Cued Speech. Communication with Leah, our 6-year-old deaf daughter, is so easy! It is not necessary to repeat over and over or grope for the understandable words. Usually something is said only once, understood, and responded to.

A great benefit of using Cued Speech is that we can say *anything* to Leah. We can talk about "squishy mud," describe something as "icky," or say "T.G.I.F." Of course, the first several times the latter was said around her we explained that it means "Thank goodness it's Friday." One day Anne, our 9-year-old daughter, came dashing into the room and shouted at Leah, "Who made a *disaster area* out of my room?!" In a case like this, Leah learns the meaning from the situation. Another time Anne said, "I have told you one million times to stay off my bed!" Since all this is cued, Leah absorbs it and stores it for future use. Most of the time, if we say something unusual, we follow up with an explanation. When I said, "Bobby's late, and he's in the doghouse," I explained that I meant he was in trouble.

This natural communication on our part makes Leah's communication with us more like that of a hearing child. When I once said, "Why did you mess up our new piece of chalk?" she replied, "I didn't." When I said, "Did you have milk?" she responded, "No, just water." During the day she'll nonchalantly say things like: "Okay." "Wait a minute." "I'm so sorry." "Be careful." When she drops food into her lap or runs into a door, she usually says, "Oops!" She will matter-of-factly say things such as: "Give me some," "I can't do it," "Let me do it."

Correction and Explanation
Another benefit of Cued Speech is that it is easy to correct Leah

when she uses poor grammar. We can do it the same way we correct Jane, 17 months younger. Once Leah said, "Bob and Jim are going *to* outside." I thanked her for telling me, then said, "But you don't say it that way. Just say, 'Bob and Jim are going outside.'" This natural error reveals a developing grasp of grammar that initially regularizes irregular verbs, as in: "I drinked my milk."

Leah Henegar, 1967

We don't have to "teach" Leah; we just do what we do with our other children—talk and explain. In this way we constantly and almost effortlessly enable her to increase her vocabulary and language facility. It is easy to build on her good language foundation. One of the other children recently used the word *invisible*. I explained it to her in relation to something she already understood: "*Invisible* is like your Guardian Angel; he's there behind you but you can't see him."

When a guest from England said to Leah, "I like your anarak," everyone in the family needed an explanation. Since the guest cued, all the Henegars learned that *anarak* is another name for a hooded coat like an Eskimo wears.

At church during Easter week, Leah observed as soon as Mass began—"two priests." I explained silently (in the only manner appropriate in church—a soundless whisper—just mouth movements and cues) that when there are two priests it is called a *concelebrated* Mass. Of course, Leah doesn't always remember words like *anarak* and *concelebrated* unless we initiate some "follow-up talk" about them. We try to remember to mention new words again, perhaps several times, so that they will become a part of her permanent vocabulary.

Discipline, Manners, Family Relationships

Periodically, we encounter behavior problems in church and elsewhere, but we handle them the same with all our children. (We can deal with any of them without sound, without causing the disturbance of whispering to our hearing children!) If Leah acts up, she is warned to behave or else! The "or else" may be the threat of a spanking or other punishment, such as sitting on a chair. It's great to be able to tell her what will happen if she doesn't line up and know that she understands completely. Understanding doesn't insure obedience, but it does help. And it eliminates the possibility of punishing Leah and then finding that she didn't understand.

At times, Leah has been described as "normally naughty," and normal discipline is what we use. We feel that explanations are important in good discipline. It is not enough to just say "no." Psychology sometimes needs to be used. When a child persists in his intent to do something undesirable, it is good to offer an alternative, which is easy to do with Cued Speech. One morning Leah wanted to wear a large, gaudy, multicolored necklace with the wildly-flowered print dress she had on. I protested and told her to take it off. She resisted. We almost had a full-scale clash until I told her: "Wear it tomorrow with your blue jumper dress; that will look better." She immediately changed her attitude, said "Okay," and dashed off to get out the jumper dress and lay it on her bed—with the necklace—for the next day.

It is also important (and easy with CS) to appeal to a child's logic and reason. One night at bedtime, Leah invented an excuse to stay up, as most children do at times. She produced an empty toy suitcase and compared it to Jane's, which was bursting at the seams with doll clothes. She insisted that she be allowed to go downstairs and hunt up some doll clothes for her doll. I was equally insistent that she get in bed. I explained that in the morning she could get up early and get dressed, then go down to the playroom to search for clothes. (I was thinking this would be an incentive for her to get up without the usual coercion in the morning.) She continued to insist, cueing "clothes," "downstairs," etc. Finally I thought of a different strategy. I said, "Look at your baby. He's sound asleep. He doesn't need any clothes tonight. He already has on his pajamas. You can get him some clothes in the morning when he wakes up. Let him sleep in peace tonight." It worked like magic. She immediately agreed, looked lovingly at "Baby Larry," and crawled into bed!

Of course, before all the stalling, she had said her prayers. Even though her prayers are memorized, she adds her own thoughts. One night she said, "Please help Great-Granddaddy—well tomorrow." (Earlier we had discussed his imminent operation.) Another time, instead of saying, "God bless Mommy and Daddy," it was "God bless Mr. and Mrs. Henegar."

Good manners are expected of Leah as well as the other children. For years she has been expected to say "May I please be excused?" when she wants to leave the table. Recently she hopefully said to me: "Sesame Street?" I replied, "Ask me nicely." So she said,

"May I see Sesame Street?" The other day, she came charging past someone, saying, "Move." Of course, I told her: "Say 'Excuse me, please.'" She did.

Leah has very normal relationships with her brothers and sisters (two each) and a lot of verbal interaction with them. Basically they all get along well, but there are times when the clashes are more frequent than desirable. Leah often shouts to the boys, "Get out of our room!," and she can trade insults with the best of them: "You are a baby." "Anne is fat." (Anne's reply:"I know *you* are!") "Bob is cuckoo." One day Jane asked me, "How do you cue, 'Leah loves mustard?'" (Leah detests mustard!)

The three girls share a bedroom, and because of Anne's repeated requests for a room of her own, we moved in a bookcase divider. She completed the division of the room by drawing her foot across the rug in an imaginary line and saying, "No trespassing!" She proceeded to explain (while cueing) what trespassing means. The next morning Leah woke Anne up by jumping on her bed. As soon as Anne's eyes opened, she said to Leah, "You're trespassing!" Leah said, "Oops!," jumped back behind the imaginary line, and hollered, "Wake up!" Once in a while it backfires on Anne. If she crosses the line, Leah and Jane chase her back with shouts of "You're trespassing!"

Leah participates in all family activities and often initiates them herself. She will say, "Let's race!" or "Let's go play in the playroom," or "Let's go downstairs and cook." One day I came into the family room and found all five children plus some friends, playing "Simon Says." Standing in front and spouting directions was "Simon" Leah.

When riding in the car, Leah is usually in the back seat, so communication between her and the driver is difficult, though the rear-view mirror is useful sometimes. If a cuer (usually Anne) is in the back seat, Leah can be kept informed.

Language and School

Leah's language development is helped considerably by Anne's frequent use of Cued Speech. She reads to Leah, plays school with her, and talks to her about anything and everything, using Cued Speech all the time. Anne's proficiency is a great help to us; it eases the burden of keeping Leah informed. The more people the task is spread among, the easier it is for everyone. Our three other hearing children use Cued Speech to varying degrees, none consistently. Bob (10 years) can cue, but since he does not do it enough to feel at ease with it, he cues only when he wants to be absolutely certain Leah understands, as when he is angry at her or when he wants to make a deal. Jim (8 years) is too busy thinking about monkeys and frogs to be bothered. Jane (5 years) plays with Leah most of the time and communicates with her constantly. They use some natural gestures but depend mostly on spoken communication. Jane cues some in imitation. All the children can read Cued Speech very well and seldom have difficulty in understanding.

Leah has been attending a program for the hearing impaired in the public school system where we live in Maryland. During the past year she has been integrated into the regular first grade for the entire morning's academic work. The teacher does not cue, but Leah's progress has been good. She lipreads phonics lessons and spelling tests, volunteers answers, and is considered a top student by her teacher. Her April 1971 report card indicated that she is excellent in reading and both written and oral comprehension, and very good in spelling and math. Her social adjustment seems to be good; she always has company on the playground.

Even though Leah is doing well, we know she could learn more if she were in a situation with a cueing teacher in a class with as stimulating an atmosphere as her present hearing class (1992 note: or if she had a Cued Speech interpreter/transliterator, unheard of in 1971.) Although Leah's lipreading ability is good enough for comprehension most of the time, she needs to be exposed to Cued Speech a greater percentage of the time 1) so that she can clearly understand all that is said in her class, and 2) so that she will continue to learn new language. In her mainstream class she frequently misses the spoken directions and is completely lost when the class sings or recites poetry. (This is so easy for her and so much fun with Cued Speech!) In addition, Leah misses much incidental discussion and learning.

Many times we have been asked how long we plan to cue to Leah or when we think we might stop cueing to her. The answer is that we never intend to stop cueing! The benefits are too great to ignore or eliminate. She is constantly learning when people cue to her. After all, learning does not end when school is over. Even adults continue to learn all their lives.

Speechreading, Hearing, Speech

As a result of exposure to Cued Speech, Leah is a very good lipreader. Though lipreading is not adequate for the classroom where it is important for everything to be clearly understood, she copes very well in situations where there are no cuers. She amazes us by understanding and responding appropriately to uncued communication.

One morning while Leah was getting dressed I asked her without cueing (my hands were full): "Did you make up your bed?" She answered, "Not yet." On another occasion Bobby (noting that she had on her poncho but not the matching hat) said without cueing, "Where's the hat?" Leah easily responded, "I don't need it."

Although her hearing loss is classified as profound, Leah makes good use of her residual hearing. She can now recognize the ringing telephone and turns around when her name is shouted (if there is no background noise). On the way to the store one day, Leah and Jane were in the back seat of the car. When they became extremely rowdy, I yelled "Stop it!" Since I was facing the front, Leah must have understood through hearing alone. She yelled to Jane, "Mommy said 'Stop it!'"

Leah's speech has continued to improve although I feel it would be much better if she had a teacher (or interpreter) who cued to her all day so she could pick up the pronunciation of new words. Also, it would be better if she had a speech therapist proficient in Cued Speech. She knows how to make most of the speech sounds correctly, but needs frequent visual reminders to use these sounds in the proper places. If she says something we do not understand, we can tell her to cue it (she does not cue all the time), and it is then usually intelligible. This is because the act of cueing reminds her where to put which sounds.

The rhythm of Leah's speech is very good. Long before she could make a lot of sounds, her speech sounded better than it really was because of the proper rhythm and inflection. She can be understood most of the time—even the cat comes running when she calls, "Here Kitty, Kitty." But good speech has come slowly for Leah.

Because of her constant exposure to spoken language through Cued Speech at home, Leah can say anything she is told to say. She readily pronounces hard-to-say words and phrases such as *Pacific Ocean, hippopotamus*, and *Kee-uh-mue-tuh*, our dog's name. Of course, she does not necessarily make all the sounds correctly in such words, though she knows which sounds they are. She can also pronounce difficult unfamiliar words on the first attempt if they are cued to her. While out shopping one day, we looked at bathing suits. When she admired the fuzzy one, I told her what it was and suggested she tell Daddy about it when we got home. She did, saying, "I saw a fur bikini." Of course this familiarity with the spoken language is the foundation for development of proficiency in reading. She reads with no trouble—even Dr. Seuss nonsense such as *splatt, blurp*, and "Grum, grum, hippopotamus chewing gum."

Expressive Language

Leah's expressive (spoken) language improves continuously. The most noticeable thing about it is that she is apt to come out with anything. Her expressive language is not based on patterns or drill received in school, such as the too-frequent use of a stilted subject-verb-object pattern. Instead, she employs many patterns, including complicated clause constructions.

Of course Leah makes mistakes in usage, but hearing children go through the same learning stage, and it is easy to correct her. She does not just imitate patterns used with her. For example, once she came to me and reported: "Jim hit me!" I said, "Tell him I want him." She went out on the porch and yelled at the top of her lungs: "Jimmy! Mommy said, 'Come here!'" Another day, when I told Leah and Jane to clean up the family room, Leah barked out the orders, "Jane! I'll clean up the floor. You clean up the chair."

Leah has a great sense of humor. I asked her a question at the dinner table one night, and she answered with her mouth so full I couldn't understand her. I told her not to talk with her mouth full and to cue it. She grinned mischievously and said: "I can't cue."

Leah continues to be a happy child who is growing and developing like her brothers and sisters. She enjoyed a recent trip to the circus so much that before she went to sleep she said, "Circus next week." To me, her normalcy was best illustrated by a typical (never satisfied) child's reaction to the piles of gifts at Christmas. The day after Christmas she said: "Easter is coming!"

The Best of Both Worlds — 1985

Now that she is on the threshold of full adulthood, Leah does have the best of both worlds. She is a full-fledged member of a hearing family and functions comfortably with everyone. Her friends include hearing and hearing-impaired people. Communication is effortless for Leah when Cued Speech is used, so she obviously prefers the natural dialogue with cuers. However, she can proficiently handle communication with non-cuers by using her speech and speechreading skills. She can also competently handle expressive and receptive sign language when she needs to communicate with hearing-impaired people who do not know Cued Speech.

Schooling

Leah has had almost every variety of schooling since 1971: totally integrated in her neighborhood school for five years of elementary school, with Cued Speech support; total reliance on her speechreading and reading skills, with no Cued Speech in the classroom, for three years of junior high school; and finally Cued Speech classroom transliterating for the three years of high school. Leah was the first profoundly deaf high school graduate of Wake County's hearing-impaired program (Raleigh, N.C.) in 1982.

Next, Leah decided on what was for her a first-time experience: attendance at a school for the deaf, Gallaudet University. She developed signing fluency during the intensive New Signers Program in the summer before entering as a freshman and even won recognition as the best in her class at reading fingerspelling. She "majored in socialization," and a year and a half later returned home to pursue her education more seriously with Cued Speech in the mainstream. She attended a local community college, completing an office and computer skills program, and also took classes at North Carolina State University, all with the aid of Cued Speech transliterators employed by the schools.

Communication Skills Evaluations

Gallaudet College's standard evaluation of student communication skills indicated Leah's abilities in 1983. On a scale of 1 (best) to 5 (worst), her hearing was rated 5 with earphones or with her hearing aids, "essentially no word discrimination ability." However, she relies greatly on her amplified hearing. She recently admonished someone who was speaking softly to her, "Speak up. I can't hear you if you don't use your voice!"

Gallaudet College rated Leah's speech as 3, or "good deaf speech," meaning the general public may have some initial difficulty in understanding her, though she can be easily understood once the listener adjusts to her voice. Her lipreading was assessed at level 2 without sound, meaning 54%-74% of the words correct, and at level 1 with sound, meaning 75%-100% of the words correct, thus demonstrating excellent use of her very limited residual hearing.

Although she understands sign language and can communicate comfortably in that mode, Leah adamantly states her preference for Cued Speech rather than sign-language interpreting because she "wants to know what the *exact* words are." She also says she appreciates Cued Speech because it helps her "understand people who don't cue."

Benefits and Adulthood

Now that Leah is grown, the greatest benefits of Cued Speech use are apparent: social development and maturity, and such characteristics as self-esteem, independence, self-confidence, adaptability, and a marvelous sense of humor, even under stress. These all contribute to good mental health and happiness.

Her self-confidence enabled Leah to handle alone the interview for her first job (at a fast-food restaurant) while still in high school. She has been courageous enough to fly alone and to brave the intricacies of the bus-subway system of the Washington, D.C., metropolitan area. She has confidently handled numerous breakdowns of her decrepit car, including one on a long journey. She has proven that she can cope with life independently with self-assurance and aplomb.

Leah avidly reads daily newspapers and news magazines and is interested in a wide range of subjects such as world affairs, ancient Egypt, television, swimming, and physical fitness, and she is the family expert on both current events and detail retention.

Leah officially reached adulthood as she turned 21 on September 12, 1985, with the immediate goal of lucrative employment and financial independence. Armed with a technical school certificate in business, she landed her first full-time job only a week after graduation. During her job interview with three strangers, she so deftly handled the meeting, relying on her speechreading abilities, that her prospective employers later reported she impressed them with her communication abilities and her self-confidence.

Dreams Do come True—1992

In looking back over 26 years of pioneering with Cued Speech, I am struck by the realization that Cued Speech has made dreams come true for Leah and for the rest of our family. Leah is now 28 years old, a happy, well-adjusted, and productive young lady. Her realized dreams involve independence, love, marriage, family, work, home, acting, and people. Cued Speech has helped her successfully pass many of the usual milestones of life.

All mothers have dreams for their children. For all five of my children, now grown and happily established, I wanted what most mothers aspire to for their offspring—rewarding work, love and wonderful personal relationships with God and people, an interesting and challenging life, the ability to handle whatever problems occur, and lots of fun along the way. My dreams for my deaf daughter were similar to those for my other four children.

The Real World of Work

A full-time, respectable, and secure job enabled Leah to achieve the independence to which she aspired. It allowed her to leave the family nest and share an apartment with a hearing, cueing friend. It gave her the satisfaction of doing important and challenging work and earning the approbation of her supervisors.

Leah is now serving her seventh year in the Corporations Division of the North Carolina Department of State. She has advanced to a position where she processes legal documents and works with people and computers. She relies totally on her oral communication abilities since no one in her office cues or signs.

In a phone conversation, Leah's immediate supervisor praised her first deaf employee:

> *Leah's fantastic! I depend on Leah a lot; she's a valuable employee, and she's a pleasure to work around. She has a special ability with the computer.... I don't have any problem understanding Leah. I forget she's deaf; I sometimes turn away when I'm talking, forgetting she can't hear.... Her sense of humor is great... she comes in every day in an upbeat manner. She's a pleasure to be around. You should be very proud of Leah.*

"Happily Ever After"

At her apartment complex Christmas party in 1986, Leah met a new resident who was, like her, alone for the evening. She and Jack Lewis spent the rest of the evening deep in conversation. A note on her door the next morning invited her to a dinner that Jack cooked and served by candlelight. A romantic courtship led to marriage a year and a half later, with both of them convinced they had found the mate of their dreams, with a relationship based on solid family values and good communication.

When Jack Lewis nervously cued his wedding vows on April 16, 1988, his bride Leah was not the only one touched by the significance of his efforts. It was the first wedding ceremony ever at which the hearing bridegroom cued his vows to his deaf bride; the first at which the bride had the services of Cued Speech transliterators in order to follow every word of the ceremony exactly as spoken or sung; and the first at which the matron of honor and the two bridesmaids were all family members able to cue what they said to the bride. The hearing-impaired guests could follow the ceremonies by watching either a cueing or a signing interpreter. Even the singing was interpreted, though when it came to rendering the Latin words to "Ave Maria," this could be done only through Cued Speech.

The bride and groom chose their own readings and memorized their vows, each cueing in turn. As the groom cued his vows to Leah, there was hardly a dry eye in the church. At the reception, the bride demonstrated her ability to communicate in whatever mode was needed at the moment, relying in turn on Cued Speech, lipreading, and signing.

Leah and Jack are very happy together, and she confided recently that she has "the most wonderful husband"; yet they know that it takes work and determination to deal with the adversities of life and the ordinary stresses of marriage. They are encountering the usual financial struggles of

Jack and Leah Lewis

most young married couples. At one point, recently, each was handling two jobs and adeptly juggling their duties and time constraints.

Leah has had much experience in coping. Her childhood determination to get up and go again after a fall or any adversity has stood her in good stead over the years as she has had to concentrate and persist to achieve communication with most of those people around her who will never learn to cue or to sign. Leah has obviously managed well with other problems or situations: those of long-term significance, like the divorce of her parents and her family's move to another state, as well as problems of shorter duration, such as the many car breakdowns she has coped with alone. She has experienced the enrichment as well as the problems of living with a stepfamily from another culture and language, and she managed well on her own when away at school. So I feel sure the problems she faces today and tomorrow will be dealt with in a mature, competent manner.

Communication Flexibility in Acting Debut

Although marriage made "spouse and house" the primary focus of Leah's life, she is not so wrapped up in her personal life and domestic pursuits that her world is narrowed to that exclusively. Her lifelong dream of being an actress was realized when she starred in "Children Of A Lesser God" at Raleigh's Theatre in the Park for 15 performances in April and May 1990.

The audition, rehearsal, and performance process meant that Leah spent two and one-half months in an intense learning experience without the aid of Cued Speech. Sign language interpreters were provided, and Leah additionally relied on her speechreading skills. She worked to improve her sign language fluency while honing her acting techniques. Leah played a deaf woman, but it was challenging to play a part so different from her real life in almost all other respects.

Jim, Jane, Leah, Mary Elsie, Anne, and Bob

Rave reviews came from far and wide, complimenting her acting and her communication skills. The theater's program elaborated on Leah's involvement with Cued Speech, citing it as the reason for her ability "to function in the hearing world independently."

After a lead role acting debut, future acting opportunities for Leah were certain to pale in comparison. But she is realistic enough to know that good roles for deaf people are very limited (other than with exclusively deaf theater companies). She has persisted in maintaining her theater involvement, enjoying work behind the scenes, learning different phases of drama and production, and occasionally landing another acting challenge.

Totally enamored with the world of the theater, Leah went to an audition for Shakespeare's "Richard II" at Raleigh's Theatre in the Park, with the intent of filling a technical role backstage. Instead she was given the role of the Queen's Lady-in-Waiting and floated away from the first rehearsal thinking that at least her non-speaking walk-on role would entitle her to the fun of prancing about in an Elizabethan costume.

Involvement in a David Wood theatrical enterprise with Raleigh's Theatre in the Park can result in many surprises, and one surprise followed another as Leah learned that her costume would be of the 1960s, and the play would be set in a fictional Latin American country. She then learned that her role, though a minor one, would involve speaking Shakespearean lines. She rehearsed tirelessly in the weeks leading up to the premiere of the play, practicing her lines on her own by cueing to help her pronounce Shakespearean English more clearly.

On opening night this mother's pride in her deaf daughter's performance in a speaking role was only eclipsed by her pride at

Leah's total involvement and pleasure at interacting with her theatrical friends. At the opening night reception after the performance it was interesting to observe numbers of her fellow actors and actresses who spoke with her, being careful that she could see their faces and pronouncing their words distinctly so she could understand. They were obviously good friends with mutual interests and many things to talk about.

"I Can Do Anything"

Leah has said many times that she feels like a hearing person, but this is never said as a way of denying her deafness. She has a healthy, matter-of-fact attitude about being deaf. She has been known to remonstrate with her siblings, "Cue—I'm deaf, you know!" Yet she feels that her deafness imposes few restrictions on her life.

In a television interview during her "Children Of A Lesser God" acting stint, Leah proudly said, with a big smile, "I can do anything—except talk on the phone." (She manages to do even that in a limited fashion, but must rely on TDD's or the telephone relay services for full telephone communication.) Her high self-esteem and good communication abilities obviously support her positive outlook on life.

Leah's "I can do anything" attitude is now helping her in her newest life phase: motherhood. She is thrilled with her new role and the beautiful son she produced on June 24, 1992. Weighing in at 10½ pounds, Michael Jonathan Lewis is already, at two months, responding with wide-eyed attention, big smiles, and cooing to the cued baby talk produced by his doting mother and grandmother. When he was born, a Cued Speech transliterator in the delivery room gave Leah access to everything said by those wearing surgical masks, and special permission to keep on her hearing aids enabled her to her her baby's first cry.

Dubbed "Super Baby" by his Uncle Jim, Leah's baby was born just a week earlier than her sister Anne's new daughter. The fun of sharing the nine months of pregnant anticipation has turned into the joy of raising close cousins for the two sisters. Younger sister Jane already has two children (and their brothers Bob and Jim, three more), so family talk now is frequently children-centered. We are trying to encourage all the "little people" to cue so that Leah's baby will pick it up naturally, as they all did, and so that Leah will also have the comfort of easy communication with her nieces and nephews.

Now this mother/grandmother recognizes that many dreams do come true. I feel a great sense of pride and accomplishment that all my children are grown, happy, self-sufficient, emotionally healthy, and productive, contributing members of society. And besides all that, they are wonderful people, and we have great fun together!

This doesn't mean that everything for us is great and wonderful all the time. We have the same problems and successes, pains and joys as any other family. And our family saga is by no means finished. We all have a lot of growing and learning to do yet. We read and interact with new people all the time and seek to expand our horizons. We all have a ways to go to reach self-actualization, becoming all that each of us is capable of being. That is why we will continue to cue whenever Leah is in our presence. Cued Speech makes it possible to raise successful deaf adults and have a normal family life in the process.

The greatest sense of satisfaction we can have as parents of deaf children is that we have raised or are raising them to be happy, independent, emotionally healthy individuals who can function at their full potential and do what they want to do, without any limits imposed by their imperfect hearing. Our Cued Speech children do not consider themselves handicapped. They feel no limits. They can do anything they want to do, and their dreams can come true!

Chapter Summary

This chapter summarizes the experiences of the first child with whom Cued Speech was used and those of her family. With the opportunity to observe hundreds of children whose families have used Cued Speech with them, we believe that Leah's achievements are typical of what can be expected when a child of average-or-better ability, and no additional disability, receives superior support with Cued Speech at home, and school support ranging from poor to somewhat less than optimum. (*Cornett's evaluation*)

Janie Abell suggests that the near-perfect outcome of this first case may contribute to over-optimism in families with children for whom the results will be less satisfactory. It is just as likely to have a sobering effect on parents' realization of how much must be done in the home if the results are to be worthy of the child's potential.

Statements by Leah's sisters are on pages 276 and 277.

Chapter 4
You and Your Deaf Child

Many parents who have excellent rapport with their hearing children are bewildered when they learn they have a hearing-impaired child. How will they convey to that child their expectations and their reasons for requests and decisions? How will they set limits on behavior or warn the child of danger? How do they make him/her a member of the family? How can they pass on their values? How can they contribute to the development of character and personality?

A Hearing-Impaired Child is a Child

Ideally, a hearing-impaired child should be treated the same way a hearing child should be treated. With clear communication this is possible. For example, if a parent warns other children in the family that they have "only one more chance," but the deaf child misses the warning, he or she should not be held responsible. If the child did understand the warning, she or he should be held accountable for his/her actions. A hearing-impaired child should have only as much indulgence as a hearing child, and no more—within the limits imposed by the lack of sufficient language and communication ability. But, if these limits result in the necessity for much greater indulgence, the child can rapidly become a spoiled and frustrated individual. The only satisfactory solution is to develop clear communication so that discipline and control can be even-handed.

The relationship between a hearing-impaired child and family members is a major factor in that child's achieving success with whatever educational approach is followed. The early years are of prime importance in any child's development, and nearly all this time is spent with family members. As children get older, more of the influence in their lives gradually shifts from family to peers, and often back and forth. If parents are to have a continuing beneficial effect on their children through these periods of less-dominant influence, strong bonding must be established early in childhood. The key to development of a good child-parent relationship is good communication.

A child's sense of security and self-confidence are in direct relation to his or her family life. These feelings grow or wane according to whether the child knows what is going on or feels left out. Cued Speech can enable the family to involve the child fully, if it is used consistently and well. If parents of a hearing-impaired child are to meet their child's needs, they must develop sufficient proficiency in Cued Speech to communicate effectively. Then they must take the time to cue everything said in the child's presence and explain everything they would explain to a hearing child.

Communication, Discipline, Sense of Family

Lack of adequate communication can result in domination of the home by a strong-willed deaf child, or in the development of severe behavior problems. In such cases deaf children are likely to become "problem children" because of their frustration. Inability to express themselves can lead to temper tantrums and related, more serious disturbances. How does the hearing-impaired child communicate feelings, specific needs and wants, daily experiences? With Cued Speech, a clear means of communication is available between parents and child. This clear communication makes it possible to exchange thoughts and ideas, and to discuss not only needs and wants, but any and all topics of interest. For example, it helps minimize fear in connection with medical treatment. Christy Nemeth relates that when John had surgery at 3 he knew exactly what to expect (shots, anesthesia, a special gown, etc.) and was never frightened about it. Twin deaf boys in New York had diametrically opposite experiences in connection with removal of tonsils. One had a terrible ordeal, before Cued Speech, because everything was unexpected and frightening. The other, a year after starting CS, had no trouble, since he knew what to expect, including the sore throat, and the ice cream to relieve it.

All normal children are demanding. Babies have frequent needs, and their built-in "I want" mechanisms develop very early. Parents soon realize they cannot let a child have his or her way in everything. They have to help children conform their behavior to the world in which they live. But too much parental domination is not good. What is expected, and why, has to be explained to a child. Parents who require blind obedience will inhibit development of self-sufficiency and delay or limit emotional and mental maturity. Three principles are important to good discipline:

1. The child must know what is expected.
2. Parents must be consistent in their expectations and requirements, as applied to the child.
3. Parents must be consistent in allowing the expression of love to permeate every aspect of living, even the disciplinary process.

Children often misbehave in order to get attention. This happens frequently with deaf children because of their sense of isolation. Parents must strive to alleviate this sense of isolation by consistently informing the child of what he or she misses because of limited hearing. The deaf child thus requires more parent time than do hearing brothers and sisters. Yet, this imbalance must be maintained without making siblings feel they are less valued or that they are receiving too little parental time and attention. The "I wish I were deaf so you would love me too" syndrome may not often come to the level of actual expression, but such feelings do occur frequently, according to interviewers of siblings. The disparity in time and attention must be compensated for by the quality of the attention given the hearing siblings as well as the deaf child. How to accomplish this is discussed at length in Chapter 16, "The Roles of Hearing Siblings and Peers." Actually the consistent use of Cued Speech during the course of normal living and family activities tends to minimize the effect of any unavoidable disparity in time and attention.

Even conversation not specifically directed to the hearing-impaired child should be cued. The deaf child should receive the continuing input of unimportant and even irrelevant information that hearing children receive automatically: weather, news, comic-strip characters, fashions, jokes, TV cartoons, etc.

The hearing-impaired child should be told the whole truth—just as would be the case if she or he were hearing. Family members often avoid doing this because it is frequently difficult and time-consuming. But, the child who is deaf deserves to be as well informed as anyone.

Affective Development of the Child

Parents have a pervasive effect on a child's personality and character. Their responsibility for the **affective** development of their deaf child is as great as for that of a hearing child. Affective development is development that relates to attitudes, beliefs, feelings, and emotions. Development in religion, the concepts of right and wrong, respect, consideration for others, social behavior, self-confidence, and a sense of security—all these are needed as much by the deaf child as by hearing children. Yet, in many ways, it is more difficult for a deaf child to develop a good self-image unless parents give specific attention to that need. It is easy for parents to neglect some of the child's needs because of the pressure on them to take care of language development, speech therapy, auditory training, and academic concerns, and time is insufficient to do it all. The key is to involve as many elements of affective development as possible in the process of communication aimed also at language development.

Children's feelings of security and self-confidence are in direct relation to the quality of their family life. These feelings develop appropriately only if a child generally knows what is going on and feels a part of it. Feeling left out is damaging to both self-esteem and development. Cued Speech can help involve the child in every aspect of the family's life, *if it is used consistently*.

The abstract concepts of God, love, right, and wrong can be conveyed to hearing children through examples and discussions at home and at a place of organized worship. But to many deaf children, a house of worship is no more than a place of mysterious, silent ritual, unless it furnishes either Cued Speech transliteration or sign language interpreting. Unless churches and synagogues offer such services, or provide special religious instruction for deaf children, virtually all the responsibility for religious instruction falls on the parents. Of course, some parents make a great difference by providing transliteration for their own child in their house of worship.

Many books and pamphlets on the subjects of child development, guidance, discipline, and behavioral modification are available through libraries, bookstores, churches, and health agencies. Most of them are directly applicable to rearing a hearing-impaired child, if there is clear communication in the home. Some of these materials that are especially helpful to parents of hearing-impaired children are listed in the Appendix.

In order to meet their child's needs, parents must develop sufficient proficiency in Cued Speech to communicate freely with their child. Then, they must take the time to explain everything they would explain to a hearing child, plus many things obvious to a hearing child that need to be explained to a deaf child. Finally, they need to be aware of the need to provide access to what is said by non-cueing people in the child's environment.

Bonding

Bonding is the term psychologists use in referring to the forming of a profound, personally directed relationship between persons. Usually this begins in a baby's bonding with the primary care-giver. Ideally, it broadens to include all members of the family. It is judged to be essential to the child's physical, mental, and emotional development. Hearing impairment can interfere with this process unless measures are taken to support it.

Mother and Child

Typically, the person with whom a baby has the closest relationship is the mother. This closeness begins with the early holding and caressing usually provided by the mother. The hearing child's first perceptions of meaning in sounds, according to psychologists, are centered in the picking up of the mother's voice tones—soothing, comforting, loving sounds that contribute to bonding. This occurs long before sounds have any specific linguistic significance. Pitch, inflection, changes in level—all of these are part of the vocal "caressing" that results from the mother's cooing, loving communication to her child. The child's first perceptions of communication as a two-way process begins with the realization that sounds he or she produces can bring responses from mother. Of course, from the time of birth screams of discomfort bring help, but it is much later that children connect their quieter vocalizations with responses from their mother or others. Expression and response, initially carrying only overtones of affection and togetherness, build a base that expands into significant linguistic communication.

The mother's touch is typically the child's first specific association of the tactile sense with comfort and pleasure. It soon develops into a rudimentary form of tactile communication. Stroking, petting, caressing of her baby, as natural to the mother as life itself, are essential to the welfare of the child. The tactile sensations associated with suckling are thought by psychologists to be intimately linked to feelings of security, affection, and extreme pleasure, for both child and mother, enhancing bonding. At least some of the same benefits are thought to be obtainable in bottle feeding if the mother holds the child, caressing and talking or singing. With this foundation in the earliest stages of life outside the womb, the child has a tendency to bond with the mother in a relationship that is natural, strong, and enduring. It is no wonder that vocal communication tends to be established first with the mother and that the first recognition of specific words and phrases by the child comes about in interaction with the mother. In many activities—bathing, changing, dressing, even playing—the mother is usually the person most involved, even though participation of fathers in care-giving is increasing.

In fact, many babies today are fortunate enough to have a fully involved father, beginning with his presence and active participation at birth. These babies can also bond early with their father if the father is fully involved in the baby's care and provides abundant nurturing.

If the child is hearing impaired, those aspects of bonding that are dependent on the reception of the mother's (or father's) voice are inhibited or delayed unless compensated for by extra tactile and visual exchange. If the hearing impairment is profound, or if the child is without amplification, it is suggested that the mother hold the baby's head against her cheek as she speaks and hums or sings, so the baby can feel the communication. A father who shares this early nurturing should do the same.

Family Bonding Builds On Parent-Child Bonding

It is essential for other family members to build on the child's usual initial orientation toward the mother and help broaden the child's perceptions of persons other than himself or herself. Fathers and siblings who participate in caring for the baby can share in the cultivation of the child's permanent bonding with all members of the family. In the case of a child with a severe-to-profound hearing deficit, this requires specific planning and coordinated effort.

A baby's earliest visual experiences tend to center on the mother's face. Perception of meaning in facial expression begins to form in connection with the face that is so consistently in view. Then the baby, as it associates different meanings with different expressions on its mother's face, gradually becomes capable of interpreting the facial expressions of others, as well as their voice quality, body language, contact, and other paralinguistic elements (actions accompanying spoken language that assist in its interpretation).

The early sensations of being touched and caressed by parents and other care-givers, and the sounds associated with those activities, are important in the early development of a baby. Early visual and tactile development can occur very naturally in a hearing-impaired child. Because of the hearing deficit, the child is likely to rely almost entirely on what can be seen and felt. The advocates of very early provision of amplification for hearing-impaired babies point out that in many cases it makes possible an orientation to the mother's voice that is similar to that experienced by babies with normal hearing. Of course, much depends on the degree and kind of hearing deficit. The provision of very early appropriate amplification is difficult, but modern audiological techniques make it increasingly feasible.

What has been presented thus far in this chapter is typical of situations in which the mother does not work outside the home. In such cases the mother will likely continue to be the primary agent in the infant's early language development through the preschool years. Especially during the early years, the activities of the home make it a veritable language-learning laboratory. Research shows that a young child learns more new language in two hours of undivided attention from a skillful mother than in a full day of school. Studies of the relative merits of use of Cued Speech in the home and at school (Hage, Alegría, & Périer, 1989) demonstrate the importance of what happens in the home. More information on the use of Cued Speech with very young children (under 3 years of age) is given in Chapter 18, "Starting With A Very Young Child." The home is also an ideal place for auditory training, which can be particularly enjoyable for the child if conducted as described in Chapter 14, "Auditory Training, Cochlear Implants."

The Two-Job Family

The modern trend toward outside employment of both parents has caused significant changes from the description above. When both have outside employment, it is essential for them to achieve a high level of cooperation, careful planning, and teamwork, in which both father and mother fill appropriate and in some respects interchangeable roles. Fortunately, the trend toward outside employment of both parents has been accompanied by a corresponding trend toward parental sharing of infant care and nurturing, followed by a sense of partnership and sharing in the process of child rearing. Though this is a relatively new trend, enough information is available to make it clear that a family with two wage earners can cope effectively with a deaf child if both parents are determined to do so.

Father and Child

Ideally, both father and mother build on all the progress that occurs as a result of the child's association with the other. Gestures used with the child by one should be picked up by the other. Each may do well initially to imitate some of the other parent's helpful and reassuring mannerisms. This is beneficial only in the beginning stages, until both mother and father begin to get consistent responses to direct efforts at communication. Then, each of their roles should take its natural course. The articles by fathers in Chapter 21, "The Greatest Problem — Time," will furnish helpful information on how the father can do his part. If the father learns to cue at the same time the mother does, and develops comparable proficiency, there will rarely be a problem. The key is for the father to increase the amount of time he spends communicating with the child, to make their bonding strong.

If the father learns to cue along with the mother, and if he then assumes his proper and distinctive share of the task of caring for the child, many wonderful things can happen. The psychological need of the child for a strong bond with the father is satisfied, language acquisition and social development are accelerated, and the father can become proud of the child's progress and his own part in it. The hearing-impaired child needs a strong sense of family identification and family unity, just as a child with normal hearing does. You will encounter many ideas and methods for achieving this in the upcoming chapters.

The modern shift toward more participation by the father in infant caretaking not only broadens the baby's bonding to the family, but lessens for the mother a load that is often almost impossible to carry alone. There simply is not enough time for her to do all that is necessary to meet the needs of a hearing-impaired child, as will be explained in detail in Chapter 21: "The Greatest Problem—Time." Since not all needs can be met, priorities must be established. Assumption of part of the load by father, siblings, other relatives, and friends is essential. The contributions of siblings, peers, baby-sitters, and others will be discussed in detail later. For now, it is important to remember the advisability of spreading the load as much as possible.

In the ideal situation, the hearing-impaired child with Cued Speech grows up in an environment in which members of the family develop a natural pattern of taking turns in communication and interaction with the hearing-impaired child. The roles of mother, father, and siblings expand to support everything that is essential to the child's growing perception of what is happening. Explanations of things that would not be noticed or understood are essential. Transliterating or summarizing (with Cued Speech) what others are saying is essential if the child is to have an opportunity to get full input. In many families this role comes naturally to a sibling who learns to cue. Parents should express appreciation and praise to make clear how important this help is to the child.

Fathers and/or siblings who do not learn to cue, and thus are unable to provide communication and support to the deaf child, often feel excluded, guilty, and resentful. This sometimes results in serious problems in family relationships, even to the point of breaking up the family.

The Need to Excel

Every child, deaf or hearing, needs to discover something at which he or she can excel, at least modestly. This is essential to self-esteem and is also a tremendous contributor to motivation in everything. Be alert to the interests of your deaf child and ready to support the development of any worthwhile activity or skill. The January 1991 issue of *Parents Magazine* has an article on how a child's play reveals basic things about him or her. The article classifies children as "organizers" or "dramatists" and describes how their play patterns differ according to their inclinations. Watching your child play, either alone or with others, may or may not tell you what that child will likely grow up to be, but it can reveal much about state of mind, frustrations, and needs.

Many deaf children show aptitude for drawing, arranging, sculpting, or arts and crafts. Parents must not look at these interests in terms of the probability that one of them will be a life pursuit, but should recognize them as instruments for development of skills and acquisition of confidence. A deaf child may very well benefit from interest in chess or checkers, or in semi-educational card games.

The following item illustrates how an aptitude discovered and developed can provide a central core of motivation and effort. A youngster who has the experience of excelling usually develops the desire to excel in whatever he or she does. This is the inevitable effect of excelling at something and applying similar standards to other interests and activities.

Matthew's Chance to Excel
by Kathy Goodall

Our son Matthew is 14. He became deaf at age 3½ after a serious illness (spinal meningitis). There are many things the doctor said Matthew would never be able to do, but with time and prayer Matthew's physical abilities and activities are not limited in any way.

We have observed over the years that individual sports have developed a lot of self-confidence in Matthew. He found a sport he truly loved when he found karate. It's a sport you can actively learn, and you can progress rapidly or slowly depending on how much time you are willing to practice. Even though you train as a group, each person is at a different skill level. Matthew has worked very hard and progressed rapidly. In his first year of competition he was a state champion and a regional champion. He went on to national competition and was fourth in the nation. Matthew enjoys competing even if it means performing in front of a thousand people. I think this all happened for several reasons. First, he found an activity he loved and was good at. Second, it took a degree of commitment from us as parents to go to every karate class and cue for him. Third, Matthew comes from a Christian home, and I feel God was using this sport to build his self-confidence and self-esteem. Not only has he learned how to compete with others, but he is comfortable performing in front of large groups.

Matthew Goodall

Matthew is currently helping to teach the beginners' class in karate. Teaching others has been a challenge for him, and he now enjoys it. At first he was worried that the students might not understand what he said to them, because his speech is very different from theirs, but he now knows that, with a lot of patience and some repetition, even very young children can understand him.

It can be very hard for deaf kids to make new friends, but I would like to encourage parents to believe that our children can overcome their fears and concerns about interacting with new people.

I've seen a great change in our Matthew in the last year. He has become more outgoing and more willing to interact with his peers. His 12-year-old sister, who has cued faithfully to him for six years, has been a great help. Just this summer we went on a Mexico mission trip for a week. I stood back and watched Matthew interact with a group of kids he had never met before, none of whom cued. He communicated as well with Spanish-speaking Mexicans as we did. None of us spoke much Spanish, but we managed to communicate well enough to help build small houses for them. Matthew found out he is able to read Spanish much better than the other children who went on the trip. I attribute this partly to the fact that he is an avid reader, but also to the fact that Cued Speech is a phonetic system.

Other sports Matthew is involved in are kayaking, soccer, and a little racketball. I hope you parents will encourage your deaf children to be bold and get involved in an activity they can enjoy, either a team sport or an individual sport. If you help them find the right one, it can do much more than keep them in good physical shape. It can help them develop socially and emotionally, too.

Mental Development of Your Child

Later chapters will give you suggestions on how to help your child acquire language, develop communication skills, acquire self-esteem and confidence, and progress in many other important ways. There is much you can do, in addition, to help your deaf child acquire specific mental skills that are needed in school and in life that are not specifically developed in school. Some of these are visualization, manipulation of mental images, efficient memorization, systematic thinking, anticipation, and creativity. Parents can do much to support the development of these mental abilities through the activities they use in the development of language. Some of them must wait until your child has acquired a good deal of language, can communicate well with you, and can play "pretend" games. Such activities are beneficial to young hearing children also. In Chapter 9, "Advanced Activities," are some specific activities that will help develop your child's ability to visualize, manipulate mental images, etc. When the child is older you can use activities for development of other mental skills. The reason many deaf children need attention in these areas is that most of them tend to experience a range of activities narrower than that available to hearing children.

In the Appendix are lists and descriptions of materials for guidance of parents, and materials to read or to use with their deaf children. At this point you will likely find particularly helpful the book *Choices in Deafness*, edited by Sue Schwartz. (See Appendix, p. 754).

Another Look at Methods

Your desire is to choose the method that will be best for your child, taking into account his/her abilities and your own, in your situation. The opinions of professionals in favor of one method or another may not be as meaningful to you as the actual experiences of other parents with similar problems.

An excellent way for you to learn what will be expected of you and what you can expect from each of the methods from which you can choose is to read the case histories in this book. You can read of the experiences of parents who started with aural/oral methods (Johndrows, p. 458; Nemeths, p. 467; Hightowers, p. 476). They can tell you what was expected of them, and what they were able to do. You can read about the experiences of parents (Maslins, p. 305; Branscomes, p. 353; Consacros, p. 480) who started out with TC. Others (McDonnels, p.

550; Engelmans, p. 362; Cottams, p. 356) used Cued Speech first with very young children. The Crosbys (p. 639) chose bilingualism from the start. The Lees (p. 222) and the Keblawi family (p. 316) used all three approaches, successively, before finding what was best. These parents tell you what worked and what didn't, what was hard and what was easy, and what they could and couldn't do.

Chapter Summary

The deaf child is first of all a child and should be treated essentially the same way as a hearing child. His or her relationships with members of the family are a major factor in success with whatever educational method is chosen.

Poor communication can contribute to domination of the home by a strong-willed deaf child. Parents must be sensitive to the types of behavior that can be caused by the sense of isolation so often associated with deafness.

Three principles are important to good discipline: 1) The child must understand what is expected of him/her; 2) The parents must be consistent in their expectations and requirements; 3) All family members must allow the expression of love to permeate every aspect of living.

The deaf child needs full access to information about what is happening, even relatively unimportant or seemingly irrelevant information. Parents should recognize that the usual aspects of affective development can be integrated with language development.

The relationship between mother and deaf child, in a majority of cases, is even more the foundation for all other relationships than in the case of the hearing child. Other family members must build on it. The father's role is vital, yet in practice it is often difficult to implement if the father does not develop communication skills. When the child's relationship and amount of communication with father and mother is well balanced, important benefits in self-esteem and emotional health result. When both parents are employed outside the home, it is essential that they share fully in meeting the needs of the deaf child.

The deaf child's behavior at play, alone or with others, can yield clues as to his or her basic needs and problems.

When the child's language capabilities permit it, development of important mental skills can be accelerated through appropriate "pretend" games and activities.

Through Cued Speech parents can provide the clear communication needed for a normal, supportive relationship with their deaf child.

Chapter 5
Getting Started

This chapter is a summary of ways to go about learning Cued Speech, how to master it, and various ideas on how to develop fluency. You may need to read it more than once. Mastering Cued Speech is not easy for everyone, but it is possible for almost anyone.

To learn the basics of Cued Speech requires up to a week or so of intensive work (three-to-six-hours a day). Development of skill sufficient for easy, natural communication takes months of actual use. Fluency comes from actual use in communication, not just from practice. Short (two-or-three-day) workshops are excellent, but must be followed by either practice with others or use of materials designed for self-instruction. The effort necessary to learn Cued Speech is more than justified by the satisfaction parents feel in their enormous contribution to their child's development and in their relief from the heartbreak associated with inability to communicate effectively with their child.

Osmond Crosby makes the following comparison:

> With cueing, you **quickly** learn to express **anything**, but at an extremely slow rate. With signs, you **quickly** learn to express a very **limited** set of ideas, at a reasonable speed. With cues, you add to the **rate** slowly, over a period of months. With signs, you add—slowly, over a period of years—to the **number of ideas** you can express.

One of the problems of educating deaf children is the fact that they are widely scattered. Since fewer than one-tenth of 1% of children have a hearing impairment that requires special education, it is only in the larger cities that enough deaf children are found to justify maintaining special, segregated classes for them. For the same reason, many parents do not have local access to instruction in the method or methods they choose to use. A great advantage of Cued Speech is that it can, if necessary, be learned and used in isolation. Chapter 22, "Going it Alone," relates the experiences of families that have had to do this. Not only have they had to learn Cued Speech virtually on their own: most of them have had to teach it to others, including teachers, transliterators, and other parents. An advantage in such situations is that children brought up on Cued Speech in the home typically qualify for mainstreaming after a few years of consistent exposure at home.

Methods of Learning Cued Speech

Several methods are available for learning Cued Speech: 1) attendance at a one-week Cued Speech workshop, or two three-day workshops, followed by self-instruction and practice with others; 2) extended sessions of individual face-to face instruction from a person who is already proficient; 3) self-instruction through use of audiocassette and videocassette lessons, preferably preceded by a workshop; and 4) self-instruction (after some face-to-face instruction) with manuals or other materials available at some service centers (see Appendix). In general, a combination of these methods is most desirable. It should be kept in mind that some of the videocassette lessons do not cover the system in sufficient depth and require additional instructional materials and/or face-to-face instruction.

Face-to-face instruction has several advantages: The instructor can adjust to your pace and problems to some extent, can demonstrate as needed, and can provide full explanation. However, fluency seems to come only from daily use, preferably with a deaf child. It is difficult to arrange for a sufficient number of hours of face-to-face instruction to achieve fluency, and the expense may be considerable unless you have a friend who is willing to provide the instruction without charge. Also, the quality of the instruction depends on the instructor. Those certified as Cued Speech Instructors by the National Cued Speech Association (NCSA) are experienced professional teachers who provide quality, standardized Cued Speech instruction. A distinction should be made between professional teachers of Cued Speech and professional teachers who use Cued Speech with hearing-impaired children. One should not depend entirely on a cueing friend, but should secure help also from professional teachers *of* Cued Speech, the audiocassette lessons, other approved materials, or attendance at a workshop.

The best way to get started (or to get a "boost" if you are already started) is to attend a weekend or full-week family Cued Speech workshop or program, or to enroll in an on-going sequence of classes at a Cued Speech service center listed in the Appendix. A one-week family program was scheduled each summer at Gallaudet University from 1978 through 1991. Attendance ranged from about 60 to nearly 350 individuals. This annual program has been replaced by regional family/professional programs, both week-end and full-week, to reduce the distances families must travel to attend. An example is the annual three-day family workshop at Camp Cheerio, North Carolina, which has continued since its beginning in 1985. The Cued Speech Center in Raleigh, N.C., offers regularly scheduled monthly classes and other workshops. Regional and state Cued Speech associations offer occasional weekend programs. For a list of organizations that regularly provide workshops, refer to the Appendix, pp. 751-752.

A great advantage of family workshops is that they provide the opportunity to get acquainted with other families, including those just beginning to learn Cued Speech and others who have used it for many years. Talking with them about the difficulties they had, the successes they have achieved, and how they worked things out is very helpful to beginning families. The opportunity to observe and communicate with children who have grown up with Cued Speech continues to be enjoyable and helpful, even to the "old-timers."

The typical family workshop offers classes for beginners, those with intermediate skills, and those who are more advanced. Classes for children are offered, and nursery services are provided. Featured professionals present lectures and discussions on subjects of interest to parents, with various types of entertainment for the children.

If you absolutely cannot attend a workshop or family program, try to arrange for several periods of face-to-face instruction. This will enable you to get questions answered and to actually see and experience the basics of cueing. After six-to-eight hours of face-to-face instruction you can probably (if determined) profit from self-instruction with audiocassette lessons, or from use of self-instructional manuals and materials of various kinds. Videocassette lessons designed for use by people who cannot arrange for adequate face-to-face instruction are available from the Cued Speech Team at Gallaudet University. Remember, though, that these videocassette lessons are designed to be used only in conjunction with the audiocassette lessons, not alone. This is because video lessons tend to "pull one through" everything, but not lead to mastery as one goes. Each of the Gallaudet video lessons is to be followed by practice on the same material in the corresponding audiocassette lesson. The audiocassette lessons may be used without the videocassette lessons by individuals who have had the necessary face-to-face instruction. Other instructional materials, including videotapes, are listed in the Appendix. Remember, though, that there is no adequate substitute for face-to-face instruction.

Memorizing the chart of the sounds to be paired with the cues (See Appendix, p. 774) is not a desirable way to learn, though many people have preferred to use the chart in conjunction with face-to-face instruction. It is important that the cues be associated with sounds, not letters. To fail to think the sounds (rather than letters) as you cue tends to delay fluency in most cases by necessitating conversion from letters to sounds in the process of cueing. Those who memorize the letters then have to struggle to keep sounds in their minds. If you practice with written material, remember to think (or preferably make) the sounds in each word or phrase just before you cue it.

While you are learning, it is a great advantage to have frequent contact (and practice, if possible) with several proficient cuers. If there is no opportunity for this, and you encounter difficulties, contact one of the sources of assistance listed in the Appendix. Attendance at periodic practice sessions or even social gatherings of parents is very helpful. You will find that the sharing of experiences with regard to both difficulties and successes adds to morale and motivation and furnishes useful information about how to deal with your child. By far the greatest boost to morale, of course, comes when the child begins to demonstrate understanding of what you say and cue. As soon as you can cue a useful word, cue that word every time you say it to your child.

Many short practice sessions are generally more effective than long sessions. This is true of practice with the audiocassette lessons, the practice sentences in the Appendix, or with other materials. Several 15-minute periods a day are excellent, and even shorter periods are still valuable. If both parents are available and can practice together, so much the better. Fathers may take longer to become fluent if they have less time for use of cues with the child. Fortunately, Cued Speech is a finite system: once a parent learns it, anything said to the deaf child can be cued.

Practice ideas can include almost anything available through vision or hearing: TV commercials, jingles, and other items you hear often; when reading, cue headlines, advertisements, or short paragraphs; in the car, use the audiocassette lessons, cue road signs, or cue slow songs with the radio. On trips, add cues to traditional car games, such as identifying and cueing each state name the first time it is seen on a license plate, or keeping track of (and cueing) how many cars are encountered from each state—Alabama, three!, Georgia, two!, Maryland 21!

The matter of which hand to use initially in cueing is optional. If you are right-handed, you may find it advantageous to be able to use the left hand for cueing. Thus, you will be able to keep the right hand free to do other things while talking, such as writing, pouring milk, etc. This alternative strategy of learning initially and achieving proficiency with only the less-dexterous hand makes it easy then to switch to the other hand as desired. Thus, with minimum effort one can becomes ambidextrous in cueing. This ability to cue with either hand is particularly advantageous when one will be cueing for prolonged periods of time, as when reading aloud, conversing extensively, or transliterating.

Many Cued Speech instructors now teach beginners to develop skill with each hand, and do so by having the learner practice with both hands at once. However, if a beginner is distracted by the effort of trying to cue with both hands, or by trying to shift, it may be best to concentrate on developing initial cueing skill with one hand.

Begin With Your Child Right Away

Once you begin learning, the best and most fruitful way to practice is by using Cued Speech with your child. It is essential that you begin using Cued Speech with your child while you are still learning it—long before you are fluent. In fact, it will likely take you much longer to become fluent if you do not begin using it with your child in the early stages of your learning. The response of your child provides the best kind of motivation to improve your cueing. Several parent reviewers point out that parents who choose to wait until they are fluent before beginning to cue much to their child never get fluent, and wind up not using it with their child. This is a tragedy, since such parents have already accomplished the hard part—getting to where they know the system and can cue anything they wish, although slowly. They need only to "jump in" and use it with their child. Fluency will come with use.

Remember that accuracy of cueing is much more important than speed; in fact, even hearing children learn language faster if they receive it at a deliberate rate. This is certainly true of a deaf child learning a new way of receiving language.

Make Lists

You may wish to make a list of 10-to-20 words, phrases, and short sentences you use (or want to use) frequently with your child. If you wish, you can learn to write the words in Funetik Speling (see Appendix) and indicate how to cue them by using Cuescript (also in the Appendix). As soon as you are well started on the fundamentals of Cued Speech, practice your word list over and over until you can cue all the words smoothly and comfortably. Then cue them every time you use them with your child. Of course, include the child's name, the names of others in the family, and simple words used every day. Add a few new words to the list every day.

A typical list of "starter" words, with the common cueing indicated, is given at the beginning of the Cuescript section in the Appendix, beginning on page 776. For assistance on other words, refer to the Cuescript Basic Vocabulary, pp. 781-805, consult a skilled cuer, or use the chart. If you refer to the chart, be sure to think the sounds, not the letters, before you cue them.

Begin to cue consistently all generative phrases such as: "Put on your ____. Get your ____. Where's your ____?" You can combine these with many words you can already cue. Practice many such phrases until they begin to be automatic.

Cue All The Words

As soon as you are able to cue words (even though slowly and with hesitation on some words), begin cueing groups of words, expressions, short sentences, and questions. Try to cue all the words in a phrase, so that your child will be exposed to the complete patterns of spoken English. If you fall into the habit of using sentences in which you may cue only one or two words, you are likely to make very little progress in cueing fluency. The deaf child needs to experience each and every element of the language, every little *a, and, the, in, off, with,* not just a word here and there. Cued Speech makes it possible for you to give your child complete language, so be sure you **use** and **cue** complete language. Only if you use complete language will your child have a chance to learn complete language instead of the fragmented language most deaf children acquire through perceiving only key words. This is why parents and teachers using Cued Speech need to reach the point, as early as possible, at which they can cue everything they want to say to their hearing-impaired children.

You should use language appropriate to the age and language development of your child, as you do with hearing children. But, as quickly as you can, get away from simplifying the language to avoid hard-to-cue words.

Slow is Beautiful!

At first, you will feel that you are cueing and speaking very slowly. Remember that the child is learning, too, and slow is beautiful to him/her. The child may need this slow rate for as much as six months or more, in order to be able to perceive each syllable. The more you cue, the faster and more fluent you will become. But don't try to cue fast—speed will come automatically. You and your child will be growing together—you in your ability to cue, your child in ability to receive and understand the spoken patterns. Be sure to learn, through face-to-face instruction or cassette lessons, how to cue consonant clusters correctly. Consonant clusters must not make your pronunciation unnatural (although it may be slow for a while).

An experienced teacher of cueing has said: "*Slow and accurate* will become *fast and accurate*, but *slow and sloppy* will become *fast and sloppy.*" Keep in mind your long-term goal of speed and accuracy, but accuracy must come first. Linda Balderson, mother of 18-year-old Tiffany, suggests an excellent way of understanding how cueing will become automatic in time:

> *Imagine a typewriter on which the keys represent sounds you can combine into syllables and words. You could easily memorize the locations of these in a short time. However, if you have ever learned to type you know the difference between learning the locations of a limited number of keys and becoming a fast, fluent typist.*

Think Sounds

Probably your most difficult problem in the early stages will be deciding which sounds you actually put in a word, or how you should pronounce words that can be pronounced two or more ways. Few people can readily identify the specific sounds they make. You must concentrate on listening to yourself to determine the exact sounds you use in many common words. You must train yourself to analyze the sounds that compose your own speech. Why? Because you should cue the way you actually speak.

To have to make a study of your own speech may seem onerous, but in a few months you will be amazed at your understanding of the details of common speech and your perception of speech sounds. This is certainly an asset to a parent of a child who has to learn or be taught to make all these sounds.

For example, do you pronounce *dog* as *dawg* or *dahg*? A few people actually say *doeg*. The word *one* is pronounced *wun*. Many people think they pronounce *lady* as *lay-dee* when they actually (as most people do) say *lay-di*. Each person should listen to himself, and follow the rule: Cue it the way you are saying it. This does not mean that you should always pronounce a word the same way. Sometimes you will say, carefully: "I don't want to." On another occasion you may say: "I doe wannuh." Won't this confuse the deaf child? *Don't underestimate your child!* With Cued Speech your deaf child can sort out, just as a hearing child does, the liberties we take with our language and the accents of different people from different parts of the country, or from other countries.

When Leah Henegar (the first child exposed to Cued Speech) was six years old, she was visited by Mrs. Winifred Tumim, from London, England. Mrs. Tumim had come to the United States to learn Cued Speech for the benefit of her two hearing-impaired children, the older of whom was also 6 years old. She had learned Cued Speech during the week and helped make recorded lessons with a British accent, to take back to England. Mrs. Tumim had no difficulty communicating with Leah. Although a bit shy at first, Leah warmed up quickly. A bit later, she looked at Mrs. Tumim and said: "You talk funny." There was no trouble with her understanding, but British pronunciations such as *cahn't, bahth, Muhthuh* sounded strange to her. What is important here is that, with Cued Speech, Leah reacted to a different accent in the same way a hearing child might react.

Do Not "Spell-Cue"

In deciding how to cue a word, be sure not to lean too much toward the spelling. This is a serious error, and one easy to make. Sometimes a beginner is tempted to cue *his* with an "s" at the end. *Think sounds!* It has been said facetiously that if the spelling of English had been designed to make life as difficult as possible for foreigners learning to read English and for deaf people, the designer could hardly have done better. At some point you should turn to the Appendix and learn about Funetik Speling, our easy system for writing words the way they sound. Doing so will probably amaze you at how far written English sometimes deviates from the spoken form (or vice versa). Witness these examples of British pronunciation: Worcestershire (Woostershur), Featherstone (Fanshaw), and Cholmondeley (Chumley).

If there is doubt or disagreement about how a word should be pronounced, refer to a good dictionary, but don't cue it as shown in the dictionary unless you are saying it that way at the time.

The 500 words in the Basic Vocabulary (Appendix, p. 781) are written in both Funetik Speling and Cuescript to show you exactly how to cue them (if you use the pronunciation indicated). In most cases the pronunciation given is according to the Merriam-Webster Dictionary, which is intended to follow General American pronunciation, but you should cue the way you speak. Also, the dictionaries don't all agree.

A hearing-impaired child needs to receive different pronunciations (in Cued Speech), so he or she can become familiar with the variations. This will make the child a better speechreader—unless, of course, he has occasion to lipread only a few people. More important, it will increase the child's insight into language. Sarina Roffé furnished this anecdote:

> *At age 7, Simon was being observed by visitors from Japan during a resource session with his teacher at Flower Valley School. The visitors were intrigued that Simon was arguing with his teacher over how to pronounce "interesting," from the three ways he had seen it cued. Cued Speech enabled him to analyze and internalize multiple pronunciations.*

From another parent: "Go easy on your spouse! Don't get hung up on correcting each other, either on cueing details or on what each thinks he says. It can get to be as pointless as bridge arguments!"

Auditory Conceptualization

According to Patricia and Charles Lindamood (1969), co-authors of the Lindamood Auditory Conceptialization Test (L.A.T.), about 10% of normally hearing people have difficulty with *auditory conceptualization*, the identification of specific speech sounds. In hearing children this often causes difficulties in the early stages of reading, especially in learning or applying phonics. Persons who have trouble learning Cued Speech because of this problem typically experience difficulty in identifying the short vowels, as in the words *bit, bet, but, bat*. They have no problems in recognizing the words, or in saying them, but only in deciding what the sounds in them (usually the vowels) are. The Lindamoods are also co-authors of an elaborate program titled *The A.D.D. Program: Auditory Discrimination in Depth*. It is designed for preventive, developmental, and remedial use with hearing children and others "who need to improve auditory conceptualization skills in order to read and spell accurately."

In instructing hearing people, teachers can usually resolve the problem of deficient auditory conceptualization sufficiently for learning Cued Speech in an hour or less of practice in "word-shaving." One can direct the learner to practice saying the word *pit*, then saying it without the *t*, as *pi*, then without the *p*, as *it*. Finally, he or she can think of saying *pi* without the *p*, and say *i* alone. He/she has "shaved" the word to *i* and can say *i* in isolation. A reasonable amount of directed practice at this activity, followed by cueing of many words containing the short vowels, will usually bring the problem to an end. In workshops I (*Cornett*) often spot the learners who have trouble with auditory conceptualization and take them out for 30 minutes of "word-shaving" while someone else practices with the class. Then, we usually return to the class with the problem solved.

Most people initially have trouble deciding whether some words ending in *y* end with the short *i* sound or the long *ee* sound. Actually, no one is really consistent on this. If I call my son, saying "Bobby!" it is natural to lengthen the final sound and make it an *ee*, because it is stressed and lengthened. But, in normal conversation: "Where did Bobby go?" the final sound in the name will be the short *i*, as in *it* or *city*. Generally, when the sound of final *y* is stressed it will tend to be *ee*, and when unstressed, *i*. You can solve this problem by listening to yourself and deciding what you actually say. Most of us do not become aware of how we actually talk until we learn Cued Speech.

A good policy to follow is to cue the way you think you speak, and let it go at that. If you are uncertain, look up the word in the dictionary, but remember that most people are not always consistent with the dictionary, especially in informal conversation. No great harm will result if you pronounce an occasional word wrong, or cue it wrong. Hearing children tend to pick up their parents' accents. Cueing parents make it possible for their deaf children to sound like them.

There is Strength in Numbers

You will find that practicing with other learners, including both beginners and more advanced cuers, will help tremendously. The benefits include increased motivation, escape from the "aloneness" of the parent who feels the weight of the world on her/his shoulders, the opportunity to share information on progress and discuss difficulties, and the sense of oneness with others who share your problems. Even one other person with whom you can practice regularly can make a great difference in the level of your morale and your motivation.

A fascinating dividend is discovery of the variety and idiosyncracies of the ideolects (individual, unique dialects) of others and yourself. Learning Cued Speech will probably make you aware of how you speak—to a degree of which you never before conceived. Sharing this with others is one of the most enjoyable aspects of practicing together.

Some Practical Tips

Take any opportunity for a few minutes of practice at cueing. Cue anything—words or thoughts that come to mind, a few lines of an item in the newspaper, a brief passage in a book you are reading, something said on television. Don't overlook the opportunity to cue when driving, especially when you make the same trip regularly and your driving can be almost automatic. Cue slow songs or other materials heard on the radio. Such regular trips are also great for practicing with audiocassette lessons and practice materials. Speak aloud when cueing, as much as you can, but remember that silent practice is helpful also if you think all the sounds as you cue. Even practice that is completely mental is helpful if you both "cue" and "speak" in your mind.

It is important to spend some practice time in front of a mirror to pick up any errors or sloppy movements and to make sure that your lip movements are natural and adequate, but not exaggerated. Your lip movements should show the differences among the vowels in a single group: open, flat-relaxed, and rounded. Proper lip movements are important because many basic words are cued identically. Examples are: *eat-meet-feet; yes-chair; sit-sat; show-low.*

Watching yourself in a large mirror as you cue will help prepare you to read your child's expressive cueing. So will silent practice with another cueing person. Some Cued Speech instructors divide instructional time between teaching cueing and reception when they are teaching parents.

Sarina Roffé suggests cueing when waiting—in the dentist's office or anywhere—if you aren't too sensitive about attracting other people's attention. Of course, this kind of practice is likely to lead to a conversation!

If you will practice with both hands simultaneously, you will develop the ability to cue with either hand alone. One hand seems to "learn" from the other. There are many situations in which the ability to cue with either hand is valuable, making it unnecessary to move an object from one hand to the other in order to cue, or having to hold the telephone to the "wrong" ear.

While you are learning Cued Speech, you may find it advantageous to use the "primer" in the Appendix. The material is designed to be directly helpful to parents in cueing the language they may normally use with a young child. This primer was developed when it was discovered that a good way to practice is to cue books written on a beginning reading level. Any elementary and repetitious material is useful for practice. Cueing as you read to your deaf child develops your fluency, expands the child's language, and prepares for reading.

Learning and using Cued Speech are simplest for the parents of young children who are just beginning to learn language. Parents and child can progress together. The parents' gradual progression to more complex language should proceed in keeping with the child's expanding understanding.

Progress to Phrases and Sentences

In the beginning, cue single words with which you feel at ease, but cue them within natural, complete phrases or sentences. You can begin by cueing only *hat* in this sentence: "Get your *hat*." After some practice you will be able to cue: "*Get* your *hat*." Eventually you will have no difficulty in cueing: "*Susie, please get your hat right now!*" Before long you will be able to cue everything you say to your child, by speaking and cueing slowly, but preserve the natural rhythm as much as possible. Do not allow the effort of cueing to reduce how much you talk to your child. Just use a bit more time. And, as soon as possible, resolve to cue every word you say to your child.

After two months or so, you should be cueing many complete phrases or short sentences, with the ability to cue any word if you have time to stop and think about how to do it. Keep in mind the fact that any suggestion as to how long it will take to achieve a particular goal or to reach a certain level is made only to give a general idea. You may reach the goal a lot sooner. It may take you longer if you do not have much time for practice. Your child may not initially be very receptive, or there may be other inhibiting factors.

Our suggestion that in the beginning it is acceptable to cue a word here and there, as you can, applies only to the very early stages of using Cued Speech. Within two months you should decide to cue every word you say to your child. Parents who yield to the temptation to continue cueing a word here and there will never cue well, and their children will not be exposed to (or learn) full, complete language.

Practice cueing as often as possible. But, don't worry about lack of sufficient time for extended periods of practice. A few minutes here and there will be just as valuable as longer periods if you can work in enough practice periods. Many parents manage to do a little practice whenever they have even a minute—when waiting, when taking a break from a tiring task, or when shifting from one task to another. Sustained motivation is the key to making progress.

Sarina Roffé offers these suggestions:

> *Commit to cueing at all meals, anywhere. Make short lists of phrases you use, no more than six-to-10 per list, and make 20 copies. Put them everywhere. Start with mealtime phrases, bedtime phrases and sentences, discipline (the six things you forbid or discourage most frequently), bathing, getting dressed.*

In all kinds of learning there tend to be plateaus—periods when progress seems to be almost at a standstill. A plateau is a temporary phase, and the best antidotes are patience and perseverance. Almost always after a plateau, there is a sudden apparent burst of improvement. A typical experience is to cue something and suddenly realize: *I cued that without even thinking!*

An encouraging thing to remember when things are not going well is that after a year of using Cued Speech you will likely be communicating automatically with it most of the time. Time will fly!

Teri Poore, who started with Michael when he was 3, furnished this helpful description of their progress:

> *Everyone stresses that CS is so easy and can be learned so quickly that people think complete success will come quickly, too. Three months was the critical time for our family. That's when Michael began to watch longer than it took for me to cue one word, and he started cueing back. After six months he asked more questions and understood the answers so he could ask additional questions. After one year we reached the point where we asked him not to talk so much and not to ask so many questions! Now, seven years later, he is so normal in conversing with people in general it's easy to forget he's deaf until there's something he can't lipread.*

Chapter Summary

Several methods are available for learning Cued Speech: 1) two-day, three-day, and week-long workshops, which are desirable, not only for learning, but for motivation and encouragement, 2) other opportunities for face-to-face instruction from a qualified person, 3) self-instruction through videotape and audiotape lessons, and 4) self-instruction through written materials (after face-to-face instruction).

Do not memorize the Cued Speech chart, even if a propensity for visual learning leads you to use it a good bit. Memorizing it may support any tendency to think letters instead of sounds. Learn to associate the sounds (not the letters) with the cues.

Have as much contact and practice as possible with other cuers. Most are willing to help because they are grateful for the help others gave them.

As soon as possible, start cueing to your deaf child—single words and short phrases—as you can. Progress as soon as possible to cueing almost everything you say to the child, even though you are slow. To cue slowly is desirable for the child, who is developing skill in decoding Cued Speech.

Despite any early difficulty in deciding what sounds you use in each word, try always to cue the way you are speaking at that moment—formally or informally, run together or with words separated, slang, or whatever. Don't cue words the way they are spelled when you know you aren't saying them that way.

Practicing while watching yourself in a mirror is very helpful, as is also practice with another person. Practicing with both hands at once will help you become able to use either hand.

Accuracy is much more important than speed; in fact, cueing slowly for several months will enable your deaf child to learn language more rapidly.

This chapter is itself a summary of ways to learn Cued Speech and how to develop proficiency. If you are just starting to learn Cued Speech, be sure to read this chapter again, carefully.

Chapter 6
Initiating Communication

This chapter deals with techniques most useful with young deaf children who know little verbal language. Included are young children just beginning to communicate, and older children with whom other methods have been used without much progress in verbal language. Techniques for use with older children who already have a good bit of verbal language are presented in Chapter 17, "Starting With An Older Deaf Child."

In Chapter 18, *Starting with a Very Young Child*, is an article by Marylou Barwell, teacher of deaf children in the Montgomery County Maryland Public Schools and a long-time Cued Speech teacher and consultant for various school systems. Entitled "There's More to Cued Speech Than Cueing," it contains a wealth of information on initiating communication with very young deaf children. Those who are now starting to use CS with children under 3½ years old should read Ms. Barwell's article, or all of Chapter 18, before reading this chapter.

Some parents assume they should use "lessons" in introducing Cued Speech to their deaf child. On the contrary, Cued Speech should not be specifically "taught" to young deaf children. They learn to understand it most naturally and easily by being exposed to it in association with specific objects, concepts, or experiences, just as a hearing child learns language. Every child is different, and children learn at different rates. Every family situation is different. In some cases the introduction of Cued Speech will be nearly effortless; in more cases it will mean lots of hard work, at least for a year or so.

Start With What The Child Knows

One way to start is to list all the words (if any) and gestures (or signs) your deaf child knows. Each word, gesture, or sign your child understands is important and useful, because you can teach him/her the Cued Speech equivalent of each very quickly by pairing it with the Cued Speech presentation. You may be surprised at the number of gestures you use with your child. One mother who came to learn Cued Speech was asked to estimate how many gestures she used, and she guessed that the number was 25 or 30. Then, she proceeded to write down 225, with increasing amazement as she continued. This mother thought her child was a good lipreader. When she returned home, she tried to communicate with her child with her hands behind her, and reported that her daughter could lipread very little.

Each gesture or formal sign the child already understands is important, since it identifies a familiar concept the child has. You can teach the Cued Speech equivalents of all the gestures (or signs) very rapidly. Just learn to cue the equivalent words or phrases, and cue and say them just ahead of the gestures. For example, cue and say *come* and follow it with the gesture, but only on occasions when you actually want the child to come. After this has happened several times, over a period of a day or so, delay the gesture a bit to see if the child will respond to the spoken-and-cued command without the gesture. If he or she does, stop using the gesture except when the child fails to respond to the verbal message. Use this procedure to replace with verbal communication all the gestures the child knows. Praise him/her for every success, even tiny ones.

After you have replaced all the gestures and/or signs with cueing, and the child understands the cueing, use natural gestures only in situations in which you are introducing new language and the context may not be sufficient for the child to get the meaning without a gesture or "prop." This is exactly the way natural gestures are used with hearing children. Be sure to phase out the formal gestures or signs.

Our recommendation that hearing parents should use neither gestures nor formal signs systematically should not be construed as being in opposition to signing. As you will see later, we recommend that most deaf children eventually learn American Sign Language, but not from hearing parents. Few hearing parents can become qualified as ASL models for a deaf child. Also, all the parents' available time is needed for development of verbal language through Cued Speech and the other things their child needs from them. Methods of helping a deaf child become bilingual will be discussed in detail in Chapter 23.

Watch for Attention

Engaging a deaf child's attention is an almost universal problem for hearing parents and teachers in initiating communication. You must have the full attention of the child, and eye contact with him/her, in order to communicate usefully. Only when children begin to realize that by watching a person's face they can experience meaningful communication will they watch consistently. The parents of a young child with little real communication experience may find that engaging the child's attention may be a very frustrating problem for a while.

Seize any opportunity to communicate. Whenever the child glances at you, be ready to say and cue something short and simple that relates specifically to something at hand. This can be either what he or she has just been looking at, or something to which you can direct his/her attention immediately. Typical examples are: "That's a ball." "That's a car." "You have a kitten." Use a sentence like the last one only if the child is holding the kitten and you can point to it.

Your child may look away while you are cueing, or at first may even close his or her eyes to discourage you from cueing. This is a common response of children before they begin to realize that they can get meaning from the cueing. Watch for what your child is interested in, and cue it when you tell what it is. Don't forget that it is better to say and cue "That's a ...." than to simply cue the name of the object to which you direct the child's attention, except in the very beginning stages of communication. If the child looks away in the middle of your phrase or sentence, don't stop. Instead, go ahead and finish it. This is to keep your cueing progress from being disrupted. Osmond Crosby put it this way:

> *We got hung up on having our child see what we cued. We broke it up, invited her to look, etc. To increase the fluency of your cueing, it's important to plow on through, whether the child continues to look or not. Then, repeat when the child looks again. As cueing gets easier, you can begin to use all the techniques of visual contact that work with a deaf child.*

Your best early opportunities to communicate are created by what the child wants at the moment. Suppose a favorite toy is on a shelf, out of reach of the child. The child is tugging at you and pointing, begging for the toy. Say and cue, "Yes, you want your doggie. Okay, here's your doggie." Try to do your cueing and speaking when the child is looking at your face. You may wish to clear or construct a high shelf for the express purpose of creating such language-learning situations.

The child's desire for something in the refrigerator is another opportunity on which you can usually capitalize, especially if it cannot be opened by a child. It is always advantageous to introduce language in connection with what the child is interested in, or what he/she wants. The next level of advantage is associated with things that have to be done every day, such as eating, bathing, dressing, brushing teeth, etc. The third level is choosing things which arouse the child's interest.

Grab any amount of attention the child will give you. Soon he or she will realize that watching your face and hand is worthwhile because it supports understanding. Then language and communication will come rapidly. An exhilarating experience for you may occur when your child suddenly realizes that everything has a name. He/she may grasp your hand and steer you to object after object, pointing to each one and then looking at you so that you will say and cue its name. In this situation the child often gets very excited, captivated by the idea that has burst upon him/her. You will be just as excited, because you will know that language will increase rapidly from then on. Of course, many children acquire name awareness more gradually and react less spectacularly.

The Child Who Looks Away

Some parents complain that their child looks away before they finish a sentence. This can happen before the child has learned that what the parent is doing is communicating. In this case the parent must continue using the techniques recommended in this chapter. When the child begins to pick up information, he or she will watch better.

Another problem of "looking away" may occur after the child has learned to understand well at the single-word or short-sentence level. There are two possible causes. One is particularly likely in a child who has developed some ability at lipreading before being exposed to Cued Speech. Such a child is accustomed to picking up only a general idea of what is meant from key words. With the added clarity of meaning conveyed through Cued Speech he is likely to decide what is being said before the parent is finished. The other possibility is that the child is not interested because he/she is understanding nothing.

We have two suggestions for remedying the first situation. One, as an alternative to the earlier suggestion that you not stop if the child looks away, is to stop when this happens, and continue at exactly the same place (no repetition!) when he or she looks back. Your child will soon realize that there was more to the message. Second, try to phrase the sentence so that the important word or idea is near the end. Don't say: "Tomorrow we will go on a picnic if it doesn't rain." This invites the child to begin celebrating after the word *picnic*. Instead, say: "If it doesn't rain tomorrow, we will go on a picnic." Here the child must watch to the end to get the important idea.

Be sure you do not actually invite the child to look away. For example, if you say, "Look at the dog. He's yellow," you have actually instructed the child to look away before you finish your statement. Instead, say, "Look at the yellow dog."

The transition from single words and very short sentences to complete and longer sentences can be supported by repeating the key word or phrase. For example, you can say, "See the bunny in the cage—in the cage." The word *see* is not as strong an invitation to turn away as the word *look*. Also, the repetition of the phrase *in the cage* will help the child learn the word *cage*, if it is a new word.

Give the child enough time to do what you ask. If you have told him/her to look at something, wait until he/she is satisfied, then say something else. Wait for the child to turn back to you.

Once the child realizes that language can carry much more explicit and complex meaning than she or he has been able to get through lipreading, the problem of failing to watch the speaker throughout a complete sentence will disappear. Rarely is slow cueing by the parent a major factor. Children who have been using Cued Speech for several years and can understand it at rapid speaking rates tend to be quite patient with adults who are still cueing slowly. Furthermore, children learn language faster when it is presented to them slowly. New language, and new connotations of already familiar words, will not be picked up as rapidly unless the rate of presentation is sufficiently deliberate for the child to decode fully and easily.

The Situation Must Convey the Meaning

It is not enough to cue everything you say to a young child and expect him/her to learn language efficiently. A young hearing child cannot learn language solely by receiving language unrelated to things around him/her. If a young hearing baby were placed in a room in which a radio played during all his waking hours, he would never learn any language unless the persons who took care of him communicated with him about the things around him. He might recite phrases heard over and over, but he would understand nothing and learn nothing. The learning of language cannot begin until the language received can be associated directly with objects, actions, and ideas.

You must use association and repetition in communicating with your child. *Show* your child what you are talking about. Point, gesture, use a picture, or act out what you mean. Point to a picture of a boy jumping, and then, when the deaf child looks at you, say and cue: "Jumping. Billy is jumping." Then, immediately, you should jump and cue and say: "I am jumping." Repeat anything you say and cue, and repeat the identification given by pointing to or picking up the object to which you are referring.

Try to make several varied, related statements about the same object: "Put on your *shoe*." "Let's tie your *shoe*." "Your *shoe* is on your foot." "Here's your other *shoe*."

In the initial stages of learning language the child must see and understand what you are talking about in order to learn new language. Later comes learning language from language. After children know a lot of language they can learn much new language from the verbal context, without having to get the meaning entirely from the situation. However, situational information will always help with new language.

Use Appropriate Games

When beginning the use of Cued Speech with a child unaccustomed to clear communication, you may need to devise special ways to attract his or her attention. One way to do this is to play little games in which a few words are repeated many times. These games help provide practice in cueing for all members of the family. They also enhance the child's sense of family if all members participate. Finally, this participation helps family members acquire a sense of responsibility for participation in the provision of benefits to the child. More activities and games are given in Chapter 10. Examples of simple games you can use or devise follow:

"Come and Go"
Have all members of the family sit on the floor in a semicircle. One parent sits in front and invites each person in turn to come to him/her. Just say and cue: "Come, Mary" or "Come, John." As each person responds to his or her name, the hearing-impaired child begins to realize that the initial word *come* is what makes each person move forward and that the second element is different in each case. Soon, he or she will begin to associate each person with the name to which that person responds. A great display of approval should be made when each person responds properly. In this game deaf children often find it difficult to wait their turn; they will be anxious to play, too. And, when it is his/her turn, the fact that the parent in control looks at him or her will help the child identify his or her turn. As the child catches on to this game, variations can be added to it. Both parents (or one parent and an older sibling) can sit in front. One gives the instructions, "Come to Mommy, John" or "Come to Daddy, Mary." This adds another concept that can be easily learned. When the child is ready, it may be a good idea to let him/her be the leader.

"Favorite Things"

An important word for the child to learn is *where* (where is, where's, where are, where're). This word provides patterns for adding many other words to a deaf child's vocabulary. Hold a toy near your face and repeat (cue and say) its name several times, when the child looks at you. Be sure the child sees your face when he/she looks at the toy. After you have repeated the name several times let the child have the toy. Then, later in the day, repeat the procedure and then say and cue:"Where's the _____?" Turn up your hands and shake your head back and forth in the familiar "Where is it?" gesture. If the child doesn't understand and show you the toy, or look for it, repeat the entire procedure. It may be necessary to try this for several days before the child succeeds. When the child understands the names of the members of the family and the names of the objects, use them together (e.g., Where are Joe's shoes? Where's Sally's doll? Where're the dogs?). Be sure to use both "Where are?" and "Where're?" Remember that where're is pronounced and cued *wheh-rur*, which is cued 4 chin, 3 mouth. Of course, the most frequent use is: "Where's the _____?" For a primer of short sentences, refer to the Appendix, p. 806.

"People and Things"

You can make games of many routine activities. For example, have the deaf child help you set the table. Identify a plate and say and cue: "Give Daddy a plate." "Give Mommy a plate." "Give Billy a plate." Then proceed to knives, forks and spoons, napkins, glasses, etc.—as long as the child remains interested. This is a good activity, because it combines repetition with variation in both names and objects.

Young children often take great delight in matching members of their family with the items that belong to them. You can initiate this by pointing out items, such as toys scattered on the floor, first saying what belongs to whom, and then asking the child. You can set the stage for a more formal "game" by bringing out a basket of clean laundry to fold. Seat family members and have the child match the items to the persons, showing approval with: "Yes, that's daddy's sock." "Yes, those are Billy's underpants." Other items that can be used are stacks of books, toys, etc. This activity can by repeated many times, with variations, providing an enjoyable way for your child to learn names and relationships.

From Teri Poore: "We made an album of polaroid pictures for Michael to look at anytime to help him remember family members and friends we didn't see often. We also used these to help him learn 'Who?' 'Where?' 'When?' 'What?' and 'Why?'" Other parents mention using photographs made on trips or at family gatherings.

"This is Me"

Many children enjoy looking in a mirror and talking about eyes, ears, nose, legs, arms, etc. You may need to use the question: "What's that?" Also, confirm with: "Yes, that's your arm." "I see your eyes." Ask "Where's your nose?" "Where's Mommy's nose?"

"Talking Back"

Take advantage of the child's own spontaneous utterances and immediately reinforce them with vocal repetition, with cues. Before your child speaks words, babble with him/her—bububu, lah-lah-lah, da-da-da. Try to imitate and cue the natural voice sounds the child makes. Also, take advantage of situations in which spontaneous utterances are habitual with hearing persons. Thus, if the child hurts a finger, imitate him/her and say and cue "Ouch!" or "Ow!"

"The Animal Says"

Animal sounds can be a source of great fun for all and an incentive to vocalization. Realistic pictures of animals, or life-like stuffed toys can be pointed at or played with in ways that stimulate vocalization. Introduce one at a time and keep the activity at the fun level. Say: "The dog says: 'Arf! Arf! Arf!'" Have the child attempt to imitate the sounds. Bark when the child sees a real dog or when you show him/her a picture of a dog. Add other animal sounds, such as: *bow-wow, moo, baa, meow, oink,* in appropriate situations. Older children will enjoy learning that people imitate animals differently in different countries. For example, in most European countries dogs supposedly say: "Wah! Wah!" instead of "Arf! Arf!" or "Bow-Wow."

"Places"

When your child accompanies you to the supermarket, immediately on returning home (if possible) capitalize on the language opportunity. Have the child help you put the items away, and *cue everything*. Cue the name of each item, and where you are putting it. Don't shy away from big words (refrigerator). Your child will, in many cases, learn these faster than short words—if you cue them consistently. Make use of everywhere the child goes with you—to a place of worship, to the drug store, to the gas station, etc. After the child is understanding well, make photos of the supermarket, drug store, etc., and use them to prepare for the visits, discussing what is on the list of things to be purchased. This will lay a foundation for the concept of future tense. Then, at the supermarket, have the child help you find the various items.

Other Games and Activities

Most of the little games and activities that parents use with their hearing children are beneficial to their hearing-impaired youngsters as well. Play peek-a-boo anytime, but always cue "peek-a-boo" when you say it. The simple form "boo" can be used at first. The important thing is to make the use of Cued Speech enjoyable to the child. Refer to chapters 8, 9, and 10 for additional ideas.

The Key is Meaning

Most young hearing-impaired children respond almost immediately to cueing when it is first introduced, because the novelty of seeing the hand moving near the face attracts attention. But, there is a danger in this novelty. Unless the child begins very quickly to perceive *meaning* in connection with the cueing (and speaking), as the novelty wears off the child may dismiss cueing as unimportant, and no longer pay attention. For this reason, it is essential that the child *understand*.

Occasionally, but not often, there will be a child who is very slow to understand that first word through Cued Speech. We cannot overemphasize the importance of trying different techniques to enable the child to associate what you are saying with what it refers to. One parent reviewer indicated that her 2½-year-old son required three months of cueing *shoe* before he (for the first time) associated the message with the object. This suggests that perhaps not enough stress was placed on *association* by using two objects, as explained below.

An easy way to increase the probability that children will attach meaning to their early encounters with Cued Speech is to use two or three of their favorite toys or objects in the following way. Be sure they are objects that have real significance to the child. For example, if one is a ball, the child should have already experienced many times the fun of playing with a ball, of rolling it, of having it rolled to him, of seeing it bounce, so that all the qualities of "ballness" are within the child's experience, although he or she has no word or sign for it.

Place two such familiar objects in front of the child. Point to the ball, pick it up, put it down, then move it near your mouth, and then say and (with the other hand) cue "Ball." Next, put the ball down, point to it and again say and cue "Ball," when the child looks back to your face. Then, pick up the other object (perhaps a doll), place it near your mouth and say and cue "Doll" or "Dollie." Then immediately put the doll down, point to it and say and cue "Doll" as soon as the child looks at your face again. Repeat the process several times, alternating between the two objects. Then, without picking up or pointing to an item, cue and say the name of one and see if the child will show that he/she knows which you said. You may wish to cue "Which?" and look back and forth between the two objects. Soon, you can dispense with picking up the object and holding it near your face; just point to it, then to your mouth, and then say and cue its verbal symbol. If the child has difficulty in perceiving the difference in the two inputs, start with two objects whose names are more contrastive (*ball* and *airplane*).

After the child can identify reliably which of two objects you designate, use three objects, being careful to go through the process of identifying each in succession, by both pointing and cueing, before asking the child to identify one of them.

A good book about toys and their use in developing communication skills is *The Language of Toys: Teaching Communication Skills to Special Needs Children,* by Sue Schwartz, Ph.D., and Joan E. Heller Miller, M. (eds.). (1988). Details are in the Appendix, p. 764.

Praise the Child

Every parent of a hearing-impaired child should endeavor to become as skillful as possible at the systematic use of approval, enthusiasm, affection, and praise to sustain motivation and a feeling of success in the child. *Applaud* your child's success. Handle failure with patience, and attempt to turn the experience into success by immediately assigning an easier task, preferably related to the one on which the child failed initially.

The Place of Faith

"Now faith is the substance of things hoped for,
the evidence of things not seen." (Hebrews 11: 1)

Few things in life require as much exercise of faith as raising a deaf child. The parents who accomplish most toward meeting their child's needs are those who decide which way to go and believe that they are doing what is best. Unfortunately, the method they choose may not be right for their child, and a long period of disappointment and limited progress may ensue before they become sure they should change to a different approach.

Even while pursuing the wrong method, if the parents are not convinced that they are doing right they are not likely to exert enough effort to prove to themselves that a change is necessary. So, faith has its benefits even when it is misplaced.

Where does faith come from? It begins with hope, not certainty, just hope. Taking action based on that hope must bring successive bits of evidence that will gradually transform hope into faith, which is hope plus a measure of belief. If results are slow in appearing, hope is taxed or even dissipated. If there is steady and accelerating progress, faith is transformed into confidence, certainty, and ultimately pride in the child's accomplishments.

Would that there were some way to spare parents the fear that the best decision they are capable of making will turn out to be the wrong one. Would that there were some way to spare them the confusion caused by conflicting opinions of well-meaning professionals. The case histories written by parents for this book should be reassuring to parents in the early stages of fear and indecision. They relate the experiences of many parents who struggled with fear and indecision, parents who were led in wrong directions, but who finally found the path that was right for their child. Not only that, but the stories all have common threads of faith, satisfaction, and pride. Yes, it takes faith, but faith is ultimately rewarded.

Parents should not choose an educational path for their deaf child simply on hope, or on acceptance of the opinions of others. They should use all the information they can get, sort out what makes sense to them and what doesn't, and choose a way to *start*. They should give their best to the path they choose to try, but all along the way they should look for evidence, positive and negative. They should study, learn, question, and test. They should let hope grow into faith only through the accumulation of evidence that what is happening is right for their child.

When a deaf child is born into a hearing family, every member of that family is damaged, at least initially and/or potentially. The deaf child himself is damaged by his deafness, as are his siblings and parents. Often the family is torn apart, disillusioned, and even ashamed. But that scenario need not endure. If the family searches for and finds a way to cope with the problems of deafness, and if they see the child progressing as a result of their efforts, then despair turns to hope, and hope to faith and expectation. Indeed, the presence of a deaf child in the family can become a blessing, not a burden. Every member of the family can become a better, stronger, and happier person by finding within depths of patience, caring, and helping he/she would otherwise never have experienced. Typically, the CS parents we know are intensely proud of their deaf children, because each child is living evidence of what the parents have accomplished through faith and love.

The Most Important Ideas

The most important ideas to keep in mind in initiating communication with your deaf child are:

1) Cue consistently—once you can cue it, *always* cue it.

2) Begin cueing everything you say to the child.

3) Reinforce the child's spontaneous vocalizations by identifying them with Cued Speech.

4) Associate what you say with what it means—through gestures, props, pointing. With Cued Speech, deaf children can see *what* you are saying; let them also see what you are talking *about*.

5) Devise games and activities that are enjoyable and which, at the same time, lead to communication and language development.

6) Demonstrate to make it easy for the child to know what you are talking about. One can talk about a ball. A child needs to be shown a ball and told, "Ball! This is a ball," thus attaching a label to it. Also, the concept (of a ball) needs to be expanded. If the ball is bounced, rolled, and thrown, the child's idea of the word *ball* is broadened.

Chapter Summary

1) Let your child learn language through natural communication in the home, in Cued Speech.

2) Make use of each occasion when you have the child's attention.

3) Make sure that the child has enough situational information to associate everything you say with what it means.

4) Use members of the family to associate names, actions, objects with the language that is used, as in the "Come and Go" game.

5) Make extensive use of props to identify concepts you express.

6) Talk to the child about what he/she is interested in, or what you can direct attention to.

7) Develop the habit of consistent use of approval, enthusiasm, affection, and other techniques of support and motivation.

8) Remember that some children are slow in getting started.

9) Have faith in your child and in yourself.

Chapter 7
What to Expect

Remember that your child will progress unevenly. He/she will encounter plateaus followed by spurts of progress. Moreover, even steady progress will give an impression of unevenness because of the inability of educators and parents to observe and evaluate everything.

Imagine yourself in a situation in which you are surrounded by people using an exotic language completely unknown to you. You would learn very little of the language if the people spoke to you as they usually did to each other. You might pick up their words for *yes* and *no* by noticing which word they said along with an affirmative nod of the head, and which word was accompanied by a negative shake of the head. You might identify a few other words from the gestures that accompanied them. But, you would be able to learn very little unless someone helped you.

In order to make any real progress, you would have to ask people to speak to you very slowly, point to objects, illustrate actions, separate the identification of objects and actions, and give you time to grasp the appropriate verbal labels for objects and actions. You would try over and over again to make the sounds and put them together like everyone else. Often the natives would not understand you, and you would understand almost nothing of what they said unless they adapted to your needs. Certainly you would require numerous repetitions and much gesturing and illustrating in order to master many of the words and grammatical forms.

Slow Down and Show

What is true in the above situation is true in the case of any young child—hearing or deaf—just coming into contact with language. Someone who knows the language must slow down in speaking and also take time to show the child objects, demonstrate actions, name objects and actions, and willingly repeat everything. That someone must also help sustain motivation and confidence in the child by providing praise and encouragement. Remember that a very young child does not even know what language is, and has no internalized connection between concepts and symbols. Thus, it is much more difficult for him or her to make a connection between an idea and a symbol than for the person who already knows another language.

There is a long period in a hearing baby's early development when he or she just absorbs bits of what is occurring and being said around him/her, not yet directly associating specific symbols with specific ideas. Psychologists tell us that some of a baby's earliest impressions are the tone and expressiveness of the mother's voice, her face, and her movements. As increasing successive impressions build up, being passively accumulated in the baby's mind, he or she begins to respond to others. Most babies' waking hours are devoted to discovery; they quietly watch and listen until they begin to develop physical abilities that enable them to begin to explore the universe around them, the world of touch-feel and look-see. At that point their discovery rate increases rapidly.

After they begin responding to movements of others, to objects presented to them, and to the objects they explore, they still continue the process of absorbing the sounds around them. They begin to associate the sounds with some of the things and happenings around them. Hearing infants listen to us for many months before expressing themselves in a simple language based on our own. A hearing child (or a deaf child of deaf parents) ordinarily enters the expressive stage of communication development at between 1 and 2 years of age.

With hearing children up to the age of 18 months, words and sentences must be supplemented with gestures and objects if the speaker is to be assured that the child will understand. One must point or gesture to support what is meant, so that the language used can be associated with its meaning in the mind of the child. For the deaf baby this 18-month period must be extended. Taking the time and effort to make sure that the child knows what is being referred to saves much time, effort, and frustration later on. With appropriate help from the parent, the child can begin to internalize the patterns of spoken English (or another language) as they are presented clearly in Cued Speech.

Everything Has A Name

A child who has no language does not know initially that anything has a name. The first several words learned are important, not only for the value of knowing those words, but because they begin to implant the idea that things and people actually have names. All this should be remembered when you begin Cued Speech with a very young child. There will be no overnight miracles. The same progression must be followed with deaf children beginning to learn language at 3 or 4 years of age, though it may proceed more rapidly because of greater maturity. There must be much input of language before you can expect a child to begin self-expression. Be willing to cue (and demonstrate) for some time before expecting expressive output. Also, accept gestures and imperfect articulation efforts on the part of the child, confirming them if you understand. Say things like:"Yes, you said 'doggie,'" or "Yes, you want to pee-pee."

Expect Progress to be Uneven

Remember that children progress unevenly. Your child will encounter plateaus followed by spurts of progress. Moreover, even steady progress will give an impression of unevenness because of the inability of parents and teachers to observe everything.

Uneven progress is particularly noticeable in the areas of language and speech. At times it will seem that your child is making little progress in one of these areas. There are phases in language growth that are "digestive" in that the child is assimilating what has already been learned while increasing in receptive understanding. Some of the most important stages in language development become apparent only after the child enters the expressive stage. The child must have *receptive* understanding (be able to understand what he/she *receives*) before becoming able to express it.

It is entirely possible that at a given time your child is making significant progress that you cannot observe until later. Try to use any "plateaus" to try new techniques and modifications of techniques already used. Also, talk with other parents about their similar experiences, which may be helpful both by reassuring you that their "plateaus" were limited in length and by picking up ideas on coping with lull periods.

Be Aware of Possible Effects of Earlier Training

Unless you are fortunate enough to get started using Cued Speech when your deaf child is under a year of age, the effects of earlier training or of your earlier efforts to communicate with him or her may complicate the situation, exerting both positive and negative effects. If at the age of 2 or 3 years your child has been trying to understand orally with some success, he or she may be distracted temporarily by the cues when they are introduced. He or she may tend to focus on them enough that his or her attention to the mouth will suffer for a week or so. The child may react very positively and tend to wave his/her hand around in meaningless patterns, in an effort to imitate. Do not be alarmed—it is normal for a deaf child to over-react to a strong new visual stimulus.

Remember that at this stage of learning, appropriate use of cues means *use of cues and speech accompanied by adequate situational information.* You and the environment must help the child understand the meaning of what you are saying and cueing. With consistent and appropriate exposure to cues the child will soon attend carefully to the lips and hands together. Children apparently learn quickly to focus on the mouth and pick up the cues with their peripheral vision. There is even some evidence that, as this skill develops further, the child's focus may even move to the eyes of the speaker, and the information from both the mouth and the hand is still picked up.

A child who has been on TC with some success may think, when Cued Speech is introduced, that the cues are new signs. This is not a problem—in fact, the easiest way to begin teaching such a child CS is to teach him/her the CS equivalent of each sign he/she knows. Simply present the Cued Speech, then the sign, and then sign "same." The TC child will soon begin to use what is seen on the mouth as part of the CS message.

If, as a result of prior training, a deaf child habitually tries to vocalize when communicating expressively, his/her first attempts to cue expressively may preoccupy him/her so much that he or she will temporarily stop vocalizing with them. This is an entirely natural phenomenon, and you should not worry about it. Just encourage the child gently to use voice, but be very patient about it. And, when the child does vocalize with attempts to cue, provide lavish praise.

You need to understand the preoccupation that is responsible for the phenomenon just described. In the beginning, cueing requires concentration, as you may already know if you have started learning. For a hearing-impaired child, vocalization also requires concentration. Thus, concentration is divided, and for a few weeks vocalization may suffer. The good side of this is that vocalization soon comes back better than ever, since the child has increasingly more language, as well as a more accurate idea of the sounds that go into the message he or she is trying to produce. The effects of Cued Speech upon speech production, and the influence of expressive cueing on speech production, are described in detail in Chapter 12, "Speech Production."

Expressive Efforts

When a child begins to try to use Cued Speech expressively, parents need to remember not to expect or try to get perfection in his or her cueing. They need to be aware of the difficulty of supporting the child's efforts at both vocal production and expressive cueing. In the beginning it is impossible to reinforce selectively two simultaneous aspects of expression. Later the child can be asked to speak and cue at the same time, or can be praised for doing so. Initially it is best to reinforce positively (with praise) both the child's attempts to speak and his/her attempts to cue. Later, when the child understands well enough, you may give lavish praise for vocalizing and cueing at the same time.

When a child begins to cue expressively, initial efforts are likely to be as inaccurate as are the early attempts at meaningful articulation. Cues will be incomplete, speech production will be defective (or may even be dropped temporarily), and language patterns will contain many aberrations. The first attempts will likely be directly imitative and approximate.

Some children will make inexact attempts at cueing very early, soon after Cued Speech is initiated with them. Others will wait longer. Some will never cue expressively unless encouraged to do so, or if they find it is needed for communication with a cueing deaf friend. Much depends on the parents' response to the first efforts of the child to cue. If the parents are supportive, praising the child for cueing, and showing him or her how to make the cues more accurately only when he/she wants help, he/she is more likely to cue.

How to Handle Incorrect Cueing by the Child

When a child cues incorrectly, do not make a big issue of it. Respond by saying: "Yes" and immediately repeating the correct form. This will avoid giving an impression of failure, but will still enable the child to be aware of the possibility of improvement.

When the deaf child does begin attempting to cue, do not expect accurate mouth movements any more than accurate cues. The initial attempts at both cues and mouth movements will be very inaccurate, as are the initial attempts of a hearing baby to talk. The same stage of (visual) "baby talk" will be encountered in Cued Speech as is encountered in hearing babies. The child may go through a period of cueing without attempting to speak, or attempting to speak without cueing. Gradually he or she will tie together the hand movements, mouth movements, and the sound production. This assumes that the child has some hearing and is receiving auditory training and speech therapy, preferably from a cueing therapist. If the child has had considerable oral training before starting Cued Speech, there may be less inclination to cue expressively at first. Also, older children who find that hearing people can understand their speech will usually prefer not to cue. They are likely to cue if they get the idea that they speak better when they cue, as is usually the case after several months of expressive cueing.

Benefits of Expressive Cueing

There are several reasons why early cueing on the part of the child is desirable:

1) Profoundly deaf children have very limited feedback on their speech efforts. After being taught by a therapist to produce a specific speech sound correctly, children may forget how to make the sound. They may not feel or hear their own production of the sound well enough to tell if they are still producing it correctly. If they master and use the cue patterns that properly accompany the sounds or groups of sounds they are trying to produce, they will find that the cueing helps them speak. The"motor" feedback (feeling of the movements of the hands) can help them retain and execute the correct sound production through association of the cueing with the habituated movements of the vocal mechanism. A hearing person can experience a similar phenomenon in dialing numbers on a touch-tone instrument. When he cannot remember the complete number, his finger can often "remember" which buttons to press. A similar experience occurs in recalling a name by trying to write it, if one has written it several times before.

Many (not all) deaf children speak better when they cue than when they do not, assuming that they cue fluently enough that it does not prevent smooth speech. In most cases cueing supports specifically to the integrity of the rhythmic patterns of their speech, as well as the accuracy of their internalized knowledge of which sounds are *supposed* to be in the words. The act of cueing often helps by slowing speech so that articulation will be done more carefully. Cued Speech does not of itself teach the child how to make the individual sounds. Speech/hearing therapy is needed for that.

2) If children's efforts at expressive communication are only partially intelligible to their parents, this can interfere seriously with language development. If the child cues when he/she speaks, the parents will be able to understand him/her much better if they learn to read Cued Speech. Reading Cued Speech is a separate skill from that of expressive cueing. In teaching parents to cue, instructors should devote some instructional effort to reception and should recommend practice in reception when they practice with friends. In fact some teachers (notably June Dixon-Millar, director of the National Centre for Cued Speech, in Canterbury, England), give roughly equal amounts of

time to expressive and receptive training in their classes for beginners.

3) Expressive cueing is essential if profoundly deaf children are to communicate among themselves through Cued Speech. For this reason it sometimes becomes necessary to press deaf children to form the habit of cueing when speaking. If the child is trying to tell you something without cueing (speaking with or without gestures) it may be wise to pretend ignorance of what he or she is trying to say. Say: "What did you say? Please cue it so I can understand." This is practical only with the child whose receptive communication is sufficient. The simple expedient of pretending not to understand by saying "What?" may work with a younger child.

Parents must be realistic about expressive cueing. The child who develops understandable speech may be less likely to cue expressively, since it does require extra effort. Even a child who has formed the habit of cueing expressively may, when approaching puberty, become very concerned about "looking different," and may even ask the parents not to cue to him/her in public. Patience, persuasion, and positive reinforcement may be needed, and even they may not be enough.

Parents may not be able to get the child to form the habit of consistent expressive cueing, except when it is specifically needed, as in communicating with deaf peers. Having hearing siblings or peers who cue help a deaf child to accept cueing in public. But, the thing that helps most, as revealed in some of the case histories by parents, is for the child to become aware that trying to understand without the cues and becoming badly confused is more painful than the fear that others will be reminded that he/she is "different."

Deaf children who have some exposure to signing friends may want to communicate among themselves through signing. This should not be discouraged. The use of signing will be considered in detail in Chapter 23, "What About Sign Language?"

Language Aberrations and "Gaps"

As a deaf child's expressive attempts increase (with or without cueing), experimentation with language can be expected. The child may employ unnatural or incorrect word order at times (e.g., Daddy me go store. Give dog me. Baby go out.). This is natural in language development and leads to true creative expression. Hearing-impaired children need to go through this normal stage just as their hearing peers do. Incorrect preposition and pronoun patterns will appear later. The transitional patterns should be of no concern unless they tend to be retained too long. Of course, it is desirable to correct them, to the extent this can be done without inhibiting the child's drive for more complex language. Typical of a precocious child is the mistake of regularizing an irregular verb: "I *rided* my bike!" This demonstrates the early stages of understanding of transformational grammar and is very encouraging. The correction, if made at all, should be very gentle: "Yes, you *rode* your bike." The child should not necessarily be asked to repeat the correct form in this case. If done at all, it should be done by posing the question: "Can you say 'I rode my bike?'"

If you are told that your child has "gaps" in his or her language, don't be alarmed. If the gaps are specific, as for example in past tense forms or incorrect pronoun usage, remember that a child tends to make progress in spurts, and in specific areas of language. This doesn't mean that you should not try to close the gaps, but don't feel too pressured about it. Work patiently to make up any specific deficits you know about. Keep in mind that there are two language deficits that are characteristic of virtually all deaf children, even those who have grown up successfully with Cued Speech, until they are well into high school. These deficits are in vocabulary and general knowledge about the world. Both are due to the fact that there is no way, even with Cued Speech, to match the *quantity* of language that a hearing child receives. This is why the time devoted to exposing your child to language must be *quality* time.

Fortunately, the deficiencies in both vocabulary and general knowledge tend to be made up completely, in the Cued Speech youngster, within a few years after he or she becomes a skilled and avid reader. From that time on, there is no limit to access to clear language, on any subject in which the child is interested. Vocabulary and knowledge usually increase rapidly. A little-known fact is that good (not average) hearing high school students, on graduation, have reading vocabularies about twice as large as their spoken vocabularies. This means that they have learned more words through reading than through all other inputs combined! This is even more likely to be characteristic of deaf children who become good readers.

What to Expect in Speech Development

Dr. Daniel Ling, one of the foremost authorities on speech in hearing-impaired children, has pointed out repeatedly that the development of good speech production in the profoundly hearing-impaired child usually takes a long time. Before spontaneous, meaningful speech can be achieved there must be inner language and understanding. Auditory training and associated speech training should begin with a deaf child as soon as the hearing impairment is diagnosed, and must continue for many years if speech production potential is to be exploited. We are aware that the term preferred by many professionals is speech/hearing/*language* pathologist. In our opinion, the child who receives Cued Speech consistently at home will not usually have a need for language correction that is acute enough to warrant taking substantial amounts of time away from the limited total usually available for speech-and-hearing therapy. For the Cued Speech child, parents, classroom teachers, and resource teachers should be expected to meet the language development needs of the child. This is not to say that a professional speech/hearing therapist should not teach some language, if it can be done without interfering with the maximum possible cultivation of use of hearing and production of speech.

Parents of deaf children often tend to judge their deaf child's progress too much by the amount and quality of his/her speech. This tendency is understandable to some extent. For young children who are being taught by traditional oral methods, speech is the only means of communication except gestures. Also, the quality of a child's speech is often, in the minds of the parents, the major factor in ability to "be like everyone else." It is more essential for a young deaf child to have good communication, self-esteem, and the ability to think and to read than to have a pleasing voice and clearly understandable speech. This is not to minimize the importance of good speech training, but only to make the point that more vital things are sometimes sacrificed in the attempt to maximize this one aspect of being like "everybody else." The goal of good speech should be a long-range goal. That goal should never be forgotten, but it should not be allowed to squeeze out other important and initially more critical needs.

The spread of Total Communication has helped dispel the initial tendency of parents toward exaggerated preoccupation with speech. It has helped parents recognize the importance of clear communication, social development, and language development. In some cases it has led to an unfortunate and extreme view that encourages parents to "give up" on the idea of speech for their deaf child. Nothing is more unwise.

With Cued Speech, parents can afford to be more patient about speech, so long as appropriate auditory and speech training are provided consistently. The reason for this is that their level of communication with the child is not as dependent on his or her expressive speech quality at the time. Before spontaneous speech can be achieved there must be internal language and understanding.

The progress of a hearing-impaired child in speech production is highly dependent on the quality of his/her hearing, as opposed to how much hearing he or she has. Many profoundly deaf children, with Pure-Tone-Average thresholds (PTA's) of 95 decibels (dB) or more, develop better speech than many children with moderate or severe hearing losses, if both receive good auditory and speech training. This is essentially because what the former hear, though very weak even with hearing aids that amplify the sound energy a million times, may be more similar to what the normal ear hears. A child with only a moderate hearing loss may have such severely distorted hearing that what he or she hears does not provide the information needed to discriminate among the sounds of speech. Thus, the child can neither understand others well nor know whether what he/she is producing is correct. This will be discussed in more detail in Chapter 12, "Speech Production."

Differences among children in rate of improvement in speech may also be due to variation in the amount of motivation. Speech improvement requires commitment on the part of the child, and his preoccupations with other things will sometimes interfere with that commitment. Often deaf youngsters become more motivated about speech as they approach puberty. However, the secret to maintenance of speech motivation is to furnish positive reinforcement to speech efforts whenever possible.

Cued Speech does not of itself teach a hearing-impaired child how to make specific speech sounds. Instead, it shows where in each word to put the sounds. This is true of both the sounds the child has been taught to make, and those he or she makes instinctively or accidentally. Cued Speech is not a substitute for audition-and-speech therapy. It is a tool that multiplies the effectiveness of audition-and-speech therapy. Equally important, it is a tool that enables parents to correct instantly errors in pronunciation that are within the articulation capabilities of the child.

Positive Reinforcement

Once children gain the necessary foundation of inner language, the key to development of expressive communication becomes *positive reinforcement*. Positive reinforcement is a technical term for what every wise parent does to support desirable behavior in a child. It includes any supportive reaction by the parent to desired performance by the child, or performance that is progressing toward the desired performance. Expressive communication in the forms of lip movements, cues, and expressive speech is likely to develop rapidly only if the response to these outputs is enthusiastic and supportive.

Discerning parents use positive reinforcement to support desired behavior of all kinds in their children. But the response to the deaf child's attempts at communication must be tailored carefully to the level of his/her capabilities and progress. Several principles should be kept in mind:

First, positive reinforcement (agreement, applause, praise, approval, enthusiasm, affection) should be used unsparingly. Negative reinforcement (disagreement, reprimand, disapproval) should be avoided whenever possible. It should be remembered that correction often comes across as negative, unless delivered carefully.

Second, without the guidance of a trained psychologist or therapist, only social/psychological (non-material) reinforcements such as those already listed should be used. Children with specific, severe behavioral problems may need the benefit of behavioral modification techniques involving food, candy, tokens, or other material rewards. Use of such techniques must be planned and directed by professionals in the field of behavioral psychology, in order to get good results without danger of undesirable and even dangerous side effects.

Third, the key to effective use of positive reinforcement techniques is the progressive and careful increasing of the performance level required for continued reinforcement. Success is achieved when the child begins to understand that the increase in the requirement is itself a confirmation of success and a new challenge. In the beginning, a child should be reinforced for any effort to cue or move his/her mouth and produce sound, no matter how rudimentary or inaccurate. As expressive output progresses, the requirements are increased gradually until only near-perfect cueing and lip movements earn reinforcement. The same is true of speech production efforts. Even gross approximations should be initially reinforced with praise. The quality required for positive reinforcement is then increased as the child's performance improves.

Only after a child can succeed consistently at the required level is the requirement increased. For example, after the child has been taught by a therapist to produce a given sound correctly, he or she is expected to produce it correctly and is positively reinforced only if he/she does. Or, he or she may be asked to repeat it if he produces it incorrectly, then reinforced for getting it right. It is essential that the child recognize when the requirement is increased because of consistent success. The child must know he or she is doing as well as before, and yet not being reinforced, after the requirement is increased. Only then will a child take the withholding of reinforcement as a challenge and a tribute to the progress made, rather than as an indication of failure.

It is usually not best to use food or candy as reinforcing agents. For children with multiple problems, food or candy may be the reinforcers that "unlock" the child in the beginning. However, they should be used only under the direction of or by specially trained personnel. Also, they should be replaced by forms of social reinforcement (praise, affection, etc.) as soon as possible. This statement should not be understood as advising against the occasional use of a special treat of food or candy, so long as it is not conditionally offered in advance, in fact or by implication.

Every parent of a hearing-impaired child should endeavor to become as skillful as possible at the systematic use of approval, enthusiasm, affection, and praise to sustain motivation and a feeling of success in the child. Parents may need some advice from a professional in learning how to use positive reinforcement in the most effective ways.

What to Do if Response Is Slow

If a deaf child is very slow in responding to language input there will be frustration on the part of both parents and child. Unless the child is demonstrating some understanding of cued input within a month or two of the beginning of its use by parents, consultations with professionals may be desirable. The child may indicate understanding, in the beginning, in any of several ways: by looking at the object mentioned, by a gesture, by vocalizing, or by performing an action. If he or she does none of these in response to cued input, the child should be checked for disabling conditions other than hearing impairment, especially aphasia and autism.

Parents should discuss with qualified professionals such matters as: the possibility of serious learning or perceptual disabilities requiring special diagnostic procedures for identification and assessment; the possible need for use of special behavioral modification techniques; and the simple possibility that in the use of Cued Speech both parents and teachers have been overlooking some steps necessary for the child in question, such as adequate praise and affection after every little success.

Occasionally a child with prior oral training may notice cueing initially, but later may look away (or even close his or her eyes) when the parents cue, indicating that he or she does not want them to cue. This usually happens because the child has been taught in school not to use the hands. Such a child is not yet perceiving any meaning in the cues. It may be possible to improve the association between input and meaning by presenting and identifying specific pairs of objects, trying only to get the child to discriminate between them. This procedure is described in detail Chapter 14, starting at the bottom of page 199.

If the child already lipreads some, but seems to get no value from the cues, one should use a pair of puppets with *homophenous* names, that is, names that look alike on the mouth, such as *Billy* and *Millie*, *Jim* and *Jip*, *Joe* and *Zoe*, *mama doll* and *papa doll*. Then, with the distinctions possible only through the cues, the child will have a better chance to pick up the fact that the cues help. Until he/she gets some meaning from cues he/she will not recognize their value. Be sure to note that the child does not have to learn any cues in these examples. He or she needs only to see a difference between the members of each pair of words to begin to perceive meaning in the cues.

Our experience is that any child who can understand natural gestures can learn to understand words and phrases presented in Cued Speech. Deaf children who are barely trainable (capable of learning no more than 30 or so words or phrases if they had normal hearing) may require different treatment. They might learn the equivalent signs and natural gestures more rapidly because of the greater ease of remembering such obvious gestures as those for eat, sleep, etc. Even children with normal hearing, with this level of intelligence, have been helped through signs and gestures. This subject is discussed in more detail in Chapter 24, "The Child With More Than One Disability." The merits of sign language as a first language for the deaf child, and its role as a second language for the child whose first language is spoken language learned through Cued Speech, are considered at length in Chapter 23, "What About Sign Language?"

Parents should remember that children have their good moments and their bad ones. Judge your child by how she/he performs during her/his good times. Try to learn what to do to increase the number of "good" times.

The deaf child's initial perception of a word in Cued Speech is as a sign made by the face and the hand in concert. Only after he/she begins to learn about sounds, their production, and their perception, does he/she begin to perceive the elements of Cued Speech in relation to spoken language. He or she may notice that the first part of the word *shoot* is the same as the word *shoe*, and the first part of *shoes* as well. Perception of the system aspects of Cued Speech by the child can be accelerated by comparing such words, after they become familiar.

Within a year or so after consistent use of Cued Speech begins in the home, the "magic of the mind" that both hearing and deaf children possess brings about a miraculous capacity for understanding increasingly complex patterns of language. It is almost always the second year of use of Cued Speech that leaves parents in awe of the mental capacity they have uncovered through the simple expedient of making the message consistently clear through vision. A sample: Oz Crosby sent a triumphant note: "Dorothy Jane (then just turned 4) has figured out homonyms. One day I asked, "Do you want to *read* something? First she gave the name sign for her friend *Reid*. Then she went for a book." On another occasion, when they went to visit Dorothy Jane's grandparents, Oz said as they got of the car, "Sky." Dorothy Jane first looked up at the sky, then realized that he was talking about her grandparents' dog, Sky. These occurrences were 20 months after she began to receive fairly consistent CS exposure.

Chapter Summary

In the earliest stages of their development, babies use observation and absorption, followed by active exploration of the world around them. Then, they begin to associate communicative input with the things and persons to which the input refers. Early communicative efforts by parents must be supplemented by gestures (especially pointing) and objects to help associate the inputs with specific objects and actions.

Remember that "Slow is Beautiful." Your child needs slow, smooth input to learn most rapidly. Don't try to cue fast.

Watch for your child's sudden or gradual recognition of the fact that everything has a name. You can prepare for this and even promote it by identifying objects in succession and in groups.

Expect uneven progress. During periods when progress appear to be slow, try to find new ways to stimulate interest. Talk with other parents about their similar experiences.

Be aware of possible effects of your child's earlier training, if any. Decide how to compensate for or take advantage of them.

Expect aberrations in language patterns used by your child. Also expect gaps in certain areas, which parents should be concerned about only if they appear to be serious.

Do not be alarmed if your child stops vocalizing with his/her first attempts to cue.

Expect speech development to be slow. Be sure that auditory training is adequate and is harmonized with speech therapy.

Make consistent use of appropriate positive reinforcement.

If your child is slow to respond, talk with professionals, but also check to make sure that nothing is missing in the exposure you give.

Chapter 8
Advancing in Language

After several months of using Cued Speech, you will probably feel that you have gotten "over the hump." Your child seems to be catching on—beginning to understand an increasing number of words, phrases, and short sentences. For you, cueing has probably become much easier, although you still have to go slowly, and now and then you actually have to stop and figure out how to cue a word (more likely, to figure out how you pronounce it!).

Once CS has enabled your child to "crash the communication barrier," it is not necessary to have special work sessions if much time is spent communicating during the course of the day. As soon as you find that you can cue almost anything by taking your time, adopt a policy of cueing everything you say to your hearing-impaired child. Only when you force yourself to do this will you begin to gain skill and fluency rapidly. More important, only when you cue every word will your child have a chance to learn complete language instead of the fragmented language that is conveyed by the key words. Also, you must remember to introduce new words every day. Don't fall into the habit of changing what you plan to say so you can use words your child already knows. This is a serious error which greatly limits language growth.

When communicating, watch your child's face for signs of confusion. Some children don't let you know if what you say isn't completely clear. So, ask a question if you suspect he or she is confused. Or, if you suspect that a specific word is causing trouble, discuss it with your child.

A parent reviewer suggests that this is a good place to remind parents to form the habit of cueing what they say to each other in the child's presence. Often the child is fascinated by this. If you form this habit your child will not feel left out of what goes on between you, and will also pick up language from "overhearing." A striking example of the value of the child's "eavesdropping" appears on page 477.

Maintain A Current Word Work List

At this point you will probably find it helpful to keep a current work list of words. On a paper or card that you can keep in a handy location, or in a small notebook, jot down words or phrases that you have introduced to your child accidentally or by design. This list will serve as a reminder (if you check it daily) of the words or phrases you should make a point of using several times a day, so they will become a part of the child's permanent vocabulary. The word list can also be of help to other cuers who spend time with your child.

Your child will frequently amaze you by learning a word in a single exposure, but this cannot be expected in the early stages. Repetition in meaningful situations is the key to vocabulary growth. When a new word is learned (or half-learned) it can easily be forgotten if not used a few more times. Even when you are sure the child understands a specific word, that word needs to be reviewed or reinforced by additional use. Your word list will naturally be short at first. Later it will be long and will include a variety of different types of words—not only those you encounter in daily communication, but also words or ideas that you think a hearing child would understand.

Vocabulary Growth Record

The natural follow-up to a current working list for new words is a comprehensive list of words you are sure your child knows. You should not struggle to keep such a list up to date if it takes much of your time. However, in most cases it can be of great value because it gives you a sense of accomplishment that can motivate you to greater achievement, and also documents your impressions of what is happening. If you use a notebook for your initial working word list you can easily make it serve also as a permanent record of your child's acquisition of vocabulary and phrases.

Start by including every word or phrase your child understands through Cued Speech without situational clues. Expand the list as he/she understands more items, and review them as suggested in connection with the word list. Then, after you are sure the child recognizes the word or phrase consistently, place a check mark after it to certify that you do not need to make a point of reviewing it any more. The check mark essentially certifies the word as a part of the permanent vocabulary. By reviewing a word we do not mean formally working on it in a work session. Instead, we mean that you should simply make it a point to use the word appropriately now and then.

You can maintain an accurate vocabulary record only if you jot down every new word your child recognizes, *at the time*. You will not be able to remember all the new words at the end of the day or week. Carry your little notebook and pen, and write down the new word or phrase *on the spot!*

A vocabulary acquisition record can be very valuable in gauging progress later on. For example, the first child exposed to Cued Speech, starting at 24 months, acquired a receptive vocabulary of 102 words in the first six months and an additional 348 words and phrases in the second six months! This furnished a first indication of the progress that might reasonably be expected of other children. It turned out to be only a normal expectation when a reasonably bright child receives appropriate exposure at home. Many children acquire vocabulary more slowly, Others learn faster, depending on ability and circumstances.

Teaching New Concepts

By the time a child knows several hundred words he or she will be very receptive to learning. The introduction of new vocabulary and new concepts is easy to achieve. Several new words can be taught in a single session if simple guidelines are followed. Follow this pattern:

1) "This is a shoelace."

2) When the child is aware of the new word, use it differently. Say: "Show me the shoelace."

3) Follow up by having the child respond to other questions such as: "Where's the shoelace." or by pointing out, "Here's another shoelace." Continue to bring the new item into discussion.

Having the child repeat the word with cues provides additional reinforcement. Try also to follow a natural continuation of progress in connection with a new concept related to the word just learned. For example, after following the shoelace sequence above, help the child install shoelaces in a shoe.

Many ideas, such as the concept of wetness, may require considerable demonstration along with the patterns suggested. Instead of seeing one example of wetness, such as a wet washcloth, let the child feel water, juice, wet clothes, wet dirt, and wet paper, as you associate the term *wet* with each of them. The child has to focus on the quality that is common to the wet items.

Big and *little*, *soft* and *hard*, *rough* and *smooth* are contrasting pairs of concepts that are easy to teach. Assemble pairs of objects that are identical except for the qualities indicated, and contrast them.

Abstract concepts will develop slowly. Some that can be taught early are "All gone!" and "More" (meaning additional). It might be argued that these are not really abstract concepts, since they relate to relationships of concrete things. At any rate, they are at a higher level than simple labelling of objects and actions. Thus, the mental processes that are involved in learning them are similar to those involved in learning abstract concepts such as future and past tenses.

Directions, Questions, and "Danger" Words

Directions, such as "Get your coat," and questions, such as "Where's your doll?," are used frequently and usually suggest immediate responses. As a result, they will probably produce the first responses of a deaf child. In the beginning, the child will need to be guided in his/her responses. After asking a question you may need to provide the answer, e.g., "Where is your toe? *Here* is your toe!" Help the child's language expand by continuing with more advanced ideas: "Is your toe on your hand? No, your toe is on your foot!"

There are many question words the child needs to master: *who, what, where, why, when, whose, which, how many, what color, how much, how, what happened?* These interrogative forms provide patterns for adding many words to the child's vocabulary, and they also give the child opportunities to respond. Once the child understands one of these interrogatives (especially *where*), they can be used extensively to test and expand his/her knowledge on a broader scale. This boosts parents' morale and the child's motivation.

Some of the interrogatives are much easier to teach than others. *Where, which,* and *what* are easiest and should be introduced first. In the initial exposures the parent should provide the answer to each question. Each interrogative will have to be used several times before understanding is firm. You should depend on repeated use rather than specific or intense teaching. *Whose* and *who* are also relatively easy for the child if you introduce them properly, giving the answer to each question, "Whose doll is this?" "This is Dorothy's doll." After *where, which,* and *what,* the other interrogatives will be picked up over time through use in everyday communication.

Sarina Roffé mentions the importance of making sure the child learns all the needed "danger" words and phrases, such as *Hot!, Sharp!, Stop! Don't move!* If possible, the child should be capable of lipreading these and other vital words, or even of understanding them without visual input when they are shouted.

Testing

It is important for parents to experience renewed motivation regularly. This is especially true in the early stages of cueing when the task of developing their own skill preoccupies them, and they are waiting for the child's language to begin picking up rapidly. There is nothing that boosts parent motivation as much as evidence that the child is beginning to understand specific words and phrases through their efforts. Simple testing to see if a child understands a word or idea can be casual and easy.

Some authorities suggest that you should feed your deaf child vast amounts of language input but should not "test" the child on what you have presented. The reasoning behind this is that you should avoid causing the child to experience a sense of failure. With Cued Speech, a child will pick up new language rapidly enough that there is not much psychological danger in testing. Also, much of the time children will not even realize they are being tested, if it is done skillfully. In fact, testing builds the child's morale when he or she succeeds. Care should be taken to spare the child feelings of inadequacy or defeat. This requires that he/she succeed most of the time.

When failure on an item does occur, it is important to follow up by testing on an item you know the child will get correctly, replacing failure with success as soon as possible. Another effective technique is to say: "We'll try that one again," when the child fails, making sure to prepare the child before testing again on the same item.

A preschool teacher whose teaching career spanned 60 years said that all children love to learn, whether they are slow, average, or bright children, if they are taught in such a way that they can succeed about three times in four. This level of success maintains enthusiasm, avoids boredom, and totally prevents frustration. When children are tested and perform successfully (receiving appropriate praise) they get a sense of accomplishment which is extremely important to their motivation and self-esteem.

Don't test the child unnecessarily. Be patient. When he/she begins asking questions spontaneously, you can be sure that sophisticated use of questions is on the way. Remember that your child's language will progress, over a period of several years, through the four steps: reception, expression, reading, and writing. There needs to be a secure foundation in each to ensure mastery of the next.

Language Awareness In Parents

In order to take full advantage of opportunities to impart language, parents must be constantly aware of those opportunities. All too often deaf children are first of all *deprived* children. As parents you must outwit this deprivation by seizing every possible chance to interpret to your child the events and things in the world around. You should constantly talk to your child about surroundings and activities as they occur. You have to train yourself to be aware and to make your child aware. Fortunately, once you train yourself in this role it is easy to maintain it.

Talk about whatever you hear, see, feel, or experience, especially the ordinary experiences you commonly take for granted. A deliberate attempt must be made to cue thoughts that do not call for a response, but which add to the child's perception of the world. (e.g., "You're angry." "The wind is blowing." These boxes are heavy." "The grass is long." "It needs to be cut." "I wonder why Dad is late." "If we go for a ride, we'll miss *Lassie*.")

Use descriptive words as much as possible. Think of possible uses for the following words and use them in as many contexts as possible: *big, little, small; lots, more, much, almost; hard, soft, smooth, rough; hot, warm, cold, chilly; yesterday, tomorrow, today; wait, later, now, soon; happy, sad, unhappy, glad; pretty, ugly, beautiful, lovely; bad, good, naughty, nice; fast, slow.*

Once you get a phrase across, expand it. Progress from "Go to bed," to "Go to Daddy," "Go to Billy," "Go to Mommy," "Go to the table," "Go to the kitchen," "Go to your bedroom." Progress from "Do you want milk? to "Do you want bread? Do you want potatoes?" Later, insert the word *more* when it is appropriate.

Parents must be always alert to the need for continuous expansion of the deaf child's vocabulary. Hearing children usually call things by the same names their family uses. But, they hear the same objects referred to by other terms and pick up the differences: *carpet, rug; sofa, couch; soft drink, soda, pop.* Such differences will likely have to be explained to a deaf child unless the family members typically use more than one word for a given object and try consciously to maintain diversity in the vocabulary they use.

An important item often overlooked is the learning of words that sound alike but have different meanings (homonyms). Parents cannot assume that this will be just picked up. Probably it will, but it may cause much confusion before it becomes straightened out. Make a list: *bare, bear (noun), bear (verb); wear, where* (if you pronounce the last two same); *led, lead (noun); chilly, chili.* When you encounter such a case, make a note of it and explain it to the child when you can.

Advancement in Language Complexity

With Cued Speech your relationship with your deaf child can be almost free of the usual limitations encountered in working with deaf children. This is not to say it will be easy—it won't—but it will be possible for you to enable your child to accomplish the things that are usually very difficult or impossible for a deaf child to achieve. More and more, you will have the feeling of speaking naturally and cueing what you say, the way you say it. This can lead to natural and desirable progression in the complexity of the language used, so long as understanding on the part of the child remains good.

Most parents and teachers of deaf children tend not to use normal conversational language with the deaf children. They have a tendency to use very simple sentences rather than complex sentences. For example they might be more likely to say, "Do you want to go out to play? Get your coat," than the conditional sentence "If you want to go out to play, get your coat." *Beautiful* and *wonderful* are greatly overworked words. Parents of deaf children tend to use *broken* to refer to anything from a flat tire to a dead hearing-aid battery. The words *brown, pink,* and *white* are often unwisely substituted for *chocolate, strawberry* and *vanilla*.

If you are using Cued Speech with your child, do not fall into the habit of using oversimplified language. When parents or teachers are proficient in cueing and understand the proper use of Cued Speech, they can communicate with a deaf child with complete freedom, using normal language patterns and concepts. Of course, the language should be appropriate for the child's age and language level. The eventual result of "cueing what comes naturally" should be that the deaf child sees the same kind of language the hearing child hears.

As a deaf child's vocabulary and knowledge of language patterns become more extensive, he/she will progress in the ability to understand abstract and intangible concepts. What a hearing child hears contributes to his or her understanding of complex and abstract ideas. When children hear a word used a number of times in a particular context, or in related contexts, they will come to understand its meaning and be able to use it correctly. For example, suppose that Mother answers the telephone and talks for a minute, then hangs up and says: "That was Daddy. He is coming home in a few minutes." Initially a young child, even though he understands the ideas of *Daddy* and *coming home*, has no idea of what *in a few minutes* means. However, when Daddy appears shortly, the first seed is sown. If the sequence occurs again, and if there are occasions when it is necessary "to wait a few minutes" the child gains an understanding of the concept of the future and an approximate idea of the meaning of "in a few minutes." Eventually, the whole concept of time and words related to it is formed and then refined over time. All this is possible with a deaf child with whom Cued Speech is used, if it is used consistently and appropriately.

Explain, Demonstrate, Fill Gaps

In addition to providing an environment that stimulates the development of ideas and concepts, parents must explain and demonstrate many ideas. For example, a child can be taught very early, by demonstration, that there is a difference between noisy and quiet. Then, when told to "be quiet," he or she will have a basis for understanding what is requested. Enforcement of the request will then be a matter of discipline to be handled as with a hearing child.

Even if the deaf child's vocabulary and language grow at a rapid rate (which is not to be expected in all cases), there will be many times when something is explained but not understood. The child may have a gap in knowledge that prevents understanding. When this happens, jot down a note to yourself. When you have time, give thought to the idea and attempt to work out a way of explaining.

Through Cued Speech hearing-impaired children can have the advantages of accelerated vocabulary growth and significant language development at an early age. After several years of consistent use, they will be thinking in spoken English, unhampered by the usual linguistic limitations of hearing-impaired children. Moreover, their internal (thought) language will be the appropriate base for learning to read, for fueling speech production, and for communicating in a meaningful way.[1] Their continuing needs will include 1) much stimulating and enjoyable communication in Cued Speech, 2) appropriate training in use of residual hearing in aural/oral reception and in speech production, 3) gradual and appropriate preparation for reading by being read to in the home, 4) a warm, active family environment, and 5) placement in an appropriate preschool program at the right time.

Preschool

The qualification "at the right time" is included above because the desirability of preschool for a deaf child, beyond the specialized audition-and-speech training all hearing-impaired children need from an early age, depends upon several factors. As was pointed out earlier, two hours with the undivided attention of the mother at home typically results in more linguistic advancement by a young hearing child than an entire day in school. Our observation strongly confirms that this is

---

[1]For research evidence supporting these assertions, refer to the research of Alegría, Dejean, Capouillez, and Leybaert, summarized on page 695.

true also of a deaf child with whom Cued Speech is used.

If both parents work outside the home, there will be more need for preschool unless a cueing nanny/tutor is available, even if the child is only 2 years of age. If there are no hearing siblings, the child will need to go to preschool or a day-care center in order to learn to interact socially with other children unless there is opportunity to interact with neighborhood children. If the abilities or schedules of the parents limit the amount of benefit that can be gained at home, preschool may be more important. If full day care is necessary, every possible attempt should be made to see that an appropriate amount of time each day is given to organized preschool activities appropriate for the needs of a deaf child—in a cueing atmosphere if possible.

The following schedule may be appropriate for a child who has excellent support at home: at 2 years of age, two to two-and-one-half hours of preschool a day, two or three days a week, with an hour or more of auditory/speech therapy included in that total. A range is indicated because children differ in readiness and need for preschool, and because a 24-month-old child is quite different from a child 6-to-10 months older. At 3 years of age, three hours three times a week is probably appropriate. At 4 the child should be ready for three hours four-to-five mornings a week, and at 5 years a child should be ready for a full school day, five days a week, including play and rest periods and therapy sessions.

The above guidelines should be regarded as very flexible. Also, attention should be given to what alternative is available if less time is spent in the preschool. If the alternative is ordinary day care, more time in preschool might be preferable. On the other hand, if the alternative is prime time at home with the undivided attention of a parent, less time in preschool would be indicated.

Except in large cities, preschool programs that have self-contained classes for hearing-impaired children in which Cued Speech is used are scarce. Parents in other locations will usually have to accept mainstreaming, which has many limitations at the preschool level, placement in an oral program, or placement in a TC program. An appropriate preschool program should include either a teacher who is equipped to cue to the deaf child as needed, or a cueing tutor/interpreter, with willingness to tune in to the needs of the deaf child. If such a program cannot be arranged, the child may benefit socially from an hour or two of interaction with other children, without any special support except that of a teacher sensitive to the needs of a deaf child. The child should be observed to make sure he or she is enjoying the program and that it is really beneficial. If the child has hearing siblings, or if there are other children in the neighborhood with whom to play, day care for socialization should not be needed. Time with family would likely be more beneficial.

There have been some remarkable cases of cooperation by preschools. Montessori schools are usually very responsive to the needs of special children, and many have cooperated with parents in meeting those needs. They place a heavy emphasis on phonics and are quick to see the implications of Cued Speech in this regard, recognizing its possible value for hearing children. In some cases the teachers have learned to cue, and have even taught hearing classmates to cue. Other private and church-related schools, and a good many public school systems, have also accommodated deaf children successfully in preschool classes through use of Cued Speech.

Before their child starts to preschool, parents should become familiar with the responsibilities of school systems, including the preparation of an Individualized Educational Plan (IEP) or the Individualized Family Service Plan (IFSP) for each child with a disability. They should be fully aware of the rights of parents in connection with the IEP developed for their child, and what they should do if they are not satisfied with it. A brief summary of the rights of deaf children and their parents is presented in Chapter 30, "Potpourri." Additional material on the rights of hearing-impaired children, and their parents' right to participate in decisions about their education, are available from the Alexander Graham Bell Association for the Deaf. Material on the function of a preschool and on desirable attributes for a preschool are available from the same source.

The Importance of a Diary

The accumulation of records for use in evaluating progress and making plans is extremely important. The easiest way to do this is to keep a diary. At least one member of the family should do so. If one person keeps a diary, other family members should submit items for inclusion. A good diary becomes a very valuable document. It can be of help in the planning of education for the child in question. Further, it can be important as a source of material useful to other families with deaf children.

A parent reviewer notes that a diary is useful also for helping you realize that progress is being made when you yourself feel "down." A diary enables you to go back and see how far you have come.

Interjections, Exclamations, and Expressions

At some time you will need to begin using (and cueing) interjections and exclamations such as "Ouch!," "Wow!," "You don't say!," "My goodness!," "Uh oh!," "Oops!", "Oh! No!," "Oh?," "Oh yeah?," (pronounced *yeuh, yow,* or *yeow*), "Really?," "Aw, go on!," etc. And, you will want to begin to cue the two statements you probably use more often than any other: "*ŭh hŭh*" and "*hŭh ŭh*." Here ŭ is the nasal neutral vowel. This sound should be cued at the throat. It is a French vowel which appears in English only in the expressions just given. Ironically, it probably appears more often in English speech than in French speech; yet it doesn't appear in our dictionaries!

You may wish to cue also the closed-mouth renditions of the same expressions—*mm hmm* and *hmm mm*. In these the "vowel" is the continuant consonant *m*, so it is cued at the side with a slight movement forward, keeping the lips tightly closed. Don't underestimate your child! These aren't hard for deaf children to learn—not even the nasal ŭ. Tell the child to say *uh* in his nose. If that doesn't work, ask the therapist to teach him. After all, it may be the second most frequent sound in *spoken* English, for many people!

In many of the items listed above, the effectiveness is increased if you can show your changes in vocal intonation as well as facial expression. (See page 169.)

Language Development Suggestions for Parents

Even though the following suggestions were developed for parents of hearing children, each item is just as important and just as practicable for the parents of a deaf child with whom they are using Cued Speech. They were written by Sheila Fridovich, language consultant to Operation Moving Ahead (funded under Title I of the Elementary and Secondary Education Act), Prince George's County, Upper Marlboro, Maryland. A few minor editorial changes have been made to increase applicability to deaf children.

1) Take time to talk with your child and encourage him to talk to you.
2) Try to give your child your undivided attention for at least several short periods each day.
3) Ask him questions and encourage him to reply.
4) Let him tell you what he has done and how he did it, or what he told others about it.

5) Listen to your child's ideas and show respect for them.

6) Answer your child's questions.

7) Reward your child with verbal praise. (That's good. You did well!)

8) Help your child become alert to sounds around him.

9) Identify sounds for your child.

10) Ask your child what he thinks or how he feels about matters he can understand.

11) Name things for your child. Help him to call things by their correct names.

12) Help your child to look at pictures and describe what he sees. Ask questions about the pictures.

13) Help your child to make up stories about pictures.

14) Tell your child stories, fairy tales, and nursery rhymes and shift later into reading stories to him.

15) Stimulate your child to speak. You may wish to put magazine pictures on the wall or give him objects to tell about.

16) Help your child to listen to and identify the sounds around him— the ring of the telephone, the television receiver, the pots and pans, the water running, the door slamming, the window closing, the clapping of hands.

17) Take your child for a walk and talk about the things you and he see and hear.

18) When you're cooking, talk to your child about the foods you are making and the things you are doing.

19) On a trip to the grocery store, tell your child what you are buying and name the foods for him. Do the same thing in other stores.

20) Whenever you go anywhere with your child, try to talk with him about where you are and what you see, hear, and do.

21) Help your child to notice the things in his environment. Point out things to him and play a game of counting how many different things he sees, or how many of one thing.

22) Take every possible opportunity to talk with your child.

A parent reviewer suggests: *Read at bedtime every night.* Another reports an important point, that reading at bedtime may get some children so stimulated that it is hard for them to get to sleep afterward. Children are different, so find your way with your own child. Another parent suggests having the reading period well before bedtime and following the reading with quiet conversation, affection, and relaxed activities.

Give Attention to Your Own Fluency

This may be a good time to take stock of your own progress in developing cueing fluency and accuracy. To this point, speed has probably not been a problem, since slow cueing is better for a deaf child in the early stages of language acquisition. It may be that your own skill has progressed so that you have little difficulty in cueing as fast as needed. You may need to begin transliterating for your child more of what other people say, or cueing in other situations that push you to cue faster.

You may need also to have your cueing accuracy checked. Going through the audiocassette lessons again for review, which will take only a few hours, will help you find errors and eliminate them. You may want to ask an expert cuer to check you out. A helpful resource is the book *Gaining Cued Speech Proficiency*, by Walter J. Beaupré (Appendix, p. 766). This manual is for people who know the basics, can cue anything they wish, but who want to make sure of their accuracy and increase their fluency. A basic evaluation of your cueing is needed to produce your "Basic Cued Speech Proficiency Rating Profile," which will let you know where you stand in accuracy and enable you to use the manual to improve. This evaluation can be obtained through face-to-face evaluation by a qualified person, or you can even make arrangements to do it by mail by making a camcorder recording of the test material and sending it to the Cued Speech Team at Gallaudet University. There is a charge for the evaluation.

How Long?

One of the questions asked most frequently by parents is: "How long will my child be dependent on Cued Speech?" or "How long will it be necessary to cue to my child?" Some parents assume that CS should be de-emphasized as soon as the child can get along reasonably well without it in informal communication. This assumption is incorrect and reflects a lack of knowledge about the functions of Cued Speech. The question should be: "How long will exposure to Cued Speech help my child?"

It is important to distinguish between the growing ability of the child to function without the help of Cued Speech when it is necessary or desirable to do so, and his or her capacity to benefit from further exposure to Cued Speech. One of the basic purposes of CS is to develop the ability of the deaf child to communicate with hearing people in general—that is, to function without CS when necessary.

How soon he or she will be able to do so, and to what extent, will depend on the child, on his/her abilities and limitations. It will also depend greatly on the quantity and quality of continuing exposure to CS, and on how effectively the use of audition and speech production are cultivated. Parents must recognize that their deaf child will *always* need Cued Speech—not that he/she can't perform increasingly well without it, but because he or she 1) *won't ever* reach the point of being able to learn new language efficiently from lipreading, 2) will need Cued Speech to relieve the *strain* of lipreading, (3) will always miss much of what goes on around him if he has to try to understand only through lipreading, and (4) needs the help CS provides in monitoring and correcting his/her own speech.

Most parents who have used CS consistently with a young deaf child have reported significant increases in understanding and communication within one to six months. We think that two-to-three years are typically required for language, speech, and speechreading to become functional as a solid base for oral communication without Cued Speech *when it is necessary or desirable to communicate without it.*

Janie Abell, mother of Holly, writes:

> *Holly is perhaps a good example for answering the question "How Long?" As she has aptly put it, she wants her family to continue to cue to her because now that she spends so much time with deaf friends she gets much less Cued Speech. She is aware that she needs continued refreshing of English words and the ways of saying things. Continued family use of Cued Speech is especially important for those kids who prefer to spend most of their social time in the deaf world after they are older. I still teach Holly new words all the time, and she helps me find the right English words for the new signs she picks up from deaf friends.*

How Long Will Continued Use of CS Be Helpful?

Sometimes we say to parents: "You may discontinue cueing to your child when you are ready for him to stop learning more language through conversation, and improving his speech and speechreading skills." The deaf person, even in adulthood, will continue to profit from further exposure to a clear, complete presentation of spoken language. Actually, a deaf child becomes progressively less dependent on having Cued Speech, in the sense that his or her ability to function without it when necessary continues to improve. On the other hand, there are at least four significant reasons why a deaf child will continue to need and prefer to have CS from those who can use it:

1) When a deaf person communicates through speechreading, he/she learns no new language unless the situation in which the surroundings are manipulated and the language stimuli reinforced (usually by written material) in such a way as to teach new language. The child needs as much exposure to CS as is possible, in both formal and informal settings, in order to acquire new language.

2) When receiving CS, children can understand clearly and with less effort. Speechreading is a stressful activity in which the brain is working furiously and attention must be concentrated. It is tiring, and the best lipreaders often become confused. Parents who deliberately deny their child Cued Speech to provide practice in speechreading are misled. They are denying their child the opportunity to understand easily, to be relaxed in communication, and thus to enjoy communication fully. The world is full of non-cueing people who will give deaf children more practice in speechreading than they need. Sometimes we say: "You can stop cueing when you are willing for your child to be under constant stress."

3) A speaking deaf person without CS is forced to depend upon hearing individuals to correct his/her errors in pronunciation and language, in order to improve. Not knowing how other people pronounce even common words (unless they cue), the deaf person has no way to improve or maintain the level of his/her own efforts unless others interrupt and correct him/her. Deaf children who have close relatives and/or friends who cue consistently receive a continuing "moving picture" of the spoken language, including pronunciation, patterns, and rhythm. This enables them to identify their own speech misconceptions and correct themselves, instead of depending on being corrected by others. Important to parents is the fact that when correction is necessary, it can be delivered quickly and easily, minimizing frustration or embarrassment.

4) Without Cued Speech (or a signing environment) deaf people are doomed to go through life in near-constant uncertainty about what is happening around them. It is difficult for hearing people to understand the crushing weight of this deprivation. It causes many deaf individuals to develop quirks of personality that are deviant from their natural selves. It causes all of them to be repeatedly discouraged, and makes many afraid to try. Understanding what is going on is a precious privilege hearing people take for granted. Parents need to remember this. They need to go to great lengths to make sure their deaf child "knows the score."

Whenever we speak to a hearing child we are showing the pronunciation of the words we use, the patterns of the language, its rhythm, stress, and timing. The deaf child also needs an accurate representation of what we say and how we say it. He or she will get plenty of exposure to people who do not use Cued Speech, and thus plenty of practice in functioning without it. A deaf person will always need the benefit of consistent, daily exposure to Cued Speech from family and friends, in sufficient amount to continue to refresh and improve the internalized phonological model of the spoken language, that is needed for speaking, lipreading, reading, and writing.

What Is *Dependence*?

Parents sometimes ask: "Will Cued Speech turn out to be a crutch on which my child will always be dependent?" An analogy might help clarify the role of Cued Speech in the life of a deaf child and defuse the pejorative term *dependent*. Suppose an otherwise normal child is born with a defective leg that, without special attention, will never become strong enough to enable that child to learn to walk. Suppose the child is fitted with an adjustable brace that can be set to provide just enough support that he or she can be taught to walk. With the increased activity of walking (with the brace) the leg becomes stronger, so that eventually the child can walk slowly without it. Because that leg will always be smaller and weaker than the other one, the child will never be able to run as fast or walk for long distances without the brace. In order to play running games with other children he or she must wear the brace. For comfort and continued physical development he/she should wear it most of the time. *But, the child can function better without the brace than if he or she had never had it at all!* And, he/she can function much better with it than without it. Is this an example of dependence, or of a tool for increased independence?

Cued Speech is not addictive. As a child becomes older and his/her major source of new language becomes reading, he/she actually needs CS less for learning new language. This does not mean, however, that those who can cue should stop cueing to the child. They should continue to make communication easy.

Osmond Crosby makes a strong point from actual experience:

> *My wife has no Anterior Crucial Ligament in one leg. Without her brace she can ski only very slowly, uncomfortably, and at some risk. With the brace she can ski powder, steep slopes, etc. Is she dependent on the brace, or does it contribute*

to her independence?

The following summarizing facts should be kept in mind:

1) The consistent use of Cued Speech with a deaf child can be expected to increase his/her ability to function without it when it is necessary or desirable to do so. There will be plenty of opportunities to function without CS. What the child needs is exposure to the full text of the spoken language, which is available to hearing children.

2) There is no possibility that Cued Speech will become a manual method of communication for the child. The information on the mouth is indispensable for receiving the full message.

3) If deaf children are not taught a method by which they can communicate clearly with each other, they will develop or find one. They do this by using gestures and mime, or picking up signs if they have access to them.

Deaf children brought up with Cued Speech often tend to communicate with each other with a combination, adding the cues to the aural/oral expression only as needed. *Parents should not do this!*

Use of CS Among Deaf Children

Deaf children who start receiving Cued Speech at an early age are often able to communicate well among themselves, particularly if as young children they are encouraged to cue expressively and especially to cue to each other. The development of expressive cueing, however, cannot be taken for granted. The development of expressive cueing will require constant and varied support from family, teachers, and peers. Of course, many deaf children using Cued Speech are the only deaf children in their programs. They are not likely to cue to hearing peers if their speech is reasonably intelligible.

Isn't Cueing A Chore for Parents?

Of course cueing is a chore, at least for a year or more. That is why deaf children who can cue don't bother to do it when they learn that others can understand them without the cues. For parents the chore becomes lighter as time goes on, because cueing becomes very natural and easy, and because they have less and less time with their child, so they don't have to cue as much.

Bill Robers makes this observation:

I don't think our child is as addicted as we are to Cued

Speech. After 13 years of cueing it feels funny not to cue. It certainly is no longer a chore to cue. To not cue would be like walking in a pouring rain with an umbrella folded up under your arm. Why not use it if you've got it?

Chapter Summary

Parents should keep in mind that as language grows in the child the balance between work sessions and more natural language development should shift in favor of language acquisition in natural conversation. Of course, parents should still remember that they must retain as an objective the introduction of new language in all appropriate situations. Accordingly, parents should maintain a current word work list, to remind them to make repeated use of new words, once they are introduced.

Parents should also maintain a vocabulary growth record and make sure that words, expressions, and idioms learned are reviewed or reused periodically. Most parents will find it easy to teach commands. Once the child begins to understand the question form, extensive use of questions can proceed rapidly.

Testing should be avoided except when occasional checks can be done in a casual way, to make sure the child has indeed learned the material well. Constant language awareness on the part of parents is essential. Specifically, parents should be always aware of the level of language complexity the child can handle, and communicate at that level, gradually increasing it.

Parents should keep notes on many aspects of behavior and communication. The easiest method of doing this is for one member of the family to keep a diary, inviting other members of the family to supply material for it.

Parents should consider whether they need to have an evaluation made of their cueing accuracy and fluency and, if the need exists, to improve it.

Parents should face up forthrightly to the necessity of cueing consistently to the child, and in his/her presence, "so long as they both shall live."

Because children who grow up with Cued Speech in the home are almost always mainstreamed by the early elementary grades, parents will need to learn as much as possible about the problems of mainstreaming. The subject is presented in detail in Chapter 20.

Chapter 9
Higher Levels of Understanding

One of the great advantages of Cued Speech is that with it understanding can be gained and language acquired through the process of living and interacting in the home. In a classroom with other children, the child must fit into a structured pattern, with specific lessons and procedures. This is the only way to handle the logistics of the learning process for a group of children. The teacher cannot make sure that every child learns what is presented. Not so in the home, where materials needed for language development are in abundance, encountered repeatedly in the necessary activities of life, and where instruction can be related directly to the child in question. The home has the resources needed for development of <u>higher levels of understanding</u>, not just of language, but of the situations and activities <u>behind</u> the language used with and learned by the child.

If the rich language development potential of the home is to be fully exploited by the parents of a deaf child, they must plan, and to some extent structure, their interaction with the child. Yet, to the child the process should seem natural, unstructured, and enjoyable. The material and its use can be structured in such a way as to assure comprehensive coverage of specific areas of language development and still be entertaining to the child. The activities in which parent and child engage together at regular intervals are "work sessions" to the parent, but they must be fun for the child, and the parent must not "come across" as a teacher.

If in reading this chapter you get the impression that proper use of Cued Speech with a child requires a lot of work on the part of a parent during the preschool years, you are right. A parent who first used a traditional aural/oral approach suggests:

> *You may want to stress more strongly that this extra home effort is not unique to Cued Speech but is required with any system you use. We have had people suggest that our success with our hearing-impaired daughter is due more to hard work than to Cued Speech. Actually it is much more work doing these exercises strictly oral. Cued Speech makes the necessary work a thousand times EASIER!*

As soon as cueing becomes meaningful to your child, it is desirable that you spend some time each day at structured or more formal activities. This is the only way to make progress occur systematically and steadily. Periods of "sit down and talk" seem to be effective in helping a child move rapidly into the communicating stage, but they must not degenerate into "sit down and teach" sessions. Keep in mind that this does not apply equally to all children. Some enjoy sitting down for "work sessions," but others resist efforts to have them sit and watch. Such sessions should be kept short and should be ended promptly when the child's interest wanes. A young child cannot endure too much of any one thing without losing motivation.

In Chapter 21, "The Greatest Problem—Time," the allocation of appropriate amounts of time to different activities is discussed in detail. Planned work sessions need to be regularly scheduled. It is helpful to have a specific spot for the planned work sessions. If they are kept at the right level of interest for the child, he or she will react enthusiastically and be ready for "business" when you go to the designated spot. It is not necessary, or even desirable, to use the same spot for all activities. But, carrying out a specific activity in the same place, day after day, is helpful. What is done during the "work sessions" should be varied and of interest to the child.

A desirable arrangement is to have the child sit in a comfortable chair facing the parent, on about the same level. You need not conduct these sessions alone. The presence of a hearing sibling or friend who is cooperative and willing to demonstrate activities and responses at your request can be very helpful. When a demonstration is needed, the hearing child can take his or her turn first. This is sometimes more effective than a demonstration by the parent. It should be made clear to the child that during these sessions the parent is the leader and controls the situation. The parent should turn the pages or change the subject, watching the child closely for clues to interest and anticipating the need for change.

One area of parent support that necessitates planned work sessions is that of auditory training, which needs to follow specific procedures in which the child performs a series of tasks, in sequence. A model suggested for coordinated use of auditory, aural/oral, and Cued Speech inputs, which parents can utilize at home with the guidance of a speech/hearing professional, is described in Chapter 14, "Auditory Training, Cochlear Implants," pp. 201-208.

The remainder of this chapter consists of descriptions of activities and materials suitable for the use of parents in increasing the sophistication and complexity of the child's internalized language, and the resultant depth of understanding of situations and events. Language should now be adequate for the child's level of understanding to increase rapidly. A goal to work toward is for your child to begin to want to know "all about" some things, rather than simply to know a little about a lot of things. This should be a long-range objective.

Scrapbooks

Scrapbooks are ideal for generating varied, interesting language development activities. Collect all kinds of good, pertinent, meaningful pictures from magazines and other sources. Select pictures of objects and activities familiar to the child. Photographs of familiar people and experiences are important. At some point it will become appropriate to have the child help collect and mount the pictures.

In your sessions proceed through the scrapbook and talk (and cue) about the pictures, emphasizing what your child shows interest in on that particular day. Remember to watch the child carefully, so that you cue when he or she is looking at you. Repeat statements about things of most interest, rephrasing what you say. Remember that the pictures generate thought in your child's mind even when no language is used. This means that judicious use of language can tie language to the child's thoughts. Talk about what you see in the pictures. Find things that are alike or different, tell what is happening and going to happen, talk about the colors of objects in the pictures. Say such things as: "I see a car. What do you see? I see something blue. What is it?"

Before a child has acquired much language, pictures are essential in talking about what has happened or what is going to happen. For example, before a trip to the grocery store, it is helpful to have a picture to show what will happen—such as a picture of a child riding in a shopping cart, a man weighing produce, or a cashier checking out an order. If you can't find a suitable picture in a magazine or elsewhere, you will need to take a camera on a trip to the store and take pictures of some of the items you will buy, for later use in the work sessions. All this should be accompanied by as much cueing as possible. Soon you will be able to say and cue to the child, without pictures or props: "We are going to the grocery store to get apples, sugar, milk, and bread," and be completely understood. Just before such a visit is a good time for discussion of what the child would like and a decision to include at least one item he or she suggests.

Scrapbooks can enable a parent to intensify the child's perception of an event or sequence of events, so that he/she understands its full scope and the relationships of things and persons involved. When the child "graduates" to the level of "experience books" his or her participation in the process can increase identification with the experience and understanding of everything connected with it.

Sarina Roffé suggests that at the supermarket you place the child in the cart, facing you, so that you can talk to him/her about each item you look at. This can become a very flexible game as the child's language level increases. You can ponder (aloud, with cues) what items to purchase, and ask the child what different members of the family prefer, and what to plan for different meals.

Linda Balderson calls attention to the usefulness of empty boxes and containers familiar to the child: "Show the child the empty container and say: 'The Cheerios are all gone. The Cheerios box is empty. We need more Cheerios. We will buy more Cheerios at the grocery store.'" Notice the build-up of language in the suggested sentences. Actual objects are usually better than pictures, though they may be less easily available.

The supermarket is a veritable treasure trove of language opportunities. But a parent shopping with a hearing-impaired child should allow extra time for so beneficial an expedition. It is occasionally best to take only the deaf child shopping, without siblings, in order to have more language-learning time.

Special Aids

There are many items that can be used effectively during your little work sessions. Some are listed in the Appendix. Simple object picture books are among the most useful. At least in the beginning, use books that illustrate only one object per page, so the child will focus on what you are talking about. Some pictures will not interest the child. Picture books containing photographs are usually better than books using drawings. Photographs are easier for the young child to recognize and relate to. If drawings are included, they should be realistic rather than stylized or fanciful.

If a picture requires a word that is difficult for you to cue, practice it before the work session, or skip the picture in question. For example, a picture of a squirrel could be skipped until a later session when you feel you could be at ease in cueing it. Of course, if a child shows particular interest in a hard-to-cue item, you should make every effort to practice the word before the next session.

If a book you are using includes the written word with each object, do not specifically call attention to the written words. If the child asks about a word, cue and say it, but do not attach emphasis to it. Do not make the mistake of pushing your child into reading before his/her language base is adequate. Why is this important? Because easy, appropriate development of reading skills requires prior knowledge of several thousand internalized spoken (but not necessarily articulated by the child) words, and even larger numbers of basic language patterns. A child who is led into reading before the language base and other elements of reading readiness are adequate is likely to 1) find reading difficult, and 2) tend to form poor reading habits that may handicap his or her reading. Suggestions regarding the child's transition into reading will be given in the chapter on that subject.

Simple lotto-type puzzles and materials (see Appendix) are invaluable because separate items can be held up and handled: animals can be made to hop, balls to bounce, kites to fly, etc. You can emphasize one item to the exclusion of all others. Also, the fact that you can manipulate each item makes it easy to make several statements about the one item.

Numerous other types of aids are available, such as games and flashcards. In addition, there are many objects and toys that are good for teaching colors, shapes, etc. It is a good idea to develop the habit of being on the lookout for such things. If you are looking for a particular book or item, it may seem to take forever to locate it. But, if you develop the habit of always watching for pertinent materials, valuable materials will pop up in the most unexpected places.

It is important that these aids be kept strictly for use during the work sessions until they have served their purposes. If the child is allowed to play with them at will, novelty and interest are likely to lag or be lost. Later, of course, the objects may be used for free play.

"Experience" Books

When scrapbooks are designed and arranged to depict an actual experience in the life of the child, they become "experience" books. Through them new and higher levels of interest and language can be achieved and maintained. For example, a scrapbook with many pictures of different animals always interests children, and they can enjoy going through it repeatedly. If the family goes to the zoo, the child actually sees and hears and smells many different animals. Through Cued Speech he or she can learn the names of many of the animals on the spot. But, if a parent helps the child make a book about the experience, preferably with photographs made during the visit, the book is unique because it represents his or her actual experience. It is not found in the library. Your child can show an experience book to others with pride in the knowledge that only he/she has it. Their real magic lies in the fact that each of them makes possible the reliving of an interesting experience and recall of everything learned.

In an essay on preparing preschoolers to read, Sarina Roffé provides an excellent description of the use of experience books. Though her essay was not aimed specifically at deaf children, it is fully applicable to them. Experience books, not found in the library, can be used effectively long before your child is ready to be read to. Here is the substance of what Sarina presents:

> The stories most interesting to young preschoolers are stories about themselves. Nothing creates more excitement in a child than having a book that tells about him/her and facilitates reliving an interesting experience.

Why are experience books so effective?

An experience book is something the child can share at nursery school or with neighborhood friends that no one else will have. It enables the child to recall an experience and retain it. It is something he or she can go back to and reflect on years later. An experience book is alive to the child. It is much less sterile and more familiar than a printed book. As the child becomes older you can allow him/her to dictate stories for you to write in the book. Then you can read them to him or her. This will help your child organize his/her thoughts and develop clarity in thinking, essential later in writing skills.

How do you produce an experience book?

Take one experience and reduce it to a series of simple steps. Use unlined paper or construction paper, pasting in pictures and souvenirs. If the child is old enough to have a language base, write one or two sentences on each page. Be careful to print, using uppercase and lowercase letters. This is important. You do not want the youngster (later) to use uppercase letters in the middle of a sentence. Use simple dialogue. Remember that it is not necessary or desirable to use written text in experience books for young children or those with meager language. The pictures and souvenirs can serve as the catalysts for repeated discussions of the experience. Incorporate text only as the child is ready for it.

It is important to have a picture or a souvenir on each page. The pictures need not require much artistry. Use stick figures and label them. If the experience was eating at a seafood restaurant, cut off part of the wrapper from the french fries and glue it in the book. Photographs taken with an instant camera are a nice addition. You can buy stickers from a museum gift shop to use instead of pictures. You can buy postcards when sightseeing and paste them into the book. If you visit relatives who live far away, paste their photos into the experience book. When they talk to you by phone, refer to the book to remind your child who is talking to you. Use mementos freely: pieces of wrappings, menus, ribbons, etc.

You can use crayons or markers to write sentences. Fasten the pages together in a binder or folder, or with yarn threaded through punched holes. If you're in a hurry, staple the pages together.

What experience books teach

These books are terrific for developing a child's *sequencing* skills. The ability to order events is important in reading readiness development. "First we did this, then we did that, and finally we...." A child who has difficulty in sequencing will have trouble reading, so it's important to make sure this skill is developed.

Experience books help develop *retention*. The child will have an easier time remembering an activity if his or her memory is supported by the preparation and use of an experience book. Ability to retain is enhanced by practice at retention. Retention is important in making the learning process rapid and efficient. It is essential also in testing. When your child reaches the point of supplying input for the making of an experience book, he or she can use you as a secretary and dictate what you are to write. This practice at oral expression (evaluation when you read the story back) helps your child learn to think sequentially and express him/herself clearly.

Finally, this activity is beneficial to your child's self-concept. If a child feels that what he/she has to say is important enough for you to write it in a book, it will help him feel good about himself. When a child feels good about him/herself the confidence needed for trying new things comes naturally.

What to write about

Family vacations, a trip to McDonald's, a birthday party, and an afternoon outing at the park are good things to write about. Visiting overnight at the home of a relative or attending a family gathering would be a natural. Choosing a toy in a store or making a gift is special to a child. Perhaps your child helped you plant something in the garden or pick flowers. A walk to observe the fall colors of the trees is good if you make pictures to support it, and then look at them and read the text after there are no more leaves. Taking a few pictures of your child at play with another child can make an excellent story for an experience book. Any activity that is of interest to your child and of sufficient duration to be resolved into a sequence of events is something to write about.

After an experience book is completed, your child will carry it proudly to share with others. Read each experience book several times with your child. You will see that he or she picks up words or expressions here and there, associating them with the pictures and the story. The words are important because they are his/her words, words about what he or she did, words about him/her. Years later your child may enjoy looking through the experience books and reminiscing. He or she may be astonished at some of the things you did together.

As your child becomes older, the experience-book procedure passes through several stages: 1) the parent's making the book, then 2) the child's dictating the experience and helping put the book together, then 3) as the child begins to write, the book can become an illustrated journal. At each stage both the child and the parent will enjoy a new level of pleasure, and the child will also develop new skills at each level of participation. Most important, the use of experience books leads right into enjoying being read to, then into the child's participation in the reading, and finally into the child's joyous discovery that he/she can read without a helper.

Sensory Training

The child will learn more from his/her experiences if you help him to be more aware of them by bringing all his senses (sight, touch, taste, smell, and hearing) into involvement with a specific experience. A parent can do much in a casual manner to involve several senses in each activity, and at the same time increase interest and variety. An orange or banana can stimulate use of all the senses. Show the child an orange and say (and cue): "It's an orange." Then suggest that he/she look at it, feel it (It's round like a ball. It has little bumps on it.), smell it (remove a piece of the peeling to increase the aroma), taste it, and shake and listen to it. (Nothing! There's no noise. I don't hear anything. Do you hear anything?) Sensory-oriented books for children are widely available. An excellent one is *The Touch Me Book* (p. 762).

You will need to demonstrate each of these sensory-related activities for the child and use the related language several times. Do not assume that at the conclusion of such a session the child will have internalized all the vocabulary and language structures you have used. Several repetitions of such a session will be required. The interest of the child will guide you as to how many repetitions (on different days) will be beneficial. The format described above can be followed with foods, toys, or other objects.

A fascinating game which extends sense-development activities consists of identifying items without seeing them: distinguishing two objects in a bag by feeling them; distinguishing items of different textures or shapes; tasting unseen foods; smelling fruits or flowers; listening to the sounds of different noise makers.

Puppets

A puppet can be a good "helper" because children readily "listen" to a puppet's statements and critical remarks, as relayed by the parent or teacher. When a puppet is used with Cued Speech it is best to have a hand puppet with a mouth that opens and closes, so that it can whisper to you, suggesting what you should "quote" to the child. The puppet also needs to have ears, one of which should be fitted with a hearing aid. A paper circle for the receiver and a piece of yarn for the cord will suffice. Such puppets can be either purchased or made.

The puppet is given a name and introduced to the child. The puppet's hearing aid should be conspicuous. This gives the deaf child an extra sense of identification with the new friend. The puppet talks to the child by whispering in your ear so that you can relay the message with cues. (The puppet has no hands with which to cue to the deaf child.) Anyone speaking to the puppet (including the deaf child) should cue, since the puppet has a hearing loss and can understand speech only when one adds cues for him. You may wish to have two puppets, one male and one female, letting the child choose.

Hand puppets can show a great deal of emotion—joy with a wide-open mouth followed by a big kiss, sadness with a crumpled-down face retreating to your shoulder, puzzlement with a screwed-up face and a questioning angle of the head. Admonitions can be delivered to the child via discussion between puppet and adult. The puppet whispers in your ear, then you reply, "Yes, I know. Julie forgot to watch. Let's do it again."

Puppets can demonstrate activities. Just say and cue the directions to the puppet and have him follow through. He can make mistakes too, as a child might. When the puppet is finished with a demonstration, it is the child's turn. The puppet can also instruct you to demonstrate. He whispers to you, and you say: "Okay, I'll bark like a dog if you want me to: Arf, Arf, ARF."

If the puppet distracts or bores the child, have them say good-bye to each other and put the puppet out of sight for a while. The puppet is your helper and not a plaything for the child. You may wish to give the child another puppet to play with outside of the work sessions. Do not allow the child to play with the puppet used for "business."

Puppets are very helpful in stimulating visualization and imagination. Start "pretending" (without using the word *pretend* at first). Example:"Joey (the puppet) is in the bathroom. What is he doing there? Is he taking a bath? Does he have some soap. Now he is washing his foot. Uh-oh! Joey doesn't have feet! Well, maybe he's washing his ears. He took out his hearing aid first." Another example: "Let's pretend Joey (the puppet) is in Mommy's bedroom, on Mommy's dressing table. What else is there with Joey, on Mommy's dressing table? Is it talcum powder? Perfume? Soap? What else?"

Children who don't seem to attend to cues may respond to a special type of puppet. A puppet consisting of a face drawn on the back of a plain-colored, stretchy glove will direct the child's attention. If you make one for each hand the puppets can talk to each other (if you will learn to cue with a light glove). We hope you have already learned to cue with each hand!

Telling Stories

As your child's attention span increases, you can begin telling stories, using non-verbal picture stories with sequential action. You may wish to collect progressive picture stories from magazines and other sources. Or, you can draw pictures using simple stick figures. You can then explain in simple terms what is happening.

When you begin to read simple books to the child it is best to have books that illustrate each important event or circumstance in the story. For example, "The Three Bears" should show Goldilocks testing each of the three porridge bowls, each of the three chairs, etc. You can begin by telling the story in the briefest possible terms and then elaborate in later renditions as your cueing gets better and your child's attention span and interest increase. Of course, children love repeated readings of their favorite stories, and this factor is very beneficial when the goal is to develop language.

There are numbers of wonderful books with only one line of text per page. Start with these. Some of these are sequential series, utilizing familiar characters and progressive related experiences. (See Appendix)

When you are first telling stories with the aid of a book or picture sequence, you can hold the materials in one hand, facing the child, and cue with the other. You then show the child the pictures at the appropriate times. In the early stages of reading books to the child, you can hold the book and read it, facing the child, since you need to decide when to show the pictures and when to resume reading.

You will find limited lists of books and materials in the Appendix. The lists are not extensive, because new and better materials are constantly appearing. Many good books and other materials (video, microfilm) are available in public libraries. It is much less expensive to borrow them than to buy them, and the selection is usually broader. Your child will enjoy helping select books and having you do sample readings from them. You can cue the samples silently (with lip movements) at the library or bookstore, without disturbing other library or bookstore patrons.

The Miracle of Reading to Children

The report of the Commission on Reading (1983) appointed by the National Academy of Education and the National Institute of Education concluded: "The single most important activity for building the knowledge required for eventual success in reading is *reading aloud* to children." The miracle that it brings about in hearing children happens as the child who is ready to read reaches the point at which he/she begins to follow *in the written text* some of what he/she is hearing. The child begins to pick out specific words, asking for verification, or even to ask to read back what has just been read. If the parent then begins to mix periods of reading to the child with periods of allowing him/her to read aloud, the child will soon become an autonomous reader, needing little or no help with appropriate material.

The same miracle can happen with a deaf child, but some adjustments are necessary. As in the case of a hearing child, the deaf child must have an adequate base of language, must have acquired a love of being read to, and must be ready for the adventure. The factor that necessitates a procedure different from that used in reading to a hearing child is that the deaf child cannot receive the message the parent is reading, and at the same time look at the written text. The parent must follow a pattern in which, after reading a sentence or two, he/she pauses to give the deaf child an opportunity to look at the text. Initially, this will be for the purpose of allowing the child to look at a picture. So, the habit of alternating can be developed with picture books, long before the child is ready to pay attention to the text. Refer to p. 252 for more details on reading to your child.

The child who is ready to begin reading will soon take advantage of the opportunity to look at the text, and may want to trace each sentence with a finger, after it is read by the parent. At first he or she may just look for a familiar word or two, especially the names of the characters, sometimes asking for verification of the written form. Soon, though, the child will begin following more closely, and may begin wanting to read aloud what has just been read to him/her.

At no point should the child be pushed to take any of the steps mentioned. The parent simply provides the opportunity, and allows the child to look down when he/she wants to look at the text, then looking up to signal the parent to continue reading. When the child expresses a desire to take the book aside and read it through himself/herself, the parent can rejoice in the knowledge that the child is on the way to becoming an autonomous reader.

"Upside-Down" Reading

You may find the usual practice of holding your child or seating him/her beside you a bit awkward for reading, since he or she will have to read your CS from the side. Once the child is accustomed to being read to, and is capable of sharing control of the book without breaking up the continuity of the reading excessively, you can change the arrangement. In one procedure the book can be placed on a small table or box in front of your child, right side up for him or her, and under his/her control. The child can then look at the pictures, look up at you when ready for you to resume reading, turn pages, etc. This procedure requires you to read upside-down copy. You may need to practice reading a story upside down before reading it to your child.

The upside-down reading arrangement serves two purposes. One is to give the child an increased sense of freedom and control of the book, for looking at pictures, etc. The other is to enable him/her to slide naturally into reading readiness, as described above. When your child is ready, he or she will begin to notice individual words and ask what they are. Next, he/she will begin to ask to read a portion of a page of the story to you after you have read it. This will happen as your child is ready (linguistically and otherwise), and will not push him/her prematurely into reading.

An Alternative to Upside-Down Reading

An ingenious alternative procedure suggested by Osmond Crosby makes it unnecessary for the parent to read inverted text, and also makes it possible for the parent to hold the child while reading to him/her. It requires the use of a large (20" by 30" or larger) mirror. The parent sits facing the mirror, holding the child on his/her lap, or allowing the child to sit or stand at one side. The child must watch the parent in the mirror, to perceive the cueing and mouth movements clearly. The child can also look at the book with the parent, when told to look at the picture. When the child is older and begins to pick out words and ask about them, he/she can do so conveniently. This procedure is very new, and not yet thoroughly tested. You may need to try both arrangements, to see which you and your child prefer.

The Calendar Game

This isn't really a game. It's a very educational and interesting activity that can add interest every day, suggested by Linda Balderson.

> *Get a wall calendar with daily spaces as large as possible. We mean large, large enough for Polaroid pictures if possible. Such calendars are provided for businesses. Or, get a giant sheet of paper or cardboard and make your own. Or, if you have to use a wall calendar of modest size, mount the pictures on a separate piece of cardboard and connect it to the square on the calendar with a piece of string.*

Paste pictures on the calendar to illustrate and record what you did on specific, important, recent days. Then, do the same thing for important coming events. One family used this technique to prepare its deaf child for the birth of a baby brother. They used pictures of the hospital, of the mother holding a baby, of the grandmother helping out, etc. Another parent reviewer reports extensive use of stick figures and drawings created for the purpose.

In addition to expansion of vocabulary and language, the activities associated with preparation and discussion of the calendar help the child refine his or her conception of time. Be sure to balance attention to the past, the present, and the future.

The "Held-HI" Videotapes

This series of videotapes of books for children to watch as an on-screen cuer reads them is a veritable "parent-saver." Once your child enjoys having you read books to him/her you can use these to supplement your own program of reading to the child. As soon as your child is able to operate the pause control on your VCR, (s)he can watch a videotaped book alone, giving you time to do other things. The books to accompany each videotape are loaned with it, and you return them when your child is through with the tape. Many children have watched the stories over and over, up to as many as 12 times. The 40 hours of stories cover a wide range of levels of interest and language complexity. Check the Appendix (p. 759) for availability and sources.

Your child holds the book as he/she watches the story being cued, and looks at each picture when told by the reader to do so. Thus, the procedure has all the advantages associated with the procedure you will have used in reading to your child. The child learns new language, enjoys the stories, and enjoys his/her own control of the procedure (stopping the VCR to look at the pictures). The only cost to parents is a modest annual fee, which is independent of how many videotapes are used, plus the cost of returning the tapes and books after they are used.

Good Manners

The development of mannerly behavior in a deaf child is very difficult if clear communication is not possible. As your child progresses in understanding, you can begin to require the same standards of conduct that you would require of a hearing child. If the child has siblings the development of mannerly behavior can occur in a very natural and relatively trouble-free way. If there are no siblings, good manners and orderly behavior will need to be a regular topic for discussion.

A deaf child must be taught to understand that his/her deafness makes it more difficult for him/her to behave considerately. Accordingly, extra effort on the part of the child and extra patience on the part of the parents are necessary. Praise for thoughtful, considerate behavior and patience in explaining problems are essential. Act on the assumption that your deaf child wants to be thought well of, and remind him/her frequently of your recognition of that fact. You may wish to reread Chapter 3, "Life With Leah," to review the many good examples of behavior-shaping techniques that are related there.

There are many aspects of mannerly behavior that children pick up, over time, that are difficult for a deaf child to acquire. Sarina Roffé suggests that it is important that deaf children learn:

1) that hearing people can hear through doors, windows, and walls;

2) that hearing individuals can hear a person speak when not looking at him/her;

3) to say "Excuse me, please!" and wait to be listened to, when trying to break into a conversation;

4) not to talk when others are speaking;

5) that it is not appropriate to talk about other people in their presence;

6) the principles of polite interaction;

7) not to be ashamed to ask other people to repeat something not understood.

Ms. Roffé adds that sometimes parents are so anxious for their child to talk that they forget to encourage manners and courtesy.

Your Child Needs to Understand

Deaf children typically suffer a great deal because they don't understand in unfamiliar or potentially frightening situations. They often don't understand what to expect, why something is happening, or when absent parents will be back. This applies to such (for them) traumatic experiences as a tonsillectomy, in which they are frightened because they don't know what to expect (except that it may be bad), to lesser matters such as why Mommy has to be gone for a few days, where she is going, and when she will be back. As soon as your child understands enough language for you to do so, try to enable him/her to understand why you have to leave, when you must leave, and when you will return. And, prepare a child thoroughly for everything from shots to surgery, visits to grandparents, arrival of a baby-sitter, telling the truth, and good manners in general.

A child's sense of security is dependent upon understanding, especially understanding what to expect when new and potentially frightening experiences are ahead. An article in the February/March, 1980 issue of *Cued Speech News*, reprinted below with permission, illustrates eloquently and vividly the importance of clear communication in this connection:

A Hospital Stay For Tiffany
by Linda Balderson

At 6 years of age Tiffany Balderson had been treated by more medical specialists than most people see in a lifetime. Profoundly deaf at birth, Tiffany also had congenital problems pertaining to: vision, balance, bladder, muscular development, gross motor delays, and allergies. She is missing a tear duct, is unable to breathe through one nostril, and was born with a constriction in her aorta which caused blood pressure inequities.

With all these factors against her, Tiffany underwent open heart surgery at the Children's Hospital National Medical Center in Washington, D.C., just before her 6th birthday, to surgically repair her aorta. She did beautifully, both medically and psychologically. Why? She understood clearly what was happening to her. I became Tiffany's interpreter as well as her mother. She could communicate her fears and receive answers to her questions.

Tiffany's clear understanding of English was and is the direct result of our decision to use Cued Speech with her when she was 18 months old. Her audiogram indicates a bilateral neuro-sensory hearing loss of approximately 105 dB in the speech range. After three-and-one-half years of Cued Speech, her communicative abilities were to be given the ultimate test. In a strange place and during a crisis, her few familiar links were her father and I, her hearing aid, and Cued Speech, which we provided for her throughout her hospitalization.

The doctors and staff at Children's Hospital couldn't have been more receptive to Tiffany's needs. Each child is assigned a "charge" nurse who has the primary responsibility for the overall physical and emotional well-being of the child. She is also responsible for involving the family in the child's treatment. Tiffany's charge nurse, Vicky, was exceptionally patient and understanding and developed a warm relationship with her. This allowed us freedom to come and go without causing Tiffany to feel deserted. Vicky had little difficulty understanding Tiffy's speech, and Tiffy speechread Vicky well, also. Vicky attached a sign over Tiffany's bed that read: "I am deaf—also, please do not put catheter in my right nostril. Please talk with me and tell me what you are doing. I CAN understand some of the things you say. Thanks, Tiffany." Everyone's willingness to communicate with her and help Tiffany through a difficult time made her heart surgery easier for all of us.

During Tiffany's hospitalizations I noted many of her questions and comments to indicate how well she understood via Cued Speech. Here are some excerpts from that journal:

June 13, 1979: Admission to Children's Hospital
1) Situation: Interpreted explanation of Tiffany's surgery was given by Vicky, her charge nurse, with procedures demonstrated on a doll. Tiffany was asked if she had any questions and was given the doll. Although Tiffany was quiet during the explanation, Vicky felt certain that she understood, as her facial expressions were appropriate

throughout.

Tiffany: "Can I give my baby a shot?"

2) Situation: In hallway, on the way to visit the intensive care unit where Tiffany would be taken after surgery.

Tiffany: "Is there a T.V. in there?"

3) Situation: In bath, scrubbing incision area well.

Tiffany: "Why are you washing me there a long time?"

My response: "That is where you will get your cut tomorrow morning."

Tiffany: "I don't wanna get a cut, Mommy. Please."

June 14, 1979: Open-heart Surgery

4) Situation: On cart outside room, just prior to leaving for surgery.

Tiffany: "I don't want a cut. I wanna stay with you, Mommy.... Get me off (the cart). I don't want to go.... You come with me, Mommy."

June 15, 1979: Intensive Care Unit

5) Situation: First visitation period.

Tiffany: "Can I go back to my other room now? I want my green room. I want Vicky."

6) Situation: A doctor, reading the sign over Tiffany's bed came over and signed (not cued): "Hi Tiffany, How are you?"

Tiffany:"What did he say, Mom?"

June 16, 1979: Back in Cardiac Unit

7) Situation: Upon awaking two days after open-heart surgery.

Tiffany: "Can I go in the toy room and ride in the fire truck?"

Tiffany's recovery period was uneventful. She has cheerfully returned to Children's Hospital several times for check-ups and even minor surgical procedures. She always insists on visiting the Cardiac Unit and seeing Vicky again. Some weeks after the surgery Tiffany spotted some Phisoderm soap high on a shelf. She nonchalantly commented, "That's the soap you used to wash my cut. My cut is all better now. You throw it away, o.k.?"

I'm not saying that Tiffany's open-heart surgery was easy for all of us. Until now, I don't think I could have written about it. She had her share of times when she hurt, times when she was angry and uncooperative, but she was spared the frustration of ambiguous communication at such a critical period in her life. For that important advantage we owe our thanks to all who have helped our Tiffany to become the bright and happy little girl she is today. (See page 547 for more details on Tiffany's "growing up.")

Chapter Summary

Balance "work sessions" with normal family activities. Remember that the work sessions are work sessions only for the parent. They must be fun sessions for the child. Have a special place for these sessions, so that the habit of getting down to business will be associated with the location without any exhortations by the parent. Remember that pictures are essential, especially in the beginning and intermediate stages of language acquisition. During the earliest stages, of course, there is no substitute for specific objects that should be seen, touched, and played with.

Make scrapbooks for use in organizing materials in sequence. When the child is ready for use of "experience" books, start making and using them.

Keep in mind the importance of utilizing as many of the child's senses as possible. Looking, touching, feeling, smelling (where applicable), listening—all should be called into play.

Make regular use of puppets. Stimulate visualization and imagination, especially with objects. And *tell* stories, *read* stories, *make up* stories, plan a trip. Do everything possible to help the child picture in his/her mind where you plan to go, what you plan to do, what you plan to take, etc. Then, take pictures on the trip and make an "experience" book on your return. The ability of a child to create mental pictures of events in the past, events planned, people, rooms in the house, etc., needs to be developed by communication that encourages visualization.

Tell stories to your child, then progress to reading simple books with lots of pictures, with only one line of text per page, and then on to the favorite books of young children. Use of a public library is desirable, and you may wish to refer to the lists in the Appendix. Use the "Held Hi" videotapes, which are available for loan, if your child is of appropriate age, language level, and experience with CS.

Use a big wall calendar, with pictures, to prepare for future events and recall past ones. If possible, get one large enough that you can mount or draw simple pictures on it.

As communication becomes easier and clearer, give attention to the development of mannerly behavior. Teach your child to respect the rights of other persons. To start this, make sure you respect your child's rights and protect his/her dignity.

Chapter 10
Advanced Activities

Initially, a child gains the building blocks of language: individual nouns, verbs, adjectives. He or she progresses to understanding combinations of these with each other and with adverbs, prepositions, and the other carriers of the richness of our language. All this language must become so well internalized and mastered that the child can move to new, higher levels of perception and understanding of increasingly complex activities and situations. This does not happen all at once, or as a result of a single activity. Rather, it comes from engaging in increasingly complex exchanges of language in connection with activities that make sense through rules, patterns, cooperation, and even planning on the part of parents and child.

This chapter includes a variety of activities provided for the benefit of parents who need specific suggestions about what to do with their deaf child in order to expand language and enhance personal development. Parents should not hesitate to improvise such activities.

Deaf children miss a lot of the fun of childhood because they are unaware of what is being said around them. Seldom do deaf girls know the verses that hearing girls everywhere recite as they jump rope. Seldom do deaf boys know the chants that hearing boys use to taunt each other. Hearing-impaired children tend to miss most of the fun of poems, singing, and verbal games. Reading experts consider these activities vital to later development of reading skills. Nursery rhymes and children's songs, presented in a form clear through vision, allow a deaf child to experience many of the pleasures associated with rhythm and rhyme in language. All these activities, and the associated benefits, are available to deaf children who are fortunate enough to have hearing friends, siblings, and parents who cue.

A parent suggests that you remember that the verses, rhymes, and sayings in this chapter 1) rhyme in spoken English, 2) have catchy rhythms, and 3) may contain nonsense syllables. A deaf child can fully appreciate and enjoy these characteristics only through Cued Speech.

Finger Fun

These activities should remind (and help) you expose your deaf child to what are universal sources of enjoyment among hearing children. Most people know the hand movements that accompany these simple verses. If they are unfamiliar, consult a book of childhood verses and/or activities at a public library, or check the lists of materials in the Appendix. You may have some problems at first with alternating the cueing and the movements. For most of the rhymes in this section, each phrase can be cued and the appropriate movement can follow. When the statement is repeated twice (as in "pat-a-cake"), you can say and cue the phrase the first time, then do the movements with speech the second time. Or, you can teach the rhyme with Cued Speech and then do the rhyme and movements. Later, you may be able to cue with one hand and make some of the movements with the other.

Tandem teaching/playing can be effective in handling some of the Finger-Fun activities and Finger-Play songs. Two people do the activities simultaneously, one cueing and the other doing the appropriate hand movements as they recite the words together. The deaf child can enjoy performing with one and then the other.

> Pat-a-cake, pat-a-cake, baker's man,
> Make me a cake as fast as you can.
> Pat it and prick it, and mark it with a B,
> And put it in the oven for you and me.
> ***
> Here's the church and here's the steeple,
> Open up the doors and see all the people.
> ***
> This little piggy went to market,
> This little piggy stayed home,
> This little piggy had roast beef,
> This little piggy had none.
> This little piggy said, "Wee, wee, wee," all the way
> home.
> ***
> Peas porridge hot,
> Peas porridge cold,
> Peas porridge in the pot,
> Nine days old.
> ***
> There were two blackbirds sitting on a hill,
> The one named Jack and the other named Jill.
> Fly away, Jack; fly away, Jill,
> Come again, Jack; come again, Jill.
> ***

Nursery Rhymes

Nursery rhymes and other simple poems for young children can be used either for recitation or for dramatic play. Here are a few of the many that can be used profitably.

Jack be nimble,
Jack be quick,
Jack jumped over the candlestick.
***

Mary had a little lamb,
Its fleece was white as snow,
And everywhere that Mary went,
The lamb was sure to go.
***

Humpty Dumpty sat on a wall,
Humpty Dumpty had a great fall;
All the king's horses and all the king's men
Couldn't put Humpty Dumpty together again.
***

Jack and Jill went up the hill,
To fetch a pail of water;
Jack fell down and broke his crown,
And Jill came tumbling after.
***

Baa, Baa, black sheep,
Have you any wool?
Yes sir, yes sir,
Three bags full.

One for my master,
And one for my dame,
And one for the little boy
Who lives in the lane.
***

One, two, buckle my shoe,
Three, four, shut the door,
Five, six, pick up sticks,
Seven, eight, lay them straight,
Nine, ten, a big fat hen.
***

Folk Sayings

These sayings are examples of the perennial favorites that are picked up and chanted or sung by hearing children everywhere to entertain themselves and others. Deaf children are seldom exposed to this material, which contains much verbal "nonsense," because it is often considered unimportant by the adults who would have to teach it. Since a deaf child's learning time is limited, there is a tendency to regard as unimportant everything that is not "strictly business."

Psychologists consider folklore, including both its wisdom and its nonsense, to be an important factor in social development. When Cued Speech is used, a deaf child can pick up sayings such as these from people around (especially hearing siblings and peers)—with much fun and little effort.

One for the money,
Two for the show,
Three to make ready,
And four to go.
***

Order in the court,
The monkey wants to speak,
Speak, monkey, speak!
***

Through the teeth,
Past the gums,
Look out, stomach,
Here it comes!
***

Rain, rain, go away,
Come again some other day,
Little Johnny wants to play.
***

Sticks and stones will break my bones,
But names will never hurt me.
***

It's raining, it's pouring,
The little old man is snoring,
He went to bed with a bump on his head,
And didn't get up in the morning.
***

Finders keepers,
Losers weepers.
***

Monkey see, monkey do,
Monkey speak -- and so do you.
***

April showers
Bring May flowers.
***

A sunshiny shower
Won't last an hour.
***

Good night, sleep tight;
Don't let the bedbugs bite.
***

Red sky at night, sailor's delight;
Red sky in the morning, sailors take warning.
***

See a pin and pick it up,
All day long you'll have good luck;
See a pin and let it lay,
You'll have bad luck all that day.
***

Little girls are made of sugar and spice
    and everything nice,
Little boys are made of snakes and snails
    and puppy dog tails.
***

I see the moon,
And the moon sees me.
God bless the moon,
And God bless me.
***

Haste makes waste.
***

What's your name?
Puddintame!
Ask me again and
I'll tell you the same.
***

Poems

When a child is older, has a good deal of language, and knows some nursery rhymes, he or she will probably enjoy learning short poems. With Cued Speech the rhythm and rhyme of poetry can be as real to a deaf child as to a hearing child.

Fishy-Fishy

Fishy-fishy in the brook,
Daddy caught him with a hook;
Mommy fried him in the pan
And baby ate him like a man.
***

Little Pussy

I like little Pussy,
Her coat is so warm;
And if I don't hurt her,
She'll do me no harm.

So I'll not pull her tail,
Nor drive her away,
But Pussy and I
Very gently will play.
　—Jane Taylor
***

The Swing

How do you like to go up
　in a swing,
Up in the air so blue?
Oh, I think it the
　pleasantest thing
Ever a child can do!
—Robert Louis Stevenson

The Little Turtle

There was a little turtle,
He lived in a box,
He swam in a puddle,
He climbed on the rocks.

He snapped at a mosquito
He snapped at a flea,
He snapped at a minnow,
And he snapped at me.

He caught the mosquito,
He caught the flea,
He caught the minnow,
But he didn't catch me.
　—Vachel Lindsay
***

Fuzzy, Wuzzy, Creepy, Crawly

Fuzzy, wuzzy, creepy, crawly,
Caterpillar funny,
You will be a butterfly
　When the days are sunny.
Winging, flinging,
　dancing, springing
Butterfly so yellow,
You were once a caterpillar,
Wiggly, wiggly fellow.
　—Lillian Schulz

Songs

A child with a profound hearing loss may not be able to carry a tune (many can be taught to do so), but he or she can enjoy singing simple songs. And, as explained on page 171, a parent can cue the approximate pitch to help the child raise and lower pitch on the right syllables. Deaf children have or can develop a sense of rhythm; most can enjoy the interaction of "singing" with someone. Initially it can be a matter of just singing together without words—la-la-la, tee-dah-too-dah—varying pitch up and down appropriately in patterns that will help lead to approximation of pitch production in actual songs. As vocabulary increases, the child appreciates the simple songs of childhood. Someone must take the time to teach the child the words, but it's a pleasurable sharing activity usually denied to deaf people. Singing encourages relaxed vocalization and can help enhance speech production. It also has the benefit of introducing words seldom encountered by deaf children (twinkle, weasel, baboon, swish, teensie, thumbkin). Best of all, it's fun!

Twinkle, Twinkle, Little Star	*Row, Row, Row Your Boat*
Twinkle, twinkle, little star,	*Row, row, row your boat,*
How I wonder what you are;	*Gently down the stream.*
Up above the world so high,	*Merrily, merrily,*
Like a diamond in the sky.	*merrily, merrily,*
Twinkle, twinkle, little star,	*Life is but a dream.*
How I wonder what you are.	

Pop Goes The Weasel

All around the cobbler's bench
The monkey chased the weasel.
The monkey thought it was all in fun,
Pop! Goes the weasel.

A penny for a spool of thread,
A penny for a needle,
That's the way the money goes,
Pop! Goes the weasel.

The Animal Fair

I went to the animal fair,
The birds and the beasts were there,
The big baboon, by the light of the moon,
Was combing his auburn hair;
You ought to have seen the monk,
He jumped on the elephant's trunk;
The elephant sneezed and fell on his knees
And what became of the monk?

Old Macdonald

Old Macdonald had a farm, E-I-E-I-O;
And on his farm he had a cow, E-I-E-I-O;
With a MOO-MOO here and a MOO-MOO there,
Here a MOO, there a MOO, everywhere a MOO-MOO,
Old Macdonald had a farm, E-I-E-I-O.

Old Macdonald had a farm, E-I-E-I-O;
And on his farm he had a pig, E-I-E-I-O;
With an OINK-OINK here, and an OINK-OINK there,
Here an OINK, there an OINK, everywhere an OINK-OINK,

> *A MOO-MOO here and a MOO-MOO there,*
> *everywhere a MOO-MOO,*
> *Old Macdonald had a farm, E-I-E-I-O.*
>   *(Repeat with duck, horse, donkey, chickens, as*
> *interest remains.)*

If you have a younger hearing child, watch for opportunities to teach your deaf child the neighborhood slang and jingles the sibling picks up. However, it may be best to instruct the deaf child as to when such jingles are appropriate. The parent reviewer who suggested this relates an illustrative incident. The hearing sibling enjoyed taunting other children with this jingle: "Baby, baby, suck your thumb. Wash your face with bubble gum." The family taught the jingle to the deaf youngster, who promptly yelled it at the adult who lived next door.

A,B,C,D,E,F,G

The A-B-C song is a favorite with all children, and the deaf child should be no exception, if it is introduced after the child is fully ready. Later, of course, the names of the letters can be associated with their written forms. After the child is receiving speech therapy, parents should discuss with the therapist the child's readiness to be taught the sounds associated with the letters. Teaching this is often very effective in encouraging expressive cueing.

Finger-Play Songs

These songs are enjoyable with or without the hand movements. After the child knows one of these songs, can understand the words, and can cue and "sing" the words, the accompanying hand motions can be taught. Of course, one cannot always cue at the same time, unless the movements require only one hand, or are not produced at the same time as the words. Usually, the movements can be made after each phrase. Or, two people can perform in tandem, as explained above.

Grey Squirrel

Grey squirrel, grey squirrel	Hands on hips, move from
Swish your bushy tail	side to side. Make swish-ing movement with hand.
Wrinkle up your funny nose,	Push up nose with one hand.
Put a nut between your toes.	Two hands together with imaginary nut between.
Grey squirrel, grey squirrel,	Repeat hands on hips,
Swish your bushy tail.	swishing.

Eency Weency Spider

Eency, Weency Spider	
Went up the water spout.	Move fingers up, climbing motion.
Down came the rain	Down-rushing movement
And washed the spider out;	with hand.
Out came the sun and	With fingers spread, move
Dried up all the rain;	hands out and up.
Now Eency, Weeny Spider	
Went up the spout again.	Move fingers up, climbing.

Where Is Thumbkin?
(To the tune of Frère Jacques)

Where is Thumbkin?	
Where is Thumbkin?	Hands behind back.
Here I am,	Bring fist forward, thumb up.
Here I am.	Other fist forward, thumb up.
How are you today, Sir?	Wiggle one thumb.
Very well, thank you.	Wiggle other thumb.
Run away.	Put one hand behind back.
Run away.	Put other hand behind back.

Repeat with Pointer, Tall Man, Ring Man, Pinky, etc.

If You're Happy and You Know It

If you're happy and you know it, clap your hands (clap, clap)
If you're happy and you know it, clap your hands (clap, clap)
If you're happy and you know it, then your face will surely
     show it.
If you're happy and you know it, clap your hands (clap, clap).
     Other verses: 2) stamp your feet 3) nod your head 4) pat
          your knees 5) wave good-bye

I'm a Little Teapot

I'm a little teapot short and stout.
Here is my handle, here is my spout,
When I get all steamed up I just shout
"Tip me over and pour me out."

Wheels on the Bus

The wheels on the bus go round and round, round and
     round, round and round
The wheels on the bus go round and round, all through
     the town, all through the town.

Other verses: 2) Baby goes wah wah wah 3) Lights go
blink, blink, blink 4) Driver says Move on back
5) People go up and down 6) Money goes clink clink
clink 7) Windshield wipers go swish, swish, swish.

Board Games

A hearing-impaired child will usually find it easier to participate in a structured situation than in free play because his or her attention can be centered on a few areas rather than many. Playing simple board and card games can be valuable activities for two important reasons: They provide good opportunities for learning new language, and they provide experience in socialization. The rules of good sportsmanship should be taught early, through use of expressions such as:

You won.	*Oh, too bad!*
Good for you.	*Better luck next time.*
Congratulations.	*Play fair.*
You lost, try again.	*No, that's not fair.*

It's best to start with simple games such as the classic "Uncle Wiggily" or its modern variations, such as "Winnie-the-Pooh" or "Candy Lane." Most of the simple games for young children require no reading or verbal language. A spinner or set of dice can be used to determine the number of spaces a player should move.

Although these games can be played by a child with little language, they are much more fun and actually very beneficial when they are accompanied by discussion of what is happening, what the game is about, etc.

An older child with more language can profit from more involved games that require reading and discussion. If a hearing cuer is playing or is nearby, anything not understood by the deaf child can be explained.

Card Games

Many inexpensive card games for children of all ages are available at local stores. Even a very young child can be taught to play and enjoy a game such as "Old Maid." Begin by teaching the child to shuffle the cards, and talk about the action as you show how to do it. Say: "I am shuffling the cards." Stop the shuffling long enough to cue, then resume. Next, teach the child how to deal the cards. Have him or her practice dealing five cards to each player, then seven cards to each, etc., until he understands the meaning of the word *deal*. Say: "*Deal* me five cards. *Deal* me seven cards." to make the process clear at first. Other instructions will vary with the game being played. Teach each rule by explanation and demonstration, repeating several times.

After a child has learned several card games, he/she should know such terms and phrases as:

The dealer.	Place all the cards face down.
A trick.	The player to the left of the
Draw from the pile.	dealer starts first.
Low man wins.	You must play the same suit.
High man wins.	It's your turn.
You keep score.	Put it on the discard pile.

"Play Cards"

Use an old deck of cards that may have some cards missing. Arrange 18 cards in sets of two (two 2's, two 3's, etc.), using the numbers up to 10. Do not include the face cards.

Count, using the deck. Ask: "What's this number?" If the child doesn't know, ask: "Can you find out?" The child can count the symbols.

"Concentration"

Mix up the cards. Place them face down in four rows of five cards. Try to find a good many sets of two cards with like numbers (two of clubs and two of hearts, etc.). Have the child turn over any two cards. If they have like numbers, he/she gets to keep them. If not, he or she turns them face down. Another child or a parent should then take a turn. The game can be continued until all sets are matched.

"Fish"

Seven cards from a complete deck are dealt to each player and the remaining cards are put in a draw pile in the center of the table. The object of the game is to get all four cards of a particular kind and lay them on the table. The player with the most sets of four at the end of the game is the winner.

The first player (the one to the left of the dealer) asks another player (by name) for a particular card (one he needs to build a set of four). Say: "Billy, do you have a two?" If the player who was asked for the card does not have it, he says, "Fish," and the first player draws a card from the pile in the center of the table. If he gets the card he asked for from the pile, he gets to take another turn. If not, the next player to the left is allowed to take his turn. The game is over when a player succeeds in putting all his cards on the table in sets.

Group Games

Some of these games require a good vocabulary and understanding of language. All of them offer opportunities to make vocabulary and language expansion enjoyable.

Circle Games

Circle games such as "Ring Around the Rosy" and "Farmer in the Dell" can contribute to language growth and also provide entertainment if someone will cue the words.

"Categories"

The leader names a category. All the children, in turn, have to name items that fit in the category specified.

Examples:	Furniture	Fruit	Wild Animals	Birds
	chair	apple	tiger	robin
	table	orange	snake	crow
	bed	peach	elephant	cardinal
	sofa	grapes	leopard	sparrow

Variation: The leader can name an item such as *chair*; then, the children have to identify the category, and name other items.

Variation: The leader can designate categories operationally: things you eat, things you use, things you wear, things that eat and drink.

"Directions"

The leader directs a designated person to do something. The object of the game is to see if each person in the group can remember what he or she is told to do and carry out those directions. Begin with one or two simple directions, and expand as the child can remember more. This game can easily be adapted to a group of varying ages (such as the members of a family) by giving directions to each child according to ability to succeed.

Example: Go to the closet and get a broom. Put the broom behind the door. Then open the door.

"I Spy"

The person who is IT says: "I spy something _____"(name a color) or "I'm thinking of something _____." The other people take turns at guessing what item in the surrounding area is being referred to. The person who guesses the correct answer is the next IT. Simple colors should be used in the beginning (red, yellow), but the game should progress to more complex hues (light blue, lavender, rose).

"Opposites"

The leader says a word. The correct response is a word with an opposite meaning.

Examples:	Leader	Answer
	up	down
	light	dark, or heavy
	small	large, or big
	day	night

"Remember It All"

The first person in the group tells something he/she did. The second person repeats what the first one said and adds something of his own. Each succeeding person must recall and repeat the full statement of the person before him, and add something of his own.

Example: Person #1 — "I went to the store."

Person #2 — "I went to the store and bought a loaf of bread."

Person #3 — "I went to the store and bought a loaf of bread and five apples."

Person #4 — "I went to the store and bought a loaf of bread and five apples, and paid for them."

Or: Person #1 — "I'm going to my grandmother's house and take my pajamas."

Person #2 — "I'm going to my grandmother's house and take my pajamas so I can stay all night.

Person #3 — "I'm going to my grandmother's house and take my pajamas so I can stay all night, and I'll take my doll, too."

"Simon Says"

The leader, "Simon," stands in front of the other players and tells them actions to perform, sometimes performing them himself: "Simon says put your left hand on your head." "Simon says stand on tiptoe." The players must imitate exactly when Simon actually says "Simon says____," but if Simon does not preface the order with "Simon says," they must not do it. Whoever gets caught performing an act without the authorization "Simon says," before the command is out of the game. The last player remaining in the game gets to be Simon in the next game.

"When Did I Do It?"

The leader states something he or she did. Everyone guesses when he/she did it. The first person to guess correctly takes the next turn. Any concept of time can be used: time of day (exact time or generality such as *evening*), month or season (*springtime*), general periods of time (*when you were a baby*), or specific occasions (*Thanksgiving*).

Example: "I hung up my stocking. When did I do it?"
ANSWER: "Christmas Eve."
Example: "I got off the school bus. When did I do it?"
ANSWER: "This afternoon." Or: "This morning when I got to school."

"Where Did I Go"

The person who starts the game says what he did. Whoever guesses where he went to do it is the next person to take charge.

Example: "I got a haircut. Where did I go?"
ANSWER: "To the barber shop."
Example: "I borrowed a book. Where did I go?"
ANSWER: "To the library."

"Who Am I?"

The person who is IT thinks of a familiar character, real or fictional. The children take turns asking questions to help them determine who he is. The leader answers their questions only with "Yes." or "No."

Examples: "I'm thinking of somebody." (Grandmother, Davy Crockett, the child's best friend, Dennis the Menace)

Questions: "Are you real?" "Are you a lady?" "Are you short?" "Do you live in this house?" "Do you live in this town?"

Variations: Use famous animals such as Lassie, Winnie-the-Pooh, or Donald Duck.

"Grocery Store"

(An activity for teaching concepts and terms of quantity.) A hearing-impaired child, even after he or she knows the names of things, usually takes a long time to learn how to express quantity other than with numbers. He may say: "I bought two candies," not knowing people usually say: "I bought two pieces of candy." Or, he might say: "Mommy bought two breads," showing that he has generalized the regular plural form, but not knowing that he should say: "Mommy bought two loaves of bread."

When a child is taken to the grocery store, these designations of quantity should be used consistently. An older deaf child can help make out the grocery list before going to the store. Mother may dictate (and cue) the list, using the proper designation of quantity in each case, and have the child write it down if (s)he is able to do so.

A card game can be made with pictures of the grocery items— or, better, with the items themselves. Each player has to give the correct phrase, such as "A dozen eggs," in order to win a card.

Here are some expressions of quantity:

```
a quart of milk (half-gallon, gallon)
a package of frozen strawberries (better use a picture!)
a pound of butter or margarine (half-pound).
a jar of jelly               a dozen eggs
a pint of whipping cream     a 5-pound bag of flour
a bunch of carrots           a can of soup
a half-dozen oranges         a bar of soap
a 3-pound can of coffee      two cans of beans
5 pounds of potatoes         a head of lettuce
a 4-pound beef roast         a box of cookies
a roll of toilet paper       a sack of sugar
```

Trips

Every trip made by a family should be a source of language enrichment—before, during, and after the trip. Any jaunt away from home can be of value—whether it's to a neighborhood store or to a distant vacation spot. Before the trip, there should be discussion about the trip—where, when, why, and what will be seen. Make the child aware of any planning that is done for the trip.

During the trip, talk as much as possible about everything that is seen and experienced. Take photographs on special trips, and collect souvenirs. When the child returns home, review the experience. Use any photos made or souvenirs collected as reminders of trip highlights. This helps the child remember the trip in detail, for later discussion.

Cueing Parties and Picnics

During the summer months, or even on weekends during the school term, it is highly beneficial to have cueing parties for the hearing children in your neighborhood. Have refreshments and FUN. Use some of the activities described in this chapter, and explore other types of cueing fun, always keeping in mind the ages and interests of the children involved. One of the most severe problems of deafness is a sense of isolation from peers. Hearing children who cue to your deaf child are of immeasurable value as sources of social and psychological benefit, and as aids to language development.

Visualization Activities

Visualization and pretending are among the most important mental skills, fundamental in developing efficient memory, imagination, creative thinking, and other important mental capacities. You can probably think of additional games and activities that are perhaps better suited to your own child and your own situation. Children love to pretend. Their ability to visualize can be developed easily and enjoyably. Be sure to have the child close his/her eyes when visualizing. This intensifies the visualization by freeing it from competition with that which is real.

Ask your child to think about Mommy's and Daddy's bedroom, and to pretend to go there. Say: "Close your eyes and see yourself going to Mommy's and Daddy's bedroom. Now, close your eyes and pretend you are in Mommy's and Daddy's bedroom. Now, close your eyes again and tell me what you can see. Can you see the bottom drawer—the one where Mommy keeps her sweaters? Pretend you open the drawer. Now pretend that when you open it there is a doll in it. Close your eyes and pretend that you are bringing the doll here, to me. Are you finished? Now, *really* go to Mommy's and Daddy's bedroom and look in the drawer. If you find a doll there, *really* bring it to me."

"Pretend" Games

Play elaborate pretend games in which the child and you go somewhere. "Go" to the zoo and "see" some animals. With a book of pictures of animals, identify three or four animals you want to visit. Then, "visit" them at the zoo. When "visiting" the zebra, "count" his stripes, and then actually count the stripes in the picture of a zebra. "Look" at the big lion at the pretend zoo, and ask the child if it is a daddy lion or a mother lion. Ask how you can tell the difference, and compare with the pictures. This facilitates learning the word *mane*. Then, discuss which other animals have a mane, and look at the pictures. Pretend that the big lion roars. Ask the child to close his/her eyes and see (and hear) the lion roar. Ask how big the lion's mouth is when he roars. Have the child show you.

The possibilities of pretend games are endless. They are valuable because they require the child to make the mental effort to visualize, which is far more conducive to mental development than the passive activity of watching TV cartoons!

Auditory Games

A bit of ingenuity is required to devise games that give good practice at recognizing names, environmental sounds, short sentences, etc. These games should be of short duration. They are great for parties at which several deaf children are in attendance. If only one hearing-impaired child is present, the stimuli may need to be muffled when a hearing person has a turn, or with a very young child a bit of deception may be in order.

Chapter Summary

In addition to selecting from the activities suggested above, devise your own activities. Children learn by *doing*. Enjoyable activities lead to much communication, much use of new language, and thus rapid acquisition of language. Such activities also make it easier to lead hearing siblings and peers to cue consistently. Additional materials are listed in the Appendix.

Chapter 11
Language Development

The power of language that develops normally in children is that it soon reaches the point at which new language can be learned through language, not limited to what can be seen and touched—language about things, people and places beyond the seas, even language about things that exist only in the mind. The power of language opens up to the child all the knowledge that is in books, magazines, newspapers, and libraries. With language the child can learn to read, and no longer has to learn everything from others. The tragedy of deafness is that it robs children of this power of language.

In Colorado in 1984 I (Cornett) met a profoundly deaf 5-year-old boy, John Nemeth, whom I decided to use in a demonstration before an audience of parents and teachers. John had understandable speech and had received Cued Speech in the home since before he was 2 years old. He seemed not to be bothered by the attention of the audience. After a short conversation in which his ability to understand and participate in intricate conversations was demonstrated, I said, "John, have you ever seen a subway?" On his negative reply, I asked, "Do you know what a subway is?" When he answered, "No," I proceeded to describe a subway, as follows:

"Well, John, you certainly know what a train is. A subway is a very big, long tunnel in the ground where a whole train can go down and travel miles and miles and miles. When it stops in a place under the ground where everything is lit up, the doors of the train open, and people get out and go up an escalator until they are out of the ground. Other people who are waiting go in the doors. They sit down on the train, and go on to another place where the train stops. Then they get off. Now, John, do you know what a subway is?" John thought a few seconds and said, "Yes." I asked: "What do you think about the subway?" He replied, "I think there might be a lot of bugs down there."

Notice that I created in John's mind, through language alone, an idea of something he had never seen or heard about, along with the word that designates it. The sequel to this story is even more dramatic. About a year later John and his mother visited me at Gallaudet University. When they came down the hall I was at the drinking fountain. When John saw me he started running down the hall, saying,

"Dr. Cornett! Dr. Cornett! I saw the subway!" "Was it like you thought it was?," I asked. "Yes," he said, "but it was a lot bigger!"

Indeed, the power of language is that it soon reaches the point at which new language is learned through language. A good (not average) high school graduate has a reading vocabulary of about 50,000 words and a speaking vocabulary of about 25,000 words. Thus, he or she has learned at least 25,000 words through interaction with written language.

Lois Hurowitz illustrates the importance of situations that impel a child to search for language to meet a specific need. Her daughter Amy was at the one-or-two-word stage in language development in an oral program, years before Cued Speech was used with her.

> *Amy owned a little brown stuffed dog of which she was particularly fond. It was her favorite toy and went everywhere with her. One afternoon, after taking a nap on my bed, she forgot her dog and left it behind. For reasons I don't remember, the bedroom door was locked and the dog was inside.*
>
> *Amy soon realized that the dog was missing. Unlike her mother, she remembered exactly where she had left it. She tried to tell me where the lost dog was located. She ran up the stairs, up and down the hall, and tried to open the bedroom door. She used pantomime and screamed, but to no avail. I had no idea what she wanted. I didn't realize the dog was missing, let alone that it was in my room.*
>
> *Amy became frantic and, out of sheer desperation, she must have reached down in her intelligence and something clicked. From somewhere—school, lessons, language reinforcement at home, whatever—things seemed to come together, and Amy communicated a vital need through speech. She pointed to the door and said "Doggie." I immediately responded by retrieving the dog for Amy and tried to reinforce this new language experience as much as possible. This was not Amy's first word, nor was it the first time she had associated an object with a word, but I do believe it was the first time that Amy used language to communicate a vital need. The experience represented a large step in her language development, which appeared to accelerate after the incident.*

To the casual observer, the deaf child's main problem seems to be limited ability to speak: he or she just can't talk much, or speak well enough to be understood. However, his/her greatest problem is lack of *language*. Our language is what we say and how we say it. Our language consists of words—vocabulary—but the power of language is the way we can arrange those words. Consider the sentence: "The boy rode a bike." Let us analyze this familiar pattern:

Who (noun) + Action (verb) + What (object-noun)
(The) boy   rode   (a) bike.

The sentence starts with the subject-agent. It continues with the action performed by that subject-agent. Then, it identifies the object on which that action is performed. The three items—subject, action, and object—are linked in a logical order that completes the idea that is being expressed. It is essential that the child learn the ways in which words are put together in our language. He or she does this through repeated, clear exposure to our language in meaningful situations.

How Hearing Children Learn Language

Hearing children learn language by interactive communication with those around them. The communication must relate to things they are thinking about, or to which their attention is directed. They absorb and use a pattern such as the one described above *because they have been exposed to it countless times, starting in infancy*. When they are very young their parents say much more to them than they expect them to understand, but they also take the time to show them individual objects and actions and to name them through speech: "ball," "run," "come." A long period of language input and gradual growth of understanding usually precedes any spontaneous use of language by a child. Children "absorb" language from others. Later, it comes out when they are ready to use it.

After months of listening and looking, associating combinations of sounds with objects and situations, the hearing child starts using a simplified, inaccurate version of the language: "Mommy bye-bye." He or she imitates adult language, but reduces it to child size, and also invents combinations. His/her parents help revise and expand his/her simple statements: "Mommy bye-bye." "Yes, Mommy went bye-bye." The child creates generalized language forms—not always correctly—such as: "I rided my bike." This illustrates an error that is not an error at all. It illustrates the ability of an intelligent child to expand grammar in a logical and creative way, later learning and substituting the exceptions of the irregular forms (e.g., *rode)*. By being able to hear every element of the language as it is spoken, he/she gradually internalizes its correct patterns. Before the age of 4 a child is able to insert new words in a familiar pattern and thus manufacture language to express his or her own ideas. By the age of 5 a child has absorbed more language through communication than he or she will learn in all his/her years of schooling. By this time, also, the child's ability to generate language of his/her own has developed to an advanced stage.

The Typical Deaf Child's Language

Since the typical prelingually deaf child cannot receive spoken language in its complete form without special help, the patterns tend to remain a mystery for a long time. At age three or four a deaf child is not likely to say "The boy rode a bike." He or she may tell about the boy on the bike by either pantomime or drawing. He/she may know some words and use them to express his/her impressions as they come to mind: "bike boy ride," "boy bike ride," or perhaps "ride boy bike." The small but important words *the* and *a* are typically omitted. They are two of the three words used most frequently in the English language. Such fragmented speech may get the idea across, but it is far from the conversations of three-and-four-year-old hearing children.

Could you understand a whole story set down in the confused language of the typical preschool deaf child? Parents want the child to speak well, but it is most important that he or she have something to say and be on the way to being able to say it in the patterns of his/her culture. A child needs to be able to understand not only the essential ideas, which can be expressed very crudely, but the nuances of the language through which meaning can be expressed with precision.

The stage in which the hearing child uses incomplete, fragmented expressive language is crucial to linguistic development. Though expression is fragmented, reception is more nearly complete. As time goes on the child absorbs more and more through reception and fills in the gaps in his/her expression. This can occur naturally and effectively only if the child is in an environment that supplies a rich input of language related to his/her interests and activities.

Like a hearing child, a deaf child must receive much language input before expressive use can occur. Concepts (ideas) and the labels for them (words and phrases) must be appropriately paired in natural situations. If the deaf child perceives only a small fraction of the language input directed at him/her, the acquisition and refinement of language come very slowly.

Spoken Language/Written Language

The users of methods other than Cued Speech have consistently resorted to written language as the primary means of teaching English to most deaf children. The exceptions are the fortunate ones able to learn English at a reasonable rate in a traditional oral program. There are several reasons why dependence on written language for the initial learning of language is undesirable: 1) It is not practical for natural, face-to-face communication. 2) It cannot provide the quantity, relevance, and flexibility of language exposure needed for learning language at an adequate rate. 3) Written English does not provide a proper foundation for speech and speechreading, since it is not consistent with the spoken form. For example, there are 12 ways to spell the single sound of long *e* in English. 4) Written English does not make clear the suprasegmentals of spoken English, such as rhythm, stress, juncture, and intonation, or even the spoken syllables themselves. 5) Acquisition of the primary first-language base must occur before reading is feasible or practical for most children.

The greatest problem in use of written language for the primary task of language acquisition is the first of the drawbacks listed above: It is not practical for the natural, face-to-face communication with parents and family through which a child can acquire language most efficiently. It lacks spontaneity, convenience, and flexibility. It is not immediately applicable to the child's interests at the moment. Only after the child becomes a reader should the written language become a dominant factor in his/her language growth.

Cued Speech and Language

The prime function of Cued Speech during the early years is language development through easy, clear communication. Its express purpose, for the early years, is to enable the deaf child to develop language in a manner and at a rate resembling the development of language in a hearing child more closely than was ever before possible. With Cued Speech the deaf child is able to perceive each element of the spoken language repeatedly and clearly. It is thus reasonable to expect, or at least to hope, that with Cued Speech the deaf child can and will learn language at the rate and in the way a hearing child does. In fact, when a child with little language begins receiving Cued Speech at 4 or 5 years of age, he/she may learn English at a rate two or more times that of the average hearing child that age, closing the language gap completely by age 8 or 9. This possibility is borne out by many of the case histories in this book (pp. 161, 310, 312, 314, 317, 416-418).

Two things are necessary for a child to learn a new word or expression, or a new meaning for a familiar word or expression. He needs to know *exactly* what is said, and also what it means. Suppose big brother finds his two little sisters, one deaf and one hearing, in his room. "Beat it! Clear out!" he yells, and shakes his fist at them, causing them to vacate the premises in a hurry. It is obvious to both girls what he *means*. The hearing girl also knows what he said, and after a few similar experiences may begin using the same idiomatic expressions. The deaf girl learns no language. She sees her brother's lips moving and senses his anger. She understands essentially what he means, but not what he *says*. She must know what is said *and* what it means in order to learn it as language.

The example above describes a situation full of meaning to the deaf girl, but without the language labels (spoken words) by which she can learn language from such situations. The solution is to make the sounds (and therefore the words) clear to the deaf person by adding the cues of the CS system. Knowing what is said, the deaf child will have the same opportunity as a hearing child to learn new language.

When a word is presented to a young deaf child with Cued Speech, the object, action, or other concept to which it refers must be made clear through the situation. To learn a new word the young child must understand its meaning through the environment. What the child is shown and what is happening must enable him/her to understand the meaning of the language used. If the language refers to an object, that object must be within the child's vision and he or she must know the reference is to it. If the word refers to an action, he/she must see the action taking place and know that the communication is about it. As the child learns more language, after a few years it becomes possible for him/her to learn new words through language alone, without the actual presence of the objects or actions to which they refer.

The Early Stages

In the early stages of language development a hearing child may learn to babble the word "daddy" if mother says it frequently when father is not present. The child will learn to use the word "daddy" to refer to her/his father, if and only if mother uses the label "daddy" repeatedly in situations in which the child can see that it relates to her father. After seeing other children use the same word in reference to their fathers she will expand her conception of the word *Daddy* and grasp the unique connotation it carries for each child. The association of the label with the person to whom it refers can occur only if the situation makes clear the relationship between the person and the label. Your deaf child cannot learn language just through your cueing every word you say. He/she must associate the visible language with the objects, ideas, and concepts you talk about, just as hearing children associate what they hear with what it means.

Many adults are slow at learning the names and faces of new acquaintances and must have the name and face of each matched several times. After several pairings of this type, one needs only the name to envision the person it identifies. The same is true of hearing children. As they are exposed to language they begin to match labels with objects and actions. They absorb the associations until they are able to react to the verbal labels alone. They can then identify a ball or shoe or hat, or whatever, without the aid of external clues furnished by the speaker. With this foundation their grasp of language becomes more and more focussed, so that they understand the significance of a *red* ball, the *other* shoe, or *Jack's* hat.

First a child learns a few hundred verbal labels representing concrete objects and verbs, such as "apple" and "run." Then he or she begins to grasp the implications of qualifying words and phrases, such as adjectives, adverbs, prepositions, phrases, etc. He/she readily learns the meanings of abstract terms (love, good) when he or she encounters them enough in context to refine his/her understanding of their meanings. Eventually the child reaches an age and language level at which such terms can be explained and defined. At this point he/she is capable of learning new language through language alone, and typically experiences a veritable explosion of language, quantitatively and qualitatively.

The developments described above occur normally and naturally in the deaf child with whom Cued Speech is used consistently, but there is a catch. Even when parents and siblings use Cued Speech consistently it is impossible to match the quantity of language input received by a hearing child. The deaf child's language development will tend to occur in direct proportion to the *amount* and *quality* of the cued exposure. Thus, the family using Cued Speech must be under constant pressure to expand the opportunities for communication under conditions that make introduction of new language interesting and natural. Relatives, friends, baby-sitters, neighbors, church associates—all are potential sources of communication and its result, natural language development. The deaf child's need is to receive enough cued input to match all the incidental language the hearing child receives, overhears, gets from TV, radio, telephone, neighborhood children, etc. This cannot happen, and parents can only do their best. Some of the difference can be made up through the quality of the cued exposure. That quality can be measured by the extent to which the cued input 1) is interesting to the child and 2) is directed at language development.

Your deaf child will take more interest in people he/she meets if you provide a chance to learn the name of each of them. When he/she meets a person for the first time, introduce that person (with cueing, of course): "Jimmie, this is Bobbie." Then, immediately, use the name in a sentence: "Bobbie lives in the big white house across the street." Use and cue names! The deaf child feels left out if he/she doesn't know everybody. This applies to delivery persons, the mail-carrier, everyone you admit to your home.

Facing and Overcoming The Awful Truth

Tragically, the typical profoundly deaf child, without a form of verbal language clear to his senses, must be taught every word specifically. With the limited exposure to verbal language this permits, it is difficult for a deaf person to go beyond the stage at which primarily concrete concepts are conveyed verbally. This has serious implications for a deaf person's education and thinking processes. Dr. Hans G. Furth (1966), a psychologist who has made important contributions to our understanding of deafness, said: "The fact is that under our present educational system the vast majority of persons, born deaf, do not acquire functional language competency, even after many years of intensive training."

Dr. William Stokoe, chairman of the English Department at Gallaudet University, stated (1963):

> When we look at the literally tons of evidence—we have files of student writing going back to 1954—just one conclusion is to be drawn. If one objective of our profession is to teach the language of his culture to the deaf child, we have failed. Looking only at the top tenth of the products of our teaching of the deaf, we can hardly see that we have tried. The language patterns of the other 90 percent hardly bear looking at.

Geers, Moog, and Schick (1984) evaluated selected English structures of 327 children from oral/aural (OA) and Total Communication (TC) programs, using the GAEL-S (Grammatical Analysis of Elicited Language--Simple Sentence Level). They reported that both OA and TC children, ranging in age from 5 to 9 years of age, scored far behind normally hearing 4-year-old children. They also reported: "The data clearly indicate that profoundly deaf children do not acquire language at a rate comparable to their normally hearing peers. This is true for those educated in aural/oral programs as well as those in total communication programs."

Language Evaluation in Deaf Children

Parents need to be aware of several pitfalls in interpreting the results of language testing. The first question the parent should ask is: "Does this test result mean what it seems to mean?" A test very widely used with deaf children is the Peabody Picture Vocabulary Test (PPVT). In the test the child is exposed to a word or sign and then asked to chose from four pictures the one represented by the stimulus. Suppose that at age 4 the child scores at the average level for a 2-year-old child with normal hearing. Most parents would assume that this means the child is delayed two years in vocabulary. Maybe not. To decide what the test result means, one must know how the test was administered. If the child has been trained orally, the test will likely be administered that way. If so, what is measured is not how much vocabulary the child knows, but how much vocabulary he can *lipread*. The teacher may repeat the test a year later, at age 5 years, and proudly announce that the child has scored at age 4 years, improving in vocabulary two years in a single year. Not necessarily, or even likely. The child may have made significant progress in ability to use residual hearing in lipreading. What the parents can be sure of is that the child is now not more than one year delayed, and may not be delayed at all! Until the child can be tested with written language, or with Cued Speech, the test result only sets a limit on the amount the child *may* be delayed in vocabulary development.

If the child is in a TC program, and the test is administered with signs, the result will likely be an accurate reflection of his or her sign vocabulary, but it will not test English vocabulary. He or she may not know the words for half the signs he/she recognizes and uses to indicate the appropriate pictures. Since the words the child does know will be known in the written form, an accurate evaluation of his/her English vocabulary can be made by testing with written material.

Parents need to be particularly cautious about the announced results of testing a child who has a cochlear implant. In the beginning the child will likely have great difficulty in using the stimuli of the implant in recognizing words. After he has made some progress he may be given the PPVT, and the test may then be repeated a year later. The therapist may then report, quite accurately, that the child's performance on the vocabulary test has improved two years in a single year. Unless a very careful explanation is given, the parent may think that this means that the child has learned two years worth of vocabulary in a single year. Not so. The child's improvement in use of the implant has enabled him to demonstrate two years more vocabulary knowledge than he/she could a year earlier. Actually, in at least the early years of using the implant, the child is not likely to learn much new vocabulary or language through the use of the implant, though it may well help in other areas, such as speech production and reception.

Consider the advantage to the parents if their child is at home with Cued Speech. Administration of the test with Cued Speech will provide an accurate measure of the child's English vocabulary level, in comparison with hearing children. Administration of an alternative form of the PPVT without cues will then show how well he or she is doing with the input from the cochlear implant. CS parents can monitor their child's progress in both these important areas. They can also guard against any neglect of language development by using Cued Speech consistently while so much attention is being directed at development of skill in decoding the stimuli from the implant. These and other problems are considered at some length in Chapter 14, "Auditory Training, Cochlear Implants." For a very helpful analysis of the problem of language assessment and descriptions of the language tests most widely used with young children, refer to Chapter 7 of *Language and Deafness*, by Quigley and Paul (1984). This book also furnishes a thorough analysis of the language problems of deaf people.

The Clarity of Cued Speech is the Key

Bell (1892, op. cit., p. 25) made it clear that the language to be learned must be the language the child receives:

> *I think there is only one royal road to the learning of a language, and that is to use it for the communication of thought without translating it into any other language. The moment you teach one language through another the pupil thinks in the one language and translates into the other. You must use the language without translation, and I hold that any language that is used in the presence of deaf children will be acquired by them by imitation if the language is clearly presented to their senses.*

Implied in his statement about translation, but not explicitly stated by Bell, is that in addition to being presented in a form clear to the senses of the child, language must be in a form that bears a simple *code relationship* to the target form (spoken or written language). A code relationship is one in which the parts of the coded transmission correspond one-to-one to the parts of the target (in this case spoken or written) form. Otherwise, the learning of language in the target form will be accomplished only when communication is interrupted for the process of explaining and teaching the target form. In order for signing deaf children to learn written words, for example, parents and teachers must stop communication to pair each sign (already learned) with either the written form or the fingerspelled form.

The only two systems that have both the characteristics specified above, clarity and coding, are fingerspelling and Cued Speech. Fingerspelling codes the written form. Cued Speech codes the spoken form. French and Belgian cuers use the verb *coder*, meaning to code, for the verb *to cue*. In Belgium Cornett was given a T-shirt bearing a drawing of a rabbit with a speech balloon indicating that he was saying: "Et tu—*tu* coder?"—meaning: "And you—do *you* cue?"

That Cued Speech presents spoken language clearly to a deaf child was shown by G. Nicholls (1979, 1982) in a study of 18 children exposed to Cued Speech for at least four years. She reported speech reception scores of over 95% on key words in sentences, with or without sound. She commented: "Equally high levels of reception by such children (profoundly deaf) have not been previously reported."

Cued Speech enables hearing-impaired children to begin learning the visual equivalent of the spoken language as early as possible so that they will understand and think in that language, even before being taught to make the sounds accurately. It requires the child to recognize each sound, or pattern of sounds, by watching the mouth and the hand.

The learning of a sign language by deaf children can occur in the same natural, easy manner, through communication. For this they must be in an environment in which sign language is used with them consistently. Of course, the language learned this way will not be English, but another language that also can be useful.

The evolution of the philosophy of manualism into Total Communication, which aims to secure some of the benefits of speech input by combining it with signing, has had a profound effect upon the education of deaf children. In practice Total Communication usually leads to almost complete dependence upon the signs and accompanying facial expressions for understanding communication. Signs are highly useful for communication among deaf persons, but inefficient for acquisition of spoken and written language. Moreover, TC fails to solve the problem of early communication with and learning from hearing parents. Fewer than 5% keep up with their deaf child in the use of signs during the first six or seven years. In a very thorough study of the language development of young deaf children using "Sign English," Bornstein (1980) reported that the hearing parents "did not advance very much beyond the beginner's level of proficiency even after three years of exposure and use."

Spectacular acceleration in the learning of verbal language often results from a change from signs to Cued Speech. Jennifer Ziebell comments as follows: "I don't know if phenomenal gains in short periods of time are unusual or not, but I found the switch from SEE to cues unbelievable in regard to the improvement."

Cued Speech is a system for transmitting the spoken language visually, not a separate language in itself. It can usually be learned in a week or two. It can enable hearing parents to use all the language they already know (the language the child needs to learn, speak, read, write, and speechread) without any inherent limits in vocabulary, grammar, idioms, or dialect. The controlling factor is motivation.

Cued Speech enables a deaf child to learn verbal language in the very early years, so that he/she will think in that language even before being taught to make very many of the sounds of speech. CS requires the child to recognize each sound, or pattern of sounds, by watching the mouth and the hand. Remarkably, children have no trouble using both the information on the mouth and that on the hand. Like deaf children using signs, they soon become able to maintain a global view, seeing both face and hand at once.

Hearing children *learn* many times as much language as they are *taught*. They learn most language through communication in which there is no thought of teaching as such; that is, they learn without specific interruption of the communication process to cause learning. In order for a deaf child to learn verbal (spoken or written) English, he/she must receive it in a form that he/she can convert into verbal English without any help. Deaf children who know Cued Speech can repeat, on first attempt, words they have never encountered before. These can include words in other languages if they contain only sounds familiar to the children. Even before they learn to speak, they can still learn the words naturally, as a hearing child does. Clear speech will have to wait until articulation skills develop.

The Learning of Abstract Language

A common impression among educators of hearing-impaired children is that it is very difficult for a deaf child to learn abstract language. Nothing is further from the truth. *Verbal* abstractions are difficult for a deaf child to understand if 1) he/she is weak in verbal language, or 2) if the verbal abstraction is visually ambiguous, as in unsupported oral/aural communication. Signs for abstract concepts are learned readily by a deaf child through communication in signs, if the child already has a good foundation in some form of sign communication. Similarly, verbal abstractions are picked up readily by a deaf child growing up with Cued Speech, just as by a hearing child.

Because typical deaf children are also weak in reading, they tend to fail to learn verbal abstractions through reading. This compounds their already serious problem with verbal abstractions.

Consider the concept of time in the future, which can be learned naturally and easily through experience associated with clear language input. Mother answers the telephone and, after a brief conversation says, "That was Daddy. He's coming in a few minutes." A three-year-old deaf child, if he knows what his mother said, will know (the first time) only that the conversation was with Daddy. If Daddy arrives a few minutes later, the first seed of the idea of the future is sown. If the sequence happens repeatedly, the child soon knows that when Mother answers the phone and then says something like "Daddy's coming," they can expect Daddy soon. Appropriate use of statements such as, "We'll go in a little while," and "We'll go to the lake tomorrow," can lead quickly to understanding of the concept of the future. In summary, the learning of abstract language is no easier and no harder for a deaf child than for a hearing child. In either case the child must have adequate language input and communication must be in a clear form.

Idioms

Most of the phrases and sentences of English are idiomatic; that is, they mean something other than what one would expect from the individual meanings of the words. There is a common impression among educators that deaf children are very weak in idiomatic language. They are typically weak in the idioms of *verbal* language. Idioms are learned in much the same way as abstractions. The problem of deaf children is the same as with abstractions: They must encounter the idioms in situations that give them an accurate idea of the meaning, and they must also know exactly what is said. Suppose Jimmie has a dog that periodically runs through the house, dodging and darting about to release pent-up energy. He will soon understand what it means to be *on a tear* if his mother says on several such occasions: "Jeff is on a tear again."

Idioms are not typically taught to hearing children in school—they are just picked up as illustrated above. Cueing parents must be sure to use idioms with their deaf child, especially those involving the common prepositions. The reason typical deaf children are weak in verbal idioms is the same as the reason they are weak in verbal abstractions: 1) they are weak in verbal language itself, and 2) they do not receive verbal language in a clear form. Thus, they do not learn the idioms they encounter in communication. They learn only those verbal abstractions and idioms that are specifically and individually taught to them.

Sign languages have their own abstractions and idioms. Deaf children who grow up with deaf parents will typically have a rich variety of sign abstractions and idioms. These will be useful to them in communication within the deaf society. They can also constitute a base for conversion into verbal equivalents if the children begin exposure to Cued Speech.

Twelve Ways Cued Speech Changes the Teaching of Language in the Home

The following changes in how language can be learned by a deaf child all result from the fact that Cued Speech presents the spoken language accurately and in full phonological detail.

1) There is a reduction in the time required for learning each item. Why? Because each word or phrase appears in a clear form and can be associated easily with the concept that is being paired with it.

2) The parent can both stimulate and follow the interest of the child. He can teach language associated with the child's interest.

3) Language can be taught quickly, through spoken communication, without writing.

4) Because the input is clear, story-telling can be more complex and more enjoyable than with traditional oral methods.

5) As language grows, parents can teach about things the child has not seen, even without pictures or props.

6) Much language is picked up, not specifically taught.

7) Parents can teach verses, poems, rhymes, songs, and puns.

8) Children can learn verses, poems, songs, and stories from cued videotapes.

9) Pretending and role-playing are enhanced.

10) Language can be learned from cueing siblings or peers.

11) Parents can use at will formal language, informal language, slang, or dialect, with complete freedom as to vocabulary.

12) Verbal abstractions and idioms can be picked up as easily and naturally as by a hearing child.

The Parents' Role in Language Development

The role of parents of deaf children in language development is to do everything that will contribute to the same result for their children that happens to typical hearing children. Most of the responsibility for language development in a young deaf child falls on the parents. For many years we have known that use of Cued Speech at home is more beneficial to a deaf child than its use at school, although both are beneficial. Hage, Alegría, and Périer (1989) reported results of studies (of 55 children) confirming that deaf children who had Cued Speech only at home performed much better with it than children who received it only at school. Children who received CS both at home and at school did better with it (but not a lot better) than those who received it only at home. Even if a child is receiving Cued Speech in preschool, the results achieved will be limited unless there is consistent use in the home.

The first responsibility of the parents in language development is to learn Cued Speech and begin using it consistently with the child. From the first, remember that the child must know what you are talking about before he will learn to recognize the language for it. Thus, one begins by noticing what the child's attention is on, and identifying it with Cued Speech. "Ball, that's a ball!" "Doggie, that's a doggie." The child will soon learn to look at something, and then at you, if he or she wants you to identify it. One of the most thrilling moments you will have, as a parent of a deaf child, is when your deaf child suddenly realizes that everything has a name. He/she may begin directing you to one thing after another, pulling you toward it and pointing, and then looking at you for its name. His/her vocabulary of nouns will literally explode at this time.

In the "How to do it" sections of this book, materials, activities, and suggested procedures for language development are provided. The purpose of this chapter is only to trace and explain in broad outline the process of language development as parents should support it. First, of course, is the learning of the names of objects and persons, which will continue indefinitely. The child will next begin to understand combinations of words. First are combinations of nouns with verbs or adjectives, as in "The ball rolled." "Daddy jumped." "Big ball." "Little ball." Here one should be sure to use a big ball and a little ball in introducing this language. Also, someone must really jump to identify the action in question. In identifying nouns, one may wish to use the single word at first, but it is important immediately to add the article. Thus, one might say: "Bug! That's a bug." Later, pointing: "A bug."

The articles *the* and *a* cannot be taught or explained to a child. Miraculously, however, the child will come to understand their significance if they are always included and cued appropriately.

When parents use Cued Speech they should not specifically teach the child. This statement can easily be misunderstood. It is made in order to emphasize the importance of using the normal interactions of family life to develop language in the child. What should be avoided is the *appearance* of formal, structured lessons. The home is the best language laboratory there is for a young child. Necessary activities—bathing, dressing, eating—all furnish situations potentially rich in language. Parents need only to make use of them. Play activities, kitchen activities, bathroom activities, and other family activities are full of opportunities for use of language focussed on what the child is thinking about. The same activities offer opportunities to lead the child's thinking in directions involving new language. All this use of the home as a language laboratory is exactly what good parents of a child with normal hearing do. Most parents do this without conscious effort except that made naturally by a loving and attentive parent. Cued Speech parents need to do the same, but with more specific attention to the introduction of new language.

Parents also need to display ingenuity in finding ways to introduce new language. Sarina Roffé, mother of Simon, suggested:

> Once he learned a new word, I found a synonym to replace it. This easily enriched his language without much effort. Sofa became couch and then davenport. I would also eavesdrop on the hearing children's play for their expressions and casually find a time to introduce this vocabulary to Simon. It was almost effortless because he usually needed only one exposure, occasionally followed by an explanation. The results gave him a language foundation for the rest of his life. We started CS when Simon was 3½. Now he is 15, and he scores in the higher percentiles (for hearing children) on all the standardized tests.

An important aspect of language development is the learning of multiple meanings for the "little" words, the *function* words. These include prepositions (by, with, for, in, on, out, off, etc.), conjunctions (and, but, as, etc.), and other words that combine with nouns, verbs, and adjectives to form the idiomatic expressions that make up most of our language. Each of the prepositions listed above, for example, has more than *40* different meanings. Reading authorities suggest that a child must know most of these to read easily and well at fourth-grade level. Parents need only to list the 20 or so most common meanings of each "little" word, from a good dictionary. Then, they should systematically introduce them in conversation, giving an explanation only if the child is confused or curious. Over a period of months the habit of doing this will make a great difference in the skill with which your child handles language. Another way of proceeding is to spend a few minutes each day in formal work on the function words.

Research on Language Development

Not much research has been done that compares language development in CS children with that of hearing children and other hearing-impaired groups. Two significant studies have been reported. One, by Hage, Alegría, and Périer (July, 1989) reported mastery of grammatical gender in French by children accustomed to Cued Speech. According to them, grammatical gender is "...generally taken to be a feature to which deaf children have limited access through traditional oral methods."

Of perhaps more direct interest to parents in the United States is a study entitled "Receptive and Expressive Language Abilities of Hearing-Impaired Children Who Use Cued Speech," by Berendt, Krupnik-Goldman, and Rupp (1990). We quote from the report:

This study examined the receptive and expressive language abilities of a group of CS learners aged 5 to 16. All subjects had a prelingual, bilateral, 80 dB or greater hearing loss, and had been using CS for a minimum of two years. The test volunteers submitted a videotaped spontaneous language sample, analyzed using the Developmental Sentence Score (DSS), the expressive measure. The receptive measure was the Rhode Island Test of Language Structure (RITLS), and there was also a questionnaire. On the DSS, the CS children correctly produced an average of 36.5 out of 50 sentences, which is essentially the same as the hearing children. Those children who were introduced to CS before age 2 scored significantly better than those who began at a later age. On the RITLS, the CS group acquired an average percentile score of 92, differing significantly from the hearing-impaired population the test was normed on.

Two facts from the study are very significant: 1) on average, the CS children performed better than 92% of the children in their age groups among those on whom the test was normed, and 2) the superior performance of the CS children who were introduced to CS before the age of 2 probably reflects the effect of their longer exposure to CS as much as their early starting age. Certainly the children whose exposure began before the age of 2 had more years of exposure than the average, since the minimum required was only two years.

Here is a teacher's story of her experience with a child, as she related it to the Mid-City Kiwanis Club, Shreveport, La., May 5, 1982. The organization had made several donations of funds to make Cued Speech instruction available for parents and teachers. The story has many implications for use of Cued Speech in language development.

Julie Lewis
by Nora McClure
Shreveport, La., 1982

She's 6 years old, blonde, can skate backwards, and loves Miss Piggy. Her name is Julie Lewis—and your organization helped save her. You didn't carry her from a burning building or pull her out of the deep end of a pool. Your rescue wasn't nearly so dramatic, but it was nonetheless important. Your organization gave Julie the key with which she has already begun to unlock her silent world of limited understanding and inability to communicate with others. That key, of course, is Cued Speech.

Julie, who was born with a profound bilateral sensorineural hearing loss, first came to my classroom in December of 1980, almost a year and a half ago. Before that she had been in school for two years and had been taught by oral methods alone.

One could easily see that Julie was a very bright child by the way she so readily grasped things shown to her. But, she understood very little of what was said to her. She didn't know the names of common, everyday objects; she could not follow oral directions; she could not understand the simple stories I read to the class each day; it was very difficult for her to learn subject matter—she could not understand the new information. Her communication with me consisted of isolated words or two-word phrases—most of which I could not understand.

Then I saw a videotape of deaf children who had been taught with Cued Speech. Soon after, I attended a workshop. By the end of the workshop I was convinced that Cued Speech was the answer. Now, after teaching with Cued Speech over a year, I **know** it's the answer.

I learned to cue in a class that Gay Wolcott taught every Tuesday night. I began using it on a limited basis with the youngest children in our summer school program last year. By fall I could cue fairly well, and I used it daily with my class of seven and with three other younger children who come to me every day for language training. In addition, the two speech therapists at our school both cue—so these children receive cued articulation and cued language therapy each day.

I began a class to teach my students' parents to cue. We met one night a week for four or five months. Four families faithfully attended, and the members learned to cue with varying degrees of proficiency. The star parent-pupil was Julie's mother, and she now cues almost all of her communication with Julie at home. She told me that, although she realizes Julie still has a long way to go, they now have a way of understanding and communicating with each other.

Needless to say, she's very pleased with this. By the way, the second star pupil was Julie's grandmother.

Recently I gave Julie a test that assessed her understanding of spoken language. The results were enough to keep me cueing for the next 40 years. On this test, which I cued to her, she scored as if she were 5 years 8 months. Her chronological age was 6 years 4 months. It had been seven months since I had given her the same test. At that time, without the benefit of Cued Speech instruction, she had scored as if she were only 3 years 1 month. Chronologically she was 5 years 10 months. In other words, in only seven months of instruction with Cued Speech she had gained two years and three months in her ability to understand spoken language.

Now, instead of pointing to things and trying to show me what she wants, Julie can ask for common objects by name. Now Julie can tell me she wants "Kool-Aid." Now she says "brave" every time she sees a picture of an Indian warrior; now she says she lives in a "trailer."

Now, instead of being unable to follow oral directions, Julie can "get her color box and go to the table"; she can "color the ball red and yellow"; she can "be fourth in the lunch line"; she can get a lazy teacher a ruler and a Kleenex and the stapler. Now, she understands what I ask her to do.

Now, instead of squirming in her chair, Julie pays close attention when I read a story. She can follow the action in a story; she can ask questions about what's going on in the stories; she can feel happy and sad along with the story-book characters. And, now that she has a means of learning language structure on which all reading is based, she will be able to learn to read these stories for herself. She'll be able to lie on her bed and read of magical places and of marvelous adventures.

Now, instead of being unable to understand about new things,

Julie can learn all about her world. She can learn about eating with chopsticks, about how mean camels are, about how salmon swim upstream in Alaska.

Now, instead of communicating by means of one or two unintelligible words, she can make herself understood to others. Since she is learning to cue herself, she can tell me about things that she does away from school. She can relate school experiences to her mother. And hopefully, with intensive speech therapy, she will be able to communicate effectively with unfamiliar people.

Now, instead of being a bright, bright child locked in a silent world, she will have the opportunity to realize her full potential—to have a rich, fulfilled life.

Julie can do many things now—things she was unable to do nine months ago. *Now* Julie understands. *Now* Julie has the key.

We thank you for that key.

This is not the Julie Lewis pictured on page 577.

Chapter Summary

Insight into how a deaf child learns verbal language through Cued Speech can be gained by considering how a hearing child learns language. The hearing child associates meaning receptively with single words and simple patterns, then begins to use them expressively, later expanding them and inventing new combinations. Consistent use for two-way communication stabilizes and conventionalizes the patterns.

A deaf child's language typically reveals an inadequate grasp of the importance of word order and word patterns, gained only through clear input. Teaching verbal language through the written form, which is the fall-back method used by oralists and manualists alike, lacks the freedom and spontaneity essential for an adequate rate of language acquisition. It is also impractical for the very young child.

The impact of Cued Speech on how parents can teach language in the home comes from the clarity of Cued Speech, its faithfulness to the sounds and syllables of the spoken language, and the fact that the parents can use vocabulary and dialect at will.

The parents' role in language development for the deaf child is to make use of every activity of the home as an opportunity for communication and introduction of new language, and to make use also of opportunities that arise elsewhere, from outings to long vacations.

Chapter 12
Speech Production

Cued Speech guides the deaf child as to which sounds to make, and in what combinations. It does not teach him how to make the individual speech sounds. They should be taught to him by a qualified speech/audition therapist[1], and the training should be supported by the parents' guided efforts at home.

Speech is "talking," but when we use the term *speech production*, we are referring to the actual articulation of the speech sounds and their patterns—the way sounds are produced and put together (syllabication, rhythm, emphasis, intonation). Every word is composed of a sound or a combination of sounds. These sounds are not clearly indicated by the way the words are spelled. For instance, there are 21 ways to spell the sound of the word *I (e.g.,* letter *y,* as in the word *my).* Becoming aware of the individual sounds that one produces in speaking is a fascinating and eye-opening experience for many parents of hearing-impaired children when they start learning Cued Speech.

Who would think that for the word *of* we do not ordinarily make the sounds usually associated with the letters *o* and *f,* but something logically written *uv?* To use Cued Speech, parents have to learn what sounds they actually make, with their accents, when they speak. This experience helps one realize the complexity of the speech a hearing child learns as a toddler through a process of trial and error, beginning with random babbling. The hearing-impaired child, on the other hand, must be taught specifically how to produce many sounds, and where they belong in the language.

Phonemes

There are 26 letters in the English alphabet, but in speaking we use up to 45 distinctly different *phonemes,* or speech sounds. In Cued Speech these are clearly differentiated through vision. Some sounds

---

[1]We are aware that ASHA prefers the term *hearing/speech/language pathologist.* A pathologist is a physician whose work is concentrated on the study of the essential nature of diseases. He/she tends to serve as a consultant regarding treatment, rather than engaging in treatment. We prefer to use the term *therapist* in referring to practitioners who, though they have knowledge of the nature and causes of speech, hearing, and language disorders, spend their time *correcting* problems associated with speech, hearing, and language.

differ from each other in their appearance on the mouth. Others differ in their appearance on the cueing hand. A *hearing-impaired* child needs to learn to produce (or at least refine) each of these sounds with the help of a specially trained speech teacher. Some of the sounds can be "captured" by the parent or teacher by a method explained below.

The qualified speech therapist (or speech-hearing-language therapist) has a firm understanding of the production of speech sounds. If trained for speech work with hearing-impaired children, the therapist will also be versed in appropriate techniques for training deaf children to produce good speech, and in how to guide parents in how to help. The therapist will teach interested parents to classify the sounds in different groups: 1) those for which the vocal cords must vibrate; 2) those that are formed by the interaction of the breath with the articulators (tongue, teeth, lips, pharynx, etc.), and 3) those produced or influenced in the nasal cavities. The speech therapist will also teach the parents about the mouth formations and movements required for the production of each sound separately and in combinations.

Will Cued Speech teach a hearing-impaired child how to produce the speech sounds and thus relieve her/him of the need for specialized speech instruction? No, but it will facilitate the work of the speech therapist by reducing the time required to clarify the target the therapist wants the child to attempt. Suppose the therapist instructs the child to say the word *man*. If the child does not know Cued Speech, and if residual hearing is insufficient to enable him/her to understand accurately, he/she must guess at the target. Assuming that the child is a fairly good lipreader, the guess will probably be one of the following: *mat, mad, bad, bat, pat, pad, pant, pan, ban, man, pal,* etc. Obviously, the therapist will have to depend upon written language, pictures, or a phonetic cue system to establish the targets for speech production. A speech therapist who can use Cued Speech can avoid time wasted when the child is aiming at the wrong targets.

Cued Speech can be used to "capture" speech sounds the child makes in play or babbling. In exploring the range of his/her own vocalizations, a hearing-impaired child may produce a good many of the speech sounds without having been taught to make them. If the child babbles "ba, ba, ba," the parent should immediately reinforce the babbling by saying: "Yes, *ba, ba, ba*—very good!"

As Alexander Graham Bell wrote in a letter on November 8, 1885, the basic problem in developing good speech in deaf children is not that of teaching them to make the speech sounds:

> *...the necessary preliminary to good speech is that the pupil should have a definite conception of how we pronounce our words—that he should have in his mind a definite model which he attempts to copy. With this model in the mind, the defects of his speech will be due not to defective aim, but to defective execution.*

With Cued Speech a deaf child receives (sees) the pronunciation of every word every time it is said to him/her, just as a hearing child hears it. Thus the deaf child acquires a mental model of the spoken language which guides him/her accurately in speaking, within the limits of his ability to articulate (make the sounds). That a child who grows up with Cued Speech does acquire such a model, called a *phonological* model, was verified by teams of Belgian researchers (Alegría, Dejean, Capouillez, & Leybaert, 1989). This is their closing paragraph (p. 8):

> *To come back to our initial point, the present work strongly suggests that the lexicon developed by the deaf with Cued Speech has properties which are equivalent to the phonology of the hearing subjects. In both cases the internal representations of the word are compatible with their ortho-graphic representations. This allows the use of phonologic coding to identify unfamiliar words and, as said before, can prime the whole process of reading acquisition.*

The researchers above were interested in the effects of Cued Speech on reading. Our point here is that the phonological model cited by them as needed in reading is also the base for speech.

Articulation

Articulation is the act of producing speech sounds, individually and in combination. Though Cued Speech does not itself show a child *how* to articulate (but *what* to articulate), it does have beneficial effects on articulation. The mouth is the focal point of communication. With Cued Speech, the child is very much aware of the visible evidences of the configurations and movements of the lips, tongue, teeth, and jaw. Because proper mouth movements are essential for communicating with Cued Speech, the child can be encouraged to imitate these movements (which he/she observes when cued to) in beginning to communicate expressively. This can be supported by mirror work (p. 333).

Consistent use of Cued Speech gives a child a foundation for the use of speech in expressive communication. The speech therapist builds on this by teaching the actual production of specific sounds and should relate those sounds and their production to the proper combinations of cue-and-mouth configurations and movements. Thus the child gains a set of specific combinations of visual symbols for the elements of spoken language, learning to recognize and use the patterns of the language without having to think of the elements themselves, just as a hearing child masters patterns of spoken language without having to think of the individual sounds.

If children cue, *psychomotor feedback* (the speaker's own feeling of his/her speech and cueing movements) provides help in articulating each sound as precisely as possible. This feedback, plus any feedback from residual hearing, helps substitute in part for the missing auditory feedback that supports the articulation of hearing children.

One family that requested CS instruction indicated that their 12-year-old deaf daughter thought they already knew it. Asked how this could be so, they replied that when they could not understand their daughter's speech, they asked her to cue what she was saying (she had been taught Cued Speech in school). When she cued, she spoke more distinctly and thus could be understood, so she thought her parents were reading her cues, though they were not. There are many cases in which a child's developing speech improves when he or she cues, because of associating articulation patterns with the movements of cueing. This can help a child avoid omission of sounds within words.

The opinions expressed in the preceding paragraph are supported by the observations of Belgian researchers Charlier, Capouillez, and Périer (1990):

> *Equally interesting is the consensus that the quality of sound articulated increases considerably when a child cues himself as he speaks. This feedback effect of CS on his articulation, a kinesthetic support to speech, can be explained in our view by the fact that CS has enabled the child to memorize the phonetically articulated parts of words, by associating the movements with labial-facial movements. This link-up, when speech is cued in return, results in secondary spin-offs in terms of speech quality—the right number of syllables is reproduced, phonemes not visible on the lips are pronounced (final consonants, double consonants, liaisons), and there is less of the vocal tension that results from fear of speaking.*

Pronunciation

Think for a moment about the problems deaf people face in knowing how to pronounce English words. Is the <u>ough</u> in <u>enough</u> pronounced like the <u>ough</u> in <u>bough</u> (*ou*), or those in <u>cough</u> (*awf*), <u>thought</u> (*aw*), <u>though</u> (*oe*), or <u>through</u> (*ue*)? None of these fits: <u>enough</u> is pronounced *inuf, unuf, or eenuf*. We learn how to pronounce such words by hearing them pronounced. English is full of differences between spelling and pronunciation. This is a serious barrier to speaking a language for a person who has clear access only to the written form. A deaf person who can produce speech sounds may know (in written form) the word he wants to pronounce, but may be uncertain about how to pronounce it.

Mervin Garretson, the first deaf adult to learn Cued Speech, stopped his tutor in the middle of his first tutoring session when he saw the word <u>sure</u> and asked: "Did you say *shure*? I always thought that word was *soo-er*." Even though he was only beginning to learn Cued Speech, he was able to see how the word was pronounced. Here was a brilliant man, well versed in English, but cut off from the spoken input by his adventitious deafness. Even a deaf person who has learned the correct pronunciation when younger, as Garretson did as a hearing child, can forget a pronunciation if it does not, as Alexander Graham Bell said (1892, p. 55), come "clearly differentiated to the eye."

> *If you are to get good speakers, especially among the congenitally deaf, they must see the pronunciation; it must not be taught simply as a school exercise; the words spoken by the mouth must come clearly differentiated to the eye again and again until the eye becomes familiar with them.*

Note the words: "...they must *see* the pronunciation." In this statement Bell practically wrote a prescription for Cued Speech. That prescription waited almost eight decades to be filled.

The deaf person who knows Cued Speech has the benefit of seeing the pronunciation of every word each time it is said to him or her. If Cued Speech is the primary means of communication, pronunciations become "second nature" as they do with hearing persons. Hearing children learn the patterns of spoken English from hearing them repeatedly in context; the deaf child can do the same through seeing them in context if Cued Speech is used.

Rhythm

One of the specifications listed for the development of Cued Speech was that the system should be consistent with and supportive of the rhythm, stress and duration patterns, intonation, and inflection of speech. These qualities are closely associated with syllables. Parents must cue in syllables, synchronizing precisely with the rhythmic patterns of their speech. This does not mean that they will cue at their usual rate of speaking. It will be many months before they can. In the beginning, slower, more deliberate speech is advantageous because: 1) as child development experts tell us, we should speak more slowly to young children so they can hear/see every word clearly, 2) there is an optimum speed for speechreading, which is considerably (perhaps 25%) slower than the rate of normal speech, and 3) we want the child to process every element of our speech so he or she can build language rapidly. At this lower rate the proper rhythm can still be maintained. When children repeat a phrase or sentence that has been cued for them, they can usually articulate more accurately by cueing as they speak.

Unless a deaf child cues very fluently, an unfamiliar phrase is likely to be articulated with cues in a labored, stilted pattern, rather than in natural rhythm. Jim Latt (certified both as a speech teacher and a teacher of the deaf) uses a technique that works wonders with this problem. After leading the child to produce the phrase or sentence accurately, so far as articulation of the sounds and syllables is concerned, he says: "Now say it in a *regular* voice." The child understands that this means to say it, without cueing, a little faster and in a more relaxed manner. He/she understands that he or she now has the phrase or sentence under control, and is ready to say it naturally.

It is important to keep in mind that in learning the patterns of spoken language through Cued Speech the child can be both precise and complete in his perception of the spoken language. Provided an accurate target for production, he/she tends to proceed deliberately and carefully in producing it, if he is cueing as he speaks. The child cannot free himself/herself from this studied and deliberate pattern of production until, through repetition, he or she has developed the vocal and physical skills required for fluent production of that pattern. The process must be judged by the final results, not the initial production of a new pattern. The priority must be given initially to accuracy. This is opposite to what happens in aural/oral learning of new spoken patterns, which must be *approximated* repeatedly before they can be produced accurately. The teacher strives to maintain a natural rate and smooth production from the first attempt at a pattern, even if the result is phonetically wide of the mark. This should not be done with CS.

Voice Quality

The voice quality developed by profoundly deaf children will be dependent upon a number of factors: 1) the level and quality of their residual hearing, 2) the training given to develop and use residual hearing, 3) the quality and appropriate level of amplification provided each child by properly fitted hearing aids, 4) each child's emotional state, which will be enhanced if communication in the home is easy and clear, 5) each child's familiarity with the patterns of spoken language, possibly including rhythm and intonation in addition to the phonological system, and 6) each child's age and experience.

Though most cuers do not cue intonation (voice pitch level), the fact that the stressed syllable is almost always given longer duration and higher pitch often enables a child to acquire appropriate intonation patterns. If this does not happen naturally, parents should consider asking the therapist to try indicating approximate voice pitch with the cues (through the angle of the hand), and teaching the child to raise and lower pitch appropriately. If the therapist decides that it is desirable, the parents may be asked to carry out some pitch-training exercises. Many profoundly deaf children can learn to hear the pitch.

Most deaf children have substantial amounts of hearing in the low frequencies (below 350 Hz.), where the fundamental intonation-determining components are located. Thus, many of them are capable of learning to hear voice pitch and thereby achieve natural intonation patterns. That capability must usually be developed, and Cued Speech can help. The improvement of voice quality through auditory training will be discussed in more detail below, and also in the chapter on that subject. In addition to the suggestions given there, the following may be helpful to parents starting Cued Speech.

If Cued Speech is begun while children are very young (under 2 years of age), many of them can begin speaking in a natural communicating environment, assuming that they are receiving auditory training and have appropriate hearing aids. At first a child may make mouth movements without voice. You should encourage such lip movements and try to stimulate use of voice in the following ways:

1. See that the child wears hearing aids (or a cochlear implant) during all periods of time in which communication is possible. Check each aid every day to make sure that it is working properly.

2. Have the child occasionally place one hand on the speaker's face, chest, or neck, and the other hand at the same spot on his own

body, to feel the vibrations. The sense of touch can often be used to help the child imitate speech sounds.

3. If the child makes a sound, immediately reinforce it by vocal imitation and cues—"buh-buh"—"you said buh-buh"—"Good girl!" If parents begin this activity with a deaf child in infancy, he/she can learn to approximate the speech and language development of the hearing child more closely than would otherwise be the case. Since this is a natural, relaxed procedure (if the parent is relaxed), the child tends to develop a natural, relaxed voice.

Speech Correction

One of the most easily demonstrated advantages of Cued Speech is its effectiveness in speech correction. An obvious advantage is the ease with which a cuer can give the child the speech *target*—that is, what the child is being asked to say. If the child pronounces a word incorrectly, repeating it immediately with Cued Speech will make the correct form clear. If the child still cannot say it correctly, this means that probably a speech therapist needs to teach the proper articulation of one or more of the sounds in the word. This avoids both wasted time and the danger of habituating incorrect patterns by continued unsuccessful attempts to correct the child's production.

Parents can easily clear up problems caused by a child's incorrect impressions of what the pronunciations of specific words should be. A great advantage in correction of pronunciation is that the correction can be given quickly and easily, without the numerous repetitions parents often require of a child.

If a deaf child cues what he or she says and approximates correct lip movements, the parent can (with a bit of practice at reading Cued Speech) understand what the child is trying to say. Thus, a parent can detect the child's misconceptions regarding pronunciations of specific words, including both choice of sounds and the patterns of rhythm and stress. Then, with Cued Speech, the parent can show the correct pronunciation in a form the child can understand clearly.

An older deaf child or an adult can correct his own pronunciation of a word by noting carefully how a hearing person cues that word—assuming, of course, that the hearing person uses an acceptable pronunciation. If the deaf person's idea of the pronunciation differs from that cued to him, he/she can change his/her own way of saying it without being corrected, or can consult a dictionary to make sure.

Intonation

As used during its first four years (1966-1970), Cued Speech clarified the patterns of duration and stress of the syllables, but did not specifically indicate higher or lower pitch. The voice pitch tends to follow stress and duration patterns, in that the stressed syllable is almost always higher in pitch and longer in duration. Cued Speech thus helps lead to natural intonation except in unusual contexts. In January 1970, the originator of Cued Speech added a slight modification (explained below) to show higher or lower pitch when such an indication is desired. Most cuers do not (and ordinarily should not) bother to do this, but it is very useful in speech therapy and by parents who are helping a deaf child learn to hear intonation, which we think most profoundly deaf children can be taught to do. We suggest that parents who are interested confer with their child's speech therapist about the possible benefits. The next four paragraphs will help any who wish to experiment with the cueing of intonation.

This innovation of showing approximate pitch has made it possible to adapt Cued Speech to tonal languages, such as Modern Chinese (Mandarin), Cantonese, Igbo, Thai, and a few others. In these languages changing the pitch of a single syllable can change the meaning of the word.

Two words in Japanese illustrate the way in which pitch differences can change the meaning of a word. Although Japanese is no longer a tonal language, it still contains some tonal distinctions. For example, the word *hah - shee*, with the first syllable at high pitch and the second at middle pitch, means bridge. With the first syllable at middle pitch and the second at low pitch, the word means edge.

There are two reasons why the intonation feature of Cued Speech may be important to a deaf child whose language is English. One is that his ability to follow appropriate intonation patterns makes his voice seem much more natural and his speech more intelligible. The other is that tonal changes also affect meaning in many English sentences. For example, "Did *he* do that?" with *he* at high pitch, means: "Is *he* the person who did that?" Conversely, "Did he do *that*?" with *that* at high pitch, means, "Is *that* what he did?"

Approximate pitch can be cued in songs, enabling deaf children to learn to follow and imitate the pitch changes indicated by the cueing. Not only do they enjoy this, but some of them thereby learn to hear intonation well enough to improve the inflections in their habitual speech production, or even to sing on pitch.

Normal pitch is indicated by the natural inclination of the hand for each of the four hand locations, about midway between vertical and horizontal. Elevated pitch is indicated by tilting the hand more toward the vertical, and lower pitch by tilting it toward the horizontal. For example, "Did *he* do that?" and "Did he do *that*?" are clearly differentiated if the stressed syllable is accompanied by elevation of the inclination of the hand toward the vertical.

Parents who wish to attempt to cue intonation should work in cooperation with a speech specialist or someone else who has utilized this feature of Cued Speech, or is willing to study it carefully. It seems awkward at first, but soon becomes relatively easy. Parents should be cueing proficiently before attempting to cue intonation.

Feedback

Deaf children's chief difficulty in developing accurate articulation is that they receive a very limited amount of auditory feedback from their speech efforts. The limited amount they can hear from other persons' speech also makes it difficult for them to identify speech targets to imitate. However, they can "feel" their own speech to some extent, and residual hearing may help tremendously if they are trained in its use. If deaf children add expressive cueing to the act of speaking, this increases the feedback available to them. Their hands presumably "remember" the cued patterns of speech in somewhat the same way the hands of a pianist "remember" music he/she has played. This does not mean that deaf children will always need to cue while speaking. It means that the process of mastering the patterns of speech can be expedited by consistent expressive cueing with speech.

A deaf child's greatest source of motivation to speak more and to try to speak well is having others actually understand his/her speech. This cannot be faked, but it can be supported. Those who are with a child the most and are most familiar with his/her speech must remember that they have the greatest opportunity to encourage his/her efforts and show that they understand his/her speech. They can try to convince the child that they can understand better when he or she cues expressively. To do this, they may have to improve their skill at receiving Cued Speech.

Speech is Not Easy for the Deaf Child

Speech does not usually come easily to a profoundly deaf child. After much work and unusual concentration as a young child, he may be continually frustrated by the difficulty hearing people have in understanding him/her. They may ask him to repeat and repeat, and may finally resort to just expecting their child to point, write, or draw a picture. Or, worse, they may simply give up on their efforts to communicate with the child beyond what is necessary. Parents must try to understand how painful all this can be to a deaf child. They must be altogether supportive, loving, and consistent.

Even deaf people with very poor speech often have fairly good lip approximations. If they cue as they speak they can be understood quite well by hearing people who develop their ability to receive Cued Speech. And, since they usually speak better when cueing, they can often be understood better by hearing persons who do not read Cued Speech. Success in being understood while cueing can give the child the confidence and motivation to communicate orally when necessary.

The speech potential of even a tiny amount of residual hearing can be great if the deaf child knows the spoken language. This fact is most obvious in children who lose most of their hearing suddenly, at ages beyond 3 or 4 years. Because they know most of the language (and its sounds) they can be trained to make maximum use of their remaining hearing in monitoring and improving their speech.

Many children who grow up on Cued Speech know the spoken language as well as the average hearing child. However, they have to be trained to make maximum use of residual hearing in both speaking and speechreading. If born profoundly deaf, they have to learn how speech sounds and feels like to them in order to improve their speech production. The information on auditory training in Chapter 14 is thus highly relevant to the development of speech production.

The Parents' Role In Speech Development

Parents should encourage use of speech, provide positive reinforcement of good speech production, and use Cued Speech to model pronunciation when their child makes a mistake.

Parents should follow closely the progress of the child in articulation, maintaining close communication with the therapist, and should make sure that speech therapy is carried out on a strong base of auditory training. Ideally, they should be informed by the therapist of each new sound the child learns to make, so that they can make sure the child inserts it consistently and appropriately in the words he or she uses. The correction of pronunciation by the parents is essential, but they should not try to teach articulation without the specific guidance of a professional. The reason is simple: they can very easily cause tension in the child's vocal mechanism, leading to habitual speech mannerisms that are very difficult to correct. Even trained therapists experience difficulty in avoiding the inducing of tension in deaf children. Many speech sounds are difficult for the child to learn to produce, in the absence of normal auditory feedback. An exception to the suggestion that parents not attempt speech therapy themselves is a situation in which the family is completely isolated and has to carry out speech therapy as best they can, with the help of manuals and advice.

One of the most important ways for parents to support speech therapy is to build upon what the speech therapist accomplishes. They should keep in close touch. The therapist should inform them when their child has mastered the production of a new phoneme or combination, so that they can remind the child whenever he/she omits it or substitutes another sound for it. This procedure can help make permanent the gains made in speech therapy sessions. One of the major frustrations of speech therapists working with hearing-impaired children is their tendency to lose most of what is gained. Cued Speech can make a difference in this respect.

Parents can also help by experimenting with variations in cueing to try to find those that solve particular articulation problems. A parent reviewer relates an experience occasioned by the fact that her child was having great trouble with *wire, tire, fire*, etc. He tended to pronounce *fire*, for example, as *fie-ruh*. She found that if she cued it 5 side, 5 throat, 5 mouth (*fie-ur*), he pronounced it correctly. Both ways of cueing—the one above and 5 side, 5 throat, 3 side—are acceptable. The former was preferable for the child in question.

Parents often face several problems in connection with obtaining good speech therapy for their child. Most speech therapists in public school systems have had little training for working with hearing-impaired children. Many have had no experience in working with hearing-impaired children. Because good auditory training and good speech therapy are essential to a deaf child, parents must be tenacious and diligent in their attempt to secure the services of a therapist qualified to furnish what their child needs.

Refer to p. 667 for Barbara LeBlanc's article on how parents and professionals should work together to achieve good speech.

The Child With Unintelligible Speech

The vast majority of profoundly deaf children are capable of developing speech that is reasonably intelligible, at least to family, friends, and others who spend enough time with them to become accustomed to their speech. Some, because of secondary problems that interfere with the use of the articulatory system, will never develop speech that is useful for communication with anyone other than immediate family, teachers, and friends. In such cases it is necessary to weigh the advantages and disadvantages of various options.

Many children who would otherwise be unable to develop intelligible speech can learn to do so with the aid of a special device. Children with hearing only below the speech range (below 500 Hz.) may be able to develop better use of audition in speech reception and better speech production through the use of a frequency-transposing hearing aid, a tactile device or a cochlear implant (see p. 209, ff.). The availability of the 22-electrode cochlear implant has already made intelligible speech possible for many children with little or no useable hearing, or with severely distorted hearing.

Through reception of Cued Speech, children who fail to develop useful expressive speech can learn spoken English as a base for reading, writing, and speechreading. In some cases the child can produce reasonably accurate lip movements, accompanied by expressive cueing, thus achieving two-way communication with others who know and use Cued Speech. However, this option alone is not likely to meet the child's needs for expressive communication with the public.

For children whose expressive speech continues to be unintelligible, methods are available that offer some possibilities. One such method is the Basic Articulation, Language, Learning program (B.A.L.L.) of Wilma Jean Tade (1991), of Arlington, Texas. This method has been successful with children who show symptoms of apraxia and/or low phonological awareness. It has reportedly been helpful to children using Cued Speech.

Families in which the deaf child simply cannot develop intelligible speech should learn at least 500 signs, so that Pidgin Sign English is available for communication with them and also with others who know signs. The child should have every opportunity to associate with deaf peers who sign, and regular access to the deaf society should be provided. A deaf baby-sitter would be an asset.

There are several alternatives for the child who has unintelligible speech after years of therapy, especially if she or he is learning language well with Cued Speech. The child may be a good candidate for a cochlear implant (see Chapter 14), which may result in dramatic improvement in speech intelligibility. Placing the child in a local public school program in which signs are used is another possibility for the child without useful speech. If this alternative is chosen, much can be still gained by continued consistent use of Cued Speech by the family for communication to the child, accepting whatever works out best as the child's means of expression to them. In such a case the consistent reception of communication in Cued Speech at home will very likely give the child the understanding of spoken English needed to 1) be a good reader, 2) become a good speechreader, and 3) write good English. For a good reader, academic success is virtually assured.

Placement of the child as a boarding student in a residential school should be considered if special circumstances make it impossible for the family to provide the needed supportive environment. Most residential schools currently use TC, but some are aural/oral.

So long as the child's exposure to speech therapy does not become too frustrating and unrewarding, it should be continued with a therapist who uses Cued Speech. Speech production often develops very slowly, and the child may eventually become able to use expressive speech at a very useful level if therapy is continued.

Chapter Summary

Cued Speech guides deaf children as to which sounds to make, and in what combinations, but it does not teach them how to make the individual sounds. They should be trained in articulation by a speech-audition therapist, and that training should be supported at home.

Cued Speech produces visual distinctions among all the speech sounds and develops in deaf children an internalized phonological model of the spoken language. Research reports cited above have indicated that this model has properties equivalent to those of the phonological model of a hearing child. This provides an appropriate base for expressive speech as well as speechreading and reading.

Cued Speech can also enhance voice and speech quality by providing clear impressions of rhythm, stress, and syllable duration. Since a stressed syllable is usually pronounced with longer duration and higher pitch than usual, children who grow up with Cued Speech usually develop appropriate rhythm and intonation patterns. If they do not produce appropriate intonation patterns, parents should consider learning how to add pitch indications to their cueing. Most deaf children can be taught to raise and lower their voice pitch in response to the pitch indications, and may even learn to hear the voice pitch.

Children whose development of expressive speech is inhibited or even prevented by problems in addition to deafness need careful diagnosis in order to determine the appropriate course of action. Even if expressive speech is impossible for them, the benefits of consistent exposure to Cued Speech at home can be substantial.

Chapter 13
Speechreading

Parents who are using Cued Speech can contribute most to the development of speechreading skill in their deaf child by doing nothing about it directly. Instead, they should concentrate on what the child needs in order to become capable of speechreading well.

The recognition and understanding of spoken language by a person with normal hearing is a very complex process. Learning language and understanding it is certainly one of the most difficult feats the human brain is called upon to perform. It is a process in which the brain sorts through its internal depository of familiar words and phrases to find "fits" with the incoming message. The ability to do this at an advanced level is one of the most important characteristics that distinguishes humans from other animals. Speechreading, or as it is more commonly called, lipreading, is an even more complex process.

Speechreading Defined and Described

The terms *speechreading* and *lipreading* are used interchangeably by most educators. Edward B. Nitchie (1930) defined lipreading as "The art of understanding a speaker's thoughts by watching the movements of his mouth." Others broadened the concept to include the use of all the visible manifestations of speech, including facial expression and even "body language." Anna Bunger (1952) did not rule out the use of residual hearing, defining lipreading as "the understanding of spoken language while attentively watching the speaker."

Most educators use the term lipreading to mean the understanding of spoken language through its visible manifestations. However, for profoundly deaf people who know the spoken language, the ability to understand through the *combination* of the visible and auditory inputs available to them is much more important than (and superior to) their ability to understand through lipreading without sound. This is particularly the case if their use of residual hearing has been enhanced through appropriate training. Speechreading (without the support of audition) is infinitely more complex than the understanding of spoken language through normal hearing. The reason is that the information available through vision is only about half of that in the speech message. As a result, a lipreader cannot reliably identify specific sounds, words, or phrases, but only probabilities. Except for a few sounds and a small proportion of really lipreadable words, the only chance for actual identification of the message is the use of the speechreader's knowledge of the spoken language to recognize a probability that a possible interpretation is the correct one. Speechreaders must use their knowledge of the language to rule out interpretations that fit what is seen on the mouth, but not the rules of spoken language and/or the situation. Lipreaders cannot lipread unfamiliar language reliably, or learn new language through lipreading.

If an average deaf speechreader is exposed to a series of 100 simple spoken syllables consisting of a consonant followed by a vowel (*na, wi, se, mu,* etc.), he/she will likely identify correctly 20 to 30% percent of them. Surprisingly, the best lipreaders are not much better at this than mediocre lipreaders, since speechreading, as it is better named, is primarily a process of recognizing *possible patterns* of *familiar* words and phrases, rather than identifying individual sounds, syllables, or words.

If a deaf person is an unusually good lipreader, knowledge of language and alertness to situations enable him/her often to select a reasonable interpretation of the incomplete message seen on the mouth. For example, consider the simple sentence: "I met Mr. Jones yesterday." The theoretical chance of identifying this sentence by identifying correctly from the lips all of the elements of the spoken message is about one in 40 million! But, the good speechreader's knowledge of language enables him or her, with the brain working like a remarkable computer, to rule out possible interpretations that do not make sense according to the rules of language and the situation. Thus, a good lipreader can select one of the interpretations that do make sense, and hope for the best. A reasonably good speechreader is quite likely to understand the sentence indicated above.

In the illustration just given the first word (*I*) is easy to lipread, since it is visually distinctive and is often used at the beginning of a sentence. The next word (*met*) is one of 72 combinations (not all words) that look almost exactly alike on the lips. No lipreader will know what the second word is until the last word in the sentence is seen (yesterday). If instead he or she sees and recognizes the words "five dollars" as a possibility for the last part of the sentence, he/she would lipread the second word as *bet,* and the sentence as "I bet Mr. Jones five dollars." The lipreader cannot reliably lipread either *yesterday* or *five dollars* at the end of the sentence, but can recognize them as possibilities and search for the most logical combination.

Lipreading Requires Knowledge of Language

Lipreading, or speechreading, is a process in which the ambiguous patterns of the mouth movements are recognized because they occur only in patterns dictated by the common usage of the language. One cannot possibly lipread reliably 1) a language he does not know; 2) new words, that is, words that are unfamiliar; 3) nonsense words or syllables; 4) unfamiliar names. Note the very sobering implication: *Your deaf child cannot acquire new language through lipreading.* We need a caveat here: A child who has a very useful amount of residual hearing, with adequate training, may become able to be *taught* new words through many aural/oral repetitions and a great deal of explanation. But, this is far from learning new language in the normal process of communication, which is the way most language must be learned if it is to be acquired at a reasonable rate.

To illustrate the process of lipreading, have another person cover a printed page with a sheet of paper and move the sheet so as to allow you to see only the top halves of the letters on a line. Notice that you can still read the line with little difficulty. By seeing only part of the pattern you are recognizing the whole—because you carry the patterns of the written language in your mind. You can do this because you know the language and are familiar with the patterns of all the words.

If you try the above with a language you do not know, you will be able to identify only a few letters here and there. This is similar to recognizing a photograph of a familiar person by seeing only part of it. The picture must be of a person familiar to you, or seeing a piece of it will not "ring a bell."

The point is that lipreading is possible only through a knowledge of the language—specifically, the spoken form of the language. In the illustration just given, the incomplete written message (the part uncovered) is really part of the written language pattern you are accustomed to recognizing. Of course, lipreading is actually more complicated than this. The lipreader must transfer from the lip motions to whatever mental model of the language he/she has (auditory, written, fingerspelling, or sign language) and search for interpretations that fit both what is seen on the mouth and what the situation suggests.

Some Wisdom From Alexander Graham Bell

In June, 1888, Dr. Alexander Graham Bell (1892, p. 26, par. 21,567) made the following statement to the Royal Commission of the

United Kingdom on the Condition of the Blind, the Deaf and Dumb:

> *I think that with the congenitally deaf to commence their education by speech reading, to commence to have the child read words from the mouth, before he knows the language, interferes with his mental development, retards progress in the acquisition of language, and thus defeats its own end, and retards the acquisition of speech-reading itself.*
>
> *So far as my observation has gone, if a pupil is taught to rely upon the mouth for communication, before the language is acquired, it interferes with the acquisition of language; but if he is taught the language before he relies upon the mouth, then that knowledge of the language enables him to acquire the art of speech reading.*

Synchronization of the cues with the mouth movements is important in connection with developing the base for speechreading. Parents should ask someone to check their cueing for accurate synchronization of cues and mouth movements. Or, they can watch themselves in a mirror, to check synchronization. It is also important to handle consonant clusters (such as *str* in the word *street*) without losing synchronization. You may wish to check both these points in Chapter 29, "The Fine Points of Cueing."

It is a mistake for parents to try to teach a deaf child to lipread by withholding the cues for words, phrases, or sentences the child obviously recognizes without the cues. Cued Speech reinforces the patterns with each exposure. Repeated impressions are essential. Failing to cue familiar patterns tends to lead parents into use of simplified language, inhibiting further language development. One of the most serious mistakes parents can make is to adapt to the language the child already knows and can usually lipread, instead of enriching language progressively by introducing new words and phrases constantly, cueing *everything*.

It is best to make a point of using sentences containing new words and new patterns, where situational context will help the child understand. This is particularly true of idiomatic uses of prepositions: "We were *in* line," "Sarah's *in* trouble." "Bobby's *on* the line." "Bowzer's *on* a tear." If the child does not understand, the parent should either rephrase or explain. This is the only way to insure maximum development of language in connection with the function words. The same point applies to cueing to your child what others are saying, providing exposure to new language you might not be as likely to use, also including the child in what is going on.

Gestures Make Parents Overestimate Lipreading

Parents often think their deaf children are lipreading more than they actually are. They may say: "My child lipreads me very well." They may be overlooking the fact that their gestures and facial expressions, and the situation, are conveying their meaning to the child. One mother, while learning Cued Speech, was asked to write down all the gestures she used with her child. She estimated that she used possibly 25 or 30 gestures that the child understood. She then proceeded to write out a list of 225! When she returned home, she (as instructed) put her hands behind her back and talked to the child, finding that the child had been reading the gestures and getting very little from her lips. Within a few weeks, she was able to replace all the gestures with verbal language by using Cued Speech. She used each gesture to clarify the concept she associated with it through Cued Speech. Once the child could understand the words and phrases through Cued Speech, she discontinued use of the gestures.

A common characteristic of people speaking to hearing-impaired children is a tendency to exaggerate lip movements. Slight exaggeration of lip movements may help the child understand because it makes the sounds look more clearly different from each other. As such, exaggeration of lip movements is, in effect, an incomplete and inaccurate system of cueing. Though it may temporarily help the child lipread his/her parents, it impedes development of the ability to lipread individuals who do not exaggerate lip movements. Another problem is that "lip-cueing" cannot make the message clear enough for efficient learning of new language. It is much sounder to supplement *normal* lip movements with cues supplied by the hand, so that when the child has to read normal lip movements he or she will be accustomed to them. Skilled lipreaders do not usually like untrained individuals to exaggerate their lip movements, which often actually confuse them. Trained oral interpreters use lip movements that are exaggerated slightly in ways that make lipreading easier.

Just as exaggeration of lip movements is a mistake (except in the case of oral interpreting), so is "tight-lipped" speech. Parents should speak clearly to their deaf child, with normal, adequate lip movements. As they use Cued Speech with their child more and more, parents who have been exaggerating lip movements gradually return to normal lip movements because the pressure to "get through" to the child is reduced as clear communication is established through Cued Speech.

Most Deaf People are Very Poor Lipreaders

Even with extensive training most deaf persons are inferior to the average hearing person in ability to speechread without sound. This has been confirmed by research at virtually all age levels. The reason is that prior knowledge of the spoken language is the most important single factor in ability to speechread.

Speechreading without sound involves using an input of about half the equivalent of the spoken message (the part visible on the mouth) to reconstruct the message by selecting (from millions of possibilities) the interpretation that best fits the patterns of the lips, the rules of spoken language, and the situation. Deaf persons who are average speechreaders can guess only about 25% to 30% of common words in isolation. In a situation in which language used is familiar, and there is a reasonable amount of situational context, a *good* speech-reader can usually understand much of a conversation with someone else. A speechreader can do better as a participant in the conversation than as a spectator, for two reasons: 1) it is necessary to lipread only one side of the conversation, and 2) the deaf person can influence (or even dominate) the conversation and thus anticipate its course.

Speechreading skill is desperately important to a hearing-impaired person, especially if he/she has fairly intelligible speech. Yet, it appears that only three groups of deaf people tend to become very good lipreaders: 1) those who lose their hearing after learning the language, 2) a very small minority of prelingually deaf children who are unusually successful in traditional aural/oral programs, and 3) practically all of the children who have grown up with consistent use of Cued Speech in the home. Note that all three groups consist of children who have a good knowledge of spoken language.

Factors in Speechreading

The following are essential to good speechreading: 1) prior knowledge of the spoken language, 2) familiarity with the patterns (on the mouth) of the sounds, syllables, and most of the words and phrases used in ordinary conversation, 3) knowledge of the relative frequencies of appearance of most familiar words, and 4) well-developed skill at finding "fits" between the patterns seen on the mouth, the auditory input, the patterns of ordinary language, and the probabilities associated with the situation and the trend of the conversation. This process is one in which the brain is searching among thousands, even millions of possible interpretations for the one that fits with the patterns seen on the mouth, the auditory signals received with those patterns, and the situation. It is certainly one of the most complex activities of which human beings are capable. The miracle is that deaf children can actually do it. A fifth and very important factor is the extent to which the lipreader can use residual hearing, in conjunction with the visual information, in the lipreading process.

Prior knowledge of the spoken language

Prior knowledge of the spoken language is probably the single most important factor in becoming able to speechread well. The average hearing person, with little or no training in speechreading, does better on standard lipreading tests than the average profoundly deaf person, despite the latter's experience and training. The reason is that speechreading, in the final analysis, is a process of selecting—from many interpretations possible for what is seen on the mouth—the one that makes sense, that is, which fits the patterns of spoken English and the situation. Deaf individuals who are average lipreaders can guess only 25% to 39% of common words *in isolation*, and most good lipreaders can do only a little better. But, in the context of language and situation the good lipreader may understand almost everything as a participant in a reasonably simple and relevant conversation.

Among profoundly deaf children, only the post-lingually deaf, the orally successful deaf, and those who have grown up on Cued Speech are likely to become good speechreaders. There are exceptions, but few prelingually deaf individuals learn spoken language well enough to be good speechreaders without the benefits of Cued Speech or the very best aural/oral training combined with unusual ability.

Familiarity with the mouth patterns of most frequently used syllables, words, and phrases

Essential to the speechreading process is an extensive familiarity with the mouth patterns associated with familiar syllables, words, and phrases of the language. This is not to say that a deaf person cannot learn to recognize (in situational context) a limited number of frequently used phrases and sentences without an extensive knowledge of either spoken language or the mouth patterns of common words and phrases. Such an ability can be of help to a deaf person who has to spend a substantial amount of time with hearing people, and who will learn to recognize and respond to greetings and simple, often-used instructions. But this is not a level of speechreading that will enable a deaf person to converse with hearing people with any degree of comfort. Nor will it make oral language sufficiently accessible for acquiring new information or new vocabulary without excessive repetition and/or contextual redundancy.

It should be understood that familiarity with the mouth patterns for individual words does not make it possible to recognize those words individually. The reason is that almost all words have many *homophenes*, that is, other words or non-word combinations of sounds that look the same on the mouth. For example, the word *met* is one of 72 *homophenous* combinations of sounds, most of them words, that look identical or almost so on the mouth. For a longer word the number of *homophenes* is much greater, often numbering hundreds or thousands. But, in order to recognize a word, a phrase, or a sentence by utilizing one's knowledge of what would make sense in the situation, one must be familiar with the patterns the words form on the mouth. Those patterns indicate possibilities for what is actually being said, and the possibilities fuel the speechreading process.

Since familiarity with the mouth patterns of most common syllables, words, and phrases is essential to speechreading, just how can such familiarity be acquired by people who lose their hearing after learning spoken language? Even they have great difficulty in learning to speechread because of the prodigious amount of time that has to be spent in laborious practice required to achieve this all-important familiarity with mouth patterns. The problem, basically, is that one must know which word he or she is seeing on the mouth at or shortly after the time at which he/she sees it, in order to associate the pattern with the word and remember it. This cannot be done efficiently by just trying to lipread: one must have the help of a person who will say something, more than once if necessary, then show what it was (by writing, fingerspelling, signing, etc.), and then remember to bring it up again later, repeating the process. Computer programs designed for such instruction can be helpful. The process is always laborious and tedious, so much so that most post-lingually deaf adults "burn out" on lessons and either give up or gradually develop some speechreading competence by simply trying and trying to speechread. This has led many traditional teachers of lipreading to conclude that good lipreaders are born, not made, and that teaching lipreading really benefits only those who have a special ability. They make the above assertion, but do not publish it. We differ with them, for the reasons below.

Traditional programs for teaching lipreading involve first the teaching of the mouth shapes and movements for specific phonemes and short syllables. Some teachers teach the mouth patterns for a number of frequently used words, avoiding homophenes (words that look the same on the mouth) at first in order to build confidence. Other teachers omit this stage, going immediately to teaching recognition of common phrases and short sentences. They also avoid sentences that look similar until confidence is developed, then begin to train the subjects in use of situational context to resolve the problem of similarity. Many post-lingually deaf individuals, particularly if deafened in middle age, are simply unable to make it through this process well enough to have any confidence in their ability to acquire good speechreading skills. Without that confidence, success is impossible.

For prelingually deaf people, particularly those with profound hearing impairments, the probability of success at developing good speechreading skills is much lower even than for post-lingually deaf individuals. Their lesser familiarity with the phonemic, prosodic, and grammatical patterns of spoken language is often an insurmountable difficulty. Highly motivated individuals may be exceptions, but only a tiny minority of the prelingually deaf get beyond rudimentary speech-reading capabilities without a background of Cued Speech.

The conditions required for becoming familiar with the mouth pattern of a syllable, word, or phrase are quite apparent. One must observe the pattern and simultaneously (or immediately thereafter) associate it with the correct spoken word or phrase, through assistance. After a few such experiences with the word, the person (on seeing the same pattern) will usually recognize it as one of a group of homo-phenes, from which a selection must be made by using his knowledge of the rules of language and the situation. Cued Speech is the only system that automatically and unavoidably produces the support required for becoming familiar with the mouth patterns of the frequent words and phrases. A deaf child accustomed to Cued Speech, when receiving it, must observe and make use of the mouth patterns in order to decode Cued Speech. Because he understands the message through Cued Speech, he *automatically becomes familiar* with the pairings of mouth patterns with spoken syllables, words, and phrases. This effect of Cued Speech is so powerful that, to date, we do not know of any profoundly deaf children who have grown up on Cued Speech in the home from an early age without becoming able to speechread signifi-cantly and obviously better than most profoundly deaf people. More research data is needed to support this claim.

Knowledge of Frequencies of Occurrence of Words and Phrases

Both research and experience confirm that a speechreader will usually guess a high-frequency word rather than a low-frequency word when uncertain. The good speechreader carries mentally an intuitive "table" of frequencies of appearance of common words and phrases, for use in guessing with the help of situational and linguistic context.

The Heart of Speechreading: Finding Most Probable "Fits"

In the final analysis, speechreading is a process in which the speechreader searches for most probable "fits" between the possibilities defined by the mouth patterns, and all that he/she knows about the words and patterns of the spoken language, the clues furnished by the situation, the characteristics of the speaker (and his/her ways of speaking and thinking), and the content of the conversation thus far. Good speechreaders do not simply recognize words, phrases, and sentences. Rather, they recognize possible interpretations of what is being seen on the mouth, and they utilize (usually unconsciously) estimates of the probabilities of the various possibilities. The speechreader is constantly dealing in probabilities. We will use an example to analyze how the speechreader deals with those probabilities in using all available sensory inputs, and all possibilities, to help formulate a meaningful interpretation of the incoming message.

It was pointed out above that there are more than 40 million combinations of speech sounds for which the average person's mouth patterns are identical (or nearly so) to those of the sentence: "I met Mr. Jones yesterday." Most of them are not sentences, and their parts not words, so that the person who knows the spoken language well will consider only the possible interpretations that make sense in terms of the words of spoken language, their phonemic content, their prosodic features, and also in terms of the common grammatical and idiomatic patterns of the language. He or she will rule out also any that do not fit the situation and the content of what has already occurred in the conversation. The miracle is that the human brain can carry on such a process, which possibly requires millions of decisions, confirmations, trials, and rejections, all in seconds. The brain is quite capable of carrying out such operations at a rapid rate, but only if it has access to the necessary information networks. There has to be in place a network of interrelated linguistic, visual, auditory, and situational components ready for use in speechreading synthesis.

Sensitivity to Situational Context

Sensitivity to situational context is essential to good speechreading ability. It is developed through practice, usually without much difficulty. In fact, the beginning speechreader depends tremendously on situational context, as does also a hearing person in situations in which he/she has to speechread. For example, if at a party with 200 people in a large room one sees a good friend at the other end where he cannot be heard, one might say: "I'll see you later," or "Wait for me," or even "How're you doing?" and be understood precisely. The situation makes it likely that anything said would be among these and a few other very familiar statements, which one is likely to have seen before under similar circumstances, and therefore may recognize.

Use of Linguistic Context and Continuity

The unfolding continuity of a conversation is extremely helpful to a speechreader by helping him/her anticipate what is likely coming and thus have more accurate ideas of the probabilities of the various possibilities defined by the mouth patterns. Skill at doing this efficiently is usually developed through practice, rather than instruction, but can probably be taught to some degree.

Prediction is used in conversation, in reading, and in lipreading. If one reads *The cat* at the beginning of a sentence, one's mind immediately predicts that what follows will have something to do with cats. Thus, one is ready for the names of kinds of cats, for words such as *fur, claws,* and *purr.* Skill at predicting, that is, setting up mentally for what is likely to come next, is essential in both lipreading and reading.

Inference is also important in lipreading and reading, as well as conversation. If a child reads :"Daddy put his slicker on and went out to the garage," he is likely to *infer* that it was raining, even though rain had not been mentioned.

Semantic closure is the contextual clue that makes the lipreader certain he is lipreading correctly. When his *most likely* candidate for what is being said makes sense grammatically and logically, he can be reasonably sure. Notice how prediction, inference, and semantic closure all come together in lipreading, reading, or simply understanding the sentence: "Out on the lake I fell out of the boat into the _____." Notice the contributors to prediction: Lake, boat, ____. The same words facilitate inference of something related. The phrases *out of the boat* and *into the* require that the last word be a noun related to lakes and boats, a noun meaning something into which one can fall. One can identify the last word of the sentence before it is spoken or seen, in conversation, in reading, or in lipreading.

Good speechreaders invariably make very skillful use of linguistic context, and, indeed, tend to control it. Many of the best of them tend to dominate conversation, so that what the other person says is often in answer to the speechreader's questions, or related to what he/she has just said. This simplifies the speechreading task and reduces strain and fatigue associated with prolonged continuous speechreading.

Use of Residual Hearing in Lipreading

The maximum possible development of skill in use of residual hearing in the process of lipreading is extremely important. In the research of Gaye Nicholls (1979, 1982) she found that the subjects, who had PTA thresholds of 97 to 122 dB in the speech frequencies, scored only 2% on identifying key words in sentences through audition alone. Lipreading without sound, they scored a respectable 30% on key words. However, when lipreading with the aid of audition they scored an amazing 45%. Thus, the auditory information that was worth only 2% alone was worth 15% when combined with the information seen on the mouth, enabling them to lipread 1½ times as much with the benefit of audition. When you read Chapter 14, "Auditory Training, Cochlear Implants," note the importance of audition to speech and lipreading.

Confidence, Patience, Self-Image, and Assertiveness

The qualities just listed tend to characterize good speechreaders, especially the exceptionally skilled ones. Early diagnosis and intervention, early success in communication with family, a stimulating environment in the home, and early development of aural/oral communication are all conducive to speechreading skills.

In the act of speechreading, understanding is often time-delayed; that is, the understanding of a specific sentence or utterance often comes after the speaker is well into, or even through, the next. Good speechreaders are invariably individuals who can "float along" and expect the meaning to become clear, who can put up with confusion, and who can maintain optimism. Noticeably poor at speechreading are people who want to get everything right as they go. Scientists, lawyers, and engineers, for example, have to restrain their natural insistence on precision if they are to become speechreaders after losing hearing.

Practice at Speechreading

The world is full of people who will furnish deaf children with ample opportunities to practice using and developing their lipreading abilities. Neighbors, playmates, friends, non-cueing relatives, and even strangers who will be patient will provide the best practice. Family members and friends who can cue should not use any of their much more valuable "cueing time" to furnish lipreading practice.

Children who grow up on Cued Speech in the home are spared most of the confusion and discouragement of early unsuccessful attempts to speechread. They quickly develop confidence in their ability to understand with the aid of cues. In the process, they develop all the attributes necessary for speechreading, and gradually develop confidence in their ability to speechread people who do not cue.

Speechreading is a difficult, stressful, and frustrating activity for the deaf person, even a good speechreader. The degree of frustration and failure is particularly high if the hearing-impaired individual's lipreading is not supported by useful residual hearing.

The Role of Parents in Lipreading Development

Parents who are using Cued Speech can contribute most to the development of speechreading skill in their deaf child by doing nothing about it directly, but by concentrating on the things the child needs in order to become able to lipread. These are:

1) consistent communication through Cued Speech,

2) much exposure to new language under appropriate conditions (with cues),

3) consistent use of amplification (including daily checks of hearing aids),

4) opportunities to associate with hearing friends (both cueing and non-cueing),

5) provision of good auditory training, which will be discussed in Chapter 14, including support at home,

6) use of normal, clear (but not exaggerated) lip movements.

Parents must remember that there is not enough time for them to do all that is needed, so that they must establish priorities for use of the precious time they do have. The world is filled with people who will furnish the deaf child more than enough opportunity to practice lipreading without the cues. Parents should use their precious time for what they can do best, and what others cannot do. They should not use any of their time to give their child practice at speechreading.

Parents must at all costs avoid the pitfall of failing to cue what they know their child can lipread. Some think that by dropping the cues when they are "not necessary" they will somehow help their child lipread better. They are making three serious mistakes, as follows:

1) The parents' time is too precious to use it in giving lipreading practice to the child. Others can do that.

2) They will inadvertently change their language to favor what the child can lipread, thereby avoiding the effort of cueing. Thus, they will not furnish the increasingly more complex, rich language that their child needs.

3) They will be ignoring the comfort and welfare of their child.

Lipreading is, for even the best lipreaders, a stressful and tiring activity. Deaf children who are lipreading have to maintain an exceedingly high level of concentration. In fact, they cannot maintain it for more than about 10 minutes at a time. When reading Cued Speech (after they become skilled at it) they can be almost as relaxed as a hearing person, except for the effort of maintaining a fixed gaze.

The last of the factors listed above is something parents need to keep in mind in connection with the school program. If the school will schedule the deaf child so that "heavy" classes are alternated with classes in which the verbal load is lower, and with activities such as lunch and recess, their child will be able to maintain concentration better throughout the day. Many school systems are hardly aware of this problem, and most make little or no effort to do anything about it.

Some fathers may have a heavy beard that covers much of the face, or a mustache that impedes the view of the upper lip and the space between it and the nose. This may be make it more difficult for their deaf child to read Cued Speech from them.

Relation of Speechreading to Intelligence

High intelligence is not requisite to good speechreading ability, although knowledge of language tends to correlate to some degree with intelligence, and thus may be responsible for a secondary limited correlation of speechreading with intelligence. Learning problems in addition to deafness do not always prevent a child from being a good lipreader. In fact some children with diagnosed learning problems are very good lipreaders. For example, Linda Balderson reports that her daughter Tiffany, who has the Charge Syndrome, ranks high on both the Utley and Tracy Clinic tests of speechreading of common sentences. Tiffany scored 100% in 1988 and 94% in 1989 on the Utley test. In spite of her learning problems and history of acute physical problems leading to many operations, Tiffany is close to the normal range in language, and expresses herself well in written and spoken language. Her speechreading is aided very little by residual hearing, since her PTA is in the range of 115 dB to 125 dB.

Effects of Cued Speech Upon Speechreading

Most of the evidence that exposure to Cued Speech has a cumulative and beneficial effect upon speechreading is anecdotal, but nonetheless persuasive. In fact, we are not aware of even one deaf child who has grown up with consistent exposure to Cued Speech in the home without becoming a relatively good speechreader.

Belgian researchers have reported their impressions, without supporting data, of the effects of long-term use of Cued Speech upon lipreading. Charlier, Capouillez, and Périer (1989), in "The Use of Signed French and Cued Speech in Combination," reported:

> *A secondary effect of intensive use of Cued Speech is that lipreading—even unsupported by cues—improves. Quite contrary to our initial fears, we have seen that CS does not make the deaf child dependent on the system but actually helps him become more autonomous vis-a-vis the person speaking. Two factors would explain this: on the one hand the child brought up with CS has been used to concentrated attention on the lips for long periods at a time. In addition, the child has attained a much higher level of language competency so that he can draw on the syntactical context and his language knowledge to aid him in lipreading. The efforts he makes to pay attention are therefore increasingly rewarded.*

Neef and Iwata (1985) reported:

> *Results indicated that subjects were able to accurately lipread cued stimuli as a function of Cued Speech training and that generalization of lipreading skills to novel nonsense syllables occurred. Cued Speech training also appeared to facilitate lipreading performance with non-cued stimuli, as well as articulation responses. Finally, students' probe performance following training compared favorably with that of an untrained (in CS) deaf peer who was considered to be a skilled lipreader.*

The finding that Cued Speech training enhanced lipreading of single phonemes and novel phoneme combinations is interesting and favorable. However, it has limited implications regarding the level of success in speechreading likely to be reached by Cued Speech children. The study above deals with only the most elementary skills involved in lipreading. Research has shown that speechreaders who are skilled at speechreading ordinary discourse do not perform much better on lipreading of individual phonemes and syllables than poor speech-readers. More research is needed on speechreading in discourse.

Because understanding with Cued Speech is much easier than lipreading, parents may ask: "Will CS cause my child not to want to lipread, since it is much harder?" Any child who can lipread well will make use of that skill when the need presents itself.

The question of dependence on Cued Speech is discussed at length in Chapter 8, pp. 106-107. The following facts should be kept in mind:

1) The consistent use of Cued Speech with a deaf child can be expected to increase his/her ability to function without it when it is necessary or desirable to do so.

2) There is no possibility that Cued Speech will become a manual method of communication for the child. The information visible on the mouth is indispensable for receiving the full message.

3) If deaf children are not taught a method by which they can communicate clearly with each other they will develop or find one, usually using gestures and mime.

Chapter Summary

1) Speechreading is one of the most complex activities of which human beings are capable.

2) One can lipread only familiar language, within a language whose vocabulary and syntax are well known.

3) Your child cannot learn new language through lipreading.

4) For your child to try repeatedly to lipread without the needed language base is damaging to him.

5) It is easy for parents to think their child lipreads more than he or she does, because of the natural gestures they use unconsciously.

6) Speechreading training is neither needed nor desirable.

7) Auditory training is needed to enable the child to become as good a lipreader as possible.

8) Parents should neither exaggerate their lip movements nor inhibit them. Clear, normal lip movements are best.

9) Parents should be aware of, and should try to lead school systems to attempt to reduce, the problem of exposing the child to consecutive "heavy" classes, that is, classes with a high verbal load.

10) A heavy beard or mustache may interfere with lipreading.

11) Cued Speech contributes to skill in speechreading, and thus to independence.

Chapter 14
Auditory Training, Cochlear Implants

Even a tiny amount of residual hearing, if properly trained for use in oral communication, and if supported by appropriate amplification, can be of tremendous value if (and only if) the child acquires a good knowledge of the spoken language.

The training of a hearing-impaired person to be aware of sounds, discriminate among them, attach meaning to them, and use them in both speech reception and speech production is called *auditory training*.[1] Auditory training is training in the use of residual hearing. Residual hearing is the hearing that remains after hearing loss is experienced, or is present initially in the case of a congenital hearing deficiency. Almost all so-called "deaf" persons have some useable residual hearing, including those diagnosed as having a profound[2] hearing loss. Not everyone who has less than perfect vision and needs eyeglasses is blind. Similarly, not everyone who has a hearing loss, and needs hearing aids, is deaf, or has to function as deaf. Maximum exploitation of residual hearing is essential in both receptive and expressive communication in spoken language. It is thus critically important in the education of a hearing-impaired child.

Hearing is the sense that protects one's privacy and safety by warning him or her that someone or something is approaching. It is our omnidirectional sense. To hear from all directions, one does not have to continually sweep the environment with one's ears. A deaf individual has to do this with the eyes, or be unaware of much that is happening. With amplification, residual hearing is often sufficient to help a great deal in this respect. Psychologists tell us that even a limited amount of residual hearing is psychologically beneficial to a hearing-impaired person. Without it he/she may have to combat severe feelings

---

[1]It is currently popular among professionals to use the term *auditory learning*, to focus on the child's role. We will use this term when it applies accurately, that is, when the reference is to what the child is doing, rather than what the therapist does. Auditory learning, of course, is the goal of auditory training.

[2]Persons classified as profoundly hearing impaired are those for whom audition is not useful for communication without both amplification and special training. They typically have a pure-tone-average (PTA) threshold of 90 dB or more. This figure is calculated in the United States by averaging the threshold levels from the child's pure-tone audiogram at 500, 100, and 2000 Hertz. In most European countries the average includes also the threshold at 4000 Hz.

of isolation and insecurity whose cause he/she may not even recognize.

Auditory training does not actually increase a child's physical ability to hear, but it helps form the habit and skill of *listening* (using residual hearing consistently). Most important, it helps develop skill at integrating the auditory signal with the information provided by the other senses.

Most Deaf Children Use Their Hearing Poorly

Most hearing-impaired children make relatively poor use of the residual hearing they have. There are several possible reasons for this. First, their knowledge of spoken language may be so limited that they do not know what they are listening for. Second, they may not have good amplification. Third, they may not have been trained effectively in the habit of using their hearing as fully as possible in understanding spoken language. Fourth, they may not know enough spoken language to support its recognition. Fifth, even if they have a substantial amount of residual hearing it may be so badly distorted that it is difficult to use in decoding auditory input. Intensive auditory training and practice are desirable for almost all hearing-impaired children. If residual hearing is so limited that a cochlear implant is advisable, training and practice in its use should be extensive.

The usefulness of even the most appropriate amplification for the child may be limited. Often a child's hearing is impaired by substantial amounts of nonlinear distortion, which does not show up in an audiogram. This distortion causes the ear itself to create spurious overtones and combinations of all incoming sound components. In this case, the child will experience excessive amounts of masking of the high frequencies by low-frequency components in the incoming signal. This can limit the usefulness of residual hearing largely to perception of the envelope of the speech signal and some suprasegmental features. No hearing aid made today will correct this problem. This is one reason why children with identical audiograms may differ widely in their ability to respond to auditory training and discriminate speech sounds.

If nonlinear distortion is a factor, a partial remedy is to use hearing aids in which amplification can be reduced at the low frequencies, below 500 Hz. In many cases this reduction can enable the child to perform much better auditorily, since the masking of the high frequencies will be reduced. Another alternative is the cochlear implant. Unfortunately, it is not known at this time whether children who have excessive amounts of nonlinear distortion before receiving a cochlear implant are hampered by similar difficulties with the implant. At some point in the future, hearing aids that compensate for nonlinear distortion in the hearing organism will probably become available.

Auditory Training And Cued Speech

For children accustomed to Cued Speech, auditory training is both crucially needed and highly advantageous. Their knowledge of spoken language, gained through Cued Speech, helps them respond efficiently to auditory training. But, if they learn language through vision (with cues) and are not given adequate auditory training, the result may be poor speech quality. Coordinating auditory *and* Cued Speech inputs through the Auditory/Visual Method (below) can maximize the child's skill at use of residual hearing and still result in the rapid language development achieved with Cued Speech.

In the last two decades there has been increasing recognition of the importance of *unisensory* auditory training; that is, training in the specific use of residual hearing without, at the moment, any access to the information visible on the mouth. A rapidly growing group among oralists is committed to the exclusive use of this method, avoiding insofar as possible, any early development of skill at using visual information. Many others recognize the value of frequent periods of unisensory auditory therapy, particularly in connection with speech development, as part of multisensory training. We feel that children growing up with Cued Speech should have regular periods of uni-sensory auditory training from the beginning of intervention, just as they need early and continued speech therapy. But, such training should involve only words already learned or recognized through Cued Speech.

The first model for *coordinated* use of unisensory auditory input, aural/oral input, and Cued Speech was presented by Cornett and Dowling at the Centennial Convention of the Alexander Graham Bell Association in Washington in July 1990 (Cornett, 1990). The purpose of the model is to maximize development of skill in use of residual hearing in oral communication and at the same time secure more rapid acquisition of language than is ordinarily obtained with traditional oral methods. The question that led to development of the model is: "Can optimum development of listening skills and rapid language acquisition be achieved concurrently?" For the method derived from the resulting model we have chosen the name *Auditory/Visual Method.*

A serious problem for both auditory/verbal practitioners and those engaged in training cochlear-implant recipients is the conflict between the trainer's desire to have the child get everything through listening, and the difficulty the child experiences in learning new language through hearing. The cochlear-implant therapist will agree readily that the child should ideally learn to decode the implant stimuli through exposure to familiar language. Exposure to unfamiliar language only confuses the child. One problem, then, is how the language is to become familiar in the first place. Another is the difficulty of avoiding serious language delay while the child's ability to decode language through hearing is being developed.

Advantages of Cued Speech for Auditory Training

Both children who are being trained to make maximum use of residual hearing and children who are being trained to decode the cochlear implant stimuli have a great advantage if their hearing loss came after learning the spoken language. When the therapist uses a prop to let the child know what he is about to say, the child who is already familiar with the word in question can most easily map the auditory stimulus to his/her internalized phonological lexicon. He/she can also make efficient use of linguistic context in the process of decoding through hearing, if he or she has a good knowledge of spoken language.

Children who have grown up with Cued Speech share this first advantage with the postlingually deafened child. Belgian experimental psychologists have made a series of studies of how Cued Speech children process spoken and written language. A report by Alegria and others (1990): "Role of Cued Speech in the Identification of Written Words Encountered for the First Time by Deaf Children: A Preliminary Report," closed with this summary paragraph:

> *To come back to our initial point, the present work strongly suggests that the lexicon developed by the deaf child with Cued Speech has properties which are equivalent to the phonology of the hearing subjects. In both cases the internal representations of the words are compatible with their ortho- graphic representations. This allows the use of phonological coding to identify unfamiliar written words and, as said before, can prime the whole process of reading acquisition.*

The interest of these researchers was in the effects of Cued Speech on reading. Ours at the moment is on improvement of ability at decoding auditory stimuli. What they learned is highly relevant to auditory decoding. The internalized phonological patterns are there in the mind of the child, ready for pairing with the incoming stimuli, whether natural residual hearing or the results of cochlear-implant stimulation, just as in the postlingually deafened child.

The child who has grown up with Cued Speech has three additional advantages not shared by either postlingually deaf or congenitally deaf children. One is that with Cued Speech either a parent or a therapist can give the child a clear phonological representation of what is going to be said, or of what has just been said. This makes props, environmental manipulation, and many of the machinations performed by a skilled therapist largely unnecessary in training audition on language the child already knows. The result is a substantial saving in time and effort, and relief from the burden of trying to remember what language is or is not already familiar to the child in question. The child is virtually spared failure and frustration. If he/she is given a word or phrase and does not understand it through audition, it can be immediately and accurately clarified through Cued Speech, then presented again through audition. If the word is new to him/her, it can be explained quickly and clearly.

The third advantage of the child who has received Cued Speech consistently in the home for several years is that he/she is typically a good speechreader. We know of no exceptions to this assertion, even among children with significant additional learning disabilities. Thus, the CS child has an important intermediate level of use of the auditory stimuli. If on first exposure to a familiar word, through audition alone, he is unable to decode, he can be given it through aural/oral input, and may succeed short of being given the answer through Cued Speech. This intermediate step is a part of the recommended training and testing phases of our model for maximum development of auditory skill along with the rapid language acquisition obtained by consistent use of Cued Speech in the home (except when the child is specifically being given auditory training). Nicholls (1989) reported that her subjects undertood only 2% of key words in sentences through audition alone, and 30% through lipreading alone, but 45% with audition and vision together. Lipreading skill thus multiplies the usefulness of residual hearing.

A fourth advantage of the young Cued Speech child is that his/her language level can be measured accurately by administering standard language tests through Cued Speech.

Both auditory/verbal practitioners and those responsible for habilitating cochlear-implant recipients have great difficulty in evaluating the language levels of pre-reading children, and of determining their language gains for specific periods of time. What they typically do is to administer the language tests aural/orally. In either case (with either aural/oral children or cochlear-implant recipients) the result obtained is lower than actual language level by an amount representing the effects of limited decoding ability. The problem is that some practitioners proudly and sincerely report to the parents, "Your child has gained six months of language in six months," or "Jimmie has gained eight months of language in six months, closing the language gap by two months." Actually, there may have been little or no language gain, but only a substantial increase in ability to speechread with the aid of the implant, or with the aid of residual hearing. Of course, the probability is that there has been some gain in both language and in decoding ability, so that neither is measurable. Unfortunately, parents may be led to think that their child is keeping up in language, or even closing the gap, when that is not the case.

If the child is accustomed to Cued Speech, administration of periodic language tests in that modality will assure accurate information on language level and its progress. Then, administration aural/orally will measure accurately any relative gain in decoding ability.

Guidelines for Early Auditory Training

Keep in mind that 1) all auditory training activities should be carried out in a quiet room, and 2) parents should be aware of the factor of distance. Speaking at a distance of 18 inches from the child's ear provides nine times as much sound input as at four-and-one-half feet.

A few decades ago great emphasis was placed on initiation of auditory training with loud, easily identifiable sounds, such as those of a drum, a whistle, a buzzer, or other noisemaker practically all profoundly hearing-impaired children can discriminate. This was intended to make the child aware of different sounds and their sources before working specifically on speech sounds. It is now generally accepted that beginning with gross sounds may direct attention away from the comparatively weak sounds of speech. Current thinking is that the first steps in auditory training should involve speech sounds that are easiest to discriminate and produce. There are many excellent books to help parents and professionals select specific goals and procedures for speech and auditory training. Best results are obtained when auditory training is administered in meaningful contexts and used as a natural and continuing part of daily activities that are of interest to the child.

Training in the use of residual hearing in oral communication requires careful procedures carried out with patience and understanding. In order to get a child to focus with maximum attention on what he/she is hearing, one must remove or minimize relevant visual stimuli at that moment. In other words, *unisensory auditory input* is the key to development of listening skills. This is true even though the goal is to lead the child to make maximum use of the combination of auditory and visual inputs. Also, even though the procedures carried out by the therapist or parent are carefully organized and proceed according to plan, they must come across to the child as natural and playful.

Unisensory auditory training belongs in the educational program of every deaf child with whom Cued Speech is being used. Parents must remember that residual hearing will not help much in oral communication until the child knows a substantial amount of spoken language. However, the growth of the child's ability to use his/her hearing will be clearly evident in the training process.

The Beginnings of Auditory Training

In early infancy the hearing child becomes conditioned to the voices of people, as used in the natural process of care-giving, caressing and communicating through touch, vision, and sound. The hearing-impaired infant needs even more exposure to the sounds of cooing and singing and the vibrations associated with being held against the face during sound production. Vowel sounds and babbled syllables should be emphasized. This conditioning process is very important in developing early awareness of auditory input.

Under the guidance of a professional, parents should carry out the earliest stages of auditory training by exposing the child to much *suprasegmental* information. Long before the child can understand speech as such, he/she can begin to perceive and respond to changes in duration, stress, intonation, rhythm, and relevant characteristics of speech conveyed in addition to the elemental speech sounds themselves. Training at this level should be provided initially by a professional and continued by the parents according to a plan that coordinates parental efforts with those of the therapist. Suprasegmental practice should be made as dramatic and entertaining as possible, in order to get and hold the child's attention.

The Perception of Differences in Paired Items

One of the most remarkable abilities of human beings, and of young children in particular, is their ability to perceive differences, even without consciously knowing what the differences are. The quickest way to get a 2-year-old, pre-language, hearing-impaired child to begin to understand Cued Speech is give him/her an opportunity to distinguish between the names of *pairs* of objects. You can point (a few times) to each of two familiar objects and give their names, in Cued Speech—and then invite the child to point to the correct one after you say and cue its name without pointing to it. A child can easily spot *differences*, either on the mouth or on the hand, before he/she can recognize individual words in Cued Speech or begin to pick up the system. The details of this procedure are given below.

The same principle applies to perception through residual hearing. The opportunity to spot differences between two auditory presentations gives the child the opportunity to make use of any perceivable difference, be it suprasegmental or phonetic. Distinguishing between two words through hearing alone is much easier for a hearing-impaired child than identifying or recognizing the individual words. When the names of objects are presented in pairs, the child succeeds at once in distinguishing them, and then proves that he/she does by identifying either presented alone. The exercise is immediately perceived as a game which the child enjoys and welcomes.

In distinguishing between pairs of words through audition, hearing-impaired infants will automatically make use of suprasegmental information and other perceived differences between individual sounds that may have been picked up in earlier auditory-conditioning activities. Not only do the children succeed; they *know* they are succeeding. The structure involved in the procedures used by therapists or parents in presenting stimuli in pairs is perceived by the children as merely constituting the rules of the game.

Discrimination Between Words Through Hearing

The following is a simple procedure to use for teaching a child to discriminate between two words through hearing alone. This is much easier than recognition of individual words. Keep it a fun-type activity. As long as the child considers it a game, he/she is likely to enjoy repeated sessions, with different pairs of objects.

1) Select two favorite items whose names sound very different. Consider both sounds and numbers of syllables (e.g., *book, pencil, doll, lollipop, dog.*) Use only items already familiar to the child, who can understand their names easily through Cued Speech. The first few pairs of words used should have different numbers of syllables, to aid in discrimination. Then you can proceed to pairs or groups of words

that have the same numbers of syllables.

2) Show the child the items in turn and name each one, *cueing*.

3) Explain or demonstrate that you want him or her to listen.

4) Say *lollipop* (with your mouth covered, unless the child is looking directly at the lollipop). Show the child the lollipop.

5) Let the child now watch as you cue and say *lollipop*.

6) Say *book* (with your mouth covered unless the child is looking directly at the book). Show the child the book.

7) Let the child watch while you cue and say *book*.

8) Show, before the next word, that you want him/her to tell you which you say, *book* or *lollipop*. Show the two objects, alternately.

9) Say (with your mouth covered, or later with the child covering his/her eyes) *lollipop*.

10) Ask "Which?" If the child says (or points to) the right one, show great enthusiasm. If he/she indicates the incorrect one, repeat the procedure to this point.

11) Repeat the procedure with the other word. Use facial expression and body language to lead the child which you said.

12) When the child can discriminate pairs of two words reliably, discuss with the therapist the advisability of attempting groups of three words.

The use of another adult to model the procedure (do what the child is to do) may help the child know exactly what is expected.

The procedure suggested above is just one early step in the continuing process of auditory development. How much of this needs to be done at home depends on whether a professional can work with the child regularly. If so, then the family can assume a supporting role under the guidance of the professional. Much depends upon whether the child enjoys the activity and will participate enthusiastically in multiple sessions. If the child fails repeatedly, becomes discouraged, or resists the activity, seek professional advice.

Coordinating Auditory Training and Cued Speech

In 1988 Cornett and Dowling (1990) developed a model for coordinated auditory aural/oral and Cued Speech training designed to produce maximum development of skill in using residual hearing (or cochlear-implant stimuli) while maintaining rapid language acquisition. In 1989 they conducted an experiment in which the procedures of the model were used in training a small group of profoundly deaf children to decode 20 Spanish words through audition. The children were first given a baseline test to establish that they did not know the words. They were tested on the Spanish words through audition alone, then on aural/oral input, and finally on Cued Speech. They scored, of course, at close-to-chance levels (25%), in choosing from four pictures. Next, they were taught the Spanish words in a total time of 45 seconds each, consisting of three 15-second exposures spaced over a total of eight days. The teaching was done by showing the child the appropriate picture and immediately repeating the corresponding Spanish word in Cued Speech. Each child was then given the pretraining test on the 20 words. The pretraining test was identical with the baseline test. The pretraining test was for the purpose of determining the effect on performance caused by simply learning the words through Cued Speech.

In the pretraining test the trainer presented each word through audition alone, and the child was allowed to choose from four pictures. The child was then tested on the 20 words by providing aural/oral input, and finally with Cued Speech. Then followed the training called for in the model, for about 5½ minutes per word, in all, over a period of eight days. After the training the post-test was administered, following exactly the same procedures as in the baseline test and the pretest.

On the pretraining test the four children averaged 79% on auditory presentation of the 20 words (just under 16 of 20 words), and 100% on aural/oral), after simply being taught the words with Cued Speech—that is, before receiving any unisensory/aural/oral training. Perfect scores after the training would not have represented statistically significant improvement with only four subjects. Thus, the 1988 experiment proved only that learning the words through Cued Speech prepared the children to recognize them at an impressive level through either auditory or aural/oral presentation.

In 1991 the experiment was repeated with a group of 11 profoundly deaf subjects who, unlike the subjects in the 1988 experiment, had not had intensive unisensory auditory training. As in the 1988 experiment, the subjects scored below chance levels (25%) on the baseline test, on the 20 Spanish words they did not know. After being taught the words with Cued Speech, in 45 seconds each, they were given the pretraining test, identical to the baseline test. Their performance with auditory input alone improved 68%, with aural/input 216%, and with Cued Speech 295%, as a result of being taught the Spanish words in 45 seconds each. After then receiving the training called for in the model, totalling about 5½ minutes per word (over an eight-day period), they improved additionally 63% on audition alone, 40% with aural/oral input, and 22% with Cued Speech.

The results suggest that the time spent in teaching the Spanish words should be increased to one minute instead of 45 seconds, with four exposures rather than three. This will be done in the next study, which will be conducted primarily with cochlear-implant recipients. It should be noted that the subjects who scored lowest with CS on the pretest finished learning the Spanish words during the training phase of the project, and thus were not handicapped in the post-test.

Some of the children were resistant to the procedures of the baseline test because they did not want to guess. Failure to respond was counted an error. This may be why the mean scores on the baseline test were below chance. The same factor may have limited performance on the unisensory phase of the pretest, for the children with little auditory training and /or very little hearing who felt insecure about audition.

The scores on the pretest show that the process of learning the Spanish words through Cued Speech prepared the subjects for unisensory and multisensory identification to a very significant degree. The effectiveness of the training procedure, of course, is shown by the improvement in unisensory and aural/oral identification of the words on the post-test.

There was a wide range in performance among the subjects. This could presumably be narrowed substantially by increasing the amount of time devoted to the training. Some subjects scored as high as 70% through audition alone, after the training, and one scored 90%. Two of the subjects were cochlear-implant recipients. All differences in the means related to the effects of training on auditory or auditory/oral performance were significant at the 0.005 or 0.001 level of confidence. A full report on the project will be submitted for journal publication.

Our conclusion is that the model evaluated in this experimental study makes it possible to secure rapid gains in auditory word identification through coordinated training with unisensory, aural/oral, and Cued Speech inputs. This leaves the way open for rapid language acquisition through consistent use of Cued Speech in the home *except during the specific training sessions and the periods of unisensory practice in which only familiar language is used.*

We commend the auditory/visual model/method to the specific attention of practitioners serving cochlear-implant recipients, for their consideration in connection with implant subjects who have had Cued Speech. We suggest they consider also the advisability of recommending and teaching CS to families of children who appear to be acquiring language too slowly while learning to decode the cochlear stimuli, or who appear to be sufficiently language-delayed to be at risk academically. If the child is sufficiently at home with written language, of course, his/her language level can be evaluated accurately with written tests. If not, the child should be tested with aural/oral input. This will yield an apparent language level below the actual level. If the apparent language delay is not more than one year, there should be no cause for concern unless it increases over time. If the apparent language deficit exceeds one year, it might be wise to consider asking the family to learn Cued Speech and follow the model we are suggesting, to ensure that language acquisition will not suffer.

We further suggest evaluation of the advisability of use of Cued Speech in the home with very young non-verbal children who are being prepared for reception of a cochlear implant. One to two years of consistent exposure in the home could endow the child with the internal phonological lexicon he/she needs to respond well to an implant.

We commend the auditory/visual model/method also to the attention of aural/oral and auditory/verbal practitioners for use with children who appear to be at risk with regard to language delay. Again, there is no cause for concern with children who can be given written language tests—assuming, of course, that they test within about one year of normal levels. For younger children, practitioners should evaluate language by testing with aural/oral input. If the child shows an apparent language delay of no more than one year, there may be no reason for concern unless a year later the gap remains or has widened.

If the apparent language delay exceeds one year in a non-reading child, we recommend that serious consideration be given to asking the parents to learn Cued Speech and use it in the manner suggested in the Auditory/Visual Model/Method.

If an aural/oral or auditory/verbal professional decides to use the auditory/visual method with a specific child, he or she should make sure that the family learns Cued Speech and uses it consistently for communication with the child in the home, except when engaging in specific unisensory training with the model, or during unisensory conversation limited to use of familiar language. Also, Cued Speech should be used as needed for clarifying auditory input not understood by the child.

Description of the Auditory/Visual Method

Some slight deviations from the procedures of the model itself were necessary in carrying out the experimental study described above. The following is a description of the procedures recommended for use of the model/method by practitioners and parents training a child in the use of either amplified residual hearing or the stimuli from a cochlear implant.

1. All new language, insofar as possible, is learned through Cued Speech, primarily from members of the family. Practitioners should, of course, teach through Cued Speech (or assign for the parents to teach) any new language they want specifically to use in training or assessment. There are two reasons for this. First, the acquisition of verbal language through Cued Speech is much more rapid than without it, for the children for whom the method is recommended. Second, the child's development of skill at decoding through audition alone, and through aural/oral input, is substantially enhanced if 1) the language used in training is already familiar in spoken form, and 2) any error on the child's part is immediately corrected and clarified through CS.

2. Language to be used in the training procedures should be checked through Cued Speech in advance, to make sure it is familiar to the child, even if it is thought to be familiar.

3. Parents should spend three or four five-minute sessions each day using Training Procedures A and B with their child. An important difference from the application of these in the experimental study is that the emphasis should be on having the child say each word, syllable, or phrase, rather than pointing to a picture or object. Training with only familiar language essentially eliminates the need to use pictures or other props—except, of course, for such use as may be desirable in the teaching of language to the child through Cued Speech. The result is that the unisensory and aural/oral training, according to our experience, can proceed much more rapidly and effectively when props are eliminated.

4. Parents should also spend 10 or 15 minutes each day in auditory conversation with the child, within the limits of familiar language on which the child has been trained with procedures A and B. This is best accomplished through guidelines from the practitioner.

5. Procedure A can often be combined conveniently with the learning of new language by the child. For example, if at the zoo the child encounters a new animal—say, an alpaca, the parent should use Cued Speech to say: "That's an alpaca" and invite the child to say and cue its name. Then the parent should be alert for opportunities to reinforce the word through aural/oral or auditory presentation. For example, if a picture of the animal is taken with an instant camera, when the picture appears, the parent can say again: "That's an alpaca." The choice of unisensory, aural/oral, or Cued Speech presentations should be made according to what the child can usually do after a single exposure to a new word with Cued Speech. Finally, the parent might ask the child to say the word, giving only the unisensory

exposure. The word *alpaca* should then join a list to be processed with procedures A and B on future days, and subsequently worked regularly into the daily sessions with Procedure B. Of course, the process just described can be implemented also in the home, using appropriate picture books and props. Parents should endeavor to proceed in as natural and unstructured a manner as possible.

6. The heart of the auditory/visual method is in the application of Procedure B after the preceding steps have been implemented. Though this procedure requires only a few minutes each day, we think it is crucially important.

Use only familiar words or phrases that have been through Procedure A at least a couple of times, or else used with Cued Speech within the last hour or so. Cue and speak the word *say* in "*Say* ___," and utter the word or phrase in question, with mouth covered. Cue and say: "Again, say ___," and again utter the word or phrase with mouth covered. If the child misses the word or is uncertain, give him/her a chance to lipread the word (with audition). Cue and say: "Now say:___," and speak the word without covering the mouth. The theory is that if the child misses the word on auditory presentation, rather than going immediately to Cued Speech to clear it up, the parent or practitioner should allow the child the possible satisfaction of using his/her hearing *and* what he/she sees on the mouth to identify the word or phrase. If the child succeeds at this, he/she is presumably using hearing with vision. Going immediately to Cued Speech would make use of hearing unnecessary, and fail to maximize use of audition. But, if the child is unable to speechread the word or phrase at this point, cue and say: "Say ___." This Cued Speech presentation will almost certainly enable the child to succeed. When he or she does, immediately repeat the word or phrase without cues (aural/orally) and then with mouth covered. Of course, the child will now succeed, since you have just cued the word or phrase for him/her. Finally, say: "Now, just listen and say ___." Make sure to repeat procedure B on any items on which the child fails, on several different occasions.

It is usually best to cue and say all the instructions given the child, except for the words to be presented through audition or aural/orally, at least until you can be sure that the child can consistently lipread those instructions reliably or understand them through audition. Cueing the instructions has the added advantage of contrasting with the inputs being tested or trained.

The procedures just described are based on three very important principles of pedagogy: 1) New material should be processed in three steps, going from the easy (Cued Speech) through the more difficult (aural/oral), to the most difficult (auditory). This is in procedure A.

2) Material on which the child has been trained with Procedure A is processed in steps going from most difficult (audition) to less difficult (aural/oral), to easy (Cued Speech). This is Procedure B. 3) Failure at any point is immediately relieved by reversing, toward the easier, to enable the child to regain a feeling of success.

Five things about the method should be noted:

1) All new language is learned through Cued Speech, and communication is normally in that mode.

2) For the initial auditory training phase, a familiar word or phrase is presented first in Cued Speech, then without cues, and finally with the mouth covered or vision diverted. For the child, the stimuli thus proceed from easy to difficult on new language.

3) For the second auditory training phase, on familiar language, an auditory-only presentation of a familiar word or phrase is made (with mouth covered or attention diverted), then a multisensory presentation (mouth visible), and finally (if needed for confirmation) a Cued Speech presentation. The progression, on familiar language, is thus from difficult to easy (auditory, aural/oral, Cued Speech). After the Cued Speech presentation, the presentations are repeated in the reverse order if the child was unsuccessful at any point.

4) As soon as the child's use of residual hearing makes it practical, some time each day (10 or 15 minutes) should be devoted to practice in conversation through audition alone, about very familiar subjects, and using only language that has been "primed" through procedures A and B. For this, the parents should follow guidelines worked out with or by the practitioner. The latter should map out the language associated with a specific story or episode that parents should process through procedures A and B. The parent should work carefully through this language with the child, using procedures A and B, over a period of days or weeks. Then, the auditory-only conversation periods should begin, starting with the story itself. When the story has been thoroughly covered, variations should be initiated and discussed. Meanwhile, the new language in the next story, episode, or subject to be used should be processed with procedures A and B, in preparation for a new series of auditory discourse sessions beginning when interest in the first story diminishes.

5) The time devoted by the parents to auditory training with procedures A and B should be 10 to 20 minutes per day, preferably consisting of several short periods. Unisensory auditory conversation in the home, using only familiar language, should take an additional 10 to 15 minutes per day. Thus, plenty of additional time should be

available for normal, language-stretching communication in the home in Cued Speech, which is essential to language development.

Ideally, the parents should be able to arrange for regularly scheduled auditory training by a competent professional trained in unisensory auditory methods and with experience in using the coordinated Auditory/Visual model described above. A professional who lacks that experience should secure orientation and assistance in following the model from the Cued Speech Center, Raleigh, N.C..

If the services described are not available from a local professional, the parents should consult the Cued Speech Center about using the Auditory/Visual method at home, following the suggestions made. They should try to obtain advice and guidance from a competent professional familiar with the model, even if it has to be supplied by telephone or correspondence. If possible, they should persuade a local professional to become familiar with the method and guide them.

Because the parents need all the time they can give to enrichment of language development, family life, and communication through Cued Speech, they should probably not devote more than the amounts of time indicated to auditory training of the types suggested. This limited amount of time can still enable them to furnish many exposures to sequences of the type suggested, each day.

Role of Hearing Siblings in Auditory Development

Several parents pointed out that most hearing siblings will provide unisensory auditory input whether parents want them to or not. Play activities create many situations in which siblings speak without making sure that the deaf child is looking at them. If siblings cue consistently, this is less likely to be the case. We hesitate to suggest that hearing siblings who can cue be asked to give auditory practice deliberately, because of the possibility of reducing their contribution to development of language. Also, there is a danger that they might not be careful to restrict auditory exposure to language that is familiar to the deaf child. All in all, it would seem to be best to encourage their cueing and let any unisensory auditory exposure that may happen be incidental and undirected.

Earl Fleetwood relates several anecdotal examples of auditory training given his deaf sister, Alisa. One was pointing out to Alisa that the floor in the house squeaked in various places. Helping her identify those spots helped her move quietly in playing hide-and-seek games. It also gave her excellent practice in listening. He also mentioned cueing ononmatopoeic representations of the sounds of birds (*chirp,*

chirp, tweet, tweet), of bees (*bzzzzzzzzz*), and of the wind (*whoosh*). Cueing the words of popular songs from the radio stimulated her interest in rhythm, rhyme, elongated vowels, and other aspects of singing. He noted that she observed from this experience: "There sure are a lot of songs about love!"

Earl also relates the interest generated by letting Alisa learn how much a person with normal hearing can pick up. By turning his back while Alisa opened and closed different drawers in the kitchen cabinet, he showed her that he could tell which drawer she had opened. Such demonstrations can cause a profoundly deaf child to push a little more in the effort to listen carefully.

Cochlear Implants

Many types of assistive devices have been developed in the effort to improve the perception of speech by hearing-impaired people. Among these are frequency-transposing hearing aids, vibrators, cochlear implants, and even single-purpose instruments such as the S-meter, a device that provides a vibratory or visual signal to indicate the presence of the phoneme *s*. Because the usefulness of cochlear implants seems to be enhanced substantially by both prior and concurrent use of Cued Speech, they will be discussed here in considerable detail.

Parents who are interested in looking into the possibility and advisability of securing a cochlear implant for their deaf child must obtain current information. The situation is changing very rapidly, as improvements in technology and evaluation of results come about. A very readable and informative article on cochlear implants, by a deaf adult with one (Patricia A. Clickener), appears in the Jan./Feb. 1991 issue of the *SHHH Journal*. However, much of the content of that article, and of what follows here, will be out of date in a very few years. We suggest that for the latest information in future years you get in touch with the organizations listed in the Appendix, and with the Cochlear Corporation, 61 Iverness Drive East, Suite 200, Englewood, CO 80112.

The use of the single-electrode cochlear implant was pioneered in the United States by Dr. William House, of the House Ear Institute, in Los Angeles, Calif. The implants were limited initially to post-lingually deafened adults. It was correctly anticipated that prior knowledge of the spoken language, as well as existing memory of specific speech sounds and phonological patterns, would put these subjects at an advantage in the use of the device. Experience supports this view.

When the House Ear Institute began implanting children with its cochlear device it continued its policy of accepting only post-lingually deafened subjects. Later it included several children who had received Cued Speech consistently for several years. Some of these parents have reported the opinion of the institute staff members that the Cued Speech children appear to have an advantage over most prelingually deaf children by virtue of their knowledge of the spoken language, even though that knowledge has been gained primarily through a visual method. We have received no direct reports from the House Ear Institute regarding observation of any specific advantage in the concurrent use of Cued Speech in training the subject in use of the implant. However, we have very definite and very favorable impressions on this point from parents, and the theoretical evidence is also substantial. Of course, continuing language development through Cued Speech would be expected to enhance continuing progress in the ability to utilize the input of the device. This would presumably also be true of the CS subjects' superior conceptualization of phonological patterns.

The advent of the 22-electrode cochlear implant appears to have changed the picture drastically. Whereas some people were helped substantially by the single-electrode implant, apparently most were helped very little. In fact, some scientists (James Pickett, 1980) reported that data available indicated that the single-electrode implant was of about the same usefulness as a vibrator. In contrast, many very profoundly deaf people have found the 22-electrode instrument of tremendous value, and most of them apparently find it of significant value. As a result, some individuals with small but significant amounts of usable residual hearing are being implanted in the anticipation that the result will be superior to the earlier hearing. This possibility should be balanced against the hope that future improvements in hearing aids may increase the usefulness of existing residual hearing.

We mention all this only to suggest that children who have already acquired a substantial knowledge of spoken language through Cued Speech will enjoy an even greater advantage in the use of the 22-electrode cochlear implant than in the case of the single-electrode units. We do not recommend that parents get a cochlear implant for their deaf child, nor do we recommend against it. They should seek the best current medical and professional guidance in the matter. We advise caution because of the risks involved, as well as the expense, and we suggest that parents using Cued Speech can afford to wait longer before resorting to the implant because their child's acquisition of verbal language will not be suffering. Case histories presented in this chapter, and some from other chapters referenced here, contain descriptions of experience with the cochlear implant that will be helpful to parents.

Alison M. Turner (*Cued Speech Center Lines*, Oct.89/Jan.90) advised caution because "...the cochlear implants are primarily useful for those who already have a grasp of the spoken language." Since her article appeared, the results obtained with the 22-electrode implants have caused a change in policy among those providing implants, so that now many children with some usable residual hearing are being implanted, if the prognosis indicates a good chance of achieving better results than those with the earlier residual hearing.

Impressions From Several Families

Dr. Turner's article reports on the experiences of several children who received implants after considerable experience with Cued Speech. All previously had little or no usable residual hearing, though one had normal hearing until the age of 3½. All the reports are favorable, and in all the progress made in learning to decode the input of the implant was judged to be due in significant part to prior knowledge of the spoken language through Cued Speech and the ability to receive clarification through Cued Speech in the learning process. The report emphasizes the time and effort expended by the families before deciding to get an implant:

> The McKendrees, for example, whose son Will received an implant at the University of Virginia in June, 1988 at age 4, talked with implanted adults as well as the parents of four children with implants over a period of two years before coming to their decision. They also corresponded with the Nucleus Corporation, makers of the unit.

> The Lees started keeping a file on cochlear implants from the time Danny lost his hearing in May 1985, at age 3½, and they also talked with the parents of other implanted children. Danny received a 22-channel implant in December, 1987 at age 6. The implant was performed at the House Ear Institute in Los Angeles.

The case of Benjamin Lachman (reported in considerable detail in the case history below) was special in that Benjamin's cochlea was not fully formed and there was no prospect of his being able to profit from all 22 channels. As it turned out, he receives input from 10, which is more than was expected. But, their decision to go ahead was made even harder by this problem.

With regard to the evaluations prior to the implant, all three mothers who wrote about their experiences say that their children's understanding of Cued Speech prior to the implant was very beneficial during the proceedings. MaryAnn Lachman writes: "As near as I can tell ... the main reason Benjamin was eligible for the implant at all was because of his strong phonetic training (thank you Cued Speech) and his strong auditory training."

Lily Lee writes that the professionals at the House Ear Institute said something to the effect that "Danny is an excellent candidate for cochlear implant because...he is already using Cued Speech....We can see better now that all other factors being equal, Cued Speech is definitely an asset for a child with a cochlear implant."

Dr. Turner's article emphasizes the importance of the "time-locked" nature of the relationship between the cues of Cued Speech and the sounds produced, as pointed out by Judith Lasensky and Priscilla Danielson in their article "Aural Habilitation Prior to Cochlear Implant in a Congenitally Deaf Child." This article appeared in the 1987 issue of the *Cued Speech Annual*. They write;

Sign language is not time-locked to spoken English even when it is signed in exact English. Therefore, with the introduction of a cochlear implant, they (the congenitally deaf) have to sort out all environmental noises. Speech becomes not only an added noise to their environment, but an entirely new language coding system. Therefore we propose that an effective plan of treatment is to introduce Cued Speech as the primary mode of communication prior to cochlear implant.

Perhaps an even greater advantage of several years of prior exposure to Cued Speech, when a child receives a cochlear implant, is that he or she resembles an adventitiously deaf child in already knowing the language to be decoded through the cochlear stimuli. Not only that, but the child knows it in its phonological, temporally sequenced form, which the stimuli of the implant follow implicitly. This is possibly responsible for a remark by a member of the House Ear Institute staff, years ago after they had implanted a few Cued Speech children, that the children with Cued Speech backgrounds reacted like adventitiously deaf children, in their response to training with the implant.

Dr. Turner's article reports also on the parents' observations regarding the function of Cued Speech in evaluation and in preparation of the child for the implant:

> *Susanna McKendree writes: "Fortunately, through the use of Cued Speech, Will's language level was close to his age, so we were able to talk with him about the possibilities, somewhat. Unfortunately, realizing all that had to take place was beyond comprehension of a 4-year-old as well as Mom and Dad."*

> *Danny's mother Lily Lee writes: "We are so glad we have found Cued Speech for Danny and for us...Cued Speech had definitely helped Danny in preserving his phonological memory of spoken language when he was totally without acoustic input. It has also allowed him to acquire language in similar fashion as a hearing child does....Cued Speech has also been a wonderful tool during the period of Danny's cochlear implant operation. Before the surgery, we were able to explain everything with cues, teaching him the proper terminology and concepts. I don't think we could have explained things that well to Danny if we only had fingerspelling and inadequate signs at our disposal."*

> *As regards the aural rehabilitation after the implant, the evidence shows that a prior knowledge of the spoken language continues to be of great benefit in the process of training the ear to be perceptive of and to understand and interpret correctly the new sounds which it "hears," especially when it comes to the subtleties of human speech. What the parents have to say on this matter is the best evidence. Mrs. Lee puts it in this fashion: "During the hookup, I could use Cued Speech to interpret everything that went on. And since the implant we believe that Cued Speech used over the first three or four months has helped Danny progress at a faster rate....It helps make meaningful connections between the sensations Danny feels and the sounds the cues represent. It clarifies speech while Danny learns to decode a new set of signals. Even though we can now communicate orally without signs or cues, we still use cues when we introduce a new expression. And at times, when the speech processor is not in use, we have Cued Speech to ensure clear and complete communication."*

> *Bill Robers' factual account of his daughter Gina's*

implant...makes it very clear that Cued Speech can be used as a valuable tool during the rehabilitation process, especially with a child such as his daughter who has never previously heard sound. She has had a profound hearing loss since birth and was 11 years old at the time of the implant in July 1987. Bill writes: "Like all implant recipients, she is having to learn to decipher the signals she is getting into a pattern which she recognizes as sound." Gina's speech therapist and audiologist learned Cued Speech to help her; so that: "...they are able to cover a lot of new concepts with Gina, with a minimum of confusion. With the multi-channel implant, it is possible (for Gina) to discern slight differences in speech, such as similar vowel and consonant combinations, and the use of Cued Speech has made this task easier. Through the use of CS, she is able to recognize which sounds they are working on, and is learning to distinguish sounds which closely resemble each other. She is very accustomed to CS, and once she hears a certain sound or vowel/consonant blend, through the use of cues she knows exactly which sound she is hearing and learns more easily to pick up that particular sound in everyday speech. It is a lot of work on everybody's part, but it has been a lot smoother because of the use of Cued Speech."

Catharine McNally, from Winston-Salem, N.C., became profoundly deaf at 8 months from meningitis. Her parents started using Cued Speech with her before she was 2. At the age of 3, Catharine received the 3-M single channel implant at the Houston Ear Research Foundation. Nearly a year later, on May 22, 1987, her mother wrote the following letter to Dr. Eric Kraus of the Greensboro Cochlear Implant Program in summarizing the benefits Catharine had gained even with a single-channel implant: "We have been using Cued Speech with Catharine for over two years. Prior to the implant, Catharine was developing great receptive language although her expressive language was lagging. Since the implant, Catharine's expressive language has soared and her receptive language has continued to grow. When we took her back to Houston in March for her first six-month follow-up, the professionals at the Houston Ear Research Foundation were amazed at her progress. The implant has definitely been a success—but I strongly believe that much of the credit for the success of Catharine's implant belongs to a strong program of auditory training combined with the consistent use of Cued Speech. To me, the two are a well-matched pair."

To summarize the implications of the information we have received from many sources, including that in Dr. Turner's article, it appears safe to make the following assertions:

1) Prior knowledge of the spoken language, either through normal hearing before loss of hearing, or through Cued Speech, is of decided advantage to a child in developing the ability to make good use of a cochlear implant. Specific training with the implant will result in more rapid progress if it employs only familiar language.

2) Communication in Cued Speech facilitates the process of evaluation of a child as a candidate, and of orientation of the child as to what to expect.

3) After the implant, Cued Speech helps the child learn to associate the implant stimulus with the sound it represents, and to discriminate between sounds that are similar, if the implant outputs are different for them. This is because CS is "time-locked" with the acoustic signal, so that it identifies each speech sound at the precise instant it is produced and the corresponding implant stimulus is received.

4) As and if the child progresses to the level of being able to understand a great deal with the aid of the implant, Cued Speech can still be used to clarify and correct, or to introduce new material.

Chapter Summary

Even a tiny amount of residual hearing, if properly trained for use in oral communication, can be of tremendous value to a deaf child. Most hearing-impaired individuals make very poor use of the residual hearing they have. Unisensory auditory training, appropriately coordinated with multisensory training and Cued Speech, may be the key to maximum use of residual hearing. The first model for achieving this was presented by Cornett and Dowling in 1990. The parents' role in auditory training, preferably with the advice of a speech therapist, involves unisensory presentation of familiar language in appropriate situations.

The development of the 22-electrode cochlear implant offers new hope for many of the most profoundly and prelingually deaf children, particularly if they are started on Cued Speech very early and come to the implant with a well developed internalized model of spoken language.

Case Histories

Several of the case histories in this section are very long. We have hesitated to shorten them much because the detailed descriptions of procedures and experiences connected with cochlear implants are likely to be of much interest and help to parents facing a decision as to the advisability of getting an implant for their child.

Ben Lachman's Cochlear Implant
by MaryAnn Lachman

The hardest thing about getting the implant was the decision to go ahead with it. This was especially difficult with Benjamin because, medically, he was not a great candidate. He was born deaf, and in the process of evaluating him for the implant we found out why; he has Mondini Syndrome which means that his cochlea did not finish forming. As near as I can tell (this has not been confirmed by the surgeon) the main reason Benjamin was eligible for the implant at all was because of his strong phonetic training (thanks to you, Cued Speech) and his strong auditory training (thank you, Northwestern University and Andy Lopacki and CID who got NW to let Ben into their program). Benjamin had gone about as far with auditory training as he could go when he was 4 years old, but what hearing he had (110 dB corner audiogram) he was using. Dr. Novak felt that Benjamin would use any tools we could give him.

Deciding to do the surgery was very difficult. Thanks to our consistent use of Cued Speech from the time Benjamin was 2 years old, his language is not delayed. He lacks some in quantity, and his speech needs help. Benjamin's only language tool was lipreading with Cued Speech. Although he does exceptionally well, I felt I would like things to be easier for Ben, and I hoped that some additional sound would give him a boost. As I watched the pre-implant testing done at Carle Clinic, it was so obvious that Ben was using every tool available to him to its utmost capability that I concluded he needed more tools. We had tried vibrotactile and electrotactile stimulation. The vibro was not significant for Ben, and he had a skin reaction to the electrotactile stimulation. We considered sign language, which we had used some before we used Cued Speech, but since Ben's delay is in speech and not language, this seemed illogical.

As stated above, deciding to go ahead was difficult. Until the surgery we were uncertain if Benjamin would get the 22-channel unit or a single-channel unit. We did not know if the 22-channel unit would fit in his little cochlea. We decided to do the surgery on his worse ear and hoped to get eight working channels. In this ear he did not even wear a hearing aid. An aid did no good in that ear.

We were most worried about the surgery. Part of the evaluation had been a surgical procedure to determine if Benjamin's auditory nerve was functional. This was supposed to be out-patient surgery, but it took twice the normal amount of time, and Benjamin got sick and needed to stay the night. Then he got ear infections in both ears. In a way, this made the surgery easier to take: he only needed to have one ear done. We expected him to stay two or three days after the surgery. We expected fluid accumulation because of the abnormal cochlear shape. We feared the facial nerve would get in the way. In the end, although the surgery took longer than normal, everything went well. There was no fluid. Benjamin was in the hospital only one night. Dr. Novak was able to place 12 channels of the Cochlear Corporation implant in Benjamin's left ear. Although he looked like the "walking wounded" from the Revolutionary War (head bandaged), Ben came through it very well.

After the surgery all we had to do was wait. Ben got a spike hair cut so that the shaved area would be less noticeable. He was thrilled with that.

After six weeks we went to the clinic and they "turned Ben on." They hooked up the unit to the computer and to Benjamin. They gave him a paper with numbers (off...1...2...3...4...5...6...7...8...9...10... comfortable...too loud) and told him to move his finger, when he heard or felt something. I was watching the computer screen as the number indicating the power going to the processor crept up higher and higher. Ben was not moving his finger, and I did not know when to expect him to react. I was afraid it would not work. Ron (my husband) had told me there was a 20% chance it would not work at all for Ben.

The numbers crept up and suddenly Ben moved his finger to 1. Jill Firzt (Ben's audiologist) turned the processor off, and Ben moved his finger back to off. The feeling was almost like having a baby; it was that thrilling. Of course the next hours were boring for Ben but not for me. Every new channel that was tested and functioning was a triumph. They gave him a "map" or program with 10 channels and we went to the hotel. Every new sound Ben listened to was incredible. The toilet sounded like an airplane, he said (airplanes were all he heard reliably before). The M&M bag made a sound. He heard the horns in the movie on TV, *Return of the Getaway*. The most exciting thing was that he liked it. He wanted to wear it. He had never wanted to wear his hearing aid.

That was May 9, 1988. Now it is January, 1989. We now call Ben Benjamin because, although *Ben* is easier to cue to a 2-year-old, *Benjamin* is easier to discriminate with an implant. The most significant thing to me is still that Benjamin likes the implant and that it gives him an awareness of sound at 45 dB, so that he can perceive the difference. I think he is happier. He knows he is deaf. But he knows that he can now function with some hearing, and he hopes to function as hard-of-hearing like his friend, Sarah, who was just mainstreamed into fifth grade with a Cued Speech interpreter. Of course, Benjamin has been mainstreamed for many years. Benjamin works on his speech and is able to produce all the sounds. I expect it to take at least two years (maybe three) to get the full childhood use from the implant. I say childhood because I think that when Benjamin matures, he'll get even more. If he takes after Ron, he'll reprogram their entire system to get the most benefit from the unit and tell them how to change it.

I'm glad for Ben that we got the implant. It is not a panacea, but it is a wonderful new tool.

Update to October, 1991

Benjamin's speech is significantly improved. Most people can understand him most of the time, although for a new person it is like listening to someone with a foreign accent. Sometimes understanding depends on effort from the listener. As of the end of 1990, I would say Ben had about topped out his usage of the implant using normal speech therapy methods.

This year we are starting a new program of intensive auditory training. Ben can already use the processor for the prosody of language and discriminate some phonetic information. He does not, however, use his hearing as one of his primary language tools. He said to me, "My processor doesn't help me understand you; it only makes my own speech better." This year we will work on helping Ben understand how he can use the sounds he is hearing to better advantage. Some of those sounds are speech, some are environmental. He still needs work to react appropriately to the sounds coming in.

Other interesting things in Ben's life: The courts never did support our contention that Cued Speech is a tool and not a methodology and that, as a result, Ben should be given access to public school through use of a Cued Speech transliterator. This may have been a blessing in disguise. Because that avenue was not open, we enrolled Ben in a parochial school when he reached second grade. Fortunately we are able to afford to pay not only the school fees, but also the salary for a full-time Cued Speech transliterator. Ben learns not only all the normal subjects, but he also has Judaic subjects which are taught in the Hebrew language about two hours each day. To make this possible, we found a wonderful woman from Israel who had been in America for several years, and taught her to cue. She cues both the English and the Hebrew for Ben. Reports are that Ben is doing well in school. At 10 years of age he is beginning to go through his own "I don't want to be deaf" stage. We'll see how we handle that one.

Ben leads a quite normal life. He was on the first-place Little League team in Morton Grove last summer. The coaches were superb. I thought I would need to stay to interpret, but after the first day they didn't need me. These things are not pointed out because I expect Ben to "outgrow" Cued Speech, but to show that the need for CS is for his academic life rather than his social life. He has two special friends who are girls and two who are boys, so he seems well balanced.

What else? Ben has a wonderful relationship with his sister Julia (7). She is just beginning to express an interest in CS. She does not really need it to communicate with Ben. She has always understood him, and she is very good at making things clear for him. They have very normal sibling fights, but most of the time they are very close. One nice thing is that their relationship is balanced. Ben is not dependent on Julia for his social life any more than Julia is dependent on Ben. *For Ben's own observations, see p. 575.*

Michael's Implant

Michael Poore, whose story is told in Chapter 23, received a 22-electrode cochlear implant in August 1990. The following statement is from Priscilla J. Michalk, M.S./C.C.C., his speech therapist.

In the two years and three months I have worked with Michael as his speech therapist, he has made significant progress in both areas, speech and language development. In my professional opinion this remarkable progress can be directly attributed to Michael's 22-channel cochlear implant and his use of Cued Speech....As a language specialist I am confident that his ability to write a creative story such as the one attached (see Chapter 25) is directly related to the fact that his use of Cued Speech enables him to use his intellectual potential to the utmost.

Michael's articulation skills have improved almost 25% since he received his implant last year, an especially significant improvement in a student of his age. Due to the increased auditory input Michael now receives he is able to produce his sounds more clearly and can, in some situations, monitor his own productions. He is also able to hear and identify more environmental sounds, making him a part of his environment and facilitating more interaction. His overall intelligibility is much improved and made it possible for him to dictate his story to me—I could understand him. This would not have been possible even a year ago."

Michael's mother, Teri Poore, comments as follows on his one year of experience with the implant:

> *It helped more than we thought but less than we hoped. ...We're very excited that his speech seems to be improving at a time when we were led to expect that it would level off and stop improving around the age of 10 without sound input. Now Michael can communicate and carry on a conversation much more easily because the person understands him and answers more appropriately. Michael's a good lipreader because of Cued Speech, but now we believe he also gets some of the speech sounds because of the implant, so the combination is the best. We still cue at home, Jerry and I, but we also practice without cues—only on the known phrases, not new language or important talks.*
>
> *Michael enjoys the sounds he's hearing and recognizing: telephone, dog barking, door bell, his name (he answers to any two-syllable word), water running, knock at the door, and more. He is more patient in learning new environmental sounds than in work on speech. I cue as fast as I talk and everyone says that's very fast. I believe Michael can do better with his listening skills if I take more time and make him be more "oral." But for that we give up our ease and speed of communication. He thrives on new language. So, we do the best we can—three hours of speech therapy a week, and some every day at home. Almost eight years ago, Dr. Orin Cornett was the only person to offer us hope after Michael had meningitis and lost his hearing. Through the years Cued Speech has allowed us to explain about death, God, and girl friends, and answer all the "whys" as we would have if his hearing were intact. Now we have hope that with the cochlear input Michael may hear and understand some of the words.*
>
> *Without the cochlear implant Michael has no usable hearing (110 dB unaided at 250 Hz., 95 dB aided, and nothing at higher frequencies). We've helped him believe he can do anything he wants to do. He'll understand the limitations of deafness later when he's mature enough. By then we hope he's experienced so much that he'll make the right choices.*

Michael's mother makes a very insightful observation: that other people did not perceive the effect of Michael's implant to be as much a "miracle" as his family did. She explains that this was because, to the others, Michael's performance already seemed miraculous, and the implant didn't cause him to suddenly improve by leaps and bounds. She and her husband could more accurately perceive the effect of the implant because they had a very accurate idea of the excellent progress he was already making because of Cued Speech and could judge the change that resulted from the combined effect.

Gina Robers
by Bill Robers (from *CS News*, Winter, 1987)

On July 13, 1987, Gina Robers was hooked up with a Nucleus 22-channel cochlear implant. Gina was 11 years old at the time, and had had a profound hearing loss since birth. She had been using Cued Speech for eight years and was in an oral self-contained classroom at Reading Hilltop School, in Hamilton County, Ohio.

Because Gina was the first prelingually deaf person to receive the Nucleus device, many variables had to be addressed by the implant team at Riley University Hospital in Indianapolis, where the surgery was performed. Up to this point, all multi-channel implant recipients had been

Trisha (19), Gina (15), and Betsy (14) Robers

adults who had been hearing at one time. These first recipients had had a good grasp of what sound is, and were able to make comparisons between the signals they were getting from the implant and the true sound as they remembered it. This was not the case with Gina, since she had never had any appreciable hearing. Everything she was getting from the implant was entirely new to her. Like all implant recipients, she had to *learn* to hear; that is, to learn to decode the signals she was getting from the implant and recognize them as sounds and words. Because she has nothing from her memory to compare the input to, as the postlingual adults do, she faced a far more different task, as did also the staff at Riley.

The need for Gina to have precise communication with the audiologist, Wendy Myres, and the speech therapist, Kathy Kessler, was crucial. Both Wendy and Kathy, as well as several others on the staff at Riley, learned Cued Speech. They were able to cover a lot of new concepts with Gina, with a minimum of confusion. Also, Gina's ability with the implant to discern slight differences in similar sounds was enhanced by use of Cued Speech to identify them and learn to pick them up in everyday speech.

In the development of skill at use of the cochlear implant there are many concepts to cover, such as loudness, pitch, duration of sound, minimum and maximum hearing levels, speech-noise discrimination, and the discrimination of the individual sounds themselves. Guesswork or confusion on the part of the implant user greatly impedes progress. I think the implant team at Riley will agree that Cued Speech has made their job smoother.

Now (1987) there are four children who use implants who have undergone implants at Riley Hospital, and the staff is becoming quite adept at cueing. We have seen CS help our family for eight years, both at home and at school, and now we are seeing enormous benefits of CS in working with the cochlear implant.

How I Feel About My Cochlear Implant
by Danny Lee (9.2)

I recieved (sic) my Cochlear Implant when I was 6 years old. It helps me to hear sounds *and* speech. I almost always understand my parents, and sometimes the new people I meet. I could even use the telephone.

At first when I recieved my Cochlear Implant I got the WSP (wearable speech processor). Then after two years I switched to the MSP (Mini Speech Processor). When I switched to the MSP the sound was smooth as cream and sounded very, very different, but not as choppy as the WSP. After a few days I got used to it. My parents had to pay $5000 (USA money) for the MSP, but it was worth it.

I began grade four in school when I was 8. I go to the regular classes on some subjects such as French, language arts, and grade five math. I really like my Cochlear Implant.

Life After Deafness With Danny
by Lily Lee
(CS News, Oct. 1988) update, 1992

Our son Danny was deafened by meningitis in May 1985, when he was about 3½ years old. Our second child, David, was only 3 weeks old at that time. It was a period of devastation, despair, and chaos. It was life-altering.

Danny was acquiring three languages prior to his hearing loss: Mandarin (my native tongue), Cantonese (my husband Donald's mother tongue), and English, the common language between us and outside the home. I had used Mandarin when communicating with Danny since he was born, knowing that he would have no difficulty acquiring the English language later on. As I was trained in linguistics with research interest in child language acquisition, Danny was the perfect subject in my research papers from the time he was 8 months old to the time he was 28 months old. For a child acquiring Mandarin in an English environment, Danny was advanced in his language development. His use of English expressively came about shortly after he entered a day-care program at the age of 2 years, 8 months. By the time Danny became deaf he was fluent in both English and Chinese.

Danny's deafness came as a total shock to us. May is the month of hearing. Ironically it is the month of deafness for us. However, because it happened to be May, there was an announcement about a John Tracy Clinic workshop in town, organized by a parent support group. Donald's sister alerted us about the article, and I contacted the John Tracy workshop that weekend. Seven days after Danny's homecoming from the hospital I was at the workshop and was overwhelmed by the flood of information. I met some parents and professionals and heard, for the first time, the controversy among various methodologies in deaf education.

Wanting to learn as much as we could as fast as we could, we started our research and weekly visits to various families with hearing-impaired children. Our "imposition" was well received by all the families we contacted. During this time we joined the A.G. Bell Association and began taking the parent correspondence course with the John Tracy Clinic.

Danny went through a comprehensive evaluation at Children's Hospital in June 1985. Within the same day, we were told by the psychologist who tested his non-verbal intelligence that Danny was the brightest child she had ever tested. We were told by the audiologist that Danny had the worst hearing loss she had ever seen in her six years of practice (105-110 dB PTA in the low frequencies and no response at more than 500 Hz). We were also told that he had no usable residual hearing, and even with hearing aids might never hear again. We were relieved that his mental ability seemed to be intact, but were totally crushed by a sense of helplessness in connection with his essentially total hearing loss. Broken ears; broken dreams.

One of the major decisions we had to face during that time was to switch to English completely. Another was to try the auditory-oral approach. After his hearing loss Danny could express himself with intelligible speech in either Chinese or English, but had difficulty receiving the speech of others. After four months, his speech had deteriorated drastically. By December 1985, six months after his hearing loss, his mean level of length of utterance was a one-or-two-word phrase or sentence.

Danny (9) and David (6) Lee

We learned about the oral program and the TC (Total Communication) program in our school system shortly after Danny's deafness and managed to visit both of their pre-school programs before the school year ended. We liked the oral program but were unsure Danny would fit in there, as most of the children in the oral program had very good residual hearing. Physically, Danny was still very weak. So we decided to let Danny return to his integrated day-care program in August and wait and see if any changes in his hearing would be revealed over the next few months.

The results of the weekly audiological testing did not vary much. Danny was fitted with the most powerful hearing aids, but could only feel the vibration at 85 dB with low-frequency sounds. The oral approach was simply not enough, even with the help of a collection of pictures and drawings. My usually soft voice turned louder and louder with the pitch getting higher and higher. Danny became more and more frustrated, and so did we. There was hardly a day in our household without yelling and screaming. My teaching job might have made life more stressful, but it probably saved my sanity at that time.

In January 1986, desperately needing to reestablish some degree of meaningful communication, we enrolled Danny in the TC program. Donald and I started taking sign language courses in the evenings. After a month, Danny regained some basic communication with us through the signs we all learned. While understanding the usefulness of sign language, we also came to recognize its limitations. We knew Danny needed a visual system, but we also knew a visual "phonetic scheme" could help Danny with his continued language development the most. There had to be some way to take advantage of the speech and language Danny had during his years as a hearing child.

I recalled that at the John Tracy workshop I attended in May 1985, a lady named Maria Kujala had talked about a method called Cued Speech, and mentioned that they used it with their hearing-impaired son. With nothing to lose, I contacted Maria for more information. She was very helpful. She gave us articles to read and also introduced us to Marianne Flanagan, a speech therapist in town who is familiar with Cued Speech. We met with each of them and discussed Danny's situation. Marianne lent us her collection of the *Cued Speech News* and the *Cued Speech Handbook for Parents*. The stories by parents in the *Cued Speech News* were captivating. They were also heartwarming and reassuring in our search for the right way.

In February 1986, we visited the Kujalas at their farm in Red Deer (a two-hour drive from Calgary). We wanted to see how Cued Speech was in operation in their family. We met Nicholas, who had been cued to for many years. After the visit, there was no doubt in our minds that Cued Speech could also work for us.

I sent out a few letters to some of the Cued Speech parents in the States. Elizabeth Hightower (in the Los Angeles area) phoned me immediately and urged us to start cueing to Danny as soon as possible. Isabelle Payonk (North Carolina) also contacted us to share her experience and to offer her support. With more information that we received from the Cued Speech Team at Gallaudet University, and from Joan Rupert of the West Coast Cued Speech Programs, we gained a thorough understanding of the logic behind Cued Speech. We knew we had discovered something really important that could benefit Danny tremendously.

I learned the Cued Speech system very quickly and, in March 1986, started cueing simple expressions to Danny, pairing them with signs. Meanwhile, I taught Donald how to cue. The first expression we cued was, "Good boy!" Danny immediately responded very well and we began expanding our cueing while still using signs for clarification.

By April 1986, we had decided to create an appropriate cueing environment for Danny for the coming school year. We found a private kindergarten that seemed to be receptive to Cued Speech. We also found an aide who was keen to learn Cued Speech and work in the kindergarten in the fall as Danny's interpreter. We taught the aide the basics of cueing, then sent her to the Cued Speech Adult program at Gallaudet in July 1986. The kindergarten teacher accepted our offer and went to the Cued Speech Family Program at Gallaudet with us in

August.

Problems with both the teacher and the aide began to surface in September 1986, when the real challenge of including a deaf child in a regular program through Cued Speech was present. In October 1986, I went in as Danny's interpreter/aide. (Luckily, I had decided in early spring to quit my job and become a full-time parent for my family's sake; it was possible for me to salvage the situation.) For the other half day (kindergarten in Canada is a half-day program), we set up a program for Danny at home.

In December, after lots of agony and many sleepless nights, we decided to re-register Danny in the TC program for the January 1987 semester. Before making that move, I met with his former TC program teacher to familiarize her with our reasons for choosing Cued Speech, what had gone on in the private kindergarten, and why it was necessary for Danny to return to the TC program. Our candid approach was met with understanding and support. In that positive atmosphere, Danny happily returned to the TC program so that his needs of direct learning and psychological stimulation could be met. Meanwhile, he continued with the private kindergarten so that we could further expose him to the age-appropriate language of the children through Cued Speech interpreting, and maintain the social contacts he had established there.

Thus, from January to June, 1987, Danny attended two kindergarten programs. He did well in both. Shortly after his return to the TC program, both the teacher and the speech-language pathologist commented on how much Danny's speech and language had improved. In the private kindergarten I continued to serve as Danny's interpreter. The challenge of cueing whatever was said benefitted both of us. By the spring of 1987 Danny could switch cues and signs back and forth without any difficulty. He also started to "pick up" on our occasional mistakes in either signs or cues and to enjoy a good laugh with us.

In June 1987, our whole family went to Los Angeles to attend a three-week family workshop at the John Tracy Clinic. By this time Danny was a happy, bright-eyed 5½-year-old who enjoyed the program, particularly in the company of a cute little girl from another part of Alberta. They were always hand in hand, and the teachers unanimously dubbed them "the lovebirds." While we were there, by fate, we got in touch with the House Ear Institute. This led to an evaluation of Danny as a candidate for a cochlear implant. The findings were very positive. Danny was deemed an excellent candidate. We were unprepared for this discovery, since we got in touch just to get information. However, the potential benefits Danny could receive were far too important for us to overlook.

We returned to Calgary to fully investigate the option of the cochlear implant. By August 1987, our decision was reached to proceed. As usual, Danny was included in our decision-making process. We kept him informed of all the steps involved in a cochlear-implant procedure, and we prepared him thoroughly for all the changes that might occur. We wanted him to have a very realistic understanding of what it is and what it could possibly do for him.

In order to prepare for the implant, we decided the TC program would be the least stressful environment for Danny for the fall of 1987. He started the level 1 (equivalent to grade one) TC program with ease. The option of mainstreaming Danny in a public school program with a Cued Speech interpreter was considered in early spring before we attended the John Tracy Family Workshop, but with a major decision regarding the cochlear implant ahead of us we felt it would be an inappropriate venture at that time.

On December 18, 1987, after completing the pre-surgery protocol requirement of testing and auditory training, Danny success-fully received a 22-electrode cochlear implant at the House Ear Institute. In January 1988, after the incision healed, we returned to House Ear Institute for the hook-up. When all the settings were established Danny could respond to his name immediately, even at a considerable distance. His detection of sound, as shown on the audiogram, was brought nicely into the speech range. Though the audiogram was impressive, it did not mean Danny could "hear" sounds the way other children do with equivalent gains from traditional hearing aids. A lot of hard work, especially with auditory training, would be necessary to help Danny learn to process the signals he perceived with the implant. We were experiencing only the unfolding of a new beginning.

After returning home at the conclusion of the two-week guidance (hook-up) period, Danny soon began to pick up some environmental sounds. The first was the sound of the cuckoo clock that we bought as a souvenir of Danny's surgery. During the first week after our return home, Danny ran to the clock or pointed to it every time the cuckoo chimed. To our delight, within days after the hook-up Danny began to wear the speech processor on a full-time basis. We started a diary recording his progress. At home we tried to include auditory training with games and activities that could involve both Danny and David.

On February 1, 1988, Danny returned to school after a two-week absence. He settled into the routine immediately. The school-bus driver told me that for a while Danny was quite a celebrity on the bus, with all the children wanting to do things for him.

Danny had been in a private auditory training program for three years. The teacher, Kathleen Camero, had helped us complete the pre-surgery testing and auditory training, and had begun seeing Danny two or three times a week after school. The thought of switching Danny to an oral environment came about in January, 1988, after observance of his response to sounds during the hook-up and realizing the potentials it opened up. However, we were advised to wait. Danny adjusted to the cochlear implant very quickly and was very comfortable with the academic aspects of the TC program—perhaps a bit too comfortable. We grew increasingly uncomfortable with his placement because of its lack of appropriate oral and auditory input and speech monitoring. It was evident that an oral environment would be crucial in helping Danny meet these needs.

After observing both the oral and TC programs, we were certain that any further waiting would be detrimental. In March 1988, we formally approached the program specialist, requesting a transfer to the oral program for Danny at the earliest possible date. Our request was well received, and the shift was scheduled for the end of March. We were fortunate to have the full support of the specialist, the teacher, and the speech-language pathologist. It was recommended that funding be sought to provide Danny with the one-on-one support that he would need for a short period of time. Due to budget cuts, the oral program had no classroom aide at that time. It was during this struggle that our involvement became a "fight all the way to the top." It was carried out to no avail. However, Danny was holding his own and was progressing remarkably well in reading and math. Because the other children in his class had good residual hearing, Danny was at a disadvantage. I volunteered two mornings a week in Danny's class to help the teacher, and we worked very hard at home to supplement his learning at school

Initially we were told that intensive auditory training in an auditory-oral program for the summer or the coming fall would be important for Danny. We don't have a local school program using the auditory-oral approach. Thus, to obtain the right training it would be necessary to divide our family for a while. In advance of the decision Danny and I visited the auditory-oral program of the Vancouver Oral Centre. In May, Danny was evaluated at the Oralingua School of Whittier, Calif., for possible summer or fall placement. The Oralingua School found Danny's academic and auditory skills to be well-developed and felt he would benefit from developing more social interaction skills in an integrated setting.

One option was for us to attend the summer session at Oralingua. It was definitely a better idea to work on the social interaction skills by staying put in Calgary over the summer, thus utilizing our local resources. That was what we decided. We also decided that for the coming year we would make the best of what we have here in the oral program. What a relief we felt with that decision. Both Danny and I needed a break from our frequent trips away from home. Further disruption of our family life would really be stressful for every one in the family.

Another important step we took after our visit to the Oralingua School was to drop cues at home. We wanted Danny to use his newly developed auditory skills in meaningful daily communication. It was a conscious effort for all of us, but as time went by it became easier.

The summer of 1988 was a busy but relaxing time for all of us. Danny took classes in ceramics, swimming, and horseback riding in an integrated setting. He also went to a summer day-camp for children his age in our neighborhood. I was also able to give more attention to David and his activities.

At the end of July, Danny was due for his six-month post hook-up appointment at the House Ear Institute. The tests showed that Danny had no difficulty with any of the vowels and some of the consonants, and was making very good use of this to aid his understanding of speech. His speech production had also improved drastically. His spontaneous speech had become more sophisticated and intelligible even to unfamiliar ears. Danny could also handle compound/complex sentences auditorily in a closed set and sometimes in an open set. It was a shared impression that he had become happier and more confident. At home, the communication between Danny and the rest of us had also been making steady and impressive progress.

During our frequent trips to Los Angeles we had met and become friends with some of the Cued Speech/cochlear implant families in the area. They have given us a lot of moral support. The staff of the House Ear Institute has also been wonderful to us. We felt very fortunate to encounter such warmth (please excuse the pun) whenever we went there.

We are so glad we found Cued Speech for Danny and for us. Even though there is only one other family in Alberta that uses it, we feel the lack of support services for Danny did not really significantly impede Danny's progress with Cued Speech. It definitely helped him preserve his phonological memory of spoken language, even though he was totally without acoustic input. It also allowed him to acquire new language in much the same way a hearing child does. It has made communication much easier and more enjoyable for us. It also enabled us to reintroduce, as well as newly introduce, some of the Mandarin and Cantonese expressions we feel are important.

Cued Speech was also a wonderful help during the period of Danny's implant operation. Before the surgery, we were able to explain everything with cues, teaching him the appropriate terms for everything and the concepts behind them. I don't think we could have explained things that well for Danny with only fingerspelling and the inadequate signs at our disposal.

Cued Speech has also been valuable for auditory training with the cochlear implant. It helps make meaningful connections between the sensations Danny feels and the sounds represented by Cued Speech. It clarifies speech while Danny learns to decode a new set of stimuli. Even though we can now communicate orally without signs or cues, we still use cues when we introduce a new expression or make a clarification or correction. And, when the speech processor is not in use, we have Cued Speech to ensure clear and complete communication.

Danny enjoys reciting nursery rhymes and singing children's songs, which we started with him after we acquired Cued Speech. Now this pastime is in full swing with the added help of the cochlear implant. His favorite bedtime activity is for me to sing songs or recite nursery rhymes in the dark for him to guess them from audition alone. He is getting really good at this. Once I tried humming a tune without the words, and he was able to identify it. It is difficult to say how well a cochlear implant child can discriminate melodies, though theoretically this should be possible with exposure and practice. Danny has also demonstrated renewed interest in learning the Chinese language. He often asks me, "How do you say that in Chinese?" A favorite expression has been "Wo ai ni", which means "I love you."

Danny entered level 2 (equivalent to grade two) of the oral program in September 1988. We again have a wonderful teacher this year and Danny continues to progress really well at school. We are also trying to establish a better balance with his extracurricular activities. Danny attends Beaver activities one evening a week (in Canada, Beavers are boy scouts aged 5-7), and really enjoys being with other boys in our community. He is also taking a drawing and sculpture class one evening a week. At home we continue to support all the academic and extracurricular activities, plus doing a physiotherapy home program to improve his balance which was affected by the meningitis three years ago.

Update, April 1992

Since our bad experience in the 1986-87 school year with the regular kindergarten program all went well except for minor problems. The implant had brought dramatic changes in our lives. We transferred Danny from the TC program to an oral program which he attended from March 1988 through June 1991, being partially mainstreamed beginning in June 1988.

Danny had been identified as gifted at 3½ years, following his hearing loss. Because at age 7 he was doing so well in all areas, he was nominated for entry into the gifted program for September 1991. We were pleased at his being one of only five children city-wide nominated to enter the gifted program at fifth grade.

Though our communication with Danny is now completely oral, as it has been for the last 3½ years, we still use Cued Speech on occasions when it is helpful. For example, Danny and I use it silently to exchange comments we don't wish to share with anyone else. It is also very helpful in a noisy situation, as in a cafeteria, or even at a circus. Of course we still use it for clarification or to introduce new language, as needed.

Our intense struggle over the years led us to Cued Speech and the cochlear implant. Jointly, they helped us break through the despair we once felt. Together they opened new doors to a better quality of life for Danny, and for us. Thus, a little voice within assures me that dreams lost can become dreams possible in the future.

Cued Speech, the Cochlear Implant, and Louis
by Joseph and Judith Weiss, 1992

On request, we have written a brief description of our experience as parents of a child who was raised on Cued Speech and utilizes a single-electrode cochlear implant for auditory input.

Our son, Louis, was deafened at the age of 10 months by meningitis and is considered pre-lingually deaf. We were residing in St. Louis, Mo., at the time and were assured by everyone that we were lucky to be in a city with two of the most outstanding oral institutions in the country, the Central Institute for the Deaf (CID) and St. Joseph's Academy. In fact, many families relocate to the St. Louis area to be near these institutions. What should have been an asset, in fact, proved to be a liability for our family. The dominance of these two oral institutions in the area had precluded the development of any other modalities of communication. It was only through extreme coincidence that we learned of Cued Speech.

Our oldest son was attending a preschool program where the only Cued Speech child in the city was enrolled in another class. A brief conversation with that child's mother convinced us that there was something to this Cued Speech. As all Cued Speech advocates know, the unbridled enthusiasm for the system can be contagious and in direct contrast to the negative outlook portrayed by advocates of other approaches under the guise of preparing the parents to deal with reality. We asked CID if we could use Cued Speech with our child and enroll him in their parent-infant program. Not only did they refuse this request, they gathered a dozen white-coated experts to sit us down and tell us what a tremendous mistake we were making by choosing Cued Speech. Their response left us no alternative but to relocate our family to Montgomery County, Maryland, where Cued Speech was already a viable alternative for communicating with and educating a deaf child, thanks to the early pioneers who worked diligently to bring Cued Speech to the county.

Judith, Joe, Louis, and Andrew Weiss

Louis was immediately enrolled in the parent-infant program and began attending school at the age of 3. He was in a self-contained CS program for preschool and then fully mainstreamed from kindergarten on with a Cued Speech interpreter. He is currently mainstreamed in seventh grade, is an honor roll student, and takes a number of classes for the gifted, as well as Spanish. Obviously, we miss our family and friends but have never regretted our decision to move to find the program our son needed.

We have come to regard discovering Cued Speech as the first milestone we passed in raising a deaf child. The second milestone was passed when Louis' brother, Andrew, learned to cue at the age of 5. Again we were advised by many well-intentioned experts not to insist or require a sibling to cue. After much thought, we concluded that the worst that could happen is that Andrew would find himself on some future shrink's couch complaining that his mother and father made him speak to his brother. We took the chance and taught him to cue. He learned quickly and was cueing to Louis within a month. One of his memorable first statements to his brother was, "You smell like a dead mouse." Establishing the communication between the boys gave each of them a release for their emotions, and they have had an incredible relationship ever since.

At the age of 3, our son had acquired an enormous amount of receptive language. He would respond beautifully to anything and everything we said to or asked of him. He cued back with great accuracy and moved his lips constantly. But he was a silent child; he seldom vocalized. He was aided in both ears with acoustic body aids, but his hearing loss was too great for them to be of any use to him. It was about that time we first learned of the research being done with cochlear implants. At that time there was only a single-channel device (the House Cochlear Implant) approved for adults and for clinical research done with children. At the age of 3½, Louis became the youngest (at that time) child to receive the cochlear implant under the research program. This was our third milestone with Louis. Our decision to use Cued Speech had not been a popular one, and now it seemed we had made another decision that was not supported by many people who knew us. Again, we have never regretted that decision.

Within six months of the surgery, our son was using his voice constantly. We could not believe our ears. We had prayed for sounds from this tiny little boy for so long and now we were wondering if we would ever get any peace and quiet again. We now had some speech to work with and Cued Speech proved invaluable in this effort. We were able to tell Louis immediately each sound he had just made and the one he needed to make if the first attempt was incorrect. Ironically, many of his initial efforts were very close to correct. We attribute this to the phonetic base of Cued Speech.

We had no preconceived ideas about what the implant would be able to provide him with. We were counting on it providing some environmental safety information (car horns, sirens, smoke alarms, etc.). We had seen our son walk up to a growling dog to pet him. Now it was a tremendous relief to be able to shout out warnings as well as to see our son's interest in sounds grow. We have seen his progress grow from mimicking sounds he was presented with to comprehending and repeating complete open-set statements without seeing the speaker's face. Louis uses the implant and his lip reading skills constantly in public, talking freely to strangers to obtain information, purchase something, or just to order dinner.

The independence Louis demonstrates at the age of 13 in dealing with the "hearing world" recalls those first discussions with deaf educators who stressed how important it would be for our son to be able to go into a McDonald's and order a hamburger. The signers had us thinking he might never read above a fourth-grade level, that

English would be a second language to him, and his home would be with the "deaf world." The staunch oralists said there was the chance he might be 12 years old and not know the concept of his own name without incredible amounts of intense training. We now believe that there is only one world, hearing and deaf, and that our son with his cochlear implant and Cued Speech skills is well equipped to handle it.

Paul Huchro

Paul Huchro was one of the earliest Cued Speech kids to receive a cochlear implant. He is unique in being the only case (of which we are aware) of a child on Cued Speech who did not profit from the cochlear implant. Paul simply received no auditory stimulation from the device, a single-electrode unit. Today methods of evaluating the probability of benefit from the implant are much more reliable.

Abraham Hakim
by Penny Hakim, 1992

In July of 1987 our 13½ month old child, Abraham, started running a fever and was diagnosed with strep throat. Though he was not displaying one of the classic symptoms of meningitis, a stiff neck, the staff performed a spinal tap. The spinal fluid indicated meningitis.

The day we found out Abraham was profoundly deaf was the most emotionally draining day of my life (and my husband's). We had really done all of our crying weeks before when we did not know if Abraham would survive or not. Now that we knew he would live, we were scared about his future. But, if his being deaf was the only way we could have him, we were going to do the best we could for him.

In the process of getting second opinions, we went to see Dr. Charles Berlin, the head of the Kresge Research Laboratory in New Orleans, whom our doctor had recommended. We very much wanted Abraham to be oral, if possible. Dr. Berlin sat down with us and told us things that we had to do if we wanted Abraham to be oral. He spent two days with us, was very encouraging, and showed us a "Beginnings" film that helped.

We went home from New Orleans with a feeling that we now had a direction in which to go, and with Abraham already fitted with hearing aids. At that point, my husband and I decided that I should quit work so I could do the things that Abraham so obviously needed done. The decision to quit work was not an easy one. I am a dental hygienist, and I loved my work. But, I could see the magnitude of my responsibility; also, I was six months pregnant with my second child.

Not only did Abraham have a hearing loss from the meningitis, but he had regressed in his gross motor skills. He could not walk or crawl. He had to relearn how to hold his head up and how to sit up.

I found out about Cued Speech through my sister-in-law's cous-in, Sarina Roffé, who lives in Maryland. At that time, her son Simon was entering 7th grade. He was profoundly deaf, like Abraham. We talked on the phone for hours—Sarina, my husband, and I.

Abraham (6), Eddie, and Jackie (3) Hakim

Sarina told how she had travelled all over the country searching for alternatives. Then she related her experiences with Simon. She told us about her decision to use Cued Speech with her child and what it has done in their lives. We really understood what she was saying and liked the idea that her child was in regular classrooms and was able to communicate with people who did not cue. The thing that most impressed us was Simon's extremely high reading level as compared to the national average of hearing children's reading levels.

Sarina told us about the up-coming National Cued Speech Association's first national convention to be in November of 1987. She suggested that we attend and find out what Cued Speech was all about.

We went to the NCSA convention in New Orleans. For one group they had a short training period for those who wanted to learn how to cue. The other groups were for small round-table discussions on different subjects. My husband and I both attended the first session of the group learning how to cue. Then he looked into the discussions that were related to research. He told me to finish learning how to cue while he went to hear about the other things we needed to know about. So I stayed in the class. It was very hard, but I struggled through it. The series of learning sessions lasted only 10 hours.

I encountered a lot of professionals at that convention and met many interesting parents. Some of them had stories similar to ours, but most had gone through more than we had at this point.

I came back home with mixed feelings. Some of Abraham's audiograms looked very good to me on paper. I was told in New

Orleans that he could probably be oral, and we wanted him to be oral. I learned how to cue but chose not to cue at that time. Our second child was due in a month. That and the effort to cue overwhelmed me, so I just talked. I did everything that I was told to do orally.

Leah (4½), Penny, and Joseph (8 wks.) Hakim

The week in December that my daughter Leah was born was the same week that Abraham learned how to walk. He was 19 months old at the time. It was a great relief. Abraham was not doing much talking, and he did not appear to respond well to what we were saying. We were told just to keep talking, so we did. We had been told that while a child is learning or relearning developmental skills, language acquisition is often delayed by concentration on motor activities.

In December the speech pathologist had to stop working with Abraham because of an illness in her family. At that time she told me she did not believe Abraham was hearing anything. She had serious doubts about what his audiogram had indicated, but I was still optimistic and felt that we had not given him enough time yet. Abraham was reassigned to another speech pathologist named Paula Aitken. She and Abraham hit it off immediately.

By February, I began to have doubts about Abraham's ability to be totally oral. I had wanted to give him every chance at pure oralism, but I did not want to lose any more time. In February of 1988, when Abraham was 21 months old, I decided to start cueing.

Among my notes that I had written down when I first learned to cue was a little chart of the vowel placements and consonant hand-shapes, which I relearned. This time the cueing system made more sense to me. Paula and I learned together. I was very, very slow. Since Paula was a speech pathologist, she was able to analyze a lot of the sounds, and we worked through them together. We were able to cue single words to Abraham, whatever the language target was. At first, we hardly knew what we were doing. I decided to call Sarina Roffé and get more advice from her. She told me about the fantastic program in Gonzales, La., that was started by Barbara Lee. I decided that I should visit that school and see what they were doing so I would know what we should do. Since there was no Cued Speech in the Monroe City school system, no one there knew much about it.

I went to Gonzales without Abraham. I watched Barbara Lee work with a child who was about a year older than Abraham, using the parent-infant training method. As I observed what they did together, it all made so much sense to me. They were covering everything from auditory training to language and speech. I wrote down notes of what the teacher did; then I met with the speech pathologist. She told me they used a lot of Daniel Ling's techniques. All of this was new to me, so I made copious notes. I had to be prepared to share all of this with Abraham's speech pathologist, and then to do it with her guidance.

We did some of the things Barbara Lee did, such as taking off our shoes and cueing, "your shoe," "my shoe," "Paula's shoe," "Mama's shoe," "Abraham's shoe." Abraham's first cued word, as a result, was *shoe*. We felt that we were finally getting somewhere. I still was not real proficient at cueing; I cued the words I could cue when I spoke, and simply said the others. I know this was wrong, but at the time I did not know. I was simply doing the best I could.

Abraham's early days of speech therapy consisted mostly of language enrichment and auditory awareness. We had to work on establishing eye contact with him. The cueing helped produce eye contact because our hands were moving near our mouth.

Every week I would work on a basic core vocabulary. By July, he was saying and cueing *bye-bye* and *da-da*. By September, he said and cued *goo* (good) and *wuh* (water). He had approximately nine different vowel sounds at that time, and the consonant sounds he made were *m, d, sh, j, zh, b, g, w,* and *p.* His expressive vocabulary in November was *dah* (daddy), *goo* (good), *eat, bye-bye, choo-choo, ahh* (airplane), *shoe, poo-poo, wah* (water), *bah* (bottle), *juh* (juice), and *buh* (book). He was constantly trying to verbalize and vocalize.

I had every audiologist in town doing audiograms on Abraham, and they would always come out with only one response, in the 500 Hz. range, at 110 decibels. I went back to New Orleans to see Dr. Berlin and questioned him concerning the hearing we originally thought Abraham would have with the hearing aids. We then changed Abraham to the most powerful hearing aids that were available at the time.

Abraham had been exposed to Cued Speech for 10 months, and he still had only a 12-word expressive vocabulary. I was quite worried about whether we would ever get past that point. Within two months, in February of 1989, the total increased to 50 words. It all happened within the last two months of that first year. Barbara Lee had said we needed to build a 50-word vocabulary within the first year to keep him on track with the Bloom-and-Lahey language program. We just made it. From that point his vocabulary expanded very consistently.

In March of 1989, I had Abraham re-evaluated by Dr. Berlin. He felt we needed a different opinion and sent me to an educational audiologist in New Orleans. She tested Abraham and told me Abraham was not hearing anything. At this point, I denied it; it hurt to acknowledge the possibility that hearing aids were not helping him. He was doing so well at vocabulary growth and vocalization.

Three months later I returned to New Orleans for another evaluation with Dr. Berlin. During this time I had time to really think about what the educational audiologist had said. I finally decided that Abraham was not deriving any benefit from his powerful hearing aids.

Why did some profoundly deaf children get unbelievable benefit from their hearing aids, while Abraham was not able to get any benefit at all? I could accept his deafness if he was going to be able to hear a little bit, but it was very hard to accept total deafness.

During the June 1989 visit with Dr. Berlin, he had some members of the cochlear-implant team meet with me and discuss the possibility of an implant for Abraham. He said that if we truly wanted Abraham to be oral, we should consider a cochlear implant as the hearing aids did not give him any useful information. I told Dr. Berlin that I had come to terms with Abraham's deafness. He was learning language and vocabulary, and he was vocalizing. I was happy with him the way he was. I knew he would be a success even without the implant because he was progressing well without any hearing.

Dr. Berlin told me that Abraham's speech would be limited, and that if I truly wanted him to be oral, the implant was the only way to go. I told him I wished to visit other implant centers and see what the cochlear implant was all about. He identified two other centers and two physicians he recommended. He also encouraged me to go to Central Institute for the Deaf (CID). They were doing a research study comparing children with cochlear implants vs. hearing aids and tactile aids. Dr. Berlin told me he would trust their opinion concerning whether they thought Abraham was a good candidate for the implant. Since they did not do implants there, their opinion should be unbiased.

I immediately called CID and talked to Jean Moog. She set up an appointment for me to go there with Abraham in November of 1989. We were scheduled for two days of tests, the first day being auditory testing with Ann Geers in charge. The audiogram they performed was consistent with Abraham's previous audiograms. Then they tested him using a Tactaid. He was able to discriminate between one-syllable and two-syllable words with the Tactaid.

They also did a psychometric evaluation on Abraham, testing his intellectual level. He scored within the average range. They performed a communication evaluation utilizing the Grammatical Analysis of Language at pre-sentence level and the CID Phonetic Inventory Test.

Before they started testing Abraham, I told them that I used Cued Speech to communicate with him, and I knew he would be able to perform much better on the test with the use of Cued Speech. They chose to test him orally. They wanted to be able to compare the results with those of the children who were enrolled in their program. Even though tested orally, Abraham outperformed 70% of the children his age with similar hearing loss who were evaluated with this procedure.

During my visit to CID, I was fortunate to be able to observe children with cochlear implants in the classroom situation and see what they were able to do. I was able to witness children who had not made any progress with the implant as well as children who were doing phenomenally well. On my return home my husband and I decided to give Abraham a chance to hear. I immediately called Dr. Berlin and told him we were ready to initiate the cochlear-implant process.

Prior to the visit to CID, Abraham was enrolled in a non-categorical pre-school class. The only hearing-impaired pre-school class at that time was a Total Communication class that I was not interested in for Abraham. I wanted him to be only cued to. The summer before he started school, I taught both of the teachers who would be in the class how to cue. Fortunately, Abraham had a very committed teacher (Kim Smith) who within two months was cueing at the same rate that I cue after a year and a half. I finally had someone I could turn my child over to. It was a great relief to me to know he was in a class-room with someone cueing to him. I did not have to worry about whether he was receiving language or not. Kim treated Abraham as if he were her own son. She pushed both him and me.

After our decision to go forward with the implant, I arranged for additional speech therapy four times a week with Denise Taylor, a speech pathologist already using Cued Speech. Denise's treatment plan included auditory training, speech production training, and a Bloom-and-Lahey-based language program for the hearing impaired developed by Barbara Lee. At this time Abraham's vocabulary was approximately 150 words, but it was weak in verbs and adjectives. He did not put two words together to form sentences with functional word combinations.

I requested a teacher in-service by Barbara Lee to train the teachers in our school system on her language program. I remembered what they were doing in Gonzales and knew we needed to do more. Kim was more than willing to learn what she needed to do to advance

Abraham in language. I must say that she took a special interest in Abraham and worked twice as hard to make him successful with cues.

Most of the testing in advance of the implant surgery was done three months before Abraham's fourth birthday. His speech at this time was primarily jargon with one-word utterances. During the testing, he used a few two-word utterances such as "big bear" and "push bus."

At the end of April, Abraham was scheduled for his surgery with Dr. Charles Parkins from LSU Medical Center in New Orleans. One thing that helped prepare me mentally for the surgery was reading a book written by another parent, Kevin R. Peterson, entitled *Our Spark of Hope*. It really helped me, but I was still apprehensive about the risks involved in surgery so close to the brain.

The surgery went well, with no complications. Abraham's hook-up with his processor was scheduled on May 31, four days after his fourth birthday. There was a room full of family and friends all eager to see Abraham's reaction to sound. As Tammy Crabtree, the audiologist, stimulated the electrodes, we all awaited Abraham's response. It took approximately 15 minutes to get a verified reaction to the new sound that he heard. Once Abraham related the sound to his task of putting a peg in the board, his responses were quite consistent.

Tammy programmed electrodes for an hour, and then gave Abraham an hour break. After the break, she completed the programming of all 22 electrodes. Abraham started getting tired but kept on working. He was doing so well that it seemed too good to be true.

After completing the programming of all the electrodes, Tammy scanned all of them at Abraham's loudest "threshold" level to make sure that he experienced no pain. He responded with a smile. At this point Tammy was able to allow him to receive speech. I will never forget when Eddie called Abraham's name; he smiled real big and tucked his head under my arm. It was a great feeling—indescribable.

It amazed me that Abraham responded to all the sounds of the Ling 5-sound test, even the "s" and "sh" sounds. He also responded to any other noise in the room. I wanted to see what Tammy could get in the way of an audiogram. Although Abraham was very tired, she felt that the test was pretty reliable at about 30 to 35 decibels across the frequencies. It was wonderful seeing an audiogram of Abraham that actually had marks on it, rather than "no response."

We left New Orleans excited for Abraham and eager to see how he was going to take to the processor. We were told not to expect too much at first. He was receiving completely unfamiliar information.

Just a month after he was hooked up to his processor, Abraham consistently started putting two words together. I cannot say it was the cochlear implant that caused this ability to develop so quickly. I think the language he had learned from the cued input was a big factor, and the implant enabled him finally to put it all together.

One of our school system's pre-K hearing impaired teachers, Margaret Berry, had been teaching hearing-impaired students for 12 years, using Total Communication. She had observed Abraham in his non-categorical classroom and had become interested in him and the use of Cued Speech. She had learned how to cue the year before at the Gallaudet Cued Speech Family Week. We spoke on several occasions, and she was very interested in getting Abraham in her classroom. I told her I was interested only if he could be in a class where there would be consistent cueing. I did not want sign language to take time from his learning of English. Barbara Lee's statement that it takes the average hearing child five years to learn the rules of English kept me very pressured for Abraham to learn English. We were already in year two.

Margaret had attended the in-service on Bloom and Lahey and seemed very anxious to implement the program. Since she had a pre-school class where the parents were just beginning to choose the methods they wanted used with their children, she was able to lead them to try Cued Speech. As a result, in the fall of 1990, Abraham was in a pre-kindergarten hearing-impaired class with five other hearing-impaired children. That September Margaret, Abraham, and I travelled to Gonzales, La., for Margaret to observe what the teachers were doing in the classroom and observe Barbara Lee testing Abraham.

At that time, Abraham was tested in Phase I and II of Bloom and Lahey's stages of language development. Then we drove on to New Orleans where Margaret was able to watch Abraham's processor being re-programmed. She learned from the implant center staff what she needed to do to work with Abraham. Abraham did very well in his new classroom. By the end of the year, he had completed Phase III of the Bloom and Lahey language development program.

One year after the cochlear implant, Abraham was saying and cueing: "Where is my other shoe?" "I hurt my foot." "She pushed my back." "They threw the witch in the fire."

Abraham remained in his self-contained hearing-impaired classroom the following year. For 45 minutes every day, he was mainstreamed in the kindergarten classroom with the teacher's cueing aide. Although he was old enough to attend kindergarten, he still did not have the language of a hearing 5 year old. We thought it was in his best interest to remain another year in his language-enriched classroom, with some practice in mainstreaming each day.

Abraham had another wonderful year, completing Phase VI of

Bloom and Lahey's language-development program. He continues to receive private speech therapy four days a week with Denise Taylor. His therapy currently involves auditory comprehension tasks leading toward progression from the Developmental Approach to Successful Listening (DASL). In the auditory comprehension strand, he is able to follow directions containing three critical elements in a closed set with a speaker using a normal rate of speech. Presently he is working toward sequencing three critical elements in a message. In the phonetic listening portion, he has discriminated auditorially among the words *book, beak, back,* and *bike.* New vocabulary is introduced with Cued Speech. Abraham is now able to follow common single auditory commands in an open set from a distance of six feet. His therapist is working with him on Daniel Ling's objectives and Barbara LeBlanc's co-articulation factors. On his two-year post-implant auditory tests, he scored 90% correct on body-part identification; 100% on open-set simple one-and-two-step commands and simple questions. On the Early Speech Perception Test (Moog and Geers), he scored in Category 4 (consistent word identification). Prior to the implant, he scored at the lowest levels on all these tests.

Abraham's intelligibility has improved to the point that even unfamiliar listeners are able to understand what he is saying most of the time. He is able to communicate fairly well one-on-one in a quiet situation, but he still heavily depends on me to interpret all conversations and movies. In fact, when he is in the room, I cue all conversation. If I do not, he will ask me to repeat it.

We have had workshops in Monroe, have attended CS camps at Camp Cheerio, and have attended Gallaudet's Family Week program. These camps have been very important to Abraham as he is the oldest child in our area who cues. He really needs and looks forward to going to camp where he can communicate with cueing children his age and older. This year at Camp Cheerio, he was able to converse with children his age without anyone else interfering or having to interpret. It was wonderful to watch him just being a child with other children.

Abraham will start kindergarten this fall (1992) with a Cued Speech transliterator. I am very excited about the new challenges that are ahead for us. None of this would have been possible if I had not learned about Cued Speech. Even though Abraham is performing wonderfully auditorially, I will never discontinue using Cued Speech unless he asks me to, as he is still hearing impaired. I am convinced that Cued Speech has only enhanced his auditory comprehension.

Currently Abraham is on a T-ball team, takes swimming lessons, loves to jet ski with his dad, is very interested in the Presidents of the

United States, and is very proud of his new baby brother. His younger sister, Leah, who is now 4½, is very interested in learning how to cue and is always asking me how to cue certain words. I have caught her imitating me on several occasions. When Abraham is in the room, and sometimes when he is not, I cue to all the children, even the baby.

My dream of Abraham being a real member of our family and community has come true. It would have been impossible for him to be where he is today without Cued Speech, even given the fact that he has the cochlear implant.

My Son at Seven—My Rock of Gibraltar
by Jane Knight
reprinted from the *SHHH Journal*

(At 22, recently married, Jane Knight suffered a tragic horseback riding accident that left her with a 5% chance of surviving a coma lasting 16 days. She awoke to a totally silent world, and to complete blindness. She recovered a part of her sight, but remains totally deaf. For an inspiring and fascinating account of her successful use of Cued Speech and a cochlear implant, refer to "Climbing Mountains," in the March/April 1992 issue of the SHHH Journal. After her son was born, two years after the accident, she learned Cued Speech in order to have a way to understand him. They have made many appearances together as advocates of both Cued Speech and the cochlear implant. Her article about him, from the same issue, appears below.)

John is just 7, but from his early childhood he has been the Rock of Gibraltar for me, his hearing-impaired and legally blind mother.

When John was born, I was a newly deafened mother, petrified by fear that my son would be a stranger to me throughout my life due to my deafness and limited sight. I started using Cued Speech with John at an early age, and when he had just turned two, he began trying to "cue" those words so important to a toddler, *bottle* and *pee*! It was the most reassuring event I had experienced since my accident—knowing John was willing to learn a way to communicate with me. Early on, when we were in a store and a clerk would try to talk to me, John would say, "My mom is deaf and please use Cued Speech with her." I feared that he would be embarrassed by my hearing loss—but not John.

When John was 5 years old, I was fortunate to receive a 22-channel cochlear implant. The first sight I saw when I awoke from the anesthesia after the surgery was that precious child smiling from ear to ear, holding his thumb up to show that everything was okay. All that day, John was my "nurse" at the hospital, bringing me water, walking the halls to see if my doctor was coming, and sitting next to me in the hospital bed, coloring. He was so loving and such a supporter of me that not once was I ever doubtful that things would be great.

Jane Knight, John Long, and Gregg Long

When John saw the incision for the implant, he laughingly said, "Mom, you've got a baseball head." (Sure enough, the implant sutures *did* look like baseball stitching monogrammed on my head!) Finally, a much-awaited day arrived, and I was hooked up to my speech processor. The first words I heard my son speak were, "I love you, Mommy." The joy those four words gave me was overwhelming.

From the beginning, John wanted to help me in telling groups about hearing loss and the benefits of Cued Speech. So, he started "helping" me with my speaking engagements. He has never shown any hesitation about getting up in front of a group—beginning with the local SHHH chapter and, from there, all the way up to SHHH's 1991 National Convention in Denver—to speak about Cued Speech and how it has helped us as a family. To see my small son so dedicated to helping others in Mom's shape is the ultimate pride for a mother.

John is always telling his classmates about Cued Speech. He has "recruited" friends into wanting to learn to cue. He even volunteered Mom to teach his classmates to cue "America the Beautiful" for a presentation at the PTA meeting. He continually shows his undying support to me in so many ways, both large and small. Never has he treated hearing loss like a handicap or an embarrassment, but always as simply a difference. Some people don't hear well—that's all (a very mature outlook for a small child).

John is very excited about the future with me. He is always asking, "When can we tell more people about Cued Speech, Mom?" And, he is an avid supporter of the cochlear implant as well. His loving support and never-ending desire to help others who have a hearing loss have helped me in more ways than I can express. He is, indeed, my 7-year-old Rock of Gibraltar.

realizing it, Robert Allen proved the power of reading to transform an individual life."

Reading is a powerful stimulus to mental development in any child. But the power of reading to transform the life of a deaf person is even greater than for a hearing person. The reason is that deaf people are typically much more dependent on others as sources of information. They lack equal access to radio, recorded material, easy conversation with anyone, etc. If they can read, they have access to almost all the information that exists in printed form. The deaf child who becomes a good reader can be the captain of his/her own destiny, a destiny limited only by native abilities, rather than by deafness.

The majority of deaf children have great difficulty in learning to read and never enjoy it enough to read for pleasure. There is a good reason for this. Most deaf children are not learning to read a language they already know in spoken form. Instead, they are trying to learn the language through learning to read. This is a slow, difficult, defeating, frustrating process that often engenders a permanent dislike of reading.

Most hearing children learn to love reading if they have access to appropriate books, are read to from an early age, and see others around them reading. Cued Speech makes it possible for the same thing to happen to deaf children through provision of the same positive environment for reading development.

How A Hearing Child Learns to Read

In learning to read, the hearing child is at first simply learning to pair written words with the spoken words he already knows and uses. Shown a written word that someone identifies by a picture, or through the spoken word, a hearing child immediately associates it with the spoken word, which already carries meaning for him or her. After a few such exposures to a written word, the child can associate it with the right spoken word each time he or she sees it. After a reasonable amount of experience at this process, and/or after having been taught the letters and the sounds they usually represent, he/she can "sound out" mentally a written word never seen before. At this point, a hearing child can recognize the written representations of most of the thousands of words he/she already knows in spoken form. This means that the child is already on the road to being an *autonomous* reader. From this point on, the child can seek out and learn anything he/she wants to learn, through the magic of reading.

Chapter 15
Reading

Books are the masters who instruct us without rods and ferule, without hard words and anger, without clothes or money. If you approach them, they are not asleep; if investigating you interrogate them, they conceal nothing; if you mistake them, they never grumble; if you are ignorant, they do not laugh at you. The library of wisdom, therefore, is more precious than all riches, and nothing that can be wished for is worthy to be compared with it. Whosoever therefore acknowledges himself to be a zealous follower of truth, of happiness, of wisdom, of science, or even of the faith must of necessity make of himself a lover of books.   Richard de Bury (1344)

Every parent, with or without a deaf child, should read the article "The Most Precious Gift," by Hank Whittemore, in the December 22, 1991 issue of *Parade Magazine*. It is the story of Robert Howard Allen, who grew up without attending school until, in 1981 at age 32, he entered college. He grew up in a tiny Tennessee hamlet (Rosser) in one of its three farmhouses. He had never had indoor plumbing, had never ridden a bicycle, had never been inside a theater, or had a date. Allen's Aunt Bevie read to him and thereby taught him to read at age 7. From then on he read books—not several books, not hundreds of books, but thousands of books..."from Donald Duck comic books to the Bible, from Homer to James Joyce—to the point where his head was filled with history and classical literature." Says Whittemore:

> When he discovered the Carroll County Library in nearby Huntington, it was like discovering gold. When on the shelves he found the complete set of Will and Ariel Durant's *The Story of Civilization*, he spent the next two years wading through its 10 massive volumes. Out of pure enjoyment he worked his way through the entire library.

At 30, Allen took a high school equivalency test and obtained his diploma. Two years later, when on a whim he applied to Bethel College, officials looked at his scores on the placement examination and gave him a work-study grant. He finished in three years (with all A's except in typing) and later earned both a master's degree and a Ph.D. degree, both at Vanderbilt University. He now writes poetry and teaches English at Murray State College.

Whittemore expresses the central truth of Allen's life: "Without

The Function Words

A prior knowledge of spoken language is particularly important to understanding the vital "little" words of our language, the *function* words, which cannot really be defined or explained for a child. At reading age the hearing child is completely familiar with these words and with dozens of their different meanings. Consider what happens in the mind of a hearing child who has been taught to recognize the written word *the*. When it is identified with the spoken form, he/she accepts it immediately and understands its connection with the next word, even though alone it means nothing. The child has experienced the word so many thousands of times, in combination with nouns following it, that he/she "feels" the difference between the specific form *the dog* and the non-specific form *a dog*. Thus, he or she experiences no confusion and no frustration in learning to read sentences containing *the, a, of, in, out, by, with, on, off,* and other little words that contribute so much to the sophistication and complexity of our language.

Most of the sentences we commonly use in conversation contain one of the function words, and are thus likely to be *idiomatic*—that is, made up of special combinations of words that cannot be understood from the meanings of the single words themselves. Failure to become familiar with at least 30 or 40 different meanings of each of the prepositions is one of the major contributors to the difficulty in reading experienced by deaf children in third grade. It may be the single most important factor in causing them to reach a plateau at a third-to-fourth-grade reading level. Parents using Cued Speech should make a point of exposing their deaf child systematically to phrases containing these words in all their common connotations (e.g., *on* guard, *on* call, *on* edge, *on* trial, *on* the team, *on* exhibit, *on* a trip, *on* notice, *on* medication, *on* tour, *on* Monday, *on* a vacation, to be cut *on* a tin can, a trip *on* an airplane, to creep up *on* someone). A good dictionary lists many meanings for each function word.

How Deaf Children Learn to Read

A typical deaf child is taught a sight vocabulary of several hundred words, through association of each written word with a picture, an object, or an action. Or, if he/she knows many signs, these can be paired with the corresponding written words in teaching them. But, a limited knowledge of spoken language leaves the child without anything to which to refer when he or she encounters a written word that isn't already familiar. He/she can seldom "sound it out" and find it in his/her spoken vocabulary. Far from being an autonomous reader, such a child has to seek help or give up. The only hope is that the skill of teachers and parents will be sufficient to protect the child from feelings of failure, so that he or she will not give up completely.

Basically, typical deaf children beginning to read must either have help always at hand or be furnished material composed primarily of words already in their sight vocabulary—already taught to them. In the latter case such children may be able to read this material well enough to pick up meanings of some unfamiliar words through context, pictures accompanying the story, etc. Thus, a small percentage of very bright deaf non-CS children become good readers, despite their lack of the language base for reading, if they get enough parental support.

Most hearing children pick up the function words without effort, over the first three to five years of life. These words cause the typical deaf child great difficulty. They convince him or her that reading is exceedingly difficult. In order to read well at above fourth-grade level, a child needs to be familiar with 20 to 40 different applications for each of the common prepositions.

When deaf children without CS are taught to recognize and pronounce the written form *the*, it has no meaning for them. It is just a word to say, a word that appears over and over. When asked to read, such children typically have to go through the process of recognizing and pronouncing many other words that mean nothing to them. Most of them become accustomed to getting meaning from only the key words, ignoring (even if they pronounce them) the little words that give them no meaning. By the time they reach high school age this pattern is so deeply ingrained that it is almost impossible to overcome. Such a child might silently read a sentence as follows: "_____ years ago, _ man ____ _ flashlight ___ prowling _____ ___ _____ ___ coral caves ____ Bonaire, ___ _____ island in ___ southern Caribbean." This illustration would probably be more accurate if the blank spaces were replaced by blurred images indicating incomplete or partial observation of meaning.

It is to be hoped that many repetitions of exposure to the written form of the word *the* in conjunction with various nouns will give the deaf child the same understanding of *the* that the hearing child already has before he or she even starts to learn to read. The same may occur with other function words that must be learned through context. In practice, this process goes so slowly that the majority of deaf students find reading a slow, difficult, tedious, and boring activity, which they never learn to enjoy. Thus, though they need to read more than hearing people to compensate for their reduced exposure to verbal language, they actually read much less than the average hearing person.

When a person born profoundly deaf becomes a good reader the result is spectacular. Reading can be the salvation of a deaf person insofar as intellectual growth and success are concerned, but only if he or she becomes a good reader. All the knowledge of the world is there—in the books, in the magazines, in the newspapers—but only for the reader. Those who lose their hearing after they learn the language, even as young as 4 or 5 years of age, are the ones most likely to become good readers, since they already know the language they need to learn to read. So do those who grow up with Cued Speech.

The Importance of Word Patterns

When learning to read, the hearing child begins to associate specific patterns of written words with the spoken patterns he/she has heard and used. Recognizing words is not enough. Most crucial is the understanding of patterns of words grouped together in particular order. No sentence is just so many words strung together. "The man sat on the elephant," and "The elephant sat on the man," are radically different in meaning. Knowing the order that gives a group of words the desired meaning is crucial to understanding and using the language. Both traditional oral and TC methods have failed to produce adequate levels of verbal language development. As a result, educators of the deaf have had to rely too much on teaching language through the written form. The child has had to be drilled on thousands upon thousands of repeated combinations that include the all-important function words, and receive explanation after explanation, in the effort to get their multiple meanings to "soak in." Reading and language have been "thrown into the same bag," with the result that neither progresses satisfactorily. In fairness, it must be recognized that innovative teachers have devised many clever ways in which to make the significance of specific language patterns clear. Nonetheless, both the pace of learning verbal language and the development of reading abilities have been far from satisfactory, even tragic.

Stages in Reading

Arthur I. Gates, a noted authority on reading, has suggested that all normal (hearing) pupils go through the same stages in learning to read the language they already use. The first stage is the development of reading readiness, for which the following are necessary:

1) A basic knowledge of the spoken language.
2) A desire to learn to read, arising from being read to, from recognizing some words, and from observing others as they read.
3) Adequate visual and neuro-visual skills.

The second stage in learning to read is the progression to sight recognition of approximately 300 words. During this stage, children simply call out the words in the written sequence, as they recognize them. They recognize the words in two ways. They recognize some words because parents or others have taught them to pair each written word with its spoken equivalent, and thus to make the association immediately on seeing the word. The other method a child may use, particularly if he or she is on the way to becoming able to read without help, is to "sound out" the letters in a written word he/she has not seen before, and recognize it as a familiar spoken word. It is this searching through his/her vocabulary of internalized spoken words and patterns, searching for the target suggested by "sounding out" the written word, that enables the child to proceed at an accelerated pace. Such a child requires very little help from others in the identification of spoken words. Ideally, this "sounding out" serves only the purpose of the initial identification of a new written word, which is soon added to the child's collection of written words he recognizes "at sight."

The third stage is one in which good oral and silent reading skills emerge, the sight vocabulary (much of it learned by the child with no help) expands to 1500 to 2000 words, and the child begins to read to satisfy curiosity and for pleasure. During this stage the child begins to recognize many phrases at sight, and begins to develop skill at using inference, prediction, and semantic closure in the process of reading. These are not reading skills as such, but mental skills that are essential to skilled reading as well as complex conversations. These skills are typically picked up by hearing children in the first five years of life, before they are used in reading.

The fourth stage in reading is marked by the emergence of mature reading motivations, interests, and tastes. It is characterized by the reader's selection of reading material to fit specific interests and to satisfy needs. A library card in the child's name is essential in helping him/her develop skill at selecting books. A child should be allowed to return a book without reading it if he/she finds too difficult, or not interesting. Children should be encouraged to read several pages of each book, at the library, before checking it out. The use of library books has advantages over purchasing large numbers of books (larger selection, low cost). However, the building of a personal library by the child is eminently desirable and highly conducive to reading.

Effects of Lack of Readiness for Reading

In the section above the requirements for readiness for the first stage of reading were identified. If a child is pushed into reading without the basic knowledge of the spoken language that is the primary requirement for reading readiness he/she is likely to: 1) find reading very difficult and unsatisfying, 2) make very slow progress in development of reading skills, and 3) fail almost entirely in developing and using the higher-level reading skills that characterize the good reader. Worst of all, it is extremely difficult to turn a child around when early attempts to read frustrate and discourage him/her.

Many young children have an early love affair with "reading" books, especially books with many interesting pictures, when what reading they are doing is calling out and understanding words that are in their sight vocabulary, words that they have been specifically taught. Reading does not really begin until the child is using linguistic context to help identify words and, above all, is sounding out and recognizing many words never seen before, adding them to sight vocabulary.

Deaf children whose language comprehension is more than a year below the norm for hearing children of the same age should be regarded as *at risk* in reading. If possible, their entry into reading should be delayed a year or more in order to make it possible to bring their language levels to that required for reading readiness. Then, they should read only material that is appropriate at that stage, not necessarily age-appropriate for hearing children. Parents should give careful attention to the development of reading readiness.

How to Develop Reading Readiness

The development of reading readiness in deaf children requires the same processes as in hearing children, with some additions and adaptations occasioned by the deafness. These include extensive early communication (which is critical), learning of verbal language through face-to-face communication (via CS), extensive reading to the child (in CS), association of sounds with letters and combinations of letters, the example of parental reading and enjoyment of books, obtaining library cards for children in the family, and making regular trips there to help them look for appropriate books. Special concerns for the deaf child should include making sure that the child's acquisition of language includes the function words and the idioms in which they appear, and use of supplementary language-development materials as needed.

HELD-HI (Home Education and Language Development for the Hearing-Impaired) is a series of videotapes featuring an on-camera cueing reader of children's books, suitable for children 3½ to 7 years old. It is an effective "parent saver" as well as an aid to language development. It is not a substitute for reading to the child, but a supplement. The child holds the actual book while the on-camera reader goes through it, cueing the text, and identifying the places where the child is to stop the tape and look at each picture. Some children have watched some of the stories through as many as a dozen times. The pay-off comes through the added orientation toward reading and the acquisition of new language. For example, Lily Lee, of Calgary, Alberta, Canada, reported on Danny's vocabulary acquisition from the stories:

> *From the Christmas tape, Danny learned antlers, red-nosed, elves, harness, and cupid. From the "G" group of books, Danny picked up more vocabulary and idioms: cozy, seasons, sap, maple syrup, tuba, not a wink, blouse, ribbons, scarf, chicken pox, hamster, porcupine, frightening, wondering, wee (as in a little wee bear), as fast as, light (not heavy), and apart. Danny contributed some opinions on the books: Seasons was too long, Rabbit is Next was too fast. While watching Big Dog, Little Dog, Danny would repeat words after the cuer, such as spinach and beets.*

Many families have reported enthusiastically on the effects of these tapes and the books furnished with them. (see Appendix, p.759)

Reading To Children

Jim Trelease, lecturer and author of books on reading, says: "The desire to read is not born in a child. It is planted—by parents and teachers." This is accomplished by enthusiasm for books and reading, and by example, encouragement, and reading to the child."

The National Academy of Education and the National Institute of Education appointed a Commission on Reading in 1983. It spent two years studying reading research and practice. Its final report, *Becoming a Nation of Readers* (1985), concluded that: "The single most important activity for building the knowledge required for eventual success in reading is *reading aloud* to children."

Trelease's popular guide for parents and teachers, *The Read-Aloud Handbook,* promotes reading aloud to children of all ages. It offers justification for doing this and guidelines on what to do and how to do it. He stresses these reasons for reading aloud to our children:

1) It builds and strengthens a positive attitude toward reading.

2) It strengthens reading, writing, and speaking skills—by improving "listening comprehension." The latter must come before reading comprehension and (in hearing children) remains above it until about age 12. In deaf children the equivalent happens through CS.

Children must "hear" words before they internalize them for accessibility in the reading process. Hearing-impaired children can "hear" words through vision with CS, processing them and committing them to auditory memory in preparation for reading.

Trelease also emphasizes the role of parents as prime "models for language" for their children. He stresses that the pace of the children's vocabulary development will be determined by the "amount and richness of the language heard."

The grown Henegar children remember the fun of being read to. Anne says: "I'm sure that's how we got a lot of our vocabulary." She remembers "those goofy poems—those long ones" that her mother read (and cued) to the whole group, such as "Custard the Dragon," "the Pirate Don Dirk of Dowdy," and "The Cremation of Sam McGee."

The miracle that allows hearing children to slide naturally into reading through being read to can also happen to deaf children. However, some special techniques must be used with deaf children in order for this to happen to them. Refer to pages 119-121.

Higher-Level Reading Skills

Inference is the drawing of a conclusion not specifically stated in the written text or a spoken narrative. For example, if the child reads (or hears): "Dad put on his slicker and went to the garage to start the car," he or she immediately *infers* that it was raining, even though the text or story does not indicate this fact. Note that the child can do the same thing if the story is being told. Inference is not restricted to reading, and should be developed well before reading age is reached.

Prediction is an inference related to something likely to happen next, or at least later. For example: "The car was going very fast. It came around a curve, on two wheels, and George saw a big truck coming toward him. It was very close, and was coming fast. Then

George..." In the mind of the child is the expectation (prediction) that 1) George will put on the brakes, or 2) George will turn sharply, or 3) there will be a crash, or at least a very narrow escape, and 4) George may be injured. The speed with which the skills of inference and prediction can be used is a determining factor in the speed and understanding with which a child reads.

Semantic Closure is recognition of the meaning of what is read or heard through the way the elements of the language fit together. When this occurs within familiar language it facilitates predication and inference. When it occurs with material that includes a new word or phrase, or a new meaning of a familiar word, it makes it possible for the reader to know the meaning of the new word or phrase (even when idiomatic) from the verbal context in which it is used. A good reader becomes very skillful at learning new words and idioms from reading, without having to look them up in a dictionary or have them explained. In fact, this probably becomes the major source of new language for deaf children who grow up with Cued Speech.

Semantic closure speeds up reading through anticipation of specific familiar words, so that the time used in processing them is reduced. An example of high predictability through semantic closure is the last word in the sentence: "Out on the lake, Bob fell out of the boat into the ____." The reader can identify the last word as *water* without even seeing it. The ability of the mind to put meanings together rapidly and anticipate what is coming reduces the amount of time required for decoding the message.

The important skills described above will ideally have already been developed by reading to the child before he/she is ready to read, and through communication in general. It is then necessary only for the child to begin employing these skills in the reading process. Parents should take specific steps to develop these language skills during the pre-reading years. Many of the games and activities in the earlier chapters can help accomplish this.

In the first grade, pupils ordinarily read orally and silently at about the same rate. In third grade, most pupils read faster when reading silently. This difference is greatest in the good readers. It results from the fact that readers who make good use of the advanced reading skills just described tend to read faster than they can talk. They also read with better comprehension than slower readers.

The Importance and Limitations of Context

Because our language is highly redundant, the meaning of a completely unfamiliar word, or at least an approximation of it, is often evident from the *context* in which it is embedded. This can be thought of as arriving at the meaning of a word from "circumstantial evidence." An important kind of test of reading and language abilities is the *closure* test. In this test every third or fourth word is replaced by a blank space, and the reader is asked to fill in the blanks. He/she should be able to insert the correct words in about 60% of the blank spaces if the material is suitable for his/her reading ability. Context makes some words easily predictable in this sentence: "Jimmie opened the ___ to the bathroom ___ turned on the ___ so he could ___."

The learning of new words without assistance from anyone else is possible for children who reach the appropriate level of reading skill and knowledge of language. If their knowledge of language and their familiarity with written words is sufficient to make this possible, their rate of language growth can skyrocket. It does not matter that the meaning inferred from context is approximate. The learning of language through reading is normally a process in which one acquires approximations or even only "hints" of the meanings of new words, and those approximations are refined by later exposures to the same word and eventually lead to precise knowledge. Of course, a child who encounters an unfamiliar word (unfamiliar in both written and spoken forms) may be able to use the dictionary to determine its meaning.

It should be kept in mind that learning new words and using context in reading are possible only if the child has already an adequate base of language and a good supply of "sight" words, immediately recognizable to him/her in written form. For the child to have to depend on context for too much of what he/she reads, that is, to guess excessively, will convince him/her that reading is too difficult.

How to Develop Advanced Reading Skills

In reading to a child, or even in conversation, one can help the child develop inference, prediction, and semantic-closure skills by asking questions. In the first example on page 253, one can ask: "Why did Dad put on his slicker?" In the second, one can ask: "What do you think George did next?" to prompt the child to make an inference or a prediction. One can use a sentence similar to the "Out in the lake I fell out of the boat into the ___ " example by covering up the last word in the sentence and asking the child to see if he can guess the last word.

This activity can be made into a game by preparing very easy text with every fourth word covered and letting the child try to read it.

How the Cued Speech Child Reads

The detailed analysis of how a hearing child learns to read was included above because a deaf child growing up on Cued Speech should learn to read in exactly the same way and at the same rate as a hearing child. This assumes that the deaf child's exposure to language in Cued Speech starts early, and the language support needed by hearing children is provided the deaf child. Assumed also is that the parents pay careful attention to the various factors involved in achievement of reading readiness, as described above.

The development of Cued Speech came about specifically because of concern over the fact that deaf children do not typically learn to read well. Ever since the first child exposed to Cued Speech progressed well in reading, parents and teachers using it with children have known that it gives them the foundation for reading. However, specific research evidence supporting this conclusion was not available until recently. Jean E. Wandel (1989) compared the reading comprehension levels of carefully matched groups (30 in each) of hearing, Cued Speech, Oral, and Total Communication pupils. Only the profoundly deaf Cued Speech pupils matched the hearing pupils in average level of reading comprehension, as measured on the appropriate sub-section of the Stanford Achievement Test. An interesting result was that the CS pupils with only a severe hearing impairment scored somewhat lower than the profoundly deaf CS pupils. We account for this because of the tendency of many parents of CS children with more hearing to cue "only what is necessary."

In 1974-76 one of the authors chaired a committee of 10 faculty members at Gallaudet College charged with the responsibility of designing a model of reading development suitable for analyzing the probable effects of different communication modes on the development of reading in deaf children. On the committee were two persons who were "pro-Cued Speech." The others were either unbiased or negative. At the conclusion of its two years of work, the members of the committee agreed that of all the communication modes considered, only Cued Speech offers the theoretical promise of enabling a deaf child to learn to read in the same way a hearing child does. The committee was not affirming (or denying) that Cued Speech actually does this, but only that it alone among the methods has the theoretical potential to do so. What the committee recognized in Cued Speech as a possibility was borne out by research results obtained a decade later. From 1985 through 1990 a series of about a dozen reports of experimental studies by Belgian psychologists and educators (among them Alegría, et al., 1986, 1989, 1990) established the role of Cued Speech in providing the deaf child with a base for reading. Here is the concluding paragraph from one of their reports, entitled: "Role Played by Cued Speech in the Identification of Written Words Encountered for the First Time by Deaf Children."

To come back to our initial point, the present work strongly suggests that the lexicon developed by the deaf with Cued Speech has properties which are equivalent to the phonology of the hearing subjects. In both cases the internal representations of the words are compatible with their ortho-graphic representation. This allows the use of phonological coding to identify unfamiliar words and, as said before, can prime the whole processes of reading acquisition.

The word *lexicon* in the statement above means the total family of (spoken) words internalized and understood by the child. Not only is this lexicon important; so are the patterns of spoken language that have become familiar to the child. Together, they are the base for speaking, speechreading, reading and writing.

A crucial factor is the extent to which the child actually *thinks* in the spoken language. In 1987 I (Cornett) wrote to 13 profoundly deaf youngsters who had grown up with Cued Speech in the home, asking them to indicate what happened in their minds when they were thinking—in addition to seeing mental images. Eleven replied: "I hear myself talking." One, totally deaf, wrote, "I feel myself talking." The other one, who had the most hearing and was very oral, wrote, "I see the words." All verified, in response to a question about their dreams, that people who didn't cue in real life often cued to them in their dreams, that they could lipread everybody perfectly in their dreams, and that other people could understand them perfectly. The parents of all thirteen indicated that they talk and cue in their sleep. Making the spoken language the thought language of the deaf child is one of the most important functions of Cued Speech.

The Autonomous Reader

The ability to recognize written words not seen before (if one knows them as spoken words) is described by Jorm and Share (1983) as characteristic of the child who is an autonomous reader, able to read (at the level which is appropriate for him) without help from anyone else. He/she is thus able to accumulate an increasing vocabulary of easily recognized sight words derived from reference to his/her internal spoken vocabulary (phonological lexicon). When necessary, the child can identify any less-familiar written word that is in his spoken vocabulary, unless its spelling is too different from its pronunciation.

The reasons why Cued Speech produces readers have been obvious to its users for a long time. Cued Speech enables the deaf child to acquire the spoken language in the same phonemic (sound) patterns a hearing child learns, but through vision rather than audition. Cued Speech thus produces autonomous readers.

"Getting hooked" on reading appears to be the norm for children with whom Cued Speech is started early. This generalization is supported by the results of the Wandel (1989) research. Practically all the case histories reported in this book describe children who have become good readers. This was not by selection or design, but the result of a tendency common to children growing up with CS. Even the case histories in Chapter 24, "The Child With More Than One Disability," support our impression that many children with another disability in addition to deafness have a good chance to become good readers if they receive consistent support, and if the secondary disability does not specifically preclude reading. An example is Tiffany Balderson, whose mother Linda writes: "As a ninth-grader (and dyslexic, learning disabled, and profoundly deaf), Tiffany passed the Maryland Functional Reading Test required to receive a high school diploma in Maryland." The students are allowed to take the test as many as four times: in ninth, tenth, eleventh, and twelfth grade, if they need to do so. Her mother adds: "We thought about mainstreaming Tiffany in a small (hearing) learning-disabled class, but learned that she didn't qualify because she read too well!"

The Role of Parents in Reading Development

The paragraphs above strongly suggest that the Cued Speech child should learn to read in the same way a hearing child learns to read. Most of what parents need to do about reading should be done before the child starts to read. Parents need to do the following:

1) Learn Cued Speech and use it consistently for all communication with the child except special auditory training.

2) Carefully practice the suggestions in this book for supporting language development and for development of good communication.

3) Begin reading books to your child as soon as he or she is understanding well with Cued Speech. Follow the procedure described in Chapter 9, page 119: "How to Read to Your Young Child."

4) Develop "experience books" that record significant experiences in the life of your child and recreate them in pictures and text. Follow the suggestions described in Chapter 9, pages 113-116.

5) Consider enrolling in the "HELD-HI" program of reading support. This program provides many hours of videotaped stories in Cued Speech. It will supplement your own reading to your child and provide you (as a parent) a welcome respite. The stories are appropriate for children 3½ to 7 years old. Check Appendix, p. 759 for source.

6) After your child begins to want to read for himself/herself, mix periods of reading to him/her with periods when he/she either reads to you aloud or reads silently. At first you will need to be easily available to help by identifying words, on request.

7) Make the acquisition of a personal library card a big event for your child. Encourage the child to select books (with a minimum of guidance) to take home and read. Enlist library staff to help orient the child to the children's collection and make suggestions. Suggest that the child read a few pages in each book before deciding to check it out. Do not insist that the child finish each book, especially if it turns out he/she may have selected something too difficult.

8) It is important to have appropriate reading materials available. These should range from an encyclopedia of appropriate readability and scope to comic books. Almost anything the child enjoys reading is beneficial. Linda Balderson writes: "I have bought such reading materials as *Soap Opera Digest, Peoples Magazine, the Enquirer, TV Guide* (she has a subscription), *Cat Magazine, Sweet Valley High paper backs,* etc. I think anything your child will read (within reason) is worth having for him. Caldecott Award winning books do no good if they gather dust on the shelves."

9) Build a personal library for your deaf child and encourage the care and enjoyment of personally owned books that can be treasured and read repeatedly.

10) Try to get your deaf child to "tell you the story" when he/she has finished each book (or chapter). Praise him/her for reading.

11) Try to maintain the practice of at least having a reading time on the weekends, to the extent possible. When the family goes on a trip, allow the child to take some books. Dr. Feisal Keblawi, who assisted Cornett in refining and recording the Cued Speech lessons in Arabic, tells of an occasion when his family was preparing to leave for California to visit grandparents. His wife told their 9-year-old

profoundly deaf boy, Nabeel, to go upstairs and pack his things. A few minutes later, Nabeel came down, all packed. His mother went up to check to see that he had included everything he needed. He had packed three sets of underwear and 33 books—nothing else!

12) Once your child is reading well, and is perhaps 8 or 9 years old, captioned TV programs, films, and videotapes (check for *cc.* or the captioning symbol on the box) can be beneficial if they are selected carefully. Now that all TV sets manufactured in the United States after mid-1993 must contain a TV captioner chip (eliminating the need for a separate closed-caption decoder), the numbers of captioned programs can be expected to increase rapidly. Most videotapes for rent are now available closed captioned. Coordinated use of transliteration and the remote control can be very effective in making good use of videotapes for entertainment and language development in combination.

13) Make a practice of observing a "reading time" each day during school vacations, when members of the family who are at home all read. This will help the child form the habit of reading each day.

14) Once your child is reading, get a TDD (Telecommunication Device for the Deaf). As CS kids approach the teen years, their relationship with peers, both deaf and hearing, is greatly enhanced if they can communicate clearly by telephone. Linda Balderson recommends that parents "spend a little more" and buy a model that produces a printout, since in most cases the child will want to keep the messages and reread them. This enhances language learning. In the haste to communicate, the child may not read with sufficient care, and may not remember the message well enough to be able to ask parents to explain any language that confuses him/her. The printer should also make it possible for copy corrected in the typing process to come out right on the final copy. This facilitates rereading the conversation. Mrs. Balderson cites the example of Tiffany's typing Tiffnry, then backspacing 3 spaces and typing any to correct her error. Her printer printed Tiffnryany instead of the corrected version. There are also printers that hold several words in memory and thus eliminate anything erased and replaced by corrected input.

15) Sarina Roffé suggests establishing (for both deaf child and siblings) a minimum of time each evening that must be devoted to homework. On days when homework is light, the children should be allowed to read materials of their choice for the rest of the time. During the summer the same parent allowed the kids to stay up past bedtime—but only if they were reading. The regular bedtime was set a little earlier to allow for this. According to Ms. Roffé, the children loved this. They thought they were getting away with something. It

also let them know that reading is important. As stated by Jim Trelease: "Letting the child do this makes the connection between print, privilege, and pleasure."

Readiness for Reading at Home and at School

A child, deaf or hearing, needs to know the spoken language in order to be ready to read. He or she needs cognitive skills, a sight vocabulary of a few hundred words, and an understanding of the relationship between the letters of the alphabet (singly and in combination) and the sounds of the language. This relationship is essential if the child is to use (in the process of reading) the thousands of spoken words he already knows through CS. He/she needs also to enjoy being read to by parents, and to realize that he/she can pick up some of the written words by following along in the text with the reader.

In her essay on experience books (Chapter 9), Sarina Roffé identifies skills a child does not necessarily have to have in order to enjoy reading at home, but which are important in reading at school. She presents them in the form of questions:

> *Can the child sit in a group quietly? Can the child wait his turn patiently behind 20 other children? Can the child be assigned homework and then remember to bring it back the next day? Can he focus his attention on an assigned task which requires him to sit at his desk? Can the child organize his activities in achieving a specific task? Does he see a task through to completion? If not, even the most gifted of children is not ready to read at school.*

The questions listed above should not be interpreted as requiring an all or nothing answer on each point. Most children are deficient to some extent on several of the criteria. If a child is ready to make good progress in reading in the school atmosphere he/she needs to have all of the abilities specified, to a degree that enables the teacher to "take it from there."

Chapter Summary

Hearing children typically begin to read by simply recognizing "sight" words that have been taught to them. Then they begin to convert unfamiliar written words into their sounds and recognize them as spoken words already known. They soon add these words to their lists of "sight words." Next, they begin to use the advanced mental skills already developed in communication: semantic closure, inference, and prediction, to make the process of reading faster and easier.

The hearing-impaired child accustomed to Cued Speech typically learns to read in exactly the same way a hearing child does. Recent research (Wandel, 1989) shows that in matched groups of hearing subjects and deaf subjects from Oral, TC, and Cued Speech backgrounds only the group of profoundly deaf Cued Speech subjects matched the hearing group in reading comprehension, as measured by the Stanford Achievement Test. Research by Belgian research psychologists (Alegría, et al., 1990) indicates that CS subjects acquire an internalized phonological model of spoken language with "properties equivalent to those of the phonological system of the hearing subjects."

There are many things parents can do to help a deaf child become a good reader. Here are a few. For others, refer to the longer list above.

1. Help him/her acquire language.

2. Make "experience books."

3. Read books to him/her

4. Participate in the HELD-HI program.

5. After your child begins reading independently, mix periods of reading to him/her with periods when he/she reads to you.

6. Set up family "reading times" on weekends, when family members all read material of their choice. During summer and other vacations, schedule extra reading times.

7. Provide reading materials with appropriate reading and interest levels. Include family reference books, such as illustrated encyclopedias, and add to each child's personal collection.

8. Ask your child to retell a story for you after he/she has just finished reading it. Praise him/her for reading and remembering it.

9. Utilize captioned programs, videotapes, and a TDD.

10. Patronize public and school libraries and help your child form the habit of using books from various sources.

11. Remember that readiness for reading at school requires some skills, mostly behavioral, that are not necessary for reading at home. Try to develop these skills in advance of need.

Chapter 16
Roles of Hearing Siblings and Peers

The deaf child's communication must not be limited primarily to interaction with his parents. His/her world of communication needs to be expanded in every way possible. A proper beginning is to have a family in which all members cue. If there are siblings, particularly older siblings, their learning to cue will solve many problems. If the deaf child has no brothers and sisters, sometimes neighborhood children, school classmates, a baby-sitter, or even cousins who come to visit can be cultivated as sources of peer cueing interaction.

One of the primary sources of information and language for a hearing child is overheard conversation. The deaf child typically misses all this. Being left out is a misfortune of hearing impairment that can be alleviated to a considerable extent. Be sure to use Cued Speech with other members of the family when the deaf child is present. A young deaf child is likely to notice if others are also receiving Cued Speech since this enables him/her to understand. Some young children are initially more observant of what is being cued to others than they are of what is cued directly to them. On this point Osmond Crosby writes:

"Our experience is that cueing to each other is what engaged Dorothy. She didn't try expressive cueing until we began to cue to each other. She was especially motivated when we started cueing to her 6-months-old sister."

Cue when calling any of your children. The deaf child may see you call and have time to wonder who will come, until he/she can recognize the names. This practice has added value because the child may be able to hear your loud call (even if profoundly deaf) and thus connect audition, speech, and cueing.

A parent's cueing to brothers and sisters furnishes added natural repetition and reinforcement. Tell the deaf child, and then tell the brother or sister. The deaf child can learn from the siblings' experiences, if he/she can follow what happens. For example, if a brother or sister is scolded and punished, the deaf child needs to know the reason. If not, he/she may be confused or frightened, fearing that he/she too will be punished. Cueing to siblings also helps avoid making the deaf child feel unnecessarily different.

Some hearing children, particularly siblings younger than the deaf child, may learn Cued Speech as the young deaf child does—through exposure. Others, on the other hand, need to be taught systematically, either sound-by-sound or by complete words and phrases. You will need to determine the best approach for your children. It will depend on their ages and attitudes. Great care should be taken to encourage expressive cueing on the part of hearing siblings without making them feel pressured. Praise and other forms of positive reinforcement are most effective.

Early in their use of Cued Speech the Henegar parents often cued silently to each other at the table, the way parents sometimes spell to each other to keep the children from knowing what they are saying. This subtly and quickly encouraged all their children to become adept at reading Cued Speech, because they wanted to know what was being said. The children's ages then were 1, 2, 4, 5, and 6 years.

It may help to teach younger siblings how to cue words and phrases associated with related items. For example, a brother could learn to cue the names of several toys and spend time using them in playing with the hearing-impaired child. A sister or brother could learn how to cue the names of various items of clothing and habitually assist the child in dressing. Someone else could learn the proper words to help the deaf child set the table.

Involve siblings in the games and activities you use with your deaf child. This may make it easier for them to respond to the opportunity to learn to cue. Also, it may encourage them to initiate games, verses, and other activities with their deaf sibling.

With a means of clear communication at their disposal, hearing siblings can provide valuable language background during their normal play experiences. In Chapter 10 are familiar verses, songs, and games that a deaf child and his/her brothers and sisters may enjoy together. Reading books to the deaf child (with cues), teaching the necessary vocabulary for a card game, introducing phrases such as "Ready, get set, go!", explaining how to do something—all these and many other interactions are things siblings can do to create a closer relationship between the deaf child and the entire family.

A hearing sibling who can transliterate or interpret for a deaf child is a veritable gateway to communication with hearing people in general. They can expand the deaf child's opportunities for social development and interaction with hearing peers. Once acquainted, hearing peers can choose to learn to cue or be satisfied with communicating orally, but the process of getting acquainted is made much easier if there is a cueing sibling. Equally important is reverse interpreting—speaking for the deaf child. Often a hearing sibling understands the speech of a deaf brother or sister better than even the parents.

The important role of cueing baby-sitter can be handled very effectively by siblings of deaf children who have become skilled at communication, understanding, and working with a deaf child. Having an opportunity to do useful (and remunerative) work outside the home, using their cueing skills, helps the self-esteem of the hearing sibling.

The Sibling Who Feels Left Out

The young deaf child has to be given more attention and support than the hearing brothers and sisters. He/she must be transported for therapy, for hearing-aid fitting and repair, for special classes, and for periodic testing. Parents typically must give the deaf child more of their time and attention than they do their hearing children. Often it seems to a sibling that the life of the family centers more and more on the deaf child. Sometimes this feeling becomes so strong that it leads to withdrawal, rebellion, or statements such as: "I wish I was deaf so you would love me too!" Several things can be done to prevent or alleviate this problem. Each child should have some special, separate time with mother and father, each day and every week, even if it is a small amount of (*quality*) time. Each sibling must be praised for participating in the family's effort to help the deaf child. If the sibling can be induced to learn to cue, this will help a great deal.

A deaf child is often a lot of trouble and frustration to a brother or sister because it is hard to make him/her understand, persuade him/her to take turns, stop him/her when he/she is doing wrong, etc. A parent sometimes needs to talk with the brother or sister along these lines: "I understand how much Jimmy bothers you. He can't understand why he can't have your toys, and he's bad about breaking them. He hits you, but I can't let you hit him. When he fusses with you, he doesn't understand what you say, so you have to do everything to solve the problem. If you will learn to cue, you can get him off your back. You can make him understand why you won't let him do something. I used to have the same problem when he didn't understand Cued Speech. I was afraid to punish him for doing something wrong because I was afraid he wouldn't understand why I was punishing him."

Parents need to be sensitive to the difficulties siblings experience in accepting the "double standard" that requires extra concessions to the deaf child, at least until clear communication makes it possible to get rid of or minimize the favored treatment. Siblings can understand and accept what is necessary, but only with patient and understanding treatment from parents.

Linda Balderson tells of a Q-club (cueing club) that helped motivate a sibling to cue:

The best idea we came up with (for getting Tanya to cue

more) was to get one of her friends interested in learning also.
I signed both girls up for Cued Speech club at Tiffany's
elementary school (the older girls were in junior high). My
daughter was pretty good at cueing already, so the club teacher
had her help with small groups. She and her friend then had a
secret code they could use in school.

When a hearing sibling is asked to teach the deaf child something, and succeeds in doing so, the "left out" syndrome is on its way
to being alleviated. One of the authors has said many times: "God's
most special gift to a deaf child, after a mother, is an older sister or
brother who cues."

On average, it is easier to get a sister than a brother to cue
consistently. Typically, if both male and female siblings learn to cue,
the sister is more likely to welcome the job of being "teacher," and
simply takes the deaf child under her wing. Brothers often learn to cue,
but more often tend to cue little more than is necessary to settle
disputes or engage in play. We theorize that this may be because the
play of boys tends to be more oriented toward physical activity, with
a lower verbal load, than that of girls. Thus, to enjoy play activities
they may need only a minimum of verbal communication, depending
more on gestures and motion. Fortunately, more and more exceptions
to this generalization are coming to light, perhaps enough to make it
suspect. Some examples are included in the following case histories.

A possible explanation of cases of consistent cueing by male
siblings is that their families have developed a tradition of family
activities enjoyed by all members of the family. Even though when left
to their own initiative, the boys may gravitate toward rough-and-tumble
(low verbal) play, substantial interaction in family activities can make
the difference. Two families come to mind in which there were two or
more male sibling cuers. In each there was a tradition of full family
participation in various activities.

The variables and dynamics of each family will influence sibling
acceptance and interaction with a deaf sibling. As pointed out by Dale
Atkins (1987) in a special issue of *Volta Review*, entitled "Families and
Their Hearing-Impaired Children," relevant factors may include: family
size, birth order, gender, family-member roles and responsibilities,
expression of feelings, economic and marital status, sibling rivalry,
parenting styles, etc.

As regards parenting styles, sibling Anne Henegar said she and
her brothers and sisters all learned to cue because they were expected
to. "It was a normal part of life. We all did it."

In regard to birth order, Charles Swadley theorizes that the likelihood of full sibling cueing is less if the deaf child is the eldest. Older siblings may be more likely to cue to aid a younger deaf sibling.

Linda Balderson reports an experience that illustrates the importance of accurate parent perception of sibling feelings: "I had the experience of leaving my older daughter Tanya with a baby-sitter while I took Tiffany to many clinical appointments. She wanted to come along, as she thought our trips were fun. The problem was solved by taking Tanya along a few times. As soon as she realized the trips were not fun, she happily stayed behind."

Osmond Crosby points out that the siblings themselves may have considerable adaptability. He reports on a seminar in which he heard a panel of siblings discuss their problems of relationship with their siblings with disabilities. As he put it, "They were very frank about their feelings and the bottom line I heard was that life was just that way for their family."

Issues that Bother Siblings Most
by Leslie Kravitz
Ms. Kravitz is a social worker with the Hearing Impaired Program, Fairfax (Va.) County Schools, with much experience in dealing with sibling relationships.

Of all the issues within the family, the one that bothers the siblings of a handicapped child the most is their perception that family rules are unfair. Not only do they feel that they have more household responsibilities than their deaf sibling, but that their parents have higher expectations for them as well. Children want and expect things in life to be fair. When they're not, they become upset and indignant. Some children harbor these feelings, rarely expressing them. Others act them out with uncooperative behavior. This situation is often challenging for parents to handle. Their deaf child may not be able to do the chore or follow the rule without much repetition, guidance, and support. Parents who must stop everything to supervise the child in doing the chore sometimes find it easier to demand less of their deaf child. This may relieve stress on the parent, but may increase it for the hearing sibling.

Siblings experience a range of feelings that impact on their relationships with their deaf sibling:

1. Jealousy. Siblings often feel that the hearing-impaired child is "loved more, given more attention and more material things than they receive."

2. Resentment. This feeling occurs when family plans are

interrupted or canceled due to the needs of the hearing-impaired child or when the sibling is given heavy child-care responsibilities.

3. Embarrassment. Pre-teen and particularly teenage siblings may be embarrassed by their deaf sibling's speech, language, and occasionally their behavior.

Appropriate and timely information about hearing loss is a vital aid in reducing stress in the sibling relationship. Parents should keep the following in mind:

1. Siblings have a need for honest, direct, and understandable information about the various aspects of their sibling's hearing loss.

2. Information needs to be presented repeatedly and ongoing throughout their lives.

3. Material presented to siblings should vary according to their age and developmental level.

The types of information needed by siblings include:
1. Information related to the hearing loss
   a. How a hearing loss impacts speech and language development
   b. How hearing aids, cochlear implants, and tactile devices work
   c. Cause of the hearing loss, if known
   d. Information about assistive devices (TV decoder, TDD)
   e. Prognosis of the hearing loss
   f. Understanding of deaf culture and values
   g. Awareness of educational methodologies (Cued Speech, Total Communication, oral/auditory)
2. Information from their parents
   a. Parents' expectations for them with regard to the hearing-impaired sibling, presently and in the future
   b. Clarification of responsibility for their deaf sibling
   c. Ways they can help out at home with the deaf child
3. Understanding about themselves
   a. Understanding that it is normal to experience a wide range of feelings toward the deaf sibling
   b. Awareness of how they will be enriched by their experience of having a deaf sibling
4. Information on how to interact with their friends
   a. Informing their friends about their sibling's hearing loss
   b. How to handle teasing and questions from their peers
   c. Bringing friends to their home

5. Information on how to handle expectations and questions from neighborhood, school, and community

Opportunities for Siblings to Learn to Cue

In some cases siblings will respond to opportunities to learn Cued Speech in the home. Often, however, other (or additional) opportunities need to be provided. If the entire family attends family learning workshops, such as the annual Camp Cheerio Cued Speech Family Program, in North Carolina, or other regional workshops, siblings are likely to get "over the hump."

The initiation of a Q-Club (cueing club) at school can produce a group of hearing peers who cue to the deaf youngster, and can at the same time give a sibling a chance to polish his/her cueing skills and assume a starring role. Some schools offer cueing classes to provide peer cueing support and lead to the starting of a Q-club. Siblings can benefit by attending such classes.

One of the most effective ways of encouraging sibling cueing is for several families to cooperate in conducting a series of cue "parties" for peers and siblings, involving games, cueing instruction, and refreshments.

Siblings will differ in the speed and ease with which they pick up cueing, and in the motivation they have to learn. Sarina Roffé suggests teaching everyone in the family how to talk to a deaf person (keep objects away from the mouth, face the person, establish eye contact, etc.). This can also help with un-cued communication and may also lead to increased motivation to learn to cue.

Parents can also add to their hearing children's motivation to cue by trying to increase their sensitivity to hearing loss. Such activities as speaking with little or no voice and turning the TV down or off can help them briefly "experience" hearing loss.

The Value of Sibling Support

The common thread running through all the stories of cueing siblings we have received, and there are many, is the fact that a deaf child can learn huge quantities of language from a cueing sibling. (S)he can also experience psychological support and companionship and acquire needed emotional balance and stability. A frequent testimony from cueing families is that the deaf child has learned more language from cueing siblings than from anyone else, even more than from parents and teachers.

All the families we know affirm that a cueing sibling is a boon to the parents, who can use their time more judiciously and effectively because of the assumption of part of the responsibility by the sibling. But, the most important contribution from the sibling is distinct from anything others can do. Siblings can furnish needed companionship along with language and social development. In many of the cases described below the deaf child was the only deaf child in his/her school, making the companionship of the cueing siblings even more essential.

All members of a hearing-impaired person's family should work together to develop sensitivity to all the implications of the disability. The most important thing family members can do is to make sure the hearing-impaired individual is included in all family conversation and activities. Some people seem to think it is important to cue only when they are saying something important or something that specifically concerns the hearing-impaired person. But hearing people in the household usually hear all that is said in their presence, not just what they "need to know" or what is said directly to them. Seemingly unimportant matters can be quite significant in adding a sense of perspective to life. Hearing members of the family hear the jokes and the trivia, and so should a hearing-impaired child. Humor constantly enriches our daily lives, but amusing comments are easy for the person with a hearing impairment to miss unless he/she has clear visual access to all that is said.

Much language is picked up in incidental conversation, including conversation overheard. *Full* inclusion of the hearing-impaired family member in the life of the family is the only means of preventing the tragic sense of isolation experienced, in varying degrees, by most of those who have a severe-to-profound hearing loss.

Jennifer Ziebell points out that cueing at the dinner table underscores the importance of learning to cue with both hands. For many people the more skilled hand is the one most needed in the process of eating. Unless one can cue with either hand, communication (for the deaf child) is likely to be inhibited.

The presence of siblings, whether or not they cue, simplifies the difficult task of teaching manners and courtesy to a deaf child. This is not to say that siblings make the task easy, but only that their interactions help produce situations that lead to instruction about proper behavior, or even force parents to "take a hand." It is easy for parents to be so anxious for the child to communicate, and to use speech, that they welcome all sorts of interruption and disregard of others.

Training a deaf child in considerate behavior is not an easy task, because deaf children are often not aware of many of the things that are involved. A profoundly deaf child has to learn to look to see if others are speaking before starting to talk, and to keep in mind that hearing people can be in the middle of a conversation without having eye contact with the speaker, can listen without looking, and can easily be disturbed by behavior that does not take this into account. The natural interactions and rivalries of siblings, especially siblings who have good communication with the deaf child, tend to produce situations that lead to understanding of the problems of getting along. This can enable parents to assume a guiding and leading role, and when necessary a controlling role, without too much nagging.

Deaf Children with Exemplary Sibling Support

Cases in which there are two or more cueing siblings are particularly interesting and revealing. These examples are followed by observations written by the siblings themselves.

Leah Henegar
Leah's sisters, Anne and Jane, cued to her consistently as long as they were together at home. The three of them played together, quarreled, and cooperated. Anne and Jane taught Leah everything from language to the facts of life, and interpreted for her in conversations, for TV, etc. Through it all, they were *sisters* and *pals*. Chapter 3, "Life With Leah," is rich in examples of the contribution of hearing siblings to the development of a deaf child.

John Nemeth
John Nemeth was mentioned in Chapter 11 in connection with the subway anecdote. When I first met him, at age 5, his 12-year-old sister Christine and his 9-year-old sister Nicole were already skilled and consistent cuers. His mother, Mary, recently wrote:

> *Nicole, in applying for scholarships and college admission this year (1991), wrote several essays on her satisfaction and feelings of accomplishment in connection with John's successes. You are so correct in saying a big sister is the greatest asset, and John has two cueing sisters!*

As in this example, cueing siblings almost invariably take pride in the accomplishments of their deaf sibling. This pride comes, in large part, from the knowledge that they have been partly responsible for those accomplishments.

Alisa Fleetwood

Alisa Fleetwood started Cued Speech very late (at age 12), after extended experience in aural/oral programs, which became increasingly difficult for her. Her entire family (parents and brothers Earl and Raymond) became skilled cuers and were fully supportive and helpful.

Scott Johndrow

Kimberly, sister of Scott Johndrow, and David, his brother, have been highly supportive, cueing siblings whose contribution has been of inestimable value to Scott. All through elementary and high school Scott has been the only deaf child in his school.

Alexander McDonnel

Anna McDonnel, at age 4, could cue anything she could say, and proudly taught words to her deaf brother, Alexander (age 22 months), using picture books. A videotape of this activity has been used in scores of workshops throughout the United States and in several countries in Europe. Annette McDonnel, their mother, confirms that a major share of Alexander's language acquisition has come from Anna.

Observations by Anna McDonnel
sister of Alexander, 1992

Having a deaf brother, Alex, has brought many different perspectives to my life that I probably wouldn't have experienced without him. Some were good, some not so good. As in any family, there were ups and downs with having a brother, deaf or not. These include responsibilities. As Alex's sister I was responsible for setting a good example for him to follow. I also interpret for him when people cannot understand him or cannot communicate with him. When he needs help, I'm there to stick up for him. Since we have a younger sister and brother, I am the one in charge as baby-sitter.

In a lot of ways Alex is like any normal kid, but whenever he needs it, he is treated differently by my parents. For a while I thought this was unfair, until I learned that fairness doesn't always mean to be treated equally.

But my life with Alex isn't only responsibilities. It's also new experiences. Because Alex is not only deaf but also handicapped, I think I have gained a better awareness about handicapped people.

Because of Alex I have also had more experience explaining and helping him understand new and different situations we encounter. For example, when I explain something to him from his science class, this sometimes gives me a clearer picture of it.

Alex is friendly, funny, and always wants to know what's going on. "Who's on the phone?" or "What did the dog hear?" are questions we hear everyday. Watching him try something new or difficult, and then seeing him light up when he succeeds, makes me very proud to be his sister. Playing on the basketball team in our school's Special Olympics, Alex has fun whether he wins or loses. After several attempts at making a basket, the ball finally makes it through the hoop and he shouts excitedly—offering his hand for a "high five."

I guess since I've lived with him all his life, I can't imagine Alex any other way. I can always talk to him using Cued Speech, and that has made us very close to each other. Alex's case history, p. 550.

Amy McGlone

The deaf youngster with the largest number of cueing siblings (insofar as we know) is Amy McGlone, of Spotsylvania, Va. Amy is 15 years old, a sophomore (1992-93) in high school, mainstreamed since the early grades. She has two brothers and three sisters, all of whom are expert cuers and have been since she was a young child. She now also has a sister-in-law who cues. All through school she has had many hearing friends and classmates who cue.

Malinda, Amy's oldest sister, supported herself while in college as a CS transliterator. She also spent a year as a live-in tutor and transliterator for a deaf boy in Thailand. Shelley is working as a transliterator at Wellesley College and is a senior at Bridgewater State University, nearby. Suzanne works with a 3-year-old deaf boy in a Montessori school. Matt fills in for her when she is not available.

Amy's parents, Kent and Peggy McGlone, attended a three-day workshop in 1978, and shifted from signing to Cued Speech. The entire family attended the first one-week family workshop at Gallaudet that summer. The next spring Mrs. McGlone telephoned to ask if there was any way her four oldest children could help out in the workshop, asserting that they didn't need class instruction and could cue as well as the teachers. We took that assertion with a grain of salt, but did promise to let them help in some way. When they arrived, and we checked them out, we found that their mother had not exaggerated at all. We let them serve at everything from assistant teacher to cueing nursery assistant. Ever since they have all worked at a professional level, teaching, transliterating, explaining, and promoting Cued Speech.

Surely the "cueing-est" family of all is the McGlones!

Amy, My Family, Me, and Cued Speech
by Malinda McGlone, 1982

I can't even begin to say how much of an influence Amy has had on my life. I do know that I am who I am today partly because of Amy and what I have learned from her.

Amy (16) and Malinda (27) McGlone

I was 12 when Amy, just an infant, was diagnosed as having a hearing loss. I remember wondering why Mom and Dad were so affected by this discovery. Okay, so she's deaf, I thought, what's the big deal? She just can't hear, but she's still the cutest little baby I've ever seen. She *acts* like a regular baby. Of course, at the time I was completely unaware of the implications of deafness and how it impacts a person's ability to communicate.

It became clearer as our family did the things I guess most families do when there is a deaf baby in the family. We took her to a special doctor who tested her hearing, had different people with very animated faces come to the house and blow bubbles with Amy and her siblings, had her fitted for hearing aids (that Amy seemed to prefer in her mouth or in the toilet rather than in her ears), and got the whole family (all eight of us) around the dining room table singing a monotone "Bah Bah Bah" until Amy joined in. Amy's deafness indeed became a family project that united our large family with a common goal: to teach Amy how to communicate and function in a hearing world, and more importantly, how to be just one of the family.

When the family learned signing (Signing Exact English) we were pleased initially with how we could communicate with her. Also, sign language was "cool," and I could teach all my friends the silent language. However, I noticed that when I spoke with Amy, I had to reword almost everything I said to her so that my message would fit within my vocabulary in sign language. The older Amy got, and the more sophisticated our conversations became, the more I realized how much I was compromising my natural flow of speech. What really bothered me was that I was confined to speaking to Amy in an unnatural, adapted way, whereas my other siblings, my parents, and my friends received the "normal Malinda Language."

I observed that everyone else in the family seemed to be doing this as well. We spoke naturally around each other, yet with Amy all the subtle nuances of the McGlone language were lost. With her there was no "Yeah, he's a real cool dude," or "Ho-ho-ho, we've really got to go, to the great big world of make-believe at KINGS DOMINION!!" Amy's language was so structured and un-McGlone-like that we became very frustrated with signing.

Fortunately, Mom and Dad had the good sense to try Cued Speech. We learned this method fast. In fact it took Shelley, Suzie, and me just an afternoon to learn the handshapes, and then we were well on our way to becoming fluent with Cued Speech.

Every problem we had had with signing was instantly solved with Cued Speech. Finally, slang terms and expressions could be introduced naturally to Amy! When the girls played "mothers," Amy could be the daughter with a country-hick accent. She could also be a part of the idiosyncratic McGlone language. For the first time we were not compromising our way of talking—we were cueing it!

Amy, now 15, has developed her own McGlone personality. Believe it or not, she probably is the most outgoing one of the group. I used to think I was, until one weekend when she came to Edenton to visit me and was the life of the party at a cook-out where she kept a bunch of strangers entertained with her funny stories, jokes, dances, and incredibly accurate imitations. I admire her confidence and her ability to get along with others. Cued Speech certainly helped mold the Amy we know and love today.

One thing is for sure—Amy is a true McGlone.

Antonia Sánchez Mompeán, 1992
(translated from Spanish)

Hola! My name is Antonia Sánchez Mompeán, I am 16 years old and have a deaf sister. She was found to be deaf when she was 2 years old, because of penicillin. When she was 3 she started going to APANDA *(the rehabilitation center operated by the Association of Parents with Children with Auditory Deficiencies)*. We are *(studying)* in the second level FP. When she doesn't understand something, I help her. In the afternoons she goes to APANDA , where she receives speech therapy. I *(go)* also in order to explain to her what we have done in the

Instituto (the hearing school), and thus to be able to explain away the uncertainties she has. When we go to some place, to the movies, for a walk, she comes with me and with my (girl) friends. The television enchants them and especially if they are subtitled films, also she enjoys listening to the radio.

Family of Pepi Sánchez
Antonia at left, Josefa front

The persons in class, they deal with her very well, because they say she is an agreeable, obliging person. She enjoys talking with Cued Speech, although in the Instituto it would be *(considered)* shameful to use it. We will enjoy ending the two years of the Administrativo and three of the Informática in order to put ourselves to work in a company, although my sister wants to remain to work at APANDA.

That which she enjoys most is to buy herself new clothes and be all day seated in front of the television set. On Saturday afternoons we go to Mass, because we are in the choir, and later we go to Confirmación. When we read or write something, the teacher of Confirmación explains that which is to be done, for example: if we read in the Bible, he says look for the page and later look for the sentence that she has enjoyed the most.

We have a little brother, who is always with her in order to, when she doesn't understand something that they have said on the television, explain it to her. She wears two headphones, although there are times when she takes them off, because she says that they bother her. If she is far away and you call her, there are times that she hears you (when she is wearing fitted headphones). There are teachers that when we are in class, place themselves in front of her so she can read their lips and understand better.

In my home we all use Cued Speech, but in the Instituto, the teachers do not know Cued Speech. *For Josefa's ideas, see p. 589.*

For Josefa's ideas, see p. 589.

Anne Henegar Huffman
older sister of Leah Henegar, 1992

Looking back I can see that Cued Speech made our lives as

normal as could be with a hearing-impaired family member. Of course, when you're a kid and you just want to fit in, you don't want to do anything to stick out in a crowd. Therefore it was a constant battle for our mom to remind us to cue all the time so Leah would know what was going on. But eventually we all came to appreciate the importance of sharing every aspect of daily life with Leah, and so we didn't mind the stares we got from people when we interpreted for her in church or at the movies. CS allows a literal word-for-word translation, not paraphrasing. So, we could convey pronunciations, slang, jokes, etc.

Growing up in a family of five kids, we always had someone to play with and occasionally fight with. And Leah had to deal with her share of good natured teasing from her siblings. We still don't let her forget the goofy "cat-eye" glasses she got or her attempts to sing the opening theme to the "Love Boat" TV show. We also laughed at her when she said she wanted to be an actress when she grew up. But she's had the last laugh after appearing successfully in several local theater productions. Cued Speech allowed Leah to attend public school along with the rest of us. I always thought how sad it was when I heard about deaf kids being sent to special schools.

There was a real advantage to me, as a sibling, to being exposed to Cued Speech at an early age. I don't remember actually having to sit down and learn it. I picked most of it up from watching my parents and doing it, much like we learn to talk. It becomes second nature.

Jane E. Dolan
younger sister of Leah Henegar, July, 1992

I believe that growing up with a deaf sibling taught me to be a more compassionate person and much more understanding of those with disabilities. There were times that I resented having to interpret an entire television show or for a whole roomful of people.

When I was much younger, it felt like a great big burden to have to be Leah's "ears" for her. However, looking back I realize how difficult it must have been to rely on others for the things we take for granted. Feeling isolated and left out is a feeling that hearing-impaired people are quite accustomed to. I hope that I at least helped to alleviate some of those feeling for Leah as she was growing up.

I always felt that being a Cued Speech family made our family extra special. It was like we had our own secret language that no one else knew. I drove the kids and teachers crazy in school when we could talk and they wouldn't know what we were saying. Not to mention that I always had the perfect subject on which to write term papers. The teachers were always so impressed and intrigued by my visual aids that I got A's.

Leah and I shared a room for 17 years. Cued Speech enabled us to have a normal sibling relationship, from sharing secrets to clothes to heartthrobs. We even had the usual verbal fights which sisters are famous for.

I am very proud of the independent and well adapted woman that Leah has become.

Kimberley Johndrow
Scott's older sister, 1991

I have an 8-year-old hearing-impaired brother who I wouldn't trade for the world. My family and I started cueing to Scott about five-and-one-half years ago. I was then 9 and Scott was 4. I was very excited about learning Cued Speech and I picked it up very easily. At the end of the week (*Gallaudet CS Family Week),* when it was time to leave, I could cue anything I wanted; all I had left to do was pick up some speed and fluency by using it more.

When we got back home, we used Cued Speech all the time with Scott and we haven't stopped yet. The speed and fluency of cueing came very quickly and Scott now understood everything we said, unlike when he was just lipreading. Now I could cue anything I wanted to him and I did. We joked with him and he understood so much that he started joking back. I taught most of the slang words I used and he picked them up and used them too. With the cueing he has become as normal as any other kid his age, and probably smarter.

The response I get from kids at school is very positive toward Scott and the cueing. Everyone wants to know what I'm doing and how they would say something to him. Scott sometimes is very shy when people he's not familiar with start cueing something to him. But most of the time he is very patient and waits for them to cue it right to him.

With such a good response I get not just from the kids but adults too, I feel very comfortable cueing in public. For instance, in eighth grade in a concert, I sang in the chorus. While I was singing I cued all the songs, and Scott got a lot out of it, lots more than if he was just sitting there and I wasn't cueing.

I've found cueing to be reward to both Scott and me, and Scott has gained so much from it.

In May, 1992, Kimberly Johndrow received a graduate degree in deaf education from Smith College. Much of her training was at the Clarke School For The Deaf. For Scott's own ideas, see p. 567.

David Johndrow
Scott's older brother, 1992

I am a 12-year-old who has a deaf brother named Scott. We started cueing in 1978. Cueing has helped my brother so much these past years. Since we learned to cue, it has been easier to make conversation with Scott. In 1979 my sister Kimberly became an aide that helped one of the cueing teachers (*at the Gallaudet CS Family Week*), and in 1981 I became one myself. When I'm cueing to Scott and people walk up to me or anyone in my family and asks what I am doing, I always feel proud. My friend Peter Watts and my brother get along real well so my friend Peter is trying to learn to cue.

Aine Clements (12)
Sinead's older sister, 1992

Being a sister to a deaf person isn't easy, and I never could have done it without my parents to teach and guide me.

But being deaf doesn't make Sinead different from any other of my friend's sisters. She and I still get in fights and share secrets. The only difference is that I get more exercise from walking up and down stairs to get her instead of yelling.

I think Cued Speech is an important tool for speech and reading for deaf people. The only thing that frustrates me is that people always assume that my family uses sign language, and when I tell them we use Cued Speech they say, "What's that?" I would like people to become more aware of Cued Speech and know about it, and stop assuming that deaf people are limited to sign language for their communication.

Sinead is a person to me, and I don't exclude her because she's deaf. It angers me that people don't consider deaf people, such as in

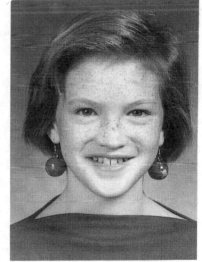

Aine Clements (12)

movie theaters and on TV shows that aren't captioned. That especially makes me angry, because some of my favorite television shows aren't captioned!

Because there's no way Sinead can understand what words are being said in a movie, she constantly shouts out questions all through it. "What's that man doing?", "Why is that woman doing that?" and more persist at my family from Sinead's little mouth.

As you can see, Sinead is as normal as any other person. She has her habits and faults. She's not considered different because she's deaf in my book. *For Sinead's letter, see p. 575; case history, p. 556.*

Betsy Robers
September, 1991

I'm Betsy, Gina Robers' younger sister. I am 14 and go to Colerain High School. This letter will be hard to write but I'll do my best to give you the information you need.

Betsy Robers

Gina is in eighth grade and is 15 years old. Physically she's older than me but mentally I'm older than her. I've always had trouble in that situation. My mom and dad would tell me "Gina needs your help!" But if I told her what to do they would say "She's older than you, don't tell her what to do." It got to the point where I didn't want to say anything to her because I was afraid I would get yelled at.

If Gina and I got in an argument, when I would say something, she would close her eyes so she wouldn't understand what I was saying. My mom would laugh and Gina would think it was okay to do that. I once closed my eyes and covered my ears with my hands. She got mad just as I did but my mom wouldn't laugh at me, she'd yell at me and tell me to listen to Gina.

Gina has trouble with her homework so my mom helps her. My mom takes 2 hours sometimes more just helping Gina with her homework. She always has time for Gina. If I ever need help I'll ask my mom and her reply usually is "Not now I'm busy. I get so confused wondering how she has 2 hrs to spare for Gina and not even 10 minutes for me.

My best friend is also a good friend of Gina's. Gina would invite her to her birthday party. We all have fun together. Sometimes I will be invited to a birthday party of a girl from my school. I would of liked to go for once without Gina. One out of every 10 parties I was invited to I would go alone. Gina didn't bother me but she sat and watched everything going on. A few times, I asked to go alone but my mom argued and Gina came anyways. I didn't mind her going to see a movie with me or going shopping but whenever Gina was invited to a party, or to see a movie, or to the mall with a friend, whatever it was, she had to go alone. I wasn't aloud to go. It made me mad sometimes that she had to go places with me but I couldn't go places with her.

I love music and I hum a lot, I was just humming now and Gina told me to shut up because it bothers her. My mom laughed so Gina figured it was funny and said it again. Every once in a while Gina will be tapping or stomping. If I tell her to stop it because it bothers me mom tells Gina she can keep doing it.

Gina can be fun to play games with and we have had good times. Overall, I like having Gina for a sister because I learned everyone is the same. At school I'm the one who doesn't rate people on their looks, money or I.Q. I judge them for the person inside, and if more people did that, the world would be a better place. *See also p. 221.*

Trisha Robers
Gina's older sister, 1991

Having a sister that is deaf is an experience I know much about. I am 19 years old and my sister is 15. We are like most other sisters our age. We are very close and would do anything for each other and as most sisters we have our days when we fight.

Gina was born deaf so I don't know her any other way. She is a normal 15 year old in my eyes. She does all the things other 15 year olds do. She is always on the phone (TDD) and goes shopping with her friends. She is also into boys! Gina has a very funny personality and likes to make people laugh. She tries very hard in school and likes to play volley ball after school with her teammates.

Gina and I have a close sister relationship. She will come to me with any problems she has and usually lets me know if anything is bothering her.

Not everything is "peachy" in our lives. Gina can get very frustrated with her school work and other things that hearing kids can learn much faster. Gina is very smart and tries very hard but she has to work ten times harder than other kids in her class.

I also get frustrated when she has a million questions to ask me.

I sometimes forget she doesn't hear everything going on around her and needs to ask so many questions.

I want to help Gina in any way I can. She has inspired me very much in my life. I've learned to acquire patience with every thing I do. I've also learned to be thankful for every thing in my life. Our family is very close and I think Gina has made all of us realize how much we need and depend on each other.

I am also going into a career of nursing in hopes to help other children with disabilities and help their families through many of the same experiences myself and family have been through.

Kimberley Perry Griffith
sister of John Perry, 1991

He had the biggest, bluest eyes I'd ever seen against fair skin and blonde hair. He was always very alert and quick to notice the slightest of movements in his line of vision. He laughed and squealed, babbled and yelled. He was very interactive. But he wouldn't always turn around when I called him.

I was forever running after John and physically stopping him to prevent a sure fall down the steps or a broken china piece. I couldn't just yell "Stop!" If he could see me, he understood perfectly what "no" meant, and his blue yes would sparkle as he continued with his actions to spite me!

I was 9 years old when my parents informed me that my younger brother, John, was hearing impaired. I don't remember ever feeling any particular emotion at that time. I'm sure I understood that he couldn't hear well, but I didn't comprehend what this meant in terms of his development. I remember overhearing fragments of the long "what to do now" discussions between my parents. I remember my mother appearing sad and my father appearing gravely concerned.

While my parents made all the pressing decisions regarding amplification, therapy and educational services, John was still John to me, hearing or not hearing, and I went about as usual. I remember thinking that it would be interesting to watch him grow. Since my other brother was just a year younger I didn't have the same opportunity to consciously observe his maturation. Little did I know how greatly I would be affected by this conscious observation of John's development.

The first step in treating John's hearing was fitting him with hearing aids. He arrived home one day with a small box strapped to his body, with wires connecting from the small box to ear plugs stuck in his ears. I was informed that these would help John hear better and that they had to be kept on him throughout the day. That was quite a challenge considering that he didn't appear to like them in the least. He would try and try until those ear plugs popped out. My mother would quickly insert them again. This "game" continued non-stop throughout the day. Eventually the entire family learned how to test the operation of the aids, put them on John, and change batteries. As long as John was around us those hearing aids stayed on his little body. When he was out of our sight he expressed his independence and dislike by removing them and disposing of them. Oh, the places a two-year-old child could find in getting rid of a hearing aid!

One day John came into the house without his hearing aids after being outside playing with neighborhood friends. Immediately the search party was organized, well rehearsed from previous experiences. The neighbors checked their houses and yards and brought in their dogs. We were told that time was a major concern because dogs have a strange attraction to hearing aids. The neighborhood children were promised monetary rewards for any "finds." A body aid has many parts: the receiver or small box, the connecting wires, the ear molds, and the batteries.

After about an hour, most of the hearing-aid parts had been recovered. The parts had trailed up the street, stretching across half the block. The receiver was the most difficult to find, because John had buried it under a neighbor's bush, three houses up the street. Burying was apparently a new technique that made the search even more challenging than usual.

Along with John's hearing aids came my first realization that hearing impairment could limit him. When John wore his hearing aids I noticed how he made more vocalizations, and he even turned to my voice sometimes when I called him. There were a few times when he couldn't wear the aids, mostly when water was involved. Of course he couldn't wear the hearing aids when swimming or going to the beach. It was at those times that I observed how John's friends had to alter their behavior to include him in their play activities, using series of gestures to show how to play the game, constantly tapping him and turning him to get his attention. I guess I had used these techniques all along, but didn't think about them until I saw others doing the same.

I remember John being very unhappy with going to school at about four-and-a-half years of age, though he had been in school since age two. It was about this time my parents decided John needed something more visually clear in order to learn more language. So, we investigated the possibility of Cued Speech. I remember going to Gallaudet University to learn Cued Speech with my parents. I was twelve years old. Mother says it took me only a few hours to learn it. I remember it was difficult at first to get John to watch me or wait for me to get the cues out.

I always thought of John's hearing impairment as making him special. I was proud of him, and once I learned to cue I cued everything to him. I'm still proud of him. I remember that once Cued Speech came into our family, things calmed down a lot and were less stressful. I know it helped me be a better sister and teacher to John. And, of course, it influenced my ambitions and my career, since I am now a Speech-Language Pathologist.

Beth Goodall (12)
sister of Matthew, 1991

My parents told me you wanted to know about me and what it's like to have a deaf brother. Well, here's a little about me. I attend Fredericksburg Christian School and I am in the 7th grade. This coming summer on August 3rd I will turn 13. I am very excited about the prospect of becoming a teenager. I *love* animals and I enjoy music. I play the piano. I am quite short for my age and i have long currly brown hair.

Beth Goodall (12), 1991

Now, Sir, I will tell you what it is like, in my opinion, to have a deaf brother. Many times it is frustrating. Sometimes when I'm depressed I'll tell myself my parents love him more than me. I sometimes feel like he gets his way because they pity him. Deep down I know this is not true. My parents love us both very much.

Matthew sometimes makes funny remarks, and not so funny, too. For example, I will be cueing to him and he will turn away when I am in the middle of a sentence. Exasperated, I will poke him trying to get his attention. He in turn becomes frustrated with me for annoying him. I'll say, "Matthew, listen to me when I am talking. I was not finished!" He will say something like, "I can't listen to you. I am deaf!" This is quite upsetting. Sometimes I give him a little kick or scream, but nothing more than a regular sister would do. I realize we should avoid fights and lately we've been doing good at that.

Sometimes while he is in class he will make a funny remark about his disability. I think this is quite strange. For example, if the teacher says, "Class, would you please quiet down. I'm trying to listen to Matthew!" Matthew might say, "Yes teacher, I am trying to listen to you, too!

Often I ask God, "Why did you let this happen to us? Don't you know it hurts enough?" The Lord gently answers, "My child, lean on me and I will give you the strength and the courage to handle this day by day, a little at a time." I know he will assure us, and give us grace, for it is only by his love and grace that we can survive the difficulties of life. I look at my brother and I realize what a blessing he is. I thank the Lord that he spared his life when he had meningitis. I put my trust in the Lord, for tomorrow is in his hands. *See also p. 47.*

Cory Fasold
brother of Brett, 1991

I will be glad to tell you about growing up with a deaf brother. First of all, it can be a real pain in the neck, like you said! It is also very challenging. My brother was announced deaf after a battle with meningitis when he was 18 months old. At that time I was 4. I didn't know what deaf meant, but I soon learned. My parents and I then decided to learn Cued Speech. I didn't have much trouble learning to Cue. I learned the real easy words (like no, go, and my name) very easily. The rest of the sounds and words took time to learn, though. Probably at age 6 or 7, I was a pretty good Cuer. I could Cue most of the words I wanted to and talk to my brother no problem.

When my brother first came home, it was weird to me that he couldn't understand me or talk back to me. I finally started to understand that he would probably never hear me again.

He didn't start to bug me until he could talk and make fun of everything I did. That was when he was 8. He started to grow up and bugged me to death whenever he could. That isn't just with deaf brothers though. I think every brother does that. But when you're deaf like my brother, he could make fun of me, and then turn his head and ignore me. He couldn't hear a word I said, so that kind of makes him invincible.

He isn't all bad though. He can be a lot of fun (sometimes), though most of the time he is bugging me. He can still play games and do all the stuff anybody else can, he just can't hear what is going on around him.

He is good at sports. Some of them are fly fishing, skiing, soccer, and karate. He likes to build things and do fly tying also. He doesn't go to deaf school or anything like that, instead he goes to a regular school with hearing kids and he has a lot of friends.

Brett also does very well in school and gets A's and B's. He also does real creative work. He loves to read books. If he starts to read a good book, he will sit there and read it until he is done, even until midnight.

Now I am 14, and he is 11. He still does all the same stuff he used to do. He does real well in school, is very active in a lot of things, but he still bugs me, and I think he always will. *p. 412, p. 571.*

Leah Diffell (12)
younger sister of Joy Diffell, 1991

When Joy first came in 1983 I didn't know what it would be like to have a deaf sister. I thought it would be similar to have a hearing sister. In many ways Joy is like a hearing sister, but in other ways not.

Joy is caring, fun, she's a good cook, ironer, and a hairstylist. She likes to do my hair such as today. We're dressed alike from head to toe. We sometimes play games together, which is always fun except when we get in fights, which is unusual. We mostly play scrabble or card games. Joy doesn't like to bake or cook, but she's good at both. And of course she's a good ironer because she does it every day. Although she dreads ironing. Joy is very good with her hands so she does a wonderful job with hair and sewing. She also enjoys painting shirts in her spare time. I enjoy having Joy as my sister and I feel God put her in this family—for a good reason.

Joy can also get on my nerves though. Often we have to explain things to her which takes a long time, and I hate doing it. Joy can also hit hard probably because she has hit me so many times (because I get on her nerves). I also do not like playing games with her when my friends are over, and my mom wants me to. But most of the time her answer is "NO." Sometimes I wonder what it would be like to have a hearing sister, but I wouldn't trade Joy in a second!

I guess all of the youngest in a family likes to be with their sister/brother when they have friends over. I do that to Joy, but she lets me be with them for a while. So to answer your question in a quicker form "What is it like having a deaf sister"? My answer "Hard but fun."

In a TDD conversation in which I (Cornett) suggested that Joy watch a certain movie on videotape, but have someone to cue to her whenever she wanted to stop and get an explanation, Joy indicated that

Leah would do it. She commented: "Leah is very patient with me."

Growing Up On Cue
by Earl Fleetwood, brother of Alisa, 1992

As a 10-year-old, like most hearing persons I was unaware of the far-reaching effects of deafness. But my 1-year-old sister, Alisa, was soon to influence my otherwise comfortable, naive perceptions.

After discovering Alisa's deafness, my family was quick to move from Vicksburg, Mississippi. They were anxious to leave behind the "She'll never talk" attitude of the local formidable professionals. They were wary of those who lower expectations as a means of redefining success, and clear in their understanding that in order to achieve freely in society, Alisa would have to answer to its requirements. The expectations of her family would have to serve as a clear window to the demands of the world.

In accord with those basic beliefs, Alisa was placed in an oral/aural preschool with other 2-and-3-year-old hearing-impaired children. This choice of methods was made with the understanding that if she were ever to compete successfully in the hearing society she must have the tools of communication and functional literacy with which that society judges success. Otherwise, she might live her life isolated from and angry at a society that perceives deafness in oversimplified terms.

Alisa's early years were devoted to speech therapy and auditory training. Speech lessons didn't end with the speech therapist. They continued at home, at appropriate times, and she acquired a sense of accomplishment as she implemented what she had learned. Auditory training was an ongoing process, too. Stimulating her to use her residual hearing was done through family exchanges such as "Listen to the phone ring!" and "Is someone knocking at the door?" Over the years these activities progressed to include more difficult discriminations until, eventually, Alisa could use the telephone to take simple messages.

When Alisa was 8 years old she was placed in a third-grade mainstream classroom with hearing children her age. Her skills at reading lips, using her residual hearing, and speaking clearly were now being tested in circumstances more typical of hearing society in general. Each time she entered this environment was a growing experience for her family. Progress and problem areas were carefully examined. It became apparent that Alisa had numerous gaps in her perception of spoken English (noun/verb disagreement, elimination or substitution of prepositions, number/mass noun errors, etc.). We continued to work with her in these areas, pointing out her errors, reviewing the rule(s) of spoken English she had violated, and supporting her each time she implemented a correction.

In hindsight, it is apparent that we were addressing her errors one incident at a time. This would not remedy the problem at its source. Alisa had internalized spoken English just as she had perceived it—ambiguously and inaccurately. Consequently, she was performing below the standards of the society with which she must compete. Those standards would not change. An alternative approach was needed.

As Alisa concluded her fifth-grade year, our mother enrolled in a class at Gallaudet University. There she learned a system that would present spoken language in unambiguous form: Cued Speech. As Cued Speech provides a visually distinct model of the meaningful units of a spoken language, **as it is spoken,** it allows the deaf viewer to internalize a clear model of the spoken words. Consequently a deaf person can speak, speechread, read, and write a familiar language, not an ambiguous one. So, it appeared that Cued Speech could close the language gaps that persisted in Alisa's perception of spoken English.

It was agreed that Alisa would use Cued Speech for six months. At the end of that time the family would discuss its benefits and detriments. During this time her progress with Cued Speech and her personal enthusiasm for its use became obvious. Early evidence of its value was her reaction: "Oh *that's* how you say that word!" Her vocabulary grew so quickly that she soon spoke like a well-versed politician, though still with some of the ambiguous English structure she had internalized prior to our using Cued Speech.

Twelve years have passed since our family first began to experience the benefits of Cued Speech. Consistent use of Cued Speech with Alisa eliminated many of the misperceptions acquired during her language-formative years. Inconspicuous prepositions are no longer misplaced or overlooked. When Alisa cues expressively her hand acts as a motor reinforcement for her speech production, which improves her already relatively clear speech. For 12 years she has seen spoken English without visual ambiguity.

Alisa has finished a baccalaureate degree with a major in accounting, and has a job in that field at the Harry Diamond Laboratory. It's nice to watch her conversing freely with people—not isolated, not angry. With the tools to challenge a competitive world, her potential seems unlimited. And if she can truly achieve without excuses, without exception, then in 20 years my family must have learned something that society already knew: deafness is nothing more than an inability to hear.

Earl Fleetwood is now co-director of the TECUnit, affiliated with the National Cued Speech Association (see Appendix). Raymond, Alisa's other brother, spent a year in Thailand as a live-in Cued Speech tutor/transliterator for a 12-year-old deaf boy, Seth Foreman.

A few years ago Alisa suffered an accident which destroyed most of her residual hearing and caused severe tinnitis. This interference with her ability to perform orally was a severe setback, but she has managed to cope with it. She began taking courses at Gallaudet University in order to experience deaf society, then finished her degree there in accounting. She is now employed in that field. See also p. 321.

The Role of Hearing Peers

The expansion of Cued Speech exposure to include hearing peers is essential. A productive summer activity is the scheduling of cueing parties or picnics for the children of the neighborhood, with refreshments, games, and (most important) cueing lessons and activities. Many cueing games can be devised to make learning a pleasure. Such parties can produce a cadre of hearing friends who will cue with the deaf child at play, include him/her in social activities, and even transliterate for him in appropriate situations. All this will contribute to both social development and language growth. Of course, many hearing peers, will not follow through and learn to cue. Many will.

If you attend a house of worship, don't overlook the opportunities available there. Teachers of church or synagogue classes may be willing to help a deaf child by learning to cue. Hearing peers may learn to transliterate in Cued Speech for the deaf child. Or, a sibling may be allowed to enter the deaf child's class in order to transliterate. The best option, of course, is for someone to teach the whole class to cue, 10 minutes or so each time the class meets.

Learning to cue can do wonders for hearing children whose auditory-conceptualization skills are limited and whose reading progress is thereby limited. *Auditory conceptualization* is the ability to identify and formulate mentally the individual phonemes of spoken language. Approximately 10% of hearing children are deficient enough in this skill to cause serious interference with their learning to read (p. 59).

Until he or she becomes a good speechreader, Cued Speech transliteration is the deaf child's clear link to people in general. If possible, it should extend to situations in which parents are not present. A brother or sister who habitually transliterates what hearing peers say in the deaf child's presence expands the child's circle of friends and increases the probability that some of those friends will learn to cue.

After a deaf child is 8-to-10 years old, the role of hearing peers can be almost as important as that of hearing siblings, especially if the deaf child is mainstreamed in school. Acceptance among his hearing peers is essential. That acceptance can be little more than token acceptance if it does not include the opportunity for clear, easy communication, the formation of lasting friendships, and healthy give and take. Hearing-impaired children, like all of us, need companionship, communication, and interaction with many people. Parents can help them in many ways to develop friendships with their peers.

During the preschool years parents should be aware of the need to cultivate their deaf child's relationships with neighborhood children or preschool and day-care classmates. Children are not likely to learn to cue much before the age of 4-to-6 years; but if the home is made a "fun" place where children can play together, there can be a beginning. "Q-parties" are fun for preschool children, who can enjoy games, refreshments, and learning to cue a few words and short sentences at each such party. CS parties can be even more effective for older children. Children of elementary-school age respond well to encouragement to cue. They can be taught intensively without destroying the fun.

The formation of a Cued Speech club (CS club, Q-club, cueing club, or I-Q club) in the school is an effective mechanism for promoting good relationships with peers. If the school has a special program for gifted children, the problem of finding a time for a group of hearing children to learn and use Cued Speech is relatively easy to solve. In many cases, the teacher in charge of the gifted children is looking for projects that will challenge them, particularly projects related to human values. Most gifted children pick up Cued Speech very quickly, and they have the confidence and assertiveness to take the lead in establishing communication and friendships with deaf children. Also, teachers who are looking for extra activities to occupy the gifted children are usually receptive to the idea of their helping, explaining, or transliterating for a deaf classmate.

Leah Henegar had many cueing friends of all abilities in elementary school. Leah's resource teacher, Ros Efron, conducted entertaining cueing sessions for Leah's mainstream class for 15 minutes at the beginning of each day for the first several months of school. All learned to cue to some degree, and 10 or 12 became proficient enough to constitute a group of communicating friends for Leah.

Jennifer Ziebell relates an example of peer support:

> *In fourth grade one of Colin's friends, Zack, joined Colin's class in learning Cued Speech. In a short time he became a fluent cuer. He could help out the transliterator and assume her role when she was out of the room. When our school board met at the school for one of its rotating meetings, there were tours for administrators prior to the meeting. The assistant special education director got Zack as a tour guide. Colin followed along, and a gentleman noticed Zack cue something to Colin. He asked Zack how much he could cue. With a puzzled look on his face, Zack replied: "I can cue EVERYTHING!" The next morning I got a call from the gentleman. He felt he had to call because he was so excited about the incident with Colin and Zack. He said it nearly brought tears to his eyes, and his final comment was: "This is what mainstreaming is all about!" Because of their ability to communicate, Zack really got to know Colin. He commented to his mother that the kids at school just didn't realize how smart Colin is.*

When Paul Swadley was mainstreamed in third grade at age 9 his teacher, Rosemary Davis Arnotts, learned Cued Speech and used it for everything she said that he needed to understand. She taught the members of the class to cue, and some of them became quite good at it. A CBS-TV news segment, shown nationwide in 1978, featured the use of CS by Paul's teacher and classmates to provide an effective mainstream educational environment. Paul had a cadre of hearing, cueing friends all the way through public school. When the family moved to Williamsburg, Va., Paul continued to have the benefit of cueing classmates. Some could even substitute for his transliterator when necessary. Paul received a bachelor's degree in mass communication from Virginia Commonwealth University in 1992.

Janie Abell writes:

> *Following your suggestion, I went to Holly's intermediate school every morning before school started for only 15 minutes to teach about 25 "volunteer" students. Within two months or less, they knew how to cue. They especially liked chants, songs, and cheerleading yells.*

Scout troops and other peer groups are also possibilities for development of peer support. There are cases in which a deaf child's interest in a specific area for which his school had a special club was accepted into the club and received peer acceptance and cueing support.

As a deaf child enters the teen years, peer support takes on vital importance. The foundation for it, however, needs to have been developed years before. The child who has not had cueing peers is likely to become self-conscious about being hearing impaired, may ask parents not to cue to her/him in public, and may exhibit signs of stress and frustration. All this will be minimized if the youngster has had cueing peers and/or siblings all along.

Early in their child's school experience, parents should initiate a dialogue about peer support in school. They should outline to school personnel what they plan to do at home about peer support, and what they want the school to do. This should fit in with their dialogue with school personnel about all other aspects of their child's educational program. They should try to get provisions for peer support into their child's IEP (Individualized Educational Program).

School personnel should be alerted to the fact that exemplary support for a deaf child by a hearing peer should be recognized as an appropriate factor for consideration in the choice of recipients of school citizenship awards and other forms of recognition.

Some deaf children, even with cueing peers, may become frustrated as early teenagers at not being able to keep up fully with social interaction. They may complain about missing some of what happens, not understanding the jokes, or being "left out." This is very likely with deaf teenagers who are a year or more behind their hearing peers in language. What should be done depends on the severity of the problem. Such youngsters should certainly have an opportunity to learn signs and interact with signing deaf youngsters to see if this helps.

Statements by Hearing Peers

Laura Hill (13)
Cousin of Michael Poore, 1992

Cued Speech has opened a whole world for my cousin, Michael. When I was 7 I learned how to cue so I could understand and communicate with Michael. Now I interpret and help people understand Michael and Michael to understand them. Just last summer our whole family was at my grandma's house in Florida. My aunt and I would sit across from Michael and interpret the whole conversation. Now that's pretty good with 17 people talking, some at the same time. We made it though and I don't think we could have done it without Cued Speech.

We rode on Wave Runners and Michael drove a golf cart with the use of lip reading, and he understood almost every word of my uncle's directions. I believe Michael will go far in life thanks to Cued Speech. He wants to be a plastic surgeon and with his determination I believe he will. I feel very lucky being related to Michael. Every year I get closer to him and more understanding towards him. Thank you for this gift that helped Michael learn English and helped us communicate together so well.

Michael's mother commented that Laura's use of "kid" language with him has benefitted him greatly. See also pp. 219, 513, 573.

Bruce Wellman, 1987

Nonchalantly I strolled into the first day of photography class. Like a typical *(high-school)* senior, time was not my major concern. I walked through a sea of staring underclassmen eyes to take my seat in the back of the room.

As I was sitting down, I noticed that two eyes, those belonging to the boy sitting next to me, were watching my every movement. I said, "Hi," and he responded with a nod and a slight wave of his hand. After sitting down, I whispered over to him, "So, what grade are you in?" No reply. Obviously this new underclassman did not realize that I, the "big senior," was talking to him, so I gave him a slight tap on the shoulder and repeated my question. He turned towards me shrugging his shoulders, shaking his head and gesturing toward his ears. His face held an apologetic expression.

This boy wasn't merely shy; he was deaf! I immediately shrank back into my seat, not knowing what to do next. This was the first time I had ever met a deaf individual.

After a brief pause, I gathered courage to again tap the boy on the shoulder. I grossly over-enunciated: "Do—you—read—lips?"

By the boy's blank expression I knew the answer to my question was, "No," or at least, "Not very well." Realizing speech would not work, I grabbed the nearest pencil and paper—hoping to pursue a written dialogue. I scribbled out my question, "What is your name?" He replied in a slightly slurred but very distinguishable, "David."

After a few exchanges, David's interpreter walked into the classroom. Her arrival took a load off my shoulders. My burdensome communication, plagued by a slow rate and numerous spelling errors, was replaced by an indirect but more fluent line of communication.

Over the next few weeks I assumed the role of tutor for David.

Being a second year photography student, I was experienced in every area of photography David would need to know for the class. He was extremely motivated so my only challenge was to find the right approach, the best words to allow David to perceive the ideas that I was attempting to convey.

As the year progressed, I learned enough sign language to enable me to give instructions without the interpreter present. I became more concerned with David's progress than with my own projects. I received all the gratification I could ever want when I saw (and I will never forget) the expression on David's face when he brought his first print from the darkroom, into the daylight for viewing. Gleaming at his creation, he looked like a new father showing off his first child.

Bruce Wellman

Soon David and I began to spend time together outside of photography class. At lunch time, I would sit with David and his deaf friends. Their conversations were totally in sign language. I was only a passive observer, never an active participant in these conversations of motion. I began to feel frustrated. I realized my "sign vocabulary" was limited to photographic situations: "Too much light," "Try a different exposure," "Maybe the picture isn't focused." My sign language was far from productive, greatly limited in its expressive capabilities. I wasn't even able to tell David things like, "Your shoe is untied," or "I hope you feel better tomorrow."

Searching for an alternative form of communication, I approached David's interpreter during our next photography class (the interpreter, I learned, was David's mother). She informed me that, although David knew sign language, his truly native language was English via Cued Speech (*which she was using*). Cued Speech? She went on to explain that Cued Speech is an augmentation to lipreading: a visualization of the "unlipped" sounds. A man by the name of Cornett had developed a system of distinct handshapes to be used simultaneously with speech. This system enables the deaf individual to differentiate between sounds that look identical on the lips.

It all sounded so complicated! However, within a few minutes she had taught me how to cue about 30 words. I grant you, these words were totally unrelated to each other; still, they had only taken about five minutes to learn! The same number of "sign words" would have taken about an hour to have learned with a much lower retention rate. Once I could master this cueing system, I would be able to cue any word in the English language—no matter how long or crazy the spelling. If I could say it, I could cue it!

After about two weeks of 15-minute "cueing sessions" immediately after school, I was fully acquainted with the entire Cued Speech system. Once I learned this system I needed to work towards increasing my accuracy and speed. Through routine practice I found myself cueing everything I heard: songs, commercials, weather reports.

One day I mustered enough courage to try cueing to David. Slowly I cued, "Can—you—understand—me?" When David quickly nodded and replied, "Yes," an incredible feeling of accomplishment overwhelmed me. Before I could continue I needed a few minutes to pull my head from the clouds. Starting again, I gradually cued more and more sentences, resulting in our first real conversation.

Suddenly it was if a door had been created where a window once stood. Before, I had been only an observer who received second hand information about David's personality. Finally I had acquired direct access to David's personal opinions, concerns and questions! With the barrier removed, our acquaintanceship molded into true friendship.

This was in 1987. Bruce Wellman became a Cued Speech transliterator and sign interpreter, serving various deaf students, and simultaneously finishing his bachelor's degree in general science at Penn State University. He is now (1992-93) doing graduate study in deaf education at the University of Rochester. He is a hall director for deaf students at NTID/RIT, where David is enrolled. See also p.310.

Kim Stitzinger
Elena Beadle's Hearing College Roommate

Dear Elena,   May 12, 1991

Thanks for letting me stay here with you! Not too wild a time, but then it's nice to have a break, eh? Hopefully you, Dave & I will all be feeling much better by the time you read this! Let me know about the 25th (oh yeah—the 27th is Memorial Day, so Dave & Jeff may have it off—maybe we could stay longer! Whatever—let me know!

Now that the excitement of graduation is over, there are a few things I'd like to say. First of all, I'm so happy that we were "assigned" to one another our freshman year. I've learned a lot from you—about *actually* studying, about perseverance, about friendship, about being neat (although I may not practice it myself!)—in general, I guess about life. We've had a lot of good times together (*really* good times) and we've had some bad times (*really* bad times). But through it all we've emerged the best of friends.

Kim Stitzinger and Elena Beadles

I don't really think of you as my best friend—I care as much about you as I care about Kerry & I know that I would do things for you that I would do only for my sister. I think that some of the other friends that we had in college will fall out of touch in the years to come, but I am confident that you and I will always keep in touch and remain close. In a way, it's sorta funny, isn't it? We're seemingly so different—who would've known that we would've become so close?

Elena, sometimes I have to remind myself that you're deaf. I just can't believe it sometimes. That's why I think I just take how well you've done in school for granted. I think it's just hard to imagine how I would've handled being deaf & in college. (I hope that I would've been like you, but how can you really know until it's you, y'know?) I really couldn't imagine *reading* my math & science books—ugh! But you really made it look so easy! You should be so proud of yourself because it was hard. I'm proud of you—but you know that. I don't know what I'm trying to say here. I think I want to say that I'm in awe of what you've done. Yeah, I guess that's it.

Well, enough of that. Hope you had fun in Florida & that you aren't so tan that I can't catch up on the 25th! *Case history, p. 467.*

Chapter 17
Starting With an Older Deaf Child

When Cued Speech is started with an older child, progress should be more rapid than with a young child because of any existing communication and language base (gestures, signs, oral language, written language). There are two serious problems in starting with an older child. First, for older children less time remains for making up existing language deficits. Second, the child is likely to have picked up and habituated incorrect language and speech patterns that will impede progress.

We are using the term *older child* to designate a child who is beginning exposure to Cued Speech enough after the optimal period from birth to 3 years, that significant adjustments in the way CS should be introduced are necessary. Children receiving Cued Speech consistently from the age of 2 years typically make up any existing language deficit by the age of 3 to 5 years and are ready for reading at the usual time of 6 or 7 years of age. Children starting at 3 years with little or no language can usually make up the deficit by age 6 if conditions are very favorable.

The problem for language-delayed children 4 years old or older is that of enabling the child to acquire language competency adequate to serve as a base for reading, speechreading, speaking, and writing, *in the time that remains before these abilities are essential in school.* A 4-year-old child whose language is at the level of a hearing 2-year-old needs to make up a two-year deficit in two or three years. This has been accomplished with many Cued Speech children, but it requires concentrated and consistent effort on the part of the family, and support in school if the child attends preschool. A 5-year-old child with a two-year deficit will almost certainly be pushed into reading with less than an optimal level of language, and techniques for accelerating language development will be needed even after reading has begun.

What often helps with older children is that such children will probably have a receptive language base of some kind—signs, gestures, sight words, or lipread words and phrases—that can be paired with spoken words through Cued Speech to produce very rapid acquisition of verbal language. Bright children who are severely language-delayed at this age because of earlier use of a method that has turned out to be inappropriate for them often achieve spectacular progress in a few years of exposure to Cued Speech, closing the language gap fully.

A child 6 years old, with severely delayed verbal language, must endure four to six (or more) years of intensive remedial effort. The miracle is that children as old as 8 or 9 years, with vocabularies below 50 words, have closed the language gap, through their own abilities and motivation, and the patient, consistent cueing and remedial support of parents and teachers. The case histories below will illustrate.

A two-way approach is usually best for beginning Cued Speech with a deaf child 5 years old or older. CS should be taught through whatever language, in any form, that the child already knows. Insofar as is possible, this should be done through unstructured communication about familiar things, with much pairing of language between Cued Speech and the language the child already knows (signs, gestures, anything). To speed up language acquisition, Cued Speech should also concurrently be taught analytically, as a system. This entails teaching the cueing of specific syllables and systematic coverage of all the handshapes and hand locations. This process can be expedited by use of large drawings of the handshapes set up for convenient use. These are included in several of the kits available, such as those of the Cued Speech Team at Gallaudet University (see Appendix, p. 751).

In order to boost motivation, the child should be exposed to cueing in natural situations, such as the communication within other cueing families. Interaction with older, experienced CS students is also likely to help.

All children are different and may require different approaches. In older children the differences are greater than in young children, since the differences in their inclinations and abilities have had time to grow. Parents and teachers must let the child's reactions and progress guide them in how to proceed. With an older child one can capitalize on greater maturity, ability to work at assigned tasks, and greater stamina. When CS is begun with an older child, it is likely that prepared materials can be used to advantage. However, it is important to find materials appropriate for instruction at the child's language level that are also suited to his/her interests. Some older children will accept materials designed for much younger children, others will not.

Begin At The Right Level

Parents should begin on the child's level. At home or school, or both, the child has developed some competency in communication, using natural gestures, signs, picture language, written language, speech, speechreading, and combinations of these. He or she should be approached through language already understood. Remember that every concept for which the child has an identifying symbol (gesture, sign, written word) is valuable, because 1) he/she already understands the concept and thus doesn't have to be taught it; 2) he or she knows a symbol that can be used to pair it with its equivalent in Cued Speech. This means that the more language (in any form) an older deaf child already knows, the more rapidly he or she can pick up or be taught language through Cued Speech. Of course, the conversion process is most rapid for any written language he/she knows.

Gesture or picture language can be converted into verbal language by associating each gesture or picture with the verbal equivalent in speech and cues. A parent who indicates *school* by symbolically clutching the handle of an imaginary lunch box should continue use of the gesture, but first say and cue *school*, before the gesture is used to confirm. After several uses, the spoken/cued symbol will be internalized and the gesture or picture can be dropped. One can easily test the child's understanding by delaying the gesture a bit to see if the child understands without it.

For students with an aural/oral background, simply add cueing to make the oral message clear. Understanding should increase rapidly since there is no change of language to bring about, only clarification. For children with a formal signing background, cue with speech, then sign or fingerspell, then repeat the cued form. Of course, this method applies only to items already familiar to the child in his manual modality. Do not introduce new signs. Late starters who are delayed in language cannot afford bilingualism at this point.

Teaching the System Analytically

Progress with an analytical approach will be enhanced by prior speech training resulting in the ability to make many of the speech sounds, by prior knowledge of a good many spoken or written words, by a substantial vocabulary of signs, or by familiarity with many words in fingerspelling. In other words, any language skills will help.

Karen Koehler-Cesa has produced the first volume of a set of manuals for use by teachers with older deaf children who have considerable knowledge of written language. An accompanying student workbook is also available. Pamela H. Beck has written a guidebook, *Discovering Cued Speech*, with a learner's workbook, an 8-hour program and a six-hour competency review. She has also written *Kids Discovering Cued Speech*. Both are designed for use by teachers, but are usable by parents. Mary Elsie Daisey's *Cued Speech Instructional Manual*, though designed for use in teaching CS to hearing people, can be used in teaching older deaf children. For descriptions and information on price and availability, refer to the Appendix, p. 758. Parents may find these and other listed materials helpful.

Pair Cued Words with Written Words

An older child may have a very useful base of written language even if his or her concepts of spoken language are erroneous and even more limited. This comes about because teaching verbal language through the written form tends to be the universal "fall-back" method for a child who is not making satisfactory progress in acquiring English through either oral or manual methods. Children who have learned to write notes or fingerspell when someone doesn't understand them have at least a limited foundation of written language to build on. They have probably passed the prime period for simply absorbing language from unstructured exposure to it, usually extending from 18 months to 5 years of age. Such children will need a program for formal, structured language instruction, along with exposure to CS communication providing unstructured opportunities for language absorption.

Keep in mind that securing rapid language acquistion through pairing known written words with spoken words through Cued Speech can last only until the child's existing vocabulary of written words is "used up." Then emphasize teaching new language with Cued Speech through the usual methods of discourse, discovery, explanation, interaction, games, and presentation of formal lesson materials.

For children who have some competence in written and/or spoken language, including some knowledge of speech sounds, it is recommended that Cued Speech be taught (in part) in terms of syllables. Parents may well proceed in a manner similar to their own initial instruction in Cued Speech, but substituting written symbols for the sounds. They can use Funetik Speling or the phonetic symbols used at the child's school, such as the Thorndyke symbols or the diacritical markings in the dictionary used at school. Single syllables can be introduced and practiced conveniently by writing each one on a separate flash card. Then they can be coupled for practice in cueing syllables and simple words. Further suggestions may be obtained from the child's school, from others who use Cued Speech with older deaf children, or from the service centers listed in the Appendix. Materials for making flashcards are included in several of the manuals listed in the Appendix. Also in the Appendix are instructions for use of Funetik Speling. Syllable flash cards (in Funetik Speling can be utilized in cueing activities that are highly enjoyable for the child.

An underlying reason for teaching analytically as well as through unstructured exposure is that it is essential that the older child learn the complete Cued Speech system as soon as possible, so that new language encountered in unstructured discourse can be perceived accurately and learned readily, both at home and at school.

As the child begins to make rapid progress in language acquisition through Cued Speech, it is critically important that speech therapy be used for the twin goals of developing speech production and tying all new language to speech as it is picked up through Cued Speech. There is a desperate need also to develop use of residual hearing as a base for speaking and for aural/oral reception.

Older Students with Very Little Written Language

For older students who have a very limited grasp of written language and speech sounds, it is recommended that a teacher or parent follow the basic suggestions for a young child in Chapters 6 and 8. However, be cautious about using with older children activities and materials suggested there that are not in keeping with the interests of older children. In some cases, however, materials and activities designed for young children can be adapted to the interests of older children. Many of the activities described in Chapter 10 are interesting to older children. Some of them are almost "age proof," appealing to children over a wide range of ages.

Every possible means (short of making the child feel pressured) should be employed to get the deaf child to cue when he or she expresses himself/herself in speech. Particularly helpful will be activities in which all the family members participate, such as reciting funny sayings, short verses, or short prayers. Older children cannot tolerate as much of a gap between receptive understanding and expression as a young child can. The repetitiveness of verses, sayings, songs, and short prayers supports understanding and ties expressive and receptive communication together.

It is easy to develop a common misconception regarding what can be expected when Cued Speech is begun with older deaf children. In most cases such children will learn Cued Speech much more rapidly than younger children, so that within a few months they can repeat accurately anything that is said to them with cues (assuming that they can make most sounds). This does not mean that one can immediately carry on a fluent conversation with them in Cued Speech, until and unless they have a good knowledge of spoken language. Conversational ability will develop as Cued Speech helps the children acquire language. The beneficial effects on reading ability will begin to be apparent much later. Frequent administration of language tests is needed to monitor progress.

The Need For Accelerated Language Development

Profoundly deaf children who start Cued Speech late, at ages such as 5 to 9 years, are usually severely delayed in verbal language. If this were not the case the parents would probably not consider a change. As soon as such children have learned the basics of the system they should be exposed in school to an intensive (two or more hours per day), structured program for accelerated language development, conducted or guided by an expert in remedial language development who can use CS, and who will guide parents in their support of accelerated language development. An excellent program is that in *Language Development and Language Disorders*, by Lois Bloom and Margaret Lahey (1978), New York, John Wiley & Sons, 689 pp. Barbara Lee, of Baton Rouge, La. has developed a program for accelerated language development in hearing-impaired children, based on the Bloom & Lahey approach to language development. Titled *Sounds to Sentences*, it will be available in September, 1993. Meanwhile, Ms. Lee will be glad to provide information and guidance to professionals and parents interested in adapting the Bloom & Lahey materials for use with hearing-impaired children. Contact her through NCSA. Ms. Lee started using and refining her adaptation in 1980.

Simple arithmetic attests the urgent need for accelerated language development in a child who starts CS late and is several years delayed in language. If a 6-year-old child is three years delayed in language, he needs to learn language approximately twice as fast as the average hearing child in order to close the language gap in three or four years. The miracle is that this can often be done. If progress so rapid as this cannot be attained, the progress that can be made is still well worth the effort it requires. If the language gap is small, it can often be closed in a few years. If it is larger, closing it will require longer or may not be feasible. The case histories in this chapter will illustrate a range of possibilities.

The choice of a program for remedial language development should depend upon the language levels and other characteristics of the children involved, and on the staff available. Most such programs are better adapted for use with a group of children than with a single child, since they involve modeling. However, modeling can be supplied by a teacher or a helping adult, if necessary. Language-delayed children should not be pushed into reading until their grasp of language is adequate. Even then they should be spared, insofar as possible, the task of trying to read language that is not easy for them to read. Thus, for language-delayed children, time is better spent at developing language than at trying to teach them to read. Ways to encourage reading without prematurely pushing it are discussed in Chapter 15.

Sustained Effort Is Necessary

Children who start Cued Speech at an early age and have the appropriate support in the home and at school during the early years usually become self-propelled learners who require less and less tutoring at home as time goes on. This is less often the case with children who start Cued Speech late, particularly if they do not close the gap in language and reading levels. Parents of late starters must remember that they must not ease up, either in providing support or in fighting for needed support at school, as the child grows older. Barbara Lee says to parents:

> When the child is mainstreamed in kindergarten, *don't relax*. When the child is in the early grades, *keep up the support.* When the child is in junior high and high school, *resist the temptation to take it easier.* And, if your deaf child goes to college, don't think you can escape the need to continue providing *whatever help is needed*.

As one parent reviewer points out: "The results are well worth the effort." Also, there are exceptions. Some late starters make amazing progress and become self-propelled learners within four or five years, reducing the load on the parents.

The progress of late starters depends a great deal on how well the program of instruction at school and the support at home are adjusted to fill the gaps in language. Much depends also on how well the children are protected from futile efforts to learn through unassisted reading when they are not yet capable of doing it. They must receive systematic help until they have the language needed for normal reading.

Chapter Summary

Although progress should be more rapid with an older child than with a younger child, two serious problems should be recognized. First, for older children less time remains in which to make up any existing language deficit. Second, the child is likely to have picked up and habituated incorrect language and speech patterns that will impede performance.

When starting Cued Speech with a child 5 years old or older, parents and teachers must balance a number of factors, including the amount and kind of language the child knows. Specifically, if the child knows a lot of signs, these should be used to accelerate the learning of spoken words through Cued Speech by using them to indicate the meanings of words. If the child knows a substantial amount of spoken or written language, tying that to the cued presentation will accelerate the mastery of Cued Speech itself. Prepared materials can be used, if they are selected properly.

Beginning at the child's language level, one should use direct exposure to the cued message in association with specific objects, situations, and actions, just as with a very young child. Concurrently, however, the Cued Speech system should be taught analytically, particularly if there is some base of oral language. The urgent need for accelerated language development should be given the first priority. So-called academic subject matter should take a back seat in favor of language development. For language-delayed children, time is better spent at language development than at trying to teach the child to read. Because an older child is likely to have been taught a good number of written words, these should be paired systematically with the spoken words through Cued Speech.

Support at home is essential. Parents should arrange their schedules so as to be able to communicate with the child as much as possible, in settings that contribute to language development without seeming to be an extension of the school day. The task of furnishing language exposure (in Cued Speech) should be spread among the members of the family as much as possible.

Experiences of Parents Starting With An Older Child

There are many cases in which a late starter has made up most of his/her deficiencies in a few years and has thereafter performed on a par with most early starters, and thus with children with normal hearing. Some are included in this chapter, and some are included in other chapters because their experiences are relevant there also by virtue of special problems or circumstances.

There are others who, though not necessarily late starters, can be described as slow starters who made modest progress for several years, then accelerated sharply. Finally, there are many who kept plugging away and eventually reduced substantially their originally severe deficiencies. Additional summaries of the experiences of parents who started Cued Speech with an older child, usually very deficient in language at the start, are given in Chapters 20, 22, 23 and 24.

Jeff Maslin
by Mike Maslin
From *Cued Speech News*, December 1982

I first heard about Cued Speech from an article that appeared in *Parade Magazine* in February 1978. Jeff, our profoundly deaf child, was six years old and in a TC program. My wife and I decided to see what it was all about, so we went to Gallaudet University for a three-day workshop. When I heard Dr. Cornett speak about Cued Speech, it made a lot of sense. When I started watching the videotapes, it was very hard for me to grasp the hand shapes, and my arm hurt. The first day was so long. We sat in a little room, watching the tapes (*5 side, 3 mouth, 5 chin,* etc.) Then we were given a tape recorder and a voice tape of more lessons on cueing. This went on for two more days. I kept saying to myself, "I can't do it." "I'll never get this." Finally, I stopped cueing and went back to signing with my son. I felt comfortable with signing, but my wife kept on cueing to Jeff.

About a year later, I was still signing and my wife was cueing to our son. He was doing both very well! I noticed that when he and I were signing, he didn't use his voice the same way he did with my wife. His speech therapist also said when he was in speech class, he would try to use his voice, but in his classroom, where they were using Total Communication, he would drop his voice and just sign. I wanted him to learn to speak as well as possible. I noticed my wife and Jeff work together at home. He was trying to use his voice with my wife. Jeff was now 7 years old, and doing well in school and with his playmates. His speech was still not getting any better in everyday use. I knew he could do better, as I heard him using Cued Speech with my wife. In May of 1979, we made plans to attend the August Family Learning Vacation. Before we left I made up my mind to do it, because I could see the results of my wife's work with Jeff.

When we arrived at Gallaudet, I met some parents that we had met at our first three-day workshop. When they told about the progress their daughter was making, I was even more determined to learn how to cue. We also met many other parents who had been using CS with great success. All I could think about was these other kids who were cueing and how well they were doing. The rest of the evening we socialized, and the main topic of conversation was our children: at what age did they lose their hearing, what caused it, what method of communication were we using, what was your school system doing, and how did you learn about Cued Speech? The next morning we all met to hear Dr. Cornett and then were assigned to a class, so that we could learn at a rate that would not totally confuse us.

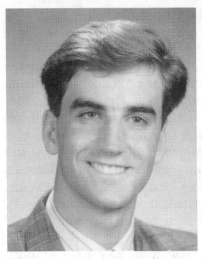

Jeff Maslin

This went on all week: listening to talks about Cued Speech and how it was working with different people throughout the world, then back to our cueing classes. At the end of each day we would meet in the dorms and talk some more and get to know each other.

On Wednesday afternoon there was a trip to the Air and Space Museum to see the movie *To Fly*. My son was sitting next to me and asking questions about the movie. I was trying my best to cue to him about what was happening. When a large herd of antelope ran across the screen, he grabbed my arm and said, "What are they?" I cued *antelope* to him and he said, "What?" I checked myself and cued antelope very slowly. He said, "Antelope." I realized he had never seen that word before, and I did not know the sign for antelope. At that time, I could really see the benefit of cueing. All I had to do was to practice and pick up speed. I would then be able to say anything that I wanted to him by cueing.

When we got home, I took advantage of many opportunities to improve my cueing. We put the cueing chart on the refrigerator, so that we always knew where it was and could check to see if we were doing it correctly. I also put a chart by my phone in my office. Many of my telephone conversations became very slow. I would take the tape and recorder in the car with me and practice on my way to and from work. I would also cue the road signs.

Jeff is now 10 years old, in a regular fourth-grade classroom, with a teacher who cues. He is on grade level in everything but his expressive language, which is improving. He also has a difficult time with reading comprehension, so he receives supplemental help in that.

Jeff is very interested in current events. It has been easy to tell him about the hostages in Iran and about the assassination of Sadat because we were able to cue. I can also talk to him freely about football games and explain the plays as we watch them on TV. Prior to baseball season we were able to discuss who was being traded and what teams we thought would do well. Jeff is an active participant in sports and can converse with his hearing friends about their games.

Even now, when cueing, my fingers will sometimes get mixed up, and Jeff will often correct me. This shows he is paying close attention to what I am saying. It takes practice, practice, and more practice; but it does get easier as time goes on, The only gap Jeff and I might have now is a generation gap, not a communication gap.

A Mother's Observations While Father Signs
by Janeane Maslin

When I started to cue to Jeff, and Mike was still signing, we had entered a transitional stage without realizing it. Since Jeff had been on Total Communication, he just seemed to think that cues were different signs. We would use the sign for something and then give him the cues. Mike was comfortable with signs, but I was not. I always felt frustrated because my signing vocabulary was so limited.

Jeff started to use cues more and more and became able to talk to me using cues. If Mike couldn't say something in signs, I would cue it, or he could cue it if he did it slowly. It never caused any arguments, and I never thought he was wrong for not using cues. He was doing what he had been told by the professionals was the best for our son. Mike's use of Cued Speech just seemed to evolve. He discovered that eventually it became easier to cue, simply by being an involved father who wanted to converse with his son. Within about a year Jeff was completely on cues. We were both using cues consistently and had taken Jeff out of the TC program and mainstreamed him.

There have been many ups and downs during the years, and we have often questioned our decisions. One thing in which we still remain confident is our decision to use Cued Speech.

Update
by Mike Maslin, 1991

When we say time flies, it really does. It seems like I just wrote the article for *Cued Speech News*. It has been nine years and so much has happened. Jeff is now 19 years old and in his second year at Western Maryland College, in Westminster, Md.

Throughout elementary and high school Jeff had a Cued Speech interpreter. As Dr. Cornett had said many times, just cue it the way you say it, and the child will understand. Well, he was right. Jeff's first interpreter was from Puerto Rico and spoke with a Spanish accent. The next one was from our home town. His last interpreter, who was with him for five years, was from Tennessee and spoke with a southern accent. As you can see, he was exposed to different variations of English. Also, while in high school he had two years of Italian and did very well, getting all "A"s and "B"s.

Jeff progressed through school totally mainstreamed, with no major problems. I guess you could say that any troubles he had were mostly age related and common to other teenagers. When he graduated from high school he was in the top 25% of his class of more than 700. He was the only student in the entire school system on Cued Speech.

While in high school Jeff earned two varsity letters in soccer and four in swimming. Swimming and baseball were also important to him during his younger years. Fortunately, he was a good athlete, and being a part of these teams was instrumental in expanding his social life. For the past five summers he has worked as a lifeguard at a local swim club and has coached the swim team for three years. Now that he is in college he is on the swim team and was selected outstanding freshman team member last year.

In my opinion, Cued Speech was the tool that gave Jeff the ability to communicate with his teachers, coaches, peers, and society. It isn't always easy, but if you set your goals high and persevere the results speak for themselves.

Amy Hurowitz
by Lois Hurowitz, 1992

Amy's case is remarkable because as a very late starter with CS she was essentially on grade level in language. See p. 626.

Amy was diagnosed with a severe-profound sensorineural hearing loss at the age of 2 years. She was raised orally and educated in that method until it was time to enter third grade.

We were introduced to Cued Speech in 1976 and started an investigation to learn about its benefits. The final decision to use the method came after a week-long Cued Speech workshop at Gallaudet College. Actually Amy, at age 8, made the decision. She loved CS and started mimicing the hand movements. While this occurred, Amy's speech slowed down and became much more intelligible. She didn't know the cues yet, and already they were helping her!! As her parent I realized by this time that Cued Speech did not distract her from the oral philosophy I held. So Amy entered the third grade in Montgomery County as a CS student.

As an older child using Cued Speech, Amy was exposed to a CS transliterator every day in the school setting. Some lessons were also presented to her, but I believe the system was assimilated mainly through daily exposure. I supported the process at home by using CS as an educational and language-building aid—for the introduction or clarification of new vocabulary words, work on spelling words, words that were confused on the lips, and words that were hard to pronounce. These are but a few examples. But I saw little frustration during this time. She liked the cues and must have been getting some reinforcement from them during this learning stage.

Amy brought a lot of language skills to Cued Speech—she was on grade level and doing quite well in school. I decided to use CS, not because Amy was failing, but because she was succeeding, and I wanted that success to continue. As an oralist, I knew the hard road ahead for both parent and child to prepare to live in a hearing world. I chose Cued Speech so that the road would be easier and the outcome would be successful. It has not failed us.

Amy remained fully mainstreamed throughout the public school years in Montgomery County, Md. She learned how to adapt to the changing classes in junior and senior high school; she learned about the ethical and educational duties of the transliterator; and she learned how to ask for information from the teacher when applicable. Amy learned that she had a responsibility to learn the best way to use her transliterator—not only to get the educational information from the teacher but to understand what the classmates were contributing, and thus to get the whole classroom environment in the learning process.

Amy was successful in getting the information and in studying her lessons. She graduated with an academic and social record that was good enough for acceptance to several top-rated colleges and universities in a mainstream setting.

Cued Speech has given Amy more than academic success. We believe that it has also helped her use her lipreading skills and develop better speech. This in turn has enabled her to live in a hearing world. Amy has successfully held down several responsible jobs that require speech. Even though the innate ability exists, we have no doubt that Cued Speech contributed to the success.

Amy is now attending the Rochester Institute of Technology and is actively involved in trying to get CS transliterators in the classrooms.

It appears to be an uphill struggle, but we both will do all we can to achieve the goal. The responsibility and battles for an oral/CS student can be demanding not only in the hearing world but, as we are discovering, in the deaf world as well. But I know that Amy agrees with me that being independent and functional in both worlds is well worth the effort. We thank Cued Speech for helping us along the way.

Louis Truett
by Freda Truett, Feb. 1991

Louis was prelingually deaf, always beyond equipment limits. At age 9, after years of exposure in an oral program, he had a vocabulary of approximately 25 words, with no intelligible speech. He is now (1991) on grade level (ninth grade) in advanced honors classes, taking a foreign language (Spanish), in which one-third of his grade is dependent on taking part orally in class. He has a Cued Speech interpreter but no other resource help. He participates in competitive athletics and seems very well adjusted to being the only deaf student in a large hearing high school. He is part of an exceptional group of hearing peers. Some cue to a limited degree.

When this mother began using Cued Speech she moved to Louisiana to put Louis in Barbara Lee's exemplary Cued Speech program in which the Bloom/Lahey curriculum for accelerated development in English was used. He made tremendous strides. After a few years she was able to move back to Houston and put Louis in mainstream classes with a Cued Speech transliterator.

Certainly Louis is very bright. But, despite this, he was unable to learn English through oral methods. He probably would have learned sign language or signed English with equal ease and speed, but with Cued Speech he learned English as his first language, through Cued Speech. He acquired English at a rate several times that of the average hearing child, making up his total deficit in five or six years.

David Sharp
by Eleanor and Richard Sharp, 1992

My husband and I first learned of Cued Speech in 1978. At that time our deaf son was 8 years old with the expressive vocabulary of an 18-month-old child. We read about a Cued Speech workshop being offered in Washington, D.C., and attended it in August 1978. It was there that we not only learned about Cued Speech, but realized that our situation was not a unique one. It was the norm for prelingually profoundly deaf children to have very low language abilities. Could the use of Cued Speech cure these language deficits and fill in all the gaps?

After more than 10 years using Cued Speech we can unequivocally reply "Yes." Even though we started cueing to our son at a later age, Cued Speech allowed him a "natural" growth of learning. It enabled us to fill in those gaps by increasing vocabulary and concepts never dreamed possible. We were able to let language flow without teaching every little word. We were able to use idioms and expressions that most deaf children never experience. There were no restrictions on what we could say. The important factors we had to remember were to cue accurately, consistently, and copiously. The successes we experienced confirmed our belief that Cued Speech works.

Persuading other parents to learn about Cued Speech was not an easy task. However, we managed to win the support and interest of four other families in our area who are still using Cued Speech with their hearing-impaired children.

We also met with school districts reluctant to provide the services we requested. We had to be persistent and often demanding when the goals we had set were in jeopardy. After much frustration with our school district, we decided to move where the services our son needed could be provided. Although I would not recommend this route for everyone, it was a welcome alternative for us. There were many adjustments. The move entailed new schools and friends for all four of our children at a time in their lives when friends were a priority. Finding employment in an economy that was at risk even then was difficult. Living at such a distance from remaining family in a different culture was not comforting. When the opportunity arose to move closer to home we seized it and met the challenges at hand. At this time we were using Cued Speech at home, of course, and in high school it was used on a daily basis. The school situation was unusual in that I (his mother) was the Cued Speech transliterator/interpreter. There were advantages to this that outweighed the disadvantages.

The four years (from 1986 to 1990) that our son spent in high school were very productive ones. He now attends a college where Cued Speech is not furnished. Once again we have encountered reluctance, but there is a bit of hope. Other students with Cued Speech backgrounds are attending this college. They also are living testimonies to the success of Cued Speech. We hope that some day CS will be recognized by all educators of the deaf for its contribution to the development of hearing-impaired children and young people.

Parents should not have to contend with the many adversities we faced in educating our son. With all the success of kids using Cued

Speech, and with all the research evidence now available, the educators should be more willing to use this tool when parents request it. We have been let down so often by school district administrators and educators that most parents in similar situations would have given up long ago. It is not difficult to understand why our educational system is in trouble when we have encountered such unwillingness to cooperate with our son's need for Cued Speech when positive results from its use were so very evident. It seemed to us that the school personnel spent more energy fighting Cued Speech than in trying to learn more about it.

Yes, we have been discouraged along the way—but never discouraged about Cued Speech itself. The content we felt in watching our son become a genuine member of the family and a successful member of society was well worth the price we paid.

We believe that hope for the future success of Cued Speech lies in our children and their willingness to support it as adults. We hope their voices will be heard to a far greater extent than those of their parents have been heard. *See also story by Bruce Wellman, p. 293.*

Jeffrey Majors

Jeffrey was started on Cued Speech at age 8, with about 25 words and no signs, according to his mother. His reading and language scores are now above the hearing mean. See p. 628 for Jeffrey's own observations.

Colin Ziebell
by Jennifer Ziebell

Colin's command of language was well beyond his 22-month chronological age when he lost his hearing in March 1981. One anecdote illustrates the level of his receptive-expressive language when he was about 18 months old. I had given him a treat. When he was just about finished devouring it, he looked up and me and said in a very bossy tone,"You better get me some more again!" At that age he was consistently using three-or-more-word sentences.

Two months after Colin's hearing loss we started him in a TC program, using SEE. His first teacher of the hearing impaired had asked me to compile a list of his receptive and expressive vocabularies. She had been impressed when he had seen a picture on her desk and said, "Mommy, a koala." She had expected him to say, "Bear." I know she didn't believe me when I gave her the list, which consisted of 500-600 words. Cued Speech later allowed all that stored language to become rapidly accessible again.

We used SEE until late 1985, or early 1986, when we started Cued Speech at home. Colin was then "going on" 7 years old. He has a typical corner audiogram, with a 90 dB threshold at 250 Hz. and then a plunge off the chart. All along, the consensus of opinion has been that his responses are tactile rather than auditory. So, the prognosis as regards oral communication has never been good.

It's difficult to remember our start with cueing. It is so much a natural part of our lives. It's easy to forget that we didn't always use it. Anyway, I learned it through a friend. When I knew the system and felt somewhat comfortable with it, I just jumped in and winged it. At the beginning, I would mostly sign something, then repeat it in Cued Speech. I got so that more and more of my communication was just cued. If he was confused I'd clarify with signs. Naturally, we started simply and moved along as we were able to.

Picture books are good for one-to-one cueing. Also, it was easy to walk around the house, the yard, a mall, or wherever and cue locations or object names. The start can be simple and still build vocabulary very rapidly. This gives a good base for building more complex phrases and then sentence structures.

It wasn't long before I phased out the signing almost completely as far as input was concerned. Colin's father and brother continued to use signs, and his sister was just a baby. About a year later the school staff began using Cued Speech also. One real plus for us all was attending a family workshop at Gallaudet in the summer of 1985. It boosted our confidence and supported our gut feeling that our decision was right. My biggest difficulty was not very significant. As a signing mom, I had trouble with confusing fingerspelling configurations with those of Cued Speech. Fortunately, the problem passed, and I'd like anyone else who has the same problem to know it doesn't last forever.

Colin's father, Tim, has a different problem. He learned the system easily enough, as he had with signs. However, he is psyched out by the phonetic aspect. He just doesn't hear the difference between a short *e* and a short *i*, as an example. As a result, he does not cue. He signs some, but mostly just talks to Colin.

Colin's language level was delayed by at least two years when we initiated Cued Speech. He was 6 years old. He did have enough spoken, written, and signed language to form a reasonable base upon which to build. Focusing on the lips was difficult for him at first. He'd gotten away from speechreading much more than we had realized. All in all, however, the process of getting back on track was much quicker and less painful than we'd anticipated. At the beginning, there was naturally some frustration, just as there had been when he was introduced to signs.

Colin, Ashley, Jennifer, Timothy, & Brandon Ziebell

Cued Speech was not used in school until the fall of 1986. That year he was repeating first grade to close up language gaps before moving on. In some areas he was doing second-grade work. The first months of school after the switch were intense. When he would overload and tire he'd ask his teacher of the hearing impaired to sign rather than cue. Before the end of that school year he asked that she cue rather than sign. It was "gang-busters" from then on.

Problems with one's school district can be difficult. Many guard their programs as one would a new baby. Despite the illegality of it, many districts insist that a child fit their program rather than the reverse. This is more likely to be the case if one is a pioneer (as to communication methodology) in that district, or if one is switching from a sign system, or especially if one is adding Cued Speech as the primary tool for language input.

Cued Speech must be the primary tool for language input at home before a school district can or should be expected to implement it. If it is, then you have your reason for requiring the school district to use it with your child. Today there are numerous sources of statistical data that support the use of Cued Speech. Also, there is an abundance of data and research evidence of the dismal failure of other techniques in their attempts to develop language and produce literacy. Most deaf people are not functionally literate, and the methods used to educate them are responsible for this result. The fact that Cued Speech makes such logical sense doesn't hurt the cause, either. Besides, what has anyone to lose with it, considering the results with the alternatives?

Colin's progress at the start was outstanding. After eight months of consistent cueing at school as well as at home, he had gained 2.4 years on the Peabody Picture Vocabulary Test. In the following year he gained 1.1 years on that same test. Naturally, once his language level caught up with his age, his gains have come at a more "normal" pace. His most recent CAT scores for language and reading, except Word Analysis, ranged from 82 to 96 in the national percentiles. Last spring (1991) he was given the Test of Syntactic Ability. The test recommends retesting any weak areas. He had no areas of failure, but out of curiosity his teacher picked out the two lowest areas to retest. His scores for both sections normed against other hearing-impaired children put him at 19-plus years, age equivalent. The test uses I.Q. to norm against hearing peers. His scores normed this way were at 130-plus I.Q.

Yes, Colin is bright—but he always was! That didn't stop him from losing ground, falling behind hearing peers in language level. Unfortunately, the brightest child on the face of the earth will not be functionally literate if he is denied access to his natural language. In our case, that language was English. It's also the language one must be literate in to succeed in our society. Cued Speech was the tool that gave Colin access to this language.

Colin will read just about anything except "girl" stories. No Baby-Sitters' Club books for him! If context doesn't provide meaning, he asks for an explanation of a word or phrase. Science fiction, the strange and unusual, mysteries, and jokes and riddles are his favorite subjects. He reads brochures everywhere he goes, as well as the newspaper, magazines of every size and subject, comics, and much more. He'll attempt just about anything in print at least once.

Any child who reads and comprehends (as well as any of us can) the book of Revelation in the King James Version of the Bible has a fair command of the English language. One year at Awana Clubs at our church, he won the boy's award at his age level for the most verses memorized. Before Cued Speech we had tried it and quit after several meetings. We'd both leave in tears, and I just couldn't stand the hurt.

Colin enjoyed a French class more than his brother did. He enjoys words and phrases, and exposure to another language was just another fun experience with them. He enjoys all the fun you can have with words, such as jokes, puns, etc. He has a terrific sense of humor.

He attends the alternative school in our district along with his brother and sister. It allows many opportunities for his creative abilities. He is fully mainstreamed with a CS transliterator. A cueing teacher of the hearing impaired works with him about three hours each two-week period. This year she will help him to improve his organizational and study skills in preparation for junior high next year.

One of Colin's recent projects is preparing a sheet of paper for each letter of the alphabet. On each he draws upper and lower case letters, with a short alliteration for each, illustrating each alliteration. For example, the *B* sheet read: "Bouncing bobcats balance on beach balls and bounce blackberries and bat basketballs." He made mention on the *Q* page that it and *X* were very hard to make something up for.

It's wonderful for Colin to have all the words he needs to ask questions, express ideas, and have his curiosity satisfied. Before Cued Speech, he had the same head-full of questions and so on, but just plain didn't have the words to get them out. He'd be so frustrated, and we'd be in tears much too often. Now his frustrations are mostly those that any child his age is likely to have.

I quit teaching after Colin lost his hearing, so I was fortunate to have some time with him. Even so, he was in school numerous hours so our time together was the more precious. One of the beauties of Cued Speech is that, once you know the system, you can just communicate with it in a natural way. Once school personnel start using it the input is maximized.

Regarding signs and signing friends, there's not too much of a problem. We started with signs, so Colin is still able to communicate with that system reasonably well. If he doesn't have the sign for something, he can fingerspell it. With his hearing peers, there is a variety. Most don't cue or sign. One of his best friends is a fluent cuer, some cue a bit, some sign a bit, and some are able to fingerspell. The rest just talk to him.

Neither of Colin's siblings cues. However, we are ready to have them learn. Both are old enough and have the desire to learn. His 6-year-old sister is not totally confident with her short vowel sounds, but can manage well enough. His brother has been in the role of interpreter many times. The role of transliterator will be a natural one for him.

An anecdote: During the scandal regarding the duo, Milli Vinilli, a bit came on TV regarding their lip-synching. Colin, with a very disgusted look, said, "That makes me very upset. They're my favorite group!" Colin never elaborated on why he likes them, but since he is apparently limited to tactile perception of sound, I'm sure it wasn't their melodies that attracted him. I suppose that he was disillusioned by the fact that the visual performance which pleased him so much was only an accompaniment to the music that had been recorded by someone else. *For Colin's views see p. 580.*

Nabeel's Story
by Suhad Keblawi, 1992

Nabeel was diagnosed with a severe-to-profound hearing loss at

17 months of age in 1981. We immediately started him in the oral program in Fairfax County, Va. We hoped the oral approach would help Nabeel to use his residual hearing and his lipreading skills.

After two years in the oral program Nabeel didn't seem to have acquired any language. Communication was frustrating for him and for his parents. We decided to move Nabeel to the Total Communication program when he was 3½ years old. The family attended the Family Learning Program at Gallaudet University to learn signs during the summer of 1983. During the school year we took sign classes at night. Nabeel was like a sponge that was very dry and that could absorb water at a fast rate. He learned signs at a rapid rate and started to communicate in a short time. We were thrilled. The frustration level went down very quickly. We took the sign book everywhere we went, building Nabeel's growing vocabulary. He started to enjoy being read to and also began to recognize written words at an early age.

After about a year and a half of exposure to signs, Nabeel was demanding more information about a lot of things. We soon hit a snag in reading books after the initial success. There were many words in English for which there was no sign, and fingerspelling didn't mean much to a 5 year old. We didn't really want to make up home signs because they would not mean much to others.

Nabeel's father, Feisal, was president-elect of the Hear Nova parent organization in Fairfax County at that time. He went to a technology fair that was hosted by the organization, and there he met Dr. Orin Cornett for the first time. Dr. Cornett was explaining Cued Speech and displaying on videotape some of the children who had succeeded with the method. One of the children was a 4-year-old deaf child who spoke in two languages, but whose audiogram was worse than Nabeel's. That made an impression on Feisal. Dr. Cornett invited us to visit him at his home to see more tapes and to learn more specifics about Cued Speech. That was the spring of 1984, and we decided to try Cued Speech with Nabeel. My feeling at the time was: "Here we go again—trying another method."

That summer we went to Gallaudet University again, this time for the Cued Speech Family Learning Vacation. Then Nabeel was moved to the Cued Speech program in Fairfax County at the start of the new school year. He was placed at kindergarten level. At home we would cue to him, then give him the same information in signs. Eventually we stopped the signs altogether.

Nabeel did so well with Cued Speech that we never looked back. He proved Dr. Cornett's theory that deaf kids and the deaf in general should enjoy reading. Nabeel became an avid reader (*Don't miss the*

anecdote about Nabeel's packing for a trip in Chapter 15, page 259.)
Within two years, at about age 7, Nabeel was preparing briefings at
home (complete with posters and pictures) to explain to us about the
solar system and how volcanoes work. He called them "shows." He
demanded that the family should make time (30 minutes to an hour) in
their schedules to watch his shows together. They usually occurred
after dinner or on weekend afternoons.

Nabeel is a sixth grader now, fully mainstreamed with a Cued
Speech transliterator. You rarely see him without a book in his hands.
His interests range from fiction to science. He loves to do experiments
in chemistry and physics. He has also become interested in rocks and
minerals through reading and started a nice collection. He reads when
he is eating breakfast, and dinner if we allow him. In the car there is
always a book, a newspaper, or a magazine that he brings with him.

Now we are in the process of trying to arrange for Nabeel to
attend his neighborhood school—with, of course, Cued Speech
transliteration, speech therapy, and any other needed support services.
We never dared dream 10 years ago that this step would be possible.
Thanks to Cued Speech and Nabeel's hard work, we believe anything
is possible. *Nabeel's scores on standard tests are impressive. His PTA
threshold of 90 dB in the better ear has been steady for many years*

John Perry
by Jacquelyn Perry, 1992

John was born November 4, 1971, diagnosed as having a severe
hearing loss in 1974 (later as severe to profound at 4 to 5 years). He
entered the Fairfax County program for the hearing impaired in March
1974 and was placed in an oral program.

John was 5½ when we started cueing to him at home. He almost
immediately seemed to understand everything we said. CS appeared to
clear up a lot of confusion that comes with lipreading alone. He was
almost 6 when he began receiving cues at school, in September 1977.

Looking back now, we have no regrets—it was the best way to
go in raising a deaf child, and it eased things a great deal at home.
John was always a happy child. His participation in all sports gave him
a good self-image and boosted his confidence. Academically, he was
mainstreamed partially at first and then at grade seven was mainstreamed completely with a Cued Speech transliterator. This continued all
through high school.

Because of John's involvement with sports he always had hearing
friends—more so than deaf friends. Now, as a freshman at Gallaudet

University, he has friends who are deaf, though more oral than he and probably with more hearing than he. By the eighth grade John had made a choice for his sports career and decided on basketball, in which he has really excelled. He was accepted by four of the five colleges he applied to and would have played basketball at any one of them. He chose to attend Gallaudet and is on the varsity basketball team.

John usually maintained a C+ to B average, never really achieving his academic potential. I attribute this to poor test-taking skills and an early delay in language that never fully caught up, though when all is considered his progress was remarkable. John is a well-adjusted, happy kid who happens to be deaf, but who doesn't consider himself handicapped. With above-average intelligence, he is able to compensate for some academic weaknesses. He functions well in the hearing world, and now in the deaf world as well. We are very proud of his accomplishments and think he is a neat kid, too!

Cued Speech has definitely contributed to John's success. Beyond that it has helped us as a family to include John in all of our functions as a family unit. I shudder to think how excluded he would have been without it. I am sure there are families that can achieve this closeness through signing, resulting in the same kind of emotional and psychological benefits. However, through Cued Speech John's verbal language has developed to a level far above that of most deaf youngsters. He is an adequate but not avid reader, preferring the newspapers and, of course, everything connected with sports, as do many hearing youngsters. He can read what he wants to read.

When John was about 12 years old he played football for a local youth organization. The coach was very supportive and allowed Bill (John's father) to help out. One of his "chores" was to stand on the sideline with the coach. As the runner came out for plays to relay back to the huddle, Bill would listen to the play designation and then cue it to John, who was waiting on the field. This was neat because John actually knew the play before his teammates in the huddle!

We are grateful to the Fairfax County school system for its cooperation in providing what John needed, especially to his elementary school teacher, Mrs. Katherine Lovette Roed, who finally got John "hooked on reading"; to Mrs. Brenda Wall, whose speech instruction and pragmatics drills are still bearing fruit; to Dr. Donald McGee, whose support kept our Cued Speech program alive and well in Fairfax County, Va.; and to all of John's swimming, soccer, baseball, football, and basketball coaches, who allowed him the opportunity to achieve his athletic potential and the associated psychological benefits, while maintaining a respectable level of academic performance.

Looking at reality, John has done well linguistically and academically in the sports-oriented environment that he chose for himself. We feel Cued Speech was the central factor in making these successes possible. *For a sister's views, see p. 282.*

Joy Diffell
by Tom and Lisa Diffell, 1992

Joy came to us in 1983 at 8 years of age, from an orphanage in Korea, with no language or formal training. After much research of deaf education prior to Joy's arrival (and encountering no mention of Cued Speech) we, like many other families, embraced the philosophy of "Total Communication." While we were pleased with Joy's initial language development, it wasn't long before we realized that while we were building communication with our new daughter, her English language skills were not developing. Despite our immersion in deaf culture, in an attempt to keep up with Joy's rapidly developing sign language skills, we soon realized that we were falling hopelessly behind. This was in addition to the constant frustration of being unable to communicate English language idioms, and having to change what we wanted to say because sign language lacked the necessary vocabulary. Even Joy experienced the frustration of sign language's limited vocabulary.

At this time we were introduced to the concepts of Cued Speech by an adventitiously deaf adult, who referred us to Dr. Cornett. After a long telephone conversation with him in May 1983, our family learned Cued Speech from Mrs. Pam Beck and started Joy on her second and greater language explosion, an explosion that is continuing to this day.

Cued Speech allowed Joy to go in four years time from a day student in a residential school for the deaf to a fully mainstreamed fifth grade classroom in our local public school, with a Cued Speech interpreter. She has gone far beyond what anyone ever dreamed she would, given her background. Now, at 16 she continues to be a happy, resilient person who has given us no trouble of any kind. Mainstreamed in ninth grade, she does good work in school and applies herself well. She still has some language gaps to fill in, and she is aware of this.

Joy has a prelingual, bilateral sensorineural hearing impairment, with a PTA threshold of 107 dB in the better ear. Her scores on standard tests demonstrate that she is still learning language at an accelerated rate. Her reading-comprehension grade equivalent was 5.8

on the SAT-8 in May 1990, when she was barely 15 years old. In the next 18 months she gained 2½ grades in reading comprehension. She is well above grade level in writing, with a writing-sample grade equivalent of 16.9 (Woodcock-Johnson) and a broad-written-language grade equivalent of 13.0. Her broad-math grade equivalent of 16.7 and her applied problems (math reasoning) grade equivalent of 16.9 demonstrate that she is superior in mathematics. Among severe/profoundly deaf students she ranked at the 83rd percentile in reading comprehension, and the 97th percentile in language. Joy's weakest area is general knowledge, as would be expected from the fact that she has had only eight years in which to acquire general knowledge. Both this and her deficiency in vocabulary must be made up primarily through reading. She also has some remaining gaps in English patterns. *See also pp. 286, 597.*

Alisa Fleetwood
by Liz Fleetwood
from *Cued Speech News,* May 1981

Alisa is in the seventh grade and is mainstreamed in her neighborhood junior high school, where she has an itinerant teacher four days a week for 45 minutes per day and a full-time Cued Speech interpreter for her major subjects. She has been on the honor roll every marking period this year, and she has accomplished this with little or no tutoring from us after school each day. Things were not always that good for Alisa before we started using Cued Speech with her.

When we discovered that our daughter was deaf, we were living in Vicksburg, Miss. Art and I started researching the area to find a good program for Alisa. After checking into many areas and into both signing and oral/aural programs, we decided to move to Montgomery County, Md., where we chose their oral/aural program. We felt that learning sign language, like learning any new language (Spanish, French, etc.), would require of us a great deal of exposure to the deaf community, hours of study, and practice for years. Meanwhile our daughter would become fluent quite rapidly through use of signs in the classroom and with peer association. We therefore felt that we as a family could help her better through communicating with her through lipreading and good auditory training in English, the language she would have to use well all her life, the language her family used.

My husband and I felt that in order that she function in society Alisa, like most persons, must learn to become independent, must be required to handle responsibilities, and must know success and how to accept failure. She must learn to become the motivating factor within herself and try to work because she believes in herself. We both felt that no matter what parents try to teach children, no matter how long one wants to work with and help them each day, they will try and learn only if they are motivated by their own goals and their own sense of self-worth and accomplishment.

With the above in all our minds, Alisa started preschool at age 3. Through kindergarten she spent half-days with hearing children and half-days with hearing-impaired children in a self-contained class. Her phonic skills were excellent (despite her 105 dB PTA threshold) and she could pronounce many written words at 5 years of age, but rarely knew the meanings of them.

As Alisa progressed each year, and the language became more complex, we found we were pre-teaching and post-teaching her all the academics. This required about two hours or more each night after a full day in school and a two-to-three-hour bus ride. By third grade she was mainstreamed all day, except for one and one-half hours in the resource classroom for language help. She was struggling to comprehend the simplest of instructions. Her written and spoken language were lacking function words and contained wrong verb tenses, and her sentences were of the most simplistic structures.

By the fifth grade we could see that despite all our effort and also the effort of her two brothers, she still could not follow simple instructions, her language was poor, and her reading level was not improving. She was beginning to realize that, despite all her effort and hard work, she was not able to keep up with her peers. She was told by the teacher of the deaf that she was doing very well "for a deaf child." This was carried over to the teacher in her regular fifth grade class, and the inference that she wasn't very smart was quickly perceived by Alisa. This realization angered her, but it also started producing some doubt in her mind as to the validity of these teachers' impressions of her.

At this point my husband and I felt that we had better step back and take another look. We realized that although Alisa was bright, she was being taught the same fundamentals over and over again. We realized that she didn't need to learn things slowly, just clearly. Here was a motivated child who had received all the help possible at home and on many occasions had been used as an example of a "successful" deaf child by the school system, but who was still unable to keep up with her peers. Knowing she had the will and the capacity to do so, we decided to try to find a way to make Alisa "more oral" by giving her a clearer input of the spoken language. That was the beginning of our interest in Cued Speech.

I immediately enrolled in a course on deafness taught by Dr. Cornett at a local college. I spoke with him after class and discussed my concerns about Alisa's writing and her lack of interest in reading. (She never read for pleasure, since her language was so limited that she couldn't enjoy reading.) He asked me to bring a sample of her writing to class and, after reading it, he felt that Alisa could be in trouble if she didn't get past the third-to-fourth-grade reading level. He stated at that point that he didn't know how much help Cued Speech would be for a child starting out at Alisa's age (10), but that if I was willing to learn it and use it consistently, it might help significantly. He also invited Alisa to his home. He realized quickly that she was both bright and highly motivated. He decided to see if he could get her more interested in reading. He told her that when she read about something she could make "pictures in her mind," and those pictures could be like a movie of her own. She said she would try, and she did begin to think about what someone, something, or some place looked like. This did stimulate her enthusiasm and she became motivated to try to read more.

Alisa said that she would be willing to learn Cued Speech and try it for one year if we thought that she would acquire language more easily and would not have as much work to do after she got home from school. We had to agree that we would not cue in public since, having been raised orally, she didn't want to "look different." At this point I knew Cued Speech and was working in the Family Cued Speech Program of 1979 at Gallaudet College. Both Alisa and her brother came to the workshop and learned. Raymond became fluent in the use of CS within a week and has used it with her consistently ever since.

That fall, with Alisa's agreement to try a new school (the fourth since she began preschool), she entered North Lake Elementary School in order to be in a program which used Cued Speech extensively. She was mainstreamed in a regular sixth grade classroom with a full-time CS interpreter, and she received one hour of resource help daily from a teacher of the deaf who was fluent in Cued Speech. In the beginning there was an adjustment period during which she had to get used to using an interpreter and to being sure how much the cues were helping her. However, there were many instances of encouragement to her and to us. For example, when given a placement test in spelling using a list of 50 uncued words she had not seen ahead of time, she was placed in a fourth-grade speller, although she had always been a good speller when she knew which words she would be tested on so she could be lipreading from a closed set of words. When given the same test with cues she placed in a sixth-grade speller. That gave her the incentive to continue trying.

After about six months with cues the entire family began to see improvement in Alisa's ability to understand new language, and she began to express herself better. At that point her dad and her brother Earl decided to learn it and use it with her so that the entire family could give her the input that she needed. As the year progressed, she was needing less and less academic reinforcement at home. As a family we realized for the first time that the time it took for us to become fluent in cueing was nothing compared with the time it took us day after day and year after year to work with Alisa to get results that were far less productive than simply giving her clear input (via CS) to learn on her own.

By the end of sixth grade, Alisa realized that she was picking up new language that was making it easier to understand what she was reading, so she began to read more. She started using slang colloquialisms in her spontaneous speech and began improving tremendously in her ability to follow instructions. She even started letting us cue to her in public as she realized what she had been missing. She now has time to socialize with the neighborhood children, some of whom know how to cue. She can now grow and develop through the experience that her new language provides and the free time it affords her.

When Alisa was 2½ years of age we were told that a hearing aid would probably be of little or no value to her except for such sounds as a car horn, and that she would probably never have intelligible speech. Nonetheless, through all the struggles, we were strong in the belief that good and constant auditory training would help Alisa's voice quality, her pronunciation of words, and her ability to lipread better by hearing bits and pieces of sound. Through her own desire to speak more clearly and her strong determination to talk with her friends on the phone, she can now use the telephone to the extent that she can understand simple instructions and relay short messages. She is getting better and better in her ability to discriminate sounds. We feel that Cued Speech and auditory training complement each other, and that auditory training will always be an ongoing process in her life.

Now, as an employee of Gallaudet College, I find sign language valuable in my everyday communication on campus. Now that Alisa is comfortable with the English language, I hope that she will learn sign language in order to be able to communicate with people who sign.

Recently Alisa wrote a letter to a hearing-impaired girl close to her age whose family was considering Cued Speech. The following excerpts are from that letter: "I don't have enough experience to tell you how Cued Speech helps. I'll try to do my best.... It took a while of using Cued Speech (about one year) before I could tell it was really helping me....(*Now*) I really love it....My language was developing because of Cued Speech....Also, I speak well because of Cued Speech....Since you see the cues you can pick up a lot of language.... When I was in 6th grade, I started using an interpreter. The CS interpreter helped me a lot to know what was going on in class. I am in 7th grade now, and I have an interpreter in Junior High School. The work is not hard. It's much easier now because of Cued Speech....It takes a while to pick up new languages. Talking is important because you can have lots of friends....They can communicate very easily because I talk and understand them....You should try Cued Speech and try hard to pick up your new languages. That's all it's about."

This summer it will have been two years since we began using cues with Alisa, and life gets better and easier for her every day. I might add that it gets better for us too, as we have more time to spend with Alisa and the boys as parents instead of our all being her teachers. We have no doubt that Cued Speech was primarily responsible for Alisa's tremendous growth and for returning our family to a more natural routine. We believe that Cued Speech can be of help to many other families. However, we feel that other parents should study all the alternatives open to them and their hearing-impaired child and then follow what they believe in. They know their child better than anyone else and, more importantly, they need to help their children believe in their own potential.

Alisa's story is brought up to date in the article by Earl Fleetwood, beginning on p. 287, in which he writes from the point of view of a sibling. An interesting angle is contributed also by Alisa's science teacher, Helen Quave, in "It's O.K. to be Curious," pp. 693. Alisa now has a bachelor's degree in accounting from Gallaudet University and is employed at the Harry Diamond Laboratory.

Daniel Koo
by Hee Sue Koo, 1992

Daniel was born November 25, 1972 in Washington, D.C. He was our first child, and we were very excited to have a son. For the first few months it was not easy for me to adjust to a new life style as a full-time working mother. About a month after his birth I noticed he was scratching behind his ears whenever he cried. I thought it was unusual. His doctor thought it was probably an irritation from the shampoo that was not cleansed well. I thought this was unlikely from the way we bathed him. I am still wondering why he did that. Daniel was very quiet and did not babble at all.

When he was 3 months old we tried one day to wake him up to take him out. No response. We called his name louder, louder, and much louder, but there was not even a blink. So frightening! I brought this to the pediatrician's attention at Daniel's 3-month checkup. He didn't see any abnormality, and said it was too early to determine. It didn't convince me. At the pediatrician's suggestion, we took Daniel to Dr. Heller at Children's Hospital in Washington, D.C., and Daniel was diagnosed hearing impaired (bilateral sensorineural impairment) when he was 6 months old. Dr. Heller advised us that nothing much could be done to correct his condition. He recommended people to contact for additional advice. I could not believe my ears and was angry at the doctor for what he said. (*Daniel's hearing impairment is profound, with a PTA average threshold of 94 dB in the better ear indicated by his audiogram of April 4, 1990.*)

Hee Sue, Wesley, Daniel, and Yung D. Koo

I learned about deafness day-by-day and little-by-little through the experience of taking care of Daniel. Soon I realized that this deafness is a serious double handicap: that hearing impairment is not the only problem he faces, but also speech.

We observed the classes in signing and oral educational programs. I believe there were no Cued Speech classes at that time in the Montgomery County, Md., public schools. We enrolled Daniel in an oral class in the Parent-Infant program in Maryland. Daniel attended school only once or twice a week with his new hearing aids, since he was only 9 months old. He was a quiet but active boy. At first he didn't like his hearing aids, which apparently felt uncomfortable. But we were thrilled to see him (with aids) respond to sound. If we called his name, he turned around to find the source of the sound.

I believed that, with Daniel's profound hearing loss, it would take every effort possible to get him to speak. So I chose the oral program for him. I was concerned that he would have less chance to utilize his residual hearing (whatever there was) and to develop his speech if he depended on sign language, which is visual. Besides, sign language is a different language from English. I felt strongly that even if it took longer and was harder, he had to learn how to speak first (the earlier, the better) and to "hear" (lip-reading with whatever residual hearing he had) in English by any method.

Daniel's progress was slower than I expected. At the end of fourth grade, his teachers and auditory staff recommended that we seek another form of communication as he was entering into a more academically advanced grade. We were introduced to sign language and Cued Speech. We observed classes for both. In the Cued Speech program, Steven Scher caught my attention during the spelling test, and caused us to consider it. The first year in the Cued Speech program, we really tried hard. We put all our efforts into helping Daniel learn Cued Speech as fast as he could so that he was able to function in the mainstream classes with a Cued Speech transliterator. We were very fortunate to have Mr. Jim Latt and Mrs. Diane Brentari to introduce Daniel to Cued Speech and assist him. I myself learned Cued Speech enough to correct Daniel's pronunciation and use the cues to introduce new vocabulary to him, even in foreign languages (Korean, Japanese, Spanish, etc.). The crucial problem, of course, was that Daniel was now being mainstreamed, and he desperately needed to become skilled enough in Cued Speech to follow the Cued Speech transliterator. He took this as a challenge and a duty, and soon became able to function well in the mainstreamed class. The good lipreading skills he already had helped him learn Cued Speech quickly. Meanwhile, we gave him extra assistance with school work at home during the time he was learning Cued Speech, so he would not fall behind academically.

As we all know, kids learn a lot from reading. Particularly, deaf children can benefit more from reading well than anyone. They learn primarily from what they see. If they read well they can "see" almost all there is to know. However, most deaf kids are noticeably naive.

Daniel loves all kinds of sports, music, art, and reading the most. Books are his companions wherever he goes. It started in fifth grade when he met his friend, Steven Scher, in the Cued Speech program. Steven had a Hardy Boy series book and that led Daniel to collect books. Daniel read books as fast as he could to fill up his book shelf. Our thanks are to Steven.

Daniel had an interest in learning sign language from peers in his junior high school. He wanted to communicate with them. As he grew he became more open and sociable with a variety of friends including sign language peers. I think it is valuable to learn many languages and all methods of communication. The more languages you know, the more you can enjoy people from all over the world.

As soon as Daniel became aware that he was different from others, he became self-conscious about being seen with his hearing aids in his ears. He preferred to keep his hair a little longer to cover up his aids. I told Daniel that no human being in this world is perfect. Some have a visible handicap, and some have an invisible handicap that nobody notices except God. The one who accepts and cares about you as you are is the real friend. In his high school years, with lots of friends, he came out of this shyness.

Daniel is a patient and religious person. When he was a child I often interrupted him to correct his pronunciation during conversation with the family. He didn't usually mind, and tried as many times as needed to get it right. I know this is rude, but it is the only way to correct his pronunciation. A mother must decide what is best for her child, and then do it or see that it is done. She must have an open mind with her child in any situation and accept him under any conditions.

Now Daniel is living in the dorm at the University of Maryland, and I have less chance to see him and talk to him. He comes home to go to church over the weekend as often as he can. Every time we have conversation, I notice how he is getting more mature and is progressing while I am staying at the same level, or even regressing. I repeatedly tell him to learn as much as he can while he is young and has full capacity to absorb knowledge.

We have all come a long way, and I am grateful for the Cued Speech program that we chose for him. I am confident that there is no way he would be able to speak and write at such an intellectual level as he does now without having had the benefit of the Cued Speech method, speech therapists, and auditory staff in the Montgomery County Public Schools who are devoted educators full of affection.

On Feb. 28, 1992, Daniel scored at the 85th percentile nationally on the language section of the California Achievement Tests, and at the 95th percentile on the mathematics section. Daniel's own observations begin on page 617.

Chapter 18
Starting With A Very Young Child[1]

A common saying among oralists is: "Oralism is not an academic exercise, it's a way of life." Much the same thing could be said about Cued Speech. At the outset, the task of learning the system and becoming fluent may be so absorbing as to make parents forget that fluency is really the beginning of the rainbow, not its end. The stories of many Cued Speech children and their families reveal a common, sometimes overlooked thread. In the end, it is not the children's remarkable achievements that stand out, though certainly these are important. Rather, it is how the experience of raising a child on Cued Speech has enriched and changed the parents' lives, turning disadvantage into advantage. (p.339)

Cued Speech and Children Under Three

It is never too soon to start cueing to a hearing-impaired baby. Maximum early benefits of natural language development can be achieved by naturally talking and cueing to a hearing-impaired baby, just as a mother does to a hearing baby. Each day of delay may be one additional day behind the optimum in language development and mental stimulation. The "cue maxim" is: "Do and say the same things with your hearing-impaired baby that you would say with a hearing baby."

With our hearing babies we begin communication and the magic process of language input immediately after birth, talking and verbally caressing them even as we do our initial inspection, counting fingers and toes, and conveying our love to our newborn. A recent theory about the effects of talking and reading to one's unborn baby *in utero* seems to be borne out by research and personal experience. However, we cannot cue to our *in utero* babies, so an unborn baby with a congenital hearing loss has a nine-month disadvantage we cannot yet remedy. We continue to talk to our hearing babies in the succeeding months, providing nearly two years of communication and language input before receiving much verbal output in return.

---

[1]Most of the material in this chapter, except for the case histories, is reproduced with permission and some adaptation from the *Parent-Infant Packet* distributed by the Cued Speech Team, Department of Audiology and Speech/Language Pathology, Gallaudet University. Our special thanks are due Barbara Williams-Scott, M.A., materials specialist for the Cued Speech team, and the authors of the material, Marylou Barwell, M.Ed., and Nancy Tepper, M.Ed.

Similar results can be achieved with hearing-impaired babies, if the supplementary visual input of Cued Speech (to deliver a clear visual representation of the language) and specific auditory training (to enhance awareness of sound and increased use of residual hearing) are included. Of course those interacting with hearing-impaired babies must learn the techniques of managing to cue and speak when the baby is watching, leading the child to form the habit of looking and listening.

What if all or part of this effort is wasted? Suppose it is found later that the child doesn't really need Cued Speech? The inescapable problem is that if you have a profoundly hearing-impaired baby and do not assume that he/she *may* need all this extra effort and input, you may wake up after a year or two to the fact that he/she needed it desperately, and that it is now too late for those early benefits.

Do it, and if it turns out to be an insurance policy you didn't have to collect on, you will rejoice in the knowledge that your child has more auditory potential than you could be sure of in the beginning. Most of what you do is needed by a baby with normal hearing: the input just needs to be stepped up a bit and supplemented visually for a hearing-impaired baby. Cued Speech won't hurt a child; in fact, there is increasing evidence that it is beneficial for children with normal hearing, especially if they have certain learning problems.

It is best for parents to seek assistance from a local teacher trained for work with very young hearing-impaired children, a speech-and-hearing specialist, usually called a speech pathologist or therapist, and/or a child-development specialist. If local assistance is unavailable or inadequate, get in touch with one or more of the organizations listed in the Appendix, starting with the National Cued Speech Association.

This chapter offers pointers on the beginning cueing-parent/deaf-child relationship. The Appendix lists helpful books and materials for use in this process. Remember that not all babies are ready for the same activities at the same age. Be prepared to come back later to activities that did not work well at the first attempt. Try to be natural when interacting with your hearing-impaired child. As a beginning cuer you may lack confidence or worry about your child's attentiveness. Don't! As the cued words become meaningful you will see a positive change. Are you wondering what to say, or how to say it? When in doubt, think *hearing*. Do you speak in complex, sophisticated sentences to a hearing baby? Of course not. Baby talk is natural and cue-able! However, do not linger at the baby-talk level too long. Use varied expressions and vocabulary as receptive vocabulary grows. Talk with your child about anything and everything of interest to him/her.

As parents gain experience in communication with their young hearing-impaired child they should learn how to isolate auditory input for the child in such a way that she/he will relate it to the cued message she/he has just understood. This *auditory learning* on the part of the child is essential to the development of maximum use of residual hearing. The auditory training furnished by the parent (preferably with the guidance of a qualified professional) is essential in the process of bringing the child's development along on all fronts. (See Chapter 14.)

Cueing Activities for Children Under Three
by Marylou Barwell[2]

Do not assume that your child will necessarily be ready to respond to all these activities. You may need to try them and, if the child does not respond, wait for a few weeks before trying them again.

Changing-Table Charmers

Keep a bag containing two or three toys near the area where you change your hearing-impaired baby. These should be toys that your child sees only when being changed. Change these toys periodically, before your baby becomes bored with them, or soon after learning their names occurs. Stuffed toys work well for this activity.

Each time you change your baby, select a toy. Holding it near your face, cue and say its name. For example, cue and say "dog," and give the dog to your baby to play with while you are doing the changing. Repeat with the other toy or toys, trying to get all three cued each time you change your baby.

Here are some tips to remember: If your baby tries to grab the toy immediately on seeing it, not waiting to watch while you cue its name even once, see if the following little game helps. Before you bring out the first toy, put your face on the baby's tummy and tickle it. Draw back immediately and bring your hands up to your face (in a cueing position). Repeat the "attack" by putting your face on the baby's tummy and tickling him, and draw back again with your hands slightly

---

[2]Marylou Barwell, trained at Clarke School for the Deaf, and a graduate of Smith College, learned Cued Speech in order to begin her teaching career in 1970 at St. Gabriel's School for Deaf Boys, in Australia. After 2 years she married and returned to the United States, where she served in a coordinating and guiding role in the program for preschool deaf children at the National Child Research Center, in Washington, D.C. Subsequently she has served in a similar capacity for the Auditory Programs Division of the Montgomery County Public Schools (Maryland).

in front of your face, pulling your hands back to your face. After a few "attacks" your child should be watching your hands come up to your face long enough for you to cue and say a word while he is looking at you. Immediately pull the toy dog out of the bag, hold it close to your face, and say and cue "dog." Then, give it to the child to play with, saying and cueing "dog" again if you can catch his/her glance.

A variation is to tickle your baby's toes with the toy dog, then pull it back to your face. Tickle the baby's toes again with the dog, and immediately pull it back to your face and cue and say "dog." Then, give the dog to your baby. Watch for signs that the baby is losing interest in the toy. When he/she does, introduce the next toy.

There are two ways you can go with this activity, depending on your child's reactions. Some babies will immediately forget the first toy when they see the second. When you want to get attention back to the first toy just pull it out again and bring it up to your face. This should be enough to get your child to watch it and you again. Other children will be so engrossed in the toy they already have that they will fail to pay attention to a new one. In this case, you can try tickling your child's tummy or toes with the new toy (as described above) to get back his/her attention and interest.

If the above doesn't work (changing toys in the middle of a session), you may need to use only one toy per session, alternating between two (or among three) toys in successive sessions. It is better to do this than to frustrate your child. In a few weeks try again to interest your child in more than one toy per changing session. Choosing toys your child does not become so engrossed in can help, also. Sometimes it will help to tickle (or otherwise play with your child) to distract him while you push the one toy out of sight and bring out a new one. In the end, of course, you have to adjust to your child and find the approach that works best.

(*Some parents have suggested that the word say in "cue and say" is redundant in an instruction to present something in Cued Speech. It is not. Cueing is only half of Cued Speech; the other half is speaking.*)

Peek-A-Boo Pop Up

The old game of peek-a-boo is a good means of getting your child to watch your face. If you pop up from behind a sofa or a doorway keeping everything out of sight except your face, and say and cue "boo," your baby will begin to look for your face, and will think it a great game.

Mirror Play

A young child usually responds well to mirror play. Seat yourself and the child, side by side, in front of a large mirror. Be sure the child can see both you and her/himself clearly in the mirror. First play the game of imitation—making faces at each other, making sounds (with and without cues), and imitating words, phrases, and sentences the child knows, plus nonsense and babbling. If the child babbles a recognizable sound, imitate it (with cues). Make sure the child learns to watch both her/himself and you in the mirror, in turn or together. Stop when the child begins to tire. Daily short periods are better than longer sessions. Don't make the novelty wear off.

Feeding-Time Frolic

When feeding your baby, say the name of what is being offered before you present a spoonful. Of course, you shouldn't do this with every spoonful, but do so with several spoonfuls at each feeding. Then, each time a new food is introduced, say and cue its name. If your child can eat without your help, put the food on the plate one item at a time, saying and cueing the name of each before you give it to your child. If getting your child to watch you is a problem, putting the spoon up to your own mouth and tasting a bit might get your child's attention. Again, if your child can eat without help, holding each item up to your mouth, saying and cueing the name, and then presenting it to be eaten will sometimes help.

Bath-Time Bag

Bath time is a regular activity into which learning time can be introduced. Sheets of foam from the fabric store (1/2" or 3/4" thick) can be cut into a variety of shapes: star, face, boat, fish, etc. Put the shapes in a bag near your child's bath. When your child is in the bath, take each item in succession, hold it up to your face, then say and cue its name. Then give the items to your child to play with in the water. Other bath toys can be used, and may be better if they are more realistic.

Two-Minute Quickies

The following are ideas for a possible time—a very short period—with your child every day. It is best to pick one or two of these and do them regularly. Don't try to do too many and feel overwhelmed.

Here are some basics that apply to all the suggested activities:

1. Seat your child on eye level with you (in an infant seat, on the sofa, with you on the floor, on a booster seat, in a high chair, walker, or whatever). Your child is more likely to look at you when your face is readily available.

2. Be sure to use lots of facial expression.

3. Plan to use these activities at the same time each day—routine is your ally.

4. It is better to perform these activities only once a day, but *every* day, than to do them several times in one day and none the next. Again, routine is the key.

5. Keep the toys for these activities separate from other toys.

6. Carry on these activities in the same place each time, preserving the routine.

7. Pick a time when your baby usually seems the happiest and most receptive—after nap-time, for example.

8. As you persevere in these activities, your child should learn that the game is "First I look, then I can have it."

What's Inside That Box?

Find a medium-sized box with a lid, and cover the lid with contact paper. Have a toy already inside the box before you start, with the lid on. Hold the box up high, under your chin and a little bit in front of your face, and open it slightly. Then close it with an excited look on your face. Cue and say the name of the toy inside. Then, give the box to your child to open and play with.

A variation on this theme is to stick your hand inside the box and pull the toy out and right up to your mouth where you immediately cue and say its name. You may be able to take the toy out of the box, pull it up to your mouth, cue and say its name, and put it back in the box before giving the box to your child.

Stop and Go

You will need a wind-up toy of some kind—one that your child cannot wind up (which gives you control). Wind up the toy, put it next to your mouth, and cue and say "Go." Then, put it down and let it go. Let your child play with it as long as it holds his/her attention. Your child will probably hand it back to you to wind up again. That is your cue to say "Wind it up" while he/she is looking questioningly at your face. Wind it up, hold it up to your face, and again cue and say "Go." If after the first time the child plays with the toy he/she does not hand it to you to wind up, you can try asking for the toy, saying and cueing "Wind it up?" if the child gives you the toy go through the original procedure. Then, usually, after the child plays with the toy a second time he or she will give you the toy for you to wind it up again.

Once this game is familiar, some children enjoy having you show them how to grab the toy before it winds down, and thus stopping it for a second. Always cue and say "Stop!" before you let it go.

Roll the Ball

Start out by teaching your child to sit down on the floor and roll a ball back and forth with you. When the child can roll it to you and wait for you to roll it back, you can quickly pick up the ball, bring it up to your mouth, and cue and say "roll it" before you roll it back.

Puzzle Pieces

Use a simple puzzle with three or four pieces, such as one in which each piece is a picture of a dog, cat, lamb, rabbit, etc. Be sure that it is a puzzle for which each piece is to be put back as a whole in a separate slot. In other words, the child has only to match the shape of the piece to the shape of the slot, not to fit pieces together.

Put all the pieces in a bag and place the puzzle board in front of the child. Take each piece out, one at a time, and hold it up to your mouth as you cue and say its name. Some children will be more interested if you make the dog jump up and down and say "arf, arf," or have the cat say "meow, meow." In any case, give the piece to the child to play with or put in the puzzle board. If the child prefers to play with the piece rather than to put it in the puzzle, let him/her play with it. Then try to get him/her to fit it into the puzzle board.

High Chair Chef

A good means of reinforcing a child's knowledge of *eyes, nose, and mouth* is to teach him to put raisins on cookies to represent them. Slice-and-bake cookies work well for this. After your child is familiar with his/her eyes, nose, and mouth, put him/her in a high chair (unless he/she is too old for this). Have some slice-and-bake cookies ready in a bag with a minimally dangerous knife and a small bag of raisins. You may need to teach the child the word *raisin* before using this activity. Wait until the child is familiar with raisins, eye, nose, and mouth.

If your child is old enough to help cut the cookies—with you guiding the knife—let him/her help you cut one. First, hold up the knife and say and cue "knife." Then, cue and say "Let's cut it" and guide your child's hand as he/she slices a cookie.

Next, take out the bag of raisins, hold one up to your eye and say "eye." Finally, put it on the cookie and say "eye." Cut another cookie and repeat the procedure with the raisin, placing it on the cookie as the second eye.

Repeat the procedure for the nose. When you are ready for the mouth, take several raisins out of the bag, hold them up and say "raisins." Then point to your mouth and say "mouth." Finally, put them on the cookie and say "mouth." Then point to the raisins on the cookie, in turn, and say and cue *eye, eye, nose,* and *mouth* in succession. Save the cookie, repeat the process each day, and when you have several cookies ready, bake them and let the child eat them, reviewing the identifications of the raisins with her/him.

Helping Young Children Adapt to Hearing Aids
by Nancy Tepper[3]

Some very young children readily accept hearing aids and wear them happily, while others reject them initially and strongly resist wearing them. Much depends on how the child is introduced to the aids and how any initial resistance is handled. The following are ideas for helping young children accept and adapt to hearing aids. There is no magic procedure that will work for all children. Feel free to adapt these ideas to fit your situation and your child.

It is important to remember that you, not your child, are responsible for deciding when the aid is to be removed. The sooner your child understands this, the better. At the same time, your child will feel more positive about wearing the aid (and about listening activities in general) if the memories of wearing the aid are positive. Pick a time when both you and your child are in your best frame of mind. The activity you plan to carry on while the aid is on should be something you both can enjoy.

Although it is natural for parents to have mixed feelings about the hearing aid, you must try to convey to your child only positive feelings about it. Look at it with interest, talk about it with enthusiasm, smile, etc. If your child starts to fuss as you put it on, create a distraction. For some children it helps to show them a toy used only in connection with putting the hearing aid on. Let your child play with this toy as soon as the aid is on, to keep attention focused on the toy

---

[3]Nancy Tepper is a specialist in working with young hearing-impaired children. She was employed for several years in the Cued Speech Office at Gallaudet University. Since that time she has engaged extensively in helping families with young deaf children get started with Cued Speech.

rather than on the aid. Other children may find it too frustrating to wait for the aid to be put on once they have seen the toy. In this case it is better to keep the toy out of sight, but near at hand, so you can draw attention to it as soon as the aid is on.

If your child tries to remove the aid, the activity at hand should stop *immediately*—until the aid is on again. The goal is to encourage your child to keep the aid on for increasingly longer periods of time. If the child resists it may be best to remove the aid for a short time, before she/he becomes really upset, to avoid developing even stronger resistance. That way, your child will be less likely to resist the aid the next time you put it on. You can gradually extend the time (which you should do as quickly as possible), continuing to watch carefully so you can remove the aid before your child's limit is reached.

You may do well to plan to put the aid on so that there will be a legitimate reason for removing the aid (such as bath time) at about the limit of the child's ability to put up with the aid. Eventually, if the child starts to remove the aid, you can say, "No, it's not bath time yet. That's when we take it off." Or, you can say: "No, let's wait until bath time." Adaptation to the aid sometimes requires a good bit of time and patience (for both parent and child), but it will become easier for you.

The following items and activities are suggested for use in teaching your child to wear the aid. The basic idea in them is to keep both the child's mind and hands occupied with other things:

• new or "rotated" old toys that absorb attention and require the child to use both hands—for example, stringing large beads, putting shapes into containers, simple puzzles, push toys, riding toys, etc.

• play dough

• water play—pouring colored water into clear plastic containers, using funnels, etc.

• simple cooking projects (making pudding or jello, slicing fruit)—if your child can do these without danger to the hearing aid.

Osmond Crosby reports that the hands-occupying activity that did the trick for his daughter Dorothy Jane was swinging. She loved swinging. Since it was an activity that required her to hold on with both hands, the aids remained in her ears. However, the problem required three months to solve, as they tried various techniques. But Dorothy Jane, after nine months of use of the aids, actually objected to their removal for a nap, insisting on sleeping with them on. Crosby offers these additional suggestions:

A little lubrication helps both insertion and acoustic seal. When the mold gets too small you can use denture-

cushioning gel for an emergency seal. Roll the gel into a string, then put it around the part of the mold to be inserted, creating a little "o" ring. This will keep you going until the replacement arrives. Insist on a good fit. It was eight months and six pairs of earmolds before we learned that you don't have to live with feedback. Don't accept less than an excellent fit. We wasted lots of time, money, and signal clarity before we found that earmolds could truly fit without feedback for more than five minutes at a time.

In the end, your child must come to realize that you view the hearing aid as crucial and that it *will* be worn on a full-time basis after a relatively short period of adjustment, whether that be a week or a month. Both you and your child wish it were not necessary for him/her to wear the aid. It is essential for you to focus on the fact that constant wearing of the aid, along with proper training, gives your child the best chance of making full use of his/her auditory potential.

Remember that, initially, your child has no reason to view the aid negatively, so long as it is introduced in a way that treats him/her with respect. The same is true of other items worn, e.g., clothing. Don't pop a shirt over the child's head without warning. Talk!

Once a child becomes accustomed to the aid, it should be accepted as a constant companion. When the child has worn it long enough (and had enough auditory training) to perceive sounds and attach meaning to them, this should cause him/her to want to wear the aids. Then, the ritual will reach the point of putting on the aid in the morning, after checking it, and taking it off for necessary activities, such as bath, naps, and bedtime. Of course, there will be kinds of play (swimming, or playing in a sand-pile, for example) for which removal of the hearing aids is justified.

Because ear molds sometimes tend to be uncomfortable, especially when new, it is sometimes difficult to distinguish between the effects of a poorly fitting ear mold and the natural resistance to having something in the ear. Be sure that the first attempts to get the child to wear the molds are made at a time when 1) everything is favorable to acceptance, and 2) you can watch carefully for any signs of discomfort or rejection. Consult your audiologist if there is any reason to suspect that an ear mold fits poorly. A parent suggests that a tiny bit of lubrication on the canal section of the earmold will help enable it to be inserted easily and without discomfort.[4]

A parent suggests that more emphasis should be given to the child's difficulties in adjusting to hearing aids as a result of the irritation of loud sounds, discomfort, etc., and to the frustration of the parents when an aid is flushed down the toilet, thrown out the car window, or chewed by the dog. She suggests buying insurance during the adjustment period when the probability of repairs or loss is highest. She also suggests tying the aids together with a bright shoelace. This hedges against loss by making it harder to pull out both aids.

Try to maintain a positive attitude. Many children accept hearing aids readily and are content to wear them all day from the beginning. Admittedly, this is most likely to be true if 1) the ear molds fit very well at the start, and 2) the child derives immediate auditory benefit. Sometimes it takes time to achieve both comfort and usefulness.

There's More to Cued Speech Than Cueing
by Marylou Barwell

A common saying among oralists is: "Oralism is not an academic exercise, it's a way of life." Much the same thing could be said about Cued Speech. At the outset, the task of learning the system and becoming fluent may be so absorbing as to make parents forget that fluency is really the beginning of the rainbow, not its end. The stories of many Cued Speech children and their families reveal a common, sometimes overlooked thread. In the end, it is not the children's remarkable achievements that stand out, though certainly these are important. Rather, it is how the experience of raising a child on Cued Speech has enriched and changed the parents' lives, turning disadvantage into advantage.

The children who are successful on Cued Speech have parents who—whether they learned quickly and easily, or slowly and laboriously—*learned*. These parents incorporated CS into their daily lives.

A philosophy of how to use Cued Speech has evolved—a philosophy rooted in parents' and professionals' conviction that a child needs (and indeed deserves) a happy and satisfying childhood, in which the emphasis is not on teaching language, but on experiencing it.

Parents want and need more than to be taught how to cue. They want to be shown how to make it work. At the very center of parents'

---

[4]A good source of suggestions and devices for keeping aids on little ears is **Huggie Aids**, 837 N.W. 10th St., Oklahoma City, OK 73106.

approach to anything is their attitude. Parents of successful deaf children somewhere along the way, manage to do four things:

- They show respect for their child, and the child knows it.
- They treat the child as any other child, insofar as possible.
- They believe in themselves, in Cued Speech, and in the child.
- They find the balance between too much and too little.

Ultimately, to treat the child as any other child is to develop a quality of communication equal to that with the hearing children (if any) in the family. It is necessary to expose the hearing-impaired child to the depth and breadth of language given to other children—not that this is easy to do. It is to expect of the child the same behavior and level of achievement (if possible) as others, and it is to be willing to give him/her the freedom to develop self-confidence and independence, by "letting go" an inch at a time.

The famous pilot/author, Richard Bach, once wrote, "To be a good pilot, one must be a believer in the unseen." To believe in yourselves as parents, in Cued Speech, and in your child is also at times to be a believer in the unseen. This is particularly so in the first year or two that CS is used. Much of what is developing in a young deaf child's mind cannot be seen or directly evidenced. Only later, when that child's expressive language, reading, and writing skills explode, can parents fully appreciate how much he/she has acquired.

To find the middle ground between failing to meet the child's needs and allowing him or her to feel that the world revolves solely around him/her is a juggling act at times. Ultimately, the judgment as to how much is enough must come as a decision for each individual family. To compare one family with another usually accomplishes nothing. Family A should not feel guilty for doing less than family B, nor feel smug for doing more. To formulate its decision as to how far they should go, a family might ask itself six questions:

1) What is a realistic assessment of our hearing-impaired child's innate potential, regardless of hearing loss?
2) How old is our child, and how far (if any) is s/he behind the norm for hearing children his/her age?
3) With the above in mind, how much do we want/expect our child to achieve, and how quickly?
4) What amount of effort (and by whom) is required, and how much are we prepared to do, to make this result possible?
5) What kinds and amount of support can we expect from the

school or other sources of professional service, and how much (if any) will this lighten our load or enable us to cope better?

6) Are we willing to make the effort required of us, even though the desired degree of success cannot be assured in advance?

Beyond what determines how high a plane will fly, is there a "minimum daily requirement" without which it won't even get off the ground? Yes, indeed. Though Cued Speech can achieve substantial benefits in a school program of good quality with no cueing support at home, particularly with a good language curriculum and skilled therapy, it can achieve far more with cueing and auditory support at home. The available research (Hage, Alegría, & Périer, 1989) indicates clearly that use of Cued Speech at home has a substantially greater benefit than its use at school. The optimum, of course, is maximum support in both the home and the school.

The acceptable minimum at home, ultimately, is to cue consistently casual conversation and communication that is age-appropriate for the child, and to cue it accurately and fluently, in the course of everyday living. Everything beyond that, such as conscious vocabulary building, specific language-development and enrichment effort, and auditory practice will help the child progress further and faster.

The parents who have the most to gain, with the least amount of effort, are those with the youngest hearing-impaired children. Nonetheless, attempting to do the elusive "enough" is taxing and bewildering at times. Cueing "casual age-appropriate conversation and communication, accurately and fluently" to a 3-year-old child who hasn't yet learned to watch well is no easy task, and it requires some neat tricks. Getting enough "pumped into" the young deaf child involves not only revving up your cueing skills, but developing the knack of inducing the child to watch you.

Getting the child to watch is not something you can accomplish in one magical moment. More likely, you will accomplish it in little steps, and perhaps even in "fits and starts." Every little success, every occasion in which the child gets meaning from looking at you, nudges the child further toward the habit of watching consistently. The deaf child wants to communicate as much as a hearing child does, and may feel the need even more. He/she fails initially to realize that the input he is receiving is the means of understanding and communicating.

Some parents tend to be the "silent type." If you are, you must try to change. Your deaf child needs lots of input, and you must become a more talkative person if it will benefit your child. Give your child lots of communication. It is important for you to talk to your deaf child, but it is even more essential that the child know what you are talking about, and eventually exactly what you mean. The principle to remember is this: What you mean must coincide with what the child thinks you mean. If you hold something up as you cue and say its name, the child eventually catches on that what you are saying is its name. This doesn't usually happen at first. Many opportunities must be provided before the child understands that everything has a name, and that what you are showing him/her with your mouth and your hand relate directly to what you are doing. When the child begins to make this connection, things start to happen very rapidly (and you get a golden glow!).

Keep in mind that a hearing child can simultaneously listen to what you are saying and continue playing with what you are talking about. A hearing-impaired child must stop playing and look at you to receive your message, or to learn language. You must watch for opportunities. The ability of a child to watch seems to develop with a "snowball" effect. The more s(he) watches, the more s(he) begins to understand. The more the child understands, the more s(he) is motivated to watch. Parents and others working with the child must learn to judge when the child has played with something long enough to be willing to pause for language input. Once you reach this point, you will find it easier to adjust your input to your child's interests. Your improvement in this respect will result in increased attentiveness from him/her.

Try to maintain a relaxed attitude. It is better to do less and make it pleasant (for both you and the child) than to push either the child or yourself too hard, possibly creating a battle of wills. Getting "up tight" accomplishes nothing, and it can quickly wear out both you and your child. Particularly at first, one-shot exposures several times a day (closely related to what is nearby) are far better than elaborate activities. Bath time, for example, offers many opportunities for teaching language with a minimum of fuss. As you run the water, splash some on your child's tummy a few times—if it's the right temperature! This gets him or her to watch your hands. When he/she looks at your face, cue and say "splash" and make another splash, then repeat the verbal message. A list of additional suggested activities for very young children appears above in this chapter, and materials for use with small children are listed on page 764, in the Appendix.

Hearing-impaired children, like all children, go through stages in their development. They also swing in pendulum fashion from intense physical development, through activities such as crawling, walking, climbing, to focusing on mental development, and back again.

You should keep these swings in the child's interest in mind, and accommodate to them by using language related to the activities he/she is most receptive to at the time.

A shifting of focus can result from one or more of the usual annoyances of teething, heat rash, hunger, fatigue, needing to be changed, etc. Any of these can reduce the child's willingness to cooperate, to watch, and to do what you want. It is better to pull back at such a time, show sympathy, or try to relieve the situation, than to continue to push for the objective you were pursuing just before you became aware of the problem. Even minor problems can cause the child to respond in fits and starts, the frequency varying from child to child. If your child becomes more resistant to your efforts to get him/her to watch, consider whether you are pushing too hard, stressing the wrong areas, failing to connect well enough what you are saying and what you are talking about, or overlooking one or more of the annoyances mentioned above.

Remember that every time you get your child to watch tends to make watching a little easier the next time, and the next. Watching must become a habit for your child. At first s(he) will watch only at optimum times—when she/he really wants to and there are not many distractions. Gradually, as watching becomes more rewarding, satisfying, and meaningful—when the child begins to recognize some of what you're saying to him—she/he will begin to watch more often, without your having to bid for attention so much. Nonetheless, sometimes you will simply have to "gut it out." Hearing-impaired children are often razor-sharp at taking advantage of the situation. In our efforts to make learning enjoyable and interesting for them we may sometimes wind up dangling on a string. One can almost imagine the child thinking, "I wonder how much of a three-ring circus she will put on, if I hold out long enough?" The key is to find the happy medium between recognizing the child's true needs and allowing yourself to be bamboozled. For this, you must rely on your instincts and your experience.

We cannot overemphasize the importance of capitalizing on the fortuitous opportunities for learning that crop up in everyday living. But, it is also necessary to have some planned activities. Everyday living may not fill all the gaps. As stated earlier, the best overall approach is to utilize many short, planned exposures during the day. A special time (10 or 15 minutes long) spent routinely alone with your hearing-impaired child offers advantages for planned activities. Doing something at the same time and in the same place each day will help the child develop the habit of watching at these times. Routine is your ally. The child will come to expect it, and not be as likely to balk as he/she might be otherwise. Use a quiet room if possible. Plan for right after a nap, right after lunch, after diaper changing—whatever works best for you and your child. Osmond Crosby reports: "Surprisingly, bedtime is a good time for us. Even though DJ is tired, she likes the routine of bedtime stories and prayer. Last night she reminded me that I had omitted one of her grandmothers."

Having your undivided attention, and free from distractions, your child is more likely to watch well and to enjoy doing so. As the habit of watching your face for information during these special times develops, it will begin to transfer to times when conditions are not optimal. Choose activities that you are comfortable with, and that are particularly interesting to your child. Having special toys and books reserved for these times works well for some children. Others especially enjoy food activities—making jello, peeling fruit, baking cookies—anything that allows opportunity to talk about what you're doing. Insofar as is possible, keep out of sight everything except what you want to talk about at the moment.

Whether you are doing a planned activity or simply responding to the events of the day, several basic things apply when it comes to encouraging your child to watch. Position the child so he/she is on eye level with you, as specified earlier. Your child is more likely to look when your face is readily available. Remember to have the light on your face, and behind the child. Another thing to check is the distance between you. You should be comfortably close. Speak at a normal, conversational level. If you tend to be soft-spoken, make sure to speak distinctly, and not too fast. Use lots of facial expression.

Put whatever you want to talk about near your mouth before you start speaking and cueing. Try different toys to find the ones that interest the child most. Try not to have anything else in sight that might distract your child. Even if s(he) has a very short attention span, you must find a way to capture your child's attention long enough for you to name the object before you give it to him/her or start the planned activity. Sometimes a little frustration is beneficial. Hand your child a box or plastic container that he/she can't quite open. After a few attempts, s(he) will probably look to you for help. That's the time you might use for a quick "open it," "wind it," or "help me." On occasion you will simply have to wait the child out. If the child wants your help or what you have badly enough, she/he will eventually learn that looking at your face is the fastest way to get help.

How much is the elusive "enough?" To give a blanket answer is impossible. Some children respond very quickly, and can be cued to all day if you're willing. Others need more prodding and get turned off if pushed too hard. Parental responsibilities, capabilities, and pressures vary greatly, influencing how much they can do. What one parent can do easily, another may find overtaxing. Sometimes, no matter how much you are doing, you will feel as if you should be doing more. Do the best you can, and be proud of your best effort.

For some parents it helps to begin with a basic minimum goal. In the early days of cueing, it may help to make a list of 20 basic words of probable interest to your child, and a few short sentences such as "Do you want _____?" or "Do you see _____?" Practice them before using them with the child, until you can cue them with reasonable ease. Then be sure to use them with your child every day, no matter what. Be sure that you pick words directly related to concrete objects and actions. For example, don't cue *cookie* unless you have a cookie at hand to show him. Also, don't cue sentences containing abstractions and grammar the child is not ready for, such as "Maybe it will rain tomorrow," when you are trying to teach the word *rain*. It is better to wait until it actually rains, or to get a picture or videotape showing rain. Of course, after the child's language has developed enough you can use words that do not refer to something actually present, and teach new language through language already known.

Basic goals might include one 10-minute planned session per day, a bath activity three times a week or more, a planned activity at one meal per day, and one table game (rotating) each day. Some experimenting will be necessary to ascertain how much you can manage each day, no matter how hectic and confused things may become. It is better to do a little less and feel good about it, than to try too much, get overwhelmed, and feel guilty about it. So find out what your basic minimum is, and tell yourself that on days when you can do more you will. You must do more whenever possible. When you can't, you should feel satisfied with the basic amount. By following a routine and giving special emphasis to a limited vocabulary for a time (though not to the exclusion of other words), you enable the child to begin to recognize some words quickly. This gives a big boost to his/her motivation to watch. Then add a little more each week, as your skills increase and your child's attention and understanding expand.

First, last, and always, remember that the ultimate goal of using Cued Speech is clear and satisfying communication as a part of everyday living, leading to command of spoken language as a base for reading, speech, and speechreading. To be fully effective, it must become a way of life. Once it is, you will see more and more visible evidence that Cued Speech is working for you and your child, and gradually your faith in the unseen will turn into celebration of goals accomplished.

Three Infants with Whom Cued Speech Was Used Early

Data Gathered by Nancy Tepper, April, 1982

Child One was diagnosed as having a severe-to-profound bilateral neurosensory hearing loss at the age of 10 months and was fitted with hearing aids shortly thereafter. This child also has a mild spasticity of the left side. The parents began cueing when the child was 12 months old. When tested at 11½ months, before he began to receive Cued Speech, his receptive language level was evaluated at 1-2 months, and his expressive level at 2-3 months. At 23 months, after 11 months of CS, he tested at age level (23 months) receptively on the SKI-HI test, at 18-20 months expressively.

Child Two was suspected of having a hearing loss at the age of 12 months. A severe-to-profound impairment was confirmed when the child was 13 months old, and hearing aids were fitted at the age of 14 months. This child also has delays in motor development. The parents began cueing when the child was 16 months old. The REEL test was administered at 12 months, before cueing, and the results indicated "severely delayed" both receptively and expressively. At age 24 months, after 12 months exposure to CS, the child tested at 22-24 months receptively and 18 months expressively, with achieved skills through 22 months.

Child Three had normal hearing until 9 months of age, when stricken with spinal meningitis. Within a month the child was diagnosed as having a severe-to-profound hearing loss and fitted with aids shortly thereafter. The parents began cueing when the child was 12 months old. On the SKI-HI test, at age 10 months, before CS exposure, the child had a receptive language score of 4-6 months, probably a low estimate, and an expressive level of 8-10 months (presumably due to development before loss of hearing). At age 24 months, after nine months of CS exposure, the scores were 22-24 months receptively and 20-22 months expressively.

The test results for the children listed above suggest that through Cued Speech it is possible for infants with severe-to-profound hearing losses to acquire age-appropriate receptive language skills by age 24 months. Certainly the families involved started cueing very quickly on learning of their child's hearing impairment, and they used it consistently with the child. And, each family had regular assistance from a parent/infant specialist who was open-minded about the family's decision to use Cued Speech. Also, each specialist learned to cue, though none had used CS before.

It should be noted that the three children for whom information and test results are given above were chosen because they happened to be the only three very young children for whom the writer had a substantial amount of test data related to hearing impairment, not because their progress was exceptional. A carefully developed study is needed to evaluate the effectiveness of CS for the majority of children in similar situations. The case histories included below in this chapter and elsewhere include additional children whose exposure to Cued Speech was also early, whose progress was comparable, and most of whom had more severe hearing deficits.

Chapter Summary

The amount of detail in this chapter makes it difficult to summarize effectively without too much duplication. We recommend simply reading the chapter several times if you are starting Cued Speech with a child under 3 years of age. You will find in Chapters 20, 22, 23, and 24 the stories of several families who started using Cued Speech with children at 24 months or younger. They are placed in those chapters because other circumstances are more remarkable for the families than the starting ages. They and the case histories below contain material that is relevant to the problem of starting with a very young child.

Case Histories

Whitney Dennis
by Deborah Dennis

I have always loved children—especially the conversations I've had with them. They have a wonderful ability to ask so many questions about so many things, and it's fun just listening and trying to answer them all. So it seemed natural that only a few hours after Whitney came into the world I told my husband, "I can't wait for her to talk to me." I had it all planned. I would read to her, talk to her, teach her. We would go to parks, the library, museums, movies, everywhere.

One day when Whitney was a little over 2 months old, I was holding her on my lap and talking to her, as I often did. On this particular day, however, I noticed that she would look at me only when she happened to catch my face with her eyes, never as a result of my talking. I thought to myself, "Can she hear well?"

When my husband came home I told him about my concerns. He assured me that she was fine and then proceeded to prove it. He got behind the couch and clapped his hands very loud. I was on the couch, holding her, and sure enough, she jumped. We didn't realize at the time that she could see his clap with her peripheral vision and could probably also feel the air brush over her. However, that was all it took for me. I went on with my life, never to think about that day for a long, long time. After all, she jumped. She *must* have heard, right?

Whitney developed like any other child. She crawled, then walked, then ran. She was constantly babbling (which most hearing-impaired children do, just like hearing children). Around her sixth month she said, "Ma-ma-ma-ma." It was wonderful, I thought. She was saying my name. Our conversations could not be far away (although we "conversed" in other ways all the time).

Around this time I also noticed that she was not responding to her name. I would call her, and she would turn around about half the time. I never knew whether she had heard or just happened to turn around.

At 9 months Whitney was still not responding to "no." I had to get up and tap her and shake my heard to get her attention. I'm sure I did this so automatically that many times when I thought she was hearing she was just responding to my head-shake. It was the same with other things. When *Sesame Street* came on I would go crazy dancing around the room to the theme song, or yell, "Look! It's Big Bird!" But unless I went and tapped her or she happened to catch the TV with her glance, she never looked.

At 1 year old, Whitney still said only "Ma-ma-ma-ma." It was at this point that the rest of my family began to think that something was wrong with her hearing. Everyone except me—that is, until one day something happened that made me see things differently. I was drying my hair while Whitney was asleep. I thought I heard her crying, and turned off the dryer. Whitney was walking down the hall looking for me. I called her name. She didn't turn around. I screamed her name and clapped my hands and stomped my feet. She continued to walk the other way, still crying. She turned around to walk back down the hall without ever looking my way. At that moment I really felt that something was wrong. Maybe the others were right.

Whitney was diagnosed as hearing impaired at 16 months of age. She had a profound hearing loss. She was *deaf*—a word I'd never used in my life unless maybe I was talking about Helen Keller.

Whitney Dennis (4½). 1989

I was numb for weeks. I had a nauseous feeling in my stomach. Millions of questions ran through my mind. How would she learn? (You hear to learn and to think. You can't think without first hearing the words to think with.) What would happen to her life? What would happen to *my* life?

I was in this state for about two weeks. Then one day I was lying on the couch crying, and my little brown-eyed girl came and gave me a big hug and just looked at me and smiled. I looked at Whitney and something happened. I'm not sure why, but the nausea left me and I started to feel better. I got up and played with her—*really* played with her, like I used to. This was still my Whitney, and we would do whatever we had to do.

After attempting to use signs with Whitney for about a month I began to get a little frustrated. I did not know all the signs. I would run to the book to recall old signs and to look up new ones. Sometimes which I found the correct gesture, it would mean two or three different words. Whether or not I signed, of course, I would always use my voice. There are very few children who are totally deaf and cannot develop any use of residual hearing.

Our audiologist had provided us with a videotape produced by Beginnings (a nonprofit organization for parents of hearing-impaired children). The tape demonstrated in a non-biased manner all the methodologies available to us. Besides signing, there was a method called Cued Speech. After watching the tape we called the National Cued Speech Center in Raleigh, N.C., for an appointment.

At the center the executive director explained the principles and demonstrated Cued Speech. Instead of fingerspelling (how do you fingerspell to a toddler?) or using symbols standing for different words, I could cue the word the way I said it. I could say any word I chose, whether it be a real word or an exclamation such as "eeeeek!" Using a total of eight handshapes in four places, in combination with the movements of my mouth, Cued Speech could enable Whitney to "see" the spoken language. It seemed to be the perfect solution especially for helping her develop good learning skills. I enrolled in the two-day class that was being offered at the center that month.

As it turned out, using Cued Speech has been nothing short of a miracle. Whitney, who at 17 months had the language development of a 3-month-old infant, is now testing at or above her age level. This happens over and over again with hearing-impaired children who use Cued Speech. I'm sure this tremendous progress has been due to the clear manner in which Cued Speech presents the English language, coupled with the consistent use of hearing aids, speech therapy, and support received at home.

My daughter is now 4 years old. Her life and mine have changed tremendously. I do read to her and talk to her and teach her, just as on the day she was born I vowed I would. The only difference between that expectation and the reality is the *extra* joy she brings me. I get all the curiosity and spontaneity of a hearing child—and *I get a little more!* It has to be because the effort of overcoming the obstacle of deafness has changed both me and my little girl.

I have had an education in life and have acquired a greater appreciation for it since Whitney was born. In our home, achievements are truly family events. The moments are savored and treasured. Each time Whitney learns how to say and use a word I've been practicing with her I not only jump for joy, I cry with delight. Living with Whitney is always wondrous. We talk about everything. I don't even open a can of peas without saying, "I am opening a can of peas. I'm turning the lid. It's almost open. I'm twisting it off. Yeah! It's open. Now we can eat peas."

Unlike hearing children, Whitney will not pick up new language by overhearing it. She needs to be exposed to new language again and again unless it is cued. When she's wearing her hearing aids (all the time except when she's asleep or swimming), I need to be close to her to be sure she's looking at my face when I'm talking. Some days it's very tiring, but it is also rewarding to all of us. Even my 2-year-old, hearing son, Brett, will say to his sister, "Whitney, look at my face!" before he talks to her.

Whitney attends a regular preschool, which she loves dearly. She is thirsty for life. She keeps our whole family going with her boundless energy and inquisitiveness. We have truly been blessed. Looking back, however, I realize I never saw her startled. I never saw her jump when the phone or doorbell rang, or when the dog barked. So many things I did see (such as the way she responded to the clapping, and her lack of response when I called her name) didn't register with me as indications of hearing loss. At that time I wasn't looking for signs of trouble. With my son it was different. On the day he was born, I noticed him jump in response to the telephone. I was watching for any sign of hearing,

I wish I had been more aware and had known what to look for during Whitney's first year. Had she been diagnosed at 2 months old, she would have been fitted with hearing aids. She would have had an extra year of hearing—her first year! Children with normal hearing are preparing for speech reception during that first year of listening, and through babbling they are practicing their approach to speech. Hearing-impaired children also babble during their first year, but it usually stops because: 1) They don't hear their babbling and thus don't get the feedback and reinforcement from their own sounds, and 2) They don't get feedback and reinforcement that comes from hearing persons who talk back to them when they babble. They do pick up on nonverbal signals of acknowledgement in response to their babbling.

Had I known what to watch for when Whitney was young, I wouldn't have spent so much time guessing. However, we were lucky. With the help of a lot of wonderful people, Whitney has made up for a lot of waste time.

On a recent trip to a restaurant, Whitney and Brett were in the back seat of the car. Every minute she would say or ask something, such as "What's that arrow?" " Let's turn left," and "Can we go to McDonald's?" It went on and on. My husband and I couldn't get a word in, much less a sentence. This was the same child whom I was so worried about. This was the same child I cried over for two weeks because I was afraid she would never speak or learn. My husband and I looked at each other with a sense of thankfulness only one who has been in a situation like ours could ever realize, and I said to him, "And Whitney is deaf?"

I am confident that we will jump the many hurdles that remain. All of us have come so far and we are all thankful for our progress.

Update, January 1992

More than two years have passed since I wrote the above. They were wonderful years in which Whitney's progress surpassed our expectations. Now she is mainstreamed in first grade and performing beautifully. In fact, she is above average in relation to the hearing children in her classroom.

Our dilemma now is how to stand prosperity! Two years ago I would have been happy at the prospect of her doing this well in the mainstream with a Cued Speech transliterator. Now that she is doing it without one I find myself wanting her to continue using and developing every possible bit of her residual hearing. I spend time with her each night to reinforce key points of her day, speech, and auditory learning. The teacher sends home major topics and goals they will discuss in the upcoming week. I find this system works well with our family and its schedule.

I have been made aware of the problem of the function words (prepositions, conjunctions, and the definite and indefinite articles) that are the key to sophistication in English and become so important in reading at about fourth grade level. I had not realized that about 85% of English sentences are idiomatic (different in meaning from what the sum total of the individual meanings of the words would indicate) and that most of them are made so by those tricky prepositions! I plan to make a list of the 30-to-40 different meanings for each of the prepositions that Whitney needs to know in order to avoid the infamous third-grade reading plateau that stops most deaf children (and many hearing children as well). Because school (especially reading) typically becomes a lot more demanding in third and fourth grades, our family will be alert for any signs of increasing stress and/or difficulty that would warrant our requesting a Cued Speech transliterator for Whitney.

So long as Whitney (with our help) can perform this well in the mainstream without a transliterator without undue stress and without having to work so hard that she hasn't enough time "to smell the flowers" (play, social interaction, discovery), we will probably continue the present arrangement. If evidence appears that she needs a transliterator in order to function well with reasonable effort, we will go all out to get one. Her welfare is our central concern.

On May 1, 1991, at age 6½ years, Whitney was given the Woodcock-Johnson Tests of Achievement. She scored at the 84th percentile on Letter-Word Identification, at the 85th percentile on Passage Comprehension, and at the 83rd percentile on Broad Reading. These tests are normed on the general school population. Whitney has a bilateral, sensorineural, very profound hearing impairment. Her last available audiogram showed a PTA threshold beyond 110 dB in the better ear. However, it showed that her hearing extended all the way to 8000 Hz.

*The first four pages of this story appeared as a Family Portrait in the October 1989 issue of **3-2-1 Contact Magazine**, Copyright 1989 Children's Television Workshop (New York, N.Y.). All rights reserved. Used with permission.*

The "Miracle" of Clear Communication
The Story of Courtney Branscome
by Amy Branscome

I will never forget the audiologist's words as I sat crying, holding my 14-month-old daughter. He said, "Your child has very little hearing—only 5% in both ears." To this day I cannot remember driving home. My husband and I were totally devastated.

At that time we were living in Rockville, Md. It is only now that we realize how very lucky we were to be in Montgomery County, because we were soon introduced to all three methodologies: Cued Speech, oralism, and signing. At the same time as Courtney's diagnosis, my husband (Lee) was in the process of interviewing for a job transfer to Charlotte, N.C.

While still in Maryland, we began working with a parent-infant teacher using signs. However, we continued to investigate and learn all we could about all three methods. Within a few months we had moved to Charlotte and put Courtney in a signing program. We also began working with

Lee, Courtney, and Amy Branscome

a home-based teacher skilled in the auditory-verbal method. We soon began to feel uncomfortable with both methods. We saw that with the auditory-verbal method it would take months and months for Courtney to process simple words auditorily. We had already lost 14 months of language-development time and felt that we were falling further and further behind.

Courtney was a quite precocious 18-month-old and began to want to know the names of everything. Lee and I would run to the sign books many times only to be frustrated because there was no sign for the word she wanted to know. We also became very frustrated about the low reading levels of many deaf adults. We felt there had to be a better way.

In July of 1987 we went to the Cued Speech Center in Raleigh and learned to cue. We were skeptical at first, but began to cue to Courtney. Within six weeks Courtney understood many words, and actually cued her first word. The amazing thing was Courtney's response to Cued Speech. She was excited about the cues. She started dropping the signs and started cueing. We also noticed that although she tended not to use her voice when signing, she always used it with the cues. Soon we began to call Courtney "the sponge." She was soaking up the language.

Although I loved Courtney's sign teachers at her school, in tears I took her out of the program. The tears really came from feeling so alone with this situation. Little did I know of the enormous support I would soon get from families all over North Carolina. I soon became friends with families in Wilmington, Winston-Salem, Statesville, and the list goes on. Courtney's speech therapist, Lou Felton, originally trained in signing, learned to cue for Courtney and is now a strong advocate of Cued Speech, besides being our friend and encourager. The people at the Cued Speech Center were always ready to answer my questions and encourage me.

Many examples come to mind as I think of Courtney's language development. The most vivid one happened on Christmas Day, 1987. Courtney had just turned 2 on December 8, and had been exposed to Cued Speech for only seven months. We were at my mother's house and there were 50 or 60 people there. There were 10 family members, some of whom Courtney sees infrequently. I began to cue the names on the gifts, and Courtney handed out all the gifts without a single mistake. I remember telling a friend what Courtney had done and she exclaimed that her hearing 2-year-old could not do that. There comes a time, deep within your heart and mind, when you know for sure that you have chosen the right methodology for your child. Our time came that Christmas, and we have never doubted our choice since that day.

Cued Speech has made our family life and Courtney's preschool years so normal. Her favorite characters are Winnie the Pooh, Piglet, Kanga, Roo, Tigger, Rabbitt, and Eeyore. She also loves Bert, Ernie, Oscar, Grover, and all the other *Sesame Street* characters. Courtney cues their names with total accuracy. These character's names do not have signs, so she would be missing a big part of childhood by not knowing who they are, if she were using signs.

A few examples of Courtney's language development stand out. I picked her up at a friend's house the other day and she pointed to their TV and said and cued, "No Pooh Bear." She then smiled and said, "Pooh Bear at home." Once my husband was reading the paper and she walked up to him and said and cued "paper." He said, "No, Courtney, **I'm** reading the paper." At this Courtney stood back, put one hand on her hip, and cued with her other hand as she said, "*I* want the paper!" Needless to say, my husband handed her the paper.

Courtney is beginning to absorb the intricacies of language just through communication with us. She is cueing many "ing" words such as playing, swinging, etc. She is using plurals such as shoes, etc., and she also cues and says possessives such as "Daddy's shoes" instead of "Daddy shoes."

At the age of 2 years 5 months, Courtney was given the Peabody Picture Vocabulary Test by her speech therapist. Courtney scored 2 years 3 months on the test. Recently, her speech therapist administered the Zimmerman preschool language test. Courtney's age was 2 years 11 months. She scored 2 years 9 months expressively and, to our absolute delight, 3 years 3½ months receptively. She has had language exposure and communication through Cued Speech for only a year and a half now, but she is quickly making up for the communication void during the first 18 months of her life.

For our family Cued Speech has turned a devastating handicap into something workable and manageable. We are so happy and thankful for clear communication in English with our daughter. We feel that we are seeing a miracle happen right before our eyes.

Soon Courtney began to say four-word sentences like "I want the juice." She was following directions such as: "Wash your hands." "Take off your coat." "Hand me the yellow one." She was very aware of ownership and used ('s) appropriately: "Daddy's shoes." She began to understand categories such as *animals, food,* and *things that go.*

It truly seemed like a miracle. My husband and I began to relax and enjoy our daughter. The pressure I felt began to ease some and we began to enjoy teaching her everything we could think of. We began to think of our daughter as a true blessing from God, a joy, and we began to find a maturity in ourselves—sort of an awakening that we would never have reached had we not had her. Cued Speech was our tool with which to tell our daughter about everything—from basic language to warning her about child abuse, and telling her about God.

At the age of 3 years 8 months Courtney was again given the Zimmerman preschool language test. She scored 4 years 7 months receptively and 3 years 8 months expressively. We had not only closed the language gap, but had gone beyond it.

My husband recently took Courtney to look at some new homes going up near us. She talked the whole time. She would say "Let's go to McDonald's." "I'm hungry, let's go eat." "I want to see another new house." "I want to see a house with a upstairs." This went on and on. When we got home, exhausted, my husband sat in a chair and began to smile. I asked what was so funny. He gave me a look that no one could read without being in a similar situation, and said, "How could we ever tell her to shut up when two years ago we wondered if she would ever talk." It was one of those wonderful moments when your heart is full of the realization that you have chosen the right way.

Courtney is now mainstreamed in kindergarten with a full-time CS interpreter. She receives speech therapy four times a week and also continued auditory training. She is on age level and above. She loves her teacher and her friends. She is beginning to read, and we all find this so exciting.

The other night I was starting to read a book to her. Just after I read the title and started to read the text she said, "Oh, Mama, stop. I want to know who that book is dedicated to." When she does not understand something we cue to her she always asks, "What does that mean?" Her teacher says she does this quite often in class. We were going to another school to get her yearly audiogram and she looked at me and said, "Mama, what does *elementary* mean?" A couple of days ago she asked me, "What does *similar* mean?"

Courtney has a little brother, Lee, who is 18 months old. He's already cueing words such as *pee-pee, shoes, Courtney,* and *ball.* Lee is already talking in four-word sentences. I can't help but believe that the cueing has helped his language development.

There are still times when the reality of Courtney's deafness hits me again, but we have overcome many obstacles and in the future we will have the tools to overcome many more. I think of Courtney as my bright, funny, inquisitive daughter who happens to be deaf. *See p. 564.* *This article was reprinted in part from Center Lines, January 1989.*

Daniel Cottam
by David Cottam, 1985, update 1992
Newtown, Essex, England.

We have two deaf children. Daniel is five, and Ben is three. Daniel has a preference for activities like reading, writing, and drawing, but has a good sense of humour and mischief. Ben is rather more restless but outgoing and extremely friendly.

Daniel has no hearing; at least he has failed to demonstrate any residual hearing for so long now that we have given up auditory training at home, although he still wears a hearing aid for school.

When his deafness was finally confirmed at 18 months, Daniel showed good situational understanding and seemed bright and alert. Although he used his voice he did not babble. He showed no understanding of language unless showered with nonverbal indicators.

I was persuaded that appropriate amplification, good interaction, and auditory training lead inevitably to the beginnings of language development, but I was worried that this might be rather slow. I did not want Daniel's mental development stunted by an inefficient means of language acquisition. The best I felt able to expect was severely retarded language which would stunt his imagination and interfere with his education.

I had a great anxiety that even if he paid attention to every word I said, and I talked to him for hours a day, he would still suffer language starvation if he could not hear.

In trying to make sense of the problem of the deaf child I read a great deal and decided that Cued Speech was just what I was looking for. I had a strong conviction that it would work.

Ben and Daniel Cottam

I learnt to cue in a few weeks but at one point I was advised to give Daniel a chance to cope on a purely auditory approach first. I decided to avoid risking failure and to persist with the cueing.

After what seemed a long period of "incubation" with Daniel interested but not really understanding he gained his first few useful words and we could see signs of success. By this time my wife Christine was cueing everything too, and he was attending nursery school part time where they also cued.

After Daniel's third birthday he was undoubtedly understanding Cued Speech very well, and other people began to notice the marked improvement. I thought, if he can read cues with lip patterns which are fleeting visual stimuli, reading the printed word must be relatively easy. I knew already that he had a remarkable visual memory.

I tried Daniel with words and pictures, and he learnt to match them quite soon. I then made him a card index of almost all the words he knew, classified under headings like: Food, Family, Clothes, Animals, etc.—each with a very small picture in the corner to help him remember what the word meant. Books and words interested him and he spent hours with a variety of picture-word books and picture dictionaries until he knew every detail in them.

Daniel started trying to form letters one month before his third birthday and managed to produce his first legible words at 3 yrs 4 mths with numbers (1-12) at about the same time. A month later he wrote his first sentence, "Here is frog," and later "Here is Daniel," both beside pictures.

By this time the house was festooned with labels for him to read. I used short sentences and changed the wording from time to time so there was always something new. For example over his bed it said, "Here is Daniel's bed," then "This is Daniel's bed," then "Daniel sleeps here," then "This is my bed," "This is where I sleep," and so on, so that he encountered different constructions. He started to write his own labels, such as "this is Daddy's room" and would stick them up with "blutak."

He began to enjoy easy readers and would insist on a book instead of sweets or an ice-cream at the sweet shop. We also joined the public library and his visits there every Saturday have long been a highlight of his week. He has requisitioned all the family tickets so that he can borrow twelve books a week.

At first I would cue books to Daniel while he followed the text with a finger and my face with his eyes but he soon preferred to keep the books to himself. Sometimes I would spy on him sitting up in bed mumbling and cueing books to himself, sometimes he would still be reading and yawning hours after he went to bed.

Because Daniel lacked intelligible speech I could not really understand him when he read "aloud." It was not possible to tell how much he was understanding or if he was missing words out, but if I knew what he was reading I could tell from the cues that most of the words were being recognised. To test his comprehension I used to play games with written instructions and he invariably followed them accurately.

At 3 yrs 9 mths he did the Hamp reading test and achieved a score about twice his age. Rather than have me read to him, Daniel has always preferred the stories I make up myself. He hangs on every word and sometimes acts out little bits, laughing and squealing.

Daniel's passion for stories led me to try a game where I started off with "Once upon a time" or some such opening and he wrote the next part. At first I would provide links to keep the ideas coming, but soon he excluded me and wrote virtually the whole thing single handed with a little advice on spelling. It was only a short step from there to his first original stories which appeared not long after his fifth birthday.

One day in November, in between sandwiches at teatime,

Daniel's first story appeared, 85 words long and completed in about four minutes. He was pleased with himself, and Christine and I were delighted, so he was soon writing more. In the next month he produced his first book consisting of about twenty-two short stories which he called "Polly Tales." We have no pets so he invented two dogs named Rover and Polly and created an imaginary world inhabited by talking animals. I was impressed with the feat of sustained concentration and the apparent ease with which the language flowed.

Up to now I had done all the talking and now at last I was getting a glimpse of what went on inside Daniel's mind. When Daniel writes he gets quite excited. He makes whooping noises and sprawls all over his writing table in different postures. He likes me to read back to him what he has written, and he is clearly pleased if he makes sense and I show appreciation. He prefers to write when I am nearby because I can give praise and encouragement—I seem to be some kind of muse or catalyst—although he resents any direct interference.

Despite a large measure of success with Daniel's receptive understanding and writing I often wonder how we can improve his speech. One of the problems is that his inner language is out of step with his voice and articulation. Because he thinks fast, he tries to cue and speak much quicker than he can control his voice, lips, and tongue, and the result is very difficult to understand. When we can't understand his speech he resorts more and more to writing instead of speaking.

It is very difficult to provide Daniel with feedback to monitor his own attempts at speech. When he can make himself understood he is very pleased and will try again. When he fails repeatedly he gives up.

Daniel has become perfectly adapted to life in the family. I fear he will not try hard to talk clearly until he needs to communicate outside the family. This experience may prove unpleasant for him.

Daniel does not have friends of his own age to talk to, although he seems well liked by other children, and I wonder whether this has contributed to his imaginative life as a compensation for the lack of social outlets.

Daniel writes very quickly and can produce pages of neat printing or large sprawling words tumbling over the page, depending on his mood and the need to get his ideas down quickly. His spelling is usually good. Sometimes it errs toward the spoken form and at other times letters occur in the wrong order as if he has visualized it incorrectly. When he starts a new sentence he uses a capital letter but he rarely uses full stops. Commas also crop up only occasionally and only in lists. He hardly ever forgets to use an apostrophe to denote possession but is less reliable in contractions like "couldn't" or "don't." He grasped the use of inverted commas for speech very early and I don't recall teaching him. He always places commas (*and quotation marks*) at the beginning and end of speech thus: [",   ,"]. Capital letters and "Fancy" script sometimes appear for emphasis and occasionally just for the hell of it. He understands how to use exclamation and question marks but sometimes forgets.

I have kept all of Daniel's original manuscripts as well as every significant picture and piece of writing from the age of 20 mths. The "archive" has grown very large and was originally kept for sentimental reasons. However as he has developed I find it fascinating to look back and see his progress.

I hope Daniel's example will serve to further the use of Cued Speech and will encourage parents to get deaf children interested in reading early since the combined effect of reading and cueing has undoubtedly helped him overcome the language barrier. I doubt if he would have learnt to read so easily without Cued Speech to relate the written to the spoken form.

Ben was diagnosed deaf at three weeks (using the Auditory Response Cradle). We cued to him even before this early diagnosis. At fourteen months he was babbling nicely and showing normal understanding for a child of his age. Following a cardiac arrest and subsequent neurological damage (both boys share a heart rhythm disorder associated with deafness), Ben had to start his development again from nothing, with added physical problems.

Ben is now nearly 4 and has made a remarkable recovery. He understands quite a lot of useful language when it is cued and can lipread familiar words without cues. He can also match words and pictures. He seems to show normal intelligence but it is hard to say how advanced he might have been without brain damage. Much of Ben's energy has been spent in acquiring basic physical skills, but I still expect him to catch up eventually with his language.

Ben lacks the motor control to cue accurately, but we can understand some of his attempts. He supplements his rather clumsy cueing with little mimes and some signs, and is also quite vocal.

One of the difficulties of having two deaf children is that they compete for your attention, so Ben will probably never get the hours of undivided time Daniel had when he was younger. Of the two boys, Ben has the greater will power and determination so he will probably achieve through hard work what Daniel does through quickness of mind.

To date (*at age 5 years 8 months*) Daniel has written enough stories (60) to fill four books. The stories vary from about 85 words to 850 in some of the later stories. I published Daniel's "Polly Tales" in a small edition of seven copies for family and friends, and it was so well received that I have produced small editions of his three other books. I thought they were very good, as a doting father, but I did not know if they merited wider attention.

Update, 1992

Daniel will be 13 this summer and Ben will be 11 in a few days time. Both boys attend the Royal School for the Deaf in Exeter. Daniel still reads a great deal, anything from Agatha Christie whodunnits to Dickens, Wilde, and Maya Angeron. He must read several hundred books a year. He still writes stories and has tried his hand at plays and pantomime scripts. A local drama group performed one of his short plays last summer.

Despite Daniel's facility with language and words, his speech is still quite difficult to understand. He is much easier to follow when he cues but he hasn't many people who can cue read him that well.

Teachers at school find that cued speech is the only way they can communicate on his level as his vocabulary and use of idiom make signed English an inadequate medium. Daniel does use sign with his deaf peers, however, and is part of the school signing choir. Daniel will take the A.C.S.E. English exam next year, two years early. His other enthusiasms are history and drawing. He has a passion for the history of costume and has a small collection of items of dress dating back to Victoria.

Daniel is happily solitary and doesn't have any particular deaf or hearing friends. But, he has begun to mix at school much more of late.

Ben has a very different personality. He is very outgoing and rather restless. He made a remarkable recovery from his cardiac arrest at 14 months and the subsequent brain damage. We continued with Cued Speech and he developed quite good receptive language. Ben learnt to read using cued speech and continues to benefit from exposure at home and school.

Ben's mobility and coordination were permanently affected by the cerebral insult he received, but he has learned to walk albeit with a slightly drunken gait and enjoys riding a large tricycle which compensates for his uncertain balance.

Ben tries to cue expressively but has a very limited vocal output and unclear mouth movements. His preferred mode is signed English, used by his teacher and peers, although not to the exclusion of Cued Speech (which we prefer because it offers a much better model of

spoken language). Ben needs an effective expressive mode and it seems likely that he will become more manual. We will try to keep pace.
One of Daniel's stories appears as the second item in Chapter 25.

Alina
Synnove Trier-Engelman and Ralph Engelman
1987, update 1992

When Alina was 17 months old, we were visiting relatives in Germany, and her grandmother noticed that Alina did not respond to her name. To us, she had seemed perfectly normal all along. When we returned to the United States, it was confirmed that Alina had a profound bilateral neurosensory hearing loss—in fact, initially there was no evidence of any hearing whatsoever. We were told by the audiologist at the hospital, "She will never learn to speak like you and me." The audiologist urged us to educate her in the Total Communication mode. We were hesitant about raising her with sign language because we had read that it might make it more difficult for her to learn to speak English.

Fortunately, friends recommended that we take Alina to the New York League for the Hard of Hearing in Manhattan, an agency that does excellent speech therapy in the oral-auditory mode. Up until this point, we had been in a state of shock, and we couldn't sleep at night. We were greatly reassured by Dr. Diane Brackett of the League, who told us that Alina probably had some usable hearing which had to be trained. So, a month after her grandmother's remark in Germany, Alina was fitted with body aids and began therapy at the League.

Ralph and Alina Engelman

The first months were hard because there was little evidence of Alina's hearing. She only responded sporadically to drums and other loud sounds. When Alina had her first hearing test with her aids, two months after beginning therapy, the audiologist told us that she had rarely seen such an extreme hearing loss. How could she do auditory training with such minimal hearing?

Fortunately, we had heard about Cued Speech. Dr. Brackett,

who had worked with Scott Johndrow (a Cued Speech child), gave us information about it. We immediately called the Cued Speech staff at Gallaudet, who referred us to the Brattners (a cueing family now living in New Jersey) in Staten Island. They taught us how to cue, and we began cueing single words to Alina. At this point she was 21 months old and had virtually no vocabulary. Around the same time, she was fitted with a Telex FM auditory trainer, which she used during waking hours. In the following summer of 1984, Alina's hearing was tested again. Her hearing loss was measured at 120 dB in one ear and 110 dB in the other. She was responding more consistently to sounds, and was making good progress in speech therapy. She learned her first words: "up," "Mommy," and "Poppy." Dr. Brackett felt she was making good use of her hearing. We decided we would stay at the League and supplement her speech training with Cued Speech.

We went to the CS Family Program at Gallaudet that same summer. It was a great experience for the whole family, especially for our 7-year-old-son, Jan. By the time Jan was 9, he cued faster than anyone else in the family. That fall we went from cueing words to whole sentences. In the winter of 1984, when Alina was 2 years and 9 months old, she began using complete sentences, only a year after we started cueing.

In the fall of 1985, Alina began nursery school at a Head Start center in our neighborhood in Brooklyn, where she was the only hearing-impaired child. She attended nursery school in the morning and went to the League for speech therapy in the afternoon four days a week. Alina made friends quickly and was very comfortable in the school. She was intellectually ahead of most of the children in her class. For example, she could recognize all the names of the children when most of them could not read their own names. We were able to convince the Head Start program to pay for a Cued Speech interpreter for the later part of the year. We had trained the interpreter ourselves.

Alina's speech therapist at the League, Liz Ying, felt that Alina was ready for a more challenging school setting for the following year. We enrolled her at Old First Nursery School in Brooklyn, a small, outstanding, cooperatively run nursery school. She had two especially warm teachers who provided a highly creative and stimulating curriculum, including many interesting trips.

Again, Alina was the only hearing-impaired child in the class. Neither teacher had worked with a deaf child before, but they were sensitive to her needs and successfully included her in all classroom activities. We had trained a new Cued Speech interpreter, Mija Clemente, who had been with us at Gallaudet in the summer. She cued for Alina four mornings a week. After a long struggle with the New York State educational bureaucracy, Mija's salary was reimbursed.

The adjustment to this new school was more difficult than in the Head Start program, perhaps because Alina was 4 years old and more aware of being different. However, after the first few months she was completely accepted and included in all activities and phantasy play.

Alina's speech is still difficult to understand. While she is able to make most speech sounds, she leaves out many in spontaneous speech, especially /f/, /s/, /sh/, and /t/. (The first four of these phonemes are fricatives, which Alina certainly cannot hear.) Also, her speech—although her language is grammatically correct—often has a chopped-up quality. Nonetheless, teachers and other adults tell us that they understand much of what Alina is saying. As parents, we understand virtually everything she says. This includes understanding her wonderful dreams. She recently told of a dream in which President Reagan was sitting next to her and her mother on a bench: "He was very nice to us, and didn't sell us any guns."

Early in 1987, Alina was evaluated by the New York City Board of Education for placement in a public school kindergarten in the fall. The psychologist who tested her was surprised that she could apply all the verbal sub-tests of the IQ battery, since she was accustomed to using only the performance sub-tests with deaf children. Alina's results on the verbal sub-tests were, with one exception, average to slightly above average for hearing children her age. The psychologist wrote, "The necessity for and benefit of Cued Speech for receptive language was very much in evidence during this examination."

At our COH (Committee of the Handicapped) meeting at the Board of Education, Alina was placed in a mainstream setting at a kindergarten level with a resource room for the hearing impaired. We were granted a full-time Cued Speech interpreter. The New York system proved to be surprisingly open-minded in accommodating to Alina's needs (*at least in part due to the influence of the New York League for the Hard of Hearing*).

Recent testing at the New York League (without Cued Speech) showed that Alina's expressive language is surprisingly one year and eight months ahead of average hearing children her age. These results are based on the One-Word Picture Vocabulary Test, and are unusual for a deaf child. In receptive language she tested six months below her age level. According to Liz Ying, of the New York League, this discrepancy is probably due to the lack of contextual clues in the test. In her judgment, Alina's functional vocabulary is at or above age expectations.

Unfortunately, Alina's minimal hearing dropped further in the fall of 1986, and is now at 117 dB in one ear and 114 dB in the other. Recently, she was fitted with stronger receivers which raised her aided hearing to a level more useful in understanding speech. She is able to understand entire sentences in a familiar context solely through her hearing. This indicates to us that, contrary to conventional wisdom, visual cues (Cued Speech) helped Alina develop her skill at using her residual hearing, instead of interfering with auditory training. (*This assertion is supported by the research of Charlier and Paulissen [1986], annotated in Chapter 28.*) We further believe that the phonetic nature of Cued Speech has helped Alina teach herself to read by age 5. She sometimes takes books we are reading to her and reads them aloud herself. Alina read a book to an audience of 25 adults as part of a Cued Speech demonstration at a hearing fair this year sponsored by the New York City school system.

This summer we went to Germany to visit relatives. We have already taught Alina some German words with the help of Cued Speech. We hope that one day she will want to speak German.

During the four years since we learned of Alina's deafness our initial despair has turned to hope. We are proud of her accomplishments and confident about her future, while recognizing her growth will have its painful periods. Alina is a bright and outgoing child, but we are convinced that Cued Speech has been instrumental in her progress.

Update by Synnove Trier-Engelman, 1992

Since kindergarten Alina has been mainstreamed at P.S. 154 in Brooklyn. She has a Cued Speech interpreter with her almost all the time. She has no difficulty keeping up with the schoolwork and is an excellent student. She receives resource-room help five times a week and speech therapy after school twice a week. While her speech is not perfect, it appears that teachers and classmates understand her pretty well, and she is a good lipreader. Several times she was chosen to sing in the holiday chorus, which she enjoys a lot.

Ever since Alina was 6 years old she has been dancing with the American Dance Theatre of the Deaf. There she has learned to sign, and she is getting pretty good at it. She loves to dance and has been in many performances, once as far away as Rochester, N.Y. Recently a German magazine printed a story about the American Dance Theatre of the Deaf with photos of Alina and other members of the group. Since she is mainstreamed we find it especially important for her to have other deaf friends in the dance class.

Alina is an avid reader. In second grade she scored at the eighth-grade level on a reading comprehension test. In third grade she did exceptionally well on the standardized reading and math tests. Her reading score was at the 99th percentile among third graders nation-wide which we know was only possible because of Cued Speech. Now that she is in fourth grade we often see her reading the *New York Times*. She loves reading biographies, books on black history, Nancy Drew, Judy Blume, and the Babysitters' Club.

Since I am from Germany we go there every other year for vacation. Alina is interested in learning German and has picked up some words and phrases through my cueing them. She even went shopping alone there a number of times and managed to make herself understood.

Twice Alina has gone to a week-long sleep-away camp for deaf children. This year, however, she wants to go to a camp for hearing **and** deaf children. Alina's friends are mostly hearing. None of them know how to cue, partly because we didn't pursue it more actively. But Alina taught fingerspelling to her friend Noel and subsequently they both taught it to other classmates. They use it as a secret language when I am around.

We have a summer bungalow in the Catskill Mountains where Alina spends much time with her best friend, Pearl, who is hearing. Throughout the year they visit each other periodically and write or talk on the phone. Alina loves the relay service. We are planning to teach Pearl how to cue this summer.

Using Cued Speech in our family has been invaluable and has made it possible for Alina to be included in all communication. Since she has such a good vocabulary and reads so much she is interested in everything, whether it is David Duke, the ozone layer, or whatever else might be going on in the world around her. She could never accept being left out, ignored, or excluded from information or activities, because she is accustomed to knowing what is going on. Thanks to Cued Speech she expects to be told and to be included. She wants to be an actress, a dancer, or a teacher when she grows up, but most of all she wants to become "famous." We'll see!

This case history could just as appropriately be in Chapter 22, "Going It Alone." The family has indeed had to find its way at every step. Note that they have trained Alina's transliterators. The first portion of this story is reprinted from CS News, Fall, 1987. Alina's own observations begin on p. 568, and her sister's on p. 286.

Chapter 19
Questions Most Frequently Asked

Where can I get additional information and advice concerning Cued Speech?
Sources are listed in the Appendix.

Who developed Cued Speech and when?
R. Orin Cornett developed Cued Speech during his first year as vice president for long-range planning at Gallaudet College, beginning August 16, 1965. The system was completed at the end of August 1966. It is now available in 53 languages and major dialects.

Why was Cued Speech developed?
Cornett's original motivation was to make it possible for deaf children to become good readers at the same age as hearing children. After studying the problem, he decided that in order for this to happen the child must learn the spoken language well by the age at which he or she would be expected to start to learn to read. This would require that the deaf child should be able to receive spoken language accurately through vision during the early years of life. Thus, the original specifications were for a system that would 1) make spoken language clear through vision, and 2) be suitable for consistent use by hearing parents with their deaf child during the child's preschool years.

Is Cued Speech a teaching method (or a teaching tool) to be used in improving speech and introducing new words?
Though Cued Speech is useful for the purposes indicated, its basic purposes are to improve communication, develop language, and lead to reading competence. Cued Speech is first of all a system that provides clear communication. It leads to language development, speechreading, and reading readiness when used consistently. Danger: If parents cue only important or new words, Cued Speech will produce the same fractionated, incomplete language that results from any "key word" approach, such as premature speechreading. Every word should be cued.

How long will it take me to learn Cued Speech?
Some people learn Cued Speech in a few days and become quite proficient (although still slow) in a few weeks. Others, especially those who find it difficult to think in sounds, must work longer to achieve fluency. The basics of the system can usually be learned very quickly

with concentrated effort, especially if one attends a CS workshop and follows up immediately with regular practice with other people, or with self-instructional materials. However, the time and amount of use necessary to become able to cue comfortably and at reasonable speed varies a great deal. Motivation and ability have a great deal to do with this. A parent reviewer reports that she has seen gifted teenagers learn to cue fast and accurately in two weeks, but others may take much longer. Motivation is the most important factor.

Parents who do best start using CS with their deaf child as early as possible, even when they are still far from fluent. The response of the child inspires them to progress in their cueing. How easily one learns Cued Speech does not appear to relate to general capability or intelligence, or even to future proficiency. Motor skills, the ability to "think" specific sounds (especially vowels), and the ability to hear the differences among the vowel sounds are all involved. Some of the most graceful and fluent cuers took much longer than average to learn CS in the first place.

Will I always have to think about my cueing?
Cueing becomes a manual/mental skill like typing or playing the piano. With practice it becomes automatic. A parent (Robers) writes: "After 13 years of cueing it feels funny not to cue. It certainly is no longer a chore. We see cues as a tool. To not cue would be like walking in a pouring rain with an umbrella folded under your arm. Why not use it if you've got it?"

From the same parent:

> *My wife is a full-time cueing interpreter, but we still review words. She can cue as well as anyone, but she has trouble <u>hearing</u> herself, particularly when pronouncing short e and short i. When she has a problem word she writes it down. In the evening we listen to each other pronounce the word and cue accordingly. Often we will wind up cueing the same word differently because we pronounce the word differently.*

Should Cued Speech be used with all hearing-impaired children?
No. If a child has enough hearing, of good enough quality, to learn verbal language efficiently through audition, he/she doesn't need Cued Speech. However, practically all children with a severe-to-profound hearing loss find it very difficult to learn new verbal language through audition and can profit from Cued Speech. Also, most children in signing programs lag in verbal language and can profit from concurrent use of Cued Speech. If their parents are hearing, consistent use of CS

by hearing parents in the home can contribute substantially to language development, no matter what is done at school.

Is it enough that just the parents cue, and not the siblings, or grandparents, or friends?
For maximum development of competence in English it is essential that as many people as possible cue to the child. The quantity of the cued input is very important. It is also important that the cued input be appropriate for language development and enrichment.

Cueing seems fast and complicated; how can a child understand it?
Cueing is no faster than the sounds and syllables of speech. Once the child learns to process them he or she can soon develop the ability to decode Cued Speech at normal speaking rates without difficulty. The language patterns become very familiar, just as spoken language does. Thus, it can be processed in "chunks."

Does the use of Cued Speech interfere with auditory/oral development because it is so visual?
Not at all—in fact it is supportive because it enables the child to learn the language he or she needs to learn to hear as well as possible. However, Cued Speech does not replace auditory training or speech therapy. See Chapter 14, "Auditory Training, Cochlear Implants."

Is Cued Speech easier to learn than sign language?
The two tasks are not comparable. Learning a language takes years. Learning a finite code like Cued Speech takes a few days. It is easy to learn a few signs quickly and use them, but that is only the first of many steps in learning sign language. After Cued Speech is learned there remains the task of using it enough to develop speed and fluency, but one can say and cue *anything* after a short time.

Will and should my hearing-impaired child cue expressively?
It is desirable for your deaf child to cue, but most children have to be encouraged. The reason is that the parents and teachers are trying to get the child to express his/her language in speech, and it is difficult to reinforce him/her for both speaking and cueing. Some children cue expressively with very little encouragement. Others do not. Circumstances have a lot to do with it.

How will my child communicate?
Most Cued Speech children communicate in several ways, depending

on with whom they are communicating. With a hearing family, a CS child is likely to communicate orally to them, and receive Cued Speech from them, unless they cannot understand his/her speech without cues. With deaf friends communication may be oral, CS, signs and finger-spelling, depending on the abilities and preferences of their friends.

Will Cued Speech isolate my hearing-impaired child from other deaf children who sign?
Not if you follow our advice to provide opportunities for your child to learn to sign. We think a deaf child should eventually be bilingual, able to communicate in both hearing and deaf environments. A problem is that time should not be taken from learning verbal language too early or in too large amounts. Thus, much depends on the child's progress.

How will my child's reading level be affected by Cued Speech?
If your child receives Cued Speech consistently from an early age, the chances are good that he/she will learn to read at the same age and on the same level with a hearing child of the same ability. Read Chapter 15, "Reading," for a more complete explanation.

Why is it good to learn to cue with either hand?
An important reason for being able to use either hand is that when you cue extensively for long periods of time, as for transliteration, reading aloud, or extended conversation, one hand gets tired, and it is good to be able to shift. Even more important is the convenience of not having to shift something from one hand to the other. If you are writing, it is convenient for you to cue with the other hand instead of having to put down the pen. Also, the relative positions of the cuer and the deaf person often make it desirable to cue with the nearer hand. If while learning to cue you make a point of practicing now and then with both hands at once, and also separately with the non-dominant hand, you will soon become able to cue with either hand at will.

What should I do when my hands are occupied?
If what you need to say is urgent, free one hand, perhaps by shifting everything to the other hand. Otherwise, let your child try to lipread, and clear up any confusion later with CS. If your child has not yet developed much speechreading ability, make every effort to free one hand for cueing. However, you should not neglect to talk just because your hands are busy. As the child develops more language and more vocabulary, you can just talk in such situations. However, you should guard against doing this when it is not necessary. If you are in the

habit of cueing everything you say to your child, such situations will probably make you aware of your child's progress in lipreading.

Bill Robers writes:

> *We have had times when the hands were free and the mouth wasn't. Our younger sibling will sometimes talk with food in her mouth and cue. Gina (our hearing-impaired daughter) thus gets the same 'mushy' information we get and tells her sister to swallow first and then talk."*

From a transliterator: "I once forgot and started interpreting with a scarf over my mouth on an outside field trip in winter."

Is it possible to cue too fast for a child to understand?

Any fluent cuer can cue faster than is best for a young deaf child, even one who understands Cued Speech very well. Parents should never try to cue fast. The wisdom of a very experienced teacher of hearing preschool children caused her to admonish parents to speak calmly and slowly to their children. Research has shown that children learn language faster when it is spoken at a deliberate pace. The reason, of course, is that discourse that contains some new language has to be analyzed a bit extra to pick up new meanings of words and patterns. *Slow is beautiful!*

At what age should a CS child learn sign language in order to communicate with signing deaf people?

No categorical answer can be given to this question. If the child starts CS early and is at a normal language level at age 6, only benefit is likely to result from beginning to learn some signs. Unless circumstances produce a specific need for development of competence in signing, the amount of time devoted to acquiring sign language should be no more than a few hours a week until the child is safely growing in reading skills, probably at age 8 or 9.

A distinction should be made between learning sign language and learning signs. A CS child can easily learn a few hundred signs and be able to communicate reasonably well in Pidgin Sign English with deaf children who know both signs and some English. This will do no harm at an early age. To learn American Sign Language, with its own grammar and idioms, is a different matter. Learning sign language does not itself do harm—in fact it has many potentially beneficial effects. However, the young deaf child can spare enough time to become truly bilingual only if it is relatively certain that he/she can still meet the deadline of adequate English by the time to begin learning to read. Learning two languages concurrently reduces the time that can be devoted to each.

A safe generalization is that the majority of deaf children should have an opportunity to become proficient in PSE (Pidgin Sign English, or signs in English word order) before the age of puberty. If they can afford the time to learn a good bit of American Sign Language as well, so much the better.

How long will it be necessary to cue to my child?
Some parents assume that Cued Speech should be discontinued as soon as the child can get along reasonably well without it in communication. The question should be: "How long will exposure to Cued Speech help my child?" For a full answer refer to the following question.

How long will continued use of Cued Speech benefit my child?
Sometimes we say to parents: "You may discontinue cueing to your child when you are ready for him to stop learning more language and improving his speech and speechreading skills." A deaf person, even in adulthood, will continue to profit from further exposure to a clear, complete presentation of spoken language. Is this continued dependence on CS? A deaf child becomes progressively less dependent on having Cued Speech, in the sense that his/her ability to function without it when necessary continues to improve. On the other hand, there are at least three significant reasons why your child will continue always to need and prefer to have CS from those who can use it. For these reasons and a full discussion, refer to page 104.

Won't Cued Speech be a crutch?
Parents sometimes ask: "Will Cued Speech turn out to be a crutch on which my child will always be dependent?" For an analysis of how a deaf individual *depends* on Cued Speech to increase his/her *independence*, refer to Chapter 8, p. 106.

Do the vowel locations of Cued Speech coincide with the places where the vowels are formed in the mouth and throat?
Not at all. The locations were chosen according to which groups of vowels are used most frequently in English words. Thus, the side location (the easiest) is for the group that appears most frequently, the throat next, etc. The group with lowest total frequency is placed near the mouth, which requires the largest hand movement. The choice of which vowels to group together was designed to get maximum visual

difference (on the mouth) among the vowels in each group.

Why should everything said to a deaf child be cued?
One of the most serious mistakes parents can make is to assume that when the child's actions show he/she understands what you mean, he/she is getting the language. The child may be able to *guess* what you mean, but needs to be able to perceive every syllable to have the same opportunity as a hearing child to add the language to his/her internal phonological base for reading and speaking. Any child, hearing or hearing-impaired, needs *hundreds* of exposures to the full text of every important pattern of language, to words, phrases, and sentences, to acquire an accurate and complete internalized model. Every word and every syllable should be cued to provide maximum opportunity to acquire this mental model, which is indispensable for reading, speechreading, and accurate speech production.

Why should the deaf child cue?
Obviously, the deaf child needs to cue to other deaf children who know Cued Speech. Moreover, most deaf children who can cue well speak better when they cue. This is apparently because the motor patterns of cueing become tied in with speech production and provide extra feedback to make the right pronunciation "feel right." Cueing supports memory. Try it! It works! One of the authors has often observed Gallaudet University students rehearsing material, to help them remember it during an exam just ahead, by fingerspelling key passages. Cueing patterns contribute to memory in essentially the same way. The deaf child who cues a great deal is less likely to slip into sloppy speech in patterns that are difficult to keep intact.

Do hard-of-hearing children need Cued Speech?
This question cannot be answered categorically. Many hard-of-hearing children need Cued Speech to help them acquire language and speech faster. Some can do without it after they have a good foundation in the spoken language and can maintain language growth through reading. Then, it may be used primarily to demonstrate or clarify pronunciation of specific words or introduce new words. But, the criterion for use of Cued Speech with such a child in the first place is whether his/her acquisition of language is progressing rapidly enough. A hard-of-hearing child who is auditorily oriented but who needs Cued Speech to learn language fast enough may be difficult to train to watch carefully. Patient effort may be required to secure the advantages of Cued Speech and auditory orientation in combination.

It should be kept in mind that some hard-of-hearing children have so much nonlinear distortion that their hearing is virtually useless in discriminating speech sounds. In such cases, CS is crucial.

How can parents know whether their child needs Cued Speech?
It is the responsibility of parents to become informed about all available options and decide for themselves and their child which route is best for them and their situation. They must continue to investigate all possibilities after they have begun using a specific method, and to evaluate their child's progress. Unfortunately, all available options come without guarantees. Basically, their child needs Cued Speech if he/she is not acquiring language rapidly enough to be at a normal level for a hearing child at six years of age.

How does a child know to make sound with the cues?
The child does not know this initially, and may have to be taught. Some sounds are made from the beginning by most children. This is true of *ah*, for example, because it is made with the natural, open position of the throat. Babbled sounds can often be "captured" easily. If a parent or teacher consistently shows pleasure when the child makes a sound spontaneously, and repeats the sound with the proper cues to reinforce it, the child may begin to associate the making of the sound (how it feels and sounds when he/she makes it) with the cued and spoken response. This can result in natural, accurate vocalization as the child builds up a group of sounds and words he/she can make.

How does a child know that he or she is making the correct sound?
The child knows in part through the reaction of the person with whom he/she communicates in Cued Speech. Also, if he/she has enough residual hearing (of adequate quality), this may help. "Motor memory" of the process of making a sound may help him/her to repeat it. All this can make the child increasingly accurate in vocalization.

Will our cue children be able to read lips?
All evidence indicates that consistent exposure to Cued Speech develops all the abilities needed for lipreading. The child's growing internal model of the spoken language is the most important factor. As explained in Chapter 13, "Speechreading," factors that contribute most to lipreading ability include: familiarity with what most of the frequent words look like on the mouth, habitual association of language with what is seen on the mouth, and development of the ability to sort among various language possibilities. A Cued Speech child should not

be *taught* to lipread. Lipreading will develop naturally when the necessary capabilities are in place.

Will Cued Speech keep my child from developing full use of residual hearing?

No. Used properly, in combination with appropriate auditory training, it will enhance use of residual hearing. Refer to Chapter 14, "Auditory Training, Cochlear Implants," giving particular attention to the model for coordinated use of auditory, aural/oral, and Cued Speech inputs.

Why is Cued Speech not as popular as oral or TC approaches? It seems so logical to me.

Popularity is not necessarily determined by logic. During the first 20 years after the introduction of Cued Speech, there was little research evidence to support the claims of its proponents. Research performed in recent years has remedied this situation. Refer to Chapter 28, "Research Parents and Teachers Need to Know About." It takes time for an innovation in education to catch on. For example, consider the history of Braille, which educators of the blind ignored for 25 years.

Will cue children become confused and frustrated when they try to communicate with hearing people who do not cue?

Typically they do not. They tend to sense what they can do and adjust to it. Cued Speech provides a communication foundation that causes most cue children to become good lipreaders, and it also helps their expressive speech. Of course, they can't understand as well when lipreading as when Cued Speech is available to them. Some will be more frustrated than others by unsuccessful efforts to lipread.

How do children make the transition from CS to lipreading?

This question implies that children will eventually give up Cued Speech in favor of lipreading, which is not the case. It will always be easier for the deaf child to understand with Cued Speech. Of course, understanding an individual who does not cue will be easiest for the CS child with good language. For information on how a Cued Speech child becomes a good lipreader, refer to Chapter 13, "Speechreading."

Will I as a hearing parent ever need to learn sign language?

If by sign language you mean the American Sign Language, the answer is that you probably will not. It is likely, however, that your deaf child will want to learn at least some ASL in order to have access to social interaction with deaf people. You should probably learn a few hundred signs so you can use Pidgin Sign English with your child's deaf friends. The time it would take you to learn ASL, on the other hand, would deprive your child of much-needed input of English.

Must students be very bright to learn this system of sounds and hand movements?

The young deaf child does not learn Cued Speech as a *system*. He/she learns it naturally, in the process of communication. The process is analogous to the experience of hearing children, who do not learn to understand spoken language by consciously analyzing the different phonetic characteristics of the sounds and the ways they are put together. Both simply acquire an understanding of which words and phrases relate to specific ideas and things. Many "slow" children, and children with specific learning problems in addition to deafness, have learned Cued Speech without trouble. There is no evidence that it is harder for a deaf child to learn Cued Speech than it is for a hearing child to learn spoken language.

Should Cued Speech be used only with children who do not respond to "pure" aural/oral methods?

Cued Speech is not needed for use with children who make adequate progress in language acquisition and other communications skills with traditional aural/oral methods. However, the vast majority fail to do this. There is danger in waiting too long to see if progress will be satisfactory. Cued Speech will not "hurt" a child. If Cued Speech is used (properly) with a child who does not need it, his/her progress in learning language orally will make that fact obvious. Of course, proper use of Cued Speech includes coordinated auditory and multisensory aural/oral training as well as Cued Speech.

Each deaf child should function according to his/her own mental capabilities. A bright child needs Cued Speech if without it he or she would function only at a level judged appropriate for average hearing children. Expectations for a deaf child of lower-than-average intelligence should be lower, but parents should let the child find his/her own limits. Parents who feel that their deaf child should make better progress than he or she is currently making with traditional aural/oral methods should consult professionals who are knowledgeable about Cued Speech and are not biased against it.

Will my child's spelling ability be affected adversely by CS?

Cued Speech children encounter only the same problems with spelling that a hearing child tends to encounter—problems caused by the irregular spelling of the English language. The initial natural tendency to spell words the way they sound, until the child learns those spelled irregularly, comes from the fact that the Cued Speech child (like the hearing child) thinks in the spoken language. His/her knowledge of the language helps him/her to spell correctly all words whose spelling is regular. This is a great advantage. Cued Speech children tend to become very good spellers because of their familiarity with language.

What if my child asks me not to cue to her/him in public?
This happens with many children at puberty when they very much want to avoid seeming "different" from their peers. It is usually best to respect the wishes of your child, whose attitude is likely to change as understanding what is happening becomes more important than appearances, or as his/her confidence that she or he can "fit in" becomes stronger. Bill Robers writes:

> *I don't think our 15-year-old hearing-impaired daughter is as addicted to Cued Speech as we are. Sometimes when we are at a crowded event she asks us not to cue. But as soon as we leave she has a thousand questions about what was said. We then have to fill in the gaps where speechreading failed.*

Should we use and cue slang with our deaf child?
Absolutely. You should use both formal and informal language, including slang, to the same extent you would with a hearing child. Bill and Diane Robers sent us two examples:

> *Gina (15) has even picked up on the word "um." This used to confuse her, because she tried to put a word in that spot when speechreading. She now understands and uses 'um' as a "hesitation" syllable. She uses many colloquialisms also, such as Ha! Ha!, Boo!, Nya! Nya!, Sh-h-h, etc.*

The other example from the Robers demonstrates how much children enjoy learning dialects:

> *We had a cueing teacher from Australia visit Cincinnati a year ago. Several cueing families got together for a cookout with our visitor. The hearing-impaired kids had a grand time listening to his colorful dialect and vocabulary. Anything they didn't understand he would Americanize for them.*

Does Cued Speech have to be used both at school and at home to produce effective results?

No, but consistent use in both places is most desirable. Research done in Belgium (Hage, Alegría, & Périer, 1989) showed that use of Cued Speech only at home helped much more than use only at school. Children who had Cued Speech in both places showed the greatest difference between comprehension through speechreading alone and comprehension with Cued Speech. Fluent communication between parents and child offers more opportunities for natural language development and more relief from frustration than use at school.

Won't a child be confused when different people cue the same word differently?

No more than different pronunciations of the same word confuse hearing children. The child's experience with speech input is like that of a hearing child. He/she will learn very early that people have different speech habits, pronunciations, and accents. The Cued Speech child reacts to different dialects (conveyed through Cued Speech) in the same way a hearing child reacts. The Cued Speech child *notices* different pronunciations (when cued), but usually understands. He/she thus gains an understanding of different dialects. The CS child will spot mistakes in the cueing of different people, and may ask about them.

What will happen to my CS child on entering primary school?

We hope that Cued Speech will be used with your child in the school he/she attends. If not, he/she will simply enter school with more language, a larger vocabulary, superior lipreading skills, and a better foundation for reading, writing, and speaking than if he/she had not had Cued Speech. Continued exposure to Cued Speech in the home and with friends will help the child continue to make good progress even if Cued Speech is not available at school.

What if my child learns sign language from deaf friends?

Great! But, it might be better to provide an opportunity before your child has to look for one. Refer to Chapter 23.

How can my Cued Speech child communicate with the many deaf people who only know signs?

By 1) learning 400 to 500 signs and communicating with them in Pidgin Sign English, or 2) going all the way and learning American Sign Language well enough to communicate with them on their own terms. Most children who grow up with Cued Speech in the home will feel a need for some interaction with deaf persons and deaf culture, at some point. Refer to Chapter 23, "What About Sign Language?"

If no one in our school system knows about Cued Speech, how can we get it into our system?
First, ask them to look into Cued Speech to explore it and consider its possible use. Approach a speech therapist and try to sell the idea of using it in therapy sessions. Try to get the school system to send the speech therapist (if interested) to a workshop. If the therapist learns it and uses it with your child, she/he can possibly teach other staff members. However, an inservice workshop should be preferred. Try to convince the school authorities that CS is not only the best approach for your child, but cheapest in the long run. If you have used Cued Speech long enough to feel confident, offer to teach staff members. But get some tips on how to teach it—from the sources of help listed in the Appendix. Refer to the last section of Chapter 28 for information on how to present Cued Speech to different kinds of people.

When can I stop using Cued Speech with my deaf child?
You may stop cueing when you are willing for your child to stop learning new language through conversation; to be under stress when communicating with; and/or be confused often. Leave it to the rest of the world to give your child practice at unaided communication.

Does a child have to have any hearing to learn Cued Speech?
No. Any residual hearing supports the development of speech and speechreading, but it is not necessary for learning the spoken language or for communication with Cued Speech.

Will use of Cued Speech at home interfere with the child's progress at school if Cued Speech is not used there?
The opposite is true. If the program at school is oral, the use of Cued Speech will support and enhance everything done at school. If the school program uses a sign system, use of Cued Speech at home will support progress in learning and using spoken and written language. This will be further enhanced if the school uses Cued Speech to work on spoken language as part of Total Communication.

Is Cued Speech harder to teach to a child who has learned signs?
No. The signs the child knows can be used to teach the meaning of new spoken words delivered with Cued Speech. Children who already have good communication with their family through signs may resist

learning a new method, but this will not happen if parents introduce Cued Speech appropriately, as a way of clarifying spoken language.

Does a child with a cochlear implant need Cued Speech?

The answer depends on whether what the child receives through the implant is sufficient for him/her to learn language efficiently and rapidly without Cued Speech. Refer to Chapter 14.

Under what conditions should a CS child get a cochlear implant?

This is a very complex question, which can be answered only after careful diagnosis. Refer to Chapter 14 for details.

Is Cued Speech effective when started with older children, 8 to 12 years old?

The results depend on the child, the parents, and the school system. If there has been limited progress in verbal language in the earlier years, not all the time can be made up except with very able children and dedicated parents. One problem is that old habits are hard to break. However, there have been cases of spectacular progress with children starting at 8 and 9 years of age. Refer to Chapter 17.

Can parents learn Cued Speech by themselves?

Yes, but it is much more difficult that way. Self-instructional materials of various kinds can be used (see Appendix for details). We strongly recommend prior attendance at a workshop or family Cued Speech weekend (or week). Contact with a skilled cuer, even by phone, can help the person who is using self-instructional materials.

What if my child is slow to speak, or speaks unintelligibly?

If speech develops very slowly, after receptive understanding is progressing well, your child may need special training in speech. For details, refer to Chapter 12 and Chapter 15.

Should a CS child continue to have a CS transliterator in college, or switch to a sign interpreter?

CS kids testify that they want to know exactly what the teacher says, which is not possible with a sign interpreter. They do not want or need a pre-digested version, which is what an interpreter can deliver. An interpreter receives the message in English and produces the nearest approximation he/she can in the vocabulary of sign language, which sometimes doesn't fit well. A CS transliterator doesn't interpret—she or he conveys exactly what the teacher says. CS kids decode the same "raw" English their classmates receive. This process causes them to develop the same degree of sophistication in understanding that their classmates get, and they want it that way. Refer to the observations of the older deaf young people in Chapter 25.

How many people use Cued Speech in the United States and elsewhere?

Actually, no one knows. Our current estimate is that it is used in 300 to 350 places in the United States, with 1,500 to 2,500 children, but this total is not reflected accurately in any broad-scale surveys. The reason is that most (perhaps all but 30 or so) of the programs where Cued Speech is used are public school programs that found themselves with a few hearing-impaired children whose parents were unwilling to send them away to a residential school. The administrators in charge looked for the simplest, most effective and least expensive way to take care of these children, and chose Cued Speech. Most of these programs are too small to appear on the lists of programs included in surveys of deaf education, and may not be counted. The Cued Speech Office at Gallaudet College has a confirmed list of only about 200 places in the United States where Cued Speech is used, but the actual number is considerably larger because of under-reporting of locations where only a few children are involved.

We know of use of Cued Speech in more than a dozen countries. By percentage of total numbers of hearing-impaired children, use of Cued Speech in such countries as France and Belgium is probably higher than in the United States. At the 1990 Centennial Celebration of the Alexander Graham Bell Association, in Washington, D.C., Brigitte Charlier (of the Laboratoric de Psychologie Expérimentale, in Brussels, Belgium) stated that 5,000 persons in France were using Cued Speech. As of August, 1991, CS had been adapted to 53 languages and major dialects, with audiocassette lessons available in 33.

Many individuals involved in the teaching and promotion of Cued Speech encounter questions with negative implications, from individuals who are opposed to it or at least very skeptical about it. One professional, also a CS parent, submitted the following questions she has had to field.

Why would you use something that is based on sounds to teach a child who cannot hear? That makes NO sense!

Oh? Does a TDD make sense? It is based on sound, using sounds conveyed by telephone to transmit the written message to a deaf individual. Ask deaf users of the 22-electrode cochlear implant, which through electronics uses sounds to stimulate nerve impulses, whether it makes sense to hear again. Talk to people whose lives have been saved by penicillin about whether it makes sense to use something that comes from a "grungy" old mold. Many miraculous innovations do not, to some people, seem to "make sense" at first. Ironically, parents just introduced to CS often observe "It makes so much sense!"

Isn't Cued Speech a denial of deafness?

Are medicines a denial of health problems? Cued Speech is designed to enable the parents of a deaf child to overcome or minimize the usual detrimental effects of deafness. Cued Speech does not deny the child the opportunity to learn sign language and have deaf friends in a signing culture. It is not a substitute for sign language.

Isn't Cued Speech something that was developed by a hearing person to make deaf children more like hearing children?

To enable deaf children to share with hearing children the advantages of reading, knowledge of the English language, and the ability to communicate in English. It is not designed or intended to keep them from sharing in interaction with signing deaf people and deaf culture.

Why do deaf adults reject Cued Speech?

Some do and some don't. The reason many deaf adults oppose Cued Speech is that they do not understand what it is and how it works. Some fear it is part of a plot to eliminate sign language. Nothing is further from the truth, as may be demonstrated in the next few years through ASL/English bilingualism projects using Cued Speech. Deaf adults have had to fight so long for the right to use their language that they tend to be apprehensive about anything that might be used against it. We don't blame them for misunderstanding about Cued Speech.

How do you justify separating deaf children from their natural language/culture?

How do you justify separating a baby from its mother's milk, and feeding it with a bottle, if it cannot digest her milk? Hearing parents cannot give a deaf child ASL, but they can give him/her the language he or she needs to learn to read, write, speak, and lipread. Most deaf children need the opportunity to learn sign language and deaf culture from deaf people. They also need to learn their parents' language.

Tamara Suiter, child of deaf parents, was asked at 8 years of age by a class at Gallaudet University: "Which is easier for you to understand, signs or Cued Speech?" She refused to choose, insisting that both are easy. There is no reason a deaf child cannot have the advantages of both English and sign language. Cued Speech can co-exist with ASL.

Whom do Cued Speech adults talk to? They don't fit in with either deaf or hearing.

You have answered your own question, incorrectly. Ask Tiri Fellows, senior at Gallaudet University, if she "fits in" with the students there, or with her many hearing friends. She grew up on Cued Speech, and now gets the best of both worlds. Ask Leah Henegar Lewis (the first Cued Speech kid) if she "fits in" with her hearing husband and their hearing friends, and with the hearing people where she works, and if she enjoyed playing the lead in *Children of A Lesser God* in 15 performances in Raleigh, N.C., using ASL. Ask the 14 Cued Speech young people at NTID/RIT if they "fit in" there.

Since few people cue, doesn't Cued Speech isolate deaf children even more than sign language does?

You are overlooking the fact that Cued Speech helps the deaf child become better able to communicate with the larger society. Cued Speech doesn't isolate a deaf child from anyone—it only helps reduce isolation from the public. Not learning signs in addition to CS will isolate a CS youngster from deaf people.

Isn't Cued Speech another kind of sign language?

No. It is not a language at all, but a code in which any spoken language can be delivered through vision. Speech is a code in which spoken language can be delivered acoustically. Fingerspelling is a code in which the written representation of a spoken language can be delivered manually. Sign languages are not codes in the same sense. Signs are symbols for concepts, just as words are, and sign languages are true languages in their own right. Stasie Jones, at Wellesley College, is receiving English, Spanish, and some Russian through Cued Speech transliteration.

What is the difference between cueing and fingerspelling? They both seem to accomplish the same thing, don't they?

Cued Speech is a code representing spoken language, whereas fingerspelling represents written language. There is a great difference. A deaf child needs to learn both spoken and written language. However, Cued Speech has the great advantage of showing how to pronounce each word, and thus provides the base for speaking, lipreading, and reading.

At what age or grade do you recommend mainstreaming?
It is not a matter of age or grade, but of readiness and available support services. The deaf child needs reading and English skills comparable with that of hearing children his/her age, within the range permitted for hearing children in the class. The majority of children brought up with Cued Speech in the home are mainstreamed by second or third grade. Almost all such children should have a trained Cued Speech transliterator. Refer to Chapter 20, "Mainstreaming."

How would you teach a young child to cue?
Refer to Chapter 18, "Starting with a Very Young Child."

Why did you choose Cued Speech instead of TC? (This question is addressed to many parents who are using Cued Speech.)
Each parent or teacher must answer this question individually. Two of them are 1) So I can use language without vocabulary limits, and 2) So my child will learn to read, speak, write, and lipread better. Chapter 2, "What is Cued Speech?" provides many possible reasons, as do Chapters 11 to 16, 20, 24, and 25.

How can you expect a young deaf child to have the fine motor skills necessary to cue?
The same way we expect the child to have the fine motor skills for signing, writing, speaking, manipulating objects, etc. They will come. Many people overlook the fact that signing and, especially, fingerspelling, require more fine motor skills than cueing. Signing requires all sorts of motions, some very complex, but a young deaf child can make approximations of signs that serve as well as approximations of words in the speech of a young hearing child. Approximation of the cues and lip movements by a young deaf child serve the same purpose.

Chapter 20
Mainstreaming

The role of parents in mainstreaming is crucial. Their responsibilities center in three areas: 1) making sure that the qualifications of their child for mainstreaming are evaluated carefully and accurately; 2) making sure that the school system arranges for the proper mainstream environment, with all of the needed support services; and 3) providing the home and out-of-school support needed by the child.

Integration, mainstreaming, and recently *inclusion* are terms used in reference to the placing of special children in school classes for regular children. The term *mainstreaming* is used in this book to mean simply the inclusion of hearing-impaired children in classes composed primarily of children with normal hearing, for any purpose, with good or bad results.

During and before the early part of this century in the United States, many public school systems practiced mainstreaming as a means to minimum effort and least expense. Many of them routinely accepted children of parents who were unwilling to send their hearing-impaired children to residential schools, with little thought of providing special services of any kind. Children were placed in regular classes because the educators could think of little else to do with them. In most cases the teachers themselves were under no pressure to provide support services of any kind, although sensitive and conscientious teachers often tried to do so of their own volition. School systems that provided speech therapy to hearing children usually expanded the therapy services to include those with hearing impairment, even though the therapists typically had little or no special training for providing therapy to hearing-impaired children. Children with mild or moderate hearing deficits, if furnished with appropriate hearing aids, sometimes did reasonably well in such situations, despite the lack of appropriate support services needed for successful mainstreaming of deaf children.

Children with severe-to-profound hearing deficits who were *integrated* (the term used then) in the public schools typically performed very poorly, and in many cases were severely and irreparably damaged by the experience. Many sat in classes, year after year, with little idea of what was going on. Some were actually diagnosed as "mentally retarded" and even committed to institutions for the mentally deficient, only to be found later to be of normal or higher intelligence.

From about 1935 to about 1965 there was a growth of sensitivity to the needs and rights of disabled persons generally. There was also growing recognition of the potential benefits of inclusion of persons with disabilities in the "main stream" of the educational process, if they could be placed in situations appropriate to the abilities of the individuals in question and provided support services designed to increase the chances of success. This movement was abetted by the publication of several important and very critical reports on the status of education of the hearing impaired. One was *Education of the Deaf — A Report to the Secretary of Health, Education and Welfare,* completed in 1965 by the Advisory Committee on the Education of the Deaf. Even more incisive was *Toward Equality, Education of the Deaf,* the report of the special Commission on Education of the Deaf, appointed to report to the President and the Congress of the United States. (See p. 7.)

Growing concern about persons with disabilities culminated in the passage in 1975 of Public Law 94-142, the Education for All Handicapped Children Act. This legislation affirmed the right of all handicapped children to be educated in the *least restrictive* environment commensurate with their needs and abilities. The term *mainstreaming* does not actually appear in this law or its accompanying regulations. However, PL 94-142 has been widely interpreted as implying that the ideal environment is the "mainstream" if with appropriate support services the handicapped child can cope in that environment.

Other important pieces of legislation bearing on the education of hearing-impaired children, some passed before P.L. 94-142 and some as late as 1990, are described and explained in Chapter 30, in the section, "The Rights of Deaf Children and Their Parents." Federal law obliges school systems to provide each child with an educational program that is *appropriate* for that child. Further, the law makes it clear that the key to providing a least restrictive environment is provision of the specific support services needed by the child.

A good resource on mainstreaming is *Hearing-Impaired Children in the Mainstream,* edited by Mark Ross, York Press, 1990. This book provides valuable information on various aspects of mainstreaming, in chapters written by noteworthy educators. Two chapters were written by administrators of large Cued Speech programs. See App., p. 755.

Requirements for Successful Mainstreaming

Children with a severe-to-profound hearing deficit can perform successfully in the mainstream only through an effective combination of several factors. These include each child's personal qualifications for mainstreaming; the support provided in the out-of-school environment, especially in the home; the maintenance of a classroom environment appropriate for the child, including an interpreter/transliterator, if needed; and the quality and appropriateness of the other support services provided by the school, such as speech/language therapy, and a resource teacher using the child's preferred mode of communication.

A deaf child's personal qualifications for mainstreaming include personality and self-image, orientation toward others, oral communication skills, language level and skill at receiving and communicating it accurately in the available modality, reading ability, and general knowledge. Of great importance among personal qualities are resilience, self-confidence, the ability to function in spite of being confused, a positive orientation toward others and a desire to communicate with them, and the drive to succeed in the mainstream.

The Most Important Requirement

In our opinion, the most important single requirement for successful academic mainstreaming of a child with a severe-to-profound hearing impairment is the ability to read at close-to-normal levels, *preferably within one grade level of the average for the children in the classroom.* This is a stringent requirement, but a deaf child in a regular classroom must learn a large share of what he or she learns through reading. Otherwise, for successful performance, the entire classroom procedure will need to be restructured for the benefit of the deaf student. This is neither practical nor desirable for the hearing children. The alternative is that the child who is profoundly hearing impaired will tend to be "lost" much of the time. A closely related requirement is that the child be highly skilled at receiving language in the form in which it will be presented in the classroom. Some children have been mainstreamed with Cued Speech soon after starting to learn it, with less-than-desirable results. Some have succeeded under such conditions, but only because of ability and outstanding home support.

The vast majority of children who grow up with CS in the home from an early age are mainstreamed, at least partially. Most are mainstreamed fully except for an hour or so of assistance each day by a cueing resource teacher. Some are mainstreamed even in preschool, many in kindergarten, and almost all by second or third grade. Mainstreaming is not appropriate for some of these children, though it may be the most desirable of the options available in the situation.

Parents using CS should give careful attention to the needs of mainstreamed children. If their child is mainstreamed under less-than-optimum conditions, they need to face the fact that the support their child needs from them is thereby increased. Applying the reading-level requirement suggested above is feasible only in programs with enough CS children to set up self-contained CS classes for those who are not yet fully qualified for mainstreaming. In many situations it is thus necessary to choose between two inappropriate alternatives, such as 1) mainstreaming a CS child whose reading-comprehension level is not adequate, and 2) putting that child in a self-contained class providing either a traditional aural/oral environment or a TC environment. The choice is often difficult.

Many CS children placed in a traditional oral program or a TC program to secure the benefits of instruction in a self-contained class have succeeded. In most cases this has happened because the parents have worked very hard at home. Most were using Cued Speech consistently, to get language levels up to the level needed to support reading at the required level. Also, they have pushed the school systems to provide the child an hour of help each day by a cueing resource teacher. This teacher helped the child keep up in the work covered in classes, and/or helped in language development and reading.

Some parents have managed to develop a cadre of cueing friends among their child's hearing friends, in the neighborhood and/or school, to increase incidental exposure to language through Cued Speech. Many CS children have succeeded under less-than-ideal circumstances. They have been able to do so only by dint of parental effort, persuasion, school cooperation, and individual aptitude.

Most profoundly deaf children are far below the reading level needed for academic mainstreaming. Moreover, the gap between reading levels of deaf and hearing children increases throughout the school years. A nationwide study by the Gallaudet University Office of Demographic Studies (Trybus and Karchmer, 1977) revealed that, for 8-year-old prelingually deaf children, the probability of reading within one grade level of hearing children is .036, or 3.6%. For 19-year-old students it was 0.001, or less than one-tenth of 1%. The role of CS in providing a base for reading is crucial for academic mainstreaming.

A deaf child is generally mainstreamed in order to provide him/her with social benefits, academic benefits, or both. In general, a hearing-impaired child who is capable of successful mainstreaming in academic classes such as English and social studies can be expected to derive social benefits as well as academic benefits. A child whose language level and academic skills are substantially below those of hearing children his/her age may benefit from being mainstreamed in one or more classes in which limited verbal and academic skills will not prevent successful performance. Classes typically selected for such children are physical education, art, and other subjects in which the verbal load can be light, or which tend to use a special language or symbol system, such as arithmetic.

Importance of Out-Of-School Learning

One of the basic problems of educating deaf children is that, typically, they learn much less during out-of-school hours than hearing children do. Few educators of deaf children would suggest that deaf children can be taught, in school, as rapidly as hearing children can be taught. Any deficiency in out-of-school learning, at home and elsewhere, causes deaf children to fall even further behind their hearing peers. For this reason, specific attention and effort must be devoted to assuring that deaf children learn a great deal outside of school, especially if they are mainstreamed in academic classes.

If Cued Speech is used consistently in the home, learning is accelerated a great deal. Out-of-school learning *outside the home* is highly dependent upon the opportunity for effective communication with peers and others. It is even more dependent upon reading ability and the motivation to read. Reading should become the major avenue of information and new language by age 10 or 12.

Needed Support Services

The support services that need to be provided by the school depend, of course, on the child in question—specifically, on the factors listed above. The needed support services tend to vary in degree rather than kind, since most mainstreamed children need all of them to some extent. They must include at least the following:

1) The school environment must be one in which the child can understand what the teacher says and also be reasonably successful in attempts to communicate with others. The child must have a "fall back" method of communication that is quite dependable. Someone must be available, whenever needed, who can communicate with him/her in the preferred modality—in this case, Cued Speech. The only fully satisfactory way of meeting this need for a CS child is for the school system to furnish the student a dedicated Cued Speech *transliterator*, whose job is to convey exactly what is said in the classroom. The importance of transliteration goes far beyond enabling the deaf child to get the information provided. The *skill* of the classroom teacher, the *logic* behind what is presented and how it is organized, and the *impact* of the presentation are all diluted unless the deaf child receives the full

equivalent of what classmates are receiving. 2) The child needs a willing classroom teacher (for the mainstream situation) who is sensitive to the problems and needs of a deaf child and willing to adjust to them as necessary and feasible. At the least this includes forming certain habits: facing the class when talking, making heavy use of written and other visual materials, and furnishing to the class (or at least the deaf student or his/her parents) copies of outlines, assignments, and plans, such as test dates and class requirements. The need for these special efforts on the part of the teacher is reduced if the student has a CS transliterator and (for older children) a note taker.

The teacher should anticipate and prepare for situations in which the deaf student may be unable to follow what is happening, as when a video is shown. Since the student is unable to watch the video and the transliterator simultaneously, he/she can get only a limited idea of the content. The teacher needs to alert the resource teacher (most mainstreamed students need one) to brief the student on the video in advance and review it after it is seen, so that initial comprehension will be enhanced and any confusion can be cleared up. This procedure can enable the student to give virtually full attention to watching the movie while it is being shown. An alternative is for the teacher to assign the student to another activity while the video is being shown, if it is not essential that he or she see it. A more desirable alternative might be for the resource teacher to view the video separately with the student, stopping to explain or clarify as needed. If a film-strip version of the material is available, the resource teacher could use it. Another possibility is for the student to view the video at home, with a cueing sibling or parent who will transliterate or explain when the student stops the tape to ask questions. Whenever ordering new videotape materials, or ordering replacements, the school should check on the availability of captioned editions, which solve the problem.

The school should provide *inservice training* for all classroom teachers who are likely to accommodate mainstreamed deaf children. Subjects covered should include briefing on deafness and its effects, use of techniques such as recitation by the children through writing on the chalk board, extensive use of overhead projectors and other media devices, furnishing the child with outlines and a simplified syllabus, writing the list of announcements on the chalk board, listing homework assignments on the board or furnishing a written copy, providing a written list of students in the class, taking care to report a noisy air conditioner or other disruptive equipment, being alert to opportunities for use of captioned video materials, etc. It may even be best to request transfer to a quieter room, exchanging with a class without a hearing-impaired student. The most striking example of school cooperation reported to us was the carpeting of the classroom for the benefit of the one deaf student in an Ellington, Conn., public school.

One of the most important areas of briefing for classroom teachers is that of teaching in a way that supports maximum effectiveness of the transliterator. Among the topics that should be included are: 1) remembering to talk directly to the student, not the interpreter, 2) being careful to watch for signs that the deaf student wants to respond or ask a question (the small time lag in transliteration makes the deaf student as much as a second behind the others, in putting up his/her hand), 3) emphasizing important items by speaking slowly or pausing, which are good techniques in teaching children with normal hearing, 4) finding the best place in the classroom for the deaf student to sit, usually on the front row, one seat to the right or left of center, 5) making sure the transliterator is in the line of sight from the client (deaf student) to the teacher, and 6) seating good cuers near the client, if possible. Other techniques for accommodating the deaf student's needs should be discussed. An example: When correcting math or English homework, the teacher may lend to the deaf student a copy of the teachers' edition of the text, which contains the answers, while calling out the answers to the class. Or, the teacher could stand beside the deaf student and grade his/her paper while calling out the answers.

Many mainstreamed students will need a period each day with a resource teacher. This teacher must be able to communicate well with the student in Cued Speech. She/he is expected to keep in touch with the classroom teacher(s) regarding the student's progress and to keep informed of any gaps that need to be made up. On days when no specific remedial or reinforcement work needs to be done, the resource teacher can use the time for language enrichment, vocabulary expansion, or general knowledge enhancement. The resource teacher should also keep in touch with the family regarding any areas in which the family can be of special help in reinforcement or remedial effort.

The resource teacher may be serving more than one student in a given hour, and must adapt to this, assigning activities to one student while working with another and finding other ways to spread the assistance. The resource teacher will also assist students who need long-term remedial work in a specific area.

The mainstream student should receive regular instruction in audition and speech production, at least three times a week. Oral communication skills are extremely important to social interaction with hearing peers who do not cue. Ideally, a group of hearing friends will become fluent cuers, able to transliterate as needed. This expands communication, not only with them, but with non-cuers with whom the deaf student's oral communication needs to be supported occasionally.

Mainstreaming With a CS Transliterator

Most children brought up on Cued Speech will reach a point at which some mainstreaming is desirable and feasible. In fact, this seems to be the norm for CS children. Though different children have different needs, practically all CS children with a severe or profound hearing loss will need a transliterator for effective mainstreaming. Exceptions may exist in a nonacademic class with a teacher who cues enough to clarify important terms and clear up confusion, and in which there may be hearing classmates who will cue as needed.

There is no substitute for a full input of information on everything that happens or is said in academic classes. Most arrangements other than the provision of a transliterator/interpreter deprive the deaf child of a great deal of needed information and opportunity for interaction. Opinions differ on the alleged value of mainstreaming without an interpreter in nonacademic classes. If mainstreamed without a cueing transliterator, the child should certainly have a cueing resource teacher to furnish pre-teaching to prepare the child (as needed) for the class period, plus post-teaching to clear up any confusion and to clarify any special terminology needed.

Mainstreaming in academic classes is a different matter. Not only should the hearing-impaired child know language on a par with most of the other children, but he/she must have a cueing transliterator in order to make progress commensurate with ability. Without a transliterator, the child cannot learn new material readily and will have to try to make up through reading and a resource teacher everything that is missed in class. In the upper elementary grades the child will also need a notetaker, since it is not possible to write notes and watch the transliterator at the same time. *To be consistently uncertain about what is being said in class is a burden few children can bear without serious damage to motivation and self-esteem.* Parents must not make the mistake of thinking that when and if their child is mainstreamed their load will necessarily be lighter because the child is receiving consistent cueing at school. The opposite may be the case. A deaf child in the mainstream situation may have difficulty in adjusting to the pace and the procedures of the mainstream classes, and may thus need more help than before. There is likely to be more homework than before, so that parents may need to provide more support at home, at least until their child becomes fully acclimated.

What if the Classroom Teacher is Reluctant?

First of all, parents should look at the problems facing a teacher who for the first time has a deaf child in the class. Good teachers have a well-developed style of teaching which takes advantage of the interests of the students and adapts to their needs and interests. They set a pace that is as fast as can be safely maintained, so interest will not lag. When the teacher learns that a deaf child is to join the class, she/he may have had no chance to participate in the decision. If he or she is a good teacher, his/her immediate concern will be about whether accommodation of the deaf's child's needs will reduce her/his over-all effectiveness. The teacher is very likely to decide that having the deaf child will interfere. Thus, the teacher is torn between desire to maintain the pace of the class as a whole and her/his response to the special needs of the deaf child. Parents should understand and be prepared for these concerns on the part of the teacher. They should also be prepared to discuss ways of meeting the needs of the deaf child with little or no impact on the class, and perhaps even with some beneficial impact. If the parents show awareness and acceptance of the problems faced by the teacher, and gratitude for supportive behavior from the teacher, effective mainstreaming will be more likely.

If the deaf child has a Cued Speech transliterator during the class and even on field trips, the problems are simpler, but there are some. If the child has no transliterator, there are almost unavoidable delays in classroom procedure unless the teacher simply decides that the deaf child must "sink or swim." If the child is doing well, he/she will want to understand everything that is said in class. No matter how well the child lipreads (with the aid of residual hearing), there will be situations in which important things are missed. For example, when a child in the class asks a question, the deaf child is unlikely to see the first part of the question, and this almost always causes a failure to understand. Then, if the deaf student asks the teacher what was said, time is consumed in the explanation. A parent should be prepared to suggest a simple way of avoiding this problem. Presumably, the teacher requires students to raise their hands and be recognized in order to speak. If the teacher will require each child to wait until his/her name is spoken, the teacher can make a practice of pointing to the child before saying the name. This enables the deaf child to look at the student before he/she starts to speak, greatly increasing the probability of understanding. This procedure requires only a fraction of a second of extra time, and avoids a choice between letting the deaf child be confused and taking time to clarify the question.

Not all the problems faced by the teacher can be solved as easily as that of the example above. Both the parents and the teacher must exercise patience and flexibility to achieve the best accommodation of the deaf child's needs along with those of the other students. Most good teachers will be alert to the benefits that accrue to the hearing children through the presence of a deaf child and the accommodations that can be made. The acceptance and appreciation of special persons should be considered an important part of the educational process.

Transliterating vs Interpreting

Parents need to be aware of the difference between *transliterating* and *interpreting*. The job of the Cued Speech transliterator is to convey to the child *everything said* by the teacher, classmates, and visitors, as well as the relevant sounds in the environment, such as a door slamming, chalk squeaking, someone sneezing, etc. A signing *interpreter*, like a person who translates from English to French, understands the message in English and expresses an approximation of its meaning in whatever sign system he/she is using, be it ASL or some form of signed English. Signs, even those of Sign English, cannot correspond one-to-one to the words of English. Nor can signs conform to letters or syllables. Transliteration can be done only with Cued Speech or fingerspelling. Unfortunately, the Registry of Interpreters of the Deaf chooses to use the term transliterate to refer to the conversion of a message in spoken English to any form of manually coded English. We say this is translation, not transliteration.

When served by a signing interpreter, the deaf child does not have to understand English words, but only the signs. The English words bypass him or her by being translated into signs by the interpreter. To understand the message, he/she does not have to think English words, or even to know them in written form.

A Cued Speech transliterator can also interpret, changing the message to make it more understandable to the child in question. This should be done only in a case in which the deaf child is confused by unfamiliar language, or in the beginning stages of CS use with children who have meager language skills. As a general rule the mainstreamed CS child should be expected to "digest" the same "raw English" his hearing classmates are receiving, and thus to develop the same sophistication in understanding English. If interpreting (rather than just transliteration) in Cued Speech is needed consistently, the child is not appropriately mainstreamed.

For additional perspectives on the differences between CS transliteration and sign interpreting, refer to the observations of persons skilled at both, in Chapter 27, "Observations from Professionals."

Two Students' Views

Steven Scher, a profoundly and prelingually deaf youngster whose views are given in more detail in Chapter 25, summarized the benefits of having a Cued Speech transliterator as follows:

1) Receiving the exact language the teacher is using, seeing exactly what the hearing students are hearing—no word changes, no word order changes, no ideas simplified. 2) If I am in class with another deaf student who has a sign interpreter, I sometimes notice how the interpreter does not repeat verbatim what the teacher is saying. Sometimes the sign interpreter substitutes words. I don't want that. I don't want an interpreted version. I want the actual message. 3) Transliterators can cue sound effects—a book dropping, a bee buzzing. They can also cue accents, like a Boston accent or a New York accent. Also, they can show you where to accent words and how to pronounce foreign words that come up.

A 13-year-old profoundly deaf boy, Simon Roffé, wrote the following under the title: "The Qualities of A Good Interpreter."

As the years went by I have learned the qualities I like in an interpreter. When I was a kid in kindergarten, first and second grade, I thought that a good interpreter was a friend and that was the only quality that a good interpreter had to have. As I got older, I learned that that's not the only quality a good interpreter needs.

One of the qualities I look for in a good interpreter is that the interpreter interprets all the sounds in the room, not just the people talking. For example, if there was a bee in the room, the interpreter should tell the client that there was a bee by saying the sound the bee is making, "bzzzzz."

Another quality in a good interpreter is the way he/she cues—like, if they cue too tightly or tensely. It should be more relaxed and loose. Most of all, the interpreter should be sitting up with good posture. Their elbow position should be slightly outward, not leaning on anything, so that the hand is straight. The fingers should not be curled.

Another good quality in an interpreter is that he/she knows the setting they are in. If they are in a junior or senior high, they should not put themselves in a position where they have to discipline students. I think the hearing students will not like the deaf kid if the interpreter disciplines them. They will think it would not have happened without a deaf kid in the class.

Female interpreters should not wear loud nail polish that will stand out, like red. Clear or light color nail polish is okay, but nothing bright. I also don't like lipstick on an interpreter.

I believe that a good interpreter should understand that a deaf child has every right that a hearing child has. For example, if the deaf child says he has to go to the bathroom and gets the pass, but doesn't go to the bathroom and makes a phone call instead, the interpreter should not tell the teacher that he lied. This is an example of privacy.

Right now they are giving a test for Cued Speech interpreters that tells what they should do. I believe if they do good on that test, then the interpreter will be a good interpreter according to my standards.

Notetaking

A mainstreamed student served by an interpreter or transliterator cannot take notes effectively. Thus, the services of a notetaker are essential unless the teacher regularly provides extensive outlines and syllabi. Notetaking can be provided most easily by a good student, enrolled in the same class, who simply uses carbon paper or some other kind of pressure-sensitive paper to make a second copy of the notes regularly produced. It is important that the student in question be one who habitually makes good, clear, complete notes for himself or herself. This procedure is so simple and inexpensive that its importance can be easily overlooked. Kathy Goodall writes after three years of transliterating for her son, Matthew, in grades 6, 7, and 8:

My client misses 50% of what goes on in a history, literature, or science class if he takes his own notes. As a result his test scores are sometimes not as high as what he is capable of. One method that has helped is to ask a good student to accept the task of note-taking, a different student in each class. At the end of the class the notes can be taken to the office and photocopied, so that the client can have a copy. An alternative is for the teacher to furnish her own notes to the client at the beginning of the class. This has the advantage that the client can read the notes as there are pauses in the class procedure. In English class, when the students read their own stories aloud, my client prefers that after each student reads his story he passes it to the client, who then reads it while the next student is reading aloud. This makes it easier for the client and the interpreter because many students are hard to understand.

A possible alternative to a notetaker is a lap-top computer, which the deaf student can use to take his/her own notes if he/she can type without looking at the keyboard. The advantage of using a computer, of course, is that it enables the deaf student to function independently. Learning to touch-type is feasible for most students by the time their classroom procedures create a need for notetaking. The possibilities of classifying the cost of a lap-top computer as an educational expense should be investigated.

Effectiveness of Communication Modes

In our opinion, there is a significant theoretical difference in problems encountered in mainstreaming children whose communication modality is strictly aural/oral, Cued Speech, or the Rochester Method, on the one hand, and children whose basic mode of communication is one of the several varieties of signed English, or American Sign Language, on the other. In any of the first group of communication modes, communication with anyone who uses it, such as the teacher, a transliterator, a classmate, or anyone, will support development of English vocabulary and grammar. In the case of any of the others, English vocabulary will not be learned unless it is specifically taught. The claims of signed English advocates that it promotes "absorption" of grammar have not been substantiated, and they do not even claim that it delivers new vocabulary. New vocabulary items can be taught only by immediate pairing with written language or fingerspelling. Of course, this interrupts the flow of communication, replacing spontaneous, interactive communication by structured teaching.

We would analyze as follows the theoretical potentials of the several communication methods as regards the learning of new language not specifically taught, in the mainstream situation:

1) For aural/oral communication, we rate the probability of absorbing vocabulary and/or grammar in the mainstream as very low for most profoundly deaf children. Research shows that speechreading of new language is virtually impossible, except for very exceptional persons whose efficient use of residual hearing makes the difference.

2) For both Cued Speech and the Rochester Method, the incidental acquisition of vocabulary and grammar is entirely possible, since each is a clear representation of verbal language. If a new word or idiom is encountered in a situation in which the meaning is clear from situational or linguistic context, it can be learned without effort. If the meaning is not clear from context, it should be noted and learned in a resource class or at home, or by asking a question on the spot.

3) For mainstreaming with any of the varieties of signed English there is minimal potential for the learning of new verbal language in the mainstream situation unless the language is specifically taught through fingerspelling or writing on the chalkboard.

Mainstreaming of Aural/Oral Children

The mainstreaming of deaf children whose basic method of communication is aural/oral has the one specific advantage that their teachers, family, and classmates are not expected to learn a special method of communication in order to provide support. Because such children typically tend to be extremely limited in their ability to learn new language through unstructured communication, the extensive use of writing and other methods of visual presentation by the teacher takes on extra importance, and the amount of time required to produce language growth tends to be excessive. This does not necessarily mean that the child is not able to communicate well within the limits of the language he/she already knows, or cannot make significant cognitive progress. The problem is that any new vocabulary or syntax must usually be presented in written form in order to make sure the child learns it. Academic mainstreaming for the child with whom only aural/oral methods are used is attended by formidable difficulties, unless oral communication skills are exceptional. An oral interpreter can sometimes increase learning of new language in the mainstream situation. This is particularly important when the child reaches a level in school in which he/she is moved from class to class and may have difficulty in lipreading several different teachers every day.

An important factor in the success with which a specific aural/oral child can be mainstreamed is how well he/she can communicate with hearing people, including both the general population and those who are especially equipped to communicate with him/her. The aural/oral child may or may not rate well on this point.

Mainstreaming of Signing Children

Academic mainstreaming of children whose basic communication method is American Sign Language or any of the manually coded sign systems used simultaneously with speech also presents formidable difficulties. If the children in question already have superior verbal language and reading skills, and have skilled interpreters, they can function in the mainstream environment, but with at least three serious disadvantages. First is the fact that they also must depend on presentation of all new English language in written or fingerspelled form in order to learn it. Second is the fact that since all English vocabulary must be converted to signs by the interpreters, the input may be limited by the lack of precise sign representations for many English words, by the interpreter's limited knowledge of signs, or by the lack of time in which to fingerspell everything new. To some extent this can be overcome by explanation, but there is really no time in the interpreting process for explanation unless the teacher pauses. A third problem is that the child in question may be *in* the class, but not really a freely participating member of the class. Communication with classmates requires an interpreter or is dependent on the deaf child's aural/oral communication skills, unless classmates learn enough signs to use Pidgin Sign English.

The acquisition of reasonable proficiency in American Sign Language by a regular classroom teacher, or by hearing classmates, is of questionable feasibility. The acquisition of a small stock of ASL signs and phrases by hearing classmates could serve as a token of acceptance and support, and might even make possible a useful amount of incidental communication in Pidgin Sign English. On the basis of information available now, it is likely that most children whose primary mode of communication is ASL would do better to be taught primarily in self-contained classes rather than to be mainstreamed. Mainstreaming of ASL students may become feasible if and when they have developed enough proficiency in written English and in aural/oral communication. No doubt experimental programs carried out during this decade will shed some light on the feasibility of mainstreaming ASL students.

The simultaneous use of speech and some form of manually coded English appears to offer more possibilities for mainstreaming than ASL—simply because it has been done. In fact, there are many examples of successful mainstreaming of TC children whose verbal language and reading skills are good. However, their mainstreaming is subject to the three difficulties listed in the first paragraph of this section. They are more likely to have useful aural/oral communication skills than ASL children, resulting in more possibilities for communication with classmates. Mainstreaming in which the deaf child depends upon a sign interpreter or a transliterator (aural, Cued Speech, or fingerspelling) will always introduce a time delay between the teacher's delivery and the deaf child's reception. This time delay tends to be much longer with an interpreter than with a transliterator, because of the time required for absorption of the meaning of the message and selection of the most appropriate combinations of signs for expressing that meaning. This time delay is a definite handicap for the child. For example, it makes it more difficult for him to understand the message in time to indicate a desire to answer, or to ask a question. The longer the time delay, the more difficult it is for the child to take part effectively.

Mainstreaming with the Rochester Method

The Rochester Method (simultaneously speaking and fingerspelling) is theoretically well suited to mainstreaming deaf children with the necessary verbal and reading skills. Its practical limitations lie in the difficulty of fingerspelling at a normal speaking rate for very long, as required for transliteration, the difficulty of reading fingerspelling if it is done at that rate, and the failure of the Rochester Method, in nearly a century and a half, to prove itself widely acceptable. Its central weakness is that it tends to degenerate, in use among children, to a mixture in which abbreviations and even signs are used to make communication easier. This dilutes the beneficial language-development effects of the method that are obtained when full fingerspelling is used. The Rochester Method has produced excellent results in at least a few individual cases in which deaf children were brought up by family and tutors. Practically all their communication was with adults, including family and tutors, who used fingerspelling exclusively and consistently for all communication with the child. Also, for a period of several decades (but not recently), a few residential schools using the method have produced graduates whose language and reading achievement appeared to be somewhat above those of most deaf children, though still far below the average of children with normal hearing. All this supports our view that the Rochester Method supplies what is needed for language learning, and even for mainstreaming, but that its use is painfully difficult to maintain at the level required. A clear advantage of the Rochester Method is that hearing classmates, given the opportunity, can easily learn to fingerspell in order to be able to communicate with the mainstreamed deaf child.

Mainstreaming of Cued Speech Children

Most children who grow up on Cued Speech tend to be mainstreamed after a very few years of elementary school. For example, in the schools of Montgomery County, Maryland, all the Cued Speech youngsters in high school are (1991) fully mainstreamed, with the exception of students who have a secondary learning disability, who are partially mainstreamed. The term *fully mainstreamed* is used here to mean mainstreamed in all classes except support service periods, as with a resource teacher or a speech/hearing therapist. Most Cued Speech high-school students are fully mainstreamed. Many have a daily period with a resource teacher.

There are at least six factors that contribute to the tendency to mainstream most Cued Speech students:

1) Students consistently exposed to Cued Speech in the home tend to be better equipped for mainstreaming because they are more advanced in language and reading than other deaf students, as shown by research with matched groups (Wandel, 1990).

2) A Cued Speech transliterator/interpreter delivers exactly what the teacher and other students say, so that the CS student has the same information to work with that hearing classmates have.

3) Cued Speech students think and communicate in the language used in the classroom by the teacher and by their fellow students.

4) Parents tend to be favorable toward mainstreaming, regarding it as evidence of the child's academic success.

5) Parents of CS students are better able to provide academic support at home because they also can communicate in the language used at school. Support at home is essential to mainstreaming.

6) Hearing classmates, given the opportunity, can learn Cued Speech and communicate clearly with the mainstreamed student. Some schools organize a cue club that meets regularly for practice. Of course, schools sometimes have sign clubs. These are usually helpful in producing a group of hearing peers who can communicate a little bit with the signing students.

A parent reviewer points out the growing evidence that CS kids tend to achieve at a higher level than most hearing-impaired children and that, as a result, parents must often face a bias against furnishing additional special services to students who are already functioning well by usual standards. The only argument we can suggest is that a high-ability child is being discriminated against if he/she is not furnished with the support services needed to function at full potential.

Qualifications of Transliterators

The profession of Cued Speech transliterator is going through the evolutionary process that characterizes all emerging professions. Until the last few years mothers usually either served as transliterators for their mainstreamed deaf children or trained others to fill the need. Standards varied with the competence of the mothers and the persons being trained. The pay for transliterators has not been sufficient in most cases to entice a qualified transliterator to move to a new location. Volunteer and mother-trained transliterators have been of great help to many children. Now Cued Speech transliteration is entering a new stage in which certification and standardization are becoming more and more widespread.

In 1980 Barbara Williams-Scott and Earl Fleetwood began studying the techniques employed by CS transliterators, with a view to defining the needs for training, standardization, and certification. In 1985 the first Cued Speech transliterator training program was established under the direction of Barbara Williams-Scott at Gallaudet University. In 1988 Earl Fleetwood and Melanie Metzger organized the Cued Speech Transliterator Training, Evaluation, and Certification Unit (TECUnit) to meet the needs for standardization and certification. In 1988 the Cued Speech Transliterator Code of Conduct was published, and in the same year the national Cued Speech Transliterator National Certification Examination was first administered. In 1990 the National Cued Speech Association (NCSA) accepted the TECUnit as a unit of the NCSA, charging it with the responsibility for "establishing and maintaining national standards for the profession of Cued Speech Transliteration."

Toward this end, the TECUnit conducts workshops, seminars, and inservice presentations, disseminates written material, and performs evaluations for local and state agencies. The TECUnit works closely with Gallaudet University's Cued Speech Interpreter Training Programs (CSITPs) to expand the CSITPs' accredited Cued Speech transliterator training curriculum.

The TECUnit is also responsible for maintaining and implementing the Cued Speech Transliterator National Certification Examination and the Cued Speech Instructor National Certification Examination.

The TECUnit works with agencies of various states, at their request, to assist in assuring that Interpreter/Transliterator Quality Assurance Screenings (QAS) and evaluations are appropriate. Toward that end, it has developed the Cued Speech Transliterator State Level Evaluation (Fleetwood and Metzger, 1991).

The certification examination tests the transliterator's knowledge and abilities as they relate to his/her proper role and function. This is accomplished through six sub-tests. These assess expressive and receptive Cued Speech proficiency, Cued Speech transliterating fluency, the ability to apply the Code of Conduct, and job-related knowledge in the areas of audiology, speech pathology, linguistics, sociology, and the field of interpreting/transliterating for deaf/hard-of-hearing people. A performance test is also administered to assess transliterating skills in a variety of potential situations and for deaf/hard-of-hearing consumers of different ages and experience.

The central role of the transliterator is to convey to the student all information that would be available to hearing students. This includes spoken information from teachers and classmates as well as information from filmstrips, audiotapes, and other live or recorded narration. In addition, the transliterator must convey environmental sounds, as they can contribute to the deaf/hard-of-hearing student's understanding of and interaction with his/her environment. Finally, the transliterator should avoid, to the extent possible, any altering of the environment, and neither assume nor accept duties that might compromise the effectiveness of his/her role and functions.

Readers who wish to examine in further depth the function of Cued Speech transliterators, their qualifications and role, and/or the Code of Conduct, should refer to *Cued Speech Transliteration, Theory and Application*, by Earl Fleetwood and Melanie Metzger., 1990, Calliope Press, Silver Spring, Md., 115 pp. It is available through the TECUnit (address on p. 752).

The Role of Parents in Mainstreaming

The role of parents in mainstreaming is crucial. Their responsibilities center in three areas: 1) making sure that the qualifications of their deaf child are evaluated carefully and accurately, 2) making sure that the school system arranges for the proper mainstream environment, taking into account all the needs of the child, and provides all of the support services needed by that child for successful mainstreaming, and 3) providing the home and out-of-school support needed by the child. Parents may have to be prepared to struggle to get the needed services for their child if they are dealing with a school system without previous experience or one that lacks willingness to adjust to specific needs, such as a Cued Speech transliterator.

In some large city public school systems several tracks for deaf children are offered. These may include traditional aural/oral, Total Communication, and Cued Speech tracks. In such systems mainstreaming a child with a Cued Speech transliterator is not likely to be a problem, although finding enough qualified transliterators is sometimes difficult. In smaller school systems or in rural areas there are likely to be serious problems, though they are usually solvable. If the deaf child in question is the only one whose parents request a Cued Speech transliterator, getting one may be difficult. Parents need to be prepared to do the following:

1) Become familiar with the rights of your child and your rights as parents. Refer to the section "Rights of Deaf Children and Their Parents," in Chapter 30, "Potpourri," beginning on p. 731.

2) Learn about the IEP (Individualized Educational Program), to

which every special child is entitled, and about your right as a parent to participate in its development.

3) Refuse to sign the IEP prepared by the school system if it does not satisfy you.

4) Study the advantages and disadvantages of mainstreaming and go through them with the help of staff.

5) With the help of staff, go through your child's qualifications for mainstreaming.

6) If mainstreaming is likely to be desirable for your child, notify school authorities that at a specified time you will push for inclusion of mainstreaming with a Cued Speech transliterator and a note taker in your child's IEP. "Early warning" is desirable.

7) If you and the staff agree that mainstreaming is desirable for the child, insist on his/her right to have a qualified, full-time CST (Cued Speech transliterator) in the classroom.

8) If the school experiences difficulty in recruiting a CS transliterator, try to help. Contact the Cued Speech Team at Gallaudet University, the regional CS centers, the National Cued Speech Association, and other sources listed in the Appendix. There have been cases in which a parent has (as a last resort) served as a temporary transliterator, or taught CS to someone who could serve as a temporary CST and go on to formal training and certification. Detailed suggestions are given in Chapter 22, "Going It Alone."

9) If the school system is reluctant to agree to mainstream your child, have the child's suitability for mainstreaming evaluated by outside qualified professionals familiar with CS mainstreaming.

10) If the school system refuses to include mainstreaming in the IEP, or to furnish a transliterator, consider initiating administrative hearings and other due-process procedures. Remember that these procedures can be expensive and time-consuming. You can afford to make some compromises, such as serving as the child's transliterator long enough to demonstrate its value, helping train a transliterator, etc., but only if it is necessary.

11) Give careful attention to the supportive services your child may need for successful mainstreaming, such as resource instruction and speech/hearing/language therapy.

12) Try to arrange for training of hearing classmates in CS, through 15-minute lessons in homeroom, inclusion of CS as an elective subject for hearing students, or formation of a cue club in the school.

13) During the summer, organize "Cue Parties" featuring games, refreshments, and cueing practice for neighborhood kids and others.

14) If your child is mainstreamed, you should be prepared to

help with homework. You should encourage the child to do all of it that he/she can, but most children will need some assistance. This assistance becomes very important if the child is not furnished a resource teacher for one period each day. If you are helping with homework you will need to keep in close touch with classroom teachers to obtain guidance on the needs of the child, even when there is no assigned homework.

15) A mainstreamed child will need specific language instruction at home in areas that are not likely to be covered in school or simply picked up in conversation. One of the most important of these is the learning of multiple meanings for the "little" words—the prepositions, conjunctions, etc. This need is discussed in some detail in Chapter 11, "Language Development." You should make up a list of multiple meanings for such words as *by, with, for, of, in, out, on,* and work them into conversation as much as possible. A few minutes of instruction on these multiple meaning, each day if possible, will add a great deal to the language-comprehension capabilities of the child. An easily-accessible source of multiple meanings is a good dictionary.

16) In dealing with the school system, keep these three things in mind: First, it is advisable to inform school personnel well in advance regarding requests you will be making. Second, use a "velvet glove" as long as you can. You may have to "pound the table" eventually, but wait until it is necessary. Third, refer to the case histories in Chapter 22, "Going it Alone," for ideas on dealing with school systems, and the section "How to Present Cued Speech," in Chapter 28.

17) Several parent reviewers point out that as your child becomes older your effort as a parent in everything from speech correction and auditory training to language development, homework, and interpreting should shift gradually to a more nearly normal parent/child relationship. Your interactions should eventually include extended discussions of many topics and mutual enjoyment of many activities, without so much of the flavor of teaching.

18) As your child approaches college age, you may need to give attention to the section "Opportunities For Postsecondary Education," in Chapter 30, "Potpourri."

Chapter Summary

A deaf child may be mainstreamed with the objective of providing both academic or social/cultural benefits, or (when academic benefits are not very feasible) primarily social/cultural benefits. The requirements for successful academic mainstreaming include appropriate abilities and qualities in the child, the adequate support provided in the out-of-school environment (primarily at home), the maintenance of an appropriate classroom environment, and the provision by the school system of support services appropriate for the child in question.

Support services that may need to be provided by the school system include: 1) a classroom environment in which the child can understand the teacher well, communicate expressively to the teacher clearly, and communicate with classmates reasonably well. For a child with a severe-to-profound hearing deficit, a qualified, full-time CS transliterator is needed for communication from the teacher, may be required also for communication to the teacher, and is essential for provision of information about "what is going on." 2) a classroom teacher who is sensitive to the problems and needs of hearing-impaired children and will make needed adjustments to them. The school should provide in-service training for all classroom teachers who will be expected to accommodate hearing-impaired children. 3) the assistance of a resource room, one period per day, for remedial and supporting instruction. 4) regular and frequent periods of therapy with a qualified auditory/speech/language therapist experienced with deaf children. 5) a notetaker and assistive devices such as an induction loop or frequency-modulated radio system, if needed.

Of all the communication methods, Cued Speech seems to offer the greatest advantages for mainstreaming except for children with a mild-to-moderate hearing impairment who may be able to succeed orally in the mainstream environment. In fact, it has become apparent that mainstreaming is the norm for Cued Speech children of normal intelligence and without an additional disability. Depending on the language level and other factors, such as the amount of support at home, mainstreaming typically begins two or three years after the use of Cued Speech begins in the home. Unfortunately, mainstreaming is sometimes begun before the child is really equipped for it, because other children with the same needs are not available to help justify a self-contained class with a cueing teacher.

Case Histories

Practically all of the children whose case histories you will read in other chapters are also mainstreamed. Their stories are placed in the other chapters because of special things about their circumstances, not because they are mainstreamed. The few case histories presented in this chapter are here because the children in question did not have or encounter the special circumstances dealt with in the other chapters.

Mainstreaming Leah Henegar
by Ros Efron, M.A., Special Education Resource Teacher
Prince George's County (Md.) Public Schools
Written 1977, published in 1985 in *Cued Speech News*
under the title
"Mainstreaming: It Can Be More Blessed To Give Than To Receive"

In June, 1976, Leah Henegar completed sixth grade at Glenn Dale Elementary School, Glenn Dale, Md. In the six months since she left, even more than while she was here, we have realized the powerful, even extraordinary impact her being with us had upon our school. It was one of the most constructive, unifying, and rewarding experiences in which we have ever been engaged. It has touched the lives of so many people and taught us so much. Among other things, we learned that providing for the mainstreaming of a deaf child was not a difficult task, that becoming aware of her special needs and learning style taught us much that was applicable to educating our hearing students. Those teachers who were directly involved in educating Leah learned a great deal about language development, individualizing instruction, developing better comprehension, and enhancing the organizational abilities of their regular pupils. The gains to the staff in terms of their own personal and professional development were great.

Leah came to Glenn Dale in second grade, and by the time she arrived there were two people who could cue: Leah's second-grade teacher and myself. In January of that year the second-grade teacher left and was replaced by another teacher. She spent several weeks learning to cue before taking over the class. Leah was very patient with us, never showing anything but good humor at our slow and deliberate efforts. During the next summer Leah's third-grade teacher learned to cue. And so it was, during every summer prior to Leah's moving to her next grade. They all did so with interest, responsibility, graciousness, and even pleasure. They look back on it now as a milestone in their personal and professional development.

The impact of the experience on the rest of the student body and on Leah's immediate classmates is particularly worth noting. When Leah was in third grade, I began teaching Cued Speech to the whole class. By the next year, as I again taught her class to cue, I saw the opportunities opening up to Leah as more people in her school environment could communicate clearly and effectively with her. I wanted as much as possible to enhance her ability to profit from incidental learning. I wanted her to move around and interact freely in an environment unhampered by the usual communication problems of the deaf. The teaching process was repeated again in the fifth and sixth grades. The classroom teacher set aside 15 to 30 minutes, four days a week, for my instruction of the entire class in Cued Speech. I started about the middle of October, and the program was completed by February. After that I went into the classroom several times a week to reinforce what we had learned and to develop speed in cueing. The children were enthusiastic about the project. They were proud of their achievements. About 50% of the children became good, effective cuers who interacted well with Leah, in both academic and social situations.

The majority of the remaining students learned cueing as if it were a foreign language and attained the level of fluency characteristic of American students speaking a foreign language after two years of study. Those students who in fact interacted with Leah, because they were in her reading group or because they were her personal friends, were constantly being reinforced by her, thereby becoming proficient.

Aside from what it did for Leah, learning to cue provided tremendous advantages to the hearing students. The refinement of their auditory abilities, the development of phonetic analysis skills, the opportunity to generalize from one situation to another—all this helped their reading, spelling, and comprehension.

All the children that I have taught to cue were rewarded tenfold for their efforts, and it turned out to be one of their most ego-enhancing activities. They knew that they were doing important work and making an important contribution to another human being. This was not make-believe or contrived, as so many other things are in children's lives. For the most part, children are asked day after day to do things that they are told will ultimately be important, or that they must do because they are important to someone else. Rarely do they have the opportunity—by their own efforts—to make an important difference in the quality of life of another human being. In addition those who cued engendered great admiration around the school, from both schoolmates and faculty. Parents of my cueing students never complained about the time taken from the regular curriculum. On the contrary, they were generous in their praise of the project, seeing much benefit for their youngsters.

Although the value of this whole experience to Leah seems obvious, I would still like to make a few points. The mainstreaming of a deaf child has important implications for her/his language development. True, but the effects upon emotional life, on feelings of belonging, on ability to model and relate in a world that more closely replicates the adult world into which the child is growing—these are even more gratifying. In the case of Leah, observing her in a class-room, in the lunchroom, or out on the playground, it was difficult to distinguish her from her peers. She was as involved in learning, play, or conversation as they were, appeared in harmony with the group, and above all functioned as a warm, healthy individual.

Professional educators and parent groups have joined together in efforts to make the currently popular concept of mainstreaming viable for all classes of exceptionality. This means that more and more "special" children will be interacting with their "normal" peers. Our experience should serve as proof-in-action that the concept is alive, well, and works!

I cannot think of a single person participating in this adventure at our school who did not benefit greatly, but no one benefitted more than myself. In teaching cueing to Leah's classmates I was responsible for and had the joy of being involved in a growing, creative enterprise, allowing and facilitating improved language development for Leah, while at the same time improving the auditory and phonetic skills of her classmates. Most importantly, the youngsters were able to *give* to another human being—for them a gratifying and rewarding experience.

Paul Swadley

One of the earliest children to be mainstreamed with Cued Speech under excellent conditions was Paul Swadley. In 1977, at age 9, Paul was mainstreamed in third grade at Beachtree Elementary School, Fairfax County, Va. His teacher, Rosemary Davis Arnotts, learned Cued Speech and used it for everything that he needed to understand. She taught the members of the class to cue, and some of them became quite good at it. When the family moved to Williams-burg, Va., they were able to see that Paul continued to have the benefit of a group of cueing classmates and a cueing transliterator all the way through public school. Some of his classmates could even substitute for his transliterator when necessary. His parents were very successful in getting the cooperation and support of school authorities and personnel.

Paul has a prelingual, bilateral auditory deficiency with a better-ear PTA of 110 dB. His parents started using CS when he was 3½, and he also received CS in preschool, kindergarten, and first grade. Paul has won several awards for outstanding performance as a writer, going all the way back to eighth grade.

Paul was employed by the United States Treasury Department during the summer of 1991, writing and editing contracts, and was invited to return for the Christmas holidays and whenever available.

Paul graduated from Virginia Commonwealth University in May 1992, with a major in mass communications, and is now (fall, 1992) employed by the U.S. Treasury Department. His personal observations begin on p. 610. His case history appears below, p. 424.

Esther Rimer
by Diane Rimer, June 1992

After an 11 day hospital stay for spinal meningitis my 2-year-old daughter, Esther, has been diagnosed as profoundly deaf. I have never felt such emotional pain. All I want to do is sleep and cry. I wake up in the morning with a feeling of dread. Something is terribly wrong. Then I remember and am unsure that I can face the day. I have visions of Esther's future as a mute and isolated child unable to communicate. I can't even recall ever having met a deaf person. Can they learn to talk? Can they learn to read?

Such was my initial reaction to the drastic change in our lives. After the first few weeks I began to read all I could find about deafness and deaf education. We enrolled in a home intervention program and got Esther fitted with hearing aids. The only communication options presented to us at that time were oralism and sign language. We felt that her residual hearing was too limited for her to learn orally so we decided to use sign language. My family and I enrolled in a signing class offered locally. For months we struggled with daily life. I was trying to teach my child a language that I did not know and would take years to learn well. I would run to my sign language dictionary to look up a word only to find that there was no sign for it. I could not fingerspell words to her because she was too young to even know the alphabet. We couldn't talk about Winnie the Pooh, Pinocchio, or even the sounds that animals make. I felt so frustrated and inadequate. After about six months Esther had begun to pick up some signs, but she had also stopped using her voice. We also began to realize that teaching her English grammar and reading was going to be a very difficult task.

About a year had gone by when I heard about a Cued Speech class being offered for the first time locally. I remembered reading about one page of information on Cued Speech in one of the books I'd read. It had sounded very complicated. None of the deaf "experts" I'd talked to so far had even suggested it as an option. I enrolled and was very impressed with Pam Gregg *(the instructor)*, and with the goal of Cued Speech. It aimed to give deaf children a mental model of the language so that they could become good readers. After learning to cue we decided to try it for six months. We had already invested nine months in sign language, but we began to feel that in the long run Cued Speech would give us the results we were hoping for.

I began cueing with Esther immediately. I had quit my full-time job to be at home with her because I knew she was at the ideal age for learning language and there was no time to waste. I pretty much dropped all the signs outright, but she never seemed confused by the switch. Over the first six months I became a better cuer and Esther a better watcher. Pam Gregg had kindly agreed to do therapy once a week with Esther so I had someone to consult when problems arose. After the first five or six weeks Esther was understanding simple words and sentences and she was using her voice again! My frustration level was much lower, too. Now I only had to worry about my hand not moving fast enough—after all, I already knew the language!

During the six-month trial period Esther had been enrolled in a preschool program at the state school for the deaf. Cued Speech was not encouraged there so we began looking at other options. Our local public school district only offered a total communication program and at that time was unwilling to offer alternatives. We decided to enroll Esther in a private church preschool. Next was the problem of finding a Cued Speech transliterator. I advertised, then interviewed, and finally hired Donna Page for the job. She learned to cue only a month before school started and then went to work in the classroom. We were very fortunate to receive money from a local Lions' club to pay for her first year's salary. During that first year we had many questions about transliterating and the correct way of doing things. At the end of the school year the evaluation team from the school district visited her classroom to observe. They were so impressed that they recommended that the district provide Cued Speech services to Esther for the following school year. She scored so well on her language test results that she did not qualify for special help in that area, although she did qualify for speech services. She would be the first profoundly deaf child they had ever had to be fully mainstreamed in kindergarten! It had been a very long two years but I felt that now we were really coming "out of the woods" thanks to Cued Speech.

Esther is 7 now. We have been cueing to her for four years and have never had any regrets. She is happy, well adjusted and a good student. Most exciting of all is her absolute love of reading! I tease her about being like Belle from "Beauty and the Beast" because she's always got her nose in a book. Her language is at or above age appropriate and she talks all the time. We have been considering a cochlear implant to improve her chances of having intelligible speech and to allow her to feel more involved with the mainstream environment. I no longer dread thinking about her future as I did five years ago. Instead, I am excited about it and about the possibilities opened up to her through this amazing communication system.

An essay written by Esther was awarded first place in her age group in the 1992 NCSA Writing Contest. It is on page 566.

The following is really a "Going It Alone" story, but only in the sense that Brett Fasold was the only deaf child around all the way through school. Like the story of Paul Swadley, it contains no horror stories about parents' struggles with "polarized professionals" or reluctant school authorities. Instead, it tells of cooperation and support, acceptance, and mutual pride. This is the way it should be.

Brett Fasold
by Patricia Fasold, 1992

In December of 1982 our son Brett, aged 18 months, contracted spinal meningitis. He was left with a profound, bilateral, sensorineural hearing loss. Also, it took him six to nine months to re-learn to sit up, walk, and otherwise regain his physical abilities.

Faced with the reality of deafness in our family and knowing very little about the subject, my husband and I had some very serious decisions to make. No one in our family or community was deaf, and we were determined to keep Brett an integral member of our family. Like most other deaf children, he would grow up in a hearing world.

We learned of Cued Speech from a wonderful speech pathologist we were fortunate enough to simply fall upon. We began using it with Brett when he was about 20 months old. It took a month or so for us to learn the basic system, and then it was just a matter of time for speed and proficiency to come. Within a short time we were fluent enough to cue every word we said to Brett. This was while he was still recovering from the physical effects of the meningitis.

Cued Speech allowed us to treat Brett in a very consistent manner, the same as his brother and sister. We used the same words, phrases, and sentences, and we enforced the same rules of behavior, including responsibility for consequences of misbehavior. Whether or not Brett already knew the words, we tried to use the same terminology with him we would with a hearing child. We spoke to him about everything and knew that, even if he did not understand it all at the time, he would retain some of the information and it would show up somewhere down the road. We did not assume that we had to teach Brett everything. He learned just as hearing children do.

Brett's first year in school was at the Governor Baxter School For the Deaf, in Portland, Maine. Though he was in a fledgling Cued

Speech program, we decided that home and our neighborhood school would be better for him. Brett was mainstreamed with a Cued Speech aide in preschool. He is now 11 years old and has a Cued Speech transliterator with him at all times. She is a wonderful, very professional person who has eased Brett's way through school with her caring, love, and support, as have all his teachers throughout his school years. There has not been one teacher who has balked at the idea of having a "deaf" child in his/her classroom. All have welcomed him.

Brett's reading ability amazes us. On average he reads about five-to-six books a week in his free time, after his school work is done. He does this strictly for pleasure and reads everything he can get his hands on, from classics to comics. His comprehension of this "outside" reading is excellent as assessed by school sources. It is an on-going project to keep him supplied with reading material.

The stories Brett writes delight us. His vivid imagination and sense of humor shine through in every one, along with healthy self-esteem and good will. He is in the top group in all his classes. His achievements are in large part due to the fact that all of us (teachers, transliterators, friends, and family) have always been able to communicate with him easily and clearly through Cued Speech.

Aside from school, Cued Speech has solidified our family. It has allowed us to fill the role of proud and happy parents. We have been able to give Brett love, affection, knowledge, and learning opportunities in his home. Brett's language skills do lead to some problems. He can disagree, argue, play jokes on us, and constantly bicker with his siblings. But, what a small price to pay!

In third grade, on the SBS level 23, Brett's rankings were as follows: composite rating, grade equivalent (g.e.) 5.4, national percentile, 83; reading total, g.e. 4.0, percentile, 53; comprehension, g.e. 4.4, percentile, 59; mechanics, g.e. 12.7, percentile, 94; language arts, g.e. 10.0, percentile, 96; vocabulary, g.e. 3.5, percentile, 45; usage, g.e. 9.8, percentile, 94; math total, g.e. 5.0, percentile, 75. The only surprise is that in his lowest area, vocabulary, he still ranked at g.e 3.5 in third grade. In fourth grade, on the Maine Educational Assessment, his percentile rank was 76 in reading and 71 in math. The optimism of his parents appears to be fully justified. They report that his fifth-grade percentiles (64th) in reading vocabulary and comprehension are increased from prior years and that he reads, reads, reads. That means, we think, that his vocabulary and reading percentiles will continue to rise. There is little room for improvement of his percentiles in language (99th) and math (94th). Bretts's own observations begin on page 571, and his brother's on page 285.

The writings of Sarina Roffé about her family's experiences with their son Simon contain so much that is relevant to the problems faced by parents that we find it necessary to include three separate articles by her, in addition to his expression of his own feelings and attitudes. The first, taken largely from <u>Cued Speech News</u>, *March, 1981, deals with Simon's life to the age of 5. The analysis of his language at age 4 is a clinic in itself. The second article is a remarkable and frank portrayal of the impact on his mother as a person. The third (in Chapter 24) is on the family's experiences in dealing with Simon's additional problem, Attention Deficiency Disorder. We are indebted to Mrs. Roffé for these helpful contributions, as well as all the suggestions she provided as a parent reviewer and the essay on "experience books" that we draw from heavily in Chapter 8, "Advancing in Language."*

Simon Roffé
"The First Five Years"
by Sarina Roffé

As I sat watching for the third time the movie *And My Name Is Jonah*, I looked from Jonah to Simon, my profoundly deaf son, now age 5, and thought how similar our early experiences with oralism were to those of Jonah's family. I was angry for Jonah's mother, Jenny, and other mothers like her. I was angry at the emotions and feelings that she and I and other mothers go through in making a decision for our deaf children. I was angry that they didn't know about Cued Speech.

Simon was in a parent-infant program for three years. We started out orally, and after one-and-one-half years, his teacher recommended that we start using signs with Simon. We began cautiously, having put up a lot of resistance to the idea. We talked to many people, and asked many questions. We came up with more and more answers we didn't like. What is the average reading level of an oral or Total Communication deaf child? Would his speech be understandable? Could he keep up with his hearing peers academically? The answers were considered adequate (by those who gave them), but did not reach our expectations of what Simon could do. After another year and a half my son still had a vocabulary of 100 words. Most of that was with sign and was not necessarily spoken or written language.

Simon is a profoundly deaf little boy. He was diagnosed at 8 months of age and had his first hearing aids at 9 months. Living in the Washington area, my husband and I had access to most any kind of educational program that we wanted for Simon. We worked very hard with him. Yet after three years all we had to show for it was 100 words (mostly signs), a lot of auditory training, and a lot of despair. Were these the best educational methods of teaching prelingually deaf children? We thought something better had to be available.

I felt very strongly that for all the effort and money going into this child, he should become able to function well in society and be able to keep up with his hearing peers academically. Simon is not stupid. He is *deaf.* There had to be a way.

We heard about Cued Speech from a

Abe, Simon, and Honey Roffé

flyer that went around the neighborhood. I called the listed number and spoke with a parent whose child was then at the National Child Research Center. She spent a lot of time explaining the advantages of Cued Speech for a deaf child. She told my husband and me how easy it is to learn and how we would be able to see quick results. She also told us that verifiable results indicate that many Cued Speech kids are able to attain or exceed grade-level reading skills. She convinced me to meet the inventor of Cued Speech. We went to the week-long workshop at Gallaudet College in August, 1979, and after the third day decided to switch our child into a Cued Speech program in Montgomery County, Md. This was the first year for the program and eight children were enrolled.

We had mixed feelings and did not quite believe that Cued Speech could deliver all that was promised for it. However, we felt strongly that the two other available methods, traditional oral and Total Communication, were not for us. We felt Cued Speech was worth a try. At this point we had nothing to lose.

We weren't sorry. Simon had been in a children's class during the August workshop, and the teacher of his class commented that by the end of the week his understanding of what she cued to him indicated that he was already making good use of the cues. Within another week he recognized the cued words for the 100 signs he had learned up to that time, and we were no longer signing at home. Within a month I was cueing sentences. For us the transition from signing to Cued Speech was smooth and swift.

Simon was enrolled in a half-day program at North Lake Elementary School starting in September, 1979. He was in a class with three other children, along with both a teacher and an aide adept at CS. Within six months Simon had learned the "over 500 words" that Dr. Cornett had indicated are possible in the first year, making his vocabulary total 600 English words. We were ecstatic. I had found a freedom with language that I could not get from the other methods I had used before to talk to my son. By the end of the year Simon was talking in sentences. By September of 1980 he was using long sentences of 10 to 12 words. His speech had drastically improved. By October, after 14 months on CS, Simon's language was like this: "That truck for people who hurt. I don't wanna eat. I'm sick. Where Daddy going? Daddy going to work. I forgot my green car."

Before entering the program Simon was two years behind his age in language development. Now Cued Speech is helping him catch up rapidly with the development of his hearing peers. I observe things like these about his spoken language: 1) Simon's subject and verb agree in a sentence; 2) he is starting to use helping verbs and articles; 3) he is starting to use prepositions; 4) he uses correctly direct/indirect objects in a sentence. For a profoundly deaf 4-year-old child, these accomplishments are uncommon. For a Cued Speech child they are the norm.

Receptively, Simon shows a good understanding of question forms. For example, he understands such questions as "Where did you put your wallet?" or "It's time to line up. Are you first?" He is able to follow commands that change context from child to child in his class. His attention to cues is excellent. Expressively, Simon is able to make the proper pronoun change to *I* when asked a *you* question. He utilizes people's names in conversation when addressing them. He carries over structures into his spontaneous commands and questions to other children. For example, he can say to another child, "Draw a cat," or "Jump over the line."

The rate of growth in Simon's language is clear from the results of tests he has taken. He was given the REEL Test in June of 1979, as he finished the parent-infant program. He scored at the 17-month level. At that time he was 3½ years old and had not been exposed to Cued Speech. When the Zimmerman Language Test was administered on his fourth birthday (after having Cued Speech for only four months), he scored at the 3 year, 1½ month level in the area of auditory comprehension and the 2 year, 2½ month level in the area of verbal ability. When the same test was administered 11 months later he scored at the 5 year 6 month level for auditory comprehension (a gain of just over two years and four months in eleven months) and at the 3-year 5-month level for verbal ability (a gain of just over one year).

It isn't just the improvement in Simon's language that excites us. It is the changes in our everyday life that this makes possible. I can say anything I want to Simon, and he understands. I can reason with him. As long as I cue, he watches me. The tension and frustration of non-communication has left our household. I can punish Simon for poor behavior and feel confident that he understands what he did wrong and why he is being punished.

On religious occasions and holidays I can explain the traditions to Simon. I think the best example of this was the holiday of Sukkos. For Jewish people, it is the festival of the harvest. My father-in-law had tears of joy in his eyes when, through the use of Cued Speech, Simon could recite the whole Hebrew blessing over the fruit used on this holiday. It gives me a very good and relieved feeling to know that Simon's deafness will not diminish his ability to be a good Jew.

An interesting thing happened on Halloween. A UNICEF box was sent home from school. I sat down and explained to Simon that some people give money away to children who have no money to buy food or clothing. We went around the neighborhood, confident that we were collecting for a good cause. Afterwards, I wanted to be sure Simon understood the money was not for him. I asked him: "Who is the money for?" He replied: "For boys and girls." I asked: "What will they do with the money?" He said, "Buy food to eat." If someone had told me a year earlier that Cued Speech would make my son understand about giving and UNICEF, I would have said they were crazy.

Simon's language development is now like that of a normal hearing child. He is able to recite the alphabet and count to 11. In school he is working on reading skills, math, science, and the usual auditory skills. Currently, he is enrolled in an all-day preschool at North Lake Elementary School in Montgomery County, Maryland. His teacher cues, the aide in his class cues, and the speech teacher cues. The curriculum used in his class includes many of the kindergarten tasks that will be used next year in kindergarten.

Would I say we are a success? Yes, though for Simon and our family the word success is hardly enough. For a profoundly deaf child to make this kind of progress in just 14 months is absolutely phenomenal. My husband and I feel we have seen a miracle happen before our eyes. Every day we are thankful for Cued Speech. Simon's unlimited progress (unlimited in the sense that the limits to his opportunity to make all the progress he was capable of making had been removed) is due to the continued use of Cued Speech both at home and at school.

I might add that he has had excellent teachers who are not new to Cued Speech. This has added to his success.

For us, Cued Speech has meant the difference between normal growth within a happy family, and the tense, depressed household we had before. That is our definition of success.

How Simon Changed My Life
by Sarina Roffé

Looking back on my 16 years as the mother of a deaf child I no longer see the pain of those first few years. Instead I see change that occurred in my life, the sense of mission that I soon felt, and how much my outlook changed.

Simon was only 9 months old when I found out he was deaf (profoundly deaf, 95 dB PTA). For me it was a time of tragedy, a period of pain, and the turning point in my life. The initial period was spent learning of all the things my firstborn son would never learn to do. The result was an inner anger that something as simple as a hearing loss would deprive my precious child of the joy of achieving.

With my anger came an adolescent resolve to prove everyone wrong, to show that deafness need not change my child, need not make him any less a person, and need not change my love for him. Once I had worked through my inner turmoil I was able to look beyond tomorrow for Simon and see to the future. That change in outlook, from tomorrow to the future, is what gave me the inner strength to try Cued Speech with Simon when he was 3½ years old. He was taught orally until he was two, and then was exposed to signing for a year and one-half, reaching a vocabulary of about 100 words when 1,000 or more would be typical of a normal child.

Cued Speech became the key to Simon's destiny, a cutting edge that severed the ties binding him to a future as a stereotypical deaf child. With Cued Speech, Simon exploded into language, recording a gain of five years in a period of only 22 months, as documented by language scores on standardized tests. Equally important, he became a normally functioning child, proving to everyone who knew him that deafness was okay and that he was and is an okay person. This transformation did not occur overnight, because he had a serious problem in addition to deafness, Attention Deficiency Disorder (p.558).

On November 11, 1986, in fifth grade, Simon tested at the 99th percentile rank on the California Achievement Test (all parts), and in sixth grade (Jan. 27, 1988), at the 99th percentile on the Stanford Achievement Test (all parts).

I must resist the temptation to brag too much about my son's accomplishments in spite of the fact that I am intensely proud of him. As it turns out, Simon is a gifted, truly remarkable person, performing accordingly. He is in the 10th grade at Watkins Mills High School, fully mainstreamed, an honor-roll student who plans to go into business. He has the services of a half-time Cued Speech transliterator for his major subjects and functions as an oral student the rest of the time. Last summer he worked for a stock brokerage firm on Wall Street that deals in junk bonds. Before that he made pizza at Little Caesar's Pizza and had his own lawn-mowing business. Simon measures his success in part by his social life, which is thriving. He is on the wrestling team and plays baseball in the spring and in the fall. I measure his success by his ability to achieve whatever goal he sets.

Now, back to my assigned subject, the effect of Simon on me. When we picked up on Cued Speech, his rapid progress turned my life around. It gave me something to live for. It gave me a mission in life, to show others that raising a deaf child doesn't have to be a cumbersome, defeating process. It can actually be as straightforward as, and much more rewarding than, raising a hearing child—if you use CS.

For me, Cued Speech changed a traumatic beginning into a happy ending. Perhaps I sound like a born-again Christian or someone new to religious fervor rather than a committed Jew, but Cued Speech was the answer to my prayers. Specifically, how did it change my life? Aside from changing Simon's life, and through him our entire family experience, it changed my feelings toward the handicapped in general. The experience of raising a deaf child with Cued Speech enabled me to write of all the wonderful, magical, impossible things that occurred to Simon. With that writing came the knowledge that I have a gift for writing. I began to speak to parent groups about cueing. With that experience came the knowledge that I like public speaking.

When Simon was small I had tried signing for a period of time and quickly saw its disadvantages. Initially, I perceived signing as a wall that would prevent my child from reading, whereas in fact it only fails to develop reading. My attitude toward signing has changed as Simon has grown and I have learned about its positive values.

Signing has advantages for social interaction among the deaf. Those who use Cued Speech need to come to recognize two things. First, they are few and far between. Thus, their child may not come into frequent contact with many children their age who can cue. Second, those in the mainstream of deaf culture *sign*. Signing is their form of language, just as English is ours. The deaf person who wants access to deaf society must become proficient in signing.

I don't mean that signing itself is all that wonderful. It has many educational limitations. But I recognize that my son is a profoundly deaf youngster who needs to socialize with other deaf people in his age group. In a given geographic area there aren't many 16-year-old deaf youngsters who cue. At his age we can forget methods and let kids be kids. We can still use Cued Speech at home. A boy who reads books by the dozens is not going to forget English.

Looking back, I think signing should have been introduced in Simon's life earlier so that he would be more fluent by now. This would make social acceptance among the deaf easier and would also make it possible for him to understand when only a sign interpreter is available. As it is, Simon struggles a bit with sign language, and it will be some time before he is good at it.

In summary, Cued Speech changed my son's life, my life, and the life of our family. It gave me a purpose in life, a goal to strive toward. With each of Simon's early accomplishments my resolve strengthened. With each hurdle he jumped, my faith grew. I had been a young, naive, idealistic woman. I became a certified interpreter, a public speaker, and a writer. After seeing my son succeed, I went back to school to earn my bachelor's degree in journalism. I graduated in May 1992. Meanwhile, I work as a journalist and columnist for the Gazette newspapers in Gaithersburg, Md. My son's need gave me a goal in life and his success gave me a career. I thank him for that.

Information about Simon appears on p. 558 because of an additional problem he had, which was eventually overcome, and his own statement is on page 595. Readers may also want to read "Simon's Story" on pp. 33-40 of **Choices in Deafness.** *(see Appendix, p. 754)*

La Floraison d'Isabelle
by Nicole Spinetta (1981)
translated by Carolyn Nachman

The subject of mainstreaming is not mentioned in this case history. Its inclusion in this chapter is justified, however, by the fact that all of Isabelle's education has been in the mainstream.
(Isabelle's PTA threshold, averaged at 500-1000-2000 Hz, is 95 dB.)

To write is not easy when everything is going wrong and it's discovered that your child is deaf. One does not feel like writing. To write is not much easier when you again discover the family harmony and the joys of your life with your child. One still doesn't feel like writing. Yet I must do it because of the harmony that we have found with our deaf daughter Isabelle (who will soon be 6 years old) and our hearing son Eric (8 years old). This harmony we owe to Cued Speech.

I am persuaded, personally, that there is no miracle nor universal method. With a deaf child, one must seek that method which suits both parent and child; that which enables them to communicate, to grow, and to be mutually enriched. For us, as hearing persons who wish to communicate in our own language with our deaf daughter, this method was Cued Speech. May our experience and our story help others.

We suspected Isabelle's deafness when she was 6-9 months old, but the diagnosis was not clearly established until the age of 14 months. She was fitted at 16 months with two hearing aids. Our feelings then? *Powerless, incompetent, helpless*—we weren't meant to have a deaf child; we knew nothing about it, and never would we be able to communicate with Isabelle; we felt so incapable.

Isabelle was rehabilitated at the rate of two sessions a week from age 18 months to 2½ years. During that period, she attended an additional educational and speech therapy program at a hearing nursery school four times a week, with a teacher of the hearing impaired.

What had she achieved? She was somewhat attentive to lip movement, recognizing some words by lipreading, but she didn't yet understand the meaning of sentences. She said a few words and only one sentence: "Where is..." followed by the name of the object she was looking for. She was 2 years and 8 months old.

Why did we begin Cued Speech? We simply had the opportunity to meet, through the course of one of her visits to Paris, the mother of Stasie Jones, and to observe the quality of Stasie's comprehension. Yet, we weren't under any illusions: Stasie was exceptionally intelligent and her mother characterized by a rare sensitivity.

Why then did we try Cued Speech, since we were persuaded that Isabelle would never understand us nor would she ever speak? First of all, because we had lost heart and were ready to try anything. Secondly, for essentially negative reasons: 1) Cued Speech could not in any way be of harm to Isabelle, as we were continuing to talk to her; and 2) if when she were older she reproached us (we were sure she would) for having not done anything specific for her, we could tell her: "We did try something ... but it didn't work." In fact, we didn't believe in it.

So what happened? A few weeks after having started to use Cued Speech with Isabelle, we observed that her attention was held more easily: she watched our lips much more attentively and for longer periods of time. Next appeared (at the end of around two months) the first words, poorly pronounced of course, but pronounced just the same. This was for us a sign of encouragement to continue.

We then began to say to ourselves, "In the end, perhaps this really will work for Isabelle, like it did for Stasie." In fact, our amazement at the possibility of an at last feasible and natural communication with Isabelle had just begun. Little by little, we saw her comprehension improve in an otherwise unhoped-for way, and her language developed just like that of her brother, Eric.

For us, the main advantage of Cued Speech was our complete and total liberation towards Isabelle: we dared to talk to her normally. We had made somewhat of a gamble on starting Cued Speech: the auditory route was going badly—let's try the visual method; and this succeeded well beyond our expectations.

As soon as we had begun to practice Cued Speech with Isabelle, our vocabulary and our sentence structures changed. For example, we risked, with Cued Speech, to tell her proper nouns; to inform her as to what we were going to do with her; to talk all the time, with all people; to use pronouns, and above all the exact terms, without worrying about which she already knew. The constant preoccupation that we'd had before, to use only the words that she already knew, disappeared. We no longer said just *meat*, but *beefsteak, ham, escalope, roast pork, calf's liver,* etc.

We could from then on say everything that came to mind without worrying about being understood or not. After all, with a newborn child, wouldn't one have the same attitude? The infant would be spoken to as soon as he was born, about everything, yet it's known that he would not understand much.

With Isabelle, thanks to Cued Speech, we have rediscovered this joy to be able to say everything; of course she didn't understand a great deal at the beginning, but we realized that she was retaining by sight, the same as a newborn hearing child retains by hearing. It was the beginning, the birth of our dialogue and our conversations. It was a little for us as though Isabelle, at 3 years of age, had just been born to oral communication.

But I must say that a most precious contribution of Cued Speech was the veritable liberation it brought us with respect to the professionals that took care of her. Before then, we had felt very guilty for not knowing, and for not being familiar with the "techniques" of speech development and habilitation. We had felt very dependent on what we were told by the specialists, and of the "work" they advised us to do with Isabelle, which we often enough did not have the desire nor the will to do.

We did not feel self-sufficient. We did not feel at ease as

parents; our parental role seemed insufficient to us—we were losing our spontaneity and our natural way. We thought continuously that it was necessary to "make Isabelle work" if we wanted her to succeed. The problem was that we did not know how.

Cued Speech returned us to our role as parents. We are happy and conscious of being able to give her warmth, affection, knowledge, and a learning opportunity—providing that the teacher of the hearing impaired who takes care of her also gives her, besides kindness and affection, every effort toward the habilitation of a deaf child.

We will content ourselves to try to fill our role as parents, as much with Isabelle as with Eric, as best we can. We have the same attitude with one as with the other. Isabelle needs, more than her brother, the precious help of a specialist; but this is no longer our field. We are only her parents, and we are satisfied in being just that, despite her deafness.

What progress has Isabelle made after three years of regular use of Cued Speech by ourselves and by her teacher? Isabelle understands practically everything. She asks a lot of questions. She wants to know everything, understand everything, and be kept abreast of everything. Little by little we have observed her language grow like that of a hearing child; articles, verb conjugations (different tenses and persons), pronouns, relatives, conjunctions, etc.

If Isabelle understands practically everything, she speaks almost equally well. Of course, in speaking she makes a lot more errors than her hearing friends of her age, but her mistakes are for us signs of accomplishment. She invents language by herself, as a hearing child would, and does not simply repeat commonly-used sentences learned by heart by dint of work and practice. Her language is very spontaneous, even if there are some mistakes in gender, tense, or agreement.

A small recent example: we read fairy tales to her for a few months, which are always written in the simple past tense. Isabelle, when she plays with her dolls or tells a story, has been using the simple past tense for several weeks now in her stories.

All of the words and all the sentence structures that Isabelle knows will be a precious aid for her, as she will be learning to read next year. She will be capable, I think, of understanding what she reads, just like a hearing child.

Cued Speech is indispensable to Isabelle. The best proof? She continuously asks us (and the few people who practice it around her) to cue to her. Why? Because Isabelle, like all children, favors the least amount of effort: she does not like to tire herself lipreading (which she otherwise must do almost all day long) when she knows that we can help her to understand easily if we cue.

How does she manage without Cued Speech? Very well, I must admit, although it is very tiring for her. Cued Speech enabled her to acquire good lipreading abilities, and she recognizes without any problem (but not without tiring) the sentence structures and the words that she has effortlessly integrated into her language, thanks to Cued Speech. Still, it is necessary that the speaker not talk too quickly.

What more is there to say about Isabelle? She's a little girl who is very active and alert, curious about everything, and who seems so radiant and happy to be alive. Is she gifted? I sincerely do not think so. Now there are times when people say she is especially intelligent. Why do they say this? Because she understands and because she speaks, and it always astonishes people that a deaf person is capable of doing that. But at 3 years old, when she didn't understand but a few words, no one ever told us she was a genius. She isn't a genius; she's a normal child, but she is deaf.

Cued Speech gave Isabelle access to comprehension and to language (thanks to her excellent prosthetic recovery and to her teacher). Cued Speech allowed us to again be happy, beaming parents.

I will add one thing: we are doing all that we can to make Cued Speech known in France. Our children are interested in our promotional work, and are proud of it, even if sometimes we become too absorbed in it, and it separates us from them. The wealth of contacts we have with other parents of deaf children, and with specialists of the deaf who are interested in Cued Speech, has changed our lives. We hope that our extraordinary experience with Isabelle may give hope, strength, and confidence to other parents of deaf children.

Yes, a deaf child can understand, without tiring, oral language in its totality. Yes, a deaf child can speak, if specialists help him. How? With Cued Speech, which will represent for him an irreplaceable aid to learn to speak and understand.

This article appeared in **Cued Speech News** *in September, 1981. We have not received a parental update on Isabelle's progress from age 6 years to her present age of 17. Readers can get an inkling of that progress, however, from the letter she wrote to a deaf girl in Texas. A translation of it begins on page 594.*

Isabelle's parents have been prime movers in the founding, growth, and success of A.L.P.C., the Association Pour La Promotion et La Développement du Langage Parlé Complété, the national Cued Speech association of France. Jean Cyril Spinetta was its first president and Nicole Spinetta its first secretary.

Paul Swadley
by Charles Swadley, 1992

Our son, Paul, is the oldest of four children. We were in Germany at the time of our discovery of his profound hearing impairment. At that time our only thoughts were that he was our child and that we loved him. We were determined that we would do whatever was necessary for him. At that time in our lives, we had no idea what was necessary. We assumed that there were programs and experts somewhere who could and would help us. We assumed that the educational system would be prepared for him and that there would be no problem about funding. All of these assumptions, however, would be called into serious question very soon after our journey began.

In this process of finding an appropriate educational program for Paul and overcoming the many hurdles to that end, one of the first traits that developed in us was a healthy sense of trusting our own instincts in areas that usually belonged to the professional community. I suppose it began with the diagnostic process. We began to realize that we seemed to know as much about our son's problem as anyone else. Though we desperately needed expert guidance from doctors, teachers, and therapists, we came to understand that each of these professions had their own set of biases that colored life in a particular way. It was up to us to make choices and to trust our own instincts and abilities to do that which we perceived as best for Paul.

Perhaps the best example of how this acquired trait worked for us occurred early in the diagnostic phase. We took Paul to the University of Maryland Hospital in Baltimore for a complete "work-up." We were young. Paul was about 2½ years old. He was having loose bowel movements and was displaying very little sense of communication skills. So, we wanted to know what was going on and what to do to help him.

After extensive testing and interviews with us, we participated in an exit interview with the staff. Their assessment was that Paul was profoundly hearing impaired, that he was of average intelligence and probably would not go to college, that he had an allergy to milk products, and that we should keep him on a very strict diet.

When we asked the team about how they determined Paul's intelligence we were told that one part of the testing at his young age involved their observation of how well he could button a shirt. It was at that point that Sue began to question their conclusions. Since she was a teacher by training, she felt that the test was not valid because Paul had never worn shirts like the type he was tested on. He always wore a pull-over shirt. So, how could firm judgments be made about his intelligence with that kind of standard? But, what did we know? In a room full of professional experts, it is fairly easy to be overwhelmed.

We were also advised that Paul's primary hearing was in his left ear. This information shocked us since Paul had undergone a thorough audiological exam at Walter Reed Army Hospital less than a year earlier and we had been told that his primary hearing was in his right ear! That kind of conflicting professional information would happen over and over again, leaving us with more questions than answers most of the time.[1] It forced us to rely on our own judgment.

When we asked the exit interview team what was available in the educational realm for Paul in the general community and in particular at Gallaudet College, we were told that Gallaudet College was only a residential school and that it only provided sign language training. We were also told that we would have to search the public school system ourselves. The exit interview team knew very little about the programs.

A few weeks later we were visiting the National Zoo in Washington, D.C. As we got out of the car, we saw another family nearby whose child had hearing aids in both ears and who appeared to be hearing impaired like Paul. Gravitating to them out of a sense of unspoken collegiality, we met the family and learned that the father was a clinical psychologist. He began to demythologize all the "truths" we had been told. At the hospital where he worked he had discovered many young children who had been diagnosed and institutionalized as mentally retarded, but who were only hearing impaired—made to appear to be mentally impaired because of their lack of communication.

This same clinical psychologist began to tell us about their search for options for their child. He was the first professional to tell us that Gallaudet was not merely a residential school and that there were other options there besides sign language. He told us that there were options for two other methodologies, which, of course, we learned to be correct. Can you imagine that these truths and realities were learned, not in a professional exit interview with a panel of experts, but from a family whom we accidentally bumped into at the zoo?

This incident burned a deep impression on us. We never forgot the misguidance we received from the professional community. Thus,

---

[1]There is also the agonizing (though perhaps remote) possibility that in the interim the hearing in Paul's right ear been damaged, making it his poorer ear. The output limits of powerful hearing aids are usually set at levels safe for speech, but not necessarily safe for continuous sounds, such as those of vacuum sweepers or airplanes. Like many parents, the Swadleys were not briefed on these dangers.

we began to question those firm and apparently absolute truths that were being foisted on us at various times. We began to trust that we could offer valid options and solutions as good as and if not even better than some of the so-called professional experts in the field.

While at the same time we would say trust your instincts and question the professional community, we would also say that it was important to us to value the persons in that community as human beings. It was relatively easy to begin to see persons sitting across the table from us as the adversary. Such a perspective, we learned, is filled with suspicion and mistrust. It does not take long for this to be translated into paranoia and isolation. We cannot say strongly enough that the role of a parent has to include the ability to trust in the humanity of the other person and to value them in a positive way no matter how threatening it is to the welfare of our child.

Paul is now (1991-92) in his last year at Virginia Commonwealth University in Richmond, Va. His major is Mass Communications. The journey for him and for us to this stage in his education was not easy. In fact, there are still hurdles every day we must face and overcome. We are still very saddened and frustrated to face the same old biases and misunderstandings both in the hearing and in the hearing impaired community about the nature of this handicap and the value of Cued Speech. But we firmly believe that we must look at the other person with a positive value judgment and hope they desire to work with us.

Each time we entered a new educational setting, we would tell the director of the program or the principal that we did not want to force Paul on them. We would also insist that only teachers who really wanted Paul should have him. We always offered our services to speak to a teachers' meeting after school or to assist in the classroom in whatever way was comfortable with the teachers. Most of the time we felt a very good rapport with the teachers. It would often be true that the so-called experts were the ones who offered the most resistance.

We can recall well a meeting that a group of us parents had in Fairfax County Virginia with the director of special education and her staff. She had a reputation for being very tough. We also knew that the oralists and the total communication teachers were very suspicious about our presence and our proposals.

When we entered the room with the other parents, I observed the non-verbal signals to see who was giving indications of the most resistance. I noticed a woman who was apparently all bound up tightly and was not giving much positive facial expression or eye contact. So I chose to give her as much attention as possible. As I spoke I would come back in her direction and try to establish some rapport with her.

Finally, she did give a sign of a positive response. As the meeting turned out, we were able to get everything we asked for, which meant a new Cued Speech program at Beechtree Elementary School.

It was a hard lesson to learn. Yet, it is important to know that people do care about kids. They are also human beings who will act quite defensively, if we put them in such a position. We sincerely believe that all the times we have been in a position of negotiation, we have tried to understand why the other persons were so opposed to the Cued Speech program. We wanted to give them every way out first, but still remain firm about what we felt was working well with Paul.

We did not try to convert others to Cued Speech, because this kind of evangelistic fervor only confused the relationships. What was most important was expressing the positive value of our son's development under the Cued Speech concept. On that basis we insisted that it continue within whatever receptive setting was available or that could be made available. We understood that they needed our help to train teachers and to set up workshops. We always attempted to align ourselves with the educational community as a friend.

I served on the Williamsburg-James City County Public Schools Special Education Committee for six years. In four of those years I served as the Chair. In that capacity I advocated for all groups with handicaps and was quite visible before the community and the school board. In fact, the school board presented me with a special "Friend of Education" award. Now, many years later, and with Paul out of the school system, Paul's mother Sue is serving on that same committee.

All this is to say that we value the system but recognize its deficiencies. We can cast stones easily enough and have done so far too many times. But, successful results seem to have occurred for us when we were able to be first of all very clear about what we wanted. Second, we had to propose our concepts in an environment in which the other persons were not viewed as simply the "bad guys." We valued the other persons in as positive a manner as we could.

Our final word is a personal testimony. We think that you must have faith. No situation is absolutely unredeemable. No person is unable to be changed, if the right circumstances occur. No obstacle is so great that there isn't a greater positive force somewhere. People and situations change everyday. Hope is essential to change. For us it is a faith perspective that nothing is impossible. Over these 23 years we have experienced many situations which were devastating and apparently impossible. Today, though not everything is perfect, we can celebrate our son's progress. He has demonstrated that those so-called experts were wrong and that Cued Speech has been right for him.

Trust your instincts. You are probably right. Trust that other people can be valued in a positive way, even though the situation may appear adversarial. Be clear about what you believe is working well for you and persistently pursue your educational goals. And, never lose faith and hope. Nothing is impossible. For us, this is our statement of faith in God, who loves creation and transforms negative into positive.

The ability of this family to interact constructively with school authorities is attested by the fact that they have managed to secure excellent cooperation and support in each environment, no matter how negative the situation may have seemed initially. See also p. 610.

Mathew White
by Deborah White
Barnes, London, England, June, 1992

Mathew was taken ill with Haemophalus Meningitis in June, 1977, at the age of 3 years 2 months. This resulted in profound deafness. Before his illness his language and speech were excellent and I would say quite advanced for his age. Within a year of becoming deaf he had lost all his speech. I think this rapid loss was due mainly at first to shock and frustrations. Much of that first year was spent screaming.

Recovering myself from shock and trying to cope with a deaf 3 year old and a younger child of 1½, it took the family quite a while to reach anything like normality. After the illness and the many tests, I first sorted out the health side of the problem, e.g., a consultant I could relate to, and getting registered at the Nuffield Centre for Speech and Hearing. Not an easy task as I had no support from my G.P. or the hospital. I had to fight for everything I wanted, or thought I wanted.

Once the health programme was underway, I turned to the problem of speech and language. Through the N.D.C.S. and the R.N.I.D. I got as much as I could on the various methods of teaching the deaf. After careful consideration I decided that Cued Speech was far and away the most logical and sensible. I contacted the Centre for Cued Speech in London, and after meeting Mrs. Dixon-Millar I set to work learning the technique. My husband was in a very demanding job, abroad a lot of the time. I therefore had very little support from the family. Once Mathew had recovered from the shock of his deafness we started with the help of his speech therapist, also familiar with Cued Speech, an intensive course of therapy which continued until he was 1. With only one half-hour session a week allotted to us with the speech therapist, a lot of the time was spent with her teaching me so that I could continue the work during the rest of the week. With this system we managed well, and Mathew progressed, with what at the time seemed alarming slowness, but which in retrospect and having taught other deaf children I now realise was quite a phenomenal rate.

I continued going to Cued Speech classes and took Mathew there once a week until with the help of Mrs. Dixon-Millar we got him into a highly academic private school at the age of 5. All credit must go to the headmaster of this school in first of all accepting Mathew, and then in making such a success of his education. The first hiccup came when he was due to move from junior to senior school and the daunting prospect of teaching him French appeared on the scene. At this stage Mathew was vocalising quite well and had managed, with infinite impatience on the part of the staff, to keep up with his peers. I worked with him constantly at home and there was no let up during the long school holidays. In fact for a long while my boys thought that all children did lessons in the holidays!

The headmaster voiced his fears to me over the French and we came to an understanding that I would teach Mathew French at home if the school concentrated on the other subjects. This didn't mean that he didn't attend the French classes at school but that I would do the bulk of the teaching. Luckily, I was a fluent French speaker. I turned once more to Cued Speech for help, and in my opinion this is the area where Cued Speech helped most in Mathew's life. I was able with the aid of Cued Speech to keep up to the required standard at school and he subsequently passed his Common Entrance Examination to St. Paul's School with a 75% pass mark in French.

Matthew is now 18 and has spent the past 5 years at St. Paul's School being the first and only deaf student to ever go there. He took 10 subjects in the G.C.S.E. examinations at 16 and passed all with A and B grades. He has just taken 4 A-level subjects—Math, Physics, Geography, and Technology and hopes to read Aeronautical Engineering at University.

He finally stopped using Cued Speech at the age of 13 when he entered his secondary school and has not had occasion to use it since. I am not sure how much of it he remembers.

Mathew's early education was an uphill struggle for all concerned. Without Cued Speech as a backup it would have been a lot worse. I am eternally grateful to Mrs. Dixon-Millar and all those people who supported me during those difficult years. Mathew would never have achieved his current status without their help and support.

Mathew's own observations begin on page 613.

Chapter 21
The Greatest Problem—Time

For parents, time is the greatest problem in raising a deaf child. Competent handling of deafness in a child requires many extra activities and special efforts beyond the normal expenditure of time in raising a hearing child. Parents need to use their time wisely, seek the assistance of other cuers, and learn to choose priorities and take shortcuts in carrying on the necessary activities.

Yes, the greatest problem in raising and educating a deaf child, for the parents, is *time*. The more they read, the more they learn about things they need to do to meet the needs of their child. The list is endless: learn and use a special communication system, help with the training of the child's use of residual hearing, work with him/her on language (use every situation to introduce new language), arrange for special experiences to help with social development, keep records, stay in touch with the school, read to the child, take him/her to the library, to speech therapy, to the clinic for testing, don't neglect the siblings, etc. There are more things to do than you can possibly get to. One trouble is that many of the things you are supposed to do are open-ended. Spend *all the time you can* teaching your deaf child language, *all the time you can* helping him listen better and speak better, *all the time you can* reading and learning about education of a hearing-impaired child.

Why Is Time Such A Problem?
There are at least four reasons why time is the greatest problem of parents of hearing-impaired children:

1) A deaf child needs many things a hearing child does not need at all. These consume much of the parents' time, some of it in actual participation, some through transporting the child (and perhaps waiting during the activity). Examples are: special testing and examinations; fitting, testing and repair of hearing aids; speech and auditory therapy. Such mundane matters as finding hearing aids when they are misplaced, or replacing them when they are actually lost or damaged, often require a good deal of time. Having to accompany the child to special events in order to transliterate takes away some of the freedom parents may have with a hearing child. Teaching others to cue may be necessary and desirable, but it takes time. Many parents have had to serve as classroom transliterators due to the unavailability of a qualified

person or the lack of school funds to use to employ one.

2) A deaf child needs more of some things (from parents) than a hearing child does. Examples are tutoring, explanation, demonstration, explanation of what others say, and assistance with homework.

3) It often takes parents longer to carry on a simple instructional activity with a deaf child than with a hearing child. For example, if the father is teaching his deaf child how to remove and replace a wheel on his/her bicycle, the child cannot receive his father's explanation and watch his demonstration at the same time. Many things must be done in sequence with a hearing-impaired child that can be carried on simultaneously in teaching a hearing child. You cannot direct your deaf child's attention to something, and then explain about it while he is looking at it. The parent cannot simply speak while demonstrating, or easily combine discussion and activity. Parents are encouraged to utilize every possible opportunity to teach new language. Almost every activity, from going to the zoo to visiting the supermarket, takes longer than with a hearing child, if new language is consistently introduced.

4) Aside from instructional activities, more parental time than for a hearing child is required for many of the routine, essential activities of living. Examples are calling the child to a meal, to bed, instructing the child to come in the house—everything that requires getting his/her attention from a distance, which in the end may make it necessary to go to him/her. This is one reason why training the child to hear and recognize his/her name from a distance can be a great help. Everything in view that is discussed or explained takes more time because he/she must focus attention alternately on the thing you are talking about, and then on what you say about it.

Communication is limited while you are driving an automobile, or at least it should be, in the interest of safety. You may sometimes actually need to stop the car in order to explain something, or to settle a difference between siblings. While the child is young the activities of dressing, bathing, undressing, preparing for bed, and even eating also take more time because you need to manipulate these activities for the sake of language development. Even conversation in the home requires extra time (more than with a hearing child) because you cannot talk to your deaf child while he/she is looking at something or someone else. And, you may feel guilty about disrupting his/her attention from something or someone else so much more than you would in the case of a hearing child, to whom you can speak without completely disengaging his attention.

5) Parents of a deaf child need to do extra reading and study, and receive extra training, in order to care effectively for their deaf

child. They need to read and study, visit programs and perhaps even to travel long distances, in the process of choosing an educational alternative. They need to continue to read and learn about the problems of deafness and about the educational approach they have chosen. They may need to master a special communication mode and learn how to use it effectively and comfortably in teaching and living. They need to read and study in order to know how to work effectively in cooperation with the professionals who will be serving their child.

Consider one of the problems of hearing parents of a child who has been placed in a Total Communication program. They are expected to learn signs and communicate with him/her, clearly and fluently. To keep up with their child in signs, after he/she is in school, they have to either spend a lot of time socially in the company of deaf people (our estimate—10 hours a week), or spend endless hours taking sign classes. Otherwise, they face the prospect of falling behind their child in their ability to communicate. Parents who use Cued Speech do not have this problem. They learn a finite system in a short time, and then acquire speed and skill in the process of using it with their child.

What Are Parents To Do?

What are you, as a parent, to do? Just do the best you can with everything that is needed? No, you must set priorities. You must allocate different amounts of time for different activities, to the best of your ability, and then readjust those allocations as you acquire experience, and as the needs change. If your child is very young (2 years old or less), recognize that you are fortunate to get started with Cued Speech at this age. Give first priority to learning to cue and becoming proficient enough to cue everything you say (slowly) to the child, or in his/her presence. Why? Because clear communication and language development are the child's most important initial needs. Other needs that should not be neglected at this time include auditory training and speech therapy. Fortunately, they require much less of your time than the other needs mentioned, since you can do your part without consumption of much time (unless you try to duplicate the therapist's role, which you should not).

Give all the time you can to language-developing interaction with your child. Also, marshal the resources of all members of the family, friends, baby-sitter—everyone you can—by teaching them to cue and thus add to the child's language input. You and your spouse should share the load—probably not equally, because circumstances will differ, but to the extent possible. Look at the possibility of adjusting your schedules so that one of you can be with the child when the other cannot. Of course, there is benefit in a three-way conversation, but it costs more in parent time. Fathers, when you are at home, communicate with the child as much as possible. You should entertain the child while the mother is taking care of other matters. You can mow the lawn, read the paper, watch sports on TV, etc., while she is with the child, or when a sibling furnishes welcome relief. Give careful attention to the article below: "Mom Can't Do It All," so that both you and your spouse can fully utilize your respective opportunities.

What About Television?

With time at a premium, parents may be tempted to rely on the "electronic baby-sitter." Unfortunately there are few regularly scheduled TV programs that are really useful for an unattended deaf child until s(he) can read well enough to profit from captioned material. Left to his/her own choices, a deaf child is likely to gravitate to programs that will entertain without requiring understanding much that is said: programs with much action (therefore, usually much violence) and car chases, and little plot. Most of the cartoons for young children fit this category.

Fortunately, television can be a means of language learning for the child and time saving for parents, if it is used appropriately. If you don't have a VCR, try to get one (or borrow or rent one). Cued Speech materials are available that will both entertain your deaf child and teach him/her new language, if he/she understands Cued Speech. The HELD-HI videotapes (see Appendix, p. 758) are for deaf children 3½ to 7 years old. These are presentations of favorite stories, cued for young children. The child sits with the book in his/her hands and follows the cued story, looking at the pictures as prompted by the reader. After the child becomes familiar with the procedure, he/she can be unattended, stopping and starting the VCR with the remote control when told by the reader: "Look at the picture!" These tapes are most effective for children 3½-to-6 years old who started CS early. Some of them can also be used effectively with older children who started CS later. Not only do they entertain the child and develop language; they give parents time to do other necessary things without reducing the language exposure of the child. These tapes, with the set of books for each tape, are available in sequence for a modest annual fee.

Another valuable use of a VCR is possible if you have or can obtain use of a camcorder to record your own cued telling and reading of stories and other material, for the child to enjoy over and over.

Until your child can use captioned video materials, it is probably best to minimize exposure to live television. Instead, record programs you think might be good, such as the Disney productions, the Lassie reruns, and other wholesome programs that teach while entertaining. They are basically morality plays in which good triumphs and which depict wholesome relationships. They have enough action for interest but almost no violence. Some cater to a child's interest in animals, and they are so interesting that your child will want to watch them enough times to learn most of the language in them—if you use them properly.

With a desirable program on videotape you can explain the story to the child in advance, and then let him/her watch it. Or, you can show a short segment, and then talk about it. Let the child stop the program at any point and ask for help in understanding. Let your deaf child operate the remote control, This encourages questions and explanations that lead directly to learning new language, on the child's initiative. Cueing members of the family can take turns at being available to help. Often a sibling is best at this.

It is impossible to transliterate an uninterrupted video program with full effectiveness because the child cannot simultaneously watch the screen and the person providing transliteration. However, one parent reviewer indicated that she spent many hours transliterating cartoons and other programs for her child before he could read fast enough to keep up with captioned materials. She thinks this helped prepare him for use of an interpreter/transliterator at school.

Recording the program before the child sees it has several advantages. First, it makes it possible to decide later whether it is a good program for the child to see. Second, it provides the opportunity to interrupt the playback at any point for questions and explanation. Third, it makes re-runs possible. In essence, it solves all the problems (except that of time!). Because the child will usually want to watch a specific recording over and over, most of the new language in it tends to be mastered in the process, particularly if the child forms the habit of stopping the tape to ask for explanation. Parent time is saved when the child has watched a tape a few times and wants to watch it again, because he/she will be satisfied to watch it without a parent in full attendance, though he/she may want to call for help occasionally.

Ideas for Managing and Saving Time

Several parents note that in the early stages it seems the time pressure will never let up, but that it eventually does. Then it is wonderful to see how independent your child can become. But what can be done in the meantime about the long list of things the parents have to do besides communicating with and instructing the deaf child? In addition to the usual load of homemaking, earning a living, and raising their family, the parents have to spend time studying and reading about deafness; communicating with school authorities and professionals about the needs of their child and what can or should be provided; transporting the child for special therapy and testing; learning about various devices and equipment: advantages, disadvantages, cost, and availability; and searching for and learning about various teaching techniques and materials. Most of this extra activity simply cannot be avoided. Yet, it must not be allowed to crowd out too much of the personal time available for the child.

An option for coping with the pressure of time is to get some extra help. Consider persuading a caring (and cueing!) relative or friend to move in with you during your child's preschool years! Such a person can share the load of transporting, helping, and even instructing your child. Or, if you can afford it during the preschool years, employ a live-in nanny who is good with young children, will learn to cue, and is a good role model for a young child.

Several parents suggest hiring a housekeeper for part of one day a week, or every two weeks. Partial relief from time-consuming housework will enable you to spend more time with your deaf child, with your other children, with your spouse, or even by yourself (for needed recuperation!).

Simplify meal preparation as much as possible. Mothers who work outside the home are accustomed to this, but the full-time homemaker may need to think about squeezing time from a formerly meticulous and satisfying job of housekeeping to one that cuts a few corners for the benefit of a deaf child. Housework *can* wait—it will be there the next day, or the next year! Don't feel guilty about it.

Encourage everyone in the family to accept a share of the responsibility for such things as: making beds, collecting laundry, taking out trash, unloading the dishwasher, putting away clothes, setting the table, straightening up. A parent reminds us that even a 2-year-old child is capable of putting his/her clothes into the hamper when taking them off to prepare for bed. Plan errands such as shopping and banking so you can coordinate them with others.

Organize your life in such a way as to save as much time as possible for your biggest job—meeting the needs of your deaf child. Life won't always be this hectic, but while your deaf child is young he/she will be your most important responsibility.

Sarina Roffé also suggests that when you take your child for an appointment you can take along things to use constructively in the waiting room. Use this time, away from the distractions of the telephone or household tasks at home, to read a book to your deaf child, do auditory training if possible, talk about environmental sounds and items in the waiting room, and look at and discuss pictures. If you forget to take anything, use what is there. If your child is small, pick him/her up and carry him/her around so that he or she can look at things on the wall at eye level. Talk about everything you see! Form the habit of using any environment as a language laboratory.

Even if you forget to bring props to use, there are ways to make the time productive. For example, if waiting in a pediatric waiting room, and there is a chalkboard, use it to play games with your child, identify letters, make sketches, etc. If he/she is too small for this, draw a line or circle and ask him/her to do the same. Draw a stick figure of your child doing an activity he/she enjoys, and talk about it. Don't waste the otherwise frustrating time in a waiting room. Use it!

Have you ever realized that you can sometimes be grateful for red traffic lights and even a few traffic jams? Sarina Roffé suggests that in the car you can seat your child in the front seat and take advantage of the fact that he/she is a captive audience while the light is red. You can talk about what the repair men at the corner are fixing, about the men who are "making the road wider," or about the holes in the road that are being patched. Don't mind if you pick up a few honks when the light catches you finishing a sentence!

Some relief from the time problem just comes along as the deaf child gets older. Robert Goodall, father of Matthew, points out that one of the most important sources of relief is the deaf child's learning to enjoy reading. Once this happens, parents can not only bask in the knowledge that their child's reading time is language-learning time, but can reassign their use of that time to meet other needs. Mr. Goodall also mentions that when Beth (three years younger than Matthew) was old enough to cue, her presence was a great help, widening the circle of communication and language input.

We are familiar with several families in which a mother with an outside job gave it up during the crucial (preschool) years. We are familiar with others in which a father cut back on his work in order to participate more fully in the nurturing of a young deaf child. In many cases a family has moved in order to place the child in a better educational setting. Such drastic measures are sometimes justified. Families have moved in order to reduce the child's time of travel to school, in order to increase the amount of time spent at home with family, even though in at least one case it increased the amount of one parent's time spent commuting to work and back.

Expanding the Cueing Environment

Both parents should be able to communicate fluently with their hearing-impaired child, and siblings should also be encouraged to learn and use Cued Speech. Extended-family members, friends, classmates, and others in the child's environment should also be encouraged to cue and assist in learning. Social skills and achievement on the level of hearing peers depends, to a great extent, on access to communication in the total environment. Obviously, the more cuers there are among his/her family and associates, the greater is the deaf child's access to the world at large. Also, adding cueing people to the child's environment will help diminish stress and the pressures of time for parents.

In earlier chapters the desirability of encouraging cueing among peers and classmates has been mentioned several times. Here we want to emphasize the specific importance of peer-and-sibling cueing to the growth of independence, self-confidence, and desirable social assertiveness in the deaf child.

A young deaf child tends to attend social and school functions almost exclusively in the presence of one or both parents. He or she depends on them to explain, to keep him/her aware of what is happening and what to expect. They protect him from feelings of confusion and vulnerability. With this security the child can enjoy social and school activities and grow in confidence and assertiveness. But he/she needs to outgrow this dependence upon his parents in time.

Hearing children can develop increasingly independent behavior gradually and comfortably, as they become increasingly dependable and confident. They can be allowed to attend social and school activities with the families of friends. Eventually they can bike to school and social functions with friends, unescorted. For profoundly deaf children this gradual, natural growth of independence is likely to be inhibited if they cannot communicate clearly with those who are with them. If hearing friends cue, they can provide explanations, answer questions, and in many ways help deaf children feel comfortable without their parents. A Q-club at school, cue-parties during the summer, and other means of stimulating cueing by peers and siblings, can be significant in the development of social adequacy in the deaf child.

The development of oral communication skills in the deaf child will enhance his/her ability to excel socially. Cueing peers facilitate this by providing backup to oral communication with others, as needed during the maturation process. Their help enables the deaf child to feel less vulnerable to confusion and misunderstanding, increases enjoyment of social activity, and undergirds development of a normal and appropriate degree of personal assertiveness and social confidence.

Aside from the desire of parents to see their deaf child develop as described above, it should be noted that such development is a great boon to the parents themselves. They can progress more easily to taking turns with other families in providing transportation to social functions, if each of those families contains at least one cuer. Most important of all, they can be assured that their child will have the same opportunity as others to understand and be understood, even if the process sometimes requires the help of a cueing peer.

More Time-Saving Ideas

Effective time management depends on setting priorities and concentrating time resources on the most important activities. Communication and language input must have highest priority for parents of young hearing-impaired children. Many other activities are indispensable, such as testing and therapy. Thus, for most families the only real possibilities for gains on the time problem involve 1) eliminating some unessential or optional activities, 2) finding ways to do some things in less time, or 3) shifting part of the load from the parents.

Many of the time-saving ideas listed below and elsewhere are impractical for some families, perhaps even most families. Many families will not be able to take advantage of those that reduce income or entail substantial expense. The suggestions that call for giving up some activities to obtain additional time to be with the deaf child may not fit the priorities of the family or its individual members. Each family should consider each of the possibilities suggested in the light of its own circumstances and priorities.

1. Do two or more things as one time, such as paying bills while helping an older child with homework, or folding clean laundry while watching TV at night. Of course, chores such as these can be used for language activities when the hearing-impaired child is present.

2. Try to do unavoidable or unpleasant tasks at an accelerated pace—to save time for activities that are more important or more enjoyable.

3. Go over a list of all the organizations in which you and your spouse participate, and to which you give a good deal of time. Check through them to see which ones you can drop out of for a few years, or in which you can participate at a less time-consuming level. Perhaps the sky won't fall in if you don't sing in the choir, manage an organizational campaign, or keep up with your golf or bridge buddies

for a few years while you help your child during the preschool and early grades. Keep activities in which your deaf child can share profitably. Drop, or cut down on, activities that your child cannot share.

4. If you get a baby-sitter, have her/him learn to cue. Pay a flat bonus for becoming proficient enough to cue everything, and make it a policy to do so. Don't pay a higher rate, or for time spent learning. Pay for *having learned.*

5. During the preschool years, hire help with housecleaning to free parents for more time with the child.

6. Try to arrange for one spouse not to hold a job outside the home during the preschool years, or cut back to part-time work. These years are critical—the results will be well worth going into debt until work can be resumed when the child reaches first grade. A debt is more desirable than a language deficiency.

7. Get a VCR (with remote control) and make use of available materials (such as HELD-HI) that develop your child's understanding and teach language, while you get other things out of the way in order to have additional time for your child.

8. Get a camcorder, or borrow one, and make your own materials to entertain and teach your child—again saving your time. Record the child as a reward for having mastered something. Tape yourself reading a book appropriate for your child, who will watch it over and over if you follow the HELD-HI format.

9. Go over all the things you and your spouse have to do to keep the house operating. Buy labor-saving (time-saving) equipment. Pay to have your lawn mowed for a couple of summers. Postpone do-it-yourself jobs unless you can make them shared experiences that will benefit your child. Pay to get out of things that will keep you from sharing time with your child.

10. After your child is in grade school, if you do secretarial work, clerical work, or health-aide work, transfer to a job with the school system so your hours will fit better with those of your child, and leave you free to be with your child more in the summers.

11. If you are a nurse, work fewer hours for a few years.

12. If you are an insurance agent, car salesman, or real estate salesperson, lower your goals for a few years to put in less time, freeing you to spend more time with your child.

13. Drop (for a few years) your memberships in some organizations that take a lot of your time, or at least lower the level of your responsibility and time investment. Explain your reason, and it won't be held against you. You can pick up when your child is "hooked on

books" and doing well in fifth or sixth grade.

14. Get others to share the load of CS input—spouse, siblings of the deaf child, neighborhood children whom you can teach to cue. Get others to provide Cued Speech input. Have cueing parties for neighborhood children during the summer or on weekends, and think of other ways to encourage peers to cue.

15. While your child is playing in the bathtub, fold your laundry. Children love to play alone in the tub and revel in the feel of the water. Bring the laundry basket into the bathroom and fold the laundry there. And, talk to your child about the clothes, about what the child is doing—but *talk and cue!*

16. Teach your child, when old enough, to fold and put away his own laundry. Or, for a younger child, fold and place the laundry on his/her bed for him/her to put away.

17. If you work outside the home, use any spare lunchtime to look through mail, pay bills, and answer correspondence. Or, use the time to read a favorite magazine you wouldn't have time to read at home. Save some time for yourself.

18. A portable telephone is a great timesaver, allowing you to tend to phone business while folding clothes, loading the dishwasher, cooking, setting the table, etc.

19. Practice cueing while doing other things: reading the newspaper, driving the car, watching TV, etc.

20. Keep in mind that every additional person who can give the deaf child regular periods of cueing time enables parents to use that time to get the other necessary things done. This extends their own time with the child. This spreading of the load begins appropriately with full participation by the father and other members of the immediate family. The examples in the next section, "Fathers and Cued Speech," illustrate the possibilities. Mike Maslin points out that cueing grandparents, if they live nearby, can be a tremendous resource. He points out that they can teach, they can baby-sit, and that they love your child. Beyond that, they are likely to have free time to give.

Not all the items in the list above will fit every family. Each set of parents needs to think about each possibility and use those that are feasible and can be fitted within their priorities.

Fathers and Cued Speech

Fathers of deaf children often experience more difficulty than mothers in doing their part in nurturing their deaf child. The mother usually has more time with the child, especially in the early years. Thus, she is likely to develop better communication with the child, who as a result may demonstrate an obviously superior response to the mother. All this can cause feelings of guilt or inferiority, as a result of the father's inability to do his part as he feels he should.

The tendency of the mother to give herself completely to the deaf infant may make the father feel deprived. He may not even be conscious of the reason, but the reduction in time and close relationship with his wife may add to his frustration, leading to resentment. Parents need to discuss any such problems frankly, without attributing any blame. Specifically, the burden of understanding in such cases usually falls most heavily on the mother, who must reassure her husband that she does not blame him for his difficulties. They must be able to share their concerns and problems, and each must be sure of the other's understanding and support.

The father's problems may extend to the learning and using of Cued Speech. It may be more difficult for him to arrange to attend classes and make use of opportunities to practice with others. All this may cause him to lag behind the mother in the learning of the system and in acquiring fluency in its use. Once he has learned the system, he may have less time with the child and thus get less of the most importance practice of all, use with the child. Nothing advances fluency like communicating with the child, and nothing contributes as much to motivation as getting a response from the child.

Fortunately, the modern trend toward more nearly equal sharing of the task of child nurture has helped many families to alleviate the problems described above. The rewards for full participation by the father in meeting the needs of a deaf child are tremendous. A strong sense of family unity, manifested in clear communication and sharing, is the ideal base for development of self-esteem and confidence on the part of a deaf child. As is shown by several of the short articles in the remainder of this chapter, fathers have much to give their deaf child that a mother cannot give.

The following brief items by fathers are reprinted, with permission from the Cued Speech Team at Gallaudet University, from back issues of the Cued Speech News. In some cases they have been amplified and/or extended by the writers in the light of what has happened since the articles were originally published (1982 and 1984).

Mom Can't Do It All
by Ken Johndrow, 1982
Ellington, Connecticut

Socket wrench, table saw, carburetor, quarterback, fishing tackle, chain saw, cord of wood, a bogie, birdie, or par in golf, solder, circuit breaker, the rules of baseball, catcher's mitt, rototiller, fertilizer, Jaguar, Corvette, film developer, acid stop bath, and so on.

There is a tremendous amount of language that your child may never experience if you depend on Mom to do all the cueing in the family. A father spends some important time with a child whether it be working around the home, enjoying a hobby, playing sports, or just watching television. Think of all the language you could give your child that Mom may never get the chance to use or even be involved with. Every normally hearing child acquires this language by just being around Dad and hearing it in normal conversation. Your child will get it only if you, Dad, give it to him directly, using clear understandable cues. Your whole relationship with your deaf child will change if you can communicate about "Dad-related" things, things that only a father-son or father-daughter relationship can share. There is no greater reward than to hear your son or daughter using language learned from you and you alone.

It is also very important that Dad be a disciplinarian along with Mom. It is important for your child to know exactly what the rules are and exactly why he/she is being punished for breaking those rules. These are the times it really pays to cue quickly and accurately so that the child gets your message right then and there. If you can't do this, then you and your child will be missing some of the important aspects of his/her behavioral development

Your child will probably want to take part in local recreational athletic programs such as Little League baseball, soccer, or basketball. Maybe you will want your child to learn to ski with the family. You're going to have to become involved in these programs, and cue instructions, rules, and strategies. If you can do this, then your child will be able to compete equally with every other kid on the block.

It's up to you, Dad! You must sit down and rank your priorities in regard to your life and your relationship with your family. If your deaf child's total development is near or at the top of that list, then it's up to you to learn to cue as well as Mom (or as near that well as you can!) and to cue everything you say when you're with your child. When you and your wife made the decision to use Cued Speech because it provides a clear, accurate representation of the English language, then you also took on the responsibility to use it all the time and to be as good at it as you possibly can. So, practice every chance you get, improve your accuracy and speed, and you will discover a whole new relationship with your child. Get with it, Dad!

More on Scott appears on pages 278, 279, 458, 459, and 567.

Kent McGlone
Spotsylvania, Virginia

What does Cued Speech mean to me as the father of a 6-year-old profoundly hearing impaired daughter? It has meant being able to contribute more fully to Amy's early years of development than would have otherwise been possible. It has meant being able to share many of her experiences through good communication. It has meant many enjoyable hours of playing "Fish" or any of several other games she loves to beat me at.

Cued Speech has meant being able to read and cue all of the children's books Amy enjoyed "hearing" again and again before she learned to read. Even more thrilling has been the joy of seeing her develop reading skills of her own.

Cued Speech has meant shopping with her in the supermarket and being able to ask her to go get a specific item. It has meant being able to take her to a circus or amusement park and share with her the various experiences encountered there. Cueing has meant all of this and much more to me as Amy's "Daddy."

Amy and her cueing brothers and sisters are discussed in Chapter 16.

Robert B. Goodall
Fredericksburg, Virginia

When my son Matthew suddenly lost his hearing at age 3½ (due to meningitis) we were fortunate to meet someone who had heard of Cued Speech and directed us to Kent and Peggy McGlone, who were using it successfully with their daughter, Amy.

We were able to learn the system and start using it in a very short period of time. Although it took most of a year to become proficient enough to feel comfortable cueing everything to Matthew, we were actually unable to communicate with him in spoken English for only a couple of months.

Matthew's vocabulary continues to grow, and he demonstrates language skills he has picked up since we began using Cued Speech, e.g., thinking of words that rhyme with a given word.

Using cues we have been working on reading readiness skills. Matthew is learning the sounds of the letters and groups of letters and is starting to associate them with pictures and written words. We expect him to use the spoken English he is receiving to learn written English as any hearing child would.

We have been delighted with the professionalism and availability of the Cued Speech staff at Gallaudet and are very pleased with our use of Cued Speech with Matthew.

More on Matthew appears on pages 47, 284, and 444.

Gerald Kujala
Eckville, Alberta, Canada

When we first heard about Cued Speech, Nicholas was 2½ years old and on an oral home program. We attended a Cued Speech workshop put on by Marianne Flanagan, of Calgary, and because of her explanation we felt CS would be a great assist to the oral program that Nicholas was on. Because of the "advice" from the "professionals" in the program, that Cued Speech was visual and would be of no use to Nicholas, we put a hold on learning it. We could see that Nicholas was making very slow progress on the oral program and that he needed something more.

This is when we decided to attend our first family Cued Speech week at Gallaudet University. At this time I had a fair idea of the hand shapes and positions and found that the week was a great help in straightening out some of the sounds. After seeing some of the parents cueing to their children, and after seeing that in a lot of cases it was the mothers who were the best cuers, it seemed very important to me that every member of the family should be able to cue well enough to carry on a conversation with the deaf child.

To gain speed in cueing I would cue things from the radio and TV and would practice short sentences and nursery rhymes over and over when I was driving or working in the field, or whenever there was an opportunity. Cued Speech was quite easy to learn; then it was just a matter of practicing to gain speed and confidence. At first we were a little self-conscious about cueing in public but now we know that it's important to give Nicholas language input at all times. It's really gratifying to have Nicholas as a more "normal" member of our family—one we can all communicate with. It has been a great asset to him.   *Nicholas died at the age of 14 in an accident.*

Malcolm Costello
Rockville, Maryland

As I look back to when we first learned that our son, Jeremy, was deaf, I have to marvel at God's sense of timing. Our pediatrician referred us to Bethesda Speech and Hearing Clinic, where the diagnosis was made. Jeremy was 19 months old at the time. David Barwell was the audiologist. A few days later, David and his wife, Marylou, came to our house and gave us a crash course on deaf education.

At this point we were really hungry for some fast information. We were in a very supportive Bible study and sharing group and knew that God would help us take care of Jeremy. We were spared the period of anguish, guilt, depression, hopelessness, and helplessness that many parents pass through. We just wanted to start doing something as soon as possible.

We liked what the Barwells said about Cued Speech, but they suggested we check out the other programs. A friend in our Bible study group is the cousin of the head of the Maryland School for the Deaf in Frederick, Md. He very graciously gave us a tour of the school, and we had very interesting discussions with him and several members of the staff. However, we chose to put Jeremy in a Cued Speech program at the National Child Research Center, in Washington, D.C.

I work for the Department of the Navy at the David Taylor Naval Ship Research and Development Center. They have a very active handicapped recruitment program, and there are many deaf employees. In the office next door to mine was a newly hired deaf mathematician. Exposure to her and other deaf professionals was very encouraging in terms of what Jeremy could aspire to in the future job market. Also just being able to discuss questions with receptive, understanding deaf adults was invaluable.

To facilitate communication between the new deaf employees and their coworkers, a beginning sign language course was held during work hours on station. I had signed up for the course, and it began the same day that Marylou Barwell came to teach us Cued Speech. Things got a little hectic because I would come home after spending two hours learning sign language, to turn around and spend another two hours or so learning Cued Speech! It struck me at the time that I learned to cue in three or four evenings, yet it took a three-month course for me to learn to sign at a basic level.

Cueing to Jeremy was very awkward at first because I was very slow, and he didn't understand that my waving my hand was supposed to tell him something. Before long, however, we both got the hang of it. Now it has become so natural that I cue to everything that is under waist high, including hearing children and pets. It cracked me up the first time I caught myself cueing to my in-laws' dog!

Jeremy is a normally curious little boy, and I find Cued Speech very helpful when I'm explaining to him what I'm doing when I'm working around the house, on the cars, or on my motorcycle. I can give him the exact name of each part I'm working on, and don't have to run to a sign language book or make up a sign. Jeremy is learning what things are and do like a hearing child, through casual exposure.

Because Jeremy is learning the English language and because he reads lips, he is able to have a normal relationship with hearing friends and relatives who don't cue. This is especially gratifying to his grandparents. We credit Cued Speech for getting the language into Jeremy.

Although I use sign language at work, most fathers of deaf children don't. If they did learn sign language and used it only at home for the few hours they see their child, they would be constantly trying to catch up with the child's sign language development. With Cued Speech, fathers already have all the language they need and the ability to express it clearly, understandably, and easily to the child. In terms of the father-child relationship, I think this is the most important aspect of Cued Speech.

Jay Fellows
Silver Spring, Maryland

Being a parent is not easy, and being the parent of a deaf child is even less easy. Cued Speech has been one of the major reasons we have been successful with our daughter Tiri.

When we discovered Tiri was deaf we were shocked and discouraged, but we soon resolved to do the best we could for her. We have tried to share the responsibilities of child-rearing equally in our marriage. We learned to cue together, and for the first month or so after the lessons we practiced together in the evenings, even if we had only a short time to do so. We kept a chart of the hand positions and configurations on the wall of the living room so we could refer to it quickly while practicing together or cueing to Tiri. Sometimes this meant running from the kitchen to the living room and back in mid-sentence.

Cueing with Tiri has meant that I have had clear communication with her since we first started, when she was 2 years old. Teaching her new vocabulary has been especially rewarding since I am an English teacher. When she needs help with a new word I can pronounce it for her and explain its meaning or help her to understand the dictionary definition. It has also been fun to teach her how to use the new words in context.

Different subjects Tiri has studied in school have been made more enjoyable and meaningful for both her and me because we could discuss them fully, thanks to CS. When she got heavily interested in tornadoes and hurricanes (the kid loves disasters) we talked at length about such storms. I told her the story of the night a tornado struck outside the small town in Wisconsin where I lived as a boy. She asked questions about it endlessly.

I don't believe a family with a hearing-impaired child can function effectively for the greatest benefit of the deaf child if only one parent learns and uses CS. Giving your child language, as you do with CS, is like giving your child food—and like food, language is a form of love when delivered by a parent.

The gift of language is the gift of culture—with its values, attitudes, ideas, and beliefs—and this is such a valuable gift that if a child receives it from only one parent when both parents are present in the home, the lack of it from the other parent could be devastating to the child's self-esteem and self-confidence.

Understandably, there are fathers who may be hard pressed for time to learn CS. But even in the case where a father lags behind the mother, it is important that he press on and continue to develop his cueing fluency, no matter how slowly it may come. The child will recognize and respond to the father's caring.

Tiri's story is especially interesting because in junior high she became very interested in learning to sign, after she was mainstreamed with CS. In high school she was allowed to have a CS transliterator in some classes and a sign interpreter in others, according to her preferences. Tiri is very much at home with both hearing and deaf people, communicating well orally, or in signs, or of course with Cued Speech. She is now a student at Gallaudet University, scheduled to graduate in 1993.)

Extended-Family Cuers

Extended-family members (grandparents, aunts, uncles, cousins, etc.) can make valuable contributions to language input and social development for a hearing-impaired child. They can also provide the parents with occasional respite from the constant pressures and responsibilities of raising the child.

A deaf child needs to feel included in family activities and discussions. This is very important at large family gatherings, such as those that occur on special holidays. But the child cannot be "included" unless he or she can understand what is said. This not possible without a clear, comfortable method of communication, used by most of the family members, and transliterated for those who cannot use it. Cued Speech is the most manageable method for extended family members to learn and use.

No matter what method of communication is used, extended family members who live elsewhere and see the deaf child only once or twice a year are likely to feel inadequate in attempting to communicate with the deaf child. In handling these feelings extended family members must consider the value of the communication, the effect of the limitations that come about as a result of infrequent use, and the "bottom line" in terms of value.

Deaf family members dread family gatherings in which most family members cannot communicate with them. They feel isolated, left out, ignored, and ostracized. Even limited communication is of value. Willingness to try to communicate in the deaf person's chosen mode of communication is recognized and accepted as an expression of togetherness. It is very important to make the effort.

If signs are used for communication, extended family members can learn perhaps 100 signs. Unless they get acquainted with signing persons in their own area who will practice with them regularly, they will forget many of the signs they learn. Their communication with the deaf child they see twice a year will tend to be extremely limited.

Advantages of CS for extended-family members include:
1) Anything in the English language can be expressed. Nothing has to be remembered except the basic code learned in the first place, 8 hand shapes and 4 hand locations, each associated with two to four sounds.
2) Cued Speech can be learned in a short time, usually 12 to 20 hours.
3) After the initial learning period, 30 minutes to an hour of practice per day for a period of a few weeks will usually raise the level of proficiency to where anything can be cued. At this point, communication with a deaf relative accustomed to Cued Speech will be satisfactory, though slow.
4) A few hours of practice, in preparation for an occasion on which there will be an opportunity to communicate with the deaf family member, will restore ability to a satisfactory level, at a slow rate.
5) About two hours of practice each month will ensure that communication ability will be adequate.

Extended family members who learn Cued Speech often feel inadequate or insecure in their cueing ability, usually because of their limited opportunity to be with the hearing-impaired child for extended periods of time. This is usually true of family members who live elsewhere and see the hearing-impaired child only once or twice a year. What is necessary to overcome this problem is to accept the fact that *slow* communication is still valuable. It does not make the deaf person feel insecure. It demonstrates the will to communicate.

A family member who learns Cued Speech does not forget it if he spends an hour or two reviewing it about once a month. Is this worth the effort? What is the deaf child's value? His/her sense of family identity cannot be completed if most of the family make no effort to communicate with him/her in the mode he/she can understand.

Extended family members who can be with the deaf child more frequently can expect to develop a higher level of proficiency, which will make communication more enjoyable and sophisticated. If there are cueing families in their own area, of course, they should have no trouble getting enough practice and benefitting those families by their interaction.

Guidelines for Learning Cued Speech—
for Extended-Family Members

Extended-family members should proceed slowly but surely to a level of proficiency that will make communication enjoyable and comfortable. To do this they need to work simultaneously on two levels: learning the basic system and acquiring a initial stock of frequently used phrases and short sentences. The following guidelines will possibly be of help.

1) Learn Cued Speech in an organized workshop or class, preferably three days or longer, so you will be saturated with the system when you return home to continue working on your own. Remember that the classes do not need to be in the area where the deaf child lives. It is possible for relatives to learn in their own home town.

2) Continue practicing on your own, preferably with a spouse or other family member, or with someone else already proficient. However, if no one else is available, solo practice is quite effective if the practice is daily. Use the audiotape lessons, videotape lessons, practice books, or other practice materials.

3) Make a list of most-used words, phrases, and sentences, and learn to cue them slowly and accurately. Practice this list daily until you can do them fluently and comfortably. Do not be discouraged that cueing materials you have not practiced forces you to cue very slowly and awkwardly. Practice and use many phrases and sentences you are

and awkwardly. Practice and use many phrases and sentences you are likely to want to use with a deaf child. Sample phrases and sentences for this purpose are included in most of the practice materials. Using these stock sentences accomplishes two things: a) It makes the deaf child realize you can communicate, so it establishes a bond between you. b) It makes you more confident and comfortable when you see the deaf child respond to your effort. See pp. 806-810 for 488 sentences.

4) Motivation and determination are the most important factors in your success. Practice every day, even if for only five minutes. Keep most in mind the importance of including the deaf child in the communication of your family, not just the parents and siblings. Be determined to enable the deaf child to be included in everything!

The rewards of having a truly communicating family are broad and fulfilling—for a hearing-impaired child—and for all members of the family. It all boils down to what value you place on the deaf child in your family. Other rewards are possible. Once an extended family member develops cueing skills, she/he may have an opportunity to be a valuable resource in his/her own area. There is a need for people with cueing skills in most areas where families are using Cued Speech. If families there are using Cued Speech, they will welcome any support that will broaden the cueing environment for their deaf children, from occasional social interaction (with cues) to volunteer or paid activity as a baby-sitter or transliterator. Even occasional social interaction with a deaf child accustomed to Cued Speech will maintain and develop skill for ready use on occasions when the extended-family member has an opportunity to be with a deaf child who belongs to the family.

Chapter Summary

Parents of a deaf child cannot possibly provide the full amount needed of each of the different things their deaf child needs. Thus, parents must assign priorities and budget their time. The most important way to cope with the time pressure on parents of a deaf child is to expand the number of cueing individuals in the child's environment. This chapter is full of suggestions from parents regarding how to deal with the problem of time. To attempt to summarize them would be simply to list them again. Our suggestion is that, every few months, you re-read this chapter, looking at all the ideas other parents have found helpful. Then you can decide whether any of them will help you at that particular time. The usefulness of different ideas and techniques such as those suggested will change as your child gets older.

Anecdotes of Patrick Gildea, age 3
by Maria Gildea

One school morning I got up early and started making pancakes from a left-over batter made the morning before. It was enough to make only four pancakes, so I said to Patrick (who was helping me), "Two pancakes for Patrick and two pancakes for Mama." Patrick said, "No, three pancakes for Patrick and one pancake for Mama." I said "No!" and repeated, "Two for you and two for me."

When I turned around to get the butter and syrup, Patrick cut my second pancake in two and put one half on his plate and the other on mine. He then said to me, "Patrick has three and Mama has two." A mathematical genius, no doubt!

One afternoon, Patrick and I went grocery shopping and I bought him a Snickers bar to eat in the car on the way home. As I was driving I asked him if I could have a bite of his candy. He said, "No. Mama is too fat." Very amused, I asked again. He said, "No, Mama has to drive the car." Running out of excuses, he finally decided to share a bite of his candy with me.

One day I was speaking to a friend on the telephone while Patrick was seated next to me "talking to himself." As I was listening to my friend, he was getting more and more animated and his conversation was becoming louder and louder. So I cued to him "Zip your lip" and made the hand motion suggesting that action. He looked at me sadly and said "Ouch, that would hurt."

Anecdotes of Elena Beadles-Hay
by Ardith Hay-Beadles

When Elena was in second grade, the whole family went to Washington, D.C., on a trip whose primary purpose was an early meeting between Elena's father and Dr. Cornett. The first morning after we arrived, while Robert and Dr. Cornett worked on research plans, Elena, her sister, and I enjoyed the swimming pool at the motel. At lunch time, Dr. Cornett and Robert dropped by the motel and came out to the pool to say hello. Elena was fascinated when Dr. Cornett cued to her. Nobody outside her immediate family had cued to her before. After they left, Elena turned to me and said, "When did Daddy teach Dr. Cornett how to cue?"

My husband Robert often picked up Elena from kindergarten and took her to a fast-food restaurant nearby for lunch, using the occasion to discuss the school day and to introduce new language where possible. Of course, he cued everything he said to her. The following year I met a lady (who later became a close friend) whose child was in the same class as our older daughter, Ardith Elyse. In the course of conversations that ensued, when we established all the family connections, she said that her husband often ate lunch at the same restaurant with Elena and Robert. Shortly thereafter, she told me this story:

On the evening of the day we met she told her husband about meeting me. She said, "You must have seen Elena and her dad in the restaurant. She is a cute little curly-haired girl, and she is deaf. Her father uses some kind of special hand signals when he talks to her." Her husband replied, "Oh, yes, now I remember seeing them. But I didn't see anything wrong with the little girl. I thought something was wrong with her father since he didn't seem to be able to talk without moving his hands around his mouth!"

Chapter 22
Going It Alone

The hard part when yours is the only child using cues is not Cued Speech itself. Rather, it is the problem of having to get an educational program set up for your child virtually on your own— sometimes having to deal with well-meaning but strongly polarized school officials—and you with no model to work from and no "push" except your own. (Diane Robers)

In summarizing their impressions of the difficulties of "Going it Alone," William Robers makes it clear that most of the administrators and teachers he and his wife dealt with were competent, caring professionals, but that they just seemed to be on a different wavelength. He amplifies their experiences as follows:

At the onset of Cued Speech we had two schools of thought in our area in regard to educating hearing-impaired children. There was the manual/total communication method and its supporters, anchored by a very fine school for the deaf, St. Rita's. There was also a strong contingent of young teachers dedicated to the idea of oral education for the deaf, mostly based on theories learned at area colleges.

Both camps thought that they had the best method for educating deaf children, and they had a lot of success with both programs. We looked at all the programs in our area, and even out of our area, and soon realized that they had some really serious shortcomings in regards to Gina's needs.

The only way to find these shortcomings in a program is to go observe them and talk to as many parents as possible. When we talked to teachers and directors we got mostly all shining examples of their star students who were doing exceptionally well. The one question they would never answer was "Where are all the children who've come through your program?"

When we started using Cued Speech, nobody had ever heard of it before. The educators we were dealing with were trained professionals who knew more about deaf education than we ever could, but who were "marching to a different drummer." We couldn't argue theory or mechanics with them because we didn't know theories and mechanics. What we did know is that Cued Speech works. That's all we knew, and that's all we needed to know. Through all of our discussions and meetings and arguments with our school district, our sole argument was that it works.

We could explain how it could work, and how it should work, but what finally got Gina a program utilizing Cued Speech was the fact that, with cues only at home, she was progressing farther and faster than anyone had thought possible. We had always been cautioned against being overly optimistic with Gina, and rightly so. Gina was a prelingually deaf child with a severe/profound hearing deficit with virtually no residual hearing—aided or unaided. In a traditional oral program, Gina could be expected to fail miserably. Yet, here she was, doing well academically, with good speech and lipreading skills, and it was obvious that Cued Speech was responsible.

Convincing the school board that Gina needed Cued Speech to maximize her potential was hard enough—we had to struggle to keep ourselves thinking clearly about what we thought was needed, and about getting it done. The school system had us to prod them, praise them for any progress, and endeavor in many ways to motivate them. As parents "going it alone" we had only ourselves as motivators. Nobody was there to remind us to cue everything we said all the time. It was easy to stay excited about cueing when we first started and we saw new language develop with every new day. When we got to the plateaus where Gina appeared to have leveled off in her progress, it would have been easy to have become complacent.

*The temptation was to slack off, to cue only sometimes, or to cue only key words. We had made good progress and, as easy as Cued Speech is, it would have been easier to stop, or to "use when needed." The thing that kept us motivated was the same thing that eventually inspired our school district—**results**. Every new day, every new year, Gina was meeting new challenges that required more complex language. Cued Speech is as effective in explaining Geometry in junior high school as it was in explaining colors to a young child.*

We have been cueing for 12 years with Gina. During that period we have taught quite a few parents how to use Cued Speech. I'm sorry to say that most parents didn't stick with it. I believe that most people are ingrained with the idea that the system dictates what is best for them. If a school system told them they must cue—they would. The parents whom we've introduced to Cued Speech who are continuing to use it are a special breed of people. They are strong, self-motivated, and proud and all of them are right now reaping the benefits of all their toils. When we get together with other cueing families, most of whom have "gone it alone" to some extent, we have a special bond, and some of the happiest kids you'll ever see.

Bill is right. "Going it Alone" does seem to take a special breed of parent—just the kind he described, as we have noted many times. In the early days of Cued Speech virtually all parents had to "Go it Alone;" hence the observation of many educators that Cued Speech is a method for the elite. Fortunately, as Cued Speech programs have become established and have flourished, there are now many places where parents don't have to be unusually confident, motivated, or strong-willed in order to obtain and use CS. On the other hand, in the United States such programs are far from numerous. For most parents the price of Cued Speech (in determination and motivation) is still high. The bottom line is that with CS such parents can succeed in relative isolation. This is not nearly as feasible with traditional methods.

Your Child's Success May be Used Against You

Sometimes a reluctant school system will use your child's success as evidence that it does not need to provide Cued Speech, a CS transliterator, or even a speech therapist using Cued Speech. CS kids whose parents have started CS with them at the age of 2 or 3 years are likely to be doing better than other deaf kids the school personnel have encountered. It is easy for them to classify your child as bright and as doing extremely well (for a deaf child, they mean). So the system may applaud your use of CS at home and propose to go merrily along with your child in a traditional oral program at school. Or, if the school uses TC, they may discount the effect of CS and recommend that you learn and use signs at home.

Mary Nemeth furnished this relevant input:

> *Years ago, you warned us that John's biggest problem in school would be his intelligence. He functions so well with his language base from CS that we've never been able to convince the school administration that an interpreter would make life much easier. John maintains a 4.0 average in junior high and is in the top spelling and math groups. It's hard to argue with that.*

Actually, it's very easy to argue the point, though perhaps it's not easy to win the argument. Do the schools actually believe that average and below-average deaf children should have every chance to perform as well as they can, but bright deaf kids should be deliberately held back by the educators' failure to provide what they need? Not with hearing kids—what about all the "magnet" schools and the programs for the gifted that are in vogue now in many school systems?

Unfortunately, in the only relevant case that reached the U.S. Supreme Court (Hendrick Hudson Central School District vs. Rowley), the Court ruled that the school system did not have to furnish support services the child in question needed in order to perform at a level above the average for hearing children. Since she was already performing at that level, and an interpreter would presumably make it possible for her to perform at a higher level, the school system was held not to be obligated. The Court made it clear that its decision was not intended to establish a precedent, but to apply to only the one child. The effect has still been to discourage parents with bright deaf children who are performing at average levels (for hearing children) from pushing the point. This point must be attacked on the grounds of constitutionality. An "appropriate educational environment" must be construed to require, when possible, the provision of all support services needed by the child in order to perform at his/her level of ability. The constitutionality of the position taken by the Court must be challenged.

A point the Court seemed to overlook entirely is that a deaf child bright enough to perform at the average level of hearing children, without needed support services, is paying a terrible price for that performance. The strain of trying all day to lipread, and then to make up for what is missed by extra study and effort, is an awful drain. Mary Nemeth's statement made that point also: "But John is wiped out after a day in school and really appreciates us cueing in the evening so he can relax his concentration. Occasionally, he'll take off his hearing aids and ignore us unless we cue."

The difference is not just the strain, but the necessity of learning everything less efficiently and less enjoyably. Additionally, the student has to spend much time in extra study to make up what has been missed in the classroom.

Parents may have to fight for their child's right to an appropriate educational program and an appropriate educational environment. It's often difficult to win that fight. Linda Balderson described how three families in Montgomery County, Md., addressed this problem:

> We insisted that the county test our children with and without cues, providing its own proof that our children did or did not need Cued Speech. The county personnel used the Carrow Test of Auditory Comprehension, presented orally with and without CS. The results showed clearly that all three children needed CS. Tiffany was 4 years 8 months old. Her raw score of 47 without cues placed here at the 4th percentile (hearing norms). Her raw score of 71 with cues placed her at the 58th percentile. Because of PL 94-142, Montgomery County decided to implement a CS program of its own rather than to pay tuition for the three children elsewhere.

Jennifer Ziebell points out that parents shifting from TC to Cued Speech often have a major problem with their school district. Where TC is firmly established, many or most educators just won't believe that anyone should consider switching from signing. The teachers have spent so much time learning and practicing signing in their deaf education programs that they feel they shouldn't be expected to learn something else in addition. Jennifer comments:

I was told that I would mess the child up, confuse him, and maybe ruin his entire life! How can they be so far off the truth? They tend to know almost nothing about Cued Speech, but do not let that deter them from forming definite opinions.

When All Else Fails

Parents who experience difficulty in obtaining what their child needs should make use of all available current information on the options open to them. Chapter 30 includes a section on the rights of deaf children and their parents, the federal laws related to those rights, and the provisions for implementation in states receiving federal funds. This material will be current for a time, but for the latest information parents should get in touch with the service agencies listed in the Appendix. Make use of the legal advisory services available from advocacy groups, some of which provide free legal assistance. Some parents will want to institute due process proceedings, or even court actions. For most this will not be practical. If parents are unable to get their school system to furnish what they believe is needed for their child through persuasion and pressure, and if they prefer not to go to formal due process, they still have other alternatives.

If the child is of preschool age and his/her mother can stay at home with him/her, the obvious solution for a situation in which a desirable preschool program is not available is to teach the child at home, obtaining materials, guidance, and help from appropriate sources (see Appendix).

Another alternative is to locate a Montessori school or a church school within reasonable distance and investigate the possibilities. Montessori schools have a tradition of putting the child ahead of their own convenience, and many of them have provided extremely well for deaf children using Cued Speech. The article "Normalizing the Deaf Child," by Anne Riley (1980), reports on her school's experience with a deaf child. The story of Sinead Clements (p. 558) describes her parents' use of this alternative and their confrontation with the schools.

Many families unable to persuade a school system to meet their needs have moved their residence, locating where a good CS program is available. Some have followed this alternative only long enough to get their child far enough along for mainstreaming, then returned to their earlier location. Dr. Raymond Hakim maintained two residences, spending Monday through Friday in one city where his son could be in a good program, and spending weekends and school holidays in his original location to keep up his medical practice.

Often the alternatives available are far from easy, but many families have felt greatly rewarded for following their best judgment. Before choosing alternatives it is usually best to make every possible effort to work with and influence the local school system. In Chapter 28 is a section entitled: "How to Present the Case for Cued Speech." Parents may find this helpful in their efforts to obtain what is needed for their children, or to choose from the options open to them.

Case Histories

Nancy Johndrow's account of the educational experience with her son Scott is placed in this chapter because it covers virtually all the factors that are involved in arranging for accommodation of a deaf child in a school in which he is the only hearing-impaired child. Don't overlook the fact that every time a teacher or interpreter learned to cue during the summer to prepare for accommodating Scott's needs at the beginning of the school year, *someone* called attention to the problem, *someone* got in touch with the right person or persons, *someone* may have had to pound the table or make threats, and *someone* trained the person or persons to cue. These things don't just happen. In this connection, remember also that the school system involved was relatively affluent. It wasn't as difficult for the administrators to agree to increase costs as it might be in many situations. All in all, this is an inspiring picture of a family and a school system that together did a excellent job of meeting the needs of a remarkable child.

Scott Johndrow is a profoundly deaf child who lost his hearing at 14 months due to meningitis. His family began using Cued Speech with him in the summer of 1978 when he was 4 years old, after several years of frustrating experience with aural/oral training. A detailed account of Scott's first one and one-half years of cueing exposure appeared in the May 1980 issue of *Cued Speech News*. Here are a few sentences from that article:

When the Johndrows first started to use CS, they decided to give it a three-year try. Four months later they found that Scott had changed from a frustrated child to an extremely happy child. His mother says that before he was exposed to CS he had a vocabulary of 200 words (good for a profoundly deaf oral child that age). By the end of the school year he was talking easily in three-and-four-word sentences and they could no longer keep track of how many words he knew. He "listened" attentively to 40-page Dr. Seuss Easy Reader Books. Additional evidence of the progress Scott was making was provided by the results of the Carrow Language Test. In June of 1979 he scored at the 3-year, 9-month level; when the test was administered at the end of the summer he scored at 4 years, 10 months, an increase of one year and four months in a period of only two and one-half months. The Johndrows attribute this progress to the fact that while he was at home with his family all summer he was exposed to CS all day every day, with both parents and both siblings cueing consistently.

One caution: in forming your impression of Scott's progress, take into account the fact that he is very bright and the fact that he received excellent support, both at home and in school.

Scott Johndrow
by Nancy Johndrow, 1987

Scott entered kindergarten at Crystal Lake Elementary School, Ellington, Conn., in Feb. 1980. From the beginning, he was to have the same curriculum, testing, and report card norms as the other children. It was our contention that with the full use of Cued Speech at home and with a full-time Cued Speech interpreter at school, Scott could function at the same level as a hearing child as long as he was given the same opportunity.

Scott's kindergarten teacher, Miss Marita Murphy, had never worked with a hearing-impaired child before. I taught her to cue so she could converse directly with Scott. Scott also had a full-time interpreter-tutor, Mrs. Adele Schwartz, who was a gifted interpreter. She interpreted everything

Scott, Nancy, Ken, David, and
Kimberly Johndrow

said by the teacher, classmates, and visitors, including questions, answers, silly jokes, slang, and announcements on the PA system. Adele has probably been the single most important influence on Scott's success in the public school setting.

Adele also interpreted Scott's speech/language therapy at the University of Connecticut as needed. The students who worked with Scott were required to learn Cued Speech beforehand.

Scott completed his first half year of kindergarten with a great deal of success. His report card and test scores proved him capable of competing on a high level with the other students. In June of that year we went into our PPT (Planning and Placement Team) meeting on "cloud nine."

The cloud quickly burst. Although we had heard glowing reports of Scott's academic success, his adjustment to his new school and to the other children, the administration of the school had concluded that they were unable to educate Scott further and that they would send him to the CREC (Capitol Region Education Council), a regional oral school, an option we had rejected earlier in the year.

We were completely devastated. It was very difficult to understand how he could be attaining every goal set for him by the professionals, and yet they could think that the educational setting could not be duplicated for another year. We refused to sign the PPT recommendation, which began the due process procedure. This meant that Scott could not be changed from his current educational placement until the school came up with an alternative acceptable to us, or the due process procedure led to a binding judgment.

We were convinced that the school's speech therapist's advice had been instrumental in the school's decision. She had not worked with Scott and had demonstrated a lack of understanding of Cued Speech. In addition, the school's reading consultant based his recommendation on opinions from several schools for the deaf around the United States, that a child with Scott's profound loss could not be taught to read using techniques employed in a public school setting. We chose to dispute those opinions and took our next step, Administrative Review.

In Administrative Review, we had to show why we had rejected the program decided upon by our PPT, as well as to propose in detail the program that we thought necessary, and explain to the Board why it was better. We told the director of Special Services that we had already engaged as our lawyer the man responsible for writing some of the laws for the handicapped in Connecticut, and that we intended to follow our claim all the way to the Supreme Court if necessary. We explained that, at that time, four Cued Speech cases had come to court, and the parents had won in every case. The Board ruled in our favor and overturned the PPT recommendation, stating that Scott could be enrolled at Crystal Lake Elementary School for the following year on a trial basis. At that moment, we realized that the responsibility had shifted to Scott. We knew inside that we had nothing to worry about.

Scott repeated a full year of kindergarten upon the recommendation of his teacher, Miss Murphy. We felt that his language (which was still delayed) would build in that year and provide a stronger foundation for first grade. This was one of the most important moves we made. Inner language development is of the utmost importance in the lower grades. Some progress in academic subject can be accomplished in the primary grades without age-appropriate language, but there is a real danger that the effect of language deficiencies will accumulate and become apparent in a higher grade.

In May 1981, we were back in a PPT meeting. After the 1980 PPT recommendation I vowed I would never walk into another without being prepared, but this year went well because Scott had proved himself. That this had been a trial year was never mentioned. Scott's first-grade class had 13 children, all hearing. Both his teacher, Mrs. Sue Stack, and his speech pathologist learned to cue during the summer, before school started. Scott received instruction in all classes in the normal classroom setting with the aid of the interpreter. In some situations, especially for spelling tests, the teacher herself cued.

Reading was taught through a phonics approach, which has been very successful for Scott. By October he was in the top reading group, where he remained the rest of the year. Scott was also one of the top math students, and had no problems with science or social studies. He attended special classes (such as music, art, and gym) with his peers. Speech and language therapy sessions were part of his regular school day. His therapist, Mrs. Pat Staszko-Kozik, easily learned to cue and worked with Scott several times a day for short intervals. She was dumbfounded at his language level.

The results of tests administered to Scott at age 7 years, 11 months, while he was in first grade, were as follows:

TEST	AGE EQUIVALENT
Peabody Picture Vocabulary Test	
PPVT Form A	8 years, 7 months
PPVT Form M	6 years, 1 month
Detroit Tests of Learning Aptitude (DTLA)	
1. Picture Absurdities	8 years, 3 months
2. Verbal Absurdities	7 years, 9 months
3. Pictorial Opposites	8 years, 9 months
4. Verbal Opposites	8 years, 3 months
5. Social Adjustment A	8 years, 3 months
6. Orientation	8 years, 3 months
7. Social Adjustment B	6 years, 9 months
8. Disarranged Pictures	15 years, 6 months
9. Oral Directions	10 years, 0 months
10. Likenesses and Differences	13 years, 9 months

Mrs. Stack was a gifted teacher who was able to bring out the very best in all children. She allowed Scott every opportunity for learning, and instilled in him what she referred to as "survival" skills. Scott discovered that making mistakes was an acceptable step to learning, that other children made them. He learned to question, to explore, and to become independent. Since he required no at-home tutoring, he enjoyed the freedom every first grader deserves after school. The first-grade curriculum was competed without a change, and Scott was duly accepted in second grade.

During that summer (1981) Scott continued his speech sessions, and was provided with three hours of tutoring a week to ensure that he maintained the skills he had developed. I taught cueing to his up-coming second-grade teacher, Ms. Watts, along with her daughter and son. Our family also returned to Gallaudet for our fourth consecutive Family Cued Speech Program. Kimberly, 13, and David, 11, were classroom aides, Ken and I assisted new cuers in the resource room, and Scott attended classes.

Scott continued to be a top math and reading student in second grade. Computers were a new addition to the school that year, and he had access to one. Speech/language therapy sessions were four per week, 45 minutes per session.

Because Scott's interpreter's family was planning to move, I began teaching Mrs. Gina Latino the basics of cueing in October of that year (1981). The school was very supportive as Mrs. Latino practiced and gained speed, paying both interpreters while the transition was in progress.

Scott is now (1983-84) in the third grade at Crystal Lake Elementary School in Ellington, Conn. He is the only hearing-impaired child in the school and has the same schedule and curriculum as the other third-graders. He enjoys skiing, swims, rides bikes, and plays on the soccer, basketball, and baseball teams. He won a third-place ribbon for his science-fair project on rainbows last year, and started organ lessons. Most people who see Scott are hardly aware that he is a very profoundly deaf child.

Third grade has been a challenge, and Scott has met it head on. Due to his high level of understanding of language and the superb job that is being done by his interpreter, third grade is becoming one of the best and most stimulating years for him. At this point it is easy to see if a child really knows how to read, to comprehend information, and give it back. Assigned reports play a major role, with emphasis on research and organizing information. Math involves multiplication, division, and word problems. He loves science. We're into volcanoes, mountain formations, and, yes, continental drift. All A's on his last report card! A major indication of his performance was his 82nd percentile score on the SRA Achievement Series.

Scott now has a man as his teacher for the first time. Mr. Wjada learned to cue over the summer, and Scott adores him completely. After reading a story Scott wrote on what he likes to do, Mr. Wjada told me that while he had seen Scott over the last three years, Scott's story had just brought him his first realization that here was just another little boy with the same hopes, likes, and dislikes as any other little boy. Scott's ability to express himself allows people to see past his deafness.

During recess, lunch, before school, and during free time Scott functions successfully on his own—that is, without an interpreter. His interaction with the other children in his classes has always been fantastic. They know he can't hear and are very courteous and try to make sure someone tells him if something is going on behind him. The kids understand most of what he says to them, and he lipreads what they say exceptionally well. Many children are learning to cue and a couple of girls are getting quite good at it.

Our school system has been quite generous and responsive in working out the best possible learning experience for Scott. The director of Special Services, Dr. McCarthy-Miller, and the principal, Mr. Frank Milbury, are both proud of Scott's success. Both are available if another school system needs information on how cueing is used in our school system. Teachers have been compensated for the hours spent learning Cued Speech. Interpreters are well paid for their services to Scott and are also paid for practice and learning time.

In our regional community of speech pathologists, audiologists, teachers of the deaf, public school teachers, and parents of the hearing-impaired, Scott is fast becoming a legend. This notoriety is due to the fact that Scott, though profoundly deaf, is being successfully educated in a public school setting. He has completely captivated persons in the school system, the town and the neighboring University of Connecticut because of his success in language acquisition, his abundant use of speech, and his academic success. Scott's mannerisms and behavior patterns are so normal that we are constantly concerned that people not forget that they are working with a profoundly deaf child.

What's it like at home? It's more often delightful than not. We have wonderful conversations at home. I know that to both Ken and me, and to our other children, Kimberly and David, our favorite times are when we each have our special times with Scott all to ourselves.

Scott and David play for hours. They talk, they laugh, they fight, they love. Kimberly is the older sister to whom Scott can turn for advice, for real tongue lashings, and for an introduction to the world of the teenager. With his dad, Scott enjoys all that is best in a father-son relationship. He respects the discipline, loves the roughhousing, and benefits so much from the talk that is special to a father and son. With me, the best are the times when we get silly, or when he tells me about what he did during the day. He excitedly discusses plans for what we'll do at Disney World, or what he and his friends did at school. He loves to remember when we did something. "Remember" turns into at least a 15-minute talk. We remember the "beautiful day skiing in Vermont" or the scary day he fell on the whale-watching boat and ended up with stitches on his forehead. We laugh, and we tell each other secrets; we call each other special nicknames, and, yes, we get angry with each other when bedtime comes too soon or promises are overlooked.

The big question: without Cued Speech, would Scott be as he is today? Our family's answer is "Definitely, no!" Cued Speech has allowed us to communicate with Scott on a level lipreading or signing would not have made possible. His entire personality reflects the comfort, the ease he feels, the understanding he has of the English language. The only barrier left between Scott and the hearing world is that he doesn't hear. Emotionally, psychologically and socially, he functions as any hearing child.

As always, I ramble, but a long time ago I realized that the big miracle of hearing might not come (or at least not soon), and I learned to appreciate all the little miracles along the way—the first sound, the first word understood, the first day I told him to please stop talking for a minute, the dedication of the teachers, the speech therapist, the principal who works with Scott, the loving, unselfish approach of both his interpreters.

Sure, it's work. I remember there were days I didn't get the floor swept, the beds made; the morning, afternoon, middle-of-the-night crying spells of utter frustration and exhaustion; the summers spent teaching cueing to those scheduled to serve Scott the next term; the fight to have him in an appropriate educational setting.

I don't think I could stand not being able to laugh, to joke, to plan, to teach, to just plain talk to my son. I know my husband and my other children feel the same way. We succeeded as a family, and we succeeded because we use Cued Speech with Scott. To those parents considering the use of cues, we offer this advice: believe in it, decide to use it as a family, and let every family member be part of the choice and the commitment to use it.

Update, 1992

Scott Johndrow turned 18 on May 22, 1992, and as I look back over the last 16½ years I feel totally at ease with our decision to use Cued Speech with him. It has provided Scott with far more than a complete representation of the spoken English language. Cued Speech has allowed Scott to function extremely successfully in the hearing world. It has allowed him to build self-confidence, humor, and a wonderful sense of self-worth. Scott is a very confident, bright young man.

Scott's success with Cued Speech and his success in his life can be attributed to a family that has as a fundamental belief that every member is loved, is special. That the strength within the family comes from all of the family members' respecting the needs of the others. We all cue when we speak to Scott for the simple reason that by doing so he understands 100% of what we say. Yes, Scott lipreads at a high receptive level, but just as we don't whisper to our hearing family members because speaking louder makes it easier to understand so we cue because it makes it easier for Scott to understand.

Our philosophy remains the same as Scott enters his senior year at Ellington High School as when he first entered kindergarten: That he have a full-time Cued Speech interpreter, that he be a full member of the class, and that all resource work be done outside of class time. A very high priority is that Scott has the right to fail just as our Kimberly and David have the same right. By this we mean that what curriculum, what musical instrument, what sport Scott wants, he has the right to try for it. We don't prejudge what he can or cannot do. Scott has never had a curriculum change; he plays a very nice saxophone, plays on the high school basketball, soccer, and golf teams. In golf he came in third in the conference and in classes made the honor roll all four times as a junior.

Except for the use of a CS interpreter, Debbie Solesky, Scott is a normal part of all classes. In place of study hall he sees a resource person who is a teacher of the deaf—a must, and a critical part of his academic program. He also has a speech therapist who has instilled in him an understanding of speech.

We make the following observations and know that the use of Cued Speech is directly responsible for them. Through the use of Cued Speech Scott has attained an extremely high level of language. His command of the English language is reinforced by the fact that he has so much inner language that he has no cutoff level on how much more language he can attain. He is able to lipread very, very well because he has language. He learned to read phonetically and reads at age level. Scott has a wonderful sense of humor, is full of interesting topics to talk about, and is aware of the world around him.

One request that we have made of our school system is that periodic testing be done on Scott's speech and language by a reputable institution. As Clarke School for the Deaf is nearby, we use their personnel to test Scott and to write recommendations for the speech teacher and resource teacher. Here are some excerpts from their 1991 evaluation:

On voice: Scott's vocal quality, resonance, intensity, and pitch were all informally judged to be within acceptable limits.

On intelligibility—80% conversational speech.

On oral expression—Scott communicated orally in a natural and spontaneous manner—used natural expressions, expanded simple sentences and well formed complex sentences, used correct word order in both statements and questions...used variety in his sentence style by using a wide variety of complex forms...successful in his use of a variety of grammatical elements...used appropriate pronouns in all instances and used prepositions correctly...varied verb tenses...inflected irregular verbs correctly in all instances...used well developed grammar.

On Semantics/Vocabulary—Scott demonstrated that he can express a wide variety of concrete and abstract ideas thru language.

On oral comprehension—In this one-to-one testing session, Scott demonstrated that he has excellent lipreading skills...showed that he is familiar with idiomatic expressions and can understand new ones through the use of contextual cues.

Scott was given selected items from the Rhode Island Test of Language Structure to test his understanding of specific grammatical forms which are often difficult for hearing impaired students to understand. This test was administered **orally**. Scott responded correctly to each of the 12 items given, showing that he can understand a good variety of simple, compound, and complex forms including Reversible Passives and Medial Relative Clauses.

On written comprehension—Scott was given a number of items from the Test of Syntactic Abilities to examine his understanding of specific grammatical forms in his reading. He answered each of the 15 items correctly, demonstrating that he can understand negation, conjunctive verb processes, pronoun usage, relative clauses, and nominals.

A letter from Scott at age 8 years is on page 567.

John Nemeth
by Mary Nemeth, 1992

There is no way to emphasize adequately the impact of Cued Speech on our family. John is a 13-year-old young person with a congenital severe/profound hearing impairment. Through tapes and a workshop, the entire family was cueing by the time John was 2½. With two cueing sisters (6 and 8) John knew the difference between a unicorn and Pegasus by the time he was 3. We have rarely felt that we could not communicate completely, which is almost unheard of in a family with a deaf child.

When John was about 3½, he had to have P.E. tubes inserted in out-patient surgery. Before that day John knew exactly what to expect—what the O.R. looked like, how staff would be dressed, etc.

Our decision to use Cued Speech has been reinforced on occasions too numerous to mention. When John was 5 we were watching a television show about handicapped children.

top: Mary, John, and Cliff Nemeth
bottom: Nicole and Christy Nemeth

When it was over, John turned to me and said: "I'm lucky. My ears are broken, but I can run, see, and talk." Yes, you are lucky, John, and I just wish that every family would have the option of being exposed to Cued Speech.

At 13 John is in the eighth grade at a local middle school. He has always been the only hearing-impaired child in his class and has had absolutely no cueing in the classroom. He presently maintains a 4.0 GPA and is in the program for gifted children. His early childhood language base from CS and his love of reading have proven to be enough to cope as a minority member of this hearing world, thanks to Cued Speech.

Elena Beadles-Hay
from information supplied by her parents

Most cases in which a young prelingually and profoundly deaf child is taught at home in the early years and then mainstreamed without support services occur because the desired services are not available. In the case of Elena Beadles-Hay, born with an auditory deficit of 110 dB (PTA), the choice was made by her parents on the basis of what they thought was best for her.

Elena was placed in an "acoustic nursery" at the age of 23 months and fitted with hearing aids. When she was 3 years old and learning language at a very slow rate, her parents learned Cued Speech and started using it with her. Her rapid acquisition of language thereafter soon convinced them that they were on the right track and they persisted in spite of the voiced concerns of the professionals at the acoustic nursery that the use of Cued Speech "might overload her eyes."

Elena remained in the acoustic nursery until age 5, at which time her parents were told that there was no reasonable place for her in the local school program. They were advised to either enroll her in a residential oral school or move to an area where an excellent oral school was located. Her father visited Central Institute for the Deaf (in St. Louis) and observed classes there at various age levels. While favorably impressed with the intensity of the school program and the dedication of the teachers, he and her mother decided that it would be better for Elena to teach her at home for a year with Cued Speech and then enroll her in a regular kindergarten at 6 years of age. This would provide a year in which to close the gap in her language skills. (*This was a crucially important decision, and a wise one, in our opinion.*)

At age 6 Elena entered kindergarten at Durham Academy, a private school with small classes. By age 7 she was in the top reading group in her class, where the average reading level was estimated at the middle of second grade. She scored at the 98th percentile on a standard reading achievement test.

Elena attended Durham Academy through high school. She had no special support and no Cued Speech there. In fact, she has never received cueing regularly from anyone except her parents. The school stresses homework every evening from first grade on. Her parents helped her regularly with her lessons each evening. Elena was always the only deaf child in her class, and until fifth grade was the only deaf child in the school. Her best teachers in most cases were those who knew no other deaf children and had no preconceived notions of what a deaf child can or cannot accomplish. Among her elective courses in high school were two years of Latin, doubtless of value in further vocabulary development.

Elena had no speech therapy until she was 19. Her father, in particular, was fearful that the speech therapy available would do more harm than good, so they helped her with speech at home. Elena graduated from North Carolina State University in May 1991, with a double major in microbiology and biochemistry, *magna cum laude,* GPA 3.56. She was awarded an R.J. Reynolds assistantship for genetic plant research during her senior year. The only special help Elena received at the University was a note-taker for her classes. The note-taker was not paid, but was a volunteer selected at the beginning of the semester by the professor. Elena is now enrolled in the clinical laboratory science program at Duke University Medical Center, preparing to go into forensic medicine.

Elena is described as witty, funny, full of puns and plays on words. As the French say, she "fits well in her skin." One cannot argue with success, though the choices her parents made would have been dangerous for a family with less able parents and a less-than-gifted child. Certainly she would have had a much easier time in school if she had had a Cued Speech transliterator and, in high school, a notetaker also. Things would have been easier also for her parents. But, who is to say that easier would have been better? A major concern of her parents, particularly for high school and beyond, was their belief that the presence of an additional person (the Cued Speech transliterator) always accompanying Elena when she went to classes might be a self-confidence reducer for Elena and a social-stigma producer in the eyes of many of her classmates.

*We can add that this is the "alone-est" case of "Going it Alone" that we know about. It is also a very spectacular illustration of the effectiveness of consistent use of Cued Speech at home. A key point is that Elena's parents recognized the danger of letting her go into first grade with a language deficit, and that they remedied this deficiency through a year of instruction **at home** before she entered kindergarten.*

Addendum
by Ardith Hay-Beadles, 1992

The above account is precise, factual, and technically correct. However, no description of bringing up a deaf child can be complete without the element of emotion, which only parents can supply.

"Your child is profoundly deaf." How can I describe the impact of that sentence? I had met only one deaf person in my 30 years of living, and that was a casual encounter. I knew neither the ramifications of deafness as it pertains to education nor its significance in everyday life.

I immediately turned to the "contributors" in every article and book I could find on deafness, and sought these people out by telephone for guidance on how to proceed. They were all extremely kind and all encouraged residential school for Elena as soon as possible. My deaf child was only 21 months old! I was also in a decision-making process for our other daughter, then 5 years old, on whether she should attend kindergarten. I have always valued the input of home and parental values as of the utmost importance to any child, hearing-impaired or otherwise.

Robert, Elena, and Ardith Beadles

Cued Speech put our child's parenting and education literally in our hands. Our whole family experience in bringing up Elena was of total normalcy due to Cued Speech. Every conversational topic was available to her. From this interaction she learned not only facts, but idioms, humor, word-play, opinions, and the personality characteristics of each member of her family.

These aspects of the process of bringing up a child, deaf or not, are as important in human development as those covered in the preceding "bare bones" description of her education and development. Elena developed as normally as her older sister. She was *Elena* (who was deaf), not a *deaf child* (named Elena). Through Cued Speech she was exposed to every family experience as fully as her older sister. There was no barrier in communication between her and her sister, so they had the closeness all siblings near the same age should experience. The pain I experienced was from watching Elena have to work harder in non-cueing situations to achieve what was so easy for her peers, at least with regard to spoken communication. She never complained, because she had never known differently. She is now 24, and I am still waiting to hear any complaints or expressions of self-pity from her about her deafness. What better proof can there be that her deafness is, or has become, nothing more than a series of temporary nuisances in some situations?

The more you invest in any worthwhile project, the more you stand to receive. In this case, I remember telling Elena last Christmas, in a close mother-daughter discussion about careers, how much I had been able to experience and to grow from having been her mother, a career I would not trade for any other. I have no doubt that one day she will pass along to her children the values she has come to know and recognize as important in her family.

Michael Poore
by Teri Poore, 1991

Our struggle to get a CS interpreter for Michael began in 1985. Michael had lost his hearing in 1984 from spinal meningitis at 2 years, 9 months. It left him with no usable hearing (unaided, 110 dB at 250 Hz., aided 95 dB at 250 Hz., no response at higher frequencies). He had been attending a private Montessori school for three months. We talked to the public school deaf education program coordinators and were told their program used total communication or signed English.

After about two months and some research (as well as talking to Dr. Orin Cornett) we chose to keep Michael in the private school and learned to cue. His teacher at the Montessori school attended a workshop given by Susan Christopher-Cofer in Fort Worth. We flew to Washington, D.C., to attend the Family Cued Speech Program that August. It really convinced us that Cued Speech was the best choice for our family.

Michael attended preschool at the Montessori school for one year; then we talked again with the public school authorities about their preschool program. After mediation with Gary Curtis from Austin with TEA (the Texas Educational Agency), Michael entered the public school preschool, where his teacher and speech therapist cued in a morning oral program. When we returned for kindergarten they denied our request for the program to continue using Cued Speech. We decided to find a different private school for kindergarten because we didn't feel Montessori was right for Michael. He needed more structure.

After many months we finally found a private school we felt would be good for Michael. Not only did they want him, but the kindergarten teacher learned to cue with me over the summer. Cued Speech made sense to her, and she had no trouble learning it. The night before the first day of school, at "parent orientation," she fell off a chair and broke her right "cueing" wrist. She practiced with her left hand at the beginning of school while I came in to interpret.

At the same school the first-grade teacher learned to cue with me the next summer. I interpreted, but she cued when she spoke to Michael. During the next year we were fortunate enough to find a young high-school graduate to interpret for part of the day. She took over full time the last two months. She was doing well, and we had second grade all set—or so we thought! Her plans changed four days before school started and we had no one to interpret. Again I made many phone calls, and after a very stressful time we were lucky and found Margie Sokolnicki, a CS interpreter who had recently moved to within 60 minutes of us. The very day I called her she had signed up to work as a sign interpreter for the Dallas schools. She said that since she preferred to interpret in CS she would meet with us. She and her husband came over, and we were very impressed with their friendliness. Margie and Michael really hit it off. She has been with us through lots of difficult times, including the due-process hearings. We hope she will be with us when Michael graduates from college.

We kept Michael in the private school through kindergarten and first and second grades. He had many friends and was doing well. We continued to talk with the public school representatives and wrote letters to the TEA in Austin. They always took the line: "The program is working well for **all** children as it is so we feel there is no change necessary." That they never listened to us is clear because after four years the director of Special Education asked this question of Wilma J. Tade (Michael's speech and language therapist at Texas Christian University) during an ARD (Administrative Review and Dismissal) meeting: "How much does he (Michael) talk in English and how much does he talk in Cued Speech?"

We finally decided we had no choice. We couldn't continue to pay for private school plus $1000 a month for an interpreter. We didn't feel it was good for Michael to have his mother go to school with him every day. We hired an attorney and tried to keep from going to court, but it seemed that's what they (the school system and TEA) wanted. We tried mediation two more times and couldn't agree.

The hearing started in Sept. 1988 and ended with the Hearing Officer's ruling in March 1989. We spent eight days in the hearing with many professionals testifying in support of Michael's continuing with Cued Speech, and three "professionals" testifying more against us as parents than against CS. It was one of the worst experiences of our lives, and I still don't know how our family has made it through Michael's hearing loss, learning a new communication method and basically changing our whole lives, much less having to go through a hearing where we're made to feel that we're "abusive" parents. The one thing that kept us strong through it all was the ease of communication with Michael. I really believe Cued Speech is what kept us together.

The Hearing Officer ruled that Michael would have a Cued Speech interpreter for one year (3rd grade) for all subjects and would also take sign language classes to prepare him for "transition" to the total communication program the next year (4th grade). We agreed, hoping to prove how well CS worked and how well Michael was doing, but also to take a break from financial stress. We were also paying for a cochlear implant that insurance did not cover ($20,000).

At the end of the year we were back in an ARD meeting asking for Cued Speech. They agreed, except for art, P.E., "programs" (presentations by policemen, celebrities discussing drugs, careers, French, etc., held in the auditorium for all grades), music, and every other area they could think of using to push sign language. We didn't feel we could afford to go to court over P.E. when most deaf students in the U.S. don't have interpreters for P.E., so we agreed. We did request later that "programs" be interpreted in cues because Michael said he was missing too much in signs. He wanted to get it "like the other kids did." The school authorities agreed reluctantly.

This year (5th grade), we finally got the break we felt we deserved after seven very long years. The special education director was out!!!!! We got a new director. After meeting with her we couldn't believe the difference. She listened and discussed! We left thinking she probably wouldn't be there the next year—just too good to be true! But she's here and so far, one month into the school year things are going well. Michael not only has an interpreter for all academic subjects, but also for P.E., art, "programs," computers, and all other areas except music. We totally agree to sign language for music. Michael doesn't hear well enough to benefit from music, and he needs to learn signs and be with other kids who sign.

We hope the new director of special education will be with us a very long time, but I believe enough people have seen how well Michael is doing that they wouldn't challenge CS again. I hope they're beginning to see that we are not the enemy; we only want what we know is BEST for Michael. Of course other kids will benefit from this program too, as well as professionals who are open-minded enough to see that not all programs work for all kids.

Our plans are to stay in the Arlington (Texas) area with Michael going through high school with a CS interpreter. Of course we'll have to find and train them constantly, but at least we're not fighting the school system at the same time.

We have copies of Michael's scores on the Stanford Achievement Test, Primary 1 Form E, in first and second grades. His first-grade scores placed him at a grade equivalent of 1.6 to 3.0 in all subjects except environmental knowledge, in which he placed at K.1 level. In second grade, on the Stanford Primary E, he ranged from grade equivalent 2.8 in listening comprehension and environmental science to grade 8.3 in reading comprehension and 7.3 in spelling. When Michael was 9 years old (in 4th grade) he was tested with the Clinical Evaluation of Language Function. His ratings were: Processing of Word and Sentence Structures, 6th grade; word classes, 3.5; linguistic concepts, 12th grade; relationships and ambiguities, 3.1; oral directions, 5th grade; spoken paragraphs, above 12th grade. Also: producing of word series, 4th grade; names on confrontation, 6.1; word associations, 5th grade; model sentences, above 12th grade; formulated sentences, 3rd grade 5th month.

At 10 Michael is a very demanding child, loves language, and wants it *all*. He constantly comes home from school with stories from Science, Social Studies, or Language Arts. He told me things about a rocket and boosters I never knew. He truly would be a different child without Cued Speech.

Excerpts from Testimony
Wilma J. Tade

In her testimony at the Sept. 1988 due process hearing for Michael his speech/language therapist, Mrs. Tade, presented a detailed analysis of the effects of Cued Speech on him. She offered the following regarding his intellectual ability:

The Test of Nonverbal Intelligence was administered to Michael by an evaluator from the Arlington Independent School District. According to the report, Michael performed at an I.Q. level of 102 and a percentile rank of 56. Note that this rank is average, not superior."

Mrs. Tade emphasized the fact that practically all the tests administered to Michael were tests normed on and usually administered to hearing children. She comments on one exception:

During an earlier examination the House Ear Institute administered to Michael a test normed on profoundly deaf children. The evaluator referred to this test in the last report, quoting, "No formal expressive language testing was administered since Michael scored on the 100 PR (percentile rank) at his last evaluation." These results were from the *Grammatical Analysis of Elicited Language—Simple Sentences,* which is normed on profoundly deaf children.

Now we should ask, "What enabled Michael to score at the 100 PR when comparing him with other profoundly deaf children?" We know it was not due to superior intelligence. In my judgment it was the use of Cued Speech that placed him at the highest percentile among all deaf children.

In her testimony Mrs. Tade also described Michael's surge in articulation and language development:

It was in late spring, 1987, a little over 3 years after Michael lost his hearing that I observed evidence of a tremendous breakthrough in Michael's articulation and also language development. I was remembering him as he was three years earlier. He then had almost wild and erratic behavior and what appeared to be a total inability to comprehend speech and language. I know he had good language, appropriate for a child nearly three years old, before the meningitis; but here was a child who appeared to have lost it all. Now just three years later Michael had again broken the code of English, this time through the use of Cued Speech; and I give you the following example:

Mrs. Poore and I were in my office discussing Michael. He kept coming in from his play and interrupting. Finally Mrs. Poore said and cued, "Michael, I'm talking to Mrs. Tade!" Michael shot back like a typical exasperated 6 year old, "Wy ah dou talkin to Mrs. Tade?" When his mother didn't give what he judged to be a satisfactory answer, he shot back again, "Wot ah dou talkin to Mrs. Tade abot?"

I understood him, and I believe you would have understood him. For a profoundly deaf 6 year old to ask such questions appropriately and understandably I judged to be phenomenal. This was a breakthrough that a short time earlier I thought would never come about. From then on it was as if all his inner language had been unloosed. In my opinion Michael was able to achieve this breakthrough because of Cued Speech which, unlike signing, had enabled him to receive all the linguistic information provided by spoken English.

Tade cited another significant item of information from Michael's performances on the Peabody Picture Vocabulary Test, at the House Ear Institute. His scores were 5 years 8 months when Cued Speech was used and 5 years 2 months when the words were written out and Michael had to read them. The examiner considered this score to be unusual and stated, "Most children tested in this clinic with this degree of hearing loss who use sign language perform very poorly on this test when presented with written cues. It is often impossible to establish a baseline and therefore the test cannot be administered. It is impressive for Michael to have the ability to process verbal vocabulary at this level."

Michael's mother concludes: Our experience with Cued Speech has been only positive except having to fight for it and convince those who don't understand. Our frustrations come from the limits deafness causes for Michael that only hearing and good speech could change. Our expectations for Michael are now limited only by what he wants to do or not to do with his life.

Michael has no usable hearing (110 dB unaided at 250 Hz., 95 dB aided, and nothing at higher frequencies.) So we know he will have a very difficult time in the hearing world. We've helped him believe he can do anything he wants to do. He'll understand the limitations of deafness later when he's mature enough. By then we hope he's experienced so much that he'll have many choices that are right for him.

A letter from Michael and an imaginative story by him appear on pages 573-575. For comments from his speech/language therapist and his mother on the effects of his use of a cochlear implant, see page 219. For comments from his transliterator, see p. 674.

Sarah Hightower
by Elizabeth Hightower, 1992

In considering what to write about the experience of rearing a profoundly hearing-impaired daughter without the benefit of a formal Cued Speech program—that is, "going it alone"—I can summarize by saying that the only things necessary to success in rearing a deaf child are to *cue everything* to your deaf child, hire the best speech teacher in your area, and rear your child the same way you would rear a normal hearing child. It really is that simple.

After 16 years of cueing to my daughter Sarah, it is almost impossible for me to remember what it was like "before Cued Speech" when I had to carefully select and/or limit what I would say to her.

The greatest compliment I now hear regarding Sarah is when my friends or acquaintances remark that Sarah's deafness "hasn't prevented her from doing anything she wants to do!"

It is true that Sarah's deafness hasn't prevented her from doing anything she wants to do—from majoring in French in college to travelling on her own in Europe—to competing in English horse shows. The reason she hasn't been prevented from doing anything she wants is the effect of Cued Speech. Sarah's language proficiency, acquired through Cued Speech almost exclusively through her home environment alone, made it possible for her to master the English language at an early age and thereby absorb all the knowledge to which she has been exposed through that language.

Sarah has never been enrolled in a Cued Speech program. Although she has had intermittent Cued Speech instruction in a school environment, the majority of her formal education has been without the benefit of interpreters.

Sarah has received Cued Speech *constantly* in her home environment. One example of what she was absorbing occurred when she was about 7 years old. We had been cueing for about 18 months. While observing a conversation being cued by her father and me, she interrupted us to ask what the word "extrapolate" meant! Since her language has been "normal" since she was approximately 12 years old, I have to believe that type of exposure to Cued Speech in the home environment alone is sufficient to develop normal language. I would have slept much better in the early years of our cueing years had I known how it would all turn out so well!

It was in April of 1976, when Sarah was 5 years old, that I first happened to hear about Cued Speech. We were living in St. Louis, Missouri, and Sarah was progressing exceedingly well in the oral program which she was attending. However, as a student in the Master's Program for Speech and Hearing at Washington University, I was aware that only a small percentage of information was available through lipreading. Sarah's hearing loss is profound (98 dB in the speech frequencies), and her father and I were concerned that she would be unable to understand the likes of Dostoevski (if she decided she wanted to understand it) if she possessed anything less than full command of the English language. I would have been content with mastery of English alone—mastery of French was her own idea. I was intrigued by the idea of Cued Speech when I heard about it from a fellow student visiting from Hong Kong!

Sarah's father and I visited with Dr. Cornett the following month. In June we wrote a letter to the oral school Sarah was attending, withdrawing her from the program there. I had three months in which to locate a placement for her. The decision to "go it alone" was frightening but not difficult because Cued Speech presented such a logical solution to the language-acquisition problem.

From the very inception of the decision to use Cued Speech, I experienced the idea as a great "liberating" experience. I believed that my job was to provide Sarah with the "tools" of language, speech, and education, so that she would have the freedom of choosing to do anything she wanted to do. I did not want any of her options foreclosed.

Childgrove, a school with a Piagetian, experience-based program for hearing children in St. Louis, was one in which I had been interested for the creative development of children. It had been a terrible loss for me to realize that Sarah, because of her hearing loss, would not have the opportunity to enjoy and benefit from the type of creative experiences offered at Childgrove. When we decided to "go it alone" with her education because of Cued Speech, Childgrove immediately became a possibility. The school was delighted and enthusiastic about accepting Sarah, so we sought an interpreter.

We hired a teacher of the deaf, Jody Haymond. Terry Vanden-bosche (Klein) came to St. Louis, and within five days Jody, Sarah's father and I, and four of the teachers from Childgrove knew how to cue! Sarah's father and I began cueing to Sarah immediately and have continued cueing to this day! Sarah took to the cueing immediately and seemed genuinely delighted at the frustration we were having tripping over our fingers!

Because Sarah was almost 6 by the time she was receiving constant cueing, we supplemented her normal school curriculum with the language program *Oral English* (the Tate Curriculum). The Oral English program and speech training were the only deviations that were necessary from the regular school curriculum. Sarah flourished both creatively and in her speech and language acquisition. Although we were well satisfied with the program and with Sarah's progress, the road was not without its difficulties.

Well into the first school year at Childgrove, the teacher we had hired moved to Minnesota with her family when her husband was transferred there. We had to find a replacement teacher, retrain her in Cued Speech, etc. Also, each year Sarah progressed to a different classroom, and the classroom teachers had to be introduced to Cued Speech. Some teachers were interested and some weren't.

When Sarah was 9 years old, it was time for her to receive a more "serious" (i.e., structured) type of instruction, and we therefore transferred her to an oral school for the deaf in St. Louis.

She had no interpretation during the school days, but because her language development was so advanced at that point, she didn't need it. She excelled in her studies with lipreading alone at school, and we continued to cue to her at home. After we moved to California in 1984, Sarah was enrolled in public schools and had signing interpretation. She has always received Cued Speech at home.

When Sarah decided that she wanted to study French, despite the fact that in California the foreign language requirement is waived for hearing-impaired students, she was frantic to have a Cued Speech interpreter. She approached her college adviser, begged and pleaded for a Cued Speech interpreter (in French), and was successful in obtaining one.

She fights her own battles for Cued Speech interpretation/transliteration now and is currently attempting to secure a transliterator for her "junior year abroad" in England through her college in North Carolina.

In conclusion, I would say that I am delighted with the results of our "going it alone." I have been surprised and made curious by people whom I have met who, after learning about Cued Speech and its potential, have nevertheless picked up and left their homes and families in order to have their children attend formal Cued Speech programs. If people want to move, that's their choice, but I firmly believe that it is utterly unnecessary to move to meet the needs of a deaf child. Cued Speech empowers parents to develop normal language in their child if they are willing to take on the responsibility of being deeply involved with their child and cueing *everything* while in the child's presence. By taking responsibility for their own child's development, they are able to support her/him to the full extent of their ability as parents.

If Cued Speech is begun early enough, there is not even the need to alter a regular school curriculum to include structured language learning, although speech training must remain a necessary adjunct to an acceptable "go it alone" program.

Cued Speech was only three years old when my daughter was born. She didn't have the advantage of exposure to it until she was 5½. We were therefore required to provide a structured language program for her. But by the time she was 8, we were able to discuss the concept of freedom, in detail, while standing at Checkpoint Charlie with her. We have been able to discuss the psychology of prejudice with her, in detail. In other words Sarah has benefitted, from the time she was 6, from whatever input we had to give to her, because the language was in a clearly decipherable form!

The triumph of Cued Speech is that it provides parents the means to give their deaf child the same opportunities for acquiring knowledge and experience that they could give to a hearing child.

In thinking back over the course of our "going it alone" my only regret is that in the beginning I was afraid! I can assure any parent consulting this resource book that there is absolutely no reason to be afraid of "going it alone." The gratification of charting your own course is great indeed.

"Going it alone" is extremely difficult for a child of average ability unless support services are adequate. Sarah would probably have encountered serious problems if she were a child of lower ability and/or determination, or her mother less able. This case history would fit just as well in the "late starter" chapter. Sarah's own observations begin on page 624, and those of her roommate on page 295.

Grace Consacro
by Donna Consacro, 1987

Imagine—or remember—discovering that all the words that you have spoken to your infant child since birth have literally fallen on deaf ears. Imagine (or remember) the confusion and disbelief that comes from learning that your child is severely or profoundly hearing impaired. Unfortunately, that confusion is only the beginning. It is not dispelled by acceptance. When acceptance does come, however slowly and reluctantly, it precipitates the search for help which leads to even greater confusion. You learn about methods and philosophies and choices that you must make.

Thus Donna Consacro, mother of Grace, started the article she wrote for the Spring, 1987 issue of Otoscope, the publication of the E.A.R. Foundation, Nashville, Tenn. Three years earlier Mrs. Consacro had summarized her experiences in an article in Cued Speech News (December, 1984), which we reproduce here with permission, and with a sequel bringing the story up to date.

It was in March 1977 that my husband and I knew for sure that our beautiful 15-month-old daughter had a severe-to-profound sensorineural hearing loss. Faced with the reality of an impairment that had to be dealt with, we turned to the people at the Chattanooga Speech and Hearing Center and enrolled Grace in their Total Communication class at the age of 19 months.

I went to class with Grace every day, observed and learned the SEE signs along with her, and went to any extra sign classes for the parents. It took only a few weeks for Grace to assimilate the idea that a sign signified an object, and her noun vocabulary began to grow rapidly. When her teacher stressed the necessity of signing complete sentences, I did the best I could. After about six months I began to be very frustrated with my limited signing. I resented always changing what I *wanted* to say into what I *could* sign.

In the spring of 1978, when Grace was 2½ I read about Cued Speech in *Parade Magazine*. I went to the first workshop close to me and met Dr. Cornett. Cueing made such good sense! I came back very enthusiastic and started cueing just the way Dr. Cornett had said *not* to use it—mixing signs and cues in the same sentence. I kept doing this for the next year. That year I tried to convince other parents and the school to use Cued Speech. Looking back, I regret all the energy and time spent which should have been directed toward Grace.

Shortly after Grace was 3, I began to realize that her baby sister Elena, at 1½ years a precocious talker, not only spoke more than Grace, but understood so much more. As this realization grew, so did another—Grace could talk with her teacher more freely than with her mother. I was very frightened and angry with the Total Communication program but lacked the confidence to commit myself to cueing exclusively.

The summer that Grace was 3½ my husband and I met Bobbi Spink, a Montessori teacher who had learned about Grace from a parent co-worker of my husband. Bobbi was very excited about having Grace at her school. It was such a relief to find her so enthusiastic after the past two frustrating years. We enrolled Grace at the Montessori school for their summer camp, on a trial basis. Everyone was pleased with her adjustment, so we enrolled her in the fall but, still uncertain, kept her in the TC program at the Center as well. The first language scores we

Grace Consacro, 1992

ever had on Grace were administered in Nov. 1979, when her age was 3 years 11 months. On the Zimmerman Preschool Language Scale her scores were: Auditory Comprehension, 3.10 years; Verbal Ability, 3.3 yrs. On Dec. 18th, Grace's fourth birthday, we met with the Chattanooga City School System. We had finally decided to remove Grace from the signing environment altogether. We asked for the school system to provide one-half hour of speech articulation therapy five days a week. We would provide the academic program through Montessori. We also asked that Grace be tested then, and again at the end of the term.

Bobbi Spink learned Cued Speech but never became fluent. I remember calling Dr. Cornett on March 13, 1980, to talk with him about my fears that we might not succeed. We had pulled her out of the Total Communication program against the advice of all those professional people we had turned to for help three years before. When Dr. Cornett asked me if I was cueing 100% of the time, I had to admit that I was still not doing that. His advice was "Cue 100% of the time; if you can't cue it, don't say it!" Finally I followed that sound advice and after only two weeks was beginning to get some real speed into my cueing. Grace became impatient if I was too slow. Right away I felt a greater rapport with my daughter.

Despite the fact that Grace Marie received cues at school only for isolated vocabulary words when a new lesson was introduced, and that I cued at 100% only the last two months, the test results show that she made rapid progress in those five months. Without an interpreter, she scored as follows:

Test scores Jan. 1980 (age 4.1)	Test scores May 1980 (age 4.5)
Receptive Language 4.9	Receptive Language 6.0
Expressive Language 3.3	Expressive Language 4.75

It was a startling leap. We were all thrilled. We asked that the school system continue to provide the Montessori program at its expense. They refused, offering instead early entry into kindergarten and insisting that Grace spend most of her day in the self-contained classroom. We could not take our daughter out of a school where she had done so well and place her in a situation we feared would be bad. Instead of initiating a due process procedure we chose to use our energy and our money for something we knew worked. We kept Grace in the Montessori school, and the school system continued to provide speech therapy.

During the following summer we went to Gallaudet for a "Family Cueing Vacation." We came home with Held-Hi video tapes in tow. There was a lot of excitement several weeks later when Grace got angry with me, saying, "I don't like it, not one little bit." She had learned that from watching *The Cat in the Hat*.

When school began in the fall, the Montessori school sent two teachers to learn Cued Speech. One of these turned out to be an excellent cuer, although she did not cue to Grace constantly. However, that year held a far greater reward for Grace. In Jan. 1981, Grace learned to read. Over the Christmas holidays she sat for long hours poring over books, and when school resumed, it all came together for her. From that moment to this, Grace has read every printed word she can lay her hands on. Her test scores for the end of that school year reflect how swiftly she began to assimilate information, now that she was no longer dependent on me or a teacher as a source. Grace was 5.5 when the next tests were given, again without an interpreter.

Tests given May, 1981	Age-equiv. Score
Utah test of Learning Development	7.1
Test of Language Development (TOLD):	
Picture vocabulary	4.0
Oral vocabulary	7.9
Grammatical understanding	5.9
Sentence Imitation	8.1
Grammatical completion	4.9
Peabody Picture Vocabulary Test	4.1

The vocabulary scores listed above are probably far below Grace's actual vocabulary at the time, because she was having to lipread individual words. Had the test material been cued, the results would have been accurate measures of her vocabulary, probably several years higher.

During Grace's third year at Montessori, some of the children began to learn Cued Speech and were able to cue simple sentences to Grace. When she was tested in May 1982, at 6.5 years, again without an interpreter, her scores continued to show progress.

Peabody Individual Achievement Test	Grade Equivalent (not age)
Math	1.8
Reading Recognition	3.6
Reading Comprehension	4.4
Spelling	4.1
General Information	3.6

During the past two years (up to mid-1984) we have lived in Nashville, and Grace has been mainstreamed in our neighborhood public school. An itinerant teacher for the hearing impaired was with Grace three hours a week last year, and now comes two hours a week. Last year Grace had no one cueing at school, yet she made mostly A's on her report card and scored at the 97th percentile on the California Achievement Test all Metro students take at the end of the year. This year her itinerant teacher began to learn cueing during the Christmas holidays. I went to Grace's second-grade classroom for a few weeks to teach cueing. Some of the children showed an interest, but for various reasons I had to stop the lessons. Again with essentially no cueing at school, Grace made A+'s on her report card and her 1984 CAT scores were impressive:

Math	88th percentile
Reading	94th percentile
Total language	97th percentile

Grace is entering third grade at the same neighborhood school this year. She has recently been certified as gifted and will be attending the enrichment classes along with the other gifted children once a week. Beginning in mid-October, I will be teaching Cued Speech for one 45-minute period each Friday as part of an enrichment program open to all the students at Grace's school. Each session will last for six weeks. As long as I have children signing up to learn, I will be teaching—I hope until the end of the school year.

If I could undo some past mistakes, I suppose they would have to do with mustering the courage earlier to take Grace out of the Total Communication program (way back in 1979). Grace has succeeded so well despite our delay in giving her Cued Speech 100%. If I can offer any encouragement to others faced with similar decisions, it would be to trust your own judgment as to what will best meet your child's needs. I have been accused many times of not "accepting" her deafness, of expecting more from her than she would be able to do. I feel I was being asked to *resign* myself to the limitations deafness can impose. Cued Speech played a large part in giving Grace the means of limiting the effect deafness could have on her development as a member of a hearing world. That world is and always will be available to her.

As a result of her insatiable appetite for reading, it is not at all uncommon for Grace to use idiomatic and colloquial expressions such as: "We don't have time for you to go gallivanting around all over the place!" or "Come here, I've got to pick a bone with you."

I asked Grace if she likes to have people cue to her. She answered, "It means lots to me when someone cues to me. I understand and can talk to him/her without saying dumb things." Puzzled, I asked her what she meant by "dumb things." She answered, "Like, 'What? What?'"

All of the tests given Grace, so far as I know, were normed on normally hearing children. Following are her scores on the Stanford Achievement Test (HI) at the end of the 1983-84 school year (end of second grade).

Vocabulary	8.8 grade level
Reading	8.6 grade level
Language	6.3 grade level
Math concepts	4.7 grade level

*Note the high vocabulary score on a test that was **read**, not lipread.*

Seven-and-a-half years have gone by since the above was written. By the end of the fourth grade it was obvious that Grace was going to need a Cued speech transliterator. The school used different teachers for different academic subjects, and Grace was having trouble coping with lipreading four or five teachers. She was coming home totally exhausted and began to show some discipline problems, not at school but at home. During the annual meeting with the school system to set up Grace's IEP (May 1986) I requested and got a transliterator. We had the teachers at her school and the principal behind us—it was not so much easy as that we were prepared, and the school system knew it. Also Ms. Georgia Robbs, who is the Metro (Nashville) system supervisor for teachers of the hearing impaired, has always been a strong advocate for children having interpreters when they need them, even if the child uses CS.

Shortly after school was out in late May, I called the school system to see how they would advertise for the job. I was informed that they would not advertise the position until after the fiscal year budget was approved. This meant that the ad would appear in the papers in mid-to-late July. Knowing full well that there was no one in Nashville (except us) who could cue, and that finding someone in late July and training them before school started in August would be impossible, I decided that I had to find Grace's transliterator myself.

We were very, very fortunate to have many friends who helped put the word out, and by late June we met Linda Cash. She agreed to my idea of being trained for the job before it was even advertised, and so we started cueing. Linda is the fastest learner I have ever encountered and is a natural interpreter. She instinctively knew a lot of things that I'm sure others have to be taught (such as allowing Grace to 'eavesdrop' on surrounding conversations). Linda even agreed to leave her 2-year-old daughter and her husband for a week to join us in a return (for us) trip to Gallaudet for the Aug. 3-8, 1986, Cueing Family Vacation. I insisted Linda go into the advanced class because school started August 21. Linda was as ready as anyone could be, and certainly more ready than any of us thought possible, when school started in August.

Linda's presence in the classroom did not cause any commotion at Grace's school. Everything went so smoothly. And the difference in Grace (more relaxed, happier, and participating much more in class) was evident very soon. Linda is still Grace's transliterator. We have had a few minor skirmishes (and one major war) with the school system over the years but I think even they know what a really outstanding transliterator Linda is. Her presence has meant so much to Grace.

Linda was out the last six weeks of Grace's seventh grade year (to have her second child). Grace had a very, very slow cuer to fill in, and told me she thought she would do better without an interpreter than with one so slow. During those six weeks Grace was involved in a peer counseling training session and the discussion got around to sex and eventually to AIDS. The substitute interpreter refused to interpret what was said when Grace asked her to clarify something (it concerned how AIDS is transmitted). When I picked Grace up that afternoon she was furious. She informed me that her civil rights had been violated. Grace felt so strongly that we made an official complaint to the school system about the incident. It was certainly a very different experience for Grace. I think both she and I were so shocked because Linda had been so good always to be completely objective.

Grace is now in the 10th grade and is enrolled in the "honors" degree program at her high school. The honors program requires extra credits in language, math, and science, and the classes are at an advanced level. Grace was able to complete her first year of Spanish and one science credit for high school while in the eighth grade. She took Spanish II last year and is taking Latin this year.

Grace has always had an interest in writing and has received several awards. She won first place two separate years for a system-wide writing contest. She continues to write and is sure that is the interest she wants to pursue in college, preferably at the University of North Carolina at Chapel Hill.

I am ashamed to admit it, but Linda Cash is the only person who cues to Grace consistently. I now cue only when necessary. Her father and her sisters have never cued. Her friends may know how to cue their own names but nothing else. Grace's speechreading ability and her patience have proven valuable assets to her in school and socially. But they have also made it unnecessary for us to cue to her. I really don't think that has been fair. I know that she has felt left out many times during lively family conversations. But when we need it, cueing is always there. If you want to be sure your 16-year-old knows what time curfew is you better *cue it*. Some people may not be above using their hearing loss as a convenient excuse!

Mrs. Consacro's letter of transmittal contains some additional important information. On the PSAT, taken in Nov. 1991, Grace scored in the 99th percentile on the verbal section (highest in the three advanced English classes, according to her teacher), but only in the 46th percentile on the quantitative section. However, her combined score of 183 [96th percentile] would have placed her in National Merit Scholarship competition had she been in the 11th (instead of 10th) grade. Her scores on IQ tests have usually been in the range of 125 to 129, and never above 135. Grace's audiogram shows pure-tone thresholds for 500 Hz, 1000 Hz, and 2000 Hz of 95 dB, 105 dB, and 105 dB, respectively, in the better ear.

Mrs. Consacro's letter of transmittal included the following:
"I know you think Grace would have succeeded even if we had not used Cued Speech. However, I shudder to think what price in emotional upheavals and feelings of isolation we [and Grace especially] would surely have paid without Cued Speech."

In dealing with parents we try to make it clear that the decision as to whether to use Cued Speech with a child who can succeed academically without it should take into account whether the success can be achieved without excessive stress and/or emotional harm. Only Grace's parents were in a position to make such decisions as whether to use CS and then whether to get a transliterator, since these decisions should be based on evidence provided through Grace's behavior, demeanor, and performance. Apparently, they made those decisions appropriately. When symptoms of the need for a transliterator became evident, they made the decision to train one. Mrs. Consacro indicates that she now cues "only when necessary." This probably does little harm now because at this point Grace learns new language primarily through reading. It would have been harmful in her younger days when she needed to learn language as rapidly as possible at home.

Patrick's Story
by Maria Gildea, 1992

He was so beautiful! No, he was perfect!! We were so thrilled and elated when God gave us Patrick a little over four years ago. He was full-term, almost nine pounds, and appeared to be what most people consider a "healthy baby." We never imagined that 20 months later we would be told that he was deaf.

There were some events and indications that led to the discovery, such as the time that Patrick cupped his hands over his ears and babbled (at about 8 months). And it's hard to forget the 1989 Fourth of July when fireworks went off right outside his bedroom window, and he never stirred in his slumber.

We weren't sure just what our expectations should be for a first child, but we sensed something wasn't right. The hardest part of discovering that Patrick was profoundly deaf was **after** we had brought our concerns and suspicions to several physicians (ear-nose-throat, pediatricians, etc.) and none gave us the satisfaction of properly testing him. It hurt us when the diagnosis (profoundly deaf, left corner audiogram, not associated with any other condition) was not made until the age of 20 months. This diagnosis could have been made as early as at 9 months if physicians had been more concerned and caring. We could have started Patrick's rehabilitation almost a year earlier! The problem was *not* a defense mechanism, it was *not* that I was an overprotective mother, it was *not* that boys are slower than girls to talk and listen.[1]

We grieved. Why me? Why him? Why us? Why deafness? It was a very shocking, chilling experience for us. No one in either family had a history of deafness. Neither of us even knew a deaf person. We felt so out of touch and out of control, especially when our thoughts turned to Patrick's probable destiny. Our plans for the future would have to take a completely different course: changes in lifestyle, friends, schools, residence, career path. It all brought new, disturbing meaning to our world. What were we going to do?

Soon after Patrick was diagnosed as profoundly deaf, we went to the library and collected books to read on the subject. The best book we read, the one that helped us the most, was *Choices in Deafness* (See Appendix). It is a parents' guide to the different modes of communication available for use with a deaf child. After reading that

---

[1] There are many similar stories—parents should trust their own suspicions enough to keep getting additional opinions, and should feel free to insist on an age-appropriate test of hearing. In 1966, in my (Cornett's) first year at Gallaudet, I talked with a lady who could not waken her 9-months-old baby by banging pots over him, but who couldn't get a firm diagnosis until he was 2 years old. But we must be fair to the physicians. Of each 10 children brought to physicians because of symptoms similar to those of hearing impairment, usually no more than one turns out to have a hearing impairment. All the possibilities that are enumerated, including "He will grow out of it; he's just not paying attention," do apply in many cases. The physicians are dealing with probabilities. Parents cannot afford to take refuge in probabilities when it is their child whose behavior suggests a possibility of hearing impairment.

was hope that Patrick could lead a very fulfilling and rewarding life with the same level of quality and opportunity available to a hearing person. However, it would not come easy by any means—for us, for him, or for Patrick's younger, hearing sister.

Patrick was quickly enrolled in an Easter Seal program, the only satisfactory program available in our area at the time. This Total Communication program included about six children who had speech and language disorders. The instructor or facilitator used her voice and basic signs to facilitate language among the group. Patrick spent about six months at Easter Seal, attending three days a week for two and one-half hours a day. During this time, he increased his vocalization skills, but much of what he had to say was unintelligible. We were told he would probably never learn to speak intelligibly. However, he continued to progress with signing. We also attended classes to learn Signing Exact English in order to communicate better with Patrick.

In the spring of 1990, when Patrick was 2½, we attended Camp Cheerio, in North Carolina. That weekend of learning Cued Speech opened up a new world to us—a much larger and brighter world! We were able to see other children who, like Patrick, were profoundly deaf, but who were communicating without any barriers. They were receiving the English language as it was spoken! It seemed miraculous to me!

From that weekend on, Daniel and I have struggled (almost two years now) to get the Virginia Beach school system to recognize Cued Speech as an option for hearing-

Patrick and Hilary Gildea, July, 1991

impaired children. They have trained one speech pathologist in Cued Speech and provided speech therapy services for Patrick five days a week, 25 minutes a day, for the past year and a half. However, we were forced to seek private educational preschool instruction elsewhere. We felt fortunate that Patrick was accepted at Montessori Children's House. Here he was in a preschool setting with hearing children and a Cued Speech transliterator, Suzie McGlone. She was a dear college student whom we "found" by getting accquanited with her at Camp Cheerio. Patrick truly excelled in this environment and adored learning and speaking! Unfortunately for us, Suzie will have to intern at two

Cheerio. Patrick truly excelled in this environment and adored learning and speaking! Unfortunately for us, Suzie will have to intern at two different elementary schools, starting in 1991, in order to complete her degree as a teacher. We faced being without a transliterator in an area where CS was not in demand.

The only appropriate course seemed to be to move to an area where Cued Speech is fully recognized and supported. So, we have made a relocation of residence in Fairfax County, Va., near Washington, D.C. Patrick will be starting school at Canterbury Woods Elementary School in Jan. 1992. We are very excited about the new prospects and opportunities that will be available to us.

In retrospect, Cued Speech is certainly the best mode of communication for Patrick. He is a testimony to the fact that it gives a child the English language and also aids in speech production and speechreading. It has "normalized" Patrick in so many respects, which is what our objective has been. We certainly still have a long way to go, but our path has been made much easier through the use of Cued Speech. And, Patrick is still as perfect as he can be to me!

Patrick's audiogram reveals a profound left-corner bilateral hearing loss, 85 dB at 500 Hz., 90 dB at 1000, and off the chart at 2000 Hz. On a patterned elicitation syntax test Sept. 24, 1991, he scored at the 10th percentile, exhibiting severely delayed receptive and expressive language skills. On October 9, 1991, at age 46 months, his auditory comprehension of language was scored at 35-37 months. The evaluator indicated Patrick had made significant progress on articulation skills as indicated by the Weiss Comprehensive Articulation Test. This was after about a year of exposure to Cued Speech. The next year will be critical as regards Patrick's readiness for being ready for reading at the appropriate age.

Some anecdotes about Patrick appear on page 452.

Chapter 23
What About Sign Language?

During the last five years the campaign for identification of American Sign Language as the most desirable first language of deaf children in this country has gathered considerable momentum. While those supporting this idea agree that a deaf child needs also to learn English, they tend to regard the learning of English as best delayed until the elementary grades, and then taught almost exclusively through the written form. This chapter is intended to examine the possible need for ASL/English bilingualism and the factors bearing on how it can and should be achieved, if it should.

The authors are not either specifically recommending ASL/English bilingualism, or recommending against it. In the novel *Tom Jones* is the statement, "Life teaches us only one great lesson, and that is not to buy at too great a price." Until experimentation reveals more about the price in time and effort, and about possible overburdening of the deaf child, parents and teachers will have to make decisions and proceed cautiously, if at all, toward bilingualism. The authors do recommend experimentation in selected situations if parents approve.

Since the board of directors of the National Cued Speech Association has taken a position on the matter of ASL/English bilingualism, we begin with their resolution, adopted July 22, 1990:

Bilingualism: A Position Statement of the National Cued Speech Association

The National Cued Speech Association recognizes advantages in bilingualism in American Sign Language and written/spoken English as an option for most children in the United States who have a prelingual, severe-to-profound hearing impairment. We therefore affirm the following:

1. The language of the home should be the language of the parents.

2. A substantial command of the phonological system of English, its vocabulary and its syntax, is critically needed by the time of

starting the elementary grades in school, as a base for reading and writing. The emphasis in preschool should therefore be on acquisition of English through Cued Speech. If children of hearing parents are to be bilingual, they will need to be provided instruction and interaction in ASL, including opportunities for association with deaf role models. Experimentation will be required to determine when to start the second language.

3. NCSA regards Cued Speech as the most desirable vehicle for a severe-to-profoundly hearing-impaired child for acquisition of a verbal language and for clear communication in that language. The use of Cued Speech must be supplemented, however, by adequate and coordinated training in audition and speech production, if speech is to be a goal for the child.

4. Insofar as is possible, each language should be learned from persons who are good models of that language.

5. NCSA favors and invites a continuing dialogue on the subject of bilingualism with and among the various organizations concerned with hearing-impaired persons.

Definition of American Sign Language

For the purposes of this chapter American Sign Language will be defined as the "more generic" ASL described by Bernard Bragg in the 1990 Deaf American Monograph: *Communication Issues Among Deaf People*: "This more generic ASL includes all of the varieties of language that deaf people employ when they sign." Thus, it includes what Bragg calls "Traditional ASL" whose grammar and idiomatic structure are influenced hardly at all by English, the "Modern ASL" that incorporates both ASL and English features, and that "adopts signs that map more directly onto English words," and even "Englished ASL" (or *Pidgin Sign English*) that follows English word order and relies considerably on fingerspelling. The implications of this definition are significant. To be competent in ASL, a person must be able to understand and use Traditional ASL, Modern ASL, and "Englished ASL." It does follow that a person who is at home with both Traditional ASL and Modern ASL will have little difficulty using Englished ASL, if he/she can follow the "Englishisms" that will crop up.

The Rationale For ASL/English Bilingualism

Many, even most, people with a prelingual severe-to-profound hearing deficiency are likely to experience the need to function in two social environments, that of the hearing and that of the deaf. This dual capability is essential if the deaf person who experiences this need is to be in full control of his/her own destiny, which is the basic requirement of freedom. However, educators and parents need to know more about how much time and effort is required to achieve this dual capability and what methods work best. Until they do, parents will have to judge whether or not their deaf child can achieve ASL/English bilingualism without being overburdened.

We have had time now to observe many young people who have grown up successfully with Cued Speech in the United States and elsewhere. Most have essentially mastered the basics of the appropriate verbal language, are good readers, express themselves well in writing, and communicate well orally within a range which depends upon many factors. These include the quantity and quality of their residual hearing, how well they have been trained to use that hearing, how well they speechread and speak, and their motivation and their personality. Some of them are able to function happily in the hearing world, without interaction with deaf individuals or any desire to take advantage of the society and culture of deaf people. The majority, however, feel a desire and need to interact with deaf society. This need typically appears during the early teen years. To satisfy the need at that point is not at all easy if the ability to communicate easily and freely in the language of the deaf community has not already been developed. Parents need to be mindful of the desirability of anticipating and meeting that need.

The choice between beginning with Cued Speech and beginning with signs should be made according to which the child needs first. The most important factor is whether the parents are deaf or hearing. If both are deaf and are users of American Sign Language, that should be the normal language of the home. However, the child's learning of spoken English should begin as early as possible through Cued Speech in a good preschool, and through additional communication with hearing people who cue. The reason is that the child needs to have acquired the same knowledge of the English language that hearing children typically have when they enter first grade.

If both parents are hearing, the language of the home should be their spoken language, delivered through Cued Speech. The age at which the child should have an opportunity to learn American Sign Language depends upon a number of factors. If the child has deaf relatives who will be with him or her from time to time, he/she should also begin learning signs early in life. If not, the parents should still consider the advantages and disadvantages of providing an opportunity for the child to acquire proficiency in ASL during the first decade of life. This would probably require some exposure to ASL during the preschool years.

If one parent is deaf and the other hearing, the child will probably need to learn both Cued Speech and signs from the beginning. The learning of verbal language could wait a few years if it were not for the fact that the child desperately needs to be at a normal level of verbal language at the time of entry to first grade. Without it the child will almost certainly be handicapped in reading.

The hearing-impaired child should probably communicate in signs with the deaf parent and in English (using Cued Speech) with the hearing parent. The only exceptions would be cases in which the deaf parent is adventitiously deaf and can also be a good model in written (and perhaps spoken) English. In these cases ASL, fingerspelled English (but usually not Cued Speech) could appropriately be used by the deaf parent. A deaf parent who is competent in written English should make it a point to use much fingerspelling with the child. If the deaf parent does not know ASL well enough to serve as a model of that language, (s)he can either make an effort to become fluent in ASL or else use Pidgin Sign English and fingerspelling with the child.

In general, hearing parents should not attempt to use ASL with the child, for two reasons. One, the child will need all the English exposure possible in order to be ready to begin to read in elementary school. Second, a hearing parent is very unlikely to become a good model in ASL and is likely to teach the child "broken" ASL by attempting to use it.

Principles For Achieving ASL/English Bilingualism

A model for acquisition of ASL/English competence should be based on these principles:

1. Each language should be learned through face-to-face interaction, communication, discourse, and play. There should be a minimum of *teaching*.

2. Each language should be learned from, and through interaction with, individuals who are *good models* of that language and the culture associated with it. ASL should be learned primarily from deaf people, and English (at least in the spoken form) from hearing people.

3. Each language should be learned through receiving it in a clear form. Since ASL in its normal form is clear, it presents no problem. If English is to be learned through natural, face-to-face communication it must be delivered in Cued Speech or fingerspelling.

4. The acquisition of each language should begin as early in life as is feasible, taking all other factors into account.

5. The child must have an adequate knowledge of English to serve as a base for reading development by the age of 5 or 6 years. This places some constraints on the division of time between English and ASL in the early years.

Application of Principles to a Theoretical Model

The application of the first three of the principles listed above, to a theoretical model for achieving ASL/English bilingualism, is reasonably straightforward.

PRINCIPLE 1

Each language should be learned through face-to-face communication, interaction, discourse, and play. Teaching should be minimized.

The normal, natural, efficient way for a child to learn a language is to be exposed to it through communication and interaction with others. ASL presents no problems here if it can be made available. Until the development of Cued Speech, educators had great difficulty in providing profoundly deaf children an easy, natural way to learn English through face-to-face communication. The only method at their disposal was fingerspelling, which has turned out to be too slow and too laborious for children to use as their major mode of communication. Fingerspelling is valuable for convenient representation of the written form, for clarification of names, and the like. It has not endured as a method of sustained communication.

It should be kept in mind that the learning of language through face-to-face communication in Cued Speech is feasible only if there is adequate exposure. Cueing siblings, other relatives, friends, baby-sitters can add substantially to the language input of parents.

PRINCIPLE 2

Each language should be learned through interaction with persons who are good models of that language and the culture associated with it.

ASL should be learned primarily from deaf people, and English (at least in the spoken form) from hearing people.

Principle 2 is borne out by all that is known about bilingualism. There are at least three reasons why hearing parents should not attempt to learn ASL and try to use it with their deaf child.

1. The first is that most of them cannot be good models of ASL.

The child needs good models in both languages. According to numerous estimates and several small surveys, fewer than 5% of hearing parents with deaf children in signing programs keep up with their deaf children in signing to the age of 6 or 7 years. To learn a complete language such as ASL is a much more formidable task than to learn enough sign vocabulary for any of the varieties of signed English. What percentage of hearing parents could be expected to devote the time and effort to learn ASL, with grammar, idioms, and vocabulary, well enough to be "good models" in that language?

Hearing parents probably should learn 400 or 500 signs so that they will be able to use Pidgin Sign English with deaf friends who know both signs and English. They should not try to learn ASL and use it with their child, who would learn inferior ASL from them.

2. The second reason that hearing parents should not spend time in learning and using ASL with their deaf child is that they need to devote as much time as possible to communication and interaction with the child in the other language he/she needs to master, the spoken language the parents already know.

The greatest problem in the education of deaf children is TIME. There simply isn't enough time to do all that needs to be done to help the child. The more parents read, the more they learn about things they need to do to meet the needs of the child. It is crucial that parents set priorities for use of the valuable time they have with their deaf children, especially during the critical preschool years. Top priority for most parents must be to spend as much time as possible providing language input, communicating with their deaf children through Cued Speech, and enriching vocabulary and understanding of the language.

3. The third reason hearing parents should not try to use ASL is that the home is the best language laboratory in the world. Most parents are capable of meeting their deaf child's needs in the language they already know, given the proper methods. They should leave the other language, ASL, to people qualified to serve as good models of ASL for their child. This does not mean that parents should not learn enough about ASL to appreciate its beauty and its value to their child.

For many years parents and professionals using Cued Speech have observed that its use by the family seems to be more important than its use in school. Most children who have had it consistently only at home have succeeded. While some who have had it only at school have done well also, the difference is clear. Hage, Alegría, and Périer (1989) reported the results of research in Belgium showing clearly that the use of Cued Speech at home is worth much more than its use at school, though it is valuable in both places.

PRINCIPLE 3

Each language must be delivered to the child in a clear form.

Since ASL in its normal form is clear, it presents no problem. If English is to be learned through natural, face-to-face communication, it must be delivered in Cued Speech or fingerspelling.

If a child is to learn two languages well, and one is as clear and understandable as ASL, the other language also must be clear and understandable. Also, it must be practical for sustained use. The only methods for delivering English face-to-face in a naturally communicating setting are Cued Speech and fingerspelling. Of the two, only Cued Speech has the great advantage of being practical for both expression and reception at an adequate speaking rate.

Cornett (1972) evaluated the accuracy with which a 15-year-old profoundly deaf girl could receive English through Cued Speech at the word, syllable, and phoneme levels, without sound. He reported 90% accuracy on isolated monosyllabic words, 96% on random nonsense syllables, and 98% on phonemes in syllables. Without cues she scored 53% on words and 42% percent on syllables.

Nicholls (Nicholls & Ling, 1982) reported on the speech reception of 18 profoundly deaf Cued Speech children in Australia. Speech reception scores were over 95% on key words in sentences, and 80% percent on random syllables, when presented with cues and lips (without sound). Studies in Belgium have confirmed high accuracy also in French.

Many people who advocate traditional aural/oral methods tend to oppose use of signs by a deaf child. They realize that if the child has an easy way to communicate, such as ASL, he/she is likely to be unwilling to work for long periods of time trying to understand a message delivered in a form difficult to understand. Cued Speech appears, therefore, to be now the only efficient and natural way for a deaf child to learn English if he or she is concurrently learning ASL.

PRINCIPLE 4

The acquisition of each language should begin as early in life as is feasible, taking all relevant factors into account.

Most children who have grown up with Cued Speech in the home have "picked up" signs, usually after they are teenagers. Most have become able to communicate reasonably well with other deaf people who use signs, but not with the ease and fluency needed to fit into and enjoy the full benefits of deaf society and culture. Children of hearing parents are not likely to become fluent in ASL without special arrangements for exposure to it. This fact supports the idea of giving deaf children an opportunity to learn and use ASL while young.

Principle 4 presents some difficult logistic questions for the education of deaf children. If the child has hearing parents and learns English at home, should he/she learn ASL at school? Perhaps so, but how much would this sacrifice progress in English? Should school time be divided between ASL and English, with some classes taught by deaf teachers, others by hearing teachers? Should team teachers be used, two to a class, one skilled in ASL, the other in English and Cued Speech, with division of class time between them? All these arrangements have been proposed by the proponents of various models.

Research on bilingualism in hearing persons verifies: 1) that a child cannot learn two languages as fast as he or she can learn one. It suggests also, however, that the bilingual child ultimately catches up to the level of a monolingual child in at least one language, and often in both. Also, there is some evidence that the bilingual child typically exhibits more "language sense" than the monolingual child. Research also suggests that 2) there is some advantage in starting one language alone, initiating the second after the child has made substantial progress in the first. This implies that if the language used by the parents is the first language, the second one could be started at school after a few years. Careful experimentation will be necessary to determine how soon and under what conditions (with a specific child) the second language can be started without seriously endangering progress in the first language. This problem is obviously greater with deaf children than with hearing children. Parents whose hearing-impaired children are making good progress in English and showing promise of succeeding academically and in reading will have justifiable concern whether their children can afford the luxury of spending time on a second language, even one that may turn out to be very much needed in the teen years.

Some ASL/English bilingualism models avoid the necessity of face-to-face communication in English by having ASL as the sole language until the child is old enough to learn English through its written form, that is, at the age of 6 or 7 years. Then English is to be taught solely or primarily through the written form, except that children with "exceptional" potential for oral communication would receive training in aural/oral communication. Such models have at least four serious defects:

1. For the 90 to 95% of deaf children who have hearing parents, these "ASL first" models insure that children following them will have very limited communication in the home during the early, formative years. They will be able to communicate far better with their teachers

and peers than with their parents. Thus these models depend primarily on situations outside the home to teach the children about life, to teach them their values, to mold their characters. Parents cannot afford to turn this job over to someone else.

2. For at least 150 years, teaching English to deaf children through the written form has tended to be the "fall-back" method used by educators of the deaf. That is, when the child failed to learn English at a reasonable rate, they have shifted to teaching it primarily through the written form. This method of teaching English to deaf children has failed consistently to bring deaf children to anywhere near typical levels for hearing children. The availability of ASL to explain the meanings of written words would presumably make it possible to teach written language with reasonable efficiency. However, one does not master a language by being taught it one word at a time. A language must be acquired through communication and interaction to develop rapidly and adequately.

3. Models that limit the teaching of English primarily to use of the written form typically doom the deaf child to be deficient in reading skills throughout all or most of his or her school experience, and probably also in adulthood. To be acceptable, a model for ASL/English bilingualism must make it possible for a deaf child to become a good reader at the age typical for hearing children.

4. The use of these models would be extremely expensive, primarily because they fail to make adequate use of the contribution available from a hearing family. They tend to require massive amounts of special teaching and training by employed personnel, and they also tend to increase residential custody of deaf children.

PRINCIPLE 5

A deaf child needs an adequate knowledge of English as a base for reading development, by the age of 5 or 6 years.

Application of this principle also places heavy constraints on the division of time between English and ASL in the early years. Hearing children start to school already knowing the language in which everything is to be taught at school. Moreover, they already know the language they are about to learn to read. When they start to read in school, they have learned or are taught the sounds of the letters. Thus, when they look at a word they have never seen before, they can sound out the letters in their minds and recognize its connection with the spoken word they already know. Thus, almost from the start, they can read autonomously, rarely needing help. If the material they are reading is appropriate for them, they will rarely encounter a word they cannot recognize. They soon becomes able to recognize thousands of words at sight, not having to sound them out once they has done so a time or two. As a result, their higher-level reading skills develop rapidly, as does reading speed.

The paragraph above describes how a deaf child exposed consistently to Cued Speech in the home reads, just as accurately as it describes the process for a hearing child.

Programs using Cued Speech in coordination with auditory and oral training are designed to achieve the language foundation needed for normal reading by the age of 6 with most children with whom Cued Speech is used consistently from the age of 2 or 3 years. Any model calling for shift of school time to ASL during the preschool years will be called into question because of the possibility of interference with this crucial objective. Experimentation will be necessary to determine under what conditions use of school time for ASL can be afforded.

A Practical Model for Bilingualism in Total Communication Programs

In most existing programs in which signs are used, it will not be practical to move immediately into ASL/English bilingualism. This model is designed to provide a gradual process in which signs are used for what they accomplish best, and Cued Speech is used for what it accomplishes best. This avoids pressures on staff to change suddenly. Likewise, the students can undergo a smooth transition.

If this model is used, a decision to go eventually to use of ASL as such need not be made until and unless the results suggest that to move on into ASL would be beneficial and desirable.

Two great advantages are claimed for this model:
1) The greatest untapped potential in deaf education, that of hearing parents with children in signing programs, is fully utilized when this model is followed.
2) Signed communication is freed from the burden it carries in Total Communication (TC) programs, that of developing competence in English, and can be used for what it is best for—communication.

Utilization of the Potential of Hearing Parents
The potential of hearing parents is grievously under-used in programs in which they are expected to learn, use, and teach signed communication. After a couple of years the child is the teacher, and the parents are no longer capable of carrying on communication in a way that will challenge their child, teach him or her about the world and him-

self/herself, and add to his/her ability to communicate. The case histories in this and other chapters amply illustrate this problem and the frustration it causes in both parents and children.

The greatest need of children, after easy, clear communication with their family, is to learn the English language in a form which will serve as a base for reading, writing, speaking, and lipreading. Parents and teachers cannot teach English words and phrases through signs. It is impossible! Suppose as a parent you give your deaf child a glass of that wonderful white liquid each morning for breakfast. Your child quickly learns the sign for it and can ask for more of it. But, learning and using the sign does not enable your child to learn the word *milk*. For that to happen you must *stop signing* and either write the word or fingerspell it. What is the implication of this? Every English word the child learns must be *taught* to him/her, and not through signs! A hearing child "picks up" the English language, without effort or specific teaching. Educators have tried for 200 years to teach deaf children through the written language. They can do it, but not fast enough. Deaf children need to know the English language at age 6—at least 5,000 words—including articles, prepositions—and innumerable idioms, verb tenses, pronoun forms, and other vital items of syntax. When a hearing parent communicates in signs, and then shifts to written or fingerspelled words to teach them, this process will work only if the parent knows enough signs to continue increasing the sophistication of the communication, and even then the learning process will be far too slow. In Signed English programs the burden falls almost entirely on the school to teach English words. Use of the model recommended can shift this to a balanced effort.

The Role of Hearing Parents In the TC Model

In this model the role of hearing parents is to do what they can do best, and what comes naturally to them. They can use the language they already know and can deliver it in a form that is clear to their deaf children. The child then learns English the way hearing children learn it, through natural communication in the course of living, without being specifically taught. Then the problem is only for parents and siblings to spend enough time with the deaf child, allowing and encouraging the child to participate fully in the activities and communication of the home. Participating fully is possible only through knowing what is happening, and being able to interject one's own personality. Only one simple tool is needed to assure this—Cued Speech. Most hearing parents can learn the basics in a one-week workshop, and then continue to practice a few minutes each day after they start using it with their child. Even while they are slow at cueing, parents can express anything they know in the English language. The child will begin to pick it up.

After learning the basic system, parents have no more lessons to take. They can profit by taking advantage of intermediate and advanced instructional opportunities, but many proceed to proficiency on their own. As they continue increasing their cueing skill, their primary task is to use this means of communicating consistently with their child, making extensive use of new experiences and situations that bring up new language. Refer to the case histories for descriptions of the feelings of freedom and optimism that come with the realization of parents that limits on communication with their child no longer exist.

Implementation of the TC Model

The first steps in the implementation of the model are 1) presenting the rationale for use of the model in a parents' meeting, and 2) providing an opportunity for the hearing parents to learn Cued Speech. Most Cued Speech instructors prefer an intensive three-day workshop or a week-long family workshop. A plan that may be more practical for parents is to schedule a weekend (Friday-evening, all-day-Saturday) workshop, followed by an identical schedule the next weekend, and then half-day sessions on the two succeeding Saturdays. The parents involved should also receive supplementary practice materials for use 15-to-30 minutes a day. These may be videotapes, audiotape lessons, or written materials.

It should be recommended to deaf parents that they use with their children the communication system they know best, and which the children also need to know. They should leave the teaching of verbal English to hearing people, just as the hearing parents will be asked to leave sign communication to deaf people. This puts the two languages on an equal basis. Ideally, all the parents can be skilled in what they use with their children. An exception could be deaf parents who are good models of written English. They should feel free to use a great deal of fingerspelling, to support English.

In general, deaf parents should feel free to use whatever sign communication they prefer, along the continuum of what deaf people use with each other. Since signing will no longer carry the major burden of teaching English to the children, it need not be bent into the patterns of English any more than is desired by those who use it.

In an existing Total Communication program, the beginning of implementation of the model would necessitate no immediate changes at school. As soon as the children are progressing well with Cued Speech at home, and the effects are beginning to be apparent in school, two kinds of staff members should learn Cued Speech and begin using it. They should use it initially for only two special purposes, speech-and-hearing therapy and the introduction of new vocabulary in class. The therapy can proceed much more rapidly and effectively with the aid of Cued Speech. The use of Cued Speech in the introduction of new language should be for the purpose of making Total Communication truly *total*. The word *total* should imply learning a sign, the corresponding written word, and the corresponding spoken word, so that the children can recognize and express the corresponding concept in all three forms. Thus, when new vocabulary is involved, the sign can be introduced and explained. Then, the written word can be paired with the same concept by pairing the word and the sign. Finally, the spoken word, expressed in Cued Speech, can be paired with the written word as well as the sign. This procedure will accelerate the learning of verbal language and the improvement of speech and lipreading.

The procedures just described can be implemented gradually. Teaching of Cued Speech, 15 minutes a day, by the teacher who will be most likely to introduce new vocabulary, will accelerate progress of the children toward knowing all their language in all three forms: sign, written word, and spoken word.

There are many possible ways to enrich the program after implementation of the model has begun. Children should be free to communicate with each other as they please. Parents and school personnel should schedule activities during the summer, or on weekends during the school year, to enable groups of the children to get together for special activities involving both sign communication and Cued Speech. Parents who schedule parties or picnics for their child's friends can include hearing children. The activities should include teaching of Cued Speech, preferably through games and enjoyable activities.

The school should make sure that follow-up is provided for the parents to make sure they maintain their progress in cueing until the point is reached at which they need little further support. Opportunities should be arranged for the parents to get together to report to each other on their progress in cueing and its effects on their children. They should be encouraged to set up such meetings in groups of three or four families. The parents should be reminded that as soon as they can cue everything, although slowly, they can quickly teach their child the spoken word to be associated with each sign the child already knows. Then, they will not need to make more systematic use of signing. However, they will find their sign vocabulary (which needs to be 400 words or so) helpful in communication in Pidgin Sign English (PSE) with any of their child's deaf friends who do not know Cued Speech.

When And If To Move All The Way To ASL

The reduction of pressure to convey English through sign communication will permit the latter to be used more naturally and easily. The school staff should decide when and whether to relax their efforts to get the children to speak when they sign. With Cued Speech taking over the responsibility for presentation of English, the use of speech with signs can be dropped at will. The pressure to follow English word order and/or to use grammatical markers will disappear. At some point, if a shift further toward ASL is desired, it may be desirable to bring in ASL specialists to accelerate this trend. However, increased use of deaf teachers to teach appropriate classes through ASL may be the proper course. As the model is implemented further, classes that are most heavily loaded with verbal terminology (such as English and social studies) should be taught through Cued Speech, for best results. In this case the sign vocabularies of the children should be updated once a week to include all the new vocabulary learned. Likewise, in classes taught in ASL there should be a weekly updating of verbal vocabulary, with Cued Speech and written presentation.

Consideration should be given to providing an immersion program in ASL for the children with hearing parents, perhaps on Saturdays, with a parallel intensive Cued Speech program for the children of deaf parents. This would be contingent, of course, on the choice of ASL/English bilingualism as the ultimate goal, if and as evidence of the desirability of that choice becomes apparent in the program. It would also be contingent on availability of funds, perhaps from a special grant.

A Theoretical Model For Achieving Bilingualism In Programs Using Cued Speech

Probably the prevailing opinion among parents of children in existing aural/oral/Cued Speech programs is that their deaf children should be allowed to "pick up" signing when and if they become aware of a need to do so, which is usually during the early-to-middle teen years. Any model calling for the formal or systematic introduction of ASL into their educational program, particularly at a preschool level, would be regarded as questionable by most of these parents. Their concern would not necessarily be based on any fear of the effects of signing, but upon the need to maintain the pace and level of the academic program already in place, for which available time is hardly adequate. Any model, to be acceptable, would have to be designed to alleviate or minimize this concern.

In offering the following model for study and possible experimentation, the authors are not specifically recommending it. Rather, we are attempting to explore the extent to which the principles delineated in this chapter can be applied to the design of a model that ongoing Cued Speech programs might safely utilize. The only sense in which we are actually recommending this model is that we suggest that it be studied carefully by those in ongoing programs using Cued Speech who have a serious interest in exploring ASL/English bilingualism.

A theoretical model for achievement of ASL/English bilingualism in the first decade of life, in accord with the principles described above, could take either of two forms in its application to existing Cued Speech programs. One is for children of deaf parents, the other for children of hearing parents. Both forms can be accommodated in a single program, with minor adjustments. Several advantages can accrue from the inclusion of both groups of deaf children in the same school program, in the same classes, to the greatest extent possible.

The basic feature of the model for deaf children of hearing parents is the furnishing of an optional ASL-immersion program on Saturdays, avoiding any interruption in or alteration of the Monday-through-Friday program. The ASL program should be conducted by deaf individuals whose competence in ASL has been checked and verified. For deaf children with deaf parents, an intensive program for English language development should be furnished on Saturdays. This would be designed to compensate in part for the fact that the deaf children with deaf parents would not receive Cued Speech at home. The ASL competence of the deaf parents should be checked, and remedial classes furnished if necessary.

Preschool Level

The program should begin at the infant level, although children can probably be accepted into it until the age of about 40 months, particularly if they have been receiving Cued Speech consistently at home. Only children whose hearing parents are using Cued Speech with them consistently should be eligible to participate in the special ASL-immersion program, and then only after making sure the child is ready. The parents' cueing should be checked to make sure that it is adequate, and classes should be scheduled for those who need extra help. Materials and suggestions for practice should be supplied.

Deaf parents should be evaluated to ascertain their competence in ASL, and ASL training should be arranged if they need it. Both deaf and hearing parents should be furnished with materials and guidance on how to maximize opportunities for language development in the home and elsewhere. Deaf parents should not be asked to learn or use Cued Speech, and hearing parents should be asked to learn only 400 to 500 signs for use in PSE with their child's deaf friends who do not know Cued Speech or communicate well orally.

The infant program should include auditory training and speech therapy sessions, conducted in Cued Speech, and counselling with parents. At the preschool level, for 3-year-old children, there should be three half-day sessions per week providing language development, interaction, and play, all conducted in Cued Speech by NCSA-certified teachers. Each day should include at least 15 minutes of coordinated auditory-aural/oral-Cued Speech training. Individual speech therapy and parent counselling should be scheduled on a fourth day.

When to Introduce ASL

It will be difficult to decide, without experience with the model to guide the choice, at what age to begin teaching ASL to the children of hearing parents. It will be necessary to experiment. Three-year-old children who are progressing well and comfortably in English with Cued Speech might attend a half-day ASL immersion program on Saturdays. Four- and 5-year-old children could attend a full day each Saturday.

If the ongoing weekday preschool program includes three half-day sessions a week for 3-year-old children, it should include three full-day sessions per week for those 4 years of age, plus individual auditory/speech therapy on a fourth day. This is in addition to an all-day-Saturday ASL immersion program for the 4- and 5-year-old children of hearing parents.

Five-year-old children should attend preschool all day, five days per week, plus the ASL immersion program on Saturday.

If possible, there should be a summer program for children in the program. Desirable additions might be family summer weekend camps featuring advanced Cued Speech training for parents, presentations by professionals, cueing classes for hearing siblings, ASL entertainment for the children by deaf individuals who are good role models, and recreational activities of various sorts. An ASL baby-sitter would be an excellent supplement for families with hearing parents.

Deaf children with deaf parents can fit into the program described above, with a few modifications for their benefit. During the ASL immersion sessions for the children with hearing parents, those with deaf parents should receive additional Cued Speech language training. If possible, they should be brought together with the children of hearing parents for part of the ASL activity. This would not only let the deaf children with deaf parents "star"—but it would stimulate communication among the deaf children in ASL. This might carry over into the Cued Speech preschool program. The children could be allowed or even encouraged to use ASL among themselves for social and incidental conversation.

Children who have a second learning disability such as dyslexia or memory problems should be placed in a bilingual program only after careful evaluation of all the factors involved and a determination that the best interests of the child would be served.

If possible, implementation of the model described should be carried out with the support of a grant, to insure 1) that all possible measures are exercised to insure appropriate and full implementation, and 2) to provide for ample evaluation of the results, documenting the results achieved and, insofar as possible, the differential effects of the various parts of the program.

The Elementary Grades

When the children reach first grade, the Saturday ASL immersion program should be continued. In addition, consideration should be given to some inclusion of ASL in the Monday-through-Friday program. However, this consideration should be done after evaluation of the experience with the preschool program, looking to the results for clues on what can and should be done in elementary school. Team teaching for some classes, using both an ASL teacher and a Cued Speech teacher, is one possibility.

Some first- and second-grade classes might be taught primarily through ASL. This would require a team teacher (serving several classes) to come in and use Cued Speech to teach the English vocabulary and language needed for the curriculum materials. It is essential that the results obtained in the preschool program be evaluated and the needs of the children for additional ASL exposure and training determined before the details of a design for the elementary grades are specified.

Some ASL advocates may be "turned off" by the proposal that ASL immersion be confined largely to Saturdays during the preschool years. However, there are many advantages to this that need to be considered carefully. One is that deaf individuals of the type needed (good role models, obviously successful and with good jobs) are not likely to be available on weekdays. They are much more likely to be able and willing to participate on Saturdays. Second, it would be very difficult to work out staff availability and scheduling for division of time between ASL and English during the week. This may very well be necessary for the elementary grades, but the model suggested avoids this problem at the preschool level.

As pointed out above, some CS advocates will question the advisability of inclusion of ASL in the curriculum of preschool children. Many CS professionals are increasingly concerned (even without any introduction of ASL) that so many young deaf children are not receiving enough exposure to clearly understandable (cued) language during the preschool years. This problem has become more pervasive as the number of job-holding mothers of preschoolers has grown. It may be that the model will need to accommodate preschool children of job-holding mothers for five full days a week, even for three-year-old children, with a substantial day-care component.

The model described will be very difficult to apply in sparsely settled areas where the availability of acceptable deaf ASL users for the Saturday immersion program is limited. Its effectiveness will probably have to be tested in areas where there are substantial numbers of deaf adults. If the results justify it, then perhaps ways of providing ASL more widely can be developed.

Examples of Multilingualism in Deaf Children

Since the specific models described above have not yet been used, we can point to no specific examples of success. However, we can identify several groups of deaf children who have achieved multilingualism through application of the five principles specified for the model. Included are the following:

1. Nearest to the model suggested for on-going TC programs is the program of the Centre Comprendre et Parler, in Brussels, Belgium (Périer, Charlier, Hage, & Alegría, 1987). In this program children learn both Signed French and Cued Speech in the preschool, learning everything in one that they learn in the other. Then, well before the beginning of first grade, Signed French is phased out, and the children begin to learn Belgian Sign Language. This program has existed since 1980 and is experiencing substantial success in producing deaf children bilingual in spoken/written French and Belgian Sign Language. It violates only the second of our principles, and that only during preschool.

2. Prelingually deaf children of hearing parents who have acquired fluency in two or more spoken languages through Cued

Speech. At least one has native fluency in two languages and substantial competence in three more.

3. Deaf children who have mastered English through Cued Speech and studied another language in high school, at the level typically reached by hearing peers. In at least two large metropolitan programs, all the Cued Speech students (except a few students with a secondary learning disability) have studied a foreign language at high school level. Several have studied two foreign languages, and at least two have studied three other languages, plus English and signing.

4. Deaf children who have mastered English through Cued Speech and "picked up" signing, either through structured teaching or immersion in a program in which signing was the primary mode of communication. Of these, the only ones who have approached ASL/English bilingualism are those who have had several years of immersion in a society of deaf students. At least a score have achieved this through attendance at NTID/RIT or Gallaudet University. These range from Leah Henegar to students now attending these institutions.

5. Deaf children who have learned ASL, fingerspelling, and (in most cases) some form of Signed English from deaf parents, but who have in school become proficient in Cued Speech and progressed well in English through it. At least one such child has been mainstreamed with a Cued Speech transliterator.

Examples of children from the groups listed above are described in the case histories below and in the observations of young people in Chapter 25.

Case Histories

Tamara Suiter

Tamara Suiter is a prelingually, profoundly deaf child of deaf parents. Her parents have used all the usual manual modes of communication with her: SEE 2, PSE, ASL, and fingerspelling. Mr. and Mrs. Suiter are well educated individuals, with excellent command of English. Mr. Suiter has reasonably intelligible speech.

Tamara attended preschool and kindergarten at Kendall Demonstration Elementary School (Gallaudet University). When she was ready for first grade her parents visited the three "tracks" for deaf children in Montgomery County, Maryland: oral, TC, and Cued Speech. They decided to put her in the Cued Speech program in order to improve her English (which was below that of an average hearing child), improve her speech, and enable her to associate more with hearing children. She was soon mainstreamed with a Cued Speech interpreter in some classes, and by third grade fully mainstreamed. Near the end of third grade she scored above the 50th percentile in all areas of the California Achievement Test, and at the 75th percentile in English and mathematics. Her speech also improved. In a videotaped interview she said she preferred to have a Cued Speech interpreter in school because "... there are so many words that don't have signs, and they have to be fingerspelled. I don't like that." Tamara appeared before a graduate class at Gallaudet University and talked with them about ASL and Cued Speech. They tried several times to get her to say which was easier for her to understand. She refused to choose—because, as she put it, "They're both easy." Tamara is now in fifth grade, 10 years old, and performing very well academically. Since she became an excellent reader by the time she was in third grade, she can function well in a TC program or in the mainstream with either a Cued Speech transliterator or a sign interpreter.

Stasie Jones

Gabrielle Anastasia Jones, daughter of an American mother and a British father, lived in France until the summer of 1991, when her family moved to California. Stasie attended only the regular French schools, with almost no Cued Speech support except at home and no school training in English, which the family used at home. Stasie was the first child with whom CS was used in France, and her progress was the initial stimulus to the widespread use that has developed there. Stasie has six brothers and sisters. She is second oldest.

Stasie's mother, Rebecca Jones, wrote the following article for the *Cued Speech News* issue of September, 1980. It is a virtual textbook on preschool bilingualism. Letters written by Stasie in 1989 and 1992 are included on pages 588 and 608..

Raising A Bilingual Deaf Child
by Rebecca Jones, September, 1980

It was four and one-half years ago that we began using Cued Speech with our daughter, Stasie, who has approximately a 90 dB PTA loss. Our expectations were high, our hopes higher. Cued Speech offered us the possibility of attempting a bilingual education with a preschool deaf child. This was not simply an intriguing experiment to be attempted at the possible detriment of the "guinea pig"; it was a necessity if Stasie were to lead the same life her siblings lead. We are an English-speaking family living in France indefinitely. There seemed little else that could be tried.

When we first began using Cued Speech, we used it in English. Stasie was about 2½ years old.[1] Her comprehension and vocabulary soared. Before six months had gone by, we were able to talk in simple terms to her about such concepts as foreign languages. We explained to her that certain of her friends spoke in French and that instead of saying "sock" they would say "chausette." We didn't know just how much of this she was taking in, but the subject came up quite naturally in the course of our daily life in France. One day before Stasie was 3 she turned to an English-speaking friend and said "bye-bye," then to a French-speaking person and said "au-revoir." What a thrill she gave us! We knew that she had acquired the basic concept of two separate language structures.

We concentrated on English, but I would cue to Stasie in French whenever we would be with French people outside the home. If she appeared not to understand, I would cue it to her in English. She became able to answer simple questions or locate items in the super-market for me. Meanwhile her comprehension and expression of English were growing steadily. During the summer after Stasie turned 3 we asked a 15-year-old girl to learn Cued Speech and to take Stasie three hours a week for informal "French lessons." Muriel's faithful play sessions helped Stasie to develop a comprehension of simple French and a basic vocabulary.

At 3½ Stasie began attending a French nursery school in the mornings. It was our idea to allow her a longer introduction to French, hoping that by the time she got to first grade she would have enough grasp of her second language to keep up with the class. Whether this was a good idea or not I am still not sure, but since almost all 3 year olds go to school in France, Stasie was more than anxious to conform! She loved it, and became more and more familiar with simple French. Her nursery teacher did not cue, but was very aware of Stasie's need for distinct and clear language spoken face-to-face. I often saw her down on her knees talking with Stasie.

In November of 1977 Muriel and I went to Paris where I addressed a group of some 120 speech therapists about Cued Speech. Very few of them had heard of the method, and none had seen it in

---

[1]Mrs. Jones learned the basics of Cued Speech in both English and French at Gallaudet College the week after Stasie reached 2 years of age. It took her a few months to get going well and to teach others to cue.

practice. We also made contact with one French family (Jean Cyril and Nicole Spinetta, parents of Isabelle, who later became the prime movers of CS in France). Having seen the freedom of communication that I had with Stasie, they decided they wanted it for themselves. That weekend was the catalyst for a surprisingly quick growth in the use of Cued Speech in France. Now, only three years later, there is a *(French)* National Cued Speech Association, there are several large schools for the deaf that have decided to use Cued Speech in some way, and there are scores of parents who are discovering the joys of unrestricted communication with their deaf children.

Zoe, Eowyn, Stasie, Miriam, Peter, Toby, Rebecca, Tessa, and Julien Jones (1989)

Stasie, meanwhile, has continued to grow in her knowledge of French and English. Though the latter is still her stronger language, she has made good progress in French. She has three 45-minute speech therapy sessions each week with a convinced and fluent cuer, who feels that with support from home Stasie will be able to follow a normal classroom education in French. She spends one afternoon each week at the home of a seminary student who cues to her in French for several hours. She attends a private French school that is very open to parent participation and to children with special educational needs.

We see the next two years as crucial ones in Stasie's development. We know we are asking a lot of her, and we realize that the strains on her are great. We are hoping to provide her this year with a Cued Speech interpreter as much of the day as possible, though this will not be easy since I am about the only person available. We trust that by the time her French friends are 8 or 9 they will be able to take over as interpreters. We also hope that her 8-year-old sister and her 4-year-old brother will help us in this task. They both can cue in English, and the 8 year old can cue in French as well. Until now they have not been willing to use their skills too often, but we hope that this will change.

We have enjoyed spending the last five months in the U.S.A. where Stasie benefitted from the excellent CS program at North Lake Elementary School in Montgomery County, Md. The whole family also took part in the two Cued Speech summer workshops at Gallaudet. The result for Stasie, who is learning to read and to cue now, has been that she suddenly expects to understand everything. For the first time since she was 2 and at home all day with me, she is receiving cued messages all day long. She now asks constantly, "What did he say? What does that word mean? I didn't understand." She asks that I cue radio programs, telephone conversations, sermons, even *Godzilla* and *Charlotte's Web*! My hand muscles are exhausted, but what joy I have. Watching Stasie's reaction to a steady diet of cues has reminded me of how crucial this is for any CS child. The more they receive, the hungrier they get for information. Stasie used to put her fingers in her mouth and daydream if she felt the conversation was above her. Now she's trying desperately to grasp everything she can.

We have every reason to expect Stasie's good progress to continue, and we look forward to continuing our promotion of Cued Speech in France.

On both counts, all reasonable expectations have been exceeded. In preparation for moving to the United States in 1990, Stasie completed, in a single year, the last two years of work for the French baccalaureate. The latter is the French grammar school diploma, considerably more advanced than the American high school diploma and earned only on the basis of comprehensive examinations lasting several days. She scored 720 on the French achievement sub-test of the SAT. In the fall of 1991, Stasie entered Wellesley College, Wellesley, Mass., as a freshman. She is taking Intermediate Russian, Beginning Spanish, English Composition, and several other required subjects. Stasie speaks English and French fluently and German to a degree consistent with several years of study in school. At Wellesley she has a Cued Speech transliterator and volunteer note-takers. The latter may be supplanted gradually by Stasie's lap-top computer.

Michael Poore
by Teri Poore

Teri Poore, mother of Michael, tells here about Michael's exposure to signs. Michael is now 10 years old and in fifth grade, mainstreamed for all classes with a CS transliterator.

Michael began to learn signs in third grade from the third-grade deaf education teacher. This was agreed to by us, but was also a part of the court ruling in our litigation for Cued Speech. The school continued to teach Michael signs in fourth grade through deaf education music. He now has a baby sitter who is deaf and signs, and one hard-of-hearing friend who is mainstreamed without an interpreter, but who also signs.

We're glad Michael has learned signs to communicate with those who sign just as we would be about his learning a foreign language. He thinks signs are fine, but he prefers to speak, and he thinks in English. He took swimming lessons from a hearing-impaired adult who has good hearing and speech (lost hearing late in life). He was impressed with Michael's language and lipreading. At first he thought Michael didn't talk or understand much, until I explained that he didn't know many signs. When Michael signs he can't talk normally, so he sounds "simple." Just let him talk in English and not sign, and he's fine. Both the swimming instructor and the baby sitter told me Michael does much better in English. Now the baby sitter wants to learn CS!

Obviously Michael is learning some signs, which is fine, but not enough to equip him to communicate well with deaf people. He needs to become proficient enough that his real abilities and personality can "show through" in communication with deaf users of signs. Of course, he may not have the opportunity to gain such proficiency in his present setting. Michael's case history begins on p. 471, his experience with a cochlear implant on p. 220, and his personal observations on p. 572.

Elizabeth Tolleson
by Connie Tolleson

Elizabeth currently attends Westwood Elementary School in the Mt. Diablos Unified School District's Deaf/Hard of Hearing program, in California. This is a SEE-based TC program. She started at Gregory Gardens Preschool the day after she was diagnosed, May 22, 1987, on the recommendation of a Children's Hospital audiologist. Elizabeth lost her hearing at approximately 14 months as a result of events surrounding her birth that caused her to spend her first two months in Children's Hospital.

At home I used SEE in conjunction with oral techniques described in the John Tracy Clinic Correspondence Course. The oral technique is basically 1) Remember that the child is a child first and needs to be treated as a total human being in developmentally appropriate ways; 2) Give the child every opportunity to see and hear spoken language under the best conditions of light, proximity to sound source, amplification, and field of vision; 3) Talk, talk, talk; 4) Do all of the above with as much love and patience as you can muster.

When Elizabeth was 2 years 8 months old we attended the John Tracy Clinic three-week summer session in Los Angeles. Her program specialist at Gregory Gardens School encouraged us to go and see for ourselves what oralism was like. After taking the summer course I started using "sequential signing," a combined oral/manual technique that integrates oralism with SEE signs. I would talk without signs or gestures and if necessary repeat with partial signs, or even with full SEE sentences.

I choose to use SEE signs, rather than gestures or pictures as a true oralist would, because: 1) We had been using SEE for over a year as a basis of our interactions; 2) The use of gestures seemed to encourage the use of "home signs" which is even more constraining than sign language; 3) I wanted her to be able to communicate freely and acquire intellectual information during her childhood regardless of her ability to speak.

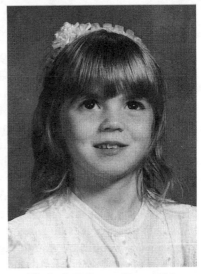

Elizabeth Tolleson, Nov. 1990

Many of the young deaf adults I have met who were brought up in either oral methods and/or TC with SEE have now turned to ASL. Some have turned their backs on both spoken language and their families. My main goal is to maintain a warm and loving relationship with my child into her adulthood. I felt (and still feel) that if I were to restrict her access to signing or deaf culture she, being the strong-willed individual she is, would be capable of becoming a rebellious teenager and rejecting the hearing world.

There followed next a very frustrating time, because I came to the end of the "Yellow Book" and was limited to a 5,000-sign vocabulary. Elizabeth's access to new vocabulary was at an end. I could not express my ideas freely to her within the framework of signing. So, for example, the "top of the bottle" is what I called the nipple. There were many other examples.

This is a poem I wrote in March 1989 expressing my frustration.

S.E.E.

She is busy
    fast moving
    wanting words **now.**

> I have English slowly
> from a big yellow book
> she stops to look.
>
> The idea lost, I wanted to share
> there is no sign
> it isn't fair.

The school year 1989-90 was marked by a terrible class composition that placed hearing language-delayed and developmentally disabled children in the Deaf/Hard of Hearing program. It stretched the school budget at the expense of the deaf/hard of hearing children. The LD and DD children verbally pushed the deaf children aside, and the hearing adult instructors had little control of the interaction. Even though they tried their best, they were simply outnumbered by the range and number of disabilities they were trying to cope with. Both teacher and aide were "burned-out" by the end of the year and left the preschool classroom. There were additional problems in the class. Elizabeth was regressing developmentally, had lost ground verbally, and had not acquired enough sign language.

In early 1990, I felt that my child was lost in a class of developmentally delayed hearing children. I decided she needed a deaf peer group and deaf role models. I sought out a deaf church and took her there. The first day she so dramatically demonstrated her need to associate with the deaf community that I will recount it here. We got there before services began, and every adult in the church gathered abound us. I explained that it was the child who was deaf, and when they introduced themselves to her they got down on their knees to talk to her! Many conversations were going on within groups of two or three adults, and each one was visible because everyone was signing. I had little idea of what was happening because they were using ASL.

During the service a woman came in late and asked if I wanted to put my child with hers in the nursery. I thought her child was deaf; later I found out that she thought my child was hearing. I agreed to her suggestion, thinking that there was a deaf Sunday School, but there wasn't. When we arrived, Elizabeth did not want to stay and play with all of her favorite things: paints and toys and books. She began to cry and sign that she wanted to go back to church. I apologized to the teacher and as we left, Elizabeth took off running ahead of me, out of the building, across the lawn, through a series of halls and back to the Deaf Church where she proceeded to pound and kick on the door until she was let in. At age 3 she sat and fidgeted through that signed sermon rather than play with hearing children.

Marked changes in Elizabeth's personality started that day, changes harking back to the way she was before she lost her hearing. On the drive home, she gave a sigh of satisfaction and settled back in her car seat, contentment written all over her face. I had not seen that expression since she had lost her hearing. Eventually a preschool Sunday School class was organized by a deaf adult and her mother for deaf/hard of hearing children, children of deaf adults (CODA), and their playmates.

Elizabeth formed a very strong bond with her Sunday School teacher, who is a powerful role model. She is a successful adult deaf woman who functions in community, job, and family. She was brought up oral and became a fluent signer as an adult at Gallaudet. She can reverse interpret, or voice, both ASL and SEE signs in spoken English.

Elizabeth turned away from me and toward the deaf community. I started to resign myself to losing my only child to this community. I could not sign fluently enough to satisfy her preference for fluent signers.

The inadequate education Elizabeth was receiving at school appeared to be especially inadequate for deaf children. Although I was fighting the system for a more appropriate class for the next year, I had pretty much resigned myself to what the literature was reporting; that the best I could hope for was that she would ultimately achieve a reading and educational level of about fourth grade. It was while researching and preparing for a confrontation at Elizabeth's IEP meeting in June of 1990 that I read an article in *Volta Review* about Cued Speech in Europe and decided to find out about it for Elizabeth.

I was impressed that Cued Speech was used in France and Belgium along with signing. Most of these children started partial mainstreaming by age 6 and most became able to read at grade level. I called the John Tracy Clinic's 800 number, and they briefly described Cued Speech and referred me to the West Coast Programs Resource Center. I began learning Cued Speech in July, 1990. It has not been easy for me to gain proficiency. They say some people can learn it in a few hours, but after 15 months I am still laboring with it. Every single one of the "easily confused sounds" was a major obstacle to me, yet I am very good at languages. In college I was fluent in both German and Russian. I do not seem to be able to break down the spoken language into individual sounds although I have a great "ear" for it.

Our opinion is that Ms. Tolleson's difficulty came from insuffi- cient face-to-face instruction. She had only two two-hour sessions. Her

CS problems are typical of individuals who do not get adequate support during the early stages of learning and practice.

My lessons gave me a head start, but I couldn't keep ahead of Elizabeth. It works so well for her; it took her only two or three days to realize how powerful CS is.

We were remodeling our home when we started Cued Speech and were camping out in my mom's back yard. It was not the best situation for starting something major, but that is how it worked out. I videotaped Elizabeth's lessons because I knew I could not devote as much time as I wanted to cueing with her. She loved her first video-taped lesson, and watched it over and over. On the morning of the third day she came into the kitchen and pretended to be cueing, then pointed to my cup of coffee and signed "coffee" and then pretended to cue again. She waited patiently while I struggled to sound out the word. "Mom, cue 'coffee,'" she signed again. I painfully sounded it out and repeated it a little more quickly. Then I realized I used the "aw" in "dawn" and it was really the "ah" in "hot" that I wanted. Before I could correct it, my 3-year-old darling child said "coffee" perfectly and walked away. She wanted to see the consonants that she couldn't hear. I sat there and cried because I knew that, even if I never became proficient at Cued Speech, my child could learn to talk because I could teach her myself.

The first major impact of Cued Speech was the improvement in Elizabeth's speech. She had lost what little speech she had during the previous school year and was a confirmed signer. Four and one-half months after starting Cued Speech, she was given a yearly speech acquisition test at school. It showed a four and one-half month improvement in her speech. She was gaining speech at a rate of one day per day with cueing.

In 1990-91 Elizabeth's classroom at Gregory Gardens included only deaf/hard of hearing children without other disabilities. Her teacher was a fluent signer, a graduate from Westwood whose childhood friendships with deaf peers had continued into adulthood. The aide was mother of two deaf girls who had attended Gregory Gardens years earlier. This was a much better environment and Elizabeth made great progress. Her academic environment, with the added benefit of Cued Speech at home, allowed for significant growth.

Knowing that Cued Speech had been used with signing in other countries, and because I was having such a difficult time becoming fluent in Cued Speech, I decided to integrate what I knew. I developed a sign system where I randomly signed some words and cued the rest. The grammar is English, the sign system is SEE, and I use Cued

Speech instead of fingerspelling. I also substitute ASL signs for SEE signs that are either offensive or laughable to ASL signers. In this way I can communicate rapidly with Elizabeth, and we can both communicate with hearing and deaf. Elizabeth has used cues on only a few occasions. The first two or three times she uses a cued word, she makes common errors, so it is tricky to know what she is saying because there is no corresponding sign to help. Most of the time I know the word she is trying to say, because I am the only person in her life who cues to her. So if she has a word without a sign, she learned it from me, and I can usually figure out what she is talking about and re-cue it. Elizabeth remembers the words better on each attempt until finally strangers can understand the words. On several occasions I have not caught on to what she was saying, then she cues back to me. "Majong," a Chinese game with beautiful thick domino pieces, was one word that she cued back because she has not had the final three lessons that include the "zha" and "ng" sounds, so she doesn't make these words reliably yet.

The second major impact of Cued Speech was on Elizabeth's speechreading. Because half of the information of Cued Speech comes from the mouth, Elizabeth soon began to focus more on the lips during conversation. Two months after starting Cued Speech she was tested at Children's Hospital. It was considered her first fully reliable test. The audiologist remarked on her improved speechreading ability. Elizabeth was 3 years 9 months at the time of this test. Beyond testing is the real-life usefulness of her being able to lipread her relatives and friends who don't either sign or cue.

The third major effect of Cued Speech was Elizabeth's increased vocabulary. Elizabeth's expressive language continues to lag behind her receptive language by a larger margin than with hearing children, but she has words like *nipple* and *sleeve*, as well as *elevator, escalator, horizontal, diagonal, labrador, dachshund, and brontosaurus* in her receptive vocabulary. She also has names for everything. During the first week of Cued Speech she asked me to name every implement in my mom's gadget drawer, and my mom collects a lot of gadgets! She has nonsense words from books like *Professor Wormbog's Search for the Zipperrumpazoo.*

The fourth major effect of Cued Speech is Elizabeth's utilization of questions. She wants to know everyone's name and all kinds of things about them. She refers to people by name and loves to know how they are related to each other. Her teacher once commented that Elizabeth asks everyone questions, including her classmates, and she expects answers. That is because she gets answers, good answers with the correct words, when she asks me questions. When we had only signs, I told her that dark was night and we sleep, and that first light was the morning of a new day and we get up. She noticed this fall that she was getting up before it was morning and was adamant that this was wrong. So, I told her about the sun and the solar system and the earth revolving tilted on its axis, and rotating angles and space. I did not look anything up. If I remembered the sign, I signed it, and cued the rest. It was really neat—just the sort of conversation I had always imagined having with my child.

The fifth major impact of Cued Speech is that both of our frustration levels have dropped. I started to be able to answer her questions, and to give her directions and explanations without stopping to look up signs in a book. Her speech has cleared to the point that I can understand much of what she is saying without signs, which is great. One problem with my being a limited signer was that she would know signs I had forgotten, or bring home signs I didn't know. We would misunderstand each other totally. Now we can communicate quite freely. I can use my own vocabulary, even though I am slow at sounding out words I have not cued before. I can continue to give her new vocabulary, and her speech continues to improve even when her hearing aids are in the repair shop.

We had almost four weeks without hearing aids this summer, but she continued to learn new words, and continued to interact with hearing people in a variety of ways. This is important because Elizabeth has a fluctuating hearing loss, and although she currently enjoys improved residual hearing in the low profound range, she may eventually have none. That will have no effect on her ability to acquire spoken language. If she can see it, she can say it!

Some of the surprises that have happened with Cued Speech were unexpectedly delightful. At Christmas she wanted me to cue the name of everyone in the family even though she had known their name signs for several years. When I cued my nephew Dale's name she signed and said "It sounds like 'tail'," and laughed at her own joke. She had independently recognized a rhyme!

The sixth major impact of Cued Speech is that Elizabeth recognizes the power of the spoken word. When she went back to school in September of 1990, she tried to revert to signing, and would request that I sign rather than cue words to her. I felt that it was because her peer group was signing and so I signed all the words I knew signs for and cued the rest. She got very insistent that I sign. So, I started looking up words in the "Yellow Book" and, if they were not there, explained that "this word has no sign." Then, I would fingerspell it, then cue it. I asked her which she preferred. She preferred cueing to fingerspelling, and stopped asking me to sign words that I cued. Elizabeth understood that there are more spoken words than signs and, being a greedy little girl, she wanted all the words.

When I cue a word that she knows a sign for, she shows me the sign. Even when she is getting a word by signing, she is lipreading well enough to recognize the word when it is cued. Amazing!

Elizabeth started to talk to me without signing—checking it out. She expected me to understand her, and most of the time I did. *The more I cued, the clearer her speech got!* The more response she got to her speech, the more she used it without signs. "No, I don't want to go." "I want to stay home!" "I don't like it!" "I am angry at you!" "Get out of my room!" "Get me a drink, now!" I joked that after years of trying to get this kid to talk, all she did was to sass me and order me about. My response to being sassed went from delighted amazement at her use of speech to dismay at her rudeness. She was translating out of signs, and in signs what she said didn't seem as rude. I had to teach her more polite ways to say things. Still, she likes to pick fights with me sometimes and now does it with her choice of words instead of dumping out the contents of her drawers.

Elizabeth talks to people on the telephone. About 50% understand her speech. Just now she came in with a scarf, saying: "Look what I found. I want to be Snow White for Halloween. Tie it on me, please." I understand her speech, maybe not everyone would. When she first meets people she checks out which language they understand (spoken English or signs) and uses it. This summer we visited a friend in southern California who has spent a lot of time around little kids, and she understood almost everything Elizabeth said.

Every day Elizabeth's speech improves; every day her knowledge of the world expands. She is a happy, confident little girl who will succeed at anything she chooses to do. Right now she wants to be an animal doctor. I have said, "Say 'veterinarian,' Elizabeth, if that's what you mean." And she said, immediately, "veterinarian."

Cued Speech is an incredibly powerful tool for the parents of deaf/hard of hearing kids. I would like to see it made available to parents of newly diagnosed kids. I think I would be better at Cued Speech if I had learned it before learning SEE. I would like to see Elizabeth in a group of peers who also use Cued Speech. I think her speech would be at age level if we had started her on Cued Speech rather than signs when she was 20 months old. It is an absolutely awesome system. It works for my child. It gives her speech!

Since writing the above I have been made aware of some of the dangers associated with the long-term mixing of signs and cued words in the same sentence. When they are mixed this way, it is impossible to develop the ability to express spoken words run together as we normally speak, using liaisons, elisions, and contractions. In addition, mixing signs and cues does not lead easily to mastery of idiomatic phrases involving different meanings associated with prepositions such as: *by, with, for, in, out, off, on, up, down,* etc. I was not aware of the fact that so many English phrases and sentences are idiomatic, primarily as a result of those tricky prepositions, and that most prepositions have 40 or more different connotations. And, I was not aware that failure to be familiar with all these different applications of the prepositions is one of the major causes of the characteristic "plateauing" of most deaf children in reading.

It is at about fourth grade that school reading materials begin to use idiomatic material on a broad scale. Multiple uses of the function words are not taught systematically in school, because most hearing children just pick them up by the time they are 8 or 9 years old. Most deaf children learn only a few of the meanings associated with each.

I am now making a strong effort to cue everything I say to Elizabeth. I am working away at the audiocassette lessons, to develop my own fluency, and using the same lessons to teach Cued Speech to other individuals. Elizabeth and I are not giving up signs, but only separating them from English. *Now, October 1992, Mrs. Tolleson is teaching Elizabeth at home, pending the outcome of negotiations with the school system. She reports rapid progress in language and speech.*

Bryan Herbert
by Carole Herbert, 1981

Of note in this record are: the late start on Cued Speech, the excellent family relationship, the spectacular academic progress considering the language level at age 8½, and the ultimate, and very late, recognition by Bryan of his need for interaction with deaf people.

Part I
In March 1978, my son Bryan was 8½ years old. He was not doing well in language development and was very frustrated. When he was 6 years of age I had withdrawn him from the oral school he had attended from 18 months of age. To continue the daily commute of 110 miles was no longer reasonable or fair to any member of the family, especially Bryan. He began to attend a private school for regular

children. After two years I realized how terribly behind he was, and took an honest look at his future. Why it took me so long to come to reality I'll never know. I'm sure I was denying his handicap, believing in the promise of the oral school, and thinking some magic moment would come when he would be functioning perfectly normally.

So, there we were....I knew I had to do something, as Bry had approximately 50 words he could understand and say. He was not learning anything in the private classroom, and the fault was not the teacher's. Bry simply could not pick up enough information with good amplification and lipreading. He was not able to learn easily. I was thinking Total Communication when a special-ed teacher brought me an article on Cued Speech. It sounded like something I should investigate, so I went to the school where Joan Rupert was teaching. I was very impressed with the children. Their language was so sophisticated and easy and natural. They were so relaxed and happy. I had worked in deaf classrooms for five years. This helped me detect something wonderful and liberating in this system.

I first learned to cue with the chart of cues. I was cueing important words to Bry within a few weeks. But three months after the class observation, we attended a workshop. From the first day I was told to cue everything to Bry, and our lives began to change. The first two weeks were hard on the whole family. However, we were accustomed to being engulfed with stress due to Bry's frustration and our sadness at not having a way to help the child we loved. After the first two weeks Bry was used to his mother's flapping her hands around, and I was becoming more comfortable with the cues.

I saw an immediate change in Bry. He watched conversation more carefully and picked up more language. He began to produce words noticeably more clearly. The job had finally begun to be what it should be, the joyous job of helping a child learn and develop. I was constantly rewarded by new speech. I found myself telling a friend:"It's like Christmas every day." And, indeed, it has been. Bry learned steadily, rapidly, and happily. He became more and more a lovely little boy, not a frustrated, distressed child. Cued Speech gave me the precious gift of watching my child grow into a precious, humorous, sensitive, charming, intelligent, inquisitive, and, maybe most of all, normal human being.

People, in their unknowing way, would say, "Bry's really changed, he's got such a good attitude." It's easy to have a good attitude if you understand what's going on and what's expected of you.

There have been many milestones along the way, these past two years and eight months. First, it was all those new words. Then it was phrases and sentences. Then it was more complicated sentence structure, with *would* and *could* and *if.* Then it was learning to write and spell phonetically, and learning five grades of math in 2½ years! Now his reading skills are growing, and he is reading currently at a grade level of 2½ to 3. He loves books and demands to be read to or to read to me every night. He can write letters to his friends, needing only a bit of spelling help.

This year Bry's greatest dream was realized. He is now attending our neighborhood school, where his brother and sister have gone. He has a full-time cueing aide in the class and one hour of language and reading with an itinerant teacher of the deaf, who has learned to cue. The classroom teacher learned to cue. Bry, though not yet on grade level (5th), has had the happiest and most rewarding year of his life.

Because of our late start at cueing, much remains to be done. Now we are concentrating on reading and language development, and trying to get Bry to cue more. His speech is more intelligible when he cues, but he cannot cue easily or readily. So, in quiet, easy moments I'm having him cue easy readers to me.

My husband, Joe, cues everything to Bry. I have watched their relationship grow to a warm and devoted camaraderie. My daughter Stephanie cues beautifully, and our son Jim is still growing in his skills. Bry's aunt Minnie cues and has just started piano lessons with him. Bry has a cousin in his class who cues. I have taught seven children in the class and will start teaching more next week. Bry has a friend on his Little League team who cues amazingly well, and there is even a playground monitor who has learned. People love learning a skill they can master easily and use to help someone. I find it fun to teach. It is so flexible and easy to use.

The great joy we are experiencing is beyond compare. As Bry was reading to me the life of Helen Keller I noted that her poor parents were so sad because they did not know how to help Helen. Bry said, "You know how to help me," with great confidence and authority in his voice. It made me feel very comfortable and warm inside. I look forward to the tomorrows with excitement. I have loved getting to know my son these past two years and eight months, and I look forward to watching him grow and finding out just who he will become. God grant me the strength and resources to do all the needed things along the way. With cueing, I feel ready for the journey.

Six months later, in the fall of 1981, Mrs. Herbert added: "We received a delightful surprise this fall. Bry had the fifth highest grade in his class in the math placement test, and was one of only four students in his class to pass the state math proficiency test. His school is an excellent one and to earn such scores is exciting. "

Part II
Added in 1987

Bry was tested at the end of his junior year in high school and his reading comprehension was 12th grade, six months, overall reading ninth grade, and his math skills were at grade level. He has many friends, all hearing, and two or three best friends. Yes, he has best friends who call him by way of the relay system and who talk to him in person as if he were hearing. He has truly made it socially. One last item: Bry took an honors course in English last year and had this poem published in the school's yearly publication *Writings on the Desk*:

SEA

In the ocean,
Huge and blue and green,
I swim,
Like flying over the fish,
I surf
And feel like becoming a bird.
Waves are the ocean dancing,
Their whitecaps are as white as clouds.
Rough sand,
Millions and millions of tiny rocks
Lie under the sky with the sun setting,
Orange, red, yellow, top-blue,
I am happy and sad.

Part III
Added in November, 1991

During the last 10 years Bryan grew up in the mainstream. He did not know another deaf boy, and only two deaf girls. They were never his close friends because it was at a time when he needed male friends and couldn't be bothered with girls, especially girls who signed (and he didn't).

A great problem that evolved was an acute identity crisis for Bryan. He really didn't know who he was, much less who he could ever be. He felt he was a bit of a freak, and certainly quite dumb. My heart aches for the pain he has had to endure. As a human being who has been around 47 years I know the experience and the pain can give him more depth, compassion, and love for his fellow man. I see that coming in my son, and I feel there may be some sunshine ahead. Of my three children, Bry is the most social, the most people-oriented.

Bry had the same interpreter from the seventh grade through high school. Because of that he did well enough academically, but he has tremendous gaps. His biggest problem, in my opinion, is that he never became an omnivorous reader. Maybe he was just not meant to be one. He knows any and all sports statistics, reads the newspaper and *Sports Illustrated* cover to cover. But, he doesn't devour books in general, which a deaf person needs to do to learn enough about the world.

Bryan was born with a very profound hearing loss, was first exposed to Cued Speech at 8½ years, and was in a mainstreamed environment from fourth grade through high school. He was accepted at the University of California at Santa Cruz where he attended for two years. He then transferred to a local junior college and took two to three classes a semester. It was there he took sign language. In April he met a deaf boy, a student at UCSC who had attended Gallaudet University. For the first time Bry knew a deaf person he really liked. Noah told Bry how wonderful it was to go to Gallaudet to meet and make friends. Bry applied immediately and now he is there. As I write, he is home for Thanksgiving and out visiting one of his buddies from high school.

As a student at Gallaudet University, Bry is recognizing his need to know and enjoy his fellow man in a comfortable environment. All of us deserve that. He has just returned from his first three months at Gallaudet Prep, and the identity crisis has disappeared. He is a calm, happy person who seems at peace with himself and the world. He signs as he speaks, and he seems to have a more concrete grasp of language. He was more comfortable in our large family gathering than I've seen him in the past.

Bry feels good about all his classes at Gallaudet Prep except English. The teacher seems very difficult and does not communicate well with the students. Bry feels he has no idea how he is doing.

I believe Cued Speech gave Bry spoken language and incredible lipreading skills for a kid with a profound loss and such a late start on language. I feel that signing has given him community, role models, and a sense of identity. I feel Bry is now emotionally strong and ready to continue his academic journey.

Only since Bry went to Gallaudet has he allowed me to cue to him in public. And, he came home wearing two hearing aids, whereas for the last nine years he would wear only one because he didn't want to look so different. Because of this new direction in Bry's life, I enrolled in signing classes this fall. I want to support Bryan and be able to enter into his world and welcome his signing friends. Learning to sign has been fun, but the culture of deafness and its history has increased my awareness of deaf reality. My teacher is deaf and very threatened by Cued Speech. After reading of the sufferings deaf people have endured over the years I begin to understand. But Cued Speech is a magical tool that gives deaf people the means of commanding spoken language and lipreading. I pray the deaf will overcome their fear of the unknown so they can open themselves to this gift as well as the gift of signs.

The Burtons in Belgium—The First Twelve Years
by Winifred Burton, 1992

The dice could hardly have been cast more badly, or so it seemed: a deaf boy born into a hearing family, living in a country with two native languages, neither of which the family used at home; almost four years later a fourth child, also deaf; no English-speaking special education on this side of the English Channel, not even any qualified speech therapy in English; neither child was willing to accept hearing aids. Indeed, with time neither boy has developed intelligible speech.

Yet as so often occurs in human history, weakness proves to be strength, the hurdle a springboard, the setback opens up a new vista—and the tale we can tell so far is in fact one of great richness. I say this with no note of complacency but with one overwhelming acknowledgement: we were armed with a first class tool without which nothing comparable would have been possible.

As you read the story please keep in mind the three particular problems we faced: We were to some extent *operating in isolation*; we had *more than one language* to cope with; and *expressive speech did not develop* as we had rather assumed it would. Our debt to Cued Speech is huge and unqualified. I shall however end with a few questions that will have to be answered before Cued Speech can take the place it justly deserves in easing communication with deaf people.

Hugh and I are hearing, English parents, living in the long term in French-speaking Belgium. Of our four children, Jamie (born 1978), Toby (1979), Katie (1981), and Emlyn (1983), the second and fourth were diagnosed profoundly deaf (third degree) in the first year of life. We presume, though we had no reason to anticipate this, that the deafness stems from a coincidence of recessive genes.

We started to notice Toby's lack of reaction to sound at around age 5 months, but he was in fact 9 months old when deafness was confirmed and aids fitted. We were extraordinarily fortunate, after plodding methodically through addresses in the phone book's yellow pages in a world with which we had never had the slightest contact, to arrive in the Centre Comprendre et Parler run by Dr. Olivier Périer in Brussels. He not only spoke fluent English to us but, being himself a parent of two deaf children, combined the professional expertise of a neurologist with the patient empathy of a parent in the advice he gave us. This was in addition to the many hours of listening time he has subsequently devoted to us.

Hugh, Kate, Winifred, Emlyn, and Toby Burton (1992)

Dr. Périer had just made the radical decision to introduce both Cued Speech (in French) and Signed French into his hitherto oralist Centre. Since he advised us to stick to one language with Toby, we wrote off to the Cued Speech Centre in the UK for tapes to help us learn to cue, whilst attending French Cued Speech lessons at Dr. Périer's Centre to boost our morale. Our start was very slow. The English cassettes took six months to work their way through postal difficulties. Then we found that learning from an audiocassette is not gratifying work. Indeed I feel it took me 18 months to feel completely at home cueing. Also, not having access to proper classes in cueing in English, I acquired bad habits that still produce mistakes in my cueing, 10 years later. (We have had *au pair* girls who have mastered CS fluently in a matter of weeks.) But take heart, parents whose fingers and mind work as lamely as mine did. A small baby is very happy with a slow, simple sentence, and there's no harm whatsoever in repeating that key word several times, till it sinks in on both sides! Our speech therapist from Dr. Périer's centre was French-speaking—and only just mastering French Cued Speech (LPC) herself, falteringly. Still, her daily visits to our home were vital to keeping us going. We withdrew Toby from his French-speaking day-care centre and on Dr. Cornett's recommendation (for I was working outside the home), enticed a dynamic young American girl, Kristie Ketchum, over the Atlantic. She was willing to do almost anything (even look after Toby) that would bring Europe to her feet and purse. Most important, she could cue more than fluently!

From then on Toby was cued to intensively morning, noon, and night. Of course this input was diluted by the fact that he was a very energetic and physical child who had his back turned to the cuer for more than half the time. By age 2½ his understanding of English cued to him in either "Standard Southern British" or broad General American was phenomenal. The difference in accent did not upset him in the slightest, although almost everything was differently cued, including the basic vocabulary elements Mummy/Mommy and Toby.[2]

Despite the best of audiological and speech-therapy attention, Toby's expressive language was not developing at all. The result of the enormous gap in sophistication between what others could get across to him and his level of response was immense frustration on all sides. The days were punctuated by lengthy, exhausting temper tantrums simply because the socks we had put on were red when he wanted blue, and he had no way of getting lips, vocal cords, or fingers round that latter word. His responses were largely single concept/word units, expressed in total body language, e.g.,"NO."

At the end of a particularly bad summer "holiday" we made the big decision: Toby must have signs, too. We embarked on learning (and giving Toby) signs. The situation relaxed almost overnight. Many other things happened around the same time: Kristie left us and was succeeded by another cheerful cueing American, Nancy; we decided the time had come to put Toby into the Belgian School for the Deaf attached to Dr. Périer's Centre, the Ecole Intégrée; at the end of September our fourth child Emlyn was born; and by Christmas Emlyn too had been diagnosed as profoundly deaf.

Nancy and Françoise, Toby's Belgian speech therapist, held Toby's hand for the first two weeks in the Belgian school, explaining to the 3½ year old that this was now "French" that was being cued to him. After two weeks he dismissed them summarily and has never looked back. Tough though it was to accept the diagnosis of profound deafness for our newborn baby who one felt should "by right" be in a state of "guaranteed in perfect working order on delivery," it in due course proved secretly great to be given a second bite at the cherry, different though the two fruits might be. By now we were much more relaxed. Gone were our theoretical worries about linguistic purity. All that was important was communication, *two-way* communication. With

---

[2]The British cue the *oe* in Toby as a diphthong, *oe-oo*, side-throat. In General American *oe* is cued as a single vowel, allowing the reader to depend upon the lip movements to recognize the second part of the diphthong.

Emlyn the language could be (and was) body, spoken, cued, signed, English, French—right from the outset.

Now in 1992 both boys (aged 12 and 8) are doing well at the Ecole Intégrée. They are as good in French as the rest of their classmates; able to understand and read English, though they have so far had no formal teaching in writing English. I hope that lack can be remedied without too much difficulty. Toby is also learning Flemish[3] (compulsory) through Cued Speech. They still have largely unintelligible speech in either language, but to our astonishment they cope on their own with the oral French-speaking world at large. Together, and with friends, they use the Belgian dialect of French Sign Language.

We are now at another turning of the ways. Neither boy is one of the "stars" pulled out of a hat at international conferences to prove the superiority of one or another method. They are bright but non-speaking deaf boys. Their early and intensive exposure to language through Cued Speech has given them an advantage over children who were diagnosed later and whose families were not in a position to give them the early support we could. They are therefore increasingly out of step with the average level of their classmates. There are only two solutions, each with drawbacks. One is to put them into a class ahead of their physical age. This entails major problems of maturity and behavior, as we have already discovered. The other is to mainstream them in hearing schools with an interpreter——a choice we would not normally make with any joy. A major part of one's school days is how you feel about yourself, who your friends are, the richness of interaction with other children and with adults at school. If you cannot make yourself understood to either the other children or the teacher without going through a third person (the interpreter) you will always be on the fringe of the classroom. We would like to think of the boys as being in the thick of it. We do not want to impose an additional burden on them. It is on this question mark that 1992 opens for us.

Let me now focus on the three specific problems I mentioned at the outset. We have indeed felt we were "going it alone" to some extent, but I think most hearing parents of deaf children have that feeling. Having a deaf child marks a hearing parent as "different." Each parent quickly gets the feeling that he/she must make the vital decisions concerning the upbringing of that child. She/he must listen to and sift through the wide range of information and advice offered from all sides by professionals and parents. She/he has to become "more

---

[3]Flemish is the dialect of Dutch that is used in Belgium.

expert than the experts" to plan wisely for his(her) deaf infant.

We certainly had new ground to explore. There were very few precedents for bringing up a profoundly deaf child bilingually. We thirstily contacted those we learned about. Rebecca Jones (mother of multilingual Stasie) was a very valuable source.

We were strongly advised against the bilingual (French/English) approach by the (hearing) English-speaking schools in Brussels, which recommended schools for the deaf on the south coast of England (for our 3-year-old!). The decision to mix signs into our purely cued English was also very controversial and frankly viewed (then) with a degree of skepticism and regret in both English and American CS circles. We were fortunate though in having Dr. Périer's enlightened support. We felt that he would not "let" anything go too far wrong. We were also fortunate in living in a country where bilingualism was not only acceptable (unlike England!) but actually compulsory! Living in Belgium has that wonderful quality of freedom about it that Hugh and I both enjoy immensely. We can taste, enjoy, or reject the cheeses, the wines, the cultures of a variety of countries in Europe, North and South, East and West, all feeding into the European Community capital. The same is true of contact with the deaf world, through encounters, journals, conferences. Exile from England has proved enriching, far from oppressive isolation.

Apart from us at home (two parents plus a series of *au pair* girls), the children have had no cued input of what was supposed to be their first language, English. The English community in Brussels is large but un-cueing. Our family in the UK were entirely supportive, and learnt to cue—but seeing the boys only two or three times a year at best makes for "rusty" fingers, however willing. Fortunately the advent of BBC television in Brussels with CEEFAX subtitles has reduced the linguistic and cultural isolation, now that the boys read.

The second of the three problems was the multilingualism itself, specifically the quadrilingualism. The school uses cued French and Signed (Belgian) French; we use cued English and signed English at home; the students pick up a good bit of Belgian Sign Language; and at age 12 Flemish (compulsory) is initiated in Cued Speech. Our boys have learned, to different degrees of proficiency, the four languages English, French, Belgian Sign Language, and Flemish. I would now call (Belgian) French sign language the boys' natural language, as distinct from their mother('s) tongue.

Most "experts" from countries where bilingualism is not the norm have always discouraged us from introducing our boys to both French and English. Here in the heart of Europe where languages are at a premium the idea is less frowned on. On balance, I would recommend strongly that anyone in a similar predicament have the courage to try it out. In our situation there was little choice. One alternative would be that we as an entire family change to speaking French together (which would have been more natural had one parent been really French-speaking). We felt the additional strain of what amounted to a cultural schizophrenia, plus the daily practical aspects of our life in the British community in Brussels, were more than we wanted to take on. The other alternative was to limit the boys to English only and sooner or later have to send them away to school in the UK (for we were not willing to contemplate moving back there as a family). A third alternative would be to gamble on multilingualism.

Initially we respected the theoretical approach. For Toby, a firm basis was established in one language first. He was introduced to French only at 3½ and indeed it did not appear to disconcert him at all. There was a clear distinction between the persons and places associated with each language. With Emlyn we were less conscientious. We now break all the linguistic rules in the book: Sometimes I speak English to the boys, sometimes French; our sentences are a mixture of signed words and cued words, with bits of French vocabulary thrown in if the word feels more appropriate.

Generally, I use more signs than cues in day-to-day conversation with the boys, though always cueing words for which there is no (known to me) equivalent sign, so that the sentence picture is completely visible, and so I do not have to simplify my language to fit my knowledge of signs. Cued Speech I keep now for English-language-based communication—homework, reading a book aloud, interpreting a TV programme. I cannot boast mastery of pure Belgian Sign Language.[4] If I try to use it, I do so in moments of intimacy when I feel it is necessary to go particularly far towards the child. The boys do occasionally mix up French and English—though not very often. They have a couple of days of difficulty in adjusting to school after two months of summer vacation in English only. Of course their input in either language, already diminished by reason of their profound

---

[4]A significant advantage of English/French bilingualism in this situation is that with the school's use of Signed (Belgian) French the family can use the same Belgian signs in the word order of either English or French and the boys can understand and express either.

deafness, is further halved as each day has its part exposure to English, part exposure to French, and there are vocabulary areas that are developed in one language rather than the other. Time will tell how high a price they will have had to pay for this gamble in terms of overall literacy.

In the last few paragraphs I may have seemed to relegate Cued Speech to a back row. Let me now pull it back into the immediate centre. Without Cued Speech we could have done none of this. As hearing parents our language is English, and only by cueing in our own language could we clarify linguistic and other concepts to our children. Only through Cued Speech could they obtain from a very early age a fundamental knowledge of the spoken patterns of both French and English that has taken the agony out of learning to read in both languages and to glean information from both cultures. Writing is still hard, but only thanks to Cued Speech have we been able to involve our deaf children in the (hearing) cultural life of our family (which, while they live with us, they are more or less obliged to share). The boys can intone the nonsense rhyme "Ging gang gooly gooly gooly watcha" at the end of the Wolf Cub Scout meeting. They can follow their older brother word for word performing on stage in a Shakespeare play or slapstick pantomime. People, places, and phenomena can be unambiguously named for them. We make no concessions to them in terms of linguistic detail, no omissions that might contribute to retarding our deaf boys in either language or their perception of the world.

In addition it is apparent to us that Cued Speech (along with their speech therapy training that is furnished at the Centre Comprendre et Parler with Guberina's verbo-tonal method) has endowed the boys with an internal phonological representation of the sounds of words in either language (and now for Toby in Flemish also), substituting for the missing input from their ears. I have stated this (for once!) in a few words, but I would not wish it to be passed over lightly. It is perhaps the most vital thing of all. Cued Speech has given them this inner impression of how, in their case, two spoken languages actually "sound." I am quite convinced nothing else could have done this, given that they have no useful input through their ears/aids.

This brings me to the third problem: *expressive language.* With the passage of time we have been able to be less emotional and less worried about the poor development of the speech of both our children. For a long time we searched for the tool that would do for expressive language what Cued Speech had done for comprehension. We now accept that whereas many profoundly deaf children do acquire comprehensible speech, some do not, and this is *not* because they have not had a purely aural/oral education. It is *not* because we have not super-glued their aids into their ears, and not because their audiograms are a few points lower than the next child's. It is because their qualitative loss in hearing (unmeasurable at present) is obviously very great. Thus, they lack the "gift" of speech, which others are fortunate to have. It has taken us all this time to get to the point where we can state this with equanimity.

Hugh has only started intensive sign language classes this year. Not only is it a big investment of time and effort, but he had always hoped that as long as the boys knew he would not understand their signs they would be forced habitually to articulate more clearly. Now he is anxious to avoid the risk of being cut off from them and their friends in adolescence, or of being reduced to having his sons pass him written notes over the breakfast table. For many years we hoped that integration with hearing children would help them catch the speech germ, or that encouraging the boys to cue as they spoke would bear its fruit. But speech is obviously immensely hard for them, and far from pleasurable. Cued Speech has given them our languages, which is obviously most important during the part of their lives when we are living in constant and close proximity. They are now in fact coming to the stage where they can enjoy spending hours chatting with their friends on the minitel (Belgian version of TDD), after having passed through a stage of rejecting everything but sign.

I am sure no one would deny that easy communication is a basic human right, and that the most pleasurable communication takes place only when both sides have comparable facility with the communication tool. Thus, on a day-to-day basis I speak in English, with cues, with the odd sign thrown in for economy or humour or emphasis; and they sign in return (with the odd cued word if that is what comes automatically to mind). Thanks to Cued Speech, which has given them access to so much that is being said or taking place around them, they are certainly motivated to communicate. Fortunately, they have not been forced into a mold where they will only open their mouths or bring out their hands to reproduce parrot-like a handful of well-polished and socially-acceptable formulae. I am moved most of all when they make jokes, for this demonstrates both the ability and the desire to "play" with language.

In conclusion, I am impatient for all deaf children to benefit from Cued Speech as ours have. I am also disappointed and dubious as I watch the spread of Cued Speech, at least in Europe. Let me list briefly my hesitations, and say how much I hope ways round them will be found to prevent them from becoming stumbling blocks.

First, Cued Speech seems generally to appeal to a particular middle-class parent rather than to everyone regardless of social or educational background. This is a pity, given how readily *anyone* can learn it. More needs to be done to give Cued Speech the image of a universally acceptable tool that is really not hard to learn, and that is *so* worth learning.[5]

Second, with the new tide of deaf awareness that is now on the rise among deaf adults, it is necessary to state clearly that Cued Speech is a tool for hearing people to use when communicating with deaf persons (especially children) in language-learning and other situations. The battle over methods must be set aside once and for all. There must be no rivalry, no competition, no mutual exclusion, no approach that is considered superior except for specific purposes. Deaf people in general do not deny the usefulness of mastering the spoken/written language of their country (and others), so long as *their* language is acknowledged and respected. Cued Speech can be a means of broadening the opportunities of deaf children without limiting their access to sign language. Some deaf adults in the UK do apparently cue themselves,[6] but I hope they will have or do have access to the beautiful richness of signed communication. As used by deaf people among themselves, signed communication has the quality we hearing people can put into our speech. Had I been a deaf parent my course would have taken a very different direction.

Lastly, I have stressed the importance of starting early with Cued Speech. It is the means by which the infant brain acquires that whole first language it is pre-programmed to do in the first four-to-six years of life. It is in my view equally important to "give" signs to a small deaf child, because this overcomes some of the possible difficulties engendered by delay in speech development. It also provides the child with the door to identification with the deaf community. Many hearing parents of newly diagnosed deaf babies are not ready to learn both to

---

[5]Note: It is the opinion of the authors that the problem is not that Cued Speech fails to appeal broadly to those who receive accurate information about it. Rather, it is that most hearing parents do not have enough confidence or documentation to go against the advice of well-meaning professionals committed to other methods. In areas where substantial numbers of families are using Cued Speech, and parents are encouraged to consider it along with other alternatives, this stereotype of the users of CS as articulate, educated parents does not seem to hold.

[6]Note: In the United States deaf adults who use Cued Speech tend to be persons who have lost their hearing late in life, or at least in adulthood, or who have grown up with Cued Speech and are just entering adulthood.

cue and to sign. Deaf parents (and some hearing parents) who go all out to sign early on will indeed give their child sign as that total, first language. But then comes the next deadline, the "normal" age for learning to read and write. There is really no time to lose if the child is going to manage this. Signs cannot claim to prepare the child for reading and writing as Cued Speech does.

It is amazing how even very young children can distinguish between the slightly varying handshapes of Cued Speech.[7] If one is lucky enough to start cueing before the child is mobile (and can probably crawl away from you at 6 months), then that child will have learned the vital importance of the movements of the mouth at the earliest possible age. We found this was a tremendous advantage with Emlyn, a captive audience at 3 months, compared with Toby, with whom we started at 9 months. This very early start is not possible in many cases because of later diagnosis, later hearing loss, a decision to use Cued Speech after other methods have been tried. *See also p. 578.*

A compelling presentation of the struggle that many deaf youngsters experience in connection with their need for interaction with deaf peers is Holly Abell's story, as she tells it, the next-to-last item in Chapter 25, beginning on p. 630. Most intriguing is her "hate-love" relationship with ASL at MSSD (The Model Secondary School for the Deaf).

---

[7]Note: Just as they can distinguish between slightly different signs.

Chapter 24
The Child With More Than One Disability

It was May, at the end of the school year. As I was watching Alexander receiving his "diploma" promoting him from preschool to kindergarten, words were coming back in my memory—words I happened to read almost four years ago in an evaluation report on our son: "Alexander is a child with hemiplegic cerebral palsy, a seizure disorder, profound bilateral hearing loss, and retinal scars in both eyes." I remember the shock and disbelief I felt seeing Alexander described in such a way and the apprehension I had about his future. But now, with these words again in my mind, I saw him walk proudly and confidently up to the teacher when it was his turn to receive his diploma. To me, these steps on the school stage were just a few steps in Alexander's long walk to success.
From "New Worlds for Alexander"— p. 550

Hearing impairment often occurs concurrently with one or more other disabling conditions that may impede communication or learning, such as memory problems, mental retardation, aphasia, dyslexia, dysarthria, cerebral palsy, Usher's Syndrome/retinitis pigmentosa, and others.

Meeting the needs of a hearing-impaired child who also has another other disabling condition that interferes with communication or learning is much more difficult and complex than dealing with a child who is only hearing-impaired. Sometimes the secondary problem can be diagnosed accurately, in which case specialists in the secondary area can be of substantial help. In many cases, however, the overlay of additional problems makes it difficult or impossible to make an accurate diagnosis of anything except the hearing deficit, so that the child is described simply as multiply handicapped. Also, even when the diagnosis is reasonably certain, the complication of an associated hearing deficit can make it difficult or impossible to use the methods of treatment commonly used for the secondary problem in question.

When a definite diagnosis of the secondary problem is not forthcoming, there is only one way to proceed. One must try different techniques until something works. Since Cued Speech will very likely solve the problem of reception of language, at least at a basic level, it may make possible the identification of the secondary problem. Also, Cued Speech may enable the child to outwit other disabling conditions, in part or even in full, especially if they are mild. Some deaf children diagnosed as having memory problems, aphasia, or dyslexia in early childhood have apparently overcome those problems after developing communication and acquiring language through Cued Speech. Of course, the likelihood of such success depends on the precise nature of the memory problem, the dyslexia, or the aphasia, and its severity. It depends also on the patience and determination of the family.

One of the most devastating effects of a second disability is the effect it has on the estimates professionals may make of the child's potential. Their desire to avoid giving the parents false hopes sometimes causes them to be so discouraging as to impair the parents' motivation to make every possible effort to help the child progress. There is pain when hopes are not realized, but it is not as severe as the guilty realization later on that opportunities were overlooked because of low expectations. We advise parents to hope for the best and be prepared to waste some effort in order to investigate every alternative. Give the child the opportunity to find his/her limits rather than allowing them to be set by others.

Since Cued Speech provides access to the spoken language for the hearing-impaired child, it is more likely to facilitate methods of treatment commonly used for a specific secondary disability for which treatment usually includes use of spoken language. Because parents of a child with a secondary disability are faced with great difficulties, we prefer to outline all the possibilities Cued Speech may offer, even though in some instances there is little actual experience to support our (in some cases) largely theoretical opinions. It should be remembered that the ideas expressed in this chapter, aside from the reports on specific children, are highly speculative. They are not all medically based, and in some cases no specific research has been done to support them. They are offered on the justification that parents whose children have other problems in addition to a hearing deficit have very little to guide them except the suggestion that different things be tried until something begins to work. Thus, we report cases in which Cued Speech appears to have helped, and we offer possible explanations of how this may have come about.

Specific Overlying Conditions

This section deals with some of the secondary problems listed above, indicating possible ways to use Cued Speech in connection with them. All of the evidence supporting the suggested approaches is anecdotal, with no available research evidence to support it. We do not want to raise false hopes, for many multi-handicapped children make very limited progress. What is given here is offered on the theory that it is better to try something that has worked in some cases than to either give up or proceed blindly.

Minor or Usually Correctable Overlying Conditions

Attention Deficit Disorder, hyperactivity, and allergic reactions may interfere seriously with communication and language acquisition in young children. Unless specifically diagnosed and treated medically or behaviorally, they may result in severe or even disastrous delays in language development and communication. Specific allergic reactions can produce or trigger hyperactivity and/or Attention Deficit Disorder, or contribute to them. These conditions are often found in highly intelligent children whose performance is far below their potential until there is appropriate treatment. Though they are not learning disabilities, they can interfere seriously with learning. Fortunately, such conditions are usually more susceptible to both accurate diagnosis and separate treatment than most of the other conditions listed in this chapter. Parents whose children exhibit symptoms that could be associated with one or more of these conditions should confer with their pediatrician and perhaps suggest referral to a specialist. In this chapter we will not discuss the symptoms or treatment of these conditions in detail, but will include some case histories that are illustrative of conditions sometimes encountered.

Cerebral Palsy

This problem may or may not constitute a specific learning disability. If it has produced damage to specific brain functions involved in learning, it can be both a learning disability and a limitation to physical performance. If the condition includes paralysis of, or lack of muscular control of, the speech organs and/or other parts of the body needed for communication, interactive learning may be inhibited in a deaf child because of limitations in expressive speech. Cerebral palsy that inhibits use of both hands/arms may keep the child from being able to cue or sign. Use of one hand is needed to cue.

A case that illustrates some of these points is that of Alexander McConnel, born in February, 1980. He was diagnosed as having a severe-to-profound bilateral hearing loss and a mild spasticity of the left side, later found to be accompanied by some lack of control of the vocal organs. The experiences of Alexander and his family are summarized in one of the case histories at the end of this chapter. Significant are these facts: 1) Alexander's mild spasticity of the left side, limiting his use of his left hand, ruled out adequate use of (two-handed) signing, but not Cued Speech. 2) The involvement of his vocal organs suggested that his speech might never be fully functional. However, as his mother explains, his speech is now intelligible to members of the family and friends who are accustomed to it. 3) Alexander is academically successful. This case illustrates the value of persistent, continuing therapy. It also demonstrates dramatically the value of sibling support, as described in Chapter 16.

Memory Problems

A good many cases have been reported in which hearing-impaired children diagnosed as having serious memory problems have responded well to Cued Speech and, indeed, have in some cases overcome those problems completely. We caution the reader to remember that these results have not been supported by any controlled research, and our speculation about how Cued Speech may have helped is not based on any broad professional competence in connection with memory. However, Cued Speech does appear to offer several advantages in coping with the needs of deaf children who have memory problems. Most important is the fact that use of Cued Speech makes it possible to use both written and spoken language in addressing the problem. A second possibility is that expressive cueing, along with speaking, can provide a "motor-memory" pattern that can sometimes be remembered better than a strictly visual one. This effect is similar to remembering a familiar but temporarily-forgotten telephone number "with your fingers" from having touch-tone-dialed it repeatedly.

Probably the most important advantage of Cued Speech in connection with therapy related to memory problems is that with it parents can possibly evaluate the length of time the child can retain in memory something just learned. In the child with memory problems, this interval is typically much shorter than in the average person. The normal mind usually retains for 24 hours or more a clearly formed image of something learned in a single set of visual exposures. If reviewed about 24 hours after the initial exposure, the image will likely last a week, and reviewing it on three successive days will make it last much longer. In persons with mild memory problems, often such an image fades out after a few hours. In such cases, material learned at school needs to be reviewed at shorter intervals. Over a period of time (by teaching and later testing new material) parents can determine at what intervals and how many times review is needed in order to make the image last indefinitely. The important thing is that, over time, such activity (if successful) may increase the length of time the mind can hold images of things learned. In some cases serious memory problems in preschool and the early grades have been overcome completely, and in others substantial improvement has occurred, as described in the case histories below.

When efforts to solve the memory problems of a deaf child through Cued Speech are successful, the child may become a good reader and may ultimately perform quite well academically. However, there is likely to be a serious deficit in general knowledge about the world, and in vocabulary, that will persist at least until the child has been a committed reader for five or 10 years.

Aphasia

Aphasia is a condition in which a sensory input cannot be decoded or understood. We are concerned here with situations in which it is the auditory input that cannot be handled properly. This is often a problem in children with normal hearing. In addition, it may cause hearing-impaired children to be unable to make use of the residual hearing they have. We have only a few reports specifically related to aphasia, and these have to do with children with normal hearing. Virginia Smith, of Lake Charles, La., reported in correspondence in 1972 that she had excellent results using Cued Speech with a group of young aphasic children. Her "before-and-after" experience with these children convinced her that Cued Speech circumvented their problem effectively. Several factors make it easy to infer too much from this case. First, the children were not thoroughly diagnosed; aphasia was the assumed problem. Second, the improvement was not quantified, so that the evaluation was subjective.

Our opinion is that cases of aphasia that respond to Cued Speech are likely those in which the aphasia is very mild and is related specifically to interference with processing of auditory input to the brain. In such cases it would seem reasonable that, by communicating the speech message through the visual channel, Cued Speech might circumvent the auditory-processing problem. We have a very limited amount of evidence to support this assertion. However, the most-used methods of treatment of aphasic children are based on the same assumptions (McGinnis, 1963).

Apraxia, or "Expressive Aphasia"

These are cases in which the problem is interference with or deficiency in the ability of the brain to communicate articulatory commands to the vocal mechanism, rather than the reception of the auditory input. Children with this problem can learn to understand spoken language, but cannot produce it. Various terms such as *apraxia, expressive aphasia, motor aphasia, developmental articulatory aphasia,* and *developmental apraxia of speech* are used to describe the condition. Wilma Jean Tade, of Texas Christian University, describes types of behavior characteristic of apraxic or apraxic-like children:

> ...*inability to imitate words, limited ability to imitate speech sounds, a poor memory for sound and word sequences, poor self-monitoring skills, a markedly reduced repertoire of phonemes, poor imitative skills for articulation, highly inconsistent articulation errors, and groping trial-and-error behaviors.*

Tade cites Jaffé (1986) as a source for this description. It should be noted that some of these behaviors (poor memory for sound and word sequences, and a reduced repertoire of phonemes) are associated also with aphasic tendencies.

Tade has developed a method, the Basic Articulation, Language, Learning (B.A.L.L.) program,[1] for using the visual channel to supplement the auditory channel in the clinical management of 4-and-5-year-old children with varying degrees of apraxic or apraxic-like difficulty (Tade, 1991). In this program the letters representing the sounds make up the visual input. She has expanded that program to include the use of Cued Speech with hearing-impaired children, and describes the results as encouraging. Tade has thus far used the approach with three CS children. She explains as follows:

> *The three profoundly deaf Cued Speech children were enrolled at the Miller Speech and Hearing Clinic of Texas Christian University in classes with seven to 10 hearing children. The classes were taught by Tade and student clinicians who cued when the deaf children were present. The hearing children were phonologically disordered, some being severely apraxic-like, language delayed, and/or language learning disabled. The program embodied an integrated approach, i.e., it facilitated phonological and meta-linguistic awareness in a setting compatible with elements of the whole language concept. It provided extensive experiences in the production of speech sounds and in learning letter/sound correspondence, word segmentation, and sound-blending. It fostered the ability to think and talk about language and to understand that thoughts are expressed by using sounds, words,*

---

[1]A revised form of the B.A.L.L. program, entitled *Children's Early Intervention Speech-Language Program,* will be available from Slosson Educational Publications, Inc., East Aurora, N.Y., in January, 1993.

and sentences. This was accomplished in an environment that encouraged learning word meanings and acquiring a knowledge of prepositional, adjectival, and numerical concepts along with providing natural opportunities for social interaction, story telling, and the development of early reading and writing skills.

All three Cued Speech children developed exceptionally good speech and sentence structure. Following their instruction with the B.A.L.L. program they were mainstreamed with Cued Speech transliterators. All three are excellent students. They excel particularly in reading, writing, and spelling. In the B.A.L.L. program, the cues were used for the benefit of the deaf children rather than as an aid for the apraxic-like children. It is possible that they might benefit the hearing children, as they seem to help aphasic hearing children.

A theoretical explanation of how Cued Speech may help with the problem of apraxia can be made by postulating that if the child repeats the cueing of specific articulatory patterns that he/she has difficulty in producing vocally, he/she may be able to remember and habituate their production. Then, by associating with the cue-plus-lip activity with each sound he/she learns to produce vocally, the child may become able to retain the sequences of vocal production. Though highly speculative, this hypothesis is similar to the assumptions underlying the method most used for dealing with apraxia, the McGinnis (1963) method, sometimes called the "association" method.

The primary idea behind this and similar approaches is to supplement the auditory input with a related visual input. In her article Tade cites a list of persons who have used this approach "...successfully in the clinical management of children with varying degrees of apraxic-like speech" (McGinnis, 1963; Rosenbek, Hanson, Baughman, & Lemme, 1974; Shelton, & Garves, 1985; Yoss & Darley, 1974). The advantage Cued Speech may have over the other means used to supplement the auditory signal is that it is a complete finite system that can be used consistently for deaf children and thus be more thoroughly ingrained and easily used than an assortment of special visual "cues" used as supplements.

Dyslexia

Dyslexia is a specific form of visual agnosia in which the brain has difficulty in perceiving shapes and spacial relationships, particularly in written language. Children afflicted with this problem typically have great difficulty in learning to read. They often transpose or reverse letters in writing, as a result of their defective brain function.

Since common methods of therapy for dyslexia depend heavily on use of the child's knowledge of spoken language, Cued Speech appears to offer unique advantages for the child who has both a hearing impairment and a dyslexic problem. We know of several cases in which specific experience has been reported, and the results have been favorable. An interesting case is that of Matthew McIntosh, a child with normal hearing. Matthew was diagnosed in preschool as dyslexic. He was exposed to Cued Speech because of its use at home with his profoundly deaf brother, Robbie McIntosh. The Montessori school that accepted Robbie in first grade decided to use Cued Speech for teaching phonics to the hearing preschoolers. Both the director of the school, Mrs. Anne Riley (1980), and Matthew's parents report that the use of Cued Speech in teaching phonics, along with its use in specific therapy for the dyslexia problem, produced rapid improvement. Matthew is now 15, reads very well, and appears to have outwitted his dyslexic tendencies completely.

Linda Balderson, in reporting on the dyslexic tendencies of her deaf daughter Tiffany (story below), points out that the Orton Society, on the basis of its research, recommends using a phonics approach to teaching reading to dyslexic children. Linda comments: "Cued Speech is the only way I know that phonics can be used with children who can't hear." Not only is CS the most direct way to use a phonic approach in teaching reading to deaf children; it is also the most efficient way to provide the deaf child with the internal phonological base of language that makes the phonics approach to reading succeed. Linda also notes that Dr. Harold Levinson, who diagnosed both Tiffany and Matthew Mcintosh as dyslexic, developed a theory that dyslexia is caused by problems related to the vestibular mechanism affecting balance. "Since this mechanism is located next to the cochlea," Linda suggests, "it seems likely to me that deaf children may be at greater risk than hearing children as regards the probability of being dyslexic. Tiffany's specific diagnosis is: Cerebellar Vestibular Dysfunction."

Linda Balderson further notes: "When Tiffany was diagnosed as dyslexic she was almost 9 years old. She exhibited many dyslexic characteristics—difficulties with handwriting, math, memory. However, her teachers were surprised at the diagnosis, as she was reading at the same level as her hearing classmates. We attribute this to Cued Speech, as she had received 'visual phonics' from the age of 20 months."

We can only speculate about the reasons why Cued Speech can apparently help overcome at least mild dyslexic tendencies in children, hearing-impaired or not. There are two possibilities: 1) With Cued Speech, the spoken language can be used as the basic instrument for therapy in the case of a hearing-impaired child, so that the procedures ordinarily used in therapy for dyslexia can be employed; 2) Expressive cueing by the hearing-impaired child, repeated and habituated, can provide memorized language patterns along with an associated kinesthetic (sensory experience derived from bodily movement) feedback. This can possibly enable a child to retain the language patterns in spite of some dyslexic confusion in connection with the written message.

Usher's Syndrome/Retinitis Pigmentosa

Usher's Syndrome is an inherited condition that produces both hearing loss and a progressive loss of vision due to retinitis pigmentosa. Sometimes the loss of peripheral vision stabilizes, at ages between 20 and 25, at a level resulting in "tunnel vision" over an area from several inches to a foot in diameter (two or three feet in front of the face). In other cases the deterioration continues to complete blindness. We know of three cases of Usher's Syndrome in which deaf youngsters have been helped by Cued Speech, especially during the stage when their field of view was too restricted for full use of signs.

Deaf-Blindness

Some individuals with a severe-to-profound hearing deficit, and suffering from very limited vision, have been able to receive spoken language through Cued Speech, usually at distances of one-to-three feet. These are people who are legally classified as both blind and deaf. Of course, they can also learn to communicate with signs.

A very promising application of Cued Speech is to those who are profoundly deaf and also incapable of receiving Cued Speech visually. We will use the term *deaf-blind* only in reference to such individuals.

Methods commonly used with deaf-blind persons include: 1) fingerspelling with the deaf-blind person's hand on top of the speller's hand. This is of limited accuracy unless the spelling is very slow; 2) the Tadoma method, in which the deaf-blind person's hand is placed on the speaker's face in such a way that the thumb and fingers can pick up information on the movements of the lips, cheek, throat, and jaw, and the vibrations of the larynx, to produce a form of tactile speech-reading; 3) placing of the deaf-blind person's hands on those of a signing person, and 4) the use of Braille, which is especially valuable in cases in which deafness is post-lingual. Two-way communication is possible between people who use a Braille writer.

Pamela H. Beck, president of the NCSA from 1989 through 1993, used Cued Speech for three years with California children who were both hearing impaired and legally blind. They could use much of the information available visually from the mouth and the cues, at very short distances. Thus, the only accommodations necessary for use of Cued Speech with them were arrangement of optimum lighting conditions and distance between speaker and receiver.

The first use of Cued Speech with a totally blind and profoundly deaf person was by Judith Lasensky-Curtin (1978). She was providing speech-language therapy (two 30-minute sessions per week) for a 9-year-old deaf-blind girl. The primary method of communication was through signs, with the deaf-blind child's hands following the hands of the signer through taction. Ms. Lasensky conceived the idea of using Cued Speech by having the child use one hand in the Tadoma position—to pick up the ordinarily visible manifestations of speech—and the other hand lightly touching the hand of the cuer. She reported that after 10 weeks of therapy totalling one hour per week, she could "make clear to the child exactly what she said." She also reported that rapid improvement occurred in the child's speech production as a result. So far as we know, this method has not been picked up by anyone else. Shortly after she reported on the case, Ms. Lasensky was transferred to a different assignment and had no opportunity to continue her work. She has now been in Saudi Arabia for several years. She is teaching Cued Speech in Arabic.

Non-Specific Learning Disability

While the term mentally retarded is no longer in vogue, it is descriptive of a situation in which no specific cause for the developmental delay can be determined, and the individual child appears to have been "held back" in mental development by an unidentified factor.

Nearly 25 years of experience and observation convince us that for a deaf child to learn spoken language through Cued Speech requires no more intelligence than for a hearing child to learn through normal hearing. However, it certainly requires more effort, time, and resourcefulness on the part of those who care for and instruct slower children. Our experience is that gifted deaf children perform like gifted hearing children, average deaf children like average hearing children, and slow deaf children like slow hearing children, when Cued Speech is used and adequate support is furnished. This seems to be true even of children with abilities as low as those of the barely trainable, though not many such cases have been reported among CS children.

In our opinion the advisability of using Cued Speech with deaf children whose capacity is at the barely trainable level is questionable. Unless the child is likely to learn to read, the advantage of using Cued

Speech is limited, and it may not be as advisable as the use of natural gestures and signs. Both natural gestures and the signs likely to be used with such children are probably easier to associate and remember than the initial Cued Speech representations because some signs have a descriptive appearance. For example, *eat, sleep, ball, come here,* and *drink* are very easy to remember once they have been associated with what they represent. Thus, if the child is capable of learning and retaining symbols for only 30 or 40 commands or phrases, it will probably be easier to use gestures and signs.

Again, our experience with the severely retarded is limited, primarily because we have not had opportunities to follow such cases for extended periods. Longitudinal studies of such children might yield significant information.

Case Histories

All except two of the case histories included here are of children who have at least one other learning problem in addition to hearing impairment. The two are included because their early years were so dominated by health problems that there appeared to be little hope for normal development of language, communication, or reading, and because their stories so well illustrate the struggles of parents against all odds to help their children. Only one of the entire group has scored below the average range on standard IQ tests. Since she is performing at grade level in spite of at least one additional disability, we think the IQ test scores (in the 70 to 80 range) are inaccurate, having been caused by interference with test performance by the disability.

Tiffany Balderson
by Linda Balderson, 1991

Tiffany has CHARGE association. This condition involves many major and minor medical problems. The problems that most affect her include: profound hearing loss in both ears, seasonal allergies, and learning disabilities. We have been using Cued Speech with her since she was 20 months of age. At that time her hearing threshold in her left ear was PTA 100 dB. She made particularly good use of this residual hearing, leading us to believe that she has a conductive component to her loss. Although this hearing level was maintained for several years, about 4 years ago there was a significant drop in her PTA (to the current level of 120 dB). She has never shown measurable hearing in the right ear. One of the ramifications of CHARGE association is a degenerative hearing loss.

Tiffany Balderson (18)

Although Tiffany's early progress with Cued Speech was slower than that of other CS children, she made good progress in preschool. At the age of 4 years and 8 months her results on the Carrow Test for receptive language showed her level to be 4 years and 8 months (hearing norms). We were very pleased. During her preschool years she received consistent cueing at home (both parents) and at a private preschool for normal hearing children. A few other hearing-impaired children attended the Cued Speech program there also.

At the age of 6 Tiffany began kindergarten in the Cued Speech Program in the Montgomery County (Md.) Public Schools. She has continued in that program since that time. She is currently in the eighth grade at Wood Mid-level School in Rockville, Md. Tiffany has not been mainstreamed very successfully throughout her school career. This is partially due to her extremely shy personality, but the major factor is her learning disabilities (memory problems and dyslexia). In April of 1984 she underwent a battery of psychological and academic tests. The results follow:

1. Average to above-average learning potential.
2. Weakness in
   a. processing visual learning material
   b. organizing at a linguistic level
   c. visual and auditory skills
   d. fine motor skills (pencil and paper)
   e. retrieving learned information
   f. not a risk taker—not feeling successful with her efforts.

These tests were administered seven years ago when Tiffany was 10 years old. I see some remarkable improvement since that time in many of her weak areas. Recently she has put more effort into school and been more successful because of her more positive attitude.

Tiffany's hardest academic subjects are World Studies and Science. Vocabulary is hard for her to learn, because of her memory problems. Compared to the other self-contained hearing-impaired students (mostly using Total Communication), her reading and language abilities are quite good—especially written language. She continues slow progress in math. Listed below are the test results from her IEP in spring 1991. In a few instances where there was significant improvement from spring 1987, I have recorded those scores as well.

STANFORD ACHIEVEMENT TEST (1991, 8th grade)
Reading—Intermediate 1 (level given)
Reading Comprehension
Grade equivalent 5.6 (hearing norms)
(3.9 in 1987)
Percentile 84% (H.I. norms for same age)

Math—Primary 2 (level given)
Concepts of Number
Grade Equivalent 8.2 (hearing norms)
(3.8 in 1987)
Math computation
Grade Equivalent 6.3 (hearing norms)
(2.0 in 1987)
Math Application
Grade Equivalent 4.2 (hearing norms)
(1.9 in 1987)

Social Studies—Primary 2 (level given) Sub-test
Grade Equivalent 3.5 (hearing norms)

UTLEY SPEECHREADING TESTS[2]
— April, 1987, 87%
(sentence level)   — 1988, 100%
(sentence level)   — 1989, 94%

Excluding the discovery of Tiffany's hearing and medical problems when she was very young, the lowest point in our dealings with her came when we were told of her learning disabilities, when she was 9 years old. Additional problems on top of a profound hearing loss

---

[2] These speechreading scores are remarkable. They not only attest the contribution of Cued Speech to speechreading skills, but suggest that Tiffany's dyslexic problems apply only to *static* visual patterns, not to serially presented visual elements such as those of the hand and the mouth in Cued Speech.

seemed like too great a burden for a child. On the positive side, Tiffany is a fairly happy child. She is not upset about being deaf. She has a few close friends who are also hearing impaired. She always tries to please us and seems to feel good about her lot in life, generally.

One of the highest points for us was when Tiffany passed the Maryland State Test of Functional Proficiency in English. This is the test all students must pass in order to be issued a high school diploma in the state of Maryland. They can take it in as many as four successive years, beginning in ninth grade. Tiffany passed it the first time she took it, when she was in the ninth grade—hearing loss, health problems, and learning problems notwithstanding.[3]

New Worlds for Alexander
by Annette McDonnel

It was May, at the end of the school year. As I was watching Alexander receiving his "diploma" promoting him from preschool to kindergarten, words were coming back in my memory—words I happened to read almost four years ago in an evaluation report on our son: "Alexander is a child with hemiplegic cerebral palsy, a seizure disorder, profound bilateral hearing loss, and retinal scars in both eyes." I remember the shock and disbelief I felt seeing Alexander described in such a way and the apprehension I had about his future. But now, with these words again in my mind, I saw him walk proudly and confidently up to the teacher when it was his turn to receive his diploma. To me, these steps on the school stage were just a few steps in Alexander's long walk to success.

We became aware of Alexander's hearing impairment when he was 10 months old. My husband held a good job as a math teacher, and I had just started on a promising career as a biologist. Best of all, we were expecting our third child in a few months. With the diagnosis of Alexander's problems, our lives suddenly changed. Learning that our little son was handicapped caught us totally unprepared, and we began to wonder how we could cope with his special needs and still be able to lead a normal life.

Since we knew next to nothing about deafness, I started reading everything related to it. The more I read, the more I realized that being

---

[3]The poignant story of Tiffany's experience with open-heart surgery and the part played in it by Cued Speech appears in Chapter 9, p. 123. It is included to illustrate the need of a child for the security provided by clear communication with caring professionals and family members.

deaf means much more than just "not hearing"—and what a crucial role we, as his parents, were going to play in his overall development. Reading my way through the literature on deafness, I came across the *Cued Speech Handbook for Parents*, by Henegar and Cornett. Cued Speech seemed to be so logical and to offer so many advantages over other communication systems, including its simplicity, that we decided to try it with Alexander.

Influencing our decision to choose Cued Speech was the fact that once we had mastered the system, we could immediately communicate with Alexander about any and everything. So, at the end of February, 1980, I set out to Gallaudet to learn CS. I had left excited, scared, skeptical, and

Kati (12), Anna(15), Annette, Elmer(10), Jerry, and Alexander(13) McDonnel (6/30/92)

optimistic all at once. I returned convinced and enthusiastic. On my return from Washington I taught my husband what I had learned, and we started cueing to 12-month-old Alexander.

It turned out that we were slow and clumsy, and he was very uncooperative, hardly giving our cueing efforts as much as a fleeting glance. The greater was our joy, when after only a few weeks of cueing he indicated he understood his first words: "light" and "candy." From then on, he has continued to acquire more and more language, receptively and also expressively. After eight months of cueing, Alexander's vocabulary had grown from no language at all to language levels appropriate to or above that of hearing kids his age. When he took the Ski HI Test, which is a language scale developed by the University of Utah, at the age of 23 months he scored 23 months receptively and 18-20 months expressively in comparison with hearing children. On the Sequence Inventory of the Communication Development Test, published by the University of Washington Press, at 23 months of age he responded accurately to 75% of the material (that would be average for a 24-month-old hearing child), and his understanding of commands was at the 28-month level. On the Peabody Picture Vocabulary Test he scored at the 26-month level when he was 24 months old.

In addition to the development in his language since we started using Cued Speech, Alexander has shown us quite a change in his personality, growing from a quiet, almost withdrawn baby to an inquisitive, outgoing little boy with a great sense of humor.

Alexander's sister, Anna, was a good cuer at 4 years of age and made few mistakes. She enjoyed figuring out how to cue "hard" words. I watched her looking at pictures and cueing "Martians" and "carriage" to herself.

When Alexander was a year old, it seemed an almost unsurmountable task to raise a handicapped kid. Thanks to CS, Alexander hardly seems handicapped any more.

When we decided to use Cued Speech with Alexander, we were aware of the fact that we might encounter problems with the public school system. Fort Lupton is a small town, and hearing-impaired children in the area are bussed to Greeley, where the University of Northern Colorado maintains an excellent on-campus school. The teachers and students there use Total Communication in all classrooms. But signs were foreign to Alexander, the bus ride was too long and tiring, and we wanted him to go to the same school his sister and the kids from our block attended.

To prepare the school for our eventual request, I joined the parent-advisory committee of the county BOCES (Board of Cooperative Educational Services), which handles all special needs children in the district. Alexander was only 3 years old then, so I did not then need to make any demands on his behalf. However, everybody knew about him and the services we would eventually request for him. When it was time to enroll Alexander in the public preschool our request to have him placed in the local school and to provide instruction in Cued Speech came as no surprise to the school.

The meeting at which Alexander's school placement was to be decided was attended by all his future teachers and the director of the local BOCES, Dr. Karl Schmidli. Throughout the meeting we felt genuine concern and a very positive attitude towards Cued Speech, among those present. It was agreed that Alexander should be mainstreamed into a regular classroom for social interaction with his peers, but that for academics and language he would benefit most in a special education classroom with a cueing teacher. Before the beginning of the school year, the special education teacher, Elena Gallegos, learned Cued Speech to be prepared for Alexander. Since then, she and her two classroom aides have become very proficient cuers. The motivation and enthusiasm with which she communicated with Alexander made his first year of school a great success. His year-end report reads in part:

Alexander is a self-confident, loving little boy. He has made tremendous progress in his spontaneous vocalization and attempts to cue. His level of receptive communication is strong—at age level or above. Use of Cued Speech with Alexander is highly beneficial. Alexander also received physical therapy and the services of a teacher for the deaf throughout the school year. Amy Winter, Kathy Jillson, and Hollis Berendt have become fluent cuers working with Alexander.

When Alexander was tested at the end of the school year (1984) at the age of 5.3 years, he scored 5.0-6.0 years in readiness, 5.0-6.0 years in receptive language, and 5.3-6.0 years in math on the Brigance test. Thanks to the dedication of his teachers and the openness to Cued Speech of Dr. Schmidli and the principal, Mrs. Martinez, the school has become somewhat of a model of how a deaf student can be successfully integrated. School administrators, teachers, and parents from out of state have visited the school. They were impressed with the quality of education that Alexander was receiving.

Whether at school or at home, we try to cue everything to Alexander. His big sister Anna is 7, and she cues effortlessly. We have always tried to keep her motivated to cue, sometimes with gentle persuasion, sometimes with not-so-gentle rules: "You cue at dinner or you don't talk." Even his little sister Kati has picked up a few cues, and Elmer (age 2) thinks that waving your fingers around your face as you talk is part of any regular conversation.

Although Alexander's receptive language has always been good, his expressive communication lags behind it considerably. About a year ago, he started to cue expressively—he now sometimes cues to himself—and recently I watched him correct Kati's crude attempts. He is also using his speech much more, talking and cueing. I usually can figure out what he wants to tell me. In general, however, he will resort to anything to get his point across. I once asked him to read a "No Smoking" sign to me and he started out saying and cueing "No." When he looked at the "smoking" part he hesitated for just a moment. Then, with a big grin on his face he picked up an imaginary cigarette and puffed away on it.

Alexander's achievements are in large part due to the fact that we were always able to communicate with him easily with Cued Speech. He knows his letters, shapes, colors, and numbers just like any other kid his age...no big deal! But, for Alexander and for us, it *is* a big deal.

Alexander had a very good first year at school. His kindergarten teacher is already preparing to have him in her class this coming fall. The future is looking good for Alexander! Some time ago I asked Kati why she thought we cue to Alexander. Without hesitation she said, "Because he was born to know Cued Speech."

Update, 1991

In a few months Alexander will turn 13. His becoming a teenager will mark a new chapter in his life and ours. As we did at other transition points, we will probably feel that we are starting over.

When we moved to a small rural town in Wyoming five years ago we left behind an excellent educational program, only to battle here with a school system that was determined to use Total Communication with Alexander. After many bitter meetings and on the advice of the Protection and Advocacy, Inc., of Wyoming, we reached a compromise allowing both signing and Cued Speech to be used for instruction. It seemed to be the best choice to work with rather than against the people who would be responsible for providing Alexander's education throughout elementary school and now junior high.

Alexander actually handles the situation pretty well, using Cued Speech at home, and speech, signs, gestures, and Cued Speech at school and in the community. For the last year he has attended junior high school. His aide knows Cued Speech and signing as well. Most of his classmates know some signs and have made his social integration into the school a reality. He goes to a special education classroom for math, reading, and language, and is being mainstreamed (with some adaptations) for science, P.E., music, and art. His science teacher commented on his report card: "Alex is amazing—he is doing so well in science—interacting with others." And, for the first quarter, Alexander has been on the "B" honor roll.

Most important of all, Alexander has a great personality, a wonderful sense of humor, and a good self-concept. Despite the fact that he has no usable hearing, we can usually understand his speech, thanks to Cued Speech. He is confident enough to go by himself to check out the latest video, place his order at McDonald's, or ask the butcher for dog bones. Just the other day, I caught him calling the Pizza Hut on the regular telephone!

In a lot of ways Alexander is just a regular kid. He loves peanut butter and pizza, Superman and the Ninja Turtles, fishing and helping on the ranch. And yet, he sees the world differently, giving us new insight into the world of the deaf. One day he drew a picture of a thunderstorm for his grandfather. It had yellow and blue lightning flashes. When I questioned him about the blue lightning, he explained in a matter-of-fact way: "That's not lightning. That's the thunder."

We live in Wyoming near the Wind River Indian Reservation. One of the most prized possessions of many Indian families is a Paint Horse. These are horses that are usually marked by patches of black and white. One day we took our mare to be bred to a Paint stallion. While we were engrossed in horse talk Alexander discovered a litter of kittens in the hay stack. He picked up a beautifully marked black and white kitten and ran up to us. "Mom," he said, holding out the cat, "I want a Paint Cat!" *Anna's "big sister" observations are on p. 272.*

Holly Abell

Holly Abell is prelingually and profoundly deaf. Her mother indicates she has memory problems, but she has made excellent progress in spite of them, in view of her early language delay and late start with Cued Speech. Refer to Chapter 23, "What About Sign Language?," for Holly's letters and the story of her experiences and feelings as a deaf youngster torn between the hearing world and the deaf culture. The following is a comment by her mother, Janie Abell:

> *Holly was aural/oral till age 8 (with little language), and then began Cued Speech. I started cueing to her (no formal lessons except at the Gallaudet CS Family Program where Tom and I learned) and she picked it up rapidly. She started making better sentences very quickly. But, she seemed to need many repetitions of the same vocabulary and sentence structures. When I tried to expand her language at times, she would become very frustrated. I've wondered about the reason for this—she's a perfectionist; she wants to understand perfectly every word that is said to her, or perhaps her learning disability caused the frustration. Now she is more open to trying harder vocabulary and sentence structures.*
>
> *Holly has not yet closed the language gap (most recent reading level was 5.3), but when she started high school with TC kids (for social needs), her teachers were astounded at the accuracy of her written language and at her ability to express herself on paper—even in comparison with the hard-of-hearing kids who could read better. They also assumed she was hard of hearing (instead of 115 dB PTA) because of her speech and her near-normal lip movements. Her biggest problem has been and still is vocabulary. Now that she is reading more I hope it will improve also. See Holly's own observations, p. 630-637.*

Sinead Siobhan Clements
by Deirdre Clements, Nov. 19, 1991

Sinead was born some 10 years ago. After her birth she appeared to be a normal little girl, but within minutes it was evident that something was wrong. She had difficulty in breathing and the doctors and nurses could not pass a small catheter through her nose to suck out her throat and nasal passages. Sinead had a condition called *choanal stresis*. In this condition the passages for air at the back of the nose are blocked. In Sinead's case they were blocked by bone. In order for her to breathe she had to have a tube placed in her throat. She was transferred to the intensive care unit and soon had an operation to open the nasal passages. She had a second surgery in 14 days. These two operations were followed by a period of two years in which repeated procedures were necessary to keep the passages open. All this culminated in an extensive and successful operation when Sinead was 2 years old. At about that time we learned that Sinead had a deficiency in her calcium metabolism called hypoparathyroidism. From that time she had to take medicine to control that problem.

Sinead and Ian Clements, 1992

As if this were not enough, when Sinead was 9 days old we suspected that she was deaf. This was difficult to confirm by audiological testing, but it was eventually found that she was profoundly deaf. She was at once fitted with a hearing aid. We decided that she would be taught using the oral approach and started teaching her English one word at a time.

When Sinead was 2½ years old she understood about nine words and could pronounce only two or three. Our options were to send her away to the local state school for the deaf where manual communication was practiced, or to the Central Institute for the Deaf in St. Louis where the oral approach was used.

In the process of considering these two options we found out that neither would necessarily lead to fluency in English for Sinead. We also found out that she would have to be exceptional to be able to read at above a third-grade level. At this point we were fortunate to find out about Cued Speech from a teacher of the deaf who had used it. We contacted the Cued Speech Office at Gallaudet University and learnt that it is a reasonable expectation for children with whom Cued Speech is used consistently to become able to use English at a level equivalent to that of their hearing peers. We decided to learn Cued Speech right away, ordered the audiocassette lessons, and booked for the family workshop at Gallaudet. The whole family, including Sinead's sister Aine (two years older) learnt Cued Speech.

Sinead's receptive language grew and eventually her expressive language developed. By the age of 5 she had the language base of a 3-year-8-months-old hearing child. We taught her to read phonetically, using Cued Speech and the techniques and word lists in the book *Why Johnny Can't Read*, by Rudolf Flesch. Thus she was taught to read like a hearing child, and we insisted that she read, write, and say the words.

During this time Sinead and we had to deal with several other health problems. Every so often Sinead would become very nauseated, and when we took her to the emergency room her blood calcium was low. This usually meant that she had to be admitted to the hospital to have her blood calcium level restored. Also she developed a weakness of the muscle of her urinary bladder. For a while we had to help her pass urine by inserting a catheter.

Cued Speech gave us a lot of advantages with Sinead. We live in a relatively small community without a lot of support for deaf children. Cued Speech allowed us to be the main teachers of English for Sinead, and we did not have to modify our language. Once we knew the Cued Speech system we could cue anything. A major advantage was that we could tell Sinead about her health problems and get her to take part in her own medical care. After all, she will have to do this anyway, all her life.

Sinead's first teacher of the deaf learnt Cued Speech with us and was very supportive. We asked our local Montessori school to take Sinead since we felt that the Montessori method of teaching language (phonics based) would be very appropriate for our child. We placed an advertisement in the local paper for someone to train in Cued Speech to become Sinead's interpreter. We had many replies and eventually found an excellent person. She took to Cued Speech right away and moreover understood the language needs of deaf children. Sinead was on the road to attaining good language skills and accumulated both receptive and expressive language.

At about this time, a decision had to be made about Sinead going to kindergarten at her local school. Although the school district had been somewhat supportive of our decisions, now that she was of school age they indicated that she could be supported only in the school district's segregated program for deaf children, in which signing was the method of communication. Thus we were faced with pressure to throw away all the progress we had made to date.

We challenged the school district's decision in a due-process hearing, and our decisions were supported by the judge and the State Commissioner for Education. This decision established that Sinead should be educated in her local school with a Cued Speech interpreter. At all stages we have maintained good working relationships with her classroom teachers, and all have been amazed by her language ability and understanding. She is now (at age 10 years) equal to any other member of her class. She is a voracious reader. Although she can cue, her method of expressive communication is speech without cues. Her speech has improved over the years. We have encouraged her to use speech exclusively with her family, friends, and strangers. She orders her own food at McDonald's. Sinead knows, however, that she must concentrate to produce good speech.

Our deaf daughter has come a long way with all her problems, and we are sure there will be more hurdles for her to jump. With Cued Speech, her family has brought language to Sinead, and as she grows up she will be increasingly capable of dealing with her problems herself. *See p. 575 for Sinead's ideas, and p.279 for her sister's.*

Raising a Child with Attention Deficit Syndrome
by Sarina Roffé, 1992

Many people look at Simon as a bright, gifted, successful deaf child. They see him as everything they want their own deaf child to grow up as. He is a gifted reader, has an amazing sense of humor, and functions and thinks as a hearing child does. But there is a side to Simon most do not know. Simon has Attention Deficit Disorder (A.D.D.).

Simon's profound deafness was diagnosed at 9 months. He was then taught orally until age 2, when his teachers recommended use of signs. When he was 3½, we started Cued Speech. At that time he knew about 100 words. Receiving Cued Speech consistently at home and school, he then made five years of progress in language in 22 months, according to his scores on standard tests.

When Simon was mainstreamed in first grade I had numerous complaints from his teacher. He didn't watch his CS interpreter. He had fights in school. He couldn't sit in a group. He spoke out. He was extremely argumentative. When involved in an activity he couldn't easily switch to a different one.

These complaints surprised me because Simon could become so involved in a book he would read it for hours. Also, these problems had not shown up in kindergarten during the half-days he was in a self-contained class of five deaf children with a skilled Cued Speech teacher, nor were they reported as serious during the rest of the day when he was mainstreamed in kindergarten. We consulted our pediatrician and a child psychiatrist who immediately diagnosed Simon as having A.D.D. We refused to believe our child was hyperactive. Instead, my husband and I became more active in behavior modification. Simon's first-grade teacher made a contract with him to correct certain behaviors. It seemed these were the appropriate things to do, but these attempts were eroding Simon's self-confidence without our realizing it. It seemed he could never do anything right. He was always being punished for something.

We attended a class to learn more about A.D.D. and learned that hyperactivity is not the same as A.D.D., but a mild form of it. A child can be hyperactive and also have an attention deficit. We soon had to face a choice between damaging Simon's self-esteem and sense of self-worth, and administering medication to control his A.D.D. in class.

Our pediatrician explained to us that when uncontrolled behaviors block the learning process it is time to control those behaviors. If the medication could be administered in a carefully controlled way, so that Simon had success in school, then learning could be fun, and he could retain his happy outlook on life and learn in school. It was a difficult decision for us. We were very reluctant to medicate our child for this condition. But it became clear on the first day of medication that it was right for Simon. Nothing we could have done to control his diet or his behavior would have the same effect.

Simon became a changed child. He was happier, more confident, and more liked by his peers. He was less argumentative and could pay attention to his teachers and interpreters. He could more easily finish an assigned task. His teacher remarked on how much Simon could accomplish now that his attention span was on a par with that of the other children in the class. By the end of first grade, Simon was identified as a gifted child. He had moved from the lowest reading group to the highest. His teacher said it was because his attention span had improved so much, and he had become able to enjoy learning so much that she could get Simon through the material at a much faster rate, in the group she had always known he should be placed in. I should point out that we never saw the benefit of the medication at home. Simon was medicated only at school because the home environment did not aggravate the problem.

By fifth grade, Simon's teacher requested that he be taken off medication. We agreed to a trial withdrawal. At that point, his body was beginning to change with early adolescence. It turned out that though there was some lessening of his attention span, he was mature enough to work through some of his attention problems by compensating in other ways.

Simon is now 16 years old and in tenth grade. He still admits to having attention problems, is still argumentative at times, and is easily bored with tedious work and note-taking. But, he has learned to compensate for his problems. He is still an intelligent and gifted person. Simon is learning to drive, which will increase his sense of independence. Last summer he worked for a stock brokerage firm on Wall Street in New York City. He was in charge of confirming junk-bond orders. Simon is entranced with the business world and looks to it as a career. See also pp. *414, 418, and 595.*

Amity Leitner
adapted from an article in *Cued Speech Center Lines*, 1987

Amity Leitner, who lives in Raleigh, N.C., was born profoundly deaf (110 dB PTA), cause not clear. She also had cardiac and vision problems and mild cerebral palsy. There seemed little chance of a normal life for Amity. But her parents never gave up hope for their child with so many problems. To cope with her deafness they tried the traditional oral approach to speech and language until age 4, but without success. In desperation, they turned to sign language for two years. Amity understood signs, but she still had no understanding of spoken or written language. When she was 6, her parents heard of Cued Speech and learned the system.

Cued Speech proved to be the breakthrough in their attempts to reach Amity through the spoken word. At last she began to understand them. They would cue and say a word or expression to her, then follow it with the sign or signs for that particular thing. Amity's understanding began to grow with such amazing rapidity that within a year they were able to stop signing altogether. From then on, Amity's language grew rapidly.

In 1981 the Leitner family moved to Raleigh, N.C. from Massachusetts to have the support of the Cued Speech Center located there. It provided the much-needed special Cued Speech services needed for Amity. The Center has also worked, in cooperation with the schools, to provide as wide a cueing environment as possible for Amity and others. Many hearing children in Amity's classes have learned to cue in order to communicate effectively with her. "Now," say's Amity's mother Jeanie, there is nothing that Amity cannot have explained to her. There are no limitations to her language."

Amity is now a vivacious and friendly young lady whose chief enjoyment is being with her peers. She overcomes her other physical problems with the same determination she has shown in overcoming the tremendous social and educational limitations of deafness. She has both hearing and deaf friends. Her best friend (at 14) is a hearing girl who does not cue, yet Amity and she understand each other very well, because Cued Speech has made her into a very good lipreader. Many deaf children are socially isolated, but not Amity. Through Cued Speech and spoken language communication Amity has acquired confidence and poise, and she enjoys looking forward to a life to which her statement "I can do anything I want to" applies.

Update January 1, 1991
by Jeanie Leitner

Amity decided during her junior year in high school that she wanted to have more interaction with hearing-impaired peers. In our search for a school placement for her we discovered that if she tested high enough she could be granted early admission to the National Technical Institute for the Deaf. She met entrance requirements and began her freshman year of college with the understanding that she would take two classes to complete her high school requirements. She is taking these classes in the Rochester Institute of Technology.

Amity's experience has been exciting and unique. She is in the process of organizing a Cued Speech club! Her friends are persons who use a variety of methodologies. She says she feels most comfortable with "oral" hearing-impaired students. She loves signs when they are used in the word order of English and is confused and frustrated by ASL. (*That may pass as she learns more ASL.*) She prefers not to ask for a Cued Speech interpreter since she enjoys the interaction with a signing teacher without receiving the message through someone else.

We feel that Amity's language has bloomed, and her speech has improved in these last five months. Speech improvement is perhaps due to the necessity of making herself understood by her "oral" hearing-impaired friends. Language growth may be due to spontaneous interaction with so many people.

When we started Cued Speech we hoped it would give her language to open the world of books to her (she hates to read!). We also hoped that it would give her intelligible speech, but it took more than Cued Speech for that. What we did get was a simple, accurate way to communicate with our child. She is a part of every conversation we are involved in. She has been provided with the social interaction within the family that so many deaf children miss.

As of May, 1991, Amity's scores on the Stanford Achievement Test were as follows: Math concepts, grade 8.7; Math computation, grade 12.9; Math application, grade 8.0; Language, grade 8.1; Reading comprehension, grade 6.1. Amity has done extremely well, even in reading, considering her combination of a very late start in exposure to Cued Speech and her additional physical problems. Her personal observations begin on page 612.

Chapter 25
Observations by Deaf Young People

The purpose of this chapter is to allow parents and teachers to "get inside" the minds of deaf young people who are growing up with Cued Speech, to learn about their feelings and attitudes, and to see the kinds of language they use in expressing themselves.

These letters and observations from profoundly deaf children and young people are *unedited,* except as noted in two specific cases, and as may be possible in the portions of the items reprinted from *CS News.* The statements of some of them contain misconceptions and over-generalizations about sign language and about signing deaf people, and evidence of various biases. Please remember that you are reading *their* opinions, which you and/or we may not share. Some reveal deep understanding of and appreciation for deaf culture and deaf language; others do not.

Parents were asked not to edit the letters, and to verify that they did not. We have made no effort to select children whose writing samples are good, but have used everything that came in from our mailing list. Thus, the samples include many from late starters and children with other problems in addition to profound deafness. We rejected only one submission, from Spain, because the child had not received Cued Speech from either parent, and very little other exposure, so he could not be considered representative of the effects of Cued Speech. Also not included were three submitted from England that reached us after the manuscript had exceeded its permissible limit of 832 pages. The only criteria for inclusion were profound deafness and consistent exposure to Cued Speech in the home for at least half their lives. A few exceptions to the latter policy were made for children who started with CS very late.

Some of the statements of the older young people are very long. They are included in full because they give the reader an unparalleled opportunity to see into the thoughts and feelings of these very expressive young people who have grown up with Cued Speech.

Courtney Branscome
Charlotte, N.C.

Courtney Branscome, prelingually and profoundly deaf, was 4 years, 10 months old when she composed this Halloween story. She had received Cued Speech since the age of 18 months. We are indebted to *the parents, to the editor of **Our Kids Magazine**, and to the Alexander Graham Bell Association for the Deaf for permission to reprint this story, which appeared in the Spring, 1991 issue. Courtney's case history begins on page 353.*

One afternoon, while her mom took a nap, Courtney went to the office with her dad. Courtney wanted to "make a story." Her dad, Butch Branscome, told her the Halloween stamps they used to make a story before were all gone. Courtney was undeterred, so her dad suggested she make up a story. Courtney found paper and pen and asked her dad to write her story down. The following is Courtney's story, *word for word*, as she dictated it to her father.

"The Pumpkin Did Not Know Who She Was"
by Courtney Branscome

One day a little pumpkin lost her mother. So, she saw a ghost. She said, "Ghost, are you my mother?" "No, I am a ghost and you are a pumpkin."

Courtney Branscome

So, the baby pumpkin saw a skeleton. "Are you my mother?" The skeleton said, "No, I am a dead person."

So, the pumpkin saw a witch and said to the witch, "Are you my mother?" "No. I am a mean witch and I will put you in my black pot." So, the pumpkin got out, the witch did not see the pumpkin. Then the witch felt in the black pot. "I do not feel a pumpkin in my pot." The witch thought the pumpkin disappeared.

And so the pumpkin hopped and hopped to a spider. And said to the spider, "Are you my mother?" "No, I am a spider and I will eat you." So the pumpkin ran away to find her mother.

So the pumpkin hopped and hopped and saw a pumpkin. The baby pumpkin said, "Are you my mother?" and the pumpkin said, "Yes."

Daniel Cottam
Newtown, Essex, England

Daniel's deafness was diagnosed at 18 months, confirmed later as total. His exposure to Cued Speech from both parents began at 2 years, and he was understanding it very well at 3. Daniel began to match pictures and words soon after his third birthday, wrote legible words at 3 years, 4 months, and wrote his first short sentences a month later. He began writing stories at 5 years, 3 months and completed 60, varying in length from 85 words to 850, in the next six months. Almost all the characters in the stories are animals. In Daniel's case history his father describes some of the activities that may have contributed to his early reading and writing. His preoccupation with composing stories was so great that at age 6 years, 2 months he happily "made up" stories on an overhead projector for an audience of 75 at the International Congress on Education of the Deaf in Manchester, England, in October 1985. Daniel wrote the following story in January 1985, when he was 5, years 5 months old. It is unedited, though a few parenthetical notes are inserted for clarification. The punctuation is Daniel's. Mr. Cottam was kind enough to furnish photocopies of many of Daniel's originals as well as four of the published booklets of stories. Daniel's case history and photo are in Chapter 18, p. 356-362.

"Polly gives her Baby Puppy a Bath"
by Daniel Cottam (5 yr., 5 mo.)

One day Polly called her baby,"Barney," She pulled off the collar and threw him in the bath

It was deep. Polly put in his boat, his playmobil diver, his Pla(s)tic care-a-lot[1] It floated. A care bear was aboard. The care bears mum was in cooking the supper and his sister

Then the door swung open it was his sister She had no collar she liked baths

She had seen the pony sink then it came up again. Its hair was wet It was a Bubble-My-Little-Pony It was a bubble bath and she got in fast.

Barney splashed his dad and mum Polly crashed into the mirror Rover [*the father*] fell on the floor. Polly broke the mirror Rover made a hole in the floor But fell in the bath SPLOSH!

---

[1]trade name

Barney laughed "HA" at Rover under water His sister kicked him out

Barney threw the Wash-My-Little-Pony to his sister She caught it in her paws and took out the care bear and put it on its back and put it down to the bottom with his diver Then it came up again Barney put the pony back in the boat on the tub and put the care bear (*in?*) the care-a-lot for supper His mum got the care bear's supper and put it on the table and he ate it all up and he said nothing and his sister got him out and put the care bear with the pony and mum pulled out the plug but he jumped out with his sister and threw the blanket over his sister "Ow" she said but Barney won and put on his pyjamas and got in his cot and fell asleep.

His sister got in her bed with her sindy doll-dog and she switched off the light and fell asleep.

Next moring Christmas came They put up the Chriistmas tree Barney put the angel on the top

He used a chair to reach and put all the balls on

His sister put the lights on and put the plug in.

The lights came on Barney wrapped the parcels with his sister Lucy and put them by the tree Barney put the parcel on the floor.

The end

Note by Daniel Cottam (12)
June, 1992

I don't care about being deaf. I never want to hear. Deafness may be a blessing in some respects—I don't have to ruin "earsight" listening to those pop songs blaring out. But I also miss nicer sounds.

I'm not keen on modern times. I'd rather go back in time! Culture is the thing. Reading is an escape and so is writing.

I like making up games and swimming. I collect costumes and old clothing and love visiting museums and old houses.

When I grow up I'd like to be a costume expert and designer and maybe work at the Victoria and Albert Museum.

Esther Rimer (7)
Greer, S.C.

This essay by Esther was awarded first place in her age group in the 1992 NCSA writing contest. Notice the freedom with which she writes because she is encouraged to spell according to sound whenever she needs to do so. Esther's case history begins on page 410.

WHALES
by Esther Rimer, 1992

Whales are mammals because they can breth air in a hole on their backs. The blue whale was the biggist of all the whales. It was biger than 30 elphants all in a straight line.

When a baby whale is near a shark the mother whale will be waching the shark. She will call other whales and they will swim around the shark soon he will be all mestup.

The killer whale can attake seals and other whales. They are black and white.

A long time a go pepeol killed whales because they wanted oil and meat to eat.

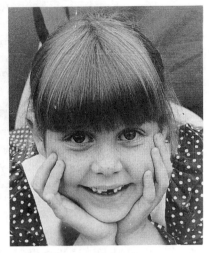

Esther Rimer

Hump back whales can jump backwards and they can make the strangist sounds. In the winter whales swim to warm waters.

Scott Johndrow (8)
Ellington, Conn., 1982

Hi Dr. Cornett,

I am doing good in school and I got all A's in my report card! I go home at 4:00 because we have Drama Club. I am singing for the play. I have a interpreter named Mrs. Latino, and she is doing good. I got a new hampter and his name is Ralph. My friend Teddy likes to call me a lot on the TTY. We went to Vermont to ski with the Schwartz. In Vermont I was in a race. Last weekend we went to Boston for my grandmother and grandfather's anniversary.

I like Cued Speech because I

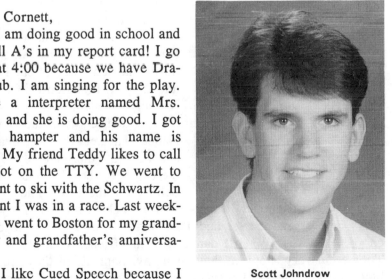

Scott Johndrow

like to see my friends and I like to see you too. My teacher's name is Mr. Wajda.

I am a newspaper reporter for Quaddington and I brought newspaper so you can read it. You can call me on the TTY. Ok Bye,

Love,　　　Scott Johndrow

For Scott's case history see page 458. A recent (1992) letter from him informs us that he is entering his senior year in high school, after being on the honor roll four times successively last year, and being captain of the golf team. He plans to become an architect.

Alina Engelman (9)
Brooklyn, N,Y., 1992

My name is Alina. I'm 9 years old and I'm starting 4th grade in P.S. 154. In class I have a cued speech interpreter, Mrs. Clemente. I'm the only deaf kid in my class which is hard but I have lots of friends. Sometimes the kids get frustrated and leave me out of stuff like games, lunch partners, etc....This only happens 25% of the time. This one kid named Jackie was especially mean. She tried to take away my friend Noel. Noel told me that she hates Jackie because she's mean and bossy and she stinks!

Alina Engelman

Sometimes Mrs. Clemente has to go to the bathroom or something and I try to make out what the teacher's saying. I make out about 92% what she's saying. I sometimes get frustrated when Mrs. Clemente is two slow or when she is busy and I'm trying to get her attention. It doesn't happen verry often. I do well and I got a high score in city-wide reading and math.

I dance with the American Dance Theater for the deaf. I've spent 3 years there already. The kids there go to St. Francis De Sales School for the deaf. They grew up with sign language. St. Francis has only 4 kids a class. They read 2 years below grade level and they write incomplete sentences. I'd choose P.S. 154. When I dance with my friends I have lots of fun. They seem very happy in their own environment but they are not too lucky in other ways. I went to a deaf summer camp (sleepaway) 2 times. Aulthough I know sign language, it's not perfect.

My speech therapist Julie Fischer had a baby! He is 2 months now. While I was in Germany for 1 month, I promised to do speech and auditory training there every morning, and when I come back, I will get a girl talk game and I will get to help Julie with her baby.

According to the New York City Board of Education, in May, 1991 Alina ranked at the 99+ percentile in reading among a "nationally representative group of 3rd grade students," and at the 98th percentile in math on the Metropolitan Achievement Test {MAT}. Her case history is in Chapter 20. Alina's entry in the NCSA 1992 writing contest earned the first award for her age group. Case history, p. 362.

Danny Lee (9)

Danny is a fifth grade student in the Gifted and Talented Education Program in Calgary, Alberta, Canada. The following is an article he wrote in connection with his application for the G.A.T.E. Program in March 1991, when he was 9 years, 3 months old. According to his mother, Danny typed it himself on an IBM PC. She explained that his British spelling of several words was due to the fact that he had a British teacher.

I am a grade 4 student at Stanley Jones School. I like to do science experiments and make things at school. Working on computers is one of my favourite activities. I don't like doing plays. I am good at computer games, reading, writing stories, math and science experiments. At home I like to play Nintendo and computer games. We have 2 computers at home. One is an Apple IIGS which I have been using since I was 4 years old. Another is an IBM That we bought several months ago. I know how to use the IBM a little bit, but not as well as I know my Apple IIGS.

I love reading at home. I like reading mystery books. Lately I have been reading Hardy Boys books. I can finish a 150 page book in one hour and half.

I like watching good programs on T.V. sometimes. My favourites are movies and cartoons with closed caption. My mom used to sit in front of the T.V. and interpret programs for me. But now we have closed caption decoders. I can read the English subtitles on the screen. The words are printed on the screen as they are said. But you have to read fast, otherwise the words will disappear. I watch News too with closed caption so that I know what is happening in the world.

I am good at fixing things. If David has a toy that doesn't work I would try to fix it. Mostly I can fix it. Sometimes I can't.

Sometimes I like to play chess and checkers. Dad taught me how to play chess when I was 7. Then I learned more from reading "Bobby

Fischer Teaches Chess." He is the best chess player in the world. My classmate and friend Daniel Taught me how to play checkers when I was in school. But I don't see much of him anymore.

Danny Lee

I also enjoy cooking. On the weekends I can cook scrambled eggs on my own. I love lasagna. but I don't know how to make lasagna from scratch.

I started clay classes when I was 5 & a half years old at the Village Square Leisure Centre. I enjoy the class very much and I took them every year. I hope I can take the clay classes this summer. I made lots of things like a mask, a bowl, a dinosaur and more. I also took art classes. In a sculpture class, I made a huge clam with a huge pearl in it.

I took my first lesson on horseback riding when I was 6 years old. I can make the horse jump small jumps. Every summer I usually take horse back riding lessons.

I *stated* taking skiing lessons about two years ago. I am doing very well now. I can make jumps about 2 or 3 feet high.

The following is a poem Danny wrote in March 1992, at the age of 10 years, 3 months. Math and science are his major interests.

"What Is Red"
by Danny Lee

Red is an apple
a rose
a shirt

Red is the blood
that the heart pumps fast

Red is the colour of the rising sun
that awakens the sky

Red is a cherry from a tree
A raspberry
Red is the nose of a

drunken man

Red is the colour of a
Lady bug shell
the sound of an alert
Red is many things.

In response to our request for his observations on life, family, school, and friends, Danny wrote as follows, at age 10 years, 4 months.

I feel good about my life because if I can hear, I could do more things and make things easier. Now I can understand what is going on. But a few years ago when we bought the van, at that time I just became deaf and had not started learning cued speech or sign language, so I didn't even know we bought the van although I rode it home!

My school is challenging but there is one thing I don't like. The teachers pound giant assignments at the same time and same due date. But I managed to survive!

At school I don't really have many friends. I only have two or three. My best friend is Daniel, a kid from the hearing impaired oral program from my old school. I don't really see him much anymore.

I like reading interesting topics, and I go to the school library after lunch to read a novel most of the time.

The cued speech is very helpful to my life. It allows me to communicate with my mom if my implant is off or the battery is dead. For us we seem to be using a mixture of cued speech and sign language. It's very useful because at times when I do not wear my implant, such as bedtime, and when I wake up in the morning, I can still talk to her. Other people with deaf children always use cued speech or sign language because they may not be able to afford the total cost of the cochlear implant and operation, US $25,000, or they may be scared because they are going to drill a hole in their child's head during the operation.

The cochlear implant has helped me a lot, mostly to hear and understand things. I think I am really lucky to have it.

Danny's case history, and also his specific opinions on his cochlear implant, are given in Chapter 14, p. 222.

Brett Fasold (10)
Raymond, Maine, 1992

Hello, deaf kids and parents, this is Brett Fasold. I'm supposed to write a story to tell you what it's like to be deaf, so here's all I know about growing up deaf, about friends, school, family and what I think about the future for deaf kids.

Brett Fasold

I think it was a little tough growing up because it was hard to know what your parents or friends were saying. I got used to it later, but I'll tell you it was hard to do. If you go to a therapist or anyone to help you improve your speech, I think that is good. I go to one, too. Her name is Suzzanne Helms. If you live in Portland or around it, you might want to go to her. She teaches me with games, for example before I move, she makes me say a rod perfectly. She gives homework, too. If I don't do it, she gives me drill. That means she gets out a box, then takes out some cards, and I have to say what is on it perfectly! Before my lessons are over, my mouth hurts! It is hard to learn how to do Sign Language, Cued Speech, or lip-reading, But if you practice alot and test it with your parents or friends, you will get it and become a master at it. I study Cued Speech, and I'm learning to read lips.

Now about friends, I know about that because I have tons and tons of friends and they are good to me. some of my friends tell me that some other people tease me about my deafness, but I just ignore it and just go on with what I am doing. I don't try to get even with them, or it might make it worse. You should be glad that you have friends because they will help you with your speech and tell you what the person is saying if you have trouble understanding. If you have a Cued Speech or Sign Language Club, I think that is great because your friends can join and learn how to sign or cue and it will be easier for you to understand.

Now, about school, if you go to a public school you must have an interpreter so you can know what the teacher is saying. I have one too. Her name is Kathy Hawkes. If you go to a Deaf school, there is not much I can tell you about that. I have never been to one. I did go to one when I was about 2 or 3 years old but I can't remember it. (the deaf school that I went is called Baxter School for the Deaf.) Do you absolutely love to read? I do. I think it's fun, plus it can help you with your education!

You must be lucky to have a family because they care fore you and will help you with your deafness. I think parents are a micracle for god. I think parents are fun, helpful, but sometimes get a little mad each day (I'm describing my mom! But this is true about all moms too, even dads.)

In the future, I hope scientists will find a way to help deaf kids or parents, like the Colear implant. (I hope this spelling is right) I hope the world will become more and more easier for deaf kids or parents.

SEE YA! (s) Brett Fasold

For Brett's case history, see p. 412.

Michael Poore (10)
Arlington, Tex., 1991

This letter was typed word-for-word by Michael's mother because he was reluctant to write, but willing to dictate. Thus, spelling and punctuation are not representative, though language is. Michael's case history starts on p. 220, with additional items on 471 and 513.

I'm having a good time in school and making lots of new friends. I have some sign language friends and more hearing friends. I have a hearing friend who's been my friend for about two years. He likes what I like. He likes to talk about shoes. He likes to talk about Michael Jordan and Magic Johnson.

I love baseball and basketball. I like to go see the Texas Rangers play.

I used to play soccer when I was six years old. I like to ride my bike and play outside alot. I like to read books; kind of. I like to read poems. I like to read adventure books. I like to read baseball card price guides to see how much the baseball cards are worth.

I like to watch "Tale Spin" on t.v. with the closed captioned machine. I like to play with Legos a lot.

I have a dog named Sugar. She likes to play ball with me and tug of war. I have a hamster named Testorosoa. I like Michael Jordan a whole lot.

The following story by Michael is submitted by his speech/language therapist, Priscilla Michalk, who comments in detail in Chapter 14 on the effects of his cochlear implant on his speech and the effects of Cued Speech on his ability to write creatively and imaginatively. Since the story was dictated to her, spelling and punctuation are not Michael's except where it is altered to show pronunciation, e.g., marshmellows.

"My Camping Trip"
by Michael Poore (10)

I went to the Central Park Camping lodge and I took my bike and my knife. I took my beebee gun along. My dad and my dog went too. We shot bullet guns and went in a boat. Then we roasted marshmellows over the fire. I would love to go again, of course.

Michael Poore

We left at five in the morning and stayed for five weeks. We got there by car because we had to take food, a grill and a T.V.—we used a trailer. We went hunting and caught a deer, then we went mountain climbing and that was my favorite part of the trip. the mountain was 2,000 feet high. We had two big adventures on our trip. The first was when we were roasting marshmellows. A grizzly bear came and tried to eat the marshmellows. My dad shot him and he still kept trying to get to my dad who shot him again and again. Then the bear's skin fell off and it was really a robot. We took the skin and made a rug on the floor. We made the robot to clean my room, do my homework, go to school for me and make Lego's for me.

Five days later when we were sleeping (we were camping on the beach) my dad woke up and saw something faster and faster spinning in the water. My dad got up and yelled, "Oh my gosh, oh my gosh!" Then we got in our racing boat that went 500 mph with 4000 horse-power. My dad put the throttle all the way down, very fast and then we went up very high. My dad almost flipped over and when we went away from the hurricane to go to California, our boat ran out of gas. The hurricane was still after us. We took the cord off and put it in the other gas tank and Dad pulled the throttle all the way down again. Then we were on the way to California again. The hurricane was still after us. We ran out of gas again but my dad found extra gas in the glove box—about 200 gallons. Then while we were going, we hit a big wave and the water came in. We kept going because if you go fast the water dries up. I was next to my dad and said "Whoa" because we were going so fast. When we got to California the hurricane was still there so we had to go all the way back to Texas! When we got back home we were so tired from the sea we went right in and told mom about our adventure. *Michael's case history begins on page 471.*

Sinead Clements (10)
Rochester, Minn., 1992

I want to talk to you about myself. I play baseball soccer and many other sports. You know I think I am the only Cued Speech kid in 4th grade. Will you please talk about sign language kids not reading books and all that. I play on the computer that's why I learn so much. we got two TTY (or TDD) it was very expensive to get them. I go to Baniber Valley Elementary School and Im in Mr. Farnhams class. My faforets are Math, D.o.2., Break, art, Phy ed (not really) reading books.
I have a tutor her name is Kim Reed. I gess you know her. I have more to

Sinead Clements

say. you know That I have two things That will help me, a bracelet and a necklas they say medic alert. Oh I like your letter thanks a lot.

Sinead Clements. *Sinead's case history and medical information are in Chapter 24. In a second letter (June 1992) she volunteered:*
I read 128 books during the school year, pretty amazing isn't it? The books I like reading are about Abraham Lincoln and some stories about "John Fitzgerald Kennedy America's 35th President" and the largest book I read was "Swiss Family Robinson" the book is about 400 pages long and I was only in third grade when I read it! I have four pets. The oldest of them is Juno, a mongrel dog, who is 12, Faline, a calico cat, who is 9, and Toffie and Honey, pupoies that are one year old. (Toffie and Honey are sisters born on April 1, 1991.) *Case hist. p.556.*

Benjamin Lachman (11)
Morton Grove, Ill., Sept. 2, 1992

Hi, my name is Benjamin Lachman. I am a deaf boy with a hearing device called a cochlear implant. It is kind of better than a hearing aid for me, since a regular hearing aid doesn't help me. With the implant I can hear soft sounds like "s" and "sh." I really like the speech processor.

I used to go to the Alexander Graham Bell elementary school, but now I go to the private school for Jewish kids. Only my friends from Alexander Graham Bell elementary school know cued speech, but some of the kids in the private school want to learn cued speech. I am doing very well in classes because they let me have a cued speech interpreter who cues in both English and Hebrew for me. This is my third year in this School, Solomon Schecter, which is fourth grade.

Benjamin Lachman

I use cued speech because it teaches you real English and also helps you learn to lipread, which is when the people's lips make shapes and (*you*) can read them. Cued speech is made up of eight hand shapes, not thousands of hand signs like sign language. It has also made me a very good reader. I read hundreds of books each year. I read eighth and ninth grade books like 20,000 Leagues Under the Sea by Jules Verne. This book is 236 pages long. I read other things like that.

I am also able to do things that the hearing kids in my class do, like reading Torah. The Torah is a religious book of our religion. It has five books all put into a big scroll written in Hebrew.

I also participate with a new system called the relay system to talk to people. You call this special phone number and then someone asks you who you want to talk (*to*), you give them your phone number and, and the person you want to call's phone number and they call that person and you type things on something called a TTY and the person who tells the person what you want to say has a TTY also, and the person you type to will call the person you want to talk to.

I have many friends. Some of them are because of my processor. When they see the magnet on my head they wonder what it is, and they ask me what it is, and I tell them what it is, and that's how I meet some of my new friends. So far all the fourth graders and most of the second third and fifth graders know about me.

During the summer of 1991 I joined the Little League team called the White Sox, and we won every game except one. We also won the championship. I really liked it, everyone on the team made friends with me very quickly, especially the coach's sons.

I get speech lessons once a week. I get them to improve my talking and listening. The speech teacher's name is Nancy, or I have Ann Bleuer sometimes. Ann have been teaching me a few card games lately. The last card game I learned helped improve my math. She's also teaching me card games to improve my talking and listening. Sometimes she covers her mouth and says something, but I can't see her, and I'm supposed to try to listen to what she says and understand it or to recognize it using the implant.

We have two dogs, one is a Sheltie, one is a Peek-a-boo. The sheltie's name is Trixie, and the peek-a-boo's name is Spindle. We have two dogs because we have a family that has a history of dogs, and also because we like animals. When I was in second grade we had two gerbils, and when I was in third grade they both died. Every year we get some goldfish from a festival we go to. But every year after a week they usually die unless they are special goldfish. *Case hist., p. 216.*

Julie Lewis (11)
Manassas, Va., Sept. 1991

Its Julie Lewis. I cue. I met you at the Cued Speech Picnic in the year of 1986. you wrote or typed me a letter. I'm just writing to you how much I really like Cued Speech. Its the main principal of my life. According to my opinion, Cued Speech is the best!! I absutley loathe sign language it takes forever to learn and I'm glad you invented CS.

Do you still have the picture of the Cued Speech Picnic? Well I'm right next to you I have Brown hair, Brown eyes. and know what I still love to Read. I have over 300 books maybe more. I heard you have a new invention. Its the glasses. It sounds neat! can you send some more information about it?? I know Cued Speech doesn't make me smarter but I'm smart thats what other people say not me!! I got 6 Honer Rolls for Straight A's and B's. School starts on Tuesday the 3rd. Well I am having a cued speech club at my school. I'm the only deaf girl at my school.

Julie Lewis

its pretty neat. Me and my mom will teach the hearing people how to cue. I bet you are pleased also cued speech is getting more popular. I bet you'll be marked down in history for inventing cued speech! Forethermore I gotta GO! your friend Julie Lewis PS Please, please write back!! Sorry so messy!!

Our reply to Julie suggested that she not think bad things about sign language, because it's a very good language and she may change her mind when she learns more about it.

We wrote to several deaf youngsters in France, Belgium, and Spain in order to elicit their feelings and observations. All are prelingually and profoundly deaf. Their handwritten letters, unedited, are relatively free of errors in spelling and punctions, which do not carry over in translation. Except as noted, translations are by Cornett.

Toby Burton (12)
Brussels, Belgium, 1992

Toby is bilingual in English and French (with CS). He also uses Signed French and Signed English, both with Belgian signs. His letter was written in English, though his schooling has been in French.

I'm Toby Burton. I am 12 years old. I have two brothers (Jamie 13, Emlyn 8) and a sister (10). We communicate very well, no poblembes.

Toby Burton

If i'm at home, I feel more English. If i'm at school I feel more Belgian. I'm very glad that I know 2 languages.

I often read a book of stories, French and English. If I'm not at school, I go swimming, going to a friend's house, going to the cinema, go for a ride on my mountain bike. I have a club: "hockey". I like listen to the musique (New Kids on the Block, Michael Jackson).

My best friend is Emmanuel. I liked to play with him (chesse, ride on bike, cinema, etc). I have also some hearing friends (par ex: at the hockey club) they are very nice to me.

I like very much to go to a deaf school because the teachers signe to us (or LPC)[2] and there is a load of deaf people there! I also like going to the holidays. I love water-skiing, windsurfing, water sports, riding on my mountain bike. The beste holidays I ever had is the last year: going to the "Maldives islands" for visit my half-brother.

I want to be a journalist when I leave school and live in a hot cuntrey. Be a famous player of hockey.

Now I feel happy to be deaf! I do not belive that "Deaf is a hadicape. I belive that I'm a normal children. *Case history, p. 527.*

Guénolé Croyere (12)
Tours, France, 1992
translated from French

My name is Guénolé Croyere. I am twelve and a half years old. I have been profoundly deaf since I was 18 months old. My parents cue very, very well. I like very much having deaf chums and hearing chums. I live at Tours in France. That is an hour by T.G.V. (*Très Grande Vitesse, the high speed train*) from Paris.

I have a brother named Jérémie. He is nine years old. He cues but not very well. But later he will cue well like my parents. My sister is named Marine. She is four and a half years old. My school is called Saint-Martin. There is a cuer in the school. I am in the sixth grade (Lisbonne). I understand very well what anyone says, except for people that I don't know, or young children. I speak very well because I go a lot to the speech therapist and the teacher. I like to listen to music. I enjoy playing football (rugby). I like playing with the computer and I watch

Guénolé Croyere

the American series and also the news, on television. I know Stasie (*Jones*). She came to a Cued Speech workshop. That was a long time ago, pretty near two years.

BONNE ANNEE! (*a good year!*)
Guénolé

---

[2]LPC, or Language Parlé Complété, means Cued Speech.

Colin Ziebell (12)
Rochester, Minn., 1992

Colin Ziebell

Dear Dr. Cornett,

Well, to start, I'm Colin Ziebell and twelve years old, and I go to Lincoln-Mann elementary school. I'm in 6th grade and will be going to Willow Creek Jr. High School. I'm the only deaf person at Mann.

I have 2 parents, a brother, a sister, three cats and a dog. I became deaf from menagatis when I was almost 2 years old. I first used sign but around when I was 7 is used cues speech. My brother and sister are learning cued and My mom is a transliterator. Some of my friends can cue, some can fingerspell, some just talk, a few know sign. school's pretty ok.

I have a tdd, a device that lets you know when the phone is ringing, 2 telecaptioners. I have a tdd at school too.

Sincerely, Colin Ziebell *For Colin's case history, see p. 312.*

Carlos Cervantes Gómez (13)
Cartagena, Spain, 1992
translated from Spanish

Family of Carlos Cervantes Gómez

I am Carlos Luis Cervantes Gomez. I am thirteen years old and was born deaf, I hear nothing. When I was seven years old I learned Cued Speech with Cori (diminutive for Corina Ruis, the directress) at APANDA). My parents and my brother Luis definitely know Cued

Speech. My deaf friends definitely know Cued Speech.

My friends and I go to a school named "MARE NOSTRUM", it is hearing but there are no deaf (*He means the school is not specifically for the deaf*). I attend the seventh (grade) of EGB (Educación General Básica -Primaria-). Also I play football on a Cartagena team. In two years I want to am going to the United States to study in a school for the deaf (*He is referring to Gallaudet, where he wants to study*), because there are many sports: boxing, motor-cycling, wrestling, basketball etc. Virgilio (*his friend*) enjoys basketball, swimming, wrestling. In the school the teachers do not know Cued Speech and I understand a little of what they say. I don't want the teacher to know Cued Speech, in APANDA yes. (*He means that he wants the hearing school to be oral, but at APANDA he likes to have Cued Speech.*)

I don't like for the hearing to speak with Cued Speech. *Apparently in the hearing school he doesn't want to call attention to the fact that he is deaf.* Carlos' father is the president of A.P.A.N.D.A., the Association of Parents of Children with Auditory Deficiencies.

Louis Weiss (13)
Kensington, Md., 1992

My name is Louis Weiss. I am 13. I go to Wood Mid Level School. I have cued since I was three. I am a mainstreamed kid. I became deaf when I was 10 months old by meningitis. I have interpreters who cue. I make all A's sometimes but no C's.

Louis Weiss

Cued speech is better than sign language. It keeps my English tip top and lets me take Spanish. I love reading.

I got an implant when I was three. It works 50x times more natural sound than regular hearing aids. I enjoy sound. Not music. Plane sounds and violent sounds are my favorite. I feel independent. I love to collect Schabak airplanes and flying. I really want to fly for Airlines like Trans World.

I am like a person no different from hearing except I have trouble understanding old people. I have some deaf friends, one hard of hearing friend and hearing friends. I speak oral and cue sometimes to them. I get arthritis if I sign for more than a minute. *See p. 231.*. *See p. 231..*

Sèbastien Jung (14)
Heerlishheim, Belg., 1992
(translated from French)

Sèbastien Jung

You asked me to speak of my life; I find that a little difficult. It appears that I made your acquaintance at Salies de Béarn when I was three years old (*in 1980*). I am actually fourteen years old. I live in a little Alsacian village. I have two sisters who are twelve and ten.

Within the family I have never had any problem making myself understood. My mother has cued for a long time; but now I ask her not to cue because I am accustomed to reading the lips.

I went to primary school in my village and now after the sixth level am in a collège (*higher school*) ten kilometers from my home (a school for hearing students). I am in the third level and have three good chums in my class; they have taken quickly the habit of speaking facing me.

Shilpa Hanumantha (14)
Springfield, Va., 1991

Shilpa is prelingually, profoundly deaf. She came to the United States from India at the age of eight years. Use of Cued Speech with her began about a year later, at age nine. She did not show her parents the letter reproduced below, which she wrote on a computer.

Even though the letter is free from both spelling and typographical errors, Schilpa says she did not use a spell-check program. The letter is in response to a request to tell about herself and her feelings about growing up deaf.

Hello! How are you doing? I would be very glad to give you some help in any way I can. But first thing, let me know when the book will be finished because I would like to have a chance to read it.

Thank you.

I really don't remember that much about how to learn to cue when I was eight years old. But I'll give you most of the information I can remember.

I was really scared and nervous when I had to leave my hometown to U.S.A. I spoke a little bit of Hindi and Tamil (regional language) by that time. I knew some of English. My parents say I only knew about 15 words in Tamil, not more than five in Hindi, and 50 to 100 in English. It was really hard for me to communicate with kids of my age at Camelot Elementary School which is my very first school in U.S.A. I learnt some English words slowly each day and did speech therapies at home and school to improve my voice and English. It was really frustrating.

When my parents first learned about the Cued Speech Program, they decided to give it a try by putting me in it at Beech Tree Elementary School. Ms. Connie Rayhill, the then Principal of Camelot (Speech & Hearing) was so helpful and encouraging me to go into this programme where I can do much better and improve a lot. I owe a lot to her. I was more scared to move to another school because I really enjoyed working with my teachers from Camelot who were very nice and I didn't want to leave them.

Shilpa Hanumantha

I was introduced to the Cued Speech staff viz., Ms. Kathy Lovette and I was so stubborn because I never talked to her but only to my parents. When I was left under the care of my teacher, Ms. Rolader, I was so confused and scared because I didn't understand what she was saying with the strange movements of her right hand. The other deaf kids who cued to me were very patient with me. I learned all the movements slowly each day and Ms. Rolader, would make me to cue to the words which she wrote on a card.

Mrs. Rolader had to leave the program and I missed her terribly because I was developing friendship with her. Ms. Kathy Lovette, known as Mrs. Roed, came and took up where Mrs. Rolader left off. She was very tough but nice and would make me to cue all the words which she wrote on the cards. She will always give me a prize for it which was why I would work hard. I learned all the subjects and slowly made friends with the deaf kids. After one or two years, I was in some mainstream classes which gave me a chance to become friends with hearing kids. It took time to do it. I was always a quick learner and wanting to learn some more. I almost knew every cue and most of English by that time.

When I was in 5th grade, I was mainstreamed for most of the subjects except one. I was learning a lot everyday and became very smart.

So now, I've come all the way through to 8th grade and I'm very anxious to go to high school next year.

I feel very happy now and I feel like one of the hearing kids. My hearing loss doesn't bother me now because I have improved a lot on my speech this year and most of the people understands what I am saying.

I like to learn new things in school but since the subjects are becoming hard, I hate classes but not my friends! I always come through with the classes with and "A" or a "B" on my report card and I sometimes think that the school is not that bad!

I am learning sign language now to use it with deaf kids who doesn't know cued speech. I also use it with hearing kids. The hearing kids are always asking me to show them how to cue or sign some words. The deaf kids also want to learn how to cue from me.

I absolutely love to read more than anything in the world! Some people tease me that I'm a bookworm which I am! (Grin!) I always check out 15 or more books at the public library each week. I almost finish one or two books each day. I never spent a day without reading a book! I read all kinds of books and I have a habit that I never leave my home unless I have book with me! You better believe it or not!

I also would like to say something. I had some interest in Indian style of dancing called "Bharata Natyam" for a long time so I decided to join it. This is my 3 and half year of dancing and I have performed on the stage before. It's a challenge for me because I have to listen to the rhythm and beats of the music very hard in order to get along on the dancing. I've done so well so far. I would like to invite you and your wife to a performance to be held on May 25th wherein my sister, Smitha and self will be there. I will send you an invitation and please do come. Mrs. Roed and her husband had a chance to see my performance before. My sister is also into it and she's hard of hearing. She helps me to follow the music which makes dancing easier for me. We're in different levels of dancing.

Boy, this is the longest letter I have ever written to you! I hope this letter of my past and present helps you. If you have any questions, please let me know.

Thanks for the compliment about my smartness. You are way off smarter than me and nicest too! (Grin!) I'm very happy that I got a chance to meet you and your wife! I hope I'll see you soon and I wish you all the best of luck on writing the book.

I owe my special thanks to Mrs. Roed because without her I wouldn't have come this far in my career.

With regards,   Sincerely yours,   Shilpa Hanumantha

Tate Tullier (14)
St. Amant, La., 1992

I am happy that Cued Speech was invented because if it wasn't, I would have never become a person like a hearing person. The only different thing between deaf and hearing people is that the deaf people can't hear and the hearing people can. Deaf people can do anything hearing people can do except hear.

Tate J. Tullier (14)

Look at me, I'm 14, I'm involved in six club activities. I'm in the 8th grade, reporter for two clubs. I'm in 4-H, Jr. Deputy, Art Club, Science Club, Journalism, and the basketball manger. I won 2nd place on my science fair project at my school and won 1st place at the Parish science fair. I go to Amant Middle School. I love the school I go to because they have a lot of friendly people there. Sometimes there are very rude people who think they can say or do whatever they want to me, but I can talk pretty good and I can stand up for myself and tell them a piece of my mind! I have lots and lots of friends. I'm the type of person who hangs out with a different group every day. I have this particular friend, Lilli Black, who is patient with me and tells me what is going on whenever I don't know. She's a very nice friend. My teachers are very nice and patient with me. I love them but hate them when they say boring lectures to us! HA - HA!

I pay attention to my interpreter most of the time. I also invented a speaking method with Cued Speech to talk to my friends in class. It is alot of fun at my school. I love my parents more than you can imagine. They are the most wonderful people in my life. I am so glad they decided to learn about Cued Speech. They are the smartest people I know. They have helped me through some rough times. I am so happy that closed caption T. V.'s were made because i absolutely love to watch T.V.! If there were no T.V.'s with closed caption on them, I would die! Also, I like the TDD, the telephone. I get called by other people before I get to call them! HA - HA!!! I am a big time reader. I love to read magazines and books. I am deaf and proud of it!

Love Ya, Tate Tullier   *Tate's entry in the NCSA 1992 writing contest earned an honorable mention.*

Rachel Wixey (15)
Wells, Somerset, England, June, 1992

I am a profoundly deaf, almost 16 year old girl. Sometimes I wish I was not deaf, because it has affected some parts of my life. For example, I need someone with me to do something with a stranger, like a job interview.

Rachel Wixey (15)

If I had to communicate with a stranger at first it would be difficult to start with, but it will gradually become easier and easier.

I have a sister called Sarah, who is over a year older than me. We get on well sometimes, but she can get fed up with me as I get in her way.

My dad is a very caring father and the best in the world. Sometimes when he tells me off about something, I disagree and even wish that I had a different father. At times, Dad can be very boring. If I had a holiday off school, sometimes my holiday is boring, because Dad either does not go out often, or he is busy doing something. Sarah is mostly out of the house, doing something. I sometimes wish that I was in her shoes, because I enjoy going out with friends.

I do not have a mother. Sometimes I wonder what life would have been like if my mother was alive, what she would have been like. I might have had a better life.

In the past, I used to go on holiday with my family quite often. Every holiday was enjoyable and we did some interesting things together, e.g. donkey rides, going to the sea-side. Nowadays we do not go on holiday together anymore.

I do not have many friends at home, in Wells. I go out with Sarah and her friends sometimes. She want me to try and make some new friends. It all started a few months ago and it takes a long while to make friends.

At school, I do not have many close friends. I have a close friend called Emma who us a year younger than me. We used to live opposite each other when we were young. She has moved to a village about 10 minutes away from my house. She has another close friend called Liz. They get along better than me, this is because of my deafness. I do not often go and visit Emma or Liz at home as they go to each others's houses often. They rarely invite me to see them at home. It makes me very angry. I find it very difficult to invite them to my house because I do not know what to do with them. I could tell that they were bored and nervous.

My friends who are the same age as me, are more difficult to get on. They belong in a group of friends. I used to be in the group a few years ago. I never got on well, because my friends spoke to each other all the way home and left me out. Sometimes I blame my deafness for making me feel left out by friends.

At school I find my work very difficult at times, but I work very hard and get very good grades for any subject. The work wears me out at the end of each day at school.

I went on work experience for a week at the accountants. I did not enjoy it, because I found it extremely difficult to communicate with the accountants. I did not understand what I had to do or why it had to be done. I had to add up figures most of the time, which was very boring. I decided not to become an accountant as a career.

When the letter arrived and I read it, I thought. "Oh, no! Not now!" It had come in the middle of my exams which ar GCSE'S. I did not have enough time to write an essay during my revision (*review*) study. I was, in fact, tired and under pressure about the letter having to be done very quickly. I wish that it did not come so very late. I would have felt much calmer if I had more time and my letter did not have to be received by Dr. Cornett by the 19th of June.

Born August 15, 1976, Rachel got a very good language foundation during 1979-1985, while she was attending the Royal School for the Deaf, Exeter, and received Cued Speech consistently both at home and at school. During middle school she received CS only at home. Since 1989 she has had Cued Speech only occasionally at home, and not at all at school. She has passed GCSE mathematics early, and is expected to obtain high grades in all subjects.

Rachel's entry in the NCSA 1992 writing contest was awarded first place in her age group.

Stasie Jones (15)
Meyreuil, France, 1989

For once I can write to you and be sure that you will recieve it. Elizabeth Cros will be giving you all my love. I met her a year ago at the Cued Speech camp (in France). She's a wonderful lady! She told me all about you this year. Oh I always remember the lovely times we had together making pop corn! You're so great. Praise the Lord that you have so many qualities .... Just because of you I can talk english and French. Now I'm beginning Russian! You will be shocked to hear that! It's already my fourth language with German. I made my big exam (*in German*), I'm so pleased.

Stasie Jones, with Toby (1989)

It has been a long time since we've seen each other! Next year, in March we're coming to the U.S.A. but maybe in Miami there is a lot of bad moments there so we're thinking of finding a good place. Anyway we'll always come by your house.

It's the time to try those cueing glasses!!! Please tell the people that I'm coming. I want to speak about France, there is so many things going on in France. I cant wait to have a speech at Gallaudet!

I'm now nearly 16 and school is going ok! Julien's in my class, he's doing very well. Mom right now is at home taking care of little Toby - Dad left yesterday for Canada, he must speeck in several churches, a kind of conference.

I'm in a restaurant with the Cros family before we go home and I profited to write to you! Give all my love to your wife! I love you both so much ... you're my "grandparents." Hope you can write back.

And please tell me wether you got my letter that I answered to yours. (You had several questions very difficult to respond!)

Next year I'll come and see you. I miss you very much! Rebecca wants me to go and study in Gallaudet but I must think before I do anything else.

Sorry for my writing I'm eating my meal at the same time! Lots of love in Jesus.   Love, Stasie. *Stasie's case history begins on p. 510. Her 1992 A.G. Bell convention presentation begins on p. 608.*

Josefa Sánchez Mompeán (15)
Cartagena, Spain, 1992
translated from Spanish

Hola! My name is Josefa Sánchez Mompeán, I am fifteen years old and I am deaf. I have two siblings: Toñi and Miguel and I live with my parents. My sister and I are in the second level FP (*Formación Profesional -Secondaria-*) and my brother is in the fourth EGB (*Educación General Básica*).

I enjoy La Palabra Complementada (*Cued Speech*) very much, and also my sister and my mother. My family helps me (in) many things so I learn everything and at the school the same. It would please me if the deaf would speak well and I would find out about everything. It would please me if the teachers would explain well and I would understand everything.

I would enjoy working with the Informática in APANDA (*the Association of Parents of Children with Auditory Deficiencies, the organization that has done most to promote Cued Speech in Spain. It operates a rehabilitation center, and La Informática is its upper division.*).

With my friends I go for a stroll, to the movies and sometimes to the record library and I enjoy myself. I remember some deaf persons who live outside of Cartagena and I would like to see them. In summer I go with my parents to the beach and I enjoy it very much and I like many kids who were on the beach. Often I was at the swimming

Josefa Sánchez Mompeán

pool with my uncles-aunts (*The word* **tios** *means uncles, uncle-aunt or uncles-aunts*). I do not remember you, anyhow I knew you when I was little at Navacerrada (*near Madrid*). My father works in FEVE (*on the railroad*). My mother is the mistress of the house and enjoys sewing clothes. My sister enjoys hearing music and reading books, my brother enjoys watching the cartoons (*on television*) and playing in the street and doesn't enjoy working. I enjoy watching the stories. Adios.

A letter from Antonia, Josefa's hearing sister, is on p. 275.

Noémi Gourhand (15)
Gers, France, 1992
(translated from French)

I am Noémi Gourhand, fifteen years old, and I live in France, in the Southwest (Gers). I was born the 8th September, 1976, full term, without problems. At the age of four or five months, my parents became aware of a striking detail. I was never disturbed by noise, no matter what it was.

Noémi Gourhand

It was then that there was a first auditory examination, not conclusive, at the age of nine months. Then at sixteen months they detected a profound deafness of the second degree, of viral origin, during the second month of my mother's pregnancy. There followed then an important orthophonic rehabilitation and the wearing of an auditory device.

When I was three years old, my parents became acquainted with Cued Speech, the aid to lipreading—very accurately used at home. I have never had its support at elementary school or the lycée (high school), but nevertheless it helped me a lot during the early years of my life, always accompanied by lipreading practice (to avoid dependence on the Cued Speech).

My parents have always considered me as a normal child, they had me taught in a private school with only hearing students. And also, I have achieved several championships in spelling, in 89 and 90! My parents have also had me participate in sporting activities; and also my teachers have not differentiated me from the other students: I have had then no right to favoritism, for example.

I lead a healthy, well rounded life with my two brothers and my sister (all hearing), of which I am the eldest. The life of the family unfolds normally, and just as at school there is no difference among my brothers, sister and me.

After that I went to high school, I did not have any problem of adjustment, and actually, I had countless friends, who always considered me as one of the group. But none of my friends know Cued Speech, they have always been interested, and actually have learned some words, but that has not become a habit.

I must confess that I have been very favored, I have had parents who were enormously occupied with me, but above all for a rigorous education, have permitted making of me a child like the others, despite the difference that separates me from them: my voice.

Actually, I am in second class (second year of lycée?), without increased maternal support, and last year, I passed my diploma successfully. I have pretty near twenty-five hours of work per week at the lycée, and I expect a "first scientific" for the next year. I would like to have a business related to horses, and eventually lucrative (money represents security...!)

Before leaving you, I would like however to drop a hint to parents of hearing-impaired children: "seek that the education that you will give to your hearing-impaired child makes him always take care that he will not be like the others. Make him feel the difference—without insisting too much, nevertheless otherwise that could degenerate into a real psychological problem.

This is the fruit of my own experience: I have been so much identified as a normal child, so well that now I myself find it difficult to accept my difference, much less to show it.   Noémi

Gina Robers (15)
Cincinnati, Ohio, 1991

Hi This is Gina Robers, 15 years old, Colerain Middle School in 8th grade but next year I'm going Colerain High School so for three years I went first school of Colerain Middle. Sometimes I was scared that I don't know what to do. When I was little, I go Beading Hill Top School, it was far away my mom don't like it because it too far away so she wants me go Colerain Middle School so it was close to my house, my mom liked it better.

Last year was 7th grade, I have a lot of friends Molly, Kelly, Kristi, Jenny, Amanda, Mike, Ryan, David, John - a lot of them and

I was very happy that I have a lot of friends. Sometimes they asked me to go out with them so my mom was happy that I really have fun with them. Who my great friends? My great friends Molly, Kelly, Jenny, & Kristi forever!

Gina Robers

Last year I went played volley-ball teams, my coach was happy that I'm very good volleyball teams and she wants me to play agan for 8th grade so this year I play volleyball teams but I can't because they think I'm too old, my friends from volley-ball teams really (want) me to play with them. I told my mom and dad about that and my dad wrote a letter for a lady who checked the rules about the ages. She will tell us or call us to see if I can play or not so if she says yes then my friends will be very happy. But if it not then I can go and watch them to play a game. I hope I can go!

I always thinking about Molly (my friend) to come over to spend the night or go out to shopping or movie sometimes my mom said no but sometimes she changes her mind I like it.

This year I worked so hard and think, it was hard but not all the time. I have a lot of tests but not everydays some of it and a lot of homework but it was easy. When I have no school this weekends if I have homework I always do it on Sun.

When I will be 16 years old I was thinking about the jobs but I don't know yet. I think I will be vets or I don't know it was hard to think about it. I always thinking about to drive a car for next year sometimes I was little scared to learn to drive! My dad told me that he wants me to asks Trisha to see if she can teach me how to drive. And she said "I will help ya." So she wants me to drive this year a lot of pratices for next year. I asked her I said "When?" She said "Maybe Later or Soon." So I can't wait to drive a car! My mom and I went walking and talked about drive a car. I knew she will day "Gina be carefull ok." I knew she will. She alway say that to me and I always remember.

My mom and dad always cued speech for me but not all the time. I always read their lips and they knows that I know what they saying. Mrs. Robers (my aunt Kathy) she cued speech for my school to help me what my teachers saying but sometimes I read their lip, sometimes I don't understand what they talking about, that what Mrs. Robers help me what they say. When my friends talks to me if I don't understand then I will say "wait please say again I don't understand" they will say again because they talk too fast. I told them to slow down then I understand what they are saying. I always read their lip when I talk to my friend, sometimes they don't understand me, they afraid to tell me if they don't understand they think that I will be so mad no I won't. I never mad at anyone never I told them to please tell me if they don't understand. Molly (my friend) She always understand me a lot. She is very good understand me I'm really happy that she understand me. Molly asked me to teach her cued speech, she likes me to teach her. She always say "Oh that cool that was fun but it hard! I told her not is hard but to be pratices sometimes she forget what she did. So she tolds her friends about it, they likes me to teach them but sometimes I forget! They love me a lot and they always say "You are funny & crazy!" Well I'm funny! I'm happy that I write a letter for you & I don't remember that you were here when I was little well thank you very much.   Gina Robers *For letters from Gina's sisters, see p. 280.*

Cheri Bell (16)
Houston, Tex., 1991

Cheri Bell asked for the name of a deaf CS girl in France to whom she could write. Here are her letter and the reply, which she sent to me for translation. Cheri has other learning problems in addition to hearing impairment, but copes exceedingly well.

Dear Isabelle: Nov. 16, 1991
     My name is Cheri Bell, and I'm from Houston Texas. I lived in Louisiana a long time ago. Then I moved back to Houston Texas. I was born in Houston Texas and I'm deaf and I use Cued Speech like you. Someone from Louisiana taught me to cue when I was eight years old. I used to sign when I was a little baby and little girl both. There's nothing signing in my old school in Louisiana we had cueing there. I'm still learning how to sign at my school. I cue and sign both. Do you know how to sign very much? I know you are from France.
     I'm sixteen years old. I go to Langham Creek High School, and I have deaf friends at my school. I have a deaf boy friend named Larry, and he goes to my school. He never learned to cue. He signs like me. I'm on the swim team every day, and I love to swim a lot. I never have gone to France before, and I would like to go to France to visit deaf people. I would like to meet you and talk to you and be your

new friend from Houston.

Cheri Bell

I have a TTY like a phone. Do you have a TTY at home? You can call me some day. I will give you my phone number and my address. I will be happy that I will be your new friend. ~~from France.~~ Are you sixteen years old? I will send you a picture of me so you can see what I look like. Do you have a boy friend and do you have deaf friends from France? How do you feel about deaf(ness) and your family?

I have to go now. I'm not learning to drive a car yet. I will have to wait to learn how to drive a car. Do you know how to drive a car? Maybe next summer you can invite me to France with you and meet you next Summer maybe. Will you please write me a letter back?

Cheri Bell

Isabelle Spinetta (17)
Paris, France, 1992
(*translated from French*)

Dear Cheri,

My name is Isabelle Spinetta. I live in Paris in France. I am born deaf and I use Cued Speech. I have used it since I was a baby. Now I will soon be seventeen years old. I will be that old in February.

I go to a school for hearing children but there are 8 deaf children who use Cued Speech like me. I have hearing friends and deaf friends. Girls and boys.

Did you have a joyous Christmas and a good vacation? For my vacation I went on a skiing trip. I love to ski. I have been showered (lit., filled) with gifts!

If you wish you can telephone me because I hear well enough. I am very happy that your wrote me that letter. It will be good if you come to France - I dream of going to the United States. That country always makes me dream. Maybe during the summer vacations this summer I will go to visit the west coast of the United States with a group of young hearing people.

I have two brothers and one sister but they are not deaf. The four (of us) have a lot of fun together. But I have a lot of work.

Normally in two years I should finish my baccalaureate.[3] But I still don't know what sort of job comes later.

So long. I will be very happy if you can answer this letter.

For the story of Isabelle's earlier years, see p. 420.

Simon Roffé
Montgomery Village, Md., 1992

Hi! I'm Simon Roffé and I'm sixteen years old. I go to Watkins Mill High School and I'm in the tenth grade. I'm what you might call a Cue Kid. Cued Speech has been very important to me in life. I owe all mu success to Cued Speech. Being able to play baseball, being on the wrestling teams, and having a thriving social life—I owe all that to Cued Speech because it taught me how to talk, which is why I have good speech. It's not perfect, but it's better than average. I get very good grades in school. I have had around a 3.6 GPA since third grade, and I owe all that to Cued Speech. And also to my mother.

Now that I've told you about myself, I'll tell you about the advantages and disadvantages of Cued Speech. Let's start with the good things first. The good news is Cue kids tend to be more successful than sign language kids. For example, Cue kids learn how to talk because Cued Speech is phonetically based, not like sign language. In sign language they sign the word but they never really learn to say it. With Cued Speech they learn how to say it. For example, you can cue a foreign accent or a Boston accent or different kinds of accents, but you can't do that in sign language. For one reason only, it (Cued Speech) is phonetically based.

Also, another advantage is that you can communicate better. You will be able to express your feelings with more passion, more love. When you sign it, it doesn't mean anything.

You can learn a (foreign) language. For example, I learned Hebrew for my bar mitzvah, but I did not learn enough Hebrew to learn how to translate the Torah, which I regret. It's possible for deaf children to learn a (foreign) language, but I would avoid it, just like any other kid would.

I like to read a lot when I was in grade school, and I still do, but I don't read as much as I did before because I'm too busy keeping up

---

[3]The baccalaureate is the French grammar school academic diploma, considerably more advanced academically than the American high school diploma, and earned only through comprehensive examinations.

with the news and reading the newspaper. One day in elementary school I went to the library and I borrowed 68 books. I read all 68 books in a two week period. That was my record. I don't read that much anymore.

I feel it's important for the mother of a Cue Kid to cue to her child, because they will learn how to read good. Sign language kids do not. I admit it takes a while for a Cue family, especially a Cue mother to get used to Cued Speech. I admit I got off to a slow start, but I made very rapid progress as I was growing up.

Simon Roffé

Now that I've told you a few advantages out of dozens of them, I will tell you a few disadvantages. One is that Cued Speech is very new and not very many people know about it. A lot of people call it a different form of sign language. It's very hard to explain Cued Speech in a way you can understand, but I will do my best.

One thing about Cued Speech which I don't like is that I never learned to sign fluently. Since Cued Speech is not that popular, not very many people cue, so it's not that simple to make a lot of deaf friends. I was not that successful with the deaf group. I did not have very many deaf friends other than the friends I had that knew Cued Speech. Since I went to Watkins Mill High School, I am one of only two deaf people in the whole school. I have made a lot of friends, which I am proud to say. Because I can communicate with them with my voice. With sign language the kids don't learn to talk. They are afraid to use their voice. They don't have confidence in it, so they become practically ASL. ASL is a form of sign language where they are completely mute. They don't mouth. It's very difficult to understand them unless you are an expert at sign language.

Another disadvantage is a lot of sign language interpreters will be dead set against it, which is not a positive for Cued Speech. You will be very lucky if you find somebody who has an open mind around. You have to know where to look. The kind of person you are looking for is a person who knows sign language but has an open mind about Cued Speech. It's important to be able to compare them both and judge for yourself.

Personally, I noticed that sign language kids have a lot more trouble communicating and getting through life than Cue Kids. Because Cue Kids can talk better. Cue Kids have some resistance, but the problems are not as big as for sign language kids.

Also, there's one more thing I want to talk to you about. That is to get assistive devices for your child. For example, a captioning decoder. That is very very important for a kid growing up. It helps you watch TV and it also helps you read. Also, a hearing aid is very important too. It's very important because you can hear loud noises like someone calling you, the class laughing at a joke, the doorbell or telephone. The deaf child will be able to get excited about things.

Also, get a TTY. That helps to be able to talk on the phone to friends. It will be possible for you to get big phone bills, like hearing kids, maybe even bigger because it takes more time to use. They have relay systems to talk to hearing people who don't have a TTY.

I've told you about Cued Speech and some advantages and disadvantages it has and I would strongly advise you to choose Cued Speech if you want your kid to be successful in life financially and emotionally. But it's your choice. I hope you make the right one.

For Simon's full case history, see pp. 414, 418, and 558.

Joy Diffell (17)
Brooklyn Park, Minn.

Dear Dr. Cornett,   Dec. 30, 1991
Hello. It was a delight talking with you on the phone(TDD). In response to what you said, I'll try to include everything in this letter. Let's go back to the year of 1983 then work on the way up to 1991-92.

In 1983 I flew from Korea to an unknown place in America with absolutely no education. More, I emerged into a new world where there was so much help coming to me such as good education, learning to speak, learning to read, etc.

Let's compare me to a chick. The chick was trying to break out of its shell into its new world. like me trying to crawl out of my silent, dark, lonely world into a new, noisy world.

Once I was in my new place, there was chaos everywhere around me. I was confusing myself a lot and my head was spinning. My mind suddenly disappeared then was replaced when I saw like different surroundings, people, strange words and everything. Of course I still remember about my life in Korea.

In a couple of months my parents were trying to teach me everything like what love is, what words mean, how to pronounce words or who my family is. After all the hard work they did, I soon understood why I'm in America and not back in Korea. My parents assumed that I was ready for school. My mother accompanied me to a deaf school in Hartford for the first time. I enjoyed learning there and made friends easily. While I was there, I received the "Yes I Can" award from the Foundation For Exceptional Children. They had a ceremony in California which I was unable to attend so they mailed the plaque to me instead. On the plaque it says, "In recognition of outstanding accomplishment in independent living skills." I had lots of living skills to learn when I came from Korea because I had never seen so many things people here use every day, like toothbrushes, flush toilets, mixers, coffee makers, vacuum sweepers, etc.

Joy Diffell

In 1985 or 1986 Cued speech rang in my parents ears and were curious to know more about it. They asked a cheerful woman, Pam Beck, to teach us C.S. I couldn't believe myself for being a rascal and naughty (sometimes) in the presence of Pam each time she came over to help me to learn how to cue. I picked C.S. up quickly.

After learning C.S. my parents decided to transfer me to a public school in my hometown, Seymour (Conn.) near New Haven. It was pretty difficult at first because I had to know how to socialize with hearing students and teachers. I also had to pay attention in classes by focusing on interpreters. Soon I grew to understand and cooperate with people pretty good. In 4th grade my mother offered to teach a small group of my friends C.S. Some successfully picked it up and used it to communicate with me. She also taught a teacher, Mr. Koehler, C.S. He's like a special education teacher who helps students get ready for regular classes. We sometimes enjoyed joking each other with C.S.

By the time I finished 5th grade, my family moved and settled in Minnesota. We had to start over again looking for interpretters or teaching C.S. My mother taught a woman, Beverly Alseleben who has been my wonderful interpreter for 4 years. During my high school years she shares the job with two women, Jenny Smith and Marcia Van Vreed who are good neighbors. Mrs. Smith worked last year and is now on a training-job in St. Paul using sign language. I have a special education teacher, Mary Shue who has been helping me to reach my goals in improving vocab words, using right tenses, writing good language, etc. for 4 years. C.S. has been a great help to me in learning to pronounce words and writing good english. But I need more practice with writing good english.

These years have flown by quickly as I learned to lipread with the help of C.S. I can lipread ok even tough I have to ask people to repeat again. If I fail I ask them to scribble down what they want to say. It's not that bad. Some people say I'm a great lipreader but I don't think so to myself. Sure I can but not *very* well.

I have many good friends who are out of state who don't know much about Cued Speech. 3-4 of them know C.S. but I'm sure they forgot how to cue today. I don't mind that. About 4-5 of my friends are deaf who don't use Cued Speech. I have some friends at school who are pretty confused about the difference between C.S. and sign language. 2-3 of them know the difference because Mrs. Alseleben taught them C.S. last year. They don't remember very well because we didn't see each other much over the summer. I went camping in Northern Iowa for a few days then went on a family vacation in South Dakota. I worked at a city Hall all summer long.

I'm active in sports—played volleyball for school for 2 years, went out for track last year; played soccer in Seymour for 5 years. I like to swim, ride and sew for pleasure. I also like to read, go shopping, baby sitting and more. I work in church nurseries and have grown to love kids. I had a lot of experience with them since I volunteered to help in 4th or 5th grade.

In the future I want to be a successful teacher teaching at a deaf school. I want to work with little, cute kids. I may teach 1st or 2nd grade.

You just mentioned on the phone that you were hoping to meet me someday. I think we will because I'm probably going to college in Virginia. During my stay there, I'll drive over and meet you or whatever.

I guess I've written enough. I hope it's what you want to know. I'm looking forward to reading the book someday in the future.

Good luck on your book! Sincerely, Joy Diffell

See p. 320 for Joy's case history, p. 286 for her sister's thoughts.

Ariane Bazureau (17)
Paris, France, 1992
(*translated from French*)

I was born profoundly deaf the 31st of July 1974: I will soon be 18 years old. I have a little brother, three years younger, Adrien, born deaf, who also received your letter. I am going to respond for the two of us: we are very close. We have had a very individualized oral education from our parents and the speech therapists, who have become close friends.

We ourselves do not often cue, though my mother, who is also a speech therapist, has used Cued Speech with us from the age of three. We communicate essentially through lipreading, sometimes without sound, and we seldom cue, since we only learned to cue systematically rather late (for me, at fourteen). We have always been mainstreamed in a hearing environment.

Ariane Bazureau

It was only in 1988 that we entered CODALI in order to facilitate our studies, though without taking away our independence: We have private tutoring from teachers, cuers in class and regular speech therapy. We have reached a point where we can make everyone understand us. But we have the same problems really integrating because real hearing friends are rare. Once introductions are made, they're happy to watch us, and let us get by on our own. The first weeks of school each year are the worst. Teachers have difficulty in giving attention to us and sometimes often forget to verify whether we have understood or written down an assignment or test. That's always my nightmare: the teacher forgets to give me the homework, then grades me down for not having done it—or I go to school not realizing that the teacher is absent that day, and poke my nose into an empty classroom! My friends have to play the role of "baby-sisters" (*she means baby-sitters)* and must keep me informed about test dates, or teacher's days off. Sometimes they forget and I have to change plans at the last minute. When I complain to the teacher, everybody chews me out; they all claim they told me. It's always hard to put up with. For me, the most important thing is not reviewing for the test, but simply keeping me informed, and this in spite of notes from my mother to the teachers, asking them to warn me of any changes. But in spite of this our schooling is going well; Adrien and I have very good grades and have never failed a class. It is important here to understand that at this age 50% of French children have repeated a grade.

At home we are very happy; it's our cocoon (*lit., protecting nest*), for everyone (*there*) knows us since we were born: they know our qualities and our faults. Our cousins think of us as special friends, funny and athletic. Our family is the only place where we easily forget our deafness, which help us overcome problems outside the home. There we have a right to speak, and everyone listens to us in contrast to school. Every time there's the telephone that rings, it's always our parents who answer and tell us who's calling; thus we are never left out of what happens at home. When we watch a movie without subtitles on T.V. my father always stops to tell us what's happening. When we watch T.V. alone, we always invent a story automatically to match the expression of the characters and the action. We try to guess the words they're pronouncing, but we only rarely can lipread a word or two to help us understand the action. We go to the movies regularly: we only watch foreign films and here in Paris we're lucky because foreign films are always in their original version with subtitles. That's what we prefer! But we are a little disappointed not to be able to watch French films, though we see them on T.V. with my father.

We read a lot: in fact, we are truly devourers of books and sometimes we talk about our reading with our parents, discussing what we liked or not. Our father is a professor of economic and social sciences and wants to know the news daily. He can't really translate the evening televised news. so we try to compensate what we miss on T.V. or radio by reading the daily paper or news magazines. We love the news and often discuss politics.

We have a lot of extra-curricular activities. Adrien and I are both members of competitive swimming clubs. We work out four times a week in addition to competition. Deafness doesn't bother us very much except for the start of a race (we have someone give us a signal). We have excellent friends, but integration is harder than at school. Adrien took three years to find good friends in his club. My club was smaller, and I found friends in just a year, but our friends here are more understanding than at school. The trainers are real friends. I also do oil painting and sculpture; these activities keep us really busy, but we like them and at least we know of which (*what*) we are capable.

Thanks to our father we have learned a lot of sports: swimming, volley ball, tennis, ski, sailboard, sailing, biking—to cite only the sports in which we are the best. We never stop doing sports during vacation. Sports mean a lot to us. I often do sports camps. I see a lot of new faces and in a week I make lots of neat friends who are interested in deafness.

We face the problem of our deafness every day: the telephone, the television, and especially the radio, our classes, friends who discuss with each other—in short, without our family we are a little excluded from life around us. We have a hard time participating in a discussion between our friends and classmates. We pretend to understand or we dream about something else. When we are asked (*to name*) our favorite singing group we can't answer—since we can't appreciate music. If I'm invited to a party I pretend to dance as if the music didn't exist. As for discussions among my friends, I am completely excluded, even if a girlfriend talks to me occasionally. I try to find other things to think, which don't exclude me: I want to be present and not look at the airplane passing, looking as if I'm not listening. This handicap is slowly becoming bothersome: how to integrate with hearing people under conditions like these! I will soon no longer be a minor and I'm worried about my future: without my family I'm only a decorative plant seen by everyone. With my family I feel very strong and feel I exist. I'm very dependent on my friends, and I hate that since I want to show them that I'm capable of living independently. It's my craziest dearest dream. We feel we don't really belong in the deaf world because we are too integrated, and yet too different for hearing people. We are suffering a lot from this as adolescents, but the goal of integration is worth it: to become autonomous. After my "baccalaureat" C (math) I want to go to university to do science and become a computer-cybernetics expert: I have lots of job ideas and I haven't the slightest fear that deafness is a hindrance for my professional life. In fact, I am neither deaf nor hearing: I'm very happy to be me.

P.S. I want to thank you for the chance to write this letter, for it has given me the occasion to minimize my problems and reflect on my life. And in spite of the ups and downs, my life is worth living.

Steven Scher (16)
Presented at the Alexander Graham Bell Centennial Convention
Washington, D.C., July 26, 1990

My name is Steven Scher and I am sixteen years old. I was born deaf and have a one-hundred-dB loss in both ears. My parents did not know I was deaf until I was two years old and they had me tested because I was not talking as a normally developing child would.

I began school in an oral preschool program and stayed until I was four years old. But, at three-and-a-half I also started with a Cued Speech tutor at home. Then, when I was four, I went to a private preschool for hearing children in Washington, D.C. which included a few Cued Speech children and two Cued Speech teachers. This school only went through kindergarten, so in the first grade, when I was six, I returned to the public school in Montgomery County, Maryland, which now had a Cued Speech program. This September, I will be in the 12th grade in Montgomery County. All through school I have been mainstreamed with a Cued Speech interpreter. I haven't needed any resource or extra help since junior high school I didn't need any extra lessons because I was learning the same way a hearing person learns. I never had to have any special lessons to teach me about English grammar rules or pronunciations. I just saw it.

For instance, I knew from cueing that even though the words "stopped" and "started" both ended in "ed," they sounded different (at the end). "Stopped" has the "t" ending (shows the cue for *t*). "Started" has the "d" ending (shows the cue for *d*). I always saw the difference, so it was easy.

Steven Scher

In school I was seeing-and-hearing all the same subjects taught that my classmates were hearing, so we learned together. I got along with my classmates by just lipreading them and using my hearing because none of them cued. Also, because Cued Speech is phonetic, I took two years of Spanish, with a Cued Speech interpreter, and learned it the same way the hearing kids in my class did, and the same thing with Hebrew.

Cued Speech makes understanding so easy that usually one time is all it takes to get something. My mother tells the story of when I was little and we were looking at an alphabet book. There was a picture of a goat and a ghost. She said them and I looked at them and pointed to both pictures again. Then she cued the difference to me (showed both words in Cued Speech) and I saw the difference.

Another example is, one day in elementary school I was reading the name of a new interpreter coming into the program. Her name was

Robin Tobin, but because the last four letters were the same, R-o-b-i-n T-o-b-i-n, I read it as Rahbin Tahbin. When I pronounced it to my Cued Speech teacher, she said it and cued its correct pronunciation, Rahbin Toebin, and I immediately got it.

Some people think Cued Speech kids are dependent on interpreters, but that is not true. My interpreter is in school to make it easier for me to understand what is being said. But outside the classroom, I use my lipreading skills. Because with Cued Speech I learned the language, I feel comfortable with it, and I believe I can understand people in everyday situations. When I go anywhere—to a restaurant, the mall, to basketball or football games, I am an oral person. The only people who cue to me are my parents and my interpreter at school.

With my brother, relatives and friends I use lipreading. This summer and for the past two summers, I have worked in a supermarket where I am involved with a lot of people. This summer I am also working as a counselor at a day camp. In all these cases I have to depend on my auditory skills and my lipreading ability.

Cued Speech makes language completely clear for me and it has helped me to function and live my life like I want to.

Linda Balderson, who was a spectator at the convention session at which Steven delivered the above, states: "After his presentation Steven was asked if his mother or any other adult helped him write his speech. He answered that his mother helped him because he needed to limit his speech to a shorter time limit. She helped him decide what to leave out. Then he thought for a minute and said, 'Yes, I guess you could say that my mother and I collaborated on this speech.' I often refer to this quote as an example of the sophistication of language a deaf youngster can acquire."

Steven has a prelingual, very profound, bilateral sensorineural hearing impairment, with a corner audiogram. His mother indicates he had negligible language and communication at 3½ years of age, when they started Cued Speech. He is now [1991-92] a freshman at the University of Maryland, Baltimore County. Our only editing of his speech was to use phonemic spelling to show in writing what he expressed through speech and cues in his explanation.

"A Trip to Boston"
by Steven Scher (18), 1992

When Daniel (Koo) and I were asked to go to Boston for a weekend to help with a Cued Speech project at MIT (Massachusetts Institute of Technology), we were both elated. We were going to fly out of Washington National Airport after classes on a Friday afternoon to Logan International in Boston where we would be met by one of the coordinators of this project. Daniel and I did not know what was expected of us but we were soon to find out at dinner the first night.

The flight in was calm and we talked most of the way between the complimentary snacks consisting of a soft drink and peanuts. We were not really nervous about the whole thing at all - we just did not know what to expect when we got there. Daniel and I planned to play the whole thing by ear. As soon as we stepped off the plane and headed into the terminal we both gave quick furtive glances around for our mysterious host. How would we recognize or even know who this person was? A minute later, a woman, the one we had corresponded with, stepped forward and gave her name and inquired, "Daniel, Steve?" We both nodded in unison and so the customary handshakes began all around. She then guided us toward the exit of the terminal and told us that her friend was waiting to pick us up outside. We stepped out into the cold Boston wind and took our first breath of Massachusetts air.

Our correspondent (Lorraine Delhorne) stepped into the car and Daniel and I climbed into the back seat after depositing our luggage in the trunk. It had not hit us yet that we were actually in Massachusetts after just being in Maryland a few hours before. The two ladies then asked us if we were hungry and after a few minutes of discussion among the four of us, they settled on an Italian restaurant in the city. To make a long story short, the dinner was delicious and they briefly ran down what the agenda would be for the next morning. We were to meet Lorraine at nine o'clock the next morning in the lobby of our hotel and she would drive us to their offices on the MIT campus. Daniel and I would then begin a long day viewing videotapes of Cued Speech transliterators interpreting sentences and saying the sentences without the benefit of cues. We were to write down each and every word they said. Briefly, the coordinators ran down what they hope to use with our data. After tallying up the correct responses versus the wrong responses we would write down, the researchers would then use the information as a "troubleshooting guide" to see what common mistakes their prototype Auto-Cuer may make in real-life situations. The night was beginning to wind down and as they drove us to our hotel, they stopped at the Boston Garden, which is the home of the NBA's Boston Celtics and the hockey Bruins. Daniel decided to see if the Garden sports store was open for browsing but, unfortunately it was closed. They then drove us to our hotel, located in Cambridge, right across the bridge from the downtown area. The hotel was within walking distance of the MIT campus and the subway station which proved to be very convenient.

When we got to the hotel, Daniel and I checked in. We each had a single room. While killing time in our rooms, we decided to take the subway into the city to the Garden to see if the store had opened yet (they open after the game is over). Having no idea which subway route to take, we walked downstairs to the front desk and asked the manager for directions. He pulled out a subway map and proceeded to show us where we were and where we wanted to get off. By then, it was about eleven o'clock and not many people were on the subway. We found our stop easily and walked over to the now-familiar building and looked inside. The same sign loomed in the dark to us - CLOSED. We concluded that we had just missed it, as it was a little bit after eleven. So Daniel and I grabbed something to eat nearby (as we were not going to go back to our hotel without accomplishing something). We took the subway back to the hotel. We became experts at this in no time.

The next morning we met Lorraine in the lobby. We were soon on our way to the MIT campus. On our way, we filled her in on our failed attempt the night before at trying to get in the sports store. She seemed amazed at how confident and independent we were in traveling around an unfamiliar city. We were soon inside the offices and after a quick tour, the coordinators reviewed what we would be doing. Daniel and I were led into a sound-proof booth with televisions. We sat down and as the coordinators sat behind us, they started the tape and we were soon writing down the exact sentences the transliterator was cueing. As time went on, we took little breaks and finally a lunch break. At the lunch break, Lorraine told us what the goal of their project was, to establish something similar to an Auto-Cuer but different in some technological fields and more advanced technically. Daniel and I had a good idea of what they were trying to accomplish by the example they gave us of what they had done so far. After lunch, we went back into the booth and the sentences got longer and harder. We went through sets of ten sentences cued and ten sentences without cues. The scripts went back and forth between two transliterators on the tape and finally after working throughout most of the day, we had finished.

Before we could decide what to do next, one of the coordinators generously offered to drive us to Boston Garden, which was now open. We accepted the offer and after saying our goodbyes to Lorraine and company, we were on our way to the Garden. Daniel and I spent a good hour browsing around and buying sports apparel in the store. After we finished, it was nearly dinnertime and we had no idea where to go for dinner. Finally, we decided on Cheers (the neighborhood bar and restaurant made popular by the television show). Because it was on the other side of town, we had to choose between the subway or our legs. Physical strength won out and we began our journey from the north end of Boston all the way into the city next to the Common. It took a good thirty to forty-five minutes in the chilly wind but we made it to the pub. We waited outside in line and talked to the "official Cheers greeter" about the city. Daniel and I ended up having a delicious meal and contemplated walking all the way back to our hotel or taking the easier way by subway. We decided we were up to the challenge once again and left Cheers. We walked down Charles Street peering into the shops lined along the street and walked over the bridge back to Cambridge. It was quite a journey by this time and we literally staggered into the hotel and up to our rooms.

The next morning Daniel and I were up at the crack of dawn to take advantage of our last hours in the city. We went over to the MIT campus cafeteria to get breakfast and browse in their campus bookstore. We went by subway to Harvard Square up north. We wanted to see the Harvard campus and catch some sights there. We spent the next two hours walking all over the square which had an abundance of college shops. It was hard to leave but we had to. After walking back to the hotel, we checked out before going to the airport, we wanted to get a quick bite to eat. We got on the subway again and rode it down to the Copley Plaza stop. We got off, and using a map figured how to get to the famed Hard Rock Cafe. Finding it successfully, Daniel and I went in, had a great lunch, and before we knew it, it was time to get to the airport. After leaving the Cafe, we jumped back onto the subway for the ride to the airport. When we got there, buses were leaving the subway station shuttling passengers to the airport terminals. We got on the bus taking us to our terminal. Getting there, we went to the airline desk, got our tickets confirmed, and sat down waiting to board. It proved to be a long wait, as our plane was delayed an hour, so we passed the time by rehashing the whole weekend. Finally, the plane arrived, we boarded, found our seats, and sat back for the ride home.

All in all, despite our hearing impairment, Daniel and I got around fine in "Beantown" without receiving any cues to help us. We relied totally on our lipreading skills learned through Cued speech. Furthermore, we felt comfortable talking to everyone we came across on our trip. Daniel and I had such a great time we are looking forward to going back.

Stasie Jones (18)
Statement at the Alexander Graham Bell
Association Convention, San Diego, Calif., June 22, 1992

When my parents discovered my deafness at the age of two, it changed a lot of their plans. Rebecca, my mother went to find a way to communicate with me since I could not get anything they were saying. My grandmother also contributed her efforts to find a system for me. When she discovered Cued Speech, a new method, she immediately informed my mother who decided to fly to the States and continue her search. Soon after, Rebecca met Dr. Cornett and started learning his new method of communication. Ten days after she started using Cued Speech, I said my first sentence at the age of two and a half: "Dog pooped". Soon after, my mother saw how fast I was acquiring language. During that first summer, she worked with me two hours a day. The results were incredible; at the age of 3, I had learned 500 spoken words in 6 months. But because we lived in France, I got frustrated one day seeing different mouths which were speaking french words. I looked at my mother perplexed. After a while, I came to realize that I was in two different languages: French and English. Not long after this frustration I said "Good Bye" to an English speaking person and "Au revoir" to a French person. This amazing experience gave hope to my parents of bilingualism. Right away I started learning French with a good friend of ours, Murielle, who was willing to cue in French. My language started to improve, especially in French where I had to learn the language at school. Whereas with English, it became my native tongue (I mean it was the language I most enjoyed speaking). Cued Speech has given me the ability to lip read better, but with Cued Speech I get 100% of the message. I believe Cued Speech is the best way to learn language in daily circumstances at home as well as at school. Reading was not my passion but my love for reading started much later during my last year of High School.

Both of my parents cue to me as well as some of my sisters and brothers. But because I was the second oldest in the family my younger brothers and sisters mostly (only) articulated. Usually the oldest children cue to their youngest and are motivated and determined to help out more than the youngest to the oldest. It was a mistake and a lack of discipline, also my impatience did have an effect on the inefficiency of the cueing, we should all have done a bigger effort including myself.

After knowing French and English fluently, I started to dream about German. I was at a German Christian Camp in Corsica and I made friends there. This made me want to learn their language. My principal and my professors objected to my idea of taking German in Middle School. After convincing them about my stubborness and that whatever I wanted I managed to get, even for the craziest idea, finally they let me learn my third language. Now it has been 5 years of German and I learned well. Going to Germany several times has also helped me to gain confidence in speaking German in spite of my deafness. I would be very afraid of speaking because I knew my deafness was causing me not to say the right sounds but with God's help and courage, I took the initiative. Like I said before, I was a very stubborn person. Everything I was determined to get; not to say I was a spoiled brat but that I always wanted to try and achieve the craziest desire. And let me tell you, I managed to succeed my French High School degree (Baccalaureat) by doing two years in one. And the Lord has blessed me and without his strength I would not have made it. The glory should be given unto Him not to me.

During my High School year I had to decide on another language to take since I was in the Languages Section. My mind came to Russian by pure curiosity. At first they were all telling me how crazy I was to take such a hard language, but when they saw I was doing well in German they knew I could do anything else. It was a big challenge. I love challenge! I took two years of Russian in High School.

I had no interpreter in my High school years (only one for a short time). She would cue in German with French sounds trying to get it close to the German sounds.

After graduating from High School early, I got into Wellesley College with the fear of not being prepared for the American schooling system. Luckily I found a full time Cued Speech transliterator who comes to my Spanish class and cues in Spanish but with an American accent, using American sounds. I guess you would be wondering why I took Spanish, well I wanted to take German and Russian the same year but my advisor objected to my so called "crazy" idea. So, since she was a Spanish teacher, I thought I could take that language. Spanish is an easier language than Russian. So finally I took Spanish instead of German. Now I miss German a lot. And I will not listen to the objections of my wanting to learn another language. Right now I am majoring in Russian studies including the Russian language itself.

My desire for the future is to have "foreign" speech therapists who could teach the deaf a foreign language the way it is supposed to be said and not using any American accent. Many colleges have native speakers who teach their native language and students learn through them the exact sounds. For deaf people we need speech therapists in foreign languages. I know this is helpful since I have a Russian tutor who is teaching me where to put my tongue and how to say the sounds of Russian. It is a big thing, but I do believe that deaf people are able to learn another language other than their own.

Now I am majoring in Russian Studies and History. My desire is to go to Russia and teach deaf students languages. Also, I want my friends to realize that they are not alone, but Jesus is and will always be our friend in our hard times. So really I did not go "out on my own." I would not have been where I am now except that God helped me all the way through.

A letter written by Stasie at age 15 appears earlier in this chapter, and her case history is on page 510.

Paul Swadley (18)
Williamsburg, Va.
(from *CS News*, Winter, 1987)

This year has been extraordinarily busy for me, since it is my senior year at Lafayette High School, where I now attend. Yet it has been in most respects a very satisfying year for me. I am eagerly awaiting the coming of fall and college after I graduate in June. Most of the courses that I am taking this year are accelerated subjects. I am in my fourth year of Latin, which was something I did not expect, but as it turned out I enjoy Latin too much and reading Virgil and Caesar as well as other Roman writers like Pliny the Younger who survived the eruption of Vesuvius and wrote about it. I am also taking Intensified U.S. Government, which is comparatively hard for me, but as in Latin, I enjoy it, and I have become more aware of current events because my government teacher talks to us quite often about the current political and international scene. Another class is AP English, in which there is quite a bit of discussion among my peers. I confess that without the help of my interpreter, I would be quite lost and unable to participate with the other guys in the discussion. In May, I have to take the AP exam for English, which I am not looking forward to. Finally, I am involved in field biology. I have been going outside the school with the class to many places like Yorktown, Jamestown Island and in small lakes and streams. Most of the time we collected bugs to label for a collection. I am currently holding a 3.5 average for the semester, and hopefully, after grades are compiled, it will get higher and my class rank, which is 41 out of 331 persons, should get close to the top tenth or in it.

I also had an internship with the Jamestown-Yorktown Foundation. The work that I did consisted of learning the elements of running a historical park and different facets of the operation of Jamestown. I did everything from running messages to different personnel to designing a display to working as an interpreter at the reconstructed fort in costume and all. Overall, it was a very positive experience for me. In addition, it gave me a valuable credential for later on in life as a history major.

I also have been involved with my school's newspaper after school. I am a reporter and a layout editor, which makes things a hassle sometimes, especially when I have swim practice. As a layout editor, I design the format of the pages and paste it up to be run off the presses. I also critique other schools' papers, looking for ideas to make the overall product even better than before. In fact, the **Ledger** is one of the top papers in the state, winning the highest awards possible. As I said before, I am also a reporter. I write at least one story for each issue. Most of the stories I have written are at least 700 words long. In fact, I am one of the most prolific writers on the staff, and in the running for the National Quill and Scroll, the honorary society for student journalists. I feel fortunate to have been given the gift of being able to write well to offset my handicap.

As I mentioned previously, I am on the swim team. I get up each morning at about 4:30 am to go to practice at 5:30 for 1½ hour(s) of grueling practice. This year we are not as strong as last year's team, but we are managing to get by with the district championship. By the time I get home from school at 3:00 pm, I fall into bed for a brief nap before dinner and homework.

I have, with all these activities and school, managed to take time to take the SAT's and achievement tests for college. The highest scores that I received for math was 500 and 670 for the verbal section. To get these scores, I had to get a studybook about 2 inches thick and take several hours a night studying for these tests. It didn't give perfect 800's on either section but I am satisfied with my performance where colleges are concerned.

I have applied to about five schools, and I should be notified in early April as to whether I have been accepted. The five schools that I have written to are: the University of Virginia, George Mason University, The College of William and Mary, and a private school in North Carolina called St. Andrew's Presbyterian College.

Of these schools, UVa is the best equipped to help the handicapped, with special help for the hearing-impaired. They have a special office designed to comply with Section 504 of the Rehabilitation Act of 1973. To this end, they will provide notetakers, transcribers for lectures, and interpreters of all kinds, including Cued Speech. So, UVa was my first choice of the five schools. Next is GMU, with lesser facilities, and excellent departments in history and communications (journalism). It is also right next to home for me, since I know the way around the school, and it has an associate dean to deal with handicapped students. Not quite so good as UVa in that respect, but it's better than nothing. The same goes for the other two schools, which have similar facilities to cope with the handicapped.

I have only five more months till I graduate from Lafayette, and a long summer for me before I go to school next fall. *See p. 409.*

Amity Leitner (18)
Raleigh, N.C., 1992

I, Amity Jean Leitner, was born in Niskayuna, New York and was officially raised as a Cued Speech person. Now I am an eighteen-year-old who has confidence due to using Cued Speech.

Amity Leitner

I used Cued Speech in mainstream schools while I was growing up. I had a lot of experiences that have some positive sides like that I got along with the teachers who knew Cued Speech. The other Hearing Impaired students in my school knew only oral or Sign Language which effected the language difficulties between us, so I picked up some signs from them and they were able to take some lessons from the Hearing Impaired teacher of the interpreters. I was more able to understand the hearing kids in my class because I mainly rely on lip-reading. I could easily understand the interpreters in the classrooms.   While I am at home, I use Cued Speech mainly with my family. I am able to know all the conversations going around the house. My brother, Carl Leitner, learned Cued speech at the age of six. Now Carl uses the Cues fluently with me and I am easily able to communicate with him, My mom, Jeanie Leitner, devoted her life to Cued Speech and is a teacher for the deaf in preschool. She helped me a lot by using clear communication in our mother-daughter conversation. Fritz Leitner, my dad, was a treasurer of the National Association of Cued Speech a few years ago. My dad uses Cued Speech to communicate with me. I am proud of my family that did that hard work for me.

As a adult, I still use Cues since I have been raised knowing it. I am in college at the National Technical Institute for the Deaf at the Rochester Institute of Technology in New York. My fiance, David King, who is oral, learned Cued Speech easily in this past year. He understands the concept and cues word by word. We both have strong communication when we use Cues and sign language, since I have also learned to sign.

Since I am in college with a large population of deaf people, I try to interact with them. When I was younger I had limited signs that I could not easily communicate with other deaf people. ASL is difficult. Now I rely on English to learn ASL as a second language.

I can understand oral deaf people easily since I have good lip-reading skills. Also I have good high reading scores due to the good English I have learned from using Cued Speech. My California score is 10.6, and my Michigan score is 79. Learning English first is important because you never know what will overcome your problems and help your future. Then, later in the future, learn Signing Exact English would be my suggestion to interact with other deaf people. Cued Speech has helped me a lot in my academic and social life. It has made it easy to be a part of both the hearing and deaf communities.

For Amtry's case history, see p. 560.

Mathew White (18)
Barnes, London, England, 1992

I was born 15th April 1974, and my hearing and speech had developed highly up until the age of three, when I fell seriously ill with a form of meningitis and recovered to find myself almost totally deaf and unable to retrieve the language skills I had gained. I then spent several years of intensive speech therapy to enable me to integrate into 'normal' society as my parents believed it to be the best option, as the standard of education at specialist deaf schools in those days was very low. I only wear one hearing aid, in my left ear as in the right ear I am totally deaf, and despite what audiologists may have suggested, I cannot hear anything with a hearing aid in my right ear. However I have a second hearing aid—the Cubex Radio Link—which I use at school. This hearing aid has its transmitter and microphone in a separate unit, and I can only hear and understand the voice of the wearer of this transmitter. Thus this cuts out the background chatter and noise in the classroom, and the power and quality of sound is far better as well—the only reason I don't wear this thing permanently is that it is far too bulky and I would have to hand the transmitter to anyone who tries to talk to me.

The shock of the loss of hearing remained with me for several years, and this did not help my parents' search for a satisfactory education which was so rare for profoundly deaf children in those days. I owe all my success to the sheer determination shown by my parents in those early days. Their drive pushed me through a tough life at a private preparatory school and having achieved satisfactory grades in my Common Entrance Examinations, I was accepted in to St. Paul's School having also impressed the Surmaster who interviewed me! Although the first couple of years presented some difficulty in an entirely different environment to that in my previous school, I gained the respect and thus the support of several of the staff there, and I went on to take 'B' grades in all my C.C.S.E.'s with an 'A' for sciences. After those, and seeing the difficulties of getting into university with my problem, I had to 'pull my socks up' and really put effort into it!

At first most of the staff found me quite a challenge, and had absolutely no idea how to handle the situation, and in fact my tutor was lumbered with me by the High Master and she wasn't too pleased about it. She promptly gave all the staff the wrong ideas and so the school took quite a long time to get really used to me. However our relationship has gradually improved with time, and now I think she actually likes me a little bit, and realises what I am capable of. I get on extremely well with all the staff, and I don't disrupt the lessons like most of the others, although I do try to put in a few witty comments.

Mathew White

I am now 18 years old and have recently finished studying A-levels in Physics, Geography, Maths and Design & Technology, and I have just completed the examinations. I feel the hard work has paid off and I am hoping for 'A' and 'B' grades at the very least. I am hoping to gain entry into Bristol University to study Aeronautical Engineering, if not then something along those lines.

I have always been one for the arts and technology, and I have a serious interest in several aspects including many forms of modelling —from radio-controlled aeroplanes to static small-scale models, and also I am fascinated by boats and cars but I am especially interested in aeroplanes—my first choice of occupation to be a fighter pilot in the RAF I have had to dismiss as a fantasy. However, I am prepared to find out about flying light aircraft such as microlites and autogyros which may not require any form of audio contact. However I collect books, magazines and information on the subject and I attend several airshows each year. On the sport side, I take sailing very seriously and I spend much of my spare time racing at the sailing club near our bungalow on the south coast, and I hope to take part in the '120' National Championships next year ('420' is the dinghy class which I race at the moment.) I suppose I would like to follow in the footsteps of my father, who was World Champion in the 'Tempest' class in 1967. However there isn't much scope for sailing here in London, although I do go to school in the summer term, so a lot of my spare time here is taken up playing squash. I find it very difficult playing team sports such as rugby or football as it is impossible for me to follow any kind of orders on the field or when training, especially if I take my hearing-aid out to prevent it being damaged. As a result, the only sport I play seriously at school is squash, and until recently I used to play every day, often on my own, and this is the important advantage of squash to me. Having played so often, I have achieved somewhat of a reputation as a squash player, and I have captained the school team several times.

My social life unfortunately has been a major flop. In fact I don't even have a social life. It is impossible for me to carry or follow any kind of conversation with more than one person at a time and even more impossible to have even a one-to-one conversation at a noisy party or disco. The intense concentration required to hear, lipread and understand another person trying to talk to me is bad enough, following a conversation between other people is simply too much. Also people who talk to me usually talk more clearly than usual, so it is far harder to listen to somebody not specifically talking to me, or somebody who has not yet realised my problem (a common situation when I meet strangers). These problems tend to leave me totally alienated at parties or any other sort of social gathering. My only hope in these situations is to find someone else standing around on their own. So you can imagine my ability to make friends and meet members of the opposite sex are extremely limited. However, having been at an all-boys school for 5 years I believe I have become something of a legend(!) in the school (probably helped by my reputation in squash), and being a large school with 750 students, they all know me but I don't know them! I receive a lot of admiration and respect from people in my age group and I don't have any enemies at all, and I am friendly with everybody but they still cannot see me as one of *them*, with the result that I never get invited to any parties or the pub crawls which I long to get involved in! Despite being on good terms with everybody, I only have one real friend, i.e. someone who doesn't feel uncomfortable talking to me and going out with me, and since we have the same strong interest in aeroplanes we can have long conversations and go to airshows together.

However as I have matured in the last couple of years, I have become much bolder and am trying much harder at my social life, and things are looking up. My membership at my sailing club allows me to meet all types of somewhat more friendly country people and I enjoy life in the country very much more than in London (nicer girls too!). As from now I believe life can only get better as I have left school, and I look forward to starting a new life at university. I am not afraid of responsibility, and I intend to take a career and do some travelling in my year before university, and look forward to life in general. I feel that all the hard work and pressure of my education has brought me my current success, confidence and strength of will (if you don't mind me saying so), I intend to get more involved in deaf people's society in the near future and probably take a course in sign language or maybe relearn Cued Speech. I am currently enjoying a new sense of freedom, having my own car (however decrepit) and having just left school.

During my prep school years I was quite severely bullied and picked on as a scapegoat for being aloof and alone, and I didn't receive any of the respect that I do nowadays, thus in early times I think I had a tendency to take things out on my younger brother, who may have resented me also because of the attention I received and possibly the fact that I went to a day school and he was a boarder. As a result, there was a great rift between us for many years, and we often fought violently over trivial matters. However in the last couple of years that has completely changed; we now get along very well, having suddenly matured and realised what nice people we really were (!). My parents have tolerated and coped with me very well; of course we had several fall-outs in the past but I think that's all a part of growing up. However I do often put them under a lot of pressure to repeat parts of their conversation if I'm trying to join in, and sometimes their impatience gets the better of them. I am eternally grateful to them for my success and their sheer determination in bringing me up. As a family we are very close and we all go on holiday every year, and our uncle (my mother's brother) often comes around to visit us. We visit my Grand-mother a couple of times a year who lives in a large house near Winchester, and 2 years ago we all went there to celebrate her 80th birthday, it was only her 79th—she didn't think she would survive long enough to celebrate the 80th birthday. *For case history, see p. 429.*

Daniel Koo (18)
Gaithersburg, Md., 1991

Daniel Koo is now (1992) a sophomore at the University of Maryland, College Park, Md. He was introduced to Cued Speech when he was in fifth grade. During his freshman year, 1990-91, the Cued Speech Team at Gallaudet University became acquainted with him. They have kindly shared with us the excerpts they obtained from his correspondence with a family new to deafness and Cued Speech. In the correspondence he answered the questions of the family by relaying his own experiences and feelings. These excerpts appeared in **Cued Speech News,** Winter, 1990, and Spring, 1991, along with some material obtained in an interview.[4] Daniel was 18 when he wrote these materials, except for the concluding update. His case history, written by his mother, is in Chapter 17.

All my life I have been enveloped in complete silence. Like a dark, cold hand, it grasps me leaving me light to "hear" only what is in front of me. I seek my light, my salvation my hearing aids. Putting on those molds, I hear a mechanical click as I flip the switch, a mo-mentary burst of static and then silence. "Hello?" I would ask myself out of habit. "Hallow" would flow through my ears...I hear distorted sounds limited to a certain low decibel (level). No matter, it is a GOOD feeling. I never realized that until now because sounds have become more a part of me than silence and in the morning all my brain cares about is, "Oh, it is 6:15 AM and I don't feel like going to school."

Being profoundly deaf does not really register in this brain of mine...I socialize with both hearing people and deaf people. I play the piano, I listen to rock and roll music, I talk on the TDD (or an amplified phone with frustrating results), I go outside and play like any normal human being. I may be exteriorly different, but my mind, heart

---

[4]Specifics on Daniel's deafness and early education appear in Chapter 17. They will help put his attainments in perspective.

and soul are just the same as any average fun-loving teenager. Sometimes I wonder what my life would be like if I was hearing. Would I be the same person as I am today? Probably not...I would be an average Asian-American who stereotypically excels in mathematics and may have a reluctant attitude towards people with disabilities—deaf people in particular. "How do I talk to them? What if they can't understand me?"...I appreciate the sensitive awareness that I have for people with disabilities because I, myself, am disabled.

Daniel Koo

But am I? Well, I consider myself fortunate to have come across ...oral(ism), Cued Speech, sign language (in English order) and some ASL. All of this does not (itself) mean that I can talk, so I am blessed with the vocal capability to communicate with the hearing world. Like my mother, I believe I must first learn how to live in the hearing world because it is everywhere—stores, taxis, salespersons, bus drivers, teachers, friends, neighbors, etc. And then, like a second language, I can integrate myself into the Deaf culture. It isn't easy doing both but it is worth the effort. And for that, I am eternally grateful to my parents. At Rockville High School (MD), I pursued my beliefs by being exposed to approximately 1,000 hearing students and 20-plus mainstreaming deaf students (5 were CS and the rest TC). A perfect ratio for the rest of the world.

When I first learned Cued Speech (fifth grade) I thought I was bilingual. Alas no, I was not. I was merely learning how to see and pronounce English. When I entered Junior high, sign language came into my life and it was then that I realized how there are no limits to my abilities. How I can soar into the two worlds! Ironically enough, I am categorized as a person with a disability. I hate that—being labeled "disabled." It makes me feel powerless to do anything I want. Yet, it is true in some ways. Being a phone, movie, TV and music teenaged addict as I am, I submit myself to captions, TDD's, and my hearing aids.

Asked if he "sounds out words" to himself, Daniel responded with "...this is the type of thing one does not ponder over often for it is a reflex...when my mother thinks, she thinks in Korean but to convey her message to me she rethinks her words into English and speaks it to me. As for me, I think it in English before translating it into sign. But when I write, or cue or speak orally, I do not have to rethink my thoughts for they are already thinking English."

Daniel reacted to a comment with a quote from Robert Frost: "Two roads diverged in a wood, and I—I took the one less traveled by and that made all the difference." This applies to me as well as to all Cued Speech advocates. Yes, it has made all the difference in my life, but there may have been some discrimination against it. Strong advocates of Deaf Power and Deaf Culture may have generated some resentment towards the growing methodology, Cued Speech...in my past experience in being exposed to TC and ASL peers, I came across attitudes ranging from curiosity to irritability. There has been a lot of misunderstandings that Cued Speech is a language and therefore threatens sign language (TC or ASL) as a language for the deaf. This is not true. Cued Speech is merely a visual tool compatible with the spoken English language thereby enabling its users to see English or any spoken language. It can be segregated from sign language and left alone like oralism. But, since it uses hands as an expressive form, it often is mislabeled as sign language or another term thereof. It does not endanger the grace, beauty, and existence of ASL like a foreign language could do to another. If only they knew that.

Daniel responded in narrative form to some questions about his experiences using Cued Speech transliterators and any differences he noticed from those in high school:

At this point in my life, I am a freshman at the University of Maryland, College Park. Life at UMCP has its typical moments ... and not-so-typical moments. Within my first week at UMCP, I discovered a message on the school's new voice mail system. I asked one of the three CS transliterators that share my classes, to interpret the message. After I pushed a series of buttons to access the message, the translitera-tor reflected the tone with an exasperated face and cued "Ohhhh." Frankly, the mysterious female caller wasn't the only one disappointed. But that is beside the point. Living alone in my dormitory, I found it to be quite an educational experience if not challenging. Ever since the brief message, I have been adjusting to my new life on campus. Of course, the transliterator can't always be with me and so, I have taken the liberty of asking the desk staff to voice out the messages for me. In addition, most of my hearing friends already know how I engage in conversation and they make minor adjustments to it like visit me instead of calling me and vice versa.

Granted, college life is by far completely different from high

school. This doesn't exclude my experiences with a CST (CS transliterator). In high school, there were a few students sharing different
transliterators and so I had different faces to look at per day. But at
UMCP, being the only CS student on campus has a different quality to
it. I see the same person the entire day, but a different person the next
day. This doesn't really bother me because I have had previous
experiences in this area. However, nothing has prepared me for the
step into a large university world where there is no resource time nor
someone to watch over me. Although, there is a program called
Disabled Student Services that caters to all disabled persons and
provides the essential services they need. Because my deafness hasn't
severely impaired my speech, I managed to get by on my own by
relying on my lipreading skills and years of speech therapy to get what
I needed.

As far as the general population is concerned, it is quite an overwhelming leap from a 1,200 high school student body to that of 38,000
men and women. But there is another dimension to consider if approximately 95 percent of them have never seen a deaf person much less a
CS advocate. On my first day of class, 200 classmates suddenly quieted
down as my CST walked in front of the class, grabbed a chair and sat
down. I would say most of them were confused as they saw their
"professor" get comfortable and face toward my seat at the far front
corner. A few moments later they figured out who's who and just what
I am. Talk about sticking out like a sore thumb! I try to be casual
about it which is kind of hard to do with eyes burning in the back of
my head or more accurately, my hearing aids. After, class, my
transliterators, as normal procedure, would introduce themselves to the
professor and add, "You can do what you normally do and just pretend
that I am not here." How ironic, I wish I could say the same for my
classmates' eyes. As days go by, the attention decreases. But now and
then, I catch people's eyes dart back and forth between me and my
faithful companion as if they were watching a tennis match. I understand and respect their lack of experience amongst deaf people. For
example, a few of my professors would talk directly to my CST with
sentences that start out like, "Tell him that..." or "Ask him..." Also,
other factors may vary from person to person. Some are lipreadable,
others aren't. For those who are clearly understandable, the third-party
in-between is unnecessary and for those who aren't, well...my sidekick
steps in.

Because of many myths on deaf people's communication
abilities, I don't get many eager questions about Cued Speech and least
of all, my deafness. If there are any questions, they are often directed

at the cueing person not wearing hearing aids. The most popular inquiry is "What kind of sign language are you using? It seems different from what I've seen before." There seems to be an unstable fear of stupid questions, offensive remarks, and communication breakdown in the air near me. So, I try to "advertise" myself by chatting with hearing people without the aid of my CST. Slowly, people seem to catch on and by the end of the semester, I have made some new friends. I will go the extra mile to present myself as who I am, not what I am in terms of the thing that I wear upon my ears. I hope they find (me) a human being who has accepted his deafness as part of him and makes no boundaries in life. But how can I reveal myself if my hearing aids and interpreters are the center of their focus.

As of this writing, I am midway through my second semester at UMCP. This time I am taking heavier classes and thereby subjecting my transliterators to fatigue at some points. I also suffer from the burden of juggling physics, Shakespeare, psych., calculus, architecture, and volleyball. They take up a lot of my time these days and I hardly have the energy to go out on social activities. But, I try my best.

Finally, I am very satisfied with my current lifestyle as it is. Living on your own in a large residential university is definitely a rare occurrence and I am reluctant to give up this privilege because it has not only taught me independence but survival skills as well. I must nurture myself with information and learn the ropes on my own for there is no one to teach me. There are times when I wish I had a roommate for a companion and someone to answer voiced phone calls. And, there are times when I am reminded with horror stories of having (a) roommate with extremely bad habits. Why change if you're happy with the way it is. So, I won't.

In an earlier letter written to the family mentioned above Daniel described his personal philosophy and situation this way:

I would like to say one of my favorite quotes from Victor Hugo, the author of "Les Miserables": "What matters the deafness of the ear when the mind hears. The one true deafness, the incurable deafness, is that of the mind." My mind hears. My eyes are my ears. my hearing aids are my salvation from insanity. And (there is) nothing more to ask for except, "Please, God, can I hear with my very own ears?" Yet, I am proud to be deaf. There are many times when I have contemplated the questions: "What am I with two different worlds inside me?" and "Am I Deaf or am I hearing?" I think deafness is an inner part of me that I cannot let go and so, I have embraced it. My other side is the hearing part and I yearn for it to accept me. With that, I consider my deafness a gift from the Lord because in time the other side will learn to accept, but it is going to be hard. What's more, it is hard enough being minority (Korean background) but a minority of a minority? I gotta just be myself and I think it is working. I like that, having the qualities that few people in the world have is a thrilling thought....

Right now I am content with my life as it is. I live alone in a dormitory room (lucky again) equipped with a phone light system. But I gotta go out and socialize, so I participate in a variety of activities: playing flag football, tennis, volleyball; taking karate classes; and being involved with a group called Intervarsity Christian Fellowship. Oh, and of course my mother's favorite word, "study."

Daniel Koo (19)
update, sophomore year, Feb. 1992

Times have changed and my life is no exception. Since my last essay, there have been two more changes in my life. One was that I have eventually decided to switch my major from architecture to sociology. The reason I went into sociology is to have a better understanding of humans and how we relate to society in general. I have a desire to teach deaf students. After all, I am deaf. Deaf teach the deaf; how appropriate. This means that I will have to go for my masters in deaf education. But, this isn't definite; some other field could come up that interests me. So, in a way, I am postponing my career decision until I graduate from UMCP. Changing to sociology is quite a dramatic change but, I came to realize my desire to impact the world around me and to come into contact with people rather than sitting behind a desk.

The other significant change in my lifestyle is the fact that I pulled in a roommate early November, an acquaintance of mine. He goes by the name of John Lee, a fellow Korean whom I can share cultural values with and a faithful Christian at heart. Not only has my room changed but, my lifestyle has changed. He answers my phone for me even when I am not there; makes calls for me; wakes me up in the morning if I oversleep; plays one-on-one Nerf hoops with me (11 wins for him and 15 for me); listens to me and various things that good friends go through. On the first day he moved in, I had to go on a weekend retreat and I had forgotten my bed vibrator. Let's just say that John got a culture shock at 8 am on Saturday morning. "What is that???" Since then, his experience with a deaf roommate has been an awakening experience. I am grateful for a great roommate and friend like John and I can safely say that the feeling is mutual. A couple of times, we'd stay up until 3 or 4 a.m. talking about life or our problems. What more can I ask for ... except for some decent sleep.

Cued Speech is still a prominent part of my college education as well as beyond. In one particular course, I am required to observe and teach a secondary classroom. My classmates are to observe an assigned middle school in Prince George county. Because my transliterator has other commitments and there is no one else to take up the job, I had to ask my professor if I could observe Cued Speech in a mainstreamed classroom. After some phone calls, I was finally assigned to Flower Valley elementary school in Montgomery County (a neighboring county of PG). Well, well, well, this is such a blessing! Cued Speech continues to be a big chapter in the life of Daniel Koo.

My social life has been just about the same but I have been putting it on the back burner for now. I have been trying to keep up with my studies and therefore, I am spending more time at my desk than outside of my dorm. I still go to Christian fellowships although I have taken a preference to two fellowships called Agape and Chosen Generation Ministry over Intervarsity. In fact, God willing, I have just taken an officer's position at CGM and that would take up more of my time. Well, like always, I'll take life day by day and play it "by hearing aid."

Daniel Koo (19)
Testimony before the House Subcommittee on Select Education, United States Congress, February 25, 1992

My name is Daniel Koo. I was born profoundly deaf for reasons unknown. I am currently a 19 year old sophomore attending the University of Maryland at College Park where I am provided with a Cued Speech transliterator for all of my classes.

My elementary education was taught in the oral program up to fourth grade when my parents transferred me to the Cued Speech program. They switched me because they felt that I had to satisfy my deficient academic needs using an alternative communication method. Prior to my transition from oral to Cued Speech, my reading and language skills were below grade level because I was having difficulty understanding instructions in the oral program. Upon learning Cued Speech, my verbal skills have significantly improved to that of on grade level. Not only has my written expression improved but my speech pronunciation has become more intellectual and comprehensible. Since then, my academic achievement has been a hierarchy of achievements with Cued Speech transliterators providing equal access in the mainstream classrooms. Because I had access to every phoneme spoken and every sound uttered, I felt I was totally integrated and that there was no limit to my educational growth nor my career possibilities. More importantly, I never felt at an academic disadvantage when compared to my peers because I was shown the exact syllables that they hear and must struggle with new vocabulary and spelling just like they do.

When I entered junior high school, I noticed that sign language is a widely used communication method among the deaf. So, I had informally picked up the language from my deaf peers and use them solely for social purposes. I still preferred Cued Speech in the classroom setting largely due to its unbiased and uninterrupted communications. I felt it was important for me to interpret verbal information as I see it, not as my interpreter hears and translates it. In achieving this, I was able to function in a society that demands English proficiency. In fact, I was able to take courses in Latin and Spanish and learn it without any difficulty.

Now, I have nothing against American Sign Language or any similar communication system because I use it myself as a communication vehicle and found it to be quite effective and expressive as a language of its own. But for me to be an active and self-sufficient member of society, I need to practice the English language.

Like it was designed for, Cued Speech has shown me the spoken language in its basic component: phonemes. But, it has also transcended beyond its original design and shown me the road to my academic success in which I believe the root lies in the English language.

Daniel's case history begins on page 325.

Sarah Hightower (19)
Hickory, N.C., March 15, 1992

I was nine months old when my parents found out that I was profoundly deaf. We moved to St. Louis from Oklahoma City so I could be in a program at an oral school for the deaf. My parents did not know sign language or cued speech at that time.

My parents learned about cued speech when I was five years old. I remember when my parents were having a meeting one night in the living room of our house. There were several people in the room and they were all learning cued speech. I was really puzzled to see that everyone in the room was moving their hands around their faces in the exact same way. I did not understand the concept of cued speech, but the more my mother used it, the more I learned from her.

Shortly after my parents started to use cued speech, I was transferred from the school for the deaf to Childgrove Elementary

School where there were only hearing students. I had my first cued speech interpreter at this school. I loved this school so much because I had the opportunity to do all kinds of creative things and fun activities with the hearing students. The teachers wanted all of the students to learn by "experience." For example, we would go someplace such as Eckerd's Farm to pick fresh apples from the trees. Then we would go back to the school and learn about math by measuring, dividing, multiplying, etc. in order to make the apples into applesauce, apple juice, apple art projects, apple muffins and other apple-related activities.

Childgrove was always exciting with new and different things. My cued speech interpreter made it possible for me to learn from all those experiences. It was so much fun and it brings back many good memories.

My mother would tutor me in speech and language and also hired tutors to teach me. One of the best tutors I ever had was a teacher for the deaf in order to teach me "oral English." She also did a lot of fun things with me such as travelling to the 1982 World's Fair in Knoxville, Tennessee and to Disney World in Orlando, cueing everything we saw all along the way!

Sarah Hightower

My mother enrolled me in a horseback riding program for hearing-impaired students when I was seven years old. The riding instructor, like myself, was hard-of-hearing. She had a lot of experience in horsemanship and was also a teacher for the deaf. She taught me the basics of horseback riding and we had a lot of fun games and competitions. I simply fell in love with horses and have been riding ever since I joined in this program.

After I left Childgrove at age nine, I went back to a school for the deaf because my mother thought I ought to have a more traditional type of education by that age. I never had cued speech interpreters after I left Childgrove but my parents always cued at home.

By the time my mother and I moved to California, I was in the eighth grade. I went to a public school for the first time with signing interpreters provided for the hearing-impaired and started learning how to sign then. I picked up the signs from watching the interpreters in class and from other deaf students who signed. I used sign language at school, but I always went home to a cueing mother! Cued speech has always been much easier for me to understand because lipreading is so easy with it, and it helps me learn the pronunciation of words.

During the summer before my sophomore year in high school, I met a family of cuers from France and realized that I could learn how to speak French with the aid of French cues! I began studying French seriously when I was in my senior year at University High School although I was unable to have a cued speech interpreter so the pronunciation of the French was lost on me.

When I started attending college I had a sign language interpreter and it was just not sufficient. I was really disappointed about not being able to learn the pronunciation of the language so I went to my French professor and she helped me find someone to interpret for me with cues. My new interpreter and I flew to Paris for spring break to learn the French cues. It was such an exciting experience for me. I began picking up the French pronunciation quickly after the cued speech interpreter started cueing to me in French in class.

Today, I am a sophomore at Lenoir-Rhyne College in Hickory, North Carolina. I am majoring in American Studies with a concentration in English. I am still studying French and have another cued speech interpreter for my French class.

I am involved with Sign Troupe—club for both hearing and deaf students. We perform songs in sign language. I am also involved with the International Club where I have met so many people from other countries. I find the people so interesting and believe I would never have had the opportunity to relate to so many different people if it had not been for cued speech making it possible for me to develop my language.

Cued Speech had helped me a great deal with my ability to communicate easily with the hearing world. I really feel fortunate to have had parents who used cued speech. It was the best thing that ever happened to me. I have absolutely no idea how I would have been able to handle my relationships with the hearing world if it had not been for Cued Speech. It is really some kind of a miracle! *Case history, p, 476.*

Amy Hurowitz (19)
Rochester, N.Y., 1992

Hello! I am responding to your letter requesting illustrations from my own experiences with cued speech. Here goes.

As far as my memory permits me, my mother, my two brothers,

and I went to the Gallaudet College's cued speech workshop in 1977. For some reason, I fell in love with cued speech! Because I was raised orally, I was fascinated by the movement of the hands and how the hands moved. I do remember, however, that I was impatient and did not want to learn cued speech that week but eventually, I came to love it! This was the beginning of a long and bumpy road to where I am. I entered Flower Valley Elementary School enrolled in the cued speech program.

I can not remember very much of those elementary school years but I do remember sitting in my fifth grade classroom with my very first cued speech interpreter and with another deaf student who also uses and still uses cued speech on the first day of school. Although I remember being nervous in a classroom full of hearing students, I had no concept of what cued speech was all about but I was really fascinated by the way my interpreter moved his hands so fast. It became a game for me, trying to figure out what (in) the world was going on with those hands! Eventually, I put the pieces together and figured out the puzzle and I believe once you learn the hand shapes, you know what the persons using cued speech are saying.

As a student in the Rochester Institute of Technology in Rochester, New York, I look back to my junior high and high school years I spent in Rockville, Maryland, and I realize how I took cued speech for granted because if it was not for cued speech, I could be one of the deaf people who

Amy Hurowitz and Sarah Hightower

believe in "deaf power" which is rapidly expanding everyday, I could not have the lipreading skills I have today, and most importantly, I could not have the ability to be aware of the sounds and the English language that is constantly around me.

Ever since I was enrolled in the cued speech program at Flower Valley, I was fortunate enough to have cued speech transliterators for the next eight years. Last year, after I graduated from high school, I attended a small private college named Lenoir Rhyne College in Hickory, North Carolina. After failed attempts to get cued speech transliterators there along with other reasons, I withdrew from this college and I decided to attend RIT in hopes of getting cued speech transliterators. People often ask me why I prefer cued speech transliterators when I already know sign language over the sign language interpreters. Well, what most people fail to notice is that in the classrooms, a cued speech transliterator transliterates EVERYTHING that is going on in the room while a sign interpreter only gives information they feel is important for the hearing impaired child. How do I know I am not getting all the information that the teacher is saying when I use a sign language interpreter. Well, I just know the English language and I read what the signing interpreters say. In other words, cued speech helps me understand the whole learning environment.

I have been at RIT three weeks now and a few students and I are still making attempts to get cued speech transliterators at RIT. I believe that each hearing impaired child deserves an interpreter of their choice of their modes of communication and I would love to see cued speech transliterators scattered across the country at various colleges/universities. I believe cued speech is an excellent tool for any hearing impaired child. I do understand that the topics of the three modes of communication, oralism, total communication, and cued speech, is a sensitive topic for the deaf community but I do know that cued speech is definitely considered to be one of the best methods of communication for hearing impaired children today and I strongly encourage parents of the deaf child to carefully consider cued speech and realize that cued speech can make a difference in many deaf children like it did for me!

In conclusion, I want to add that I deeply appreciate cued speech now and if it was not for it, myself and many other students who used cued speech would not be where we are today. I have watched myself and other cued speech kids grow academically and socially, and it is all because of cued speech.   Sincerely, Amy Hurowitz
The following is an excerpt from a later letter dated Feb. 8, 1992.

You asked for a picture of me—I couldn't find one of myself but I found one of me & Sarah Hightower (another cued speech user). We went to Lenoir Rhyne College in North Carolina for one semester together & we're really good friends. The cued speech situation up here at RIT is progressing slowly—but we shall wait and see what happens in the future with getting CS transliterators. *See p. 308.*

Jeffrey Majors (19)
Conroe, Tex., Sept. 30. 1991

I became deaf when I was five months old due to measles. Once my parents discovered that I didn't respond to sound, they were concerned and took me to a doctor. The doctor diagnosed me as profoundly deaf and recommended me to attend Houston School for the Deaf. My parents studied about the deaf world and decided to raise me orally because they expected me to learn to speak. They didn't want to use sign language because they feared that I might not be able to speak.

Eight years later, growing up orally had not produced any significant improvement in my study skills and I barely knew twenty words, according to my parents. When Cued Speech was introduced in Conroe (a suburb of Houston, Texas), my mother was skeptical at its benefits, but changed her mind soon. When I was exposed to Cued Speech I thought the movements of handshapes was beautiful and graceful, yet looked complicated. I was willing to learn. I immediately picked (up) the spoken words and learned quickly. Five years later I began to mainstream in sixth grade and still do very well in my subjects.

I instructed my interpreter not to interpret everything a teacher says because most teachers tend to repeat or superfluously explain their lectures. I wanted few words that would be understood clearly. My interpreter transliterates when it's important or when I want to know (exactly) what a teacher is saying.

Jeffrey Majors

I love to read. I read all the time. Books are nutrients for my mind. I've always enjoyed reading books about philosophy, religion, ethics, and other human-related subjects. It's the real joy of learning.

A lot of my friends are in college or working. I have several hearing friends as well as hearing-impaired friends. I prefer to be with anybody who can sign or cue so I can see what they are saying. It doesn't matter whether they are hearing or deaf.

This year is my senior year and I can hardly wait to graduate and go to college. I'm optimistic that I'll succeed in my business and write books.

Without Cued Speech I would not have been able to read like I do now nor mainstream in regular classes. I sincerely believe Cued Speech (English) should be the first language for a deaf American. As a child comprehends the grammar, it would enable him to learn other languages including ASL and still fit in a hearing world. Some people say that Cued Speech is not for everyone. I found this to be irrelevent. It's like saying English is not for everyone in America.

Anybody can learn anything if they make it clear and concise. Cued Speech is just a visual aid to spoken language. It has helped me a great deal and I feel so fortunate. I still cannot believe nobody thought of a method like Cued Speech!

With the above Jeffrey sent an essay written as a "letter to the editor" of a publication in which there were letters from persons he considered "narrow-minded Christians." We reproduce part of it to show the depth of his thinking and reading, and how far he has come linguistically from his condition at nine years of age. We are assured that the ideas in his essay came from his own reading, not his parents.

"I've been reading 'Letters to the Editor' for several years and I want to respond to Christian letters. I've met several Christians and studied Christianity for years. Based on my research, I've concluded that the New Testament is a myth, just like Gilgamesh or Greek myths. There is nothing wrong with myths, but the problem is that people should not depend on myths to justify their actions."

Jeffrey goes on to expound on evolution versus creation, and delineates clearly and forcefully his humanistic philosophy in which moral codes evolve from experience as he says they do in all religions.

Jeffrey has recently become more interested in Deaf Culture and is now (1992) considering attending a college in which he can mix with deaf signers. He is a skilled speechreader and has clearly intelligible speech. Thus, if he proceeds with his plan to choose a college in which he can have extensive social interaction with signing deaf young people, he will be seeking "the best of both worlds."

Holly Abell (19)
Commerce, Tex., 1991 and 1992

Holly is a prelingually and profoundly deaf (PTA 115 dB) girl who was in an oral program until the age of 8 years, when her parents and the local school started using Cued Speech. When she was 13 years old her family moved from Conroe, Texas, to Wharton, and then to Commerce. She was mainstreamed for part of this time with a CS transliterator, and was in a TC program for two years. Her parents continued to use CS with her at home. In the fall of 1990 she entered (for her senior year) the Model Secondary School for the Deaf (MSSD), at Gallaudet University. She was graduated in May, 1991, and was accepted for the prep program at Gallaudet University. However, feeling a need to be at home more for Cued Speech exposure, and also avoid the hassle of flying back and forth to Washington, she decided to spend one semester in a technical program in Waco, Texas.

Holly's accomplishments are remarkable in view of the fact that she started being exposed to Cued Speech very late, at 8 years of age, and with a very low language level. Also, she has had symptoms of memory problems all along, but has outwitted them to a substantial degree by family support. ingenuity, effort, and determination.

We invited Holly to write a paper for us because we knew she could describe the experiences of a deaf youngster who felt a need for access to the deaf culture and could express her feelings well.
Holly received help from her mother in reorganizing the first draft of her paper. We are therefore including copies of her letter of transmittal and one of her informal letters (which we copied from her longhand original) as a sample of her unedited output. Holly's feelings about deaf culture and ASL may help parents to know what their deaf child may eventually feel and want to do.

Dear Mom   May 21, 1991
        Thanks very much for doing the bank stuff for me. I am proud of myself that now I have a savings account. Makes me feel like I'm older now. This bank sounds a good one for me. I like the idea about 5% interest in one year and I can withdraw money three times for 3 each months—that way I can save money better—instead of withdraw too much. I don't want to withdraw more than 3 sometimes unless if its important. Can I use the card in Washington, D.C.? What kind of card it is?
        How much did you get cash for me for the summer. I need to know how much money I have in the bank. I also would like to put the graduation gift (money) from Daddy-grand in the bank. Same with stock money. Thanks. How do you do that anyway? (Putting them in bank!). I will put all money from Graduation if I get some, in the bank. I'm in hurry. It's in the morning right now—I'm mailing this soon. Michelle already asked me if I could be her roomate for prep Gally. I told her "Yes." But what if I want to go TSTI! That's a problem.
        I want to go home now! Can't wait for 4 more weeks! - Holly

The next letter, not edited by anyone, reveals writing ability that is remarkable in view of the language and reading deficits indicated by Holly's scores on standard tests.

Dear Dr. Cornett,   July 12, 1991

I hope you like my paper that I wrote. I hope it's what you want and that it answers your questions. I was going to make a book about some of this because I had so many ideas, but I remembered that you need for me to write something so I decided to do it first.

I was thinking so much about what to write for the book so that's why I have so much to say in this paper. In the first draft I said all the important things and feelings. Then my mom and I corrected it and moved things around to fit right together.

Mom told me about your new plan and I was very surprised. I'm glad you are doing that (*the ASL/English bilingual model*). I hope it works. Good Luck. I really have a hard time telling people about ASL and Cued Speech. They won't listen and they don't understand. They would rather use one thing, ASL, so that's why I'm telling you good luck. I hope this letter helps   helps.   Love,   Holly Abell

Perspectives on Deaf Culture, CS and ASL
by Holly Abell
Note the progressive change in Holly's attitude toward ASL during her year at the Model Secondary School for the Deaf.

I grew up in the hearing world until I was eighteen years old. Then I decided to go to MSSD at Gallaudet for my senior year. When I first got there, I was so frustrated in the fall because I didn't know ASL at all. I used Cued Speech for ten years and I used Signed English for three years in high school, but ASL was so different, not at all like the sign language I was used to. I started out in a volleyball camp the first week before school and I thought it was just for fun. The coach used ASL all the time and I couldn't understand him at all. I had to just follow the team like a watching a tennis ball in a game, back and forth, without understanding what was going on. I felt like the pressure was getting stronger and stronger, and harder and harder and then one day I finally asked another girl if this was the team and she told me of course it was. I was shocked. I didn't even know I was on the team. I went to talk to the coach in his office alone. I was signing my English words so awkwardly so the coach didn't really understand what I was trying to say. I couldn't take it any more. I had to have a break. It was my first time in Deaf Culture. I couldn't join any more activities because I was too lost. I couldn't do it because of ASL. I needed Cued Speech badly, but there was no one to help me.

But I was very lucky because there was a boy named Harvey from a strong deaf family and we became friends. Harvey taught me ASL from watching him talk to me. He helped me also by telling me about deaf people and about the students at MSSD so I would know what was going on. He began to tell me a lot of stories and jokes. I usually don't laugh at jokes, but when he told me his jokes, I laughed and laughed. His ASL was very fluent. His hands were flying and his face had vivid expressions. At first I had to interrupt him a lot in the middle of his stories and then he explained slowly. He told me not to talk too much while I'm signing. He said if you close your lips you improve your ASL so I closed my lips, but I was stuck. I thought people had to read my lips with signs, but I realized if I signed without talking I improved, making better summaries of language in ASL. When I talk and sign, I feel like I am signing every word and like I have no expression. It's another language. Deaf people don't have speaking or lips for communicating with other deaf people and their language doesn't need that. That belongs to the hearing world. Since I liked Harvey so much I wanted to learn ASL for him so I tried even though it was a struggle for me. But I gradually learned a little bit every day until after about six months, I began to understand. I learned then that if you stay in Deaf Culture for one week you won't realize what it's really like. You have to stay for at least six months before you start to enjoy it and begin to use ASL better, but the longer you stay, the more you will like it. When my graduation finally came, I felt like Deaf Culture was my home.

Before I went to Deaf Culture, my parents or friends would cue to me about what's going on and talk to me and I thought it was enough information. But when I went to MSSD, I couldn't believe all the information I got coming at me all the time. It overwhelmed me, like my mind didn't have enough room to accept it all. I got tired easily, but finally I realized that the world is an exciting place and that conversation with friends can be fun. Of course, I had some very good times with close friends who I grew up with and who cued to me, but when we grew up it got worse because my friends could hear and they would turn or interrupt, and make me feel uncomfortable. I felt like I couldn't fit in and that I didn't hear enough information. They told me things and talked to me, but I felt like I was getting less and less. When I found Deaf Culture, I learned that I needed to be with deaf people to know more about the world, what's going on, and to believe in myself. I needed to know I was not a cheap and boring person. In Deaf Culture I feel so good, so special, and excited about the future, like I want my life for a long time.

In my opinion and for me, if a deaf person lives in the hearing world and has a few deaf friends, that still is not enough. You will see the same people every day and it doesn't work. Those people might not know Deaf Culture either. An example is that I went to a mainstreaming school where there were about seven deaf students, but I still felt lousy because they didn't know either. Now I would love to bring all of them, even the teacher, to Deaf Culture to show them. They would be so surprised. Maybe some deaf people can be happy in the hearing world only, but I think they are missing the best part of their lives.

Holly Abell

Now I'll talk a little about Cued Speech. I don't want you to think I didn't use Cued Speech enough. I really used it every day for many years with no sign language at all. I had interpreters who used Cued Speech and my family, mom, dad and brothers, and friends used Cued Speech. It is very important for me also because my family only knows Cued Speech and I need to communicate with them. Some of my family want to learn ASL but I won't teach them because I still want them to use Cued Speech all the time, not ASL, because when I'm gone to Deaf Culture, there's no Cued Speech, so I don't have to worry about losing Cued Speech because my family knows it. Then I know I won't forget all the English words and the way to talk and use English. It's like Cued Speech reminds me of all the little words like "the" and "a" and "adverbs," etc. I'm used to them using Cued Speech. When they try to say something in ASL they look goofy.

And another thing also drives me crazy. I learned a lot of new words in sign language, and I didn't have time to ask how do you spell it or I forgot how to spell it and I didn't know how to say it. When I came home I wanted my mom to know the new signs I learned, but I didn't know the words to tell her. It shocked me that I realized I didn't know the English words to explain the signs to her. That makes me so mad because sometimes I need to use those words to say or write them. I think it would be good for deaf people to know Cued Speech for when they use ASL, so I could stop them and ask, what is that in English and they could cue it for me and then go back to ASL in the conversation.

I don't blame my parents that I missed so much in my life. They heard from the wrong people. My parents heard bad things about ASL when I was a little baby, so they tried to make me talk and read lips without cueing or signing, until I was eight years old. Finally my parents learned Cued Speech from Dr. Cornett. I was very lucky to have Cued Speech, but I wish they would have told mom the best things when I was a little baby, like to use Cued Speech *and* ASL.

Now I do have Cued Speech for English and I'm glad, but my favorite is ASL. When I'm at MSSD or Gallaudet, I use ASL all the time and I don't talk or don't use my voice at all. I love communicating like that with no voice. We can talk faster and understand each other more and we never misunderstand. It feels like we are a close family. When I come home my family is easily misunderstood, but not too bad. Some times I feel like it takes longer for them to understand because I have to talk slowly, use my voice so that every word is loud and perfect. I have to think about my speech and not about what I am saying so I get tired easily. Often they don't understand me as well as deaf people. I know they don't really understand me fully, but it's O.K. Sometimes I wish I could talk to them like deaf people so they would know me more. They don't know me enough because of communication. Too bad deaf people know me and they are not my family. I just met them and they understand me more than most of my family.

Another way ASL has helped me is in my writing. It's very true that Cued Speech helps make my English more perfect when I write, but it seemed like my stories were boring. Now when I write it's more fun and interesting to explain more by thinking in ASL, thinking about the expressions and explanations so much improves my stories or letter writing, because there is more feeling from all the things I've learned in Deaf Culture and by using ASL. (Also my English teacher at MSSD was very good at helping me learn to write stories by explaining things in ASL.)

One of my friends told me that ASL is primitive and that deaf people in Deaf culture are stupid. He thinks they don't like Cued Speech because it's too hard for them and that ASL is easier so they prefer it. This is not true at all. That makes me laugh. ASL is really very complicated and can do many things that English cannot do. People like him don't know what ASL is like enough. And they act like they might want to try to take our language away from us. It's just like other groups in America, like the people from Mexico. They speak English but when they are at home with family, friends, and other Mexicans, they love to speak in Spanish. It's just the same in Deaf Culture. We love to use ASL. You can't tell Mexicans to stop speaking Spanish. I hate when people tell others that ASL is very bad or that it's not as good as English. It is our first language. How would you feel if they tell you to stop using English in America? That's why most of the deaf people are mad about Cued Speech. They don't understand and they got the wrong idea. They think people who use Cued Speech think ASL is bad or that Cued Speech is better. Don't say that. But I'm afraid it's too late; it already spread. I appreciate ASL, and I do not want to lose our first language or maybe there will be no Deaf Culture where we can belong. You know that's one reason that deaf people are a little private about using ASL with hearing people. They are so worried that they will lose it (because hearing people have always tried to take it away in the past).

One other thing might help you learn what I am trying to say about Deaf Culture. I think it is very interesting that many hard-of-hearing people, who can talk very well, even on the phone, hear music, etc. would rather be in Deaf Culture and they love ASL. Karen is hard of hearing and she talks very well. She didn't know ASL, because it was her first year to be at MSSD like me. She was learning some and she liked it but she started having problems with all the strict dorm rules, like a prison. That made her want to go back to her hearing school. She stayed there for two weeks and she realized how much Deaf Culture was important to her and how it helped her so much so she went back and learned more ASL. She fell in love with ASL completely. Right now you can't tell she's hard-of-hearing. She uses ASL so beautifully. She decided it was better to be in a prison with deaf people because they were worth it.

All of the things I have learned in my life have made me feel like helping deaf people because they need a lot of help. I want to be a psychologist and to work with little deaf kids so I can use ASL before they grow up, and I will tell their parents how to develop their kids with ASL and Cued Speech. I am going to Gallaudet to get a degree in psychology or counseling and I will tell everyone about these things. That's my goal.

For now, I would like to say a few things of advice to parents and to deaf kids. I would suggest if you have a deaf child, please take them to meet deaf people who use ASL and let them be with them when they are young so they can learn more. They need to grow up with them in their lives. And use Cued Speech for English and reading so the English will improve so they will know hearing words also. And for deaf parents, it would be different. If you have a deaf child, of course, you will use ASL when they are babies. When they grow up some, tell them about Cued Speech, why it's important, so they would love to learn it because it's new and for the hearing world. They would love to know about the interesting hearing world. It would be like learning about another country.

For those deaf people or kids who don't live in the Deaf Culture, read books, a million books, because you are missing a lot because you are not with deaf people. If you are with deaf people you have to read books still. Hearing people hear and hear and they learn from hearing and reading; that's double. But deaf need to read more than hearing because they can't hear. But if you are with deaf people you still have to read and watch TV with captions to have better English. I am very, very behind because I didn't read many books, and I grew up in the hearing world. When I came to MSSD, I noticed I was too far behind. Many times I didn't know what the people were talking about, and I would get embarrassed. It was terrible. I wish I knew reading books was that important. I've been hearing that books are important from my parents and from my teachers, but I didn't understand why. The teacher at MSSD made me read or I would fail so I was stuck. When I read I noticed I was learning so much from books. When my parents told me about reading, I didn't really get it, but if a deaf person tells me to read a book and explains why, my mind really accepts the information. They explain so much deeper, and I would understand then. I believe when they explain and tell me what to do.

For most of my life, I did not know there was a Deaf Culture. I thought the world was just a round place with people on it, and they all went to school, to see movies, to Six Flags, or on a date, and it was just always a little bit sad. But then at MSSD, I found a whole new world where people had fun communicating and talking together so much. I learned a lot about deaf people and about myself too. In the hearing world I didn't know who I was or what I was going to do with my life. When I started communicating with the Deaf, my real personality came out and I knew who Holly was. It was like a gift to me, like going to heaven. I feel sorry for many deaf kids who don't know where they are born or where they belong, and they might be in the wrong place. But I know I found my place, where I belong.

Janie Abell, mother of Holly, writes: "Holly is perhaps a good example for answering the question 'How Long?' As she has aptly put it, she wants her family to continue to cue to her because now that she spends so much time with deaf friends she gets much less Cued Speech. She is aware that she needs continued refreshing of English words and the ways of saying things. Continued family use of Cued Speech is especially important for those kids who prefer to spend most of their social time in the deaf world after they are older. I still teach Holly new words all the time, and she helps me find the right English words for the new signs she picks up from deaf friends."

Leah Henegar Lewis (27)
Cary, N.C. Aug. 24, 1992

I want to say how fortunate I am in using Cued Speech all my life. I can't imagine *not* using Cued Speech. I could either be a signer or an oralist, but still not able to get jobs like a hearing person—which I feel like. Cued Speech has done a great deal for my life, growing up with a hearing family, marrying a hearing guy, and my latest development, a hearing infant son (I am cueing to him so he will learn to cue.

Leah Henegar Lewis

Growing up with a hearing family has given me a lot of wonderful memories. My siblings learned how to cue when we started with Cued Speech. Everybody in my family had to be sure I was included in conversations all the time. Now, all of us are grown up, and when we all get together, they still make sure I am not left out.

Not only did Cued Speech help me with my family, but it helped me tremendously at school. I went to public school all through my school years. While I was in elementary school, all my teachers learned how to cue, and even my classmates, some who would sit with me in class and help me out. In junior high school, I didn't have very much Cued Speech in school, because none of my teachers learned how to cue, and I had to depend on lipreading, and it was the most difficult time I ever went through, and I didn't really do very well in school. When I entered high school, I had an interpreter attending classes with me, and I progressed a whole lot better than without interpreters. I also had a Cued Speech interpreter for my business classes at Wake Technical Community College.

Now I am married to a hearing man, but I can lipread him very well. He is easy to understand, but there are times when I cannot understand what he's trying to tell me, so then he cues for me.

It is real important to keep on cueing in the family while the child is growing up so he can turn out to be happy and well adjusted. It is also important to keep cueing whenever deaf adults who use Cued Speech are around. *Chapter 3 is devoted to Leah and her family.*

Chapter 26
ODYSSEY, One Family's Story
by Osmond Crosby

Shattered Dreams
Diagnosis to Four Months Post Diagnosis

When your dreams shatter, there is no sound, just the slow-motion vision of icebergs sliding off a glacier, making huge soundless waves and looking so calm—unless you happen to be swimming under the iceberg.

That's what it was like the day Debbi and I learned that our beautiful 2-year-old had a hearing problem. It was hard to wrap our minds around the word "deaf" immediately, even though in recent months we had become increasingly aware that Dorothy Jane didn't seem to hear. The moment of knowing, really knowing, that our lives had taken an unexpected turn came in the audiometry booth, when DJ sat in my lap cheerfully playing with a colorful puzzle and showing no response to the sounds that came over the speakers—louder and **louder** and **LOUDER**. This wasn't happening to us; these things happen to other people; this was not happening! *God, are you really sure you've picked the right family? Can we talk?*

It was 10 more days before we could get the definitive test—a measurement of her brain wave response to sounds. When the nurse stopped her animated chatter and became all business, we knew our fears were real. A few minutes later the doctor gave us the devastating news: no response had been detected at any volume or frequency. Our child was deaf. Cause unknown.

Somehow we drove home and began the process of grieving. We spent Mother's Day weekend asking how this could be true, searching for strength, blaming ourselves for not knowing sooner, imagining what the future would bring, crying over our shattered dreams, and mourning for our poor little girl whose life, we thought, could not possibly be happy or "normal."

I'm glad to say that time was to prove us wrong on many counts. Also, we were fortunate enough to trust in the power of prayer, and we had previously learned something about grieving. So when feelings of denial, shock, anger, and more denial washed over us, we tried to accept them as early stages of the healing process. Our knowledge didn't make the experience any less intense or wounding, but with time we were able to move through the initial emotional firestorm toward acceptance and a pragmatic plan for the future.

Osmond, Debbi, Dorothy Jane (3), and Corina (2) Crosby

Night after sleepless night during those first weeks I found myself making mental lists of pleasures I thought my deaf daughter would not experience: music, dancing, movies, piloting an airplane, singing, talking after lights out. I tried to focus on the myriad of opportunities still open to her, but positive thinking just didn't help. Then I began to list some things that I probably will be unwilling or unable to do in the rest of my lifetime: learn to draw and paint, compete in the Olympics, fly on the space shuttle. When I realized with a shock that these things weren't on my list of "impossibles" for DJ, the whole issue evaporated in a flash!

Sometimes I awake and have to remember: "Oh yes, Dorothy Jane will be deaf again today." It's not something she will eventually get over, like chicken pox. When I dream, Dorothy Jane still speaks. But life continues, and DJ is interested in getting on with it even when we are not. You can attempt to cling to your own sense of tragedy, but it doesn't work when the central character isn't playing her part.

We're fortunate we had time to know DJ before we got the diagnosis. We had already come to know and love her as a beautiful, bright, inquisitive child with a sunny personality. If we had received the news sooner, we probably would not have appreciated these qualities as fully. It's comforting to realize that they didn't switch children on us when we went to the audiologist.

From her viewpoint, her parents and a bunch of their friends were pretty dumb until she finally took them to the hospital. All of a sudden, they got much smarter and started to communicate in a way that made sense.

But life doesn't give us what we can't handle. In a surprisingly short time we were back to facing the same issues all parents face. We just didn't have the luxury of making the necessary decisions unconsciously. Our child was the first deaf person we had known; we had no role models, no peer support. How could we best nurture this bright, inquisitive intelligence? I feared that one of my shattered dreams would be the hope that Dorothy Jane could soar in the realms of learning. It seemed to take so much work, so much pushing, for deaf people to excel in this arena. And when they do, at what cost to a balanced, rounded personality? Clearly, this was more of an issue for me than for DJ, but it hurt so much to let go of those dreams so soon! It felt like a part of me had been ripped away.

We began to realize that the educational decisions we would make for her (whether for Oral Communication, Signing, or Cued Speech) would also be cultural choices that would influence her whole future life. But, after all, isn't that exactly what parents do when they consider the relative benefits of an inner city magnet school, a private school, or a church school? On the other hand, sometimes our alternatives seemed more dramatic—more like choosing to raise a child as a Christian rather than a Moslem, or to live in South Africa instead of Sweden. Dorothy Jane's condition brings a lot of issues into sharper focus. Conscious parenting has become inescapable—and that's probably good.

Questions, questions, questions...But then I sit on the floor with Dorothy Jane and she signs "cat" for the first time and I smile/cry/laugh. We are explorers together in an unknown land. The maps are nonexistent, contradictory, or confusing. What adventures await us? What secrets will be revealed? Will there be treasure? Magic? Will she push back the borders of the known world? How far will we journey together?

Now those are the real questions, and the answer sleeps in my arms, dreaming silent dreams.

One Day at a Time
Months Five and Six Post Diagnosis

In the few short months since those first painful days of adjustment, Dorothy Jane taught Debbi and me more about hope and optimism and love than we ever thought possible. We met so many successful deaf adults that we stopped worrying so much. Learning that there are deaf pilots, accountants, and college presidents was a big help in putting things into perspective. The women's land speed record is held by a deaf person. (Don't go trying to break it, DJ!)

So the challenge is no longer dealing with our shattered dreams. Instead we find ourselves pondering the best educational strategies, deciding on how to help her crack the code of language, and spending a great deal of very normal time with a wonderful child.

I'll share a few entries from my journal. They reflect what I felt at the time—many opinions and perspectives have changed as our personal odyssey continues to unfold:

- Saw Dr. Charles Berlin in New Orleans. Everyone says he is the best research audiologist around. He changed the time window on DJ's brain stem test and found a little residual hearing (at 80-90 dB). This has tremendous implications for language development. To see how much a tiny bit of a sense helps, close your eyes completely and try writing something. Then, close them so far that you see only dim shapes and try writing the same thing.
- Just received a card from a good friend. The legend says "Don't Look Back," and it shows someone taking a fork in the road. The way being taken is labeled "Your Life." The other road says "No Longer an Option." What an apt description of recent months.
- Now when I dream, Dorothy Jane, Debbi, and I are signing to each other. Lots of our hearing friends are signing in my dreams too. Hope DJ will also talk.
- Sometimes people say how lucky Dorothy Jane is to have us, and we reply that we're lucky to have her. Today I realize that the Deaf community will be lucky to have her too.
- Dorothy Jane has a new, beautiful baby sister, Carina! One will grow up in the hearing world and the other in deafness. What a special relationship lies before them. (Eight months later we learned that they will have a special relationship of a different sort, as Carina has a hearing loss too.)
- We look forward to our adventure with Dorothy Jane. We didn't choose it; but since it chose us, we might as well embrace it wholeheartedly.
- This afternoon, I put a few raisins in front of Dorothy Jane. When I glanced her way a moment later, she was quietly signing grace over her tiny little snack all by herself.

And yet, and yet...At times the emotions just blindside you. Today I found DJ looking under the dining room table for our cat. Lucy was only four feet behind her and meowing her head off, but DJ kept searching intently under the table. Suddenly, I was crying like a baby. You think you're doing so well—looking at schools, having great debates about the principles of language acquisition, learning signs, learning cues—and then it just hits you, out of nowhere.

Silent Dancing

We are gathered in the family room. Tiny Carina is asleep in the swing and Dorothy Jane snuggles under a blanket, squeezed into her sister's baby basket. For the last few days DJ has been exploring the life of a 7-week-old baby with great interest bordering on envy; perhaps she dreams of leaving her 2-year-old world and returning to that earlier, simpler time.

Suddenly all sounds stop as communication inexplicably shifts to hands and touch. DJ and Debbi begin a silent hand dance. DJ's movements are purposeful as she patiently guides Debbi's hands into desired patterns. When she has Deb's index finger pointing nicely, DJ starts playing a fingertip game, fast and precise, to which only she knows the rules. Swiftly her fingers dart about, touching Debbi's hand here, then there, then pausing to invite her hand into the dance.

From my perspective, lying on the floor looking upwards, it's like scuba diving and watching fish bump noses as they devour some unseen morsel above. Dorothy Jane's movements are quick, precise, incomprehensible, and delightful. Next she takes my hand and forms it into the same shape. Patiently she leads our hands through an intricate ballet that gives each of us pleasure.

Dorothy Jane's hands dance with one of us, then the other. For weeks I've been obsessed with what we can teach her. Tonight she reminds me that she will teach us too.

A Journey of Discovery
Seven to Nine Months Post Diagnosis

At this time, our personal goal is to raise our daughters with access to both Deaf and hearing cultures,[1] with fluency in the language of each: American Sign Language and English. We will use Cued Speech to model the language we already know, while Sign Language (ASL) will be learned by all of us from native Deaf signers. There is much to investigate while making these decisions, and we respect each

---

[1]Deaf Culture uses uncapitalized "deaf" to refer to someone who is biologically deaf. Capitalized "Deaf" refers to someone who is "deaf," but has also assimilated the culture associated with deafness. Since culture is transmitted largely through language, the natural, visual language of American Sign Language (ASL) is the vehicle for passing on Deaf Culture in the United States. Therefore, many people are deaf but not Deaf (e.g., someone who loses hearing with old age).

family's individual choice.[2] There are many different kinds of success stories in deaf education. This is simply our personal experience as we learn more each day about deafness, language acquisition, bilingualism, educational methods, and pressures to "do it" a certain way.

The first thing we had to learn was that speech is not language, nor is language speech. Speech is one way of expressing a language, but it is not the only way. Language can also be expressed through writing, signing, Cued Speech, and Morse code. But before ideas can be exchanged, a language must be acquired, and therein lies the need for a major decision.

When I first read about Cued Speech in *Choices in Deafness*, it didn't interest me. It looked like an oralist approach, and oralism seemed to have serious drawbacks for a child who was profoundly deaf before acquiring language. For a deaf child to learn language when traditional Oral techniques are used can be compared to trying to learn Japanese by watching people talk to you from outside a soundproof glass booth. The task is even more difficult for a child who has been hearing impaired since birth. Unlike one who has lost hearing early in life, they don't know that all those facial movements are associated with sound, much less meaning. If a little understandable sound is available, or if one has the vaguest concept of sound and language, the task is very different.

Immediately after Dorothy Jane's diagnosis, Debbi and I began to learn signs from a deaf woman. We were quickly rewarded with basic communication, and were thrilled to have some two-way conversations at last. It was natural for us to use signs in English word order, the way signs are used in most Total Communication programs. Without realizing it, however, we began to stop signing words that were not necessary to getting the point across. Although we were speaking full sentences, the language coming off our hands went like this: "We go market. What you want buy? This pretty, you like?" I call it Tarzan Speak. It has no resemblance to the sparse beauty of ASL, which is truly a different language with its own grammar and structure. It will take us years to learn ASL. These initial forays into the thicket of communication methods made us concerned about the quality of the language DJ would internalize. This clearly had major implications for reading skills later.

While many deaf parents are already equipped to teach their

---

[2]We found two publications to be excellent starting points for information: *Beginnings,* by J. Craig Greene, and *Choices in Deafness: A Parents Guide,* Edited by Sue Schwartz, Ph.D.

children a signed language, most hearing parents are not. And because almost all early education comes from the parents, it seems reasonable for the "home language" to be the language of the parents. Debbi has used the Japanese language analogy mentioned earlier to explain what it would be like for us to try to teach Dorothy Jane ASL as her first language:

Imagine that you are suddenly and unexpectedly given two options: Either learn Japanese, which you don't speak, in order to communicate with your infant child, or let her learn language primarily from native Japanese speakers, with the hope that she may also learn to read and write English at some later time.

When we learned that Cued Speech is English presented in a form that is totally visible and unambiguous, we decided it deserved closer examination. With Cued Speech, one can understand without having to hear the verbal message; without having to guess at it (as in speechreading); without having to switch codes (as in Signed English).

For hearing parents, learning Cued Speech is not learning a new language; it is just learning a new physical way of expressing the language they already know. In this respect, it is more like learning typing or shorthand. Cued Speech accurately transposes every sound of spoken English into visual form, making each syllable accessible to deaf people. Deaf children of hearing, English-speaking parents who learn English through this tool learn the language of their parents.

Signing, on the other hand, expresses concepts in the symbols and syntax of a distinct language (American Sign Language) or in a code system (Sign English) that does not show the phonology of English. For speaking parents who think in English, or for participants in a mainstream classroom, the need for translation means that all communication must be interpreted. It moves the deaf child one layer further away from the culture of the parents and the larger society.

The strongest case I have seen for presenting a verbal language using Cued Speech is the observation by Dr. Cornett that new vocabulary cannot be picked up by speechreading alone. That is, when one relies solely on lipreading, new verbal language must be formally taught, as opposed to incidentally learned. We are grateful that Cued Speech is there to unlock the soundproof booth, providing full access to the code of English.

Just as English will be important to Dorothy Jane's educational progress, Sign Language will be important to her social development. Therefore, we plan to continue studying and using Sign (ASL, as we learn it) in appropriate contexts. Dorothy Jane will grow up seeing us sign to her deaf friends who use signs. She already has had deaf baby-sitters and a deaf playmate with Deaf parents. We hope that the number of Deaf role models in her life will continue to increase as time goes on.

Fluency in English won't make DJ a hearing person, but it will give her maximum flexibility in life's choices, access to the educational system, and participation in the daily activities of a hearing family and the larger world. By the same token, we expect that the Deaf world will be an important part of her life, and ASL will give her the best possible access to that culture too.

After a long hard look at what was available locally, it was clear that Florida just didn't have the range of options we felt we needed to support our emerging goal of bilingualism for DJ. We decided to move to an area where there was an appropriate infrastructure of deaf educators, speech therapists, deaf peers and role models, audiologists, pediatric hearing specialists, and cueing kids in the mainstream.

We identified several areas that met our needs and finally settled on Fairfax County, Va., just south of Washington, D.C. There are enough deaf children in this area and such a commitment to deaf education that a child using any of the three methods—Cued Speech, Total Communication, or Oral—can attend an elementary school with all the other deaf students in the county who are using that approach. They are mainstreamed for as many classes as feasible but also have specialized training in language skills, made possible by the concentration of resources in each location.

While visiting schools in the Washington area, we met Daniel Koo, an articulate young man who is the first Cued Speech student to go to the University of Maryland. He signs with many of his deaf friends and watches a Cued Speech transliterator in class. Daniel is a remarkable young man, a joy to meet, and certainly a source of pride to his family and teachers. Shortly after we returned home, he wrote to me. Let his inspirational words speak for themselves:

> *I consider myself very fortunate to have come across the three deaf languages[3] (Oral, Cued Speech, and Sign Language) and some ASL. All of this does not automatically mean I can talk, so I am blessed with having been able to develop the vocal capability to communicate with the*

---

[3]Although these are generally regarded as ways of expressing language rather than actual languages, I have left Daniel's terminology intact.

hearing world. Like my mother, I believe I must first learn how to live in the hearing world because it is every-where—stores, taxis, salespersons, bus drivers, teachers, friends, neighbors, etc. And then, like a second language, I can integrate myself into the Deaf culture. It isn't easy doing both but it is worth the effort. Having the qualities that few people in the world have is a thrilling thought.

When I first learned Cued Speech, I thought I was bilingual. Alas no, I was not. I was merely learning how to see and pronounce English. When I entered junior high, Sign Language came into my life, and it was then that I realized how there are no limits to my abilities. How I can soar into the two worlds!

What skills will take root and flourish in Dorothy Jane remains to be seen. If she can have the chance to realize her potential in the areas that are ultimately important to her, that will be sufficient. Certainly there are inherent limits defined by native abilities. The best track coaching in the world may get you down to 10.6 seconds in the 100 meters, but you'll never go under 10 seconds unless you are born with the natural potential of an Olympic sprinter. But you won't reach even 10.6 in the 100 unless you have both good coaching and plenty of desire. It's a delicate balance to provide a variety of opportunities for our children while letting them create their own vision of their lives. If it ever comes down to a choice between good speech and good language, however, we want Dorothy Jane to have the tool of language, in whatever form she can develop it.

Blood, Sweat, and Fears
Nine to Twelve Months Post Diagnosis

Slow, slow, slow. Sometimes it seems like we're running in place. Not every day is a good day, but we will get there.

Shortly after we moved to Virginia, it became clear that the time had come to stop considering the theoretical aspects of raising a deaf child and get on with the reality of doing so. That initial, intense period of learning was important, but now I needed to remember why I had become a student again: not to get another degree, but to map unknown terrain. Accordingly, our emphasis shifted from thinking about what we might do, to practicing our skills and exposing our children to as much language as possible.

In Virginia, our first priority was to find a family-oriented neighborhood with little traffic. We soon moved into the house where we hope to raise our family, put up a "Deaf Child at Play" sign, and started to make a home for ourselves. Two preschool children share a driveway with us, three little girls live across the street (their mother is an audiologist), and there are many other children in the neighborhood. The neighbor kids next door are already picking up some signs and cues. When we have races, I cue the ready, set, go without voice and everyone has an even chance.

The National Zoo is only 20 minutes away. There the value of Cued Speech is apparent as we cue the animals' names (orangutan, Ling-Ling the panda, python) rather than categories (bear, monkey, snake). The first time we were at the zoo, I was cueing for the video camera so DJ would be able to follow the narrative in later years, and I was introducing the South American Sloth Bear. My cueing was so slow, that by the time I'd finished and Debbi panned the camera over to the display, the bear had gone back into his cave!

Although we've made considerable progress in the last year, some lessons are emerging only now. For instance, I realize that I fell into a common, perhaps universal, trap of seeing my children as unique. When we went to the Cued Speech National Center for our initial training last year, another parent in the course said that one difficulty in raising her 11-year-old deaf child was the need to teach her everything, and that this required "a thousand repetitions." I just smiled and nodded, knowing that it would be different for us because of the secret I held deep in my heart: that DJ was different from the other kids and wouldn't encounter the same difficulties because she was smart(er). I'm ashamed of the judgment, prejudice, and plain blind ignorance these thoughts implied, but that is what I believed.

Sure my children are smart, but they have no monopoly on brainpower. When our classmate's daughter learned Cued Speech in only a few weeks and went on to win an award for the most improved student in her whole school, deaf or hearing, it demolished my secret fantasy that our brilliant child would somehow do an end run around the challenges all deaf children face. The plain fact is that being quick at problem solving doesn't allow one to skip over the need for lots of repetition in learning language.

Now I realize that everyone has to be exposed to a word "a thousand times" before they learn it. The difference, of course, is that for hearing kids most of the exposure is incidental rather than deliberate. The dialog of a Saturday morning cartoon, the chatter of children playing a game, comments at mealtimes—even everyday sounds like telephones or doorbells that provide context for re-marks—are always there for the hearing child but are not automatically available to the child who relies on visual information. It's easy to see how much learning goes unnoticed in a typical sound-saturated environment.

A Time for Faith
Twelve to Eighteen Months Post Diagnosis

Exactly one year after learning that Dorothy Jane is deaf, we confirmed that 9-month-old Carina has a 60-dB loss in both ears. To our surprise we weren't immune to another round of grieving. Angry and hurt, my first reaction was that we had already "given enough" of our children.

Carina was fitted with much less powerful hearing aids than her sister's and adjusted to them almost immediately. Within about a week, she was wearing them all the time with few problems except for occasionally using them for teething. Now that she has her aids, we are getting a clearer picture of what she was missing before. Without them she was often simply aware of sound; with the aids in she is much better at discriminating sounds, including those of speech. For example, without her aids, she would turn around when I called out "Daddy's here"; now she answers "Da-di" without looking up when I call out.

Thank God we ended up in Fairfax County where we can have one child in the Oral program and another in Cued Speech without needing to move again.

We felt we had adjusted to the reality of Carina's hearing loss until the day the new aids arrived. The simple act of putting those tiny devices into her ears somehow intensified our perception of the road ahead. DJ's Cued Speech program picnic happened to be that day. We set off in the car, trying to be cheerful, not entirely succeeding.

As we arrived, 12-year-old Jennifer Dietz came over and asked to hold Carina. Jennifer didn't know about Carina's recent tests. She was surprised and delighted at the sight of the new hearing aids. She showed Carina her own, then ran into the crowd of young people, proudly introducing her tiny friend. As we watched a group of deaf kids fussing over our baby and exclaiming how cute her little aids were, I turned to Debbi and said, "Kind of hard to maintain a sense of tragedy here, isn't it?"

During our first summer in Virginia, we went to the Family Learning Vacation presented at Gallaudet by the Cued Speech team. There we finally began cueing fast enough to actually say something before DJ looked away. Seeing kids who have been cueing for 10 to 15 years gave me much optimism about our decision to accept less communication in the short term in exchange for fluency in reading and writing English later—actually by about the same time hearing kids achieve it. Although I have met deaf adults who feel the educational system failed them and that time was wasted on certain unproductive methods, I have never met a Cued Speech student who has expressed regret or resentment about having that option selected for them.

However, it is becoming increasingly apparent that Cued Speech is not the path to pursue if you need external validation for your decisions. Sometimes I jokingly say that 50% of deaf education uses signs, 50% uses oralism, and the rest cue! There is certainly no shortage of educators, doctors, parents, and deaf people who will tell you your decision is all wrong, even though many of them don't understand Cued Speech and how it is used. But the opportunity to enlighten the world about Cued Speech will probably be around for quite a while; so for the time being we choose to focus on the immediate issues affecting our kids.

But when does perseverance turn into stubbornness, courage fade to foolishness, faith become intransigence? My intensity and tenacity have gotten us lots of help and information in a short time, but when that same focus is applied to DJ, I sometimes lose sight of *her* priorities. If I could repeat the last few months, I would wait more often for her to lead. I would do more learning and less teaching, more watching and less showing. I would search for her rhythm rather than impose my own.

DJ too is caught in a dilemma. Since she doesn't realize how she is caught, it becomes our dilemma to resolve. Dorothy Jane is blessed with qualities that will serve her well in the years to come—independence, self-sufficiency, and tenacity to match my own. But to the extent that they allow her to create her own little isolated world today, it interferes with her learning. For example, one way to teach language to hearing children is by reminding them to use words when they want something, rather than accepting gestures accompanied by noise. But Dorothy Jane is an independent soul. As often as not, if we encourage her to use her cues when she points to something, she will drag over a chair, put a stool on top of that if necessary, and climb the bookcase to get the video, crayon, or book she wants, rather than responding with sign, cue, or voice. If we wait for a clear request, she will sometimes go off in a corner and entertain herself for an hour rather than engage in a dialog. While these qualities will serve her well in many situations, they severely challenge our creativity as we try to promote a natural exchange of language, be it signed, cued, or spoken.

It is now about 16 months since we learned that DJ is deaf and a year since we began to cue. We may finally be seeing the first bit of light at the end of the first tunnel. I hope so, because the last few months have included many discouraging times. It's hard to confront our powerlessness day after day and keep plugging away with no evidence of results. I've never heard of a child going to college in diapers, and I've never heard of Cued Speech not working when there was persistence and no other physical difficulties, but some days I feel we might be raising the first candidate in both areas.

Actually, toilet training isn't such a bad analogy. Ask the parents of a sixth-grader how they managed to get it done and their answers are often vague and indifferent: "I don't know, it just finally happened." Ask the same question of any parent who is in the middle of the experience and he/she can speak volumes about the frustrations and setbacks.

Dorothy Jane, like any child, has progressed on her own schedule, not ours. She has finally started to communicate constantly, usually with Cued Speech. We understand almost none of it until we replay it a few times. But most of us have experienced a child in the language-learning stage who gets our attention, looks us straight in the eye, and earnestly says something totally incomprehensible. When they rock back on their heels and wait for a reply it is clear that they knew exactly what they said, regardless of our deficiencies in comprehension.

Today's report from DJ's teacher, Jim Latt, is encouraging:

> *Very good day today ... Lots of vocalizations all morning, easy to stimulate.... We said, "Time to go outside." DJ pointed to the window.... I said, "Where is Cajal?" DJ shrugged "don't know" and proceeded to look for her.... We said, "We will blow," and DJ immediately blew air.*

When Dorothy Jane came home with this report in hand, she watched me for such long stretches that, for the first time, I ran out of things to cue while she was looking my way. So the good times are more and more frequent. The recent unsatisfactory pace probably seems like a crisis largely because we have been dealing with the results on a daily basis.

This is a time for us to have faith that we are on a path many others have successfully trodden. First, I had to accept that Dorothy Jane was not so unique that she could avoid all of the repetition involved in learning English. Now I can take comfort in the thought that this same lack of uniqueness means that the ability to learn and express English will come, just as it has for the multitude of young people I have gotten to know over the last year.

A Christmas Miracle
Nineteen Months Post Diagnosis

Remember when the Berlin Wall came down? First there were indications that big things were going to happen, but no one knew when or how fast. Then, just before that unforgettable Christmas, everything happened at a pace that challenged our ability to adjust. One day people were being allowed to cross the border in greater numbers, then anyone could obtain a visa, finally none were needed. Before we knew it, The Wall was down, and we were witnessing history being made moment by moment. Although our little Christmas miracle wasn't reported live on the evening news, it was every bit as dramatic in the small circle of our family.

Shortly after 1-year-old Carina began her first school year and 3-year-old Dorothy Jane her second, we were fortunate to have Leah Minghenelli come into our lives as the children's nanny and teacher. Leah is an expressive, energetic young woman who was Mickey Mouse at Disney World for several years and then a children's counselor on a cruise ship. As a result, she is comfortable communicating without words and seems to know every children's song or story in existence.

Leah learned Cued Speech astonishingly quickly—she seems to have a knack for it. When both the neighbor mothers also learned Cued Speech, we felt as if our language horizons had tripled. When people ask where we found Leah, I simply reply, "God sent her." Now the children are constantly getting good language stimulation both at home and at school, and excellent progress has been our reward in recent weeks.

On Carina's first birthday, we received some good news. Her retesting showed there had been no drop in her hearing over the past three months. That gives us considerable optimism that her loss is not progressive. Although we will do our best to be sensitive to her different needs, her test indicates that she may well be just a kid with hearing aids. By this I mean that much of what she needs from us comes as a byproduct of what we are already doing with Dorothy Jane. Sometimes I wonder/worry about Carina not being more present in this story. The reason may simply be that we aren't exploring as much unknown territory with her.

As the second Christmas since starting Cued Speech drew near, we began to notice that Dorothy Jane was paying more attention to our cueing, understanding more, and trying to cue more herself. We cued dozens of Christmas videos. and she began to show interest in our cued condensations. Leah had been working on carrier phrases like "Pick it up .... and Help me ...." At last the hard work started to pay off: DJ began making the three consecutive handshapes for help when she needed something, and she would pick things up when asked. Small victories, but at last we were communicating in words rather than gestures. It was like watching an icicle begin to melt. You had to pay close attention to know the process was accelerating, but it was.

We had no idea what a wonderful scene was about to unfold. At Thanksgiving, I had promised Leah that Carina would say her name by Christmas. Turns out that the *luh* sound was a tough one to master. Although we worked repeatedly on words like *Leah, light, Lucy Cat, lunch,* and even *luh luh luh,* we were getting nowhere. Dec. 24 came and my foolish promise was unfulfilled. Three hours before we were to get on planes for separate destinations, I admitted to Leah that we wouldn't be hearing her name from Carina this Christmas. Then, from behind us, we heard a soft but perfectly clear **Lee-ah** in Carina's sweet voice.

As we went to the airport on Christmas Eve, Debbi and I joyfully discussed how DJ was responding to instructions and nodding when we used cues to explain what was coming next. Of course, it's sometimes difficult to know how much our deaf child understands, because she has already picked up the knack of bobbing her head as if she understands, even when she clearly doesn't. But when she nods and makes some sort of reply or does what you ask (or emphatically refuses), the connection is certain. Over the next couple of days, we could see her comprehension rapidly increasing. I noticed that she paid attention particularly when I was naming things. They say the realization that everything has a name is an important one.

By the time we returned home five days later, Dorothy Jane was understanding all sorts of phrases and responding appropriately: *Time to go.... Let's go swimming.... Do you want to go for a walk? ... Sit down, buckle up .... Time for your bath.* Sometimes she would indicate that she didn't want to do something, or suggest something else (e.g., the car instead of a walk), but the communication was taking place without pantomime or gesture on our part. As her cueing gets more precise, we understand much more. It really is an accelerating process, just as we were told it would be. At Christmas, DJ knew one color and no numbers. During a two-week period in February, she learned 12 colors and her numbers 1 to 5. I'm awed by what is happening, and want to share our experience with anyone who is newer than we are in this process. There have been times of serious doubt, and surely there will be again, but patience can bring wonderful results. (Patience continually eludes me, however, so persistence and the passage of time have had to suffice instead.)

And now Carina is really starting to talk. New words and short phrases come every day in a flood. Hearing each new word is like being present at a little birth—a true miracle. Often, as we work with DJ on a word, repeating it over and over, Carina will also repeat it from across the room. It's so cute to hear her attempts at *yellow, elephant*, and *rhinoceros* in her little voice. Since Carina does so well with her hearing, we haven't tried to "teach" her to cue, but she is starting all on her own. She tries to cue the *grr* of tiger, *DJ, please,* and a few others. Vowel placement is startlingly accurate. Her signs continue to crack me up, you should see her shiver and shake as she signs cold. As for her progress with speech, I can summarize it in a word: Today she has had fun going around saying *Alligator*!

Although we acknowledge no "better" or "worse" between our two children, it is amazing to watch the difference in expressive communication between Carina, with her 60 dB loss, and Dorothy Jane, with her 90 dB loss. Carina often tries to repeat every word, and it seems so effortless. On the other hand, developing Dorothy Jane's expressive communication requires much more persistence. At this stage, she uses her cues without coordinated mouth movement or voice, so it requires concentration to understand her. The good news is that we are understanding, and her communication is exploding!

Rocket Ride
Jan. 1992, Twenty-One Months Post Diagnosis

We just can't keep up with how fast Dorothy Jane's going now. If we hang in there, we can usually get what she is cueing. Words are usually still "stand alone"—she strings stuff together, but often haphazardly. When she makes combinations, it is frequently giving the color of something: *blue ball, red hat, yellow bird.* If we get a longer utterance it is often disjointed: *Carina...sleeping...pretty*; or perhaps *Turtle* ... (on skis on her shirt) ski...Daddy...me...(We did lots of skiing together this winter.) I'm trying to be rigorous in transcribing what she says, ruthless in eliminating any translating or dressing it up.

We are delighted at the present situation. There is plenty of communication to build on—lots of intent and lots of looking from DJ. It's not like turning a page; it's more like going to a new volume; not like rounding a corner so much as entering a new dimension.

It's especially nice when DJ is right and I am wrong.[4] One day, she kept cueing what I thought was *bead* and pointing into Carina's closet. Finally I saw what she was looking at and corrected her, *"No, that's not a bird, it's a duck."* This went on for a while, and DJ would not change

Dorothy Jane Crosby (4)

her cue as she often does now when corrected. It turns out we were looking at the back of Sesame Street's *Big Bird* (I misread *bead*), and I had to tell her that I was wrong. What a thrill!

So the bottom line is that we are heaving a big sigh of relief around here. It's the little things that tell me she is truly beginning to understand. When she finally began to use the cue for *turtle*, I knew that we were getting somewhere, because that is such a fun sign to make. DJ is trying long cue strings like *elephant* and *rhinoceros*, too. Cued Speech lets her easily enjoy some of the subtleties of English. DJ enjoys pointing out fine differences in colors like <u>pink</u>, <u>fuchia</u>, and <u>peach</u> in people's clothing. She has even tried rhyming a little. She cues *bread*, then finds something *red* to point out. For a while she had a cute way of pluralizing. *Shoes* became *shoe* done with both hands!

---

[4]For readers who don't cue, *bead* and *bird* look the same on the hand; it's the mouth that differs. Since most of Dorothy's expressive information is handshape and location right now, we often have to guess at the correct mouth shape. We have the same type of ambiguous information as in lipreading, but her hands are providing the "clear" input, we are "cuereading."

Now she uses both hands for emphasis, her way of cueing louder.

Everything seems to be clicking all at once rather than gradually. Last year I was frustrated because Dorothy Jane wouldn't look at us for months on end. Now when she wants our attention, she grabs our face and turns it towards her. At other times, she continues to cue something until we cue it back. She insists on that degree of confirmation, rather than letting us respond appropriately or just nod. Sometimes DJ has trouble sleeping because she's so excited about naming things. She woke me up one night to show me she could cue *red boots*.

A year and a half ago I wrote in my journal, "It's reassuring to know that they didn't switch kids on us when we went to the audiologist." This was my way of saying that DJ is beautiful, bright, inquisitive—*and* she is deaf. Now it seems that the elves of language are switching kids on us every few nights. Dorothy Jane's expressive language is appearing so fast that I call it our rocket ride.

As the new year begins, we find ourselves full of optimism. I'm so proud of our little girls for their progress, grateful to Debbi and Leah for their hard work, and hopeful that Dad can turn the burner down a notch and enjoy the ride.

****

Note by Cornett: About six months after writing the above, Osmond Crosby sent me an update. Carina, with the moderate hearing loss, had just turned 2. She could read his cues almost as well as DJ, even when he cued with his voice turned completely off. She was clearly internalizing a phonetic code, because he cued nonsense syllables voicelessly (e.g. "lah-poo") and she said them out loud.

Meanwhile, Dorothy Jane had figured out homophones. One day her father asked, "Do you want to *read* something?" First she gave the name sign for her friend *Reid*. Then she went for a book. He also noted that they were cueing to DJ with the expectation that she would understand, rather than waiting for an indication that she did.

Crosby concluded the update with this observation: "Sometimes it takes a stranger to remind us how far we have come. Recently, we were admiring a kinetic sculpture and discussing the colorful ramps and balls and gears with the kids. A lady came up said: 'It's so nice seeing you communicating with your daughters. My daughter is deaf too, but she's also retarded.' That comment yanked me out of my narrow perspective and reminded me that we <u>do</u> have real communication now—not yet as easy as some families, but real nonetheless."

Chapter 27
Observations From Professionals

These essays by professionals deal with those aspects of what they do that parents need to know about and support. If parents and professionals work together, it is the deaf child who profits. We have selected two professionals with extensive classroom teaching experience, two speech/language therapists, and two transliterators. We have also asked a few professionals with extensive experience and unique perspectives on the needs of deaf children to give their views.

Thoughts on Cued Speech After Twelve Years
by Barbara Lee, M.A., 1992

"I know you won't believe me," she stated, but when you use Cued Speech you can just talk to your children, and they can understand you."

I was walking with Barbara Williams-Scott down the corridor at Kendall Demonstration Elementary School at Gallaudet University in August, 1980. It was the day before the beginning of the Cued Speech Workshop. She made that statement just as we went through one of the double doors. I remember being glad that she was ahead of me and couldn't see my face. My thoughts, communicated through my facial expression, would have told her, "You're right. I don't believe you."

At that point in time, Barbara Williams-Scott was to me the voice of experience when it came to Cued Speech, and I was the novice getting ready to incorporate Cued Speech in the Ascension Parish Deaf Education program at the beginning of the next school year. Yes, I was enthusiastic about using Cued Speech in the program. Yes, I had initiated the decision to use it. But, I only hoped it would make it somewhat easier to teach language to the children. Based on my experience in working with profoundly deaf children in an oral nursery and preschool I absolutely could not comprehend that there would come a time when I could just talk to my children with cues and they would understand me.

The Students

In September 1980, six children, ages 2 to 7, made up the first group of deaf children to learn to cue in our program. At least one parent of each child learned to cue proficiently. For one child both parents learned to cue fluently. The teacher, classroom aide, and speech therapist learned to cue. In 1992, five of the six students are still enrolled in Ascension Parish. The two oldest are juniors in high school, two are eighth graders, and one is a sixth grader. Four of the five are fully mainstreamed; the sixth grader is partially mainstreamed. All have teachers who cue and experienced Cued Speech transliterators. The parents of three of the children have cued consistently. Parents of two of the children have cued only intermittently, for various reasons.

During the years parents, teachers, and students have experienced the heights of exhilaration, as when for the first time a child achieved a language test score on the level of his chronological age, and the depths of despair, as when the possibility of an auditory nerve tumor threatened one of the students. But through it all, the children have succeeded to academic and linguistic levels I only dreamed of before Cued Speech became my ally. I have encountered the skepticism of fellow professionals who questioned the entire concept of the Cued Speech system and the accuracy of the data I reported. They dismissed our language program that was based on learning language the way hearing children learn it, with an all-knowing, "Deaf kids can't do that." But through it all, I say again, the children have succeeded to academic and linguistic levels I only dreamed of before Cued Speech became my ally.

To the skeptics, whose frame of reference on what deaf children can do and my frame of reference are light years apart, I can only say, "You have to see it to believe it. You have to have the Cued Speech experience in your life and your own child's life before you can really understand. I know that what I say deaf students can accomplish sometimes sounds too good to be true. I remember when I was skeptical also. But, if you are willing to give it an honest trial, then it is highly likely that you too will have children who will succeed to academic and linguistic levels you only dreamed about before Cued Speech became your ally.

Myself

After 12 years of using Cued Speech, if I had to describe its effect on me as a teacher in one word, the word would be *liberating*. As a teacher in an oral program, I remember trying to carefully control the syntax and the vocabulary of the sentences I said to the students, in order to avoid talking "over their heads." Now their linguistic levels are so much higher that I just talk to them. If I happen to use a structure or say a word that they do not understand, they know exactly what to do. They tell me, I explain, and we go from there. *Liberating*!

I remember the first time I gave the students the General Knowledge sub-test of the Woodcock-Johnson Psycho-Educational

Battery. Their scores were below the bottom level of the norms. I initiated an extensive program to insure that our educational intervention included opportunities to acquire general knowledge of the world—both at home and at school. The latest scores for the students are *liberating*—for both me and the students.

I remember planning lesson units while sitting under the hair dryer, only to abandon them with the thought that it would be so long before my students would really be able to understand all that—if they ever did—that it was not worth pursuing. After Cued Speech that ceased to be a concern. I plan lessons based on topics and including activities that I think are appropriate, interesting, and applicable to the students' future. *Liberating*!

Before Cued Speech, I remember asking myself, "Am I teaching to their handicap or to their intellect?" The answer was obvious and sobering, my teaching was limited by their handicap—not by the deafness *per se*, but by the severe language delay that was the result of their deafness. Now, when I am teaching the students who are truly Cued Speech kids, meaning that they have cueing all day at school and at least one parent cues fluently and consistently at home—I teach to their intellect at whatever language level is appropriate. Degree of hearing loss is an almost irrelevant consideration. They are more like hearing kids who can hear only when they are looking at me, as Dr. Cornett says, than typical deaf kids. *Liberating*!—for them and for me.

Parents

After 12 years of Cued Speech experience, the one thing I would tell parents who want the benefits of Cued Speech but are cueing minimally is "*Increase your intensity!*" There are parents who, as I perceive them, seem to expect that a good school program will "fix' their child, and that they will pick him or her up 15 years later, after high-school graduation, in fine shape. To them I would say, "*Increase your intensity*, or it won't happen."

I have never seen a school program, the one I work in included, that can "fix" a child without consistent involvement and support from the parents. The education of a child is just too difficult and too involved. The child needs both parents and teachers on his team in order to succeed to the levels we all want for him. Parents, if you really want your child to understand, speak, read, and write the English language at age-appropriate levels, then change your life style if you have to, but *increase your intensity*!

After 12 years of Cued Speech experience the one thing I would say to parents who are already cueing fluently and consistently to their deaf child is, "*Maintain your intensity*." I have seen parents start out at full speed, only to lose their intensity once their child is mainstreamed long before I thought their child was academically or linguistically safe. I have followed students who met our guidelines for mainstreaming in the first grade but who fell below the guidelines a little more as academic learning became more demanding. Their language skills did not keep pace because of too little home support.

Parents who want their child to get a regular high-school diploma, who want that child to get an education and not just pass each grade, should plan to maintain their intensity all through high school. It is absolutely necessary that they maintain their intensity through the middle school years and on into high school. They must not assume that because their child is or has been successfully mainstreamed full time in first grade that he is on automatic for full-time academic mainstreaming in high school. First he must get past what is referred to by deaf education coordinators in my state as "the third grade wall" and "the middle-school moat."

Parents, visualize yourself walking with me down any school hallway, anywhere. Now, I am the voice of experience where Cued Speech is concerned. I'm going to stop, turn, look you full in the face and say, "I know you may not believe me, but when you use Cued Speech like the experts tell you to use Cued Speech, *you can just talk to your deaf child and (s)he will understand you—and LEARN*!" What is there to lose? Try it, and find out.

See p. 302 for information on Barbara Lee's accelerated language development program for hearing-impaired children.

A Cuer Looks at Auditory-Verbal
by Marianne Flanagan, M.A.
From *On Cue*, July/August, 1991

At the end of April, 1991, I spent two weeks in Engelwood, Colorado, at the Auditory-Verbal (A-V) clinic established a couple of years after Doreen Pollock retired from Porter Memorial Hospital, where she had built up her clinic. The Listen Acoupedic Center clinic is supervised by Mary Mosher-Stathes, whom Doreen Pollock trained, and has other Pollock-trained people on the staff.

The experience was really a mind-opener for me. I had been trained as a speech pathologist in the late sixties, and although I bought Mrs. Pollack's book, *Educational Audiology for the Limited Hearing Infant,* all my classes in auditory rehabilitation-habilitation were based on developing lipreading skills as the only way most deaf and hard of hearing children would be able to comprehend spoken language. I knew hearing aids were important for even the profoundly deaf because of the need to be warned about impending danger, but I had never said to myself, as did the early auditory/verbal people such as Pollock, "Why do we put hearing aids on kids and then tell them to use their eyes?" Certainly my constant demand of children was "Look at me!" not "Listen to me!" I was taught that it is only logical to work on the strongest sense rather than the weakest one. But should you ignore a powerful sense such as hearing just because it isn't whole?

Let's say that your child has a profound loss bilaterally. What does s/he gain from listening, without hearing a great deal, even with the best amplification possible? Your child gets a lot of what we call speech suprasegmentals: rhythm, pitch variation, loudness, stress, and duration. These are the things that allow you to understand what your hearing child is telling you long before you can understand the words s/he is saying. You can tell from the "melody," the expression in his/her voice, the intonational pattern. Perhaps you have played a game where you had to carry on a conversation with someone without using real words. So you "babbled," or used nonsense syllables or even the same syllable over and over. But you could carry on a simple conversation, taking your turn to talk, saying how happy or angry you were. It is surprising how much information you can pass along without words! This is not to say that words are not important, but rather that these other parts that go along with the words are also very important. Try saying that last sentence slowly, as though each syllable were the same length, and keep your voice in a monotone. Now, even you will be hard to understand, just because you don't have normal suprasegmentals. If you have more hearing, you get a lot of the actual speech sounds along with these important suprasegmentals, and you can actually monitor your own speech as well as the speech of others.

I have always held that language is much more important than speech. What is the point of having a child you can understand perfectly, if s/he has nothing to say? With Cued Speech we seem to have overcome the greatest problem of being deaf: providing deaf children with the language they need. Now, perhaps it its time to think also of the next problem, letting other people know, in face-to-face conversation with our children, just how competent those children are. To do this, our children need to have understandable speech. And to get this, we need to teach our kids to *listen*. I don't think we do this very much in our homes or our classrooms. It's funny how "other people" think that all Cued Speech is about is *speech*, and they say speech is really unimportant when compared to language, so Cued

Speech is unimportant. But, really, Cued Speech is about learning language through communication with others, using speech. Maybe we should call it something like Cued Communication so people would understand what we mean!

So why am I even talking about speech, if language is the most important thing? Because our kids do get the language. Now let's work on the second most important thing: intelligible speech. Kids raised on Cued Speech have a lot of information about the words—number of syllables, beginning and ending sounds, sequence of the sounds, etc. Let's start thinking about sound again, like some Cued Speech professionals are doing. Let's not put those expensive hearing aids on our kids and then leave them to use only their eyes. There is a lot of valuable information out there about the *sound* of speech for us to take advantage of, too, and our kids won't have to beat their heads against so many brick walls if they sound as good as they really are. What do you think?

Most profoundly deaf children can hear pretty well at frequencies below 300 Hz. That is where the fundamental pitch of the voice is. So, many children who can't hear enough to pick up many speech sounds as such can learn to hear the intonation patterns Ms. Flanagan is talking about.

Communication Between Home and School
by Barbara Williams-Scott, M.A.

Early childhood education focuses on development of the whole child—physically, emotionally, and intellectually. Within this context a teacher plans lessons, guides student activities, and composes correspondence with parents. This concept has stayed with me through my years of teaching deaf children of all ages, as well as in my communicating with parents.

Parents are people with deep concerns and strong feelings who are learning through trial-and-error about the specifics of communicating with a deaf or hard-of-hearing child. They are also in the process of learning to deal with the myriad of professionals that go with a special child! The school is sometimes thought of as a service agency whose employees may be taken for granted. The consumers of the educational process (the students themselves and their parents) may not realize that they need to play a very active role in the planning and fine tuning of the educational process.

Teamwork
Teamwork is essential, not only among professionals and

supporting staff members, but also with parents. In my experience I have found that, unless mutual respect and the habits of sharing and listening are established at the outset, there tends to be a gap in communication between teacher and parent. The inevitable result of a gap in communication is a defensive air that inhibits teamwork.

Parents and teachers have a common interest in the welfare of the child. They also have a common goal—nurturing a positive academic experience appropriate for the child's current skill level and potential for development. The relationship between parent and teacher should be based on trust that both are trying to serve the best interests of the child and both are working consistently toward the same educational goals. The relationship must be such that each is responsive to suggestions from the other.

The Individual Educational Plan for each child contains a column labelled "person responsible." Everyone involved with a student's educational plan has some level of responsibility. The concept of teamwork implies that there is a team. The child should be included in that team. If the child can see that the adults cooperate and participate in what is planned on his/her behalf, s(he) will begin to perceive her/his appropriate role in the whole picture and will be motivated to behave accordingly.

The concept of teamwork implies working together toward a common goal. In order for a team to be successful, there need to be open channels of communication that are honest and flexible, and that lead to acceptance of responsibility by individual members. Each member of the team must be committed to doing his/her share to the best of his/her ability. The teacher plans and implements instruction, guiding parents on educational objectives. You can support those objectives by following through daily at home as well as by providing additional information about your child that you feel might influence his/her development at school. Your child puts forth his/her best effort to learn, and should be viewed as a respected team member who is entitled to some input. If specific duties are too burdensome or some strategies are ineffective, the team should discuss alternatives together and come up with a viable solution, acceptable and fair to the team as a whole. Of course, the continuous underlying guideline is the most appropriate placement for your child.

Clear Home-School Communication

Clear communication is essential. Although teachers should not underestimate your understanding of what is expected of you, they should take care that their messages do not seem vague or confusing.

They should avoid "educational lingo" as much as possible. If teachers speak or write to parents in terms that are not common in conversation, they can inadvertently confuse or even alienate parents. If this happens to you, identify the misunderstanding and ask for clarification as needed in written and verbal exchanges.

Try to take notice of how information from school is worded. It should be helpful to you. See if expectations are stated in positive language, if accurate descriptors of your child are used in reports on behavior and/or progress, if specific vocabulary and goals for activities are included, and if time/space is provided for comments from home. Please do take the time to respond, whether by agreement or by expression of concern.

Bear in mind that teachers appreciate feedback from you—not necessarily on the quality of the reporting (although it is nice to know that at least it was read with interest and discernment!), but on any carry-over happenings at home, any similar behaviors or progress, or any inconsistencies with what the teacher describes. Is your child using the vocabulary indicated? Does your child demonstrate comprehension of the concepts covered in the school unit? Does your child know you are communicating with the teacher, and that this correspondence is out of concern and cooperation, not judgment of his/her performance alone? Do you write down your observations of your child or your reactions to the report in the space that should be provided?

If you feel that your child's teacher is not giving you practical advice on what to do at home, you might request something similar to what I used to share with the home front when I taught elementary-aged children. For example, on days that our class was scheduled for physical education, art, or music (giving me time to plan) I would send home a sheet outlining key vocabulary, activities or projects emphasized by the teachers, concepts (implied or direct) that were the object of the lessons, and suggestions for carry-over at home. The latter might include a repeat or review of the same exercises performed at school, a related idea that would reinforce the class objective from a slightly different perspective, or one that might occur in the home setting through daily chores/errands/activities. Feel free to ask your child's teacher for pointers on what to do or look for at home. Continually share with the teacher what progress you see or concerns you have about what you do not see. Inform the teacher if you feel you need assistance in what to look for. As adults, it is often easy to assume children think the same way we do. We forget how much our life's experiences influence our conclusions about events around us. Sometimes it is a matter of realizing that learning has stages, which include set-backs, plateaus, as well as improvement, when noting our children's growth.

Traveling "News-Book"

Using a spiral bound "news-book" for daily connection between home and school is a technique that I found to be very useful. It gives the child the responsibility to deliver the news-book to his/her parents and me. It also encourages all of us: teacher, student, parent, to be involved and to communicate on a daily basis in a positive manner.

At first, the "news" from school may consist of a simple statement about the special activity of the day, "We learned about ball bouncing, creating green from yellow and blue, and playing different kinds of drums for different sounds." News from home might be, "Today we planted a vegetable garden in the back yard. We used a hoe to dig the soil." It is important that appropriate descriptions accompany the news to expand vocabulary and vary language structures. In the beginning the adults should initiate ideas for the news-book or at least guide the child through specific questions toward a news topic. Eventually, the children themselves can generate what they want to write about in the news-books and illustrate the stories. They learn to stand in front of their classmates and recite or read their news, and share the picture. At home, they enjoy reading their school news to their families.

The news-book provides a routine upon which all can rely, and which helps us focus on spontaneous, frequent communication. The children enjoy it, and the parents benefit from the opportunity to model English and to recognize how important early experiences with language are in learning to (and wanting to) read. Sometimes the news was, "During my vacation I read my book over and over. It was fun!"

Progress Reports

Continuous reporting to and from home can be accomplished through weekly reports on your child's progress, and bi-weekly outlines of plans, in addition to entries in the news-book. You should receive reports based on your individual child and his/her grasp of concepts, specific strengths or needs in speech/auditory training, any noteworthy praise or concern for the week, and suggestions for follow-through. This paper work can be time-consuming and may not occur as frequently as suggested here. However, if you do not have regular contact with or feedback from your child's teacher, you might want to initiate the idea.

As a team member, you can develop a form that highlights

measures or milestones, with headings for unit concepts and vocabulary pertinent to the curriculum, as well as alternatives for the reinforcement expected to occur at home and space to list them. These variations might include introducing synonyms for primary vocabulary items, using idiomatic expressions adults often take for granted. It is a good idea to take the time to read books to your child or go on excursions related to the subject matter—all the while cueing profusely! You can also create a "report" from home in the form of a checklist indicating what was noticed, practiced, worked on, and questioned in the areas mentioned above. Regular feedback from home to school is just as important as information transmitted from school to home. Audiocassette tapes can replace paper (and provide another form of permanent record) if written exchanges become too cumbersome. Children love to make recordings of themselves. You may let your child add a few brief comments on the "business" tape, and encourage him/her to make a separate recording for entertainment to be shared.

Communication and teamwork include paying attention. Active listening is an effective technique that involves attending—with sensitivity—to details. Every person arrives at a given event with a personal agenda and participates in a conversation from a different perspective. That is why it is critical to try to understand the other person's viewpoint, no matter how different it may be from your own. Avoid defensive listening, during which one prepares only to explain his/her position of disagreement. Instead, practice active listening, as exemplified by the response, "This is what I understood you to say and what I think you meant. Am I correct?"

Quality Two-Way Communication

Communication is a two-way process that involves time. You can expect your child's teacher, who has presumably been trained in facilitation techniques, to foster communication between home and school in a comfortable, supportive, and professional manner. Ask him/her to help you learn how to make objective observations of your child's actions at home and to have realistic expectations of your own involvement as well as your child's progress. Share with the teacher what your findings are or any concerns you may have. Make suggestions, join in on a school activity that you design or that is planned for you, and try to be available at reasonable hours for the teacher to confer with you, in person or by phone, as he/she should be for you.

Invite your child's teacher to your home for a conference and/or for dinner. Show your commitment to your child's educational experience and academic career by listening carefully to the teacher.

In turn, demonstrate that you know your child best as you allow the teacher to listen to you. Your child needs to witness this kind of open communication among the important adults in his/her life. He/she will see that the "connection" between home and school is based on friendliness, genuine concern, and give-and-take. This opportunity also lets your child see that caring means sharing and that both professionals and parents feel he/she is worth every minute of it!

Parents Collaborating with the Professionals in Their Child's Speech Training Program
by Barbara M. LeBlanc, M.A., CCC-SLP

Parent involvement and collaboration in the child's speech training program is an integral part of the planning, educating, integrating, and generalizing processes. Therefore, the "parent must be taught how to do all the things that the (speech) therapist (and teacher) do" and be a major participant in the collaborative team decisions (Air & Wood, 1985).

With appropriate guidance parents can do much more than professionals to help the child develop verbal skills in early infancy. It is during early infancy that the development of spoken language requires abundant verbal interaction between the parent and the child on a one-to-one basis. The parents spend much more time with their child during his/her waking hours than the other team members (Ling & Ling-Phillips, 1978). Moreover, the parent has the best opportunity to make sure that what is said to the child relates to his/her specific interests and activities at the moment. This enhances both speech development and language acquisition.

Helping their hearing-impaired child acquire a native mastery of spoken language is a full-time occupation for the parents during the first three or four years of opportunity. This is a very important time frame for optimal spoken-language learning. For this reason it is strongly suggested that the professional train the parents to participate as full partners in the effort to develop good spoken language (Ling & Ling-Phillips, 1978). Parents need to be instructed in detail regarding how to use cueing for speech development, so that they can support and apply what the professionals accomplish with the child.

Throughout the training of speech skills, the parent and the speech therapist can correspond daily with the use of a notebook or folder. This means of communication will provide activities from the speech therapist for the parents to be involved in with the child at home. In addition, the notebook will provide a means for the parent to let the speech therapist know how the child performed, if the parent had any problems eliciting the appropriate speech skills, and about the child's performance at home and at school.

Parents should take time to observe in the school. They can observe how the speech therapist elicits correct productions from the child. "The therapist should verbalize the principle being demonstrated after the parents have observed it (lesson) in action." Parents should also learn what other sense modalities, besides audition, are being used to train speech skills. Finally, each parent should be asked to "practice the principle" while observed by the therapist (Air & Wood, 1985).

In order to familiarize parents with the details of speech development, the speech therapist should arrange for or conduct in-service training for the parents. In addition the therapist should provide for the parent written material supporting what is being taught at school. For example, a one-page summary of the speech training program being employed (such as the Ling program), carry-over strategies to be used at home, and an outline of the child's speech program would be very helpful to parents.

Early Vocalizations

An integral part of language learning for the severely hearing-impaired child is the need to train the child to discover that oral speech is a necessary and natural part of communicating. This starts when the infant begins to develop the foundations of communication involving his/her voice. Professionals should make parents aware of these early vocalizations produced by their infant. In addition, the parent should be trained by the speech therapist so that these vocalizations will be naturally attended to and reinforced appropriately to encourage further development. The therapist should include a "pragmatic assessment" of the child's auditory response to voice because many early aided and unaided audiograms are not always reliable. Parental input on the child's performance is very important to the therapist, too.

The kinds of vocalizations that will develop further during language-learning opportunities provided by the parent might include:
1) vocalizations stimulated by play and in daily activities (peek-a-boo, eating time, bath time, story-reading time, etc.);
2) consistent use of voice to attract attention (at eating time, diapering time, trips outside the home, etc.);
3) vocalization in response to a question ("Are you wet?" "Are you hungry?" "Where's your shoe?" etc.), and
4) vocalization when asked to imitate ("Say mamma." "Say daddy.") and imitating nursery rhymes, finger play activities, children's songs,

counting, ABCs, etc.) (Ling, 1976).

Activities involving much spoken language will also provide opportunities for practicing variations in duration, intensity, and pitch. Professionals should coach parents on developing these contributors to the "personality" of spoken language. At first, because of the degree of hearing impairment, these parameters may develop largely involuntarily. They, too, must be identified, attended to, and reinforced naturally by the parent, so that the child develops them as a part of his/her spoken language.

The child's perception and use of pitch, duration, and intensity in spoken language should be developed through the training of residual hearing, if possible. However, tactile cues should be employed if "...it is evident that the child does not use audition" (Ling, 1976). All of this information about the child's best learning capabilities must be made clear to the parents. Sometimes children begin to respond through audition following the paired stimulation of tactile cues (touching the parent's face, using vibrotactile instruments, etc.) with audition. This paired-stimuli approach is used to bring the child to an awareness level. Then tactile cues can be faded out quickly to emphasize the need for the child to use his/her residual hearing instead. Also, the optional pitch indication of cueing can be used, with guidance from the speech therapist.

> *Parents need to allow the child sufficient time to respond. Hearing-impaired children in the early stages of oral speech development do not necessarily have the pragmatic skills or oral skills (i.e., turn-taking) that are needed for quick, sure responses (Ling, 1989).*

Vowels and Diphthongs

The speech therapist should guide the parent in the development of vowels and diphthongs (a, e, i, o, u, etc.). Vowels and diphthongs provide loudness, rhythm, stress, and meaning to spoken language. Natural reinforcement for vowels and diphthongs should precede any development of consonants. The child who produces only consonants will still have poor speech that will be difficult to understand even at the one-word level. Emphasis for clear vowel and diphthong productions in speech can be illustrated in these words, where only the vowel or diphthong is different: *bit, boat, bite, bet, bait, beet, boot,* etc. This stage of spoken language development cannot be over-stressed. It is important that the parent be trained carefully.

What to reinforce as a correct vowel and diphthong production should be defined and demonstrated to the parent by the speech therapist on the team. Parents can ". . . introduce an enormous range of vocabulary and language structures at home" (Ling & Ling-Phillips, 1978). This will provide the multiple opportunities needed to train and reinforce good production. If guided, parents can also provide the opportunities needed to practice the vowels and diphthongs in natural situations. The child will then receive positive reinforcement as a natural part of learning oral language in an oral world. Examples of vocabulary and language structures used frequently at home for vowel and diphthong training might include the following: "off/on, hot/cold, wet, dress, shoe," etc. at a one-word level and "too big," "that's mine," "I want," "all gone," etc. at the phrase level.

Simple Consonants

It has been shown that the simple consonants can be learned more easily if they are taught in a particular order (Ling, 1976). The simple consonants with the most visual cues (most redundant) are encouraged first. Then the speech skills learned to produce these simple consonants are used to lay an adequate foundation for teaching additional simple consonants. The additional simple consonants are more complex and have fewer visual cues when lipread. The parent needs to be trained so that the correct consonants can be attended to and reinforced appropriately at home.

The speech therapist can demonstrate for parents the expected antecedent behaviors that the child should be able to perform for each simple consonant. This will include that the sound(s) be produced in an accurate, rapid, and automatic manner, that is, correctly, smoothly, and without conscious effort. As the child increases his/her repertoire of simple consonants, so will the child's ability to co-articulate these consonants with other consonants increase. Taking care to develop the target sounds with sounds he/she can already say will encourage the child and provide abundant opportunities for the him/her to be successful more frequently.

In addition to following the most effective order of teaching and practicing the vowels/diphthongs and consonants, parents need to be aware of special ways to teach the correct production of these targets from the very start. The parent may be asked to reinforce some sounds at the beginnings of words. Then they may be asked to reinforce them in other positions in syllables as they occur in spontaneous speech. Some target sounds are best taught initially at the end of a syllable where they terminate a vowel (i.e., /s/ as in bus). Then, the child can easily learn to produce the same sound at the beginning of a syllable, where it releases a vowel (i.e., /b/ as in ball). Visually illustrating this with Cued Speech will not be difficult for the parent. The speech therapist should guide the parent through this process carefully so that time is not wasted and so that success for the child is immediate. This kind of parent participation in speech development is essential to the child's best interests. Obviously, it calls for much communication between the parent and the professional.

Since parents can use Cued Speech to provide a clear input, they need to be trained in a co-articulation approach for teaching words and phrases. This should be included in the speech training as soon as the child has learned to produce the individual sounds and syllables. Co-articulation refers to spoken utterances that are at least two to three syllables in length. Co-articulation emphasizes the natural articulation of speech in terms of syllables, not word units alone (Hudson, 1980).

Amplification and Communication

Good amplification cannot be stressed enough. Amplification should be used in all speech training situations as well in the community. The parent and speech therapist should keep the audiologist posted after the amplification fitting as to the child's use of and benefit of the amplification. Daily checking and maintenance of the amplification system by all who work with the child are very important aspects of the speech training program.

> *Efficiency demands that the child with useful residual hearing be taught as far as possible through audition. Those who are totally deaf should be provided with effective tactile and visual means of receiving the speech patterns we wish them to (re)produce (Ling, 1976).*

Parents should be reminded and guided by the therapist not to lower their volume, reduce the speech rate excessively, exaggerate pitch changes, or exaggerate their speech postures when talking or cueing to hearing-impaired children. Because hearing-impaired children do have some residual hearing, it is important that they always be exposed to oral speech at normal rate, loudness, and pitch. The speech therapist emphasizes good amplification and good speaker communication skills because this audible information regarding the speech features helps the hearing-impaired child recognize, comprehend, and discriminate the speech sounds and language patterns more readily.

Summary

This article has dealt with what kinds of information and instruction should go from the speech therapist to the parent. It has also described the parents' role on the collaborative team. There is a definite process that must be followed to develop spoken language for the hearing-impaired child. The process begins with the speech therapist instructing the parent, with the parent observing the child with the speech therapist, with the parent and speech therapist sharing information about the child on a daily basis, and then with the speech therapist guiding the parent through the process as the child progresses and develops spoken language. Parents become more sophisticated in their communication with the speech therapist by reporting changes in the child's performance; in his/her disposition to communicate with neighbors and friends, or even strangers; in the amount and kind of his vocalizations; and in the extent to which sounds mastered are being used consistently. Parents should report any difficulties or successes they encounter as they follow through on what they are asked to do by the professional.

Parents, take the time to talk with your speech therapist and discuss the topics listed above. In many cases the graduate training of specialists in speech and language pathology includes very little preparation for meeting the needs of a hearing-impaired child. If the professionals available to you are not familiar with the appropriate methods and techniques for teaching speech to hearing-impaired individuals, demand that they be properly trained. Your child deserves and needs appropriately trained professionals. Also, take the time to be in-serviced yourself, so that you can receive and use the guidance you need to give your child the best opportunity to develop oral language. According to Ling (1984), "When parents and families take a very active role in the habilitation process it is more likely to succeed than when the task is left mainly to the professionals."

Providing Access—With Signs Or Cues
by Margie Sokolnicki, 1992

In the past 15 years, depending on where we lived, I have flip-flopped back and forth between sign language interpreting and Cued Speech transliterating. My career began in 1976 as an interpreter in a junior-high hearing-impaired class in Fredericksburg, Va. In 1979 I transferred (in the same school system) to a preschool hearing-impaired program. Two children were cuers, and three were signers.

By the end of my first day I knew I could not work in an

environment in which I was not able to communicate with all the children. The school system agreed and sent me to Gallaudet University to learn Cued Speech. How wonderful it was to finally understand the system! The "Mork and Mindy" show must have been popular at the time because my first impression of Cued Speech was that it looked like something Mork might have used on his planet, Ork.

The first couple of months in this preschool class were interesting, to say the least. I can remember the cuers trying to sign and the signers trying to cue. It was complicated and confusing at times, yet it was good to experience first-hand the differences in the two modes of communication. The classroom teacher and I, with the permission of the parents, gradually switched all the children to cues.

Several years later, my husband and I were transferred to New Mexico. We were there for three years. During that time I sign interpreted for a junior high class. The children had a lot of hearing, so the interpreting served as a reinforcement rather than as a necessity.

Another transfer in 1987 took us to Fairfax, in Northern Virginia. There I had the privilege of transliterating for two eighth-grade students. At the end of the year, both boys received the Presidential Academic Achievement Award for their studies.

The next summer we moved to Dallas, Texas. I spent the first six months as a sign language interpreter in a large high school. There were 18 other full-time interpreters. It was so interesting to compare signs that we had all made up to avoid fingerspelling the same words over and over. I found out very quickly that many words in high-school classes have no established signs.

It seems to me that Texas has its own sign system. I once asked six different interpreters how to sign "inch" and "foot." Would you believe I got six different answers? We do have a book, "Texas Preferred Signs." I am sure it was published in order to avoid some of this confusion. Apparently not everyone has read it yet. Maybe it doesn't matter so long as the child understands his own interpreter.

Call it fate or whatever, on the very day I was to sign a contract with the Dallas Public Schools I received a message from Teri Poore,[1]

---

[1]The code of ethics of Cued Speech transliterators and sign interpreters precludes their release of information (by name) regarding specific clients. In this case Michael's mother specifically asked that we let Ms. Sokolniki identify Michael (with his permission) in order that her experiences with him can be related to his own statement (page 573) and that of his mother (page 471). This apparent breach of the code of conduct of certified transliterators is thus for the specific benefit of the readers, and is done with the permission of all the persons involved.

a Cued Speech parent in Arlington, Texas. She needed someone to cue to her son, Michael. Michael and I have been together ever since.

At first Michael and I were in a private school with another Cued Speech child, whom I shall call Sarah. Then we were all accepted into the public school system, which was adamantly TC. I must say it was extremely uncomfortable there for the first cueing children and their cueing interpreter/transliterator. We are now in our third year in the public school. The controversy has abated, and we are accepted.

"Hearing" Through Cues

It is much easier for me to transliterate with cues than to interpret with signs. I believe that a hearing-impaired child mainstreamed in a regular classroom should be able to "hear" the same things as the hearing students. For example, the other day a third-grade teacher told the class to show the homework assignment to their "folks." Had I been signing, I would have just signed "parents." When I cued "folks" Sarah mouthed the word "folks" with a questioning expression, showing that she didn't understand. I immediately explained that in this case it is just a less formal way of saying "parents."

One day a child in the class told a joke in which the punch line contained the word "vomit." When I cued that, Sarah did not know what was meant. She was familiar with the term "throw up," but not "vomit." Since then, she has come to me with other words for "vomit," such as "barf," "toss your cookies," etc. Though this is not a typical textbook example, it illustrates the enthusiasm children have for acquiring vocabulary, especially slang used by their hearing classmates.

Last year the children had a test in which they were asked to identify unfamiliar words. The teacher said, "Circle the object which is *blunt*." Later I asked the sign interpreter how she signed blunt. She signed, "Circle the thing that is not sharp." Unfortunately, that gives the child the answer, and he scores as if he understood the word *blunt*, even though he doesn't. A class in Physical Education is a great place to let a skeptic see the value of cues. There are several deaf children in a mainstreamed fifth-grade P.E. class for which I transliterate. Of course, I transliterate exactly what the teacher says. During a volleyball and soccer skills lesson I was cueing the exact information the hearing children were receiving. Out of the corner of my eye I could see the sign interpreter beside me gesturing and using body language for words such as *dribbling* and *spike* used by the teacher. One day I asked her the sign for dribbling. She said, "Oh, I change it every day." Even though the children did fine in the tournaments, I feel that the signers missed a lot of the actual terminology of the rules and regulations.

Access to Languages, Accents, Specialized Vocabulary

Last year after the Christmas assembly I was approached by one of the sign interpreters. The sixth-grade class had just finished singing a collection of songs in several different languages. She seemed a little upset and asked me why I kept "interpreting" when the kids didn't know what I was saying. My reply was simple: "The hearing kids didn't know what the words meant, either! Both they and the cueing kids knew the sounds that were being sung, and could pick up the rhythm and the rhyming words, too."

Michael Poore loves for me to cue his fifth-grade teacher's Texas accent. She says so many cute things like "goan" instead of "going." Cued Speech leaves me free to say absolutely anything, even Michael's new geometry words such as *equilateral triangle, truncated tetrahedron, trapezoid,* and *rhombus.*

Michael talks about baseball cards to the boys in his class—every chance he gets. They all know the names of all the team members and the value of each card. The boys also talk about football teams. Michael likes to tell me the names of vehicles of all kinds, and all their statistics—especially how fast they go and how much they cost. I have never experienced carrying on conversations like this with signing children, especially about topics not related to school.

I have been on both sides of the fence. I love working with hearing-impaired children. I believe they deserve a chance to know everything they possibly can about what goes on in the hearing world. To me it is frustrating at the elementary-school level to "interpret," or change what the teacher has said because the child is too young to read fingerspelling or because there isn't time. Also, it is nice to cue the actual sounds instead of signing (as accurately as I can) only the meaning behind the sounds. Signing is beautiful. I find myself signing songs to the car radio while commuting. But, if I had my choice I would want everyone to experience the precision and the educational benefits of Cued Speech. In my mind, it is the only method which allows the hearing-impaired individual to become a part of the hearing society. That way, he has a choice. Or, he can belong to both the hearing society and the deaf society.

Reflections on Cued Speech from "Down-Under"
by Sr. Caterina Heffernan

Sr. Caterina is a truly remarkable woman with more than 35 years of service to hearing-impaired children, their families, and teachers. One of her distinctive contributions has been in the use of music with Cued Speech. She continues a busy schedule, currently serving as a member of the cochlear-implant team of her school.

Beginnings

When I first read an article about Cued Speech I was not convinced of its potential. There was no way in the world my "pure" oralism would be "tainted" by what I thought was just another form of manualism.

A couple of years later a group of us Dominican sisters heard a talk given in Sydney by Dr. Cornett, in November, 1969. His explanation of Cued Speech was so lucid and so convincing that we decided to take it up. At that time the Dominican sisters had two big schools. One was in Waratah, a suburb of Newcastle, and the other at Portsea, 90 kilometres from Melbourne. We also had a high school unit at Strathfield in Sydney and an early intervention programme in the same suburb.

On the way home from Dr. Cornett's talk someone suggested that maybe one of the two schools should experiment with Cued Speech while the other waited to see the results. No one would agree to this because we were all so enthusiastic about beginning. Although November is at the end of our academic year I was determined to start cueing immediately. After attending two three-hour learning sessions at St. Gabriel's School, Castle Hill, where CS was already being used, I began teaching it to my high school pupils at Strathfield, their parents, and the parents involved in the early intervention programme. What Cued Speech revealed at once was that even the successful oral/aural teenage girls in my class had many misconceptions about the pronunciation of common words, e.g., they thought that *sugar* was *suegah*, that *soldier* was *sol-dee-er*, and that *shoulder* was *should + er*. The two schools began using Cued Speech in February, 1970. Because St. Mary's, the school at Portsea, was so far from Melbourne, and also had pupils from as far away as Darwin and Rockhampton, plus those from country areas, many parents were not able to attend CS lessons. However, they reported a remarkable improvement in their children's speech. If a child's utterance was not intelligible a parent would say "Cue it." The parent might not be able to read the cues but could understand the (improved) speech. We used to go up to Melbourne to give Cued Speech lessons in the evenings as it was impossible for many parents to go to Portsea for lessons. I remember one group in which most parents were hearing impaired or of an ethnic background.

When I was attending the first Catholic international conference on deaf education in Dublin, in 1971, I met Fr. Cyril Axlerod, a convert from Judaism educated by the Dominicans in South Africa. He was one of the four congenitally, profoundly deaf priests in the world. He was interested in Cued Speech and was intrigued to find that, like my high school pupils, he had misconceptions about the pronunciations of simple words; e.g., he thought that *century* was *sen-tue-ri*.

Teaching Cued Speech

After trying different methods and time schedules for teaching parents, other family members, educators, and audiologists, we found that "crash" courses were much more effective than weekly lessons spread over several months. At first we used *The Mind File*, lessons produced by Terry Finn. Later, we devised our own course of lessons which expedited the cueing of words; that is, we began with the long vowels, then gradually introduced the consonants and other vowels and diphthongs. We produced two series of videotaped lessons: *Cued Speech with Donna Taylor (1971)* and *Cued Speech with Margaret Brown (1983)*. Both have been used extensively in teacher-training courses throughout Australia. The second one is in colour, has accompanying work-sheets using Cuescript, and includes songs. (Margaret Brown is a professional singer.)

We have found that the videotapes facilitate the learning of Cued Speech, making it unnecessary for parents and other learners to attend so many lessons. Each person can work at his/her own pace and review lessons as often as is needed. We find that 12 hours of instruction and six months of daily use of CS can produce fluency. In two cases, just for interest's sake, I taught all the cues and the method of using them in two hours and then asked a third person to check that the learner could cue any word in the language—not quickly, but accurately. One student was an Australian audiologist and the other a young Japanese student who was spending a year in Australia before beginning a university class at home. She had a good mastery of spoken English, having been taught by an American who used a phonics-based method. During more than 20 years' experience in teaching cueing I have concluded that two main factors influence the ease and the speed of learning: motivation (usually strong in parents and in teachers wanting a job) and educational background. Cued Speech is obviously easier for a person who is familiar with phonetics. Several times when a learner showed special aptitude I asked, "Have you done shorthand?" The answer was always affirmative.

With due respects, I have to say that women seem to learn Cued speech more quickly and easily than men do. A highly qualified male audiologist, for example, had great difficulty. (*Cornett agrees with this generalization, though there are numerous exceptions to it. He also thinks that teaching the men separately seems to reduce the difference.*)

We have not specifically taught the children to cue expressively but have expected them to learn gradually and finally to cue expressively. When they begin reading and having other formal lessons we have insisted on accurate cueing. The children at St. Mary's are no longer expected to cue expressively, mainly because many of them have come from early intervention programmes which do not use Cued Speech.

I believe that we should check as to whether the children are reading the cue/lips combination accurately. This is best done by asking for the correct repetition of a syllable, word, or sentence and/or giving dictation. We can't just "cue our merry way" assuming the children are reading us. Dictation enables us to diagnose mistakes. For example, when a teacher cued the word *bush* a child wrote *push* and another wrote *bull*. The teacher was able to say to the first, "You did not look at the cue," and to the second, "You did not look at the lips." The other six children in the class wrote the word correctly.

Before we introduced Cued Speech I always taught upper primary pupils the International Phonetic Alphabet and gave them passages to write in the I.P.A. script. This was no longer necessary, but in the early stages of using Cued Speech it was helpful to ask them to write cued nonsense syllables in I.P.A. This exercise called for accurate cue-reading and was not contingent on knowledge of vocabulary. The mistakes mentioned above seemed to indicate that the pupils sometimes wrote a word they knew without bothering to watch carefully. They would have had the words correct if they had been presented in context. However, the aim of the particular exercise was to test cue-reading, not spelling or language. The value of specific training in the reading of Cued Speech and in the use of the I.P.A. script was evident when Mrs. Leah Grammatico (director of Penninsula Oral School For the Deaf, in California) visited our school at Waratah. I asked her to say a sentence in Italian. She did so. I cued it and the pupils wrote it correctly in phonetic symbols and read it back.

Groups of tertiary (*college*) students frequently visit our schools for an hour or so. There is not time for a lengthy explanation of Cued Speech, so we generally demonstrate its value as follows. We ask some of the visitors to say their names or any word they choose, preferably an unusual proper noun. Then we show first how a profoundly deaf child would hear it by asking him to repeat it. Secondly, the child is asked to say it after using listening and speechreading. Finally he is asked to say it after simultaneously hearing and seeing it presented in Cued Speech. The results are very convincing—first, an approximation probably with the right number of syllables, and with vowels fairly accurate; and then an improvement still containing the confusions characteristic of speechreading, and then a reproduction accurate to the level permitted by articulation skills.

Inner Language

Three anecdotes will serve to show that cued language becomes internalized and is used subconsciously as a means of self-expression.

1) Jane, a 5-year-old, was put in the corner of the room for some misdemeanor. She sat there cueing angrily what she thought about it!

2) An experienced cueing teacher was doing a post-graduate course. She wondered why people were staring at her as she walked down the street. Suddenly we realized that, like Jane, she was "letting off steam" by talking to herself with cues about something that had upset her at College.

3) Two of us were staying with a family in a country town while we attended a Kodaly music seminar. A hearing girl who shared a room with her hearing-impaired sister called us to the bedroom to watch her cueing in her sleep. Some parents have reported this phenomenon, which proves that the cuers think in Cued Speech. *Our finding, based on many interviews, is that they think in spoken language, talk and lipread in their sleep, cue in their sleep, with or without audible speech, and even report that they hear and lipread perfectly in their sleep! Refer to the report on page 257.*

Cued Speech and Music

Since the founding of Waratah School in 1875 music has had an important place in the curriculum. Manual communication was used until 1948. The girls used to do beautiful eurythmics to the accompaniment of music, instrumental or vocal. I recall seeing a group of teenagers in long, flowing robes giving a moving interpretation of the poem "Trees" while a lady sang it, in 1939. They had no hearing aids and so depended on vibration, on vision, and on a memory for movement. Both boys and girls played well in percussion bands.

Auditory training, especially in music, was begun seriously in our school in 1957. One of our sisters who was studying at Manchester

(England) and at Sint Michielgestel in Holland wrote and told us that the children should not be allowed to feel vibration and that they should be playing wind instruments to develop their breath control. We began to give all music lessons in a room with a concrete floor and to teach them to play the recorder (English flute). Later, we used the Dutch "wind-instruments" specially developed for hearing-impaired children. The amount of breath required to play them was designed to be the same as that used for speech. In the 1960s we had impressive orchestras in which the children played keyboards, recorders (descant and alto), Dutch organs, and melodicas. However, although there was a carry-over to the rhythm and intonation of speech there was little effect with regard to breath control. The reason became clear when in the late 1970s we studied Ling's speech programme. He pointed out that what was wrong with the breath control of hearing-impaired children was not the inability to breathe normally but the lack of synchronization of the breathing and speech organs. This knowledge supported our placing more emphasis on singing than on instruments.

Until the two boarding schools closed down in 1977 and 1984, respectively, the girls learnt ballet and did well in Royal Academy ballet exams. Our archives contain a handwritten letter from Margot Fontaine supporting our petition to the examination board for hearing-impaired students to do the exams. Some splendid public performances were given. There was time to enjoy the many musical activities, mainly in the evenings. Ballroom dancing, both old time and modern, folk dancing, and Scottish dancing were taught by professionals and thoroughly enjoyed. The children learnt the latest popular songs—those of the Beatles; Peter, Paul, and Mary; and the Seekers being great favourites. They went to musical shows such as *The Pirates of Penzance* and *The Sound of Music*, after learning most of their songs.

Our music programme was radically modified in 1974-75 when we introduced the Kodaly programme. This is song-based, sequential and developmental, and is ideal for hearing-impaired children. The emphasis on singing rather than on the playing of instruments in Kodaly makes it relevant to speech and language. By this time Cued Speech was well established in our schools. The cueing of the words of a song during the first lesson forestalled any mispronunciations and, as in other school subjects, made communication between teachers and pupils relaxed and accurate. Mistakes made by pupils in an oral/aural school (with no Cued Speech) where I teach music now would never occur in a Cued Speech school, e.g., *We Wish You American Christmas* for *We Wish You A Merry Christmas*, or *Tebby Bear, Tebby Bear* for *Teddy Bear, Teddy Bear*.

The use of Cued Speech for songs leads to perfect beat and rhythm because it is possible to emphasize syllables or words while preserving the synchrony of song and music. Stress is shown in speech by three means—changes in duration, in intensity, and in pitch. Van Uden advises the use of duration when teaching stress to hearing-impaired children, assuming that changes in intensity and in pitch will follow. In a stressed syllable such as *fast*, in which vowel duration is clearly evident because of the consonant following it, the lengthening of the vowel that is associated with stress can enable a profoundly deaf youngster to identify the stress even if she or he is unable to sense the stress through audition. The phenomenon is clear with either "long" or "short" vowels. For example, in the words *missed* and *mist*, the so-called "short" vowel [*I*] is lengthened perceptibly because it is stressed. This lengthening is very evident in singing, e.g., "Ah, Sweet Mystery of Life...." In this song the first vowel in *Mystery* contrasts strongly in duration with the preceding and following vowels.

Cueing shows clearly the duration of a vowel or a consonant continuant, such as *s, z, sh, zh, f, v,* etc. This is why it supports accurately timed articulation in speech, poetic repetition, or song. Children with whom Cued Speech is used should be taught to notice and take advantage of the information on duration that is provided.

A cue can show clearly the duration of a phoneme or syllable in speech and in song. Likewise, more forceful cueing can indicate greater intensity. Most of the early Kodaly songs have one syllable per note so they are ideal for cueing. Some teachers find that they can indicate pitch through cues. (A syllable that requires two different notes can be cued.) All agree that cueing can express the mood of a song.

The "deaf choir" at Waratah School visits homes for elderly people and entertains them. It gives public performances in "Deafness Awareness Week" and is in demand for carol singing at Christmas time. New pupils have been enrolled as a direct result of parents' listening to their singing (in tune) and watching the graceful, precise, rhythmical cueing.

Cued Speech has been beneficial in church services, both Catholic and ecumenical. It is advantageous in readings, prayers, sermons, and hymns, and also in teaching liturgical dance. During one sermon in which the preacher was repeating himself I took the opportunity to teach a new word. I cued silently, "He's waffling now. That means saying the same thing over and over, repeating himself." The children cued and said softly, "waffling." I later told the preacher in question. The incident served a double purpose. It added to the children's vocabulary and stopped him waffling! If ever he did so after that he would say, "Sorry! I'd better stop. I seem to be waffling."

Hearing and Cued Speech

Having used Cued Speech consistently for 23 years I am convinced that it can improve listening skills, even with cochlear implant children—or perhaps specially with them. When we began using Cued Speech I asked Eddie Keir, an eminent audiologist and teacher of hearing-impaired children, if, because Cued Speech gave a perfect visual input of spoken language, it might lead to over-dependency on vision with a consequent neglect of the use of hearing. After asking for time to think about it he replied that the opposite should happen, e.g., the cue for the *s* in the word *swim* would alert the brain to the fact that the sound was present and thus lead to the hearing of it. However, in working with teachers I have stressed that we must do even more auditory training, since beginning cueing, to make sure that the children are making the best use of their residual hearing.

My reasons for claiming that Cued Speech improves listening skills are as follows:

1) It enables the child to identify and classify the phonemes of a given language.

2) There is a closer link between audition and articulation than between audition and an acoustic event. There is no doubt that Cued Speech improves articulation, pronunciation, and the rhythm of speech (see below in the comments on speech). So, it develops better listening. A simple diagram I use in lectures to educators and parents is:

Hearing <--------> Speech

Many educators realize that, normally, better listening leads to better speech, but do not realize that better speech leads to better listening because of the reciprocal effect they have on each other. The work of Tomatis on this auditory-vocal link is well worth studying.

3) There is a close relationship between hearing and language. Because Cued Speech improves both receptive and expressive language by providing consistent, accurate input and by facilitating communication, it improves listening. It is our knowledge of vocabulary, syntax, and semantics that enables us to interpret what we hear.

Cued Speech and Speech

I have specialized in teaching speech to hearing-impaired children since 1975 and have found Cued Speech to be an invaluable aid in the following ways:

1) It makes communication between teacher and pupil easy and clear. The pupil understands what is wanted and receives unambiguous

feedback. I have observed so many speech lessons where the method used was oral, oral/aural, or auditory/verbal in which the pupil looked confused. He didn't seem to understand what was expected of him or what sounds he had produced.

2) The cues (plus the lips) specify the target phonemes, syllables, words, phrases, and sentences. Thus the pupil **aims** at the right target and the teacher knows that any errors represent something to be worked on, not the result of aiming at the wrong target.

3) Duration and relative intensity are clearly indicated. (See above comments on music.)

4) The confusion of voiced and unvoiced consonants that is so common in the speech of hearing-impaired children can be prevented or remediated. Simply telling the children to be sure to use voice with a final consonant that is supposed to be voiced is often ineffective, and sometimes may cause excessive or exaggerated voicing, or even an added syllable, because many of them cannot hear the voicing. They can be taught to take advantage of the fact that a vowel preceding a final voiced consonant is lengthened because of the voicing. For example, show your pupils the words *bus* and *buzz*, cueing them carefully as you speak. Then, present them silently, again cueing them carefully in synchronization with mouth movements. Ask your pupils to notice which vowel is longer. Finally, present the words audibly without cues, and without vocalizing the final consonants, but making the appropriate mouth-jaw movements for *s* and *z* at the appropriate times. Explain that your pupils can tell the difference without hearing the final consonants, and can thus discriminate between *bus* and *buzz* visually if their audition is incapable of detecting the voicing in the final consonant. Other useful examples are *piece* vs *peas*, *niece* vs *knees*, *loose* vs *lose*.

The cues show quite clearly the difference in relative length between the all-important vowel/diphthong and the final consonant. The same technique can be used in teaching the visual voice/voiceless distinction in final stop/plosives, if you demonstrate with them as stops, e.g., *feet* vs *feed*. I no longer teach in a cueing school but have a variety of jobs in Sydney—developing listening skills and speech in cochlear implant children (with or without cues), teaching music in an oral/aural school, giving oral/aural support to a fully integrated pupil, and, most exciting of all, transliterating with Cued Speech for a fully integrated, profoundly deaf boy in his first year in high school. I am with him for one-and-one-half days a week. The Special Education teacher, who is Academic Tutor on the staff, gives help at other times when needed. The boy is among the top 10 in a class of 32 students and shows particular aptitude in French. The Academic Tutor, who has an excellent French accent and has learnt to cue, is amazed at the success of her Australian cues in producing an authentic French accent in her pupil. His family members have cued to him since he was deafened by meningitis at 10 months. He attended St. Gabriel's School, Castle Hill, NSW, till the end of third grade, and has been fully integrated since then.

As well as doing the work outlined above, which entails travelling daily to different parts of Sydney, I have private pupils, children and adults, in the evenings and on Saturday mornings. Not all of them need Cued Speech.

In conclusion, it seems to me that Cued Speech is the greatest thing that has happened to "deaf" education this century. I only wish that it were better understood and more widely used. As someone said: "It is too manual for the oralists and too oral for the manualists."

What a commentary on the breadth of the separation among educators of hearing-impaired children! The comment quoted above was made first by Dr. Powrie Doctor, of Gallaudet College, in March, 1966, when Orin Cornett first described it to him. He also advised: "Never give up. You will be shot at from both sides, but you have here the first system that shows the syllabication of the spoken language. This is what the deaf have needed from the beginning."

Cued Speech Transliterating:
The Sign of Success in a Mainstream Classroom
by Melanie Metzger

I learned Cued Speech in 1986, despite initial misgivings, while I was working in a mainstream public school program as a sign language interpreter/transliterator.[2] Like many signers, I understood very little about Cued Speech except that it was not supposed to be a "good thing." However, I disliked my inability to communicate freely with the cueing students or to provide services for them, so I learned.

At the time that I learned Cued Speech, I had known sign language for about eight years. I figured that as an experienced sign

---

[2]The term *transliterator* is used by the Registry of Interpreters for the Deaf in reference to the role of a signing interpreter when translating from English into one of the forms of Signed English. Unfortunately, this established terminology is an inaccurate description of what is actually being done. The important difference between transliterating with Cued Speech and translating from English into Signed English will be explained in full below.

language interpreter, I could just learn to cue and then start working as a Cued Speech transliterator. In retrospect, I believe that learning to cue taught me at least as much about sign language interpreting as it did about Cued Speech transliterating. I had thought Cued Speech was just another way of signing English. What I discovered, however, challenged my understanding of language, my understanding of deaf people, and the truth of I. King Jordan's famous words: "Deaf people can do anything...except hear!"

In order to share my perspective, it might be helpful to see where I was coming from in terms of my experience. An interpreter, of course, translates messages from one language into another. As a sign language interpreter, my job is to translate between the English language and American Sign Language. However, when I was hired to interpret in the public school system, I was not really hired as an interpreter, per se. I was hired to "transliterate" between the English language and signed English. Basically, this means that I was to use sign language vocabulary in English word order in an attempt to visually convey English to the deaf students. This differs from Cued Speech, of course, in that cues clarify the consonant-vowel syllables of English. What is the significance of this difference?

I have said that as a sign language transliterator my job is to listen to a spoken message and select the best signs to represent it (or vice versa, of course). This task is not always as simple as it might seem. For example, consider the sentence: "She went down the hall and right into the kitchen." In this sentence, does the word *right* mean the direction "not left" or the act of "not taking her time" as in "immediately"? In this context, the meaning of the word right is left open to interpretation. As a sign language transliterator (note, not just as an interpreter, but as a transliterator), I must first interpret the meaning myself, in order to select the appropriate sign vocabulary. As a Cued Speech transliterator it is not I who interprets the message. I simply cue the phonemes (which sound like *rite*), and the deaf student must decide whether the meaning is *right* as in "not left," *right* as in "immediately," *right* as in "Americans have certain inalienable rights," *write* as in "on paper," or *rite* as in "rites of passage." Herein lies one significant difference between the process of sign language transliterating(so-called) and Cued Speech transliterating; with the use of Cued Speech, the deaf student, and not the transliterator, interprets the meaning of the message, and must thus "digest" English.

A second fact of significance is that most public school classes, be they English, biology, or physical education, use some form of technical vocabulary. English classes cover metaphors and similes, predicates, and dangling modifiers. Biology addresses endocrine systems, amoebas, and cerebral hemispheres. P.E. classes include discussions of downs and huddles, forward passes, and interceptions. As a sign language transliterator, I must know the meanings of these terms (or at least the spelling) in order to select the appropriate signs. I must know the signs as well!

I once had the opportunity to experience a glimpse of what it must be like to receive the services of a sign language transliterator in a mainstream classroom. It was the middle of the school year and I was scheduled to substitute for a sign language transliterator in a science class. Although I was unfamiliar with the subject, and therefore unprepared for the assignment, the deaf student, teacher, and interpreter coordinator all preferred that I accept the assignment and do my best rather than leave the class with no sign language transliterator at all. Given the situation, I agreed to transliterate. At one point during the lecture, an English word came up with which I was unfamiliar. I heard the word uttered rapidly in the midst of the lecture (the students in the class, of course, were familiar with the subject matter, though I was not), and it sounded something like STOYKEEUHMEHTRIK. I could not sign the word; since I was unfamiliar with its meaning, I could not find the correct signed counterpart. So I began to fingerspell the word, but hesitated after the first letter or two; confronted by a new and unusual word, I was not certain of the correct spelling. The deaf student, however, was quite familiar with the word and the context, and recognizing my dilemma, showed me a sign to use and asked me to continue. I did not want the student to fall behind as the teacher lectured on. I did as I was asked and all was well. Eventually, the teacher asked the class a question which the deaf student answered. I was expected to voice the student's message for the class and teacher, and I did so until the student used the unfamiliar sign. I knew what the student was saying, that the student was using the word that I didn't know. But I couldn't recall the unfamiliar English word in order to share it with the class! In that instant, I understood something of what it must be like for a deaf student who is expected to learn English vocabulary through sign language. The student might sit through lectures and understand the content of what is being taught, but when it is time for the test, the student may not recognize the English words on paper any more than I could when faced with my predicament.

With Cued Speech, of course, the deaf student has access to the English word itself, not a signed counterpart. Therefore, if I need to voice for the deaf student, I pronounce the sounds being cued, and thus, I convey the English word without having to decide or even know its meaning. Also, when it comes time for a written test, the student is as capable of reading the technical word, and recognizing it, as anyone.

A third significant area involves a common classroom occurrence. Teachers often give spelling/vocabulary tests. This can pose a problem for the sign language transliterator. Consider, for example, a spelling pre-test in which the students are told English words and are expected to provide the correct spellings and definitions. If, for instance, the English phrase is "premeditated homicide," the transliterator could sign *pre-considered murder*. However, that gives the deaf student the definition of the word. So, the transliterator might spell the word; but then the student is provided with the correct spelling. When cueing the word, however, neither the meaning of the word nor the spelling of the word is conveyed. The word is simply cued in consonant-vowel syllables, and the deaf student faces a task equal to that of his/her hearing peers.

Another issue facing sign language transliterators became clear to me when I was sent to substitute sign language transliterate in a Spanish class, one day. Again, I was relatively unprepared for the spontaneous assignment, and again the choice was made that I would do better than no one at all. I walked into the Spanish class and sat down waiting for the bell to ring. When class began, the teacher immediately began lecturing. My difficulty, however, was that he was lecturing in Spanish! Fortunately, I knew enough Spanish so that I was able to understand most of what he was saying. I began to transliterate into sign vocabulary, when I realized that the deaf student did not have access to the Spanish if I signed the message. In other words, once again I was deciding on the meaning of what was being said and representing that meaning with appropriate signs. The deaf student did not have access to the Spanish words any more than the deaf student had access to English when I was transliterating the science class. There is nothing quite like the school of hard knocks to teach a transliterator how to cope in a foreign language class! In fact, I remembered this experience vividly when I substituted in a foreign language class at a later date, as a Cued Speech transliterator. I did not need to understand the language to cue it, nor did I need to know the spelling of the words. I simply cued the message as it was spoken, sound for sound, and the deaf student was able to have regular access to class, despite the absence of the regular transliterator. It is very clear that the deaf student was the one "interpreting" the message, and not the transliterator. In fact, I know of a Cued Speech transliterator who spent a year transliterating a French course. The student did just fine in the course, although the transliterator never really learned

French! (I'm not sure the transliterator should take pride in that!)

Humor is important in the classroom. Humor is often based on plays on words through rhyming and puns. Because sign language vocabulary is not English vocabulary, plays on words do not translate easily, if at all. Take, for example, the following riddle:

"The sun rose and the wind blew." What colors are the sun and the wind? In English, puns are based on double meanings of words, or on different spellings of English words that sound alike. *Rose* is both a color and the perceived movement of the sun in the morning; *blue* sounds like both the color and the act of the moving wind. In signs, however, no such pun exists with these words. Although sign language is rich in puns, its puns are not related to English words. A sign language transliterator must either interpret the pun and explain it, or try to find a counterpart in signs. With Cued Speech, the rhythm and rhyme of the spoken syllables and words are made clear. Therefore, puns and other plays on words are accessible. The deaf person has access to the pun or joke and interprets the meaning for him/herself.

Cued Speech shows rhymes. It represents the spoken language phoneme by phoneme, visually conveying the patterns of spoken sounds that form rhymes. In addition, a Cued Speech transliterator can cue a speaker's dialect or foreign accent. At first, the thought of cueing this information to a deaf student may seem irrelevant or overwhelming. However, experience has shown me that a speaker's accent or dialect is often of interest and significance to students. For example, once when I was Cued Speech transliterating for a substitute teacher (and we have all experienced the behavior of an average class with a substitute teacher!) who had a British accent, I remember the class chuckling over the sound of some of the substitute teacher's pronunciations. When cued, these "unusual" pronunciations apparently seemed equally unfamiliar to the deaf student. When the class laughed or copied the British pronunciation, the deaf student did the same, and was, therefore, a part of the entire interaction. Just like everyone else, the deaf student had the opportunity to learn that people pronounce words differently, that and how people sometimes react to these differences, and even what the differences are. Most of us can recognize a British accent without being told what it is. These deaf students, through the information conveyed by the Cued Speech transliterator, can make such determinations for themselves.

A related incident occurred one day when a teacher was calling roll. The teacher read the name "Andrea" (pronouncing it AN' DREE UH). The student quickly corrected the teacher's pronunciation to match her preference, AHN DRAY' UH. The class, upon hearing this distinction, immediately responded to the situation. The students apparently believed that Andrea's preferred pronunciation sounded rather snobbish. Some of the students may not have agreed, or even understood the nature of the reaction of others in the class. Other students had the opportunity, for the first time perhaps, to recognize that the things they say can evoke intense reactions from the class. Some students don't like the idea of evoking such a response, others pursue it. As a sign language transliterator, I could explain the pronunciation difference, or even explain that it sounded snobby. But again, I would be the one interpreting the meaning of the information and resulting situation, and then passing it along to the deaf student. When a Cued Speech transliterator cues the pronunciation, and the comments which followed it, the entire event is left for the deaf student to interpret, based on his/her personal background and stage of development, just as it is for everyone else in the room.

The situations I have described share a common theme; when Cued Speech is used, the deaf person does all the interpretation of the message—including the meaning and intent of the speaker. In other words, the deaf person can do everything except hear! The job of the Cued Speech transliterator is to provide access to the audible information and, consequently, the deaf person receives the same information as everyone else. Thus, a deaf person who understands English as conveyed through Cued Speech is not dependent upon an interpreter's personal decisions regarding the meaning and intent of a message; the message is received exactly as it originated from the speaker.

It was only after I learned Cued Speech, what it is designed to do, and what it is capable of providing, that I began to really recognize what sign language is designed to do and what sign language is capable of doing. American Sign Language (ASL) is a natural language used in this country by many people who can't hear. ASL, like any language, has evolved to meet the needs of the people who use it. ASL was not designed to represent the sounds or pronunciations of a spoken language, nor the grammar which is inextricably a part of that spoken language. ASL represents the full language and grammar of deaf people in their communication with each other. In a school that uses ASL in the classroom, no other signing system or spoken language can do what ASL is designed to do. In a school where spoken English is used in the classroom, no signed language or signing system can do what spoken English does.

In addition to providing uninterpreted access to the linguistic environment in a public school classroom, Cued Speech transliterators also cue the non-verbal sounds in the environment. Imagine a third grade classroom in which the teacher is very strict. She always stops talking when she is angry with someone and waits for them to stop the offensive behavior. One day, the teacher is talking to the class. A bell starts ringing from the hallway to indicate to the school that grades four through six are to go to lunch. The teacher suddenly stops talking.

The students in the class wonder why the teacher is angry. Some of the students are probably afraid that they are guilty of some offense. Everyone looks to see who has made the teacher angry. As the students ask themselves, "Is she mad at me?" or "Who did it this time?" no one is there to answer their questions for them. It is through such heart stopping experiences as these, that people learn to make sense of the world around them. Some students might answer the questions with, "Oh, she stopped to wait for the bell to ring. It was too loud to talk over." Other students might respond to themselves, "I think she knows I was chewing gum. But she didn't say anything this time. I'll never do it again!" Still other students might not find an answer to their questions, at least not this time.

The key is to recognize that many seemingly insignificant experiences contribute to our awareness of the world and our development within it. Essentially, the only information that is readily accessible to hearing students and not to deaf students is what a sound sounds like and where it originates. Because of this, Cued Speech transliterators are careful, once again, to provide deaf students with access to the environment and not to interpret it for them. Experience then allows the hearing-impaired student to begin to recognize and identify a variety of sounds, such as pencil sharpeners (the use of which is sometimes permissible and sometimes forbidden), bees (which can sting if you don't know to avoid them!), growling stomachs (which students are happy to know is a common experience), and so forth. Cued Speech transliterators have a variety of techniques to use in conveying such environmental sounds.

Being aware of the sounds in the environment provides countless opportunities for any student to interact with peers (to say "Bless you" to a sneeze, for example), to be aware of the passing of time (as when a bell means 10 more minutes until lunch!), and to practice decision making skills (for instance, if a bell means 15 minutes left to finish the test, one might skip the tough questions in order to finish the rest).

By transliterating the uninterpreted sounds of the environment (what a sound sounds like and where it originates), a Cued Speech transliterator provides access to developmental aspects of a classroom beyond the academics of school. Not only is linguistic information accessible in its original form, but cultural information is accessible.

When I learned Cued Speech, the importance of language and cultural access became irrevocably clear to me. I already knew that any deaf person in this country has the opportunity at some point in life to experience American Sign Language and the culture of the people who use it. What I did not know, however, was that deaf people also have the opportunity to experience the English language and the culture of the people who use it. Now, I. King Jordan's words ring clear and true to me—Deaf people can indeed do anything, except hear.

It's O.K. To Be Curious
by Helen Quave

Ms. Quave was Alisa Fleetwood's science teacher in seventh grade, during the second year of her exposure to Cued Speech. She wrote the following to describe what it was like to start the school year with a CS student mainstreamed in her class. Alisa's case history is in Chapter 17 and her own observations are in Chapter 25.

"You were curious when you were younger," I told my seventh-grade class the first day of school. "I want you to practice being curious this year so you don't lose the skill." Then I proceeded to allow the students to be curious about me. In order to learn more about my students, I made up "All About Me" an information sheet for each child to complete and started trying to match this information with a name on a seating chart and a visual image of each person.

Within the first week of school Alisa, who comes to class with her Cued Speech interpreter, Mrs. Roffé, sent word to me that she was ready for the class to be curious about her. My spine fairly tingled with admiration for her courage. Until this time the students had watched with open or embarrassed curiosity as Mrs. Roffé mouthed words and signaled with her hand to Alisa. Students had spoken to her only in forced small-group situations.

I inserted a "Being Curious About a Classmate" objective onto the blackboard with the day's science agenda. I invited any students to allow the rest of the class to find out more about them. Time for this would be a part of each class schedule for a while. Alisa, I told them, had volunteered to be first.

Alisa sat across the lab table from Mrs. Roffé with her hands folded in front of her, ready for what might come. And did it come! At first students on the far side of the room were half out of their chairs, straining to hear Alisa answer questions in her faltering, timid speech. The first question held no risk to the questioner, "How old is

Alisa?" Mrs. Roffé cued the question and Alisa voiced her answer. A few similarly simple questions followed, directed to the interpreter. The flutter of a butterfly's wing would have been a clap of thunder in the silence. Then Jay asked a question that startled the group, "Have you always been deaf?" Alisa received the cued question with unruffled composure. She answered more clearly, "Since I was very young."

Now that Alisa had allowed her classmates to be curious about her handicap, the questions poured in. "Do you ever wonder what it would be like to hear?" "Do you feel weird having someone (*the interpreter*) follow you around all day?" "How did your parents feel when they found out you were deaf?" Alisa's answers were a brief yes or no or a shrug of the shoulders in an "I don't know" gesture.

Then Sharon wanted to know if Alisa played softball. "Yes," Alisa replied, "my mother coaches a team." A new line of questioning followed, questions that implied, "You are one of us." "What other sports do you like?" "Do you go to movies?" Alisa was responding easily now. Her speech was louder and more confident. Her answers volunteered more information than was asked for and everyone relaxed.

Ron was curious to know if Alisa liked being at Bannaker Junior High with "us." Others wanted to know if she got teased in the halls. With her positive responses Alisa let her peers know that **she** liked **them** and felt comfortable in this school full of hearing people.

When asked how hard it was to learn sign language, Alisa informed the class that she didn't know sign language. Disbelief spread across the faces while Mrs. Roffé and Alisa explained that Cued Speech was what they used and that anyone could learn it. The obvious curious question came next, "Can we learn Cued Speech?" Alisa and Mrs. Roffé assured us that we could. I asked the class if they would like to spend some time each day in science learning this communication method. The excited faces told me the answer. I asked Mrs. Roffé if she would be our teacher. Of course, she didn't hesitate to say yes.

The questions wore down after 25 minutes, and we picked up the science work for the remainder of the class period. The next day there was another student requesting that he be the one that the class interviewed. And on it went, as curiosity about classmates began each class period on Tuesday and Thursday, and a Cued Speech lesson began each Monday, Wednesday, and Friday class period. Yes, a few science activities were omitted or adjusted. I do not apologize for this.

Alisa has established meaningful relationships with her classmates, and I know this has benefitted her. Only time will tell how many lives eventually will be affected by these 34 students whom Alisa allowed to be curious about her.

Chapter 28
Research that Parents of Deaf Children Need to Know About, and How to Present Cued Speech

For the last 20 years most educators of hearing-impaired children who have taken a good look at Cued Speech have been impressed by its theoretical soundness. But, because of the fact that most of the evidence cited by its advocates was based on "success stories," the majority either expressed skepticism or decided to reserve judgment until more evidence is available. Solid data-backed research that documents the effects of Cued Speech on language development, reading, and oral communication skills is now available, and merits the attention of all parents and educators of deaf children.

During the last six years a substantial amount of important research has been done on the effects of Cued Speech, much of it by experimental psychologists in Belgium. As a result, the 1990 issue of the *Cued Speech Journal* was devoted entirely to research on Cued Speech. It contains copies of the complete reports of seven studies by Belgian researchers, plus the 1990 annotated bibliography of research on Cued Speech, with 23 entries. For ordering information, check the materials section of the Appendix.

Parents who want to be able to present the case for Cued Speech effectively need to be familiar with the basic findings of researchers who have studied its effects on language and reading. They do not need to be technically familiar with the methods used or the details of the studies. They need to be able 1) to identify the important fact or facts that each piece of research listed in this chapter establishes or supports, and 2) to make available a copy of a summary or annotation of each of the studies, for professionals or others who want or need the details. To that end we present a one-or-two-sentence statement of the results of each study, for parents to remember. Following each summarizing statement is a full annotation of each study, for use as needed in dealing with professionals or others. Parents do not necessarily need to read or study the full annotations, though some will want to do so.

Annotations of Significant Research

1) The 1979 thesis of Gaye Nicholls revealed that 18 prelingually deaf children aged 9 to 16 years scored 96% on key words in cued sentences, without sound. Thus, she proved that CS is clearly

and accurately readable to deaf children who have had at least three years of CS experience.

Annotation: *Cued Speech and the Reception of Spoken Language*, by Gaye Nicholls (1979) under the supervision of Daniel Ling, settled all reasonable doubts about the readability of Cued Speech. Nicholls used as subjects 18 prelingually deaf children, aged 9 to 16 years, and having PTA thresholds ranging from 97 dB to 120 dB. On key words in sentences they scored 96% with Cued Speech, without sound. On sound alone they scored below 2%. With lipreading alone they scored 30%. Lipreading with sound, they scored an amazing 45%, showing excellent use of hearing in the process of lipreading. On cues alone they scored 49%; with cues and sound, 68%; cues and lips, 96%; and cues, lips, and sound, 95%. Both surprising and important was the effectiveness with which the subjects used their residual hearing in the presence of the cues, without seeing the mouth. The scores given were for high-predictability sentences. Scores with low-predictability sentences were lower except when the subjects saw both mouth and cues, when it made no difference whether the sentences were predictable or not. The Nicholls' thesis was the only important evidence at the disposal of Cued Speech advocates, except case studies, until about 1986. It was summarized in the *Journal of Hearing and Speech Research* (Nicholls and Ling, 1982).

Cued Speech was developed primarily to make it possible for even profoundly deaf children to become good readers. Thus, the next item is probably the most important and useful of the annotations for parents and teachers to have at their fingertips.

2) The doctoral dissertation of Jean E. Wandel (1989) reported that, on the 1982 reading sub-test of the Stanford Achievement Test, carefully matched groups of profoundly deaf CS children and hearing children scored at statistically equivalent levels. The other matched hearing-impaired groups scored lower.

Annotation: *Use of Internal Speech in Reading by Hearing-Impaired Students in Oral, Total Communication, and Cued Speech Programs,* by Wandel (1989). Wandel evaluated 213 children in order to select 120, aged 7 to 16 years, to fit into carefully matched groups of 30 each: hearing, oral, TC, and CS. Each group of 30 hearing-impaired students included 15 profoundly hearing-impaired and 15 severely hearing-impaired subjects. Dr. Wandel tested all of them on internal speech ratios, replicating Conrad's work (1979); on the Raven Standard Progressive Matrices, for cognitive functioning; and on the

1982 reading sub-test of the Stanford Achievement Test. This was the first research to make specific comparisons of the reading of CS subjects with hearing, oral, and TC subjects.

The TC group performed significantly poorer than the oral and CS groups on all measures: cognitive function, internal speech ratio, and reading comprehension. There was no statistically significant difference between the average score of the Cued Speech-profound students and the average score of the hearing group, on the reading sub-test of the SAT; that is, the two groups attained essentially the same scores on the reading sub-test.

The CS-severe group scored lower than the hearing and CS-profound groups, but higher than the oral and TC groups. Why did the CS students with more hearing score lower than the profoundly deaf CS students? Probably for the reason we have been giving to parents for 20 years: many cueing parents of children with more hearing are tempted to cue inconsistently. They may cue only what the child can't lipread, or what he or she doesn't understand in a particular situation, or what they think is unfamiliar language. This will not develop the clear, accurate internal language model needed for skilled reading.

3) Researchers in Belgium reported in 1989 that Cued Speech develops in a deaf child an internal phonological model of the spoken language that "... can prime the whole process of reading acquisition."

Annotation: *Role played by Cued Speech in the Identification of Written Words Encountered for the First Time by Deaf Children,* by Alegría, Dejean, Capouillez, and Leybaert (1989). Research on *how* Cued Speech causes deaf children to become good readers appears in several of the Belgian papers. The studies build up evidence in series, and additional studies on the effects of CS are in progress. It is this paper in which the evidence really became conclusive. This is the concluding paragraph:

> *To come back to our initial point, the present work strongly suggests that the lexicon developed by the deaf with Cued Speech has properties that are equivalent to the phonology of the hearing subjects. In both cases the internal representations of the words are compatible with their orthographic representation. This allows the use of phonological coding to identify unfamiliar (written) words and, as said before, can prime the whole process of reading acquisition.*

In simple terms: just as the hearing child who is ready to read looks at a written word he/she has not seen before, sounds it out, and recognizes it as a spoken word he/she already knows and uses, so does the deaf child who grows up with Cued Speech. The important thing about this research is that it uses an experimental procedure that yields scientific evidence of the phonological tie-in used by a deaf child. The authors argue, with supporting evidence, that Cued Speech makes the deaf child an *autonomous* reader, who doesn't need help from anyone else to read appropriate material.

4) Hage, Alegría, and Périer (July, 1989) reported that children who receive CS both at home and in school demonstrate the greatest gain in performance over lipreading alone, that those who have CS only at home perform slightly lower, and those who have CS only at school perform substantially lower.

Annotation: At the Second International Symposium on Cognition, Education, and Deafness, Washington, D.C., Hage, Alegría, and Périer (July 1989) reported on a study entitled *Cued Speech and Language Acquisition*. In it they extended the work reported under 3), above, using a larger number of subjects (55), and evaluated the relative values of use of Cued Speech at home and at school. Their results confirm what CS advocates in this country have said for many years. The children who received CS both at home and at school received most help from it in understanding Cued Speech, followed closely by those who received it only at home, and distantly by those who had it only at school. The home is more important to language acquisition than the school, if it is a cueing home.

In the same paper the authors report on the first of a series of studies they have planned on the effects of Cued Speech on mastery of grammar. This report was on the effects of CS on mastery of grammatical gender in the French language. They state: "...it is generally taken for granted that this is a feature to which deaf children have limited access through traditional oral methods." The authors report that their results indicate that the CS students, for words they know,

> ...master grammatical gender and correctly utilize the corresponding article. This result by itself does not allow us to know whether the child determines the word's gender with the help of phonological cues or whether he knows it by heart. To establish the possible phonological origin of these responses, the results concerning the unfamiliar items have to be considered.

On unfamiliar words, the subjects failed completely in guessing the gender of items for which there were no phonological clues to gender; that is, they scored at chance (50%) in guessing the grammatical gender of unfamiliar words carrying no phonological gender markers. However, when tested on unfamiliar *marked* items, that is, words characterized by phonological clues as to gender, such as typically masculine and feminine word endings (*-ille, -ine,* and *-ette* for feminine nouns such as *la paille, la farine,* and *la chausette,* and *-oir, -eau,* and *-on* for masculine nouns such as *le couloir, le manteau,* and *le mouton*), they were consistently capable of giving the correct answer. This shows that their superior knowledge of grammatical gender was indeed due to their use of phonological clues.

5) Marilyn Peterson, on the basis of research data on 36 children 5 to 11 years old, stated: "It is very apparent to me that children receiving Cued Speech surpass the majority of signing and oral children in verbal language skills."

Annotation: Marilyn Bourne Peterson, M.A., deaf educator/speech therapist at the Houston Ear Research Foundation for three years, tested more than 75 profoundly deaf children for the cochlear implant center where she worked. She compiled data on a subgroup (36 children who were in the age range of 5 to 11 years) based on the results of three tests that measure proficiency with the American-English language. These included an informal question test, the Maryland Syntax Evaluation Instrument (MSEI), and the Expressive One Word Picture Vocabulary Test (EOWPVT). She tabulated the results for those children who met the following criteria on at least one of the three measures, children who:

1. Answered the question forms with at least 85% accuracy;
2. Formulated at least six perfect sentences (of 10 possible) on the MSEI;
3. Achieved at least the 20th percentile on the EOWPVT.

Of the 36 children whose scores Ms. Peterson used, 20 customarily received some form of signed English (most SEE-2), seven Cued Speech, and nine the speechreading (oral/aural) approach. Since the EOWPVT was normalized on children through 11 years old, older children were not included in this study. Ms. Peterson's findings:

1. Most of the children receiving cues did well on all three tests.
2. Only 12 of the 36 children had at least one "high" score.

Three of 20 signers, six of seven cuers, and three of nine oral children met the criterion level for at least one of the three test measures:

Question Test	EOWPVT	MSEI
6/7 (86%) of the cuers	4/5 (80%) of cuers	5/7 (71%) of cuers
1/8 (13%) of oral	2/9 (22%) of oral	1/9 (11%) of oral
3/18 (17%) of signers	2/20 (10%) of signers	1/20 (5%) of signers

Ms. Peterson comments:

> *It is very apparent to me that children receiving Cued Speech surpass the majority of signing and oral children in verbal language skills. Additionally, I have been pleasantly amazed to witness the early ages (5 and 6 years) at which some profoundly deaf children have achieved superior language proficiency via Cued Speech. I have not witnessed this advanced level of American-English language achievement with young children receiving language via other methodologies. "*

Ms. Peterson concludes by explaining that her teaching background was primarily with signing:

> *Prior to my employment at the cochlear implant center I taught/assessed hearing-impaired children for 11 years in a Total Communication program. I was a firm believer in the importance, for both parents and teachers, of signing (and speaking simultaneously) each and every word and morphological ending. But, as time passed, I became increasingly frustrated by the limitations of signed/spoken English. Specifically: a) nothing intrinsic in the sign helps the child pronounce the word or even know how many syllables it contains; b) the phonics approach to reading cannot be used without excessive use of additional, time-consuming steps; c) often the same sign has to be used for different words (e.g., choose/pick); d) often a word does not have any sign assigned to it and has to be fingerspelled. Prior to accepting the necessity of fingerspelling the word, however, one has to go to the effort of looking up the word in one or more sign books only to discover that it must be fingerspelled; e) more than 95% of parents of deaf children in signing programs are poor signers and fail to contribute significantly to the language development of their deaf children.*
>
> *I began using Cued Speech as a supplementary tool in my TC classroom my last two years and found it to be extremely helpful. My students liked Cued Speech, too. However, it*

was not until I came to the Houston Ear Research Foundation and assessed children exposed solely to Cued Speech that I came to grasp its true potential[1] for allowing the profoundly deaf child total access to our language.

6) Berendt, Krupnik-Goldman and Rupp (1990) reported that on the Rhode Island Test of Language Structure, the average CS subject scored better than 92% of hearing-impaired children generally.

Annotation: *Receptive and Expressive Language Abilities of Hearing-Impaired Children Who Use Cued Speech,* by Berendt, Krupnik-Goldman, and Rupp (1990). We quote from the report:

> *This study examines the receptive and expressive abilities of a group of CS learners aged 5 to 16. All subjects have a prelingual, bilateral, 80 dB or greater loss, and have been using Cued Speech for a minimum of two years. The test volunteers were required to submit a videotaped spontaneous language sample, analyzed using the Developmental Sentence Score (DSS), the expressive measure. The receptive measure was the Rhode Island Test of Language Structure (RITLS), and there was also a questionnaire. On the DSS, the CS children correctly produced an average of 36.5 out of 50 sentences, which is essentially the same as the hearing children. Those children who were introduced to Cued Speech before age 2 scored significantly better than those who began at a later age. On the RITLS, the CS group acquired an average percentile score of 92, differing significantly from the hearing-impaired population the test was normed on.*

Note above that the *average* CS child scored better than 92% of hearing-impaired children generally, on the RITLS. The fact that the children who started CS before the age of 2 performed better reflected in part the simple fact that the early starters had been exposed to CS longer, since the minimum CS exposure requirement for the study was only two years.

(7) Charlier and Paulissen reported on the effects of Cued Speech on use of residual hearing: "The subjects of this research

---

[1]Ms. Peterson's use of CS as a "supplementary tool" is typical of the practice of using Cued Speech in TC programs for (only) speech therapy and reading/English or introduction of new vocabulary. As she explains, this produces some favorable results, but does not reflect the potential of CS.

were effectively able to utilize the support of the cues to improve their auditory recognition. And far from diverting the auditory attention of the children, the presence of the cues of CS was able to support in them a better phonetic discrimination through audition."

Annotation: *Speech Audiometry and Cued Speech.* Charlier and Paulissen. Audiometrie vocale et language parlé complété (L.P.C.). *Otica* 10 (19) 1986. This study addresses a question raised at the Cued Speech Workshop in Paris, April 1984. The specific problem raised concerns, the utilization of residual hearing by children regularly supported by Cued Speech. Dabout and Descourtieux call attention to the possible danger that the extent to which the child has the benefit of a superior visual way of understanding may lead the child to fail to use his or her residual hearing spontaneously or to neglect that contribution to information. The authors theorize that the grouping of the phonemes in Cued Speech tends to arrange them so that their acoustic and articulatory characteristics, within groups, are as far separated as possible. This, they postulate, may facilitate auditory discrimination among the members of a group, when the cue is present. They tested this hypothesis experimentally.

Nine prelingually and profoundly hearing-impaired subjects were used, five whose impairment was of the second degree[2] of profoundness, and four of the third degree. They had experienced 52 months of exposure to Cued Speech. Mean age was 13 years 11 months for the first group and 13 years 5 months for the second. The material presented included five lists of phonemically balanced words, covering the 50 phonemes of French (21 vowels and 29 consonants). The five conditions of presentation were: audition alone, audition plus cues without lipreading, audition plus cues plus lipreading, audition plus lipreading without cues, and lipreading alone.

The researchers were surprised at the high level of performance on lipreading alone, and raised a question as to whether lipreading is easier in French than in English, which they identified as a question needing further investigation. Their conclusion read as follows:

---

[2]In Belgium and France deafness is classified according to the standard of the Bureau Internationale d'Audiophonologie (BIAP), using the average of the thresholds at 500, 1000, and the better of the 2000 Hz. and 4000 Hz. thresholds. An average greater than 90 dB denotes a profound loss. The profoundly deaf are divided into three groups by including the threshold at 250 Hz. in the average. The groups are: < 90 dB, first degree; > 100 dB, third degree; between these, second degree.

The subjects of this research were effectively able to utilize the support of the cues to improve their auditory recognition. And far from diverting the auditory attention of the children, the presence of the cues of L.P.C. supported in them a better phonetic discrimination through audition.

Abstract: *Language Parlé Complété (Cued Speech) is a helping tool for receiving speech, facilitating the lipreading process. By design, it offers the possibility of exercising the audition of hearing-impaired children. In fact, the hypothesis of a carelessness for the residual hearing, by deaf children using this method, is discussed and disproved through research ...using a vocal test of logatomes jointly presented with complementary manual cues.*

8) Neef and Iwata (1985) reported that a minimal amount of CS training for deaf children caused improvement in the ability to lipread without the cues.

Abstract: "The Development of Generative Lipreading Skills in Deaf Persons Using Cued Speech." Nancy A. Neef and Brian A. Iwata, in *Analysis and Intervention in Developmental Disabilities,* Vol. 5, pp. 289-305, 1985. The authors' complete abstract follows:

This study evaluated the effects of Cued Speech, a system of manual cues used in conjunction with spoken words, on lipreading performance of two congenitally and profoundly deaf males. Students received sequential Cued Speech training via a multiple base-line design across groups of phonemes (responses). Prior to and following training on each group, two types of probes were administered. Individual phoneme probes assessed acquisition of lipreading skills and generalization to expressive articulation responses. Novel phoneme combination probes assessed generalization of training to untrained phoneme combinations. Results indicated that subjects were able to accurately lipread cued stimuli as a function of Cued Speech training and that generalization of lipreading skills to novel nonsense syllables occurred. Cued Speech training also appeared to facilitate lipreading performance with non-cued stimuli, as well as articulation responses. Finally, students' probe performance following training compared favorably with that of an untrained deaf peer who was considered to be a skilled lipreader. Advantages of Cued Speech over other methods of communication training are discussed.

It should be kept in mind that the study described above deals with only the most elementary skills involved in lipreading. Research has shown that speechreaders who are skilled at speechreading discourse do not do much better on lipreading of individual phonemes and syllables than poor speechreaders. This is apparently because the visual identification of individual phonemes and syllables is a very small part of the total process of speechreading. The finding of the study described above, that Cued Speech training enhances lipreading of single phonemes and novel phoneme combinations, is interesting and favorable. A study by N.A. Sneed (1972) reported similar results in 14 hearing college students given about 15 hours of instruction in Cued Speech. They scored significantly higher at lipreading CV syllables after the training than they did before. However, both studies have limited implications regarding the levels of success in speechreading likely to be reached by Cued Speech children. More research on the effects of Cued Speech on ability to speechread *conversation* is needed to support the anecdotal and theoretical evidence of the potential of Cued Speech for development of high-level speechreading skill.

9) Périer and other researchers in Belgium reported in 1985 that Cued Speech is clearly readable in French. They also reported that they encountered no serious difficulties in making deaf children bilingual in Belgian Sign Language and spoken/written French when they used Cued Speech for French.

Annotation: "Evaluation of the Effects of Prolonged Cued Speech Practice Upon the Reception of Spoken Language." Périer, Charlier, Hage, and Alegría, (1987). This paper, delivered by Périer at the International Congress on Education of the Deaf in 1985, in Manchester, England, describes the program at the Centre Comprendre et Parler, in Brussels. In its preschool they introduce both Cued Speech and signs. The authors reported no serious problems in making the children bilingual in Belgian Sign Language and spoken/written French. They also showed that Cued Speech in French is clearly readable, as Nicholls did for CS in English.

For updates on research on Cued Speech refer to the publications and reports available from the National Cued Speech Association, including the *Cued Speech Journal*, the *Annotated Bibliography of Research on Cued Speech,* and the newsletter *On Cue*.

How to Present Cued Speech

Most people involved with Cued Speech encounter the need at some point to present or "sell" Cued Speech to individuals or groups for one of two or three purposes: to persuade someone or some agency to provide a specific service, to generate financial support for various projects or purpose related to its use, or simply to expand its use among parents and professionals. Many parents do this in a variety of ways, ranging from formal consultations with representatives of school systems to informal or chance encounters with other parents or professionals.

The key to presenting and "selling" Cued Speech is basically the same as selling almost anything: reasoning with people to show them why they need personally to learn, or use, or understand, or support financially something new or different—in this case a (to them) new tool for use with deaf children.

"Selling" Cued Speech requires specific knowledge and understanding, as well as the flexibility to adjust to different individuals, audiences, or constituencies. Each of them has specific interests and needs that will influence their potential interest in Cued Speech. Being aware of and sensitive to those interests and needs can make presentation of Cued Speech more effective, for two reasons: 1) information can be presented most appropriately, and 2) the presentation can be supported with information and assistance designed to help the individual use Cued Speech successfully to address his/her interests.

How you should present Cued Speech depends on two things: to whom you are presenting, and what you are trying to achieve. Included here are approaches suggested for use with 1) parents who have recently learned their child's hearing is impaired, 2) parents who have been using signing with their deaf child, 3) parents who have been using a traditional oral approach, 4) signing teachers, 5) oral teachers, 6) speech therapists, 7) administrators, 8) deaf adults, and 9) the general public. It will be easier, of course, if you have had several years of successful use of Cued Speech with your deaf child, so that you can speak from experience as well as on theoretical grounds. *If this is not the case, seek advice or help from experienced parents or professionals, or enlist an advocate to assist you.*

1) *New Parents*

With parents of a child recently diagnosed as deaf, your emphasis should be on their need to look at all available options before choosing one. Stress that the choice should be what is best for their child and them, not necessarily what is convenient for the professionals. Make the point that their first choice, once they have looked into the available options, is what method of communication to use with their child at home. This does not necessarily have to be the method used with the child in preschool or elementary school, though certainly it is best for the same method to be used both at home and in school, if possible.

If the child is under 3 years of age, the parents can choose a method and use it for a time before the child enters preschool. Of course, they should take the child for regular auditory training and speech therapy, and to get guidance on working with a young deaf child at home. Stress that they should visit programs for deaf children and be sure to observe the older children in each program, not just the younger ones the program directors will suggest they observe. They should also be sure to obtain audiological information (an audiogram or at least a PTA, plus age at onset), and seek assistance in understanding its implications. Young children in all programs can appear to be doing well and having a good time, but this is no assurance that they will achieve appropriate levels of language, reading, and communication by the time they finish school. Parents can judge the effectiveness of a program most accurately by observing the children who are finishing grade school or high school, and by obtaining information about their language and reading levels. It may also be helpful to consult parents who have children in the program.

With parents new to CS, use the information in Chapter 1 to describe the typical language and reading attainments of deaf children. Then stress the fact that, after visiting programs and looking at the facts about the attainments of typical deaf children, parents should look at the research data available. Before telling them about research results, tell them what the use of Cued Speech has meant to you and your child. Emphasize these points:

1.1) With Cued Speech you can communicate easily and freely with your child. If others in your family can cue also, say so, and indicate that this leads to a sense of family identity and self-confidence in the child. Stress the fact that you don't have to search for vocabulary (signs or lipreadable words)—that you can say anything to your child that is appropriate for him/her. If you used traditional oral methods or signing before learning and using Cued Speech, compare the effectiveness of your communication with your child during the use of each method. If you have witnessed any effects on your child's frustration level or sense of well-being, describe them.

1.2) Summarize your impressions of your child's rate of

learning verbal language since you started Cued Speech.

1.3) If you have seen the effects of CS on your child's ability to lipread, say so, repeating the claim that receiving CS makes children into lipreaders without specific training in lipreading.

1.4) If your child can "parrot" what you say with Cued Speech, even nonsense words, tell about it or demonstrate with the child. Let the other parent give you some nonsense words or phrases for your child to say.

1.5) Stress your confidence that your child is on the way to becoming a good reader. Or, if he/she is already a good reader, cite any test results that support this impression.

1.6) Summarize the results of the research reports annotated in this chapter. Be sure to include the findings comparing the reading comprehension levels of matched groups of Cued Speech, hearing, oral, and signing children. Cite the focal points of each of the studies: Nicholls' proof that CS is clearly readable; Wandel's comparison of reading comprehension levels of matched groups of hearing, CS, signing, and oral students; the Belgian experimental psychologists' explanation of why deaf children accustomed to CS read the same way hearing children do; the study (Hage, et al.) showing that use of Cued Speech at home is more important than its use at school; the finding of Peterson (a TC teacher for 11 years) that CS children " ... surpass most signing and oral children in verbal language skills, and the finding of Berendt, Krkupnik Goldman, and Rupp that on the Rhode Island Test of Language Structures the *average* CS child in their group of subjects scored better than 92% of hearing-impaired children on whom the test was normed. If at any time the interest of the parent in the research findings seems to wane, revert to your own experience with Cued Speech, summarizing the difference it has made. Invite questions.

Linda Balderson reminds us that "There is nothing like the real thing." She suggests setting up two times to meet with new parents. One should be in your home—very informal—with your deaf child present. Make sure it is a time when your child is likely to be rested and cooperative. Do something your child can participate in. The other meeting should be in the home of the potential CS family, preferably at a time that precludes the presence of the children, so that information can be presented efficiently and questions answered.

To illustrate that even minimal communication can impress parents, Linda Balderson furnishes this example:

When Tiffany was 3 we went to visit a potential CS family with a deaf child the same age. Tiffany, who was very shy, did not talk at all, and we were worried that perhaps she did not make the kind of positive impression she could have made. Later we were told by the other child's mother that she was astounded when I asked Tiffany to go upstairs and get her shoes, and Tiffany did. Since then we have invited families to meet Tiffany at our home, on the theory that she will be more willing to talk there.

2) Signing Parents

With a parent who has been using signs with his/her deaf child, start by stressing the fact that signs are clear, easy for the child to learn, well suited to effective communication, and needed for access to the deaf society. Stress that Cued Speech is not a substitute for sign language, which almost all profoundly deaf children will need. Next, ask if the parent is considering other methods because the rate of acquisition of *verbal language* is inadequate, or if the parent is running out of signs and finding that this limits communication. Explain that a sign is not a spoken or written word, and when learned does not teach the child how the word is spoken or written. That is the problem. Signs do not cause a child to pick up words. Instead, if signs are the only method of communication used, every word has to be specifically taught to the child with fingerspelling or writing. There simply isn't enough time for parents and teachers to do that fast enough to keep up with the child's needs.

Ask the parent how many signs the child knows. Say: "Do you realize that every sign your child knows makes it possible for you to teach him or her the spoken word that means the same thing, almost instantaneously?" For a hearing child to learn a new word it has only to be said to the child in a situation that makes clear what it refers to. Thus, if you want to teach the word *gorilla* you have to get either a gorilla or a picture of one, point to it, and say *gorilla*. The same thing—no more, no less, has to be done with CS to teach a deaf child the word *gorilla*. But, if a child already knows several hundred signs, you can teach him/her the equivalent words very rapidly with Cued Speech, since you do not have to manipulate the environment (get a picture of a gorilla!) to show what you are talking about. This does not mean that the child should be taught new signs in order to use them to teach words with Cued Speech. It is faster to teach them directly.

Make the point that very few hearing parents (fewer than 5%) keep up with their signing child in sign vocabulary for more than a few years. Then the child becomes the sign teacher for the parents, and both their relationship and influence on language learning may suffer.

Now pick up section 1) at "With parents new to CS, use the information in Chapter 1 to...." The rest of the material in Section 1 should be useful with a parent who has been using signs with a deaf child and has some concerns. You may find it helpful with some parents to get into the "two-stage process" required for teaching a written word with signs, and the "three-stage process" required for teaching a spoken word through signs.

3) Oral Parents

With a parent who has been using traditional oral methods, first provide him/her an opportunity to explain why he/she is considering a change. This information may reveal the best place to start. You should make it clear that Cued Speech is an oral method, needed by most profoundly deaf children in order to succeed orally. Suggest that the basic question a parent should face is whether the child needs the support of Cued Speech in order to succeed. Your key point should be the child's rate of verbal language acquisition and whether it is rapid enough for the child to be ready for reading at age 6. If you first used oral methods and became disenchanted with them, it was probably because you felt language and communication were coming too slowly. If so, make that point. It is not usually best to attack or criticize oral methods. An inoffensive statement is that if a child can keep up with the normal spoken language acquisition rate for children of the same level of ability with only "pure oral" methods, that is fine: otherwise, the oral approach alone is not adequate for the child in question.

Next consider the value of what can happen at home. The Belgian research psychologists reported that Cued Speech at home is much more important than its use at school, though its use in both places is most effective. We have said this for 20 years, but without research data to support the assertion. The reasons are simple. First, the home is the best language laboratory there is, and the parents have the greatest opportunity to "get through" to the child because of their special relationship to him or her. There is another important reason. Many parents can do a good job of teaching their child one-to-one in the environment of the home, without training as teachers of the deaf. Many of them rapidly acquire the skills of the best teachers through reading and experience. Also, they have a very special motivation to help their child learn. Lastly, Cued Speech makes it unnecessary for the parents (as teachers) to deviate much from what the parents of a hearing child do, except to cue and to remember that the child can understand only when looking. They must do more of some things than is necessary for a hearing child, such as correction of pronunciation and language and making an effort to introduce new language consistently. Parents must budget their time in order to provide the necessary amount of interaction with the child. The parents' role requires willingness, patience, and dedication, but not as much special training as is needed with oral methods. Some of the most successful Cued Speech children have been taught entirely by their parents during the preschool years, and have reached the age of 6 with language levels well above the median for hearing children. This is not to denigrate the role of teachers, but to emphasize the value of a system that makes communication easy in a form that automatically causes phonological internalization of spoken English.

Now, pick up section 1) at "With parents new to CS, use the information...." The rest of the material in 1) should be useful for use with the concerned parent who has been using traditional oral methods.

4) Signing Teachers

With signing teachers, begin as with the signing parent, enumerating the good things about signs and the fact that Cued Speech is not a substitute for signs. Then get to the fact that signs do not teach spoken or written words. Do this by asking the teacher how words are taught to the deaf child in a signing program. Use the fact that the sign does not show how the corresponding word is pronounced or written to get the teacher to agree that the word is actually taught to the deaf child by writing it or fingerspelling it. If the spoken word is then to be learned, it is taught from the written form and accompanying oral presentation. This makes learning a written word a two-stage process (learning the sign, then using the sign with writing or fingerspelling to teach the written word), and learning a spoken word a three-stage process (sign, written word, spoken word).

Next, come to the verbal language learning rate. If every word has to be taught—in the written form by a two-stage process, and in the spoken form by a three-stage process—there isn't enough time to get words learned at the rate required for readiness to read at age 6 or 7. Stress the research results comparing language levels of CS children with other hearing-impaired kids on the RITLS. Furnish a copy of the annotations at the first of this chapter. Call attention to the program in Brussels that uses signs and Cued Speech together in preschool.

Finally, bring up the subject of how few hearing parents are able to keep up with their deaf child in signing, and for how long. Explain that this means that the contribution of the home to communication, language, values, information—everything that parents can give their child—is inhibited, limited, and distorted.

At this point pick up section 1) again at "With parents new to CS, use the information in Chapter 1 to...."

5) Oral Teachers

With oral teachers, start as with oral parents. Make the point that being a good oral teacher requires great skill, plus careful study of each child and awareness of individual speechreading abilities, vocabulary, etc. Several oral schools that took up Cued Speech have reported that its use"...made our better teachers into superb teachers and our ordinary teachers into excellent teachers." It takes skill to teach deaf children with any of the available methods, but Cued Speech makes it easier to do a good job with modest skills. Why? Because the aural/oral message is delivered to the children in a clear form. Emphasize the research results.

Stress the fact that Cued Speech is a system in which the aural/oral input is supplemented to the extent necessary to make the spoken message clear so the child can learn and understand well. In 1985 the board of directors of the Alexander Graham Bell Association for the Deaf passed a resolution affirming that "... Cued Speech is a viable supplement to oral communication." Actually, its basic goals are identical with those of persons who use aural/oral methods. Its purpose is to make those goals attainable by most profoundly deaf children. However, it is not a substitute for sign language, which many or perhaps even most deaf children need for access to the deaf society.

At this point pick up section 1) at the point specified above.

6) Speech Therapists

With a speech therapist, begin by explaining that using Cued Speech does not eliminate the need for speech therapy, since it does not teach the child how to make the sounds of speech. It shows the child which sounds to make and when to make them. However, the role of the speech therapist is changed if the parents use Cued Speech, especially if the therapist also uses it. The change does not apply to the basic function of the therapist, but to the increased rate of progress the therapist can achieve and the amount of support the parents can provide. Its effects are as follows:

6.1 Cued Speech causes the child to think in the spoken language. As a result, his/her response to speech therapy is typically more motivated and perceptive than would otherwise be the case.

6.2 With Cued Speech the therapist can work faster because the target for the child to aim for can be communicated instantly. Thus, the therapist knows that the child is trying to articulate that target, and not some confused version of it. When the child errs, the therapist can immediately demonstrate what the child produced and what he/she should produce. This minimizes frustration due to uncertainty.

6.3 The therapist can communicate well in explaining what to do with the vocal organs, at least with children with sufficient vocabulary.

6.4 When the therapist succeeds in getting the child to produce a new sound, a note to that effect can remind the parents to prompt the child to insert that sound in all the right places. Parents can correct pronunciation with ease, and without frustrating the child. They should not attempt to correct articulation without professional guidance.

6.5 The therapist can work with a child whose knowledge of the spoken language is much greater than that of most deaf children. As a result, the therapist has access to a wider range of vocabulary and word combinations to use in testing, practicing, and developing the child's speech production.

At this point, pick up section 1) at the same point as before.

7) Administrators

We can offer no convenient formula for use in talking with administrators. They have their own agendas, and a parent has to be prepared to take several different approaches. Fortunately, many of the conversations with administrators will be about something the parents want for their child. This provides a starting point and may suggest a line of discussion. Our suggestion is to have in readiness all the material suggested for use with people in the other categories, and to use it as prudence dictates. Mike Maslin suggests marking in advance key items you think you will need to use. Parents need to be familiar with as much as possible of the information on the rights of deaf children and their parents, as described in Chapter 30. They need also to keep in mind that, though the law is clear on many points, administrators inclined to resist change can use a multitude of delaying tactics. Parents need the wisdom of Solomon and the tact of a diplomat.

We can offer a few guidelines that may be helpful:

7.1 Notify school authorities or administrators as far in advance as possible concerning what you will be requesting for your child. We know of cases in which notification was presented, tactfully but firmly, more than two years in advance. Also make sure to reiterate the request and suggest actions to be taken to move toward meeting the need. For some requests, such as a CS transliterator, at least a year's notice is usually necessary because of the widespread difficulty of locating qualified transliterators nearby, and/or the time required to train them if that is determined to be necessary rather than to recruit a qualified transliterator. A recruitment problem is that the pay for transliterators is not sufficient to entice people to move across the country, or to lead large numbers of persons to secure the necessary training. What works best is to teach potential transliterators to cue and encourage the school to provide transliterator training.

7.2 Be very familiar with your rights as a parent in connection with the IEP (Individualized Educational Program) that must be prepared for your child each year. If you let the school personnel write it and adopt it without any input from you, you will not be protecting your child's interests. Obtain copies of IEP's for other children (from their parents) and study them. Obtain advice from competent people outside your district. Seek help from the sources listed in the Appendix. Above all, remember not to sign the IEP if it is not acceptable, or sign with a notation that you refuse to accept it.

7.3 In negotiating with administrators, stress the economies possible with Cued Speech, resulting from the following. Some of these assertions can be documented. Most are supported only by observation and anecdotal evidence.

7.31 The cost of training school personnel and parents to use Cued Speech is much less than the cost of teaching signing. Aides, resource teachers, mainstream teachers, and others can be taught Cued Speech in a small fraction of the time required to acquire even minimal competence in signing. A vulnerable point is that CS children tend to be mainstreamed, and a transliterator is expensive. The counter is that a sign interpreter is just as expensive.

7.32 Parental contribution to the development of language is higher than with other methods, thus enabling the school to apply more of its resources to teaching content material.

7.33 Reduces the need for resource teaching.

7.34 CS students can typically learn more for themselves, through reading, home work, special assignments. What they learn for themselves does not have to be taught to them.

7.35 Self-contained classes can be larger when Cued Speech is used, in comparison with traditional oral classes.

7.4 Pick up section 1) at the same point as suggested in the preceding sections. Present the advantages Cued Speech has for the parent and call attention to the research evidence available to support the claims made for CS. Give administrators a copy of it.

8) Deaf Individuals

Use entirely different approaches for a person who has grown up deaf and a person who has become deafened in adulthood. With both, demonstrate cued words that look alike on the mouth, such as *met, bet, pet, mit, bit, pit, mid, bid, pin;* or *do, new, loo, you.* Let the deaf person suggest pairs of "look-alike" words for you to cue to show that they are cued differently if they look the same on the mouth.

With a person deafened in adulthood who knows little or no sign language, stress how quickly Cued Speech can be learned, and that there is no new language to learn. Stress that the problem for the deafened adults is not learning Cued Speech—that's easy for them—but getting some hearing friends or relatives to learn to cue and then to do it consistently. A spouse, for example, is often so accustomed to repeating things more than once to a hearing-impaired spouse that at first this is less effort than cueing. Videotape instructional lessons for deaf adults are available (see Appendix). However, if you can be available, teach the deaf person to read CS yourself. Face-to-face instruction and practice are still best. Don't worry about the deaf person's learning to cue expressively. Put any deaf adult who shows interest in learning CS in touch with the Cued Speech National Center.

With a deaf person who has grown up signing, how you should proceed depends upon how much verbal language he/she knows, and why he/she is interested in learning CS. He/she may want to learn to speak better (by learning spoken language more accurately); to use it with a deaf child (not usually a good reason); to communicate with friends who cue; or simply to learn another communication mode for possible use with deaf or hearing persons. Few deaf people who have grown up with signing will want to learn Cued Speech if they spend most of their time with deaf people.

9) The General Public

When presenting CS to groups that include assortments of people, whether in a formal presentation or a casual one, it is usually best to begin with a general discussion of the different kinds and degrees of hearing loss, the implications of deafness, and the traditional communication and education approaches used with deaf children. This provides a base for presenting the need for Cued Speech and usually generates interest in the benefits and results of use of Cued Speech.

New ideas imply a need for change, so they usually stimulate controversy and resistance. Those who react negatively when CS is presented may exhibit anger, defensiveness, fear, or rejection. They may feel threatened and may respond emotionally. Those who envision a better way for the future are often not appreciated in the present. Be positively persistent and expect eventually to make progress.

Chapter 29
The Fine Points of Cueing

Some of the "fine points" below are "finer" than some readers will want to study in detail. We suggest that you look through them carefully and then work through the ones you think will be of most help, as you find time to do so. <u>Many of the items are not for beginners, and should be left until fluency is well along.</u> The perfection of your cueing should be regarded as a long-term project.

It is helpful to emphasize the following fundamentals and fine points in teaching Cued Speech to hearing people, or when practicing cueing in preparation for an evaluation of your own cueing, such as the Basic Cued Speech Proficiency Rating, designed by Beaupré (1984). Some points listed below are needed to furnish clear timing indications in the cueing with a minimum of motion and complexity. Others are clarifications or restatements of instructions given in the most basic lessons that need repeated emphasis. Some have been mentioned in workshops and articles, but have not hitherto been published together.

1) Use as little wrist motion as possible when learning to cue or when teaching others to cue. It is unwise for beginners to bend the wrist more than is absolutely necessary. Beginners should try to use small motions, without flourishes. Small motions make it easier to maintain synchronization, and allow fluency to develop faster. The side location should be kept to no more than four inches from the tip of the chin. The throat location should be at the larynx, not on the chest. The mouth location should be an inch or less from the corner of the mouth. Beginners should be sure to form the habit of touching at the mouth, chin and throat locations.

2) Cue a word the way you think you are saying it at the time. Your pronunciation of some words will vary. For example, most people say *dir, deer, di ur,* or *di uh,* for both *dear* and *deer.*

3) Cue the words *water* and *thirty* with a *t,* not a *d.* To understand why, refer to the section on page 723, entitled "Wahdur."

4) Rehearse run-together words aloud (or mentally) before cueing them. Your vocal mechanism will help remind you how you say them.

5) Move your hand forward only about one inch in the side location for *ah* and *oe,* with or without a preceding consonant.

6) Move down no more than one inch (½ inch unless stressed) in the side location for the schwa (as in *the* and *other*).

7) In both 5) and 6), the hand must move back to the original

location (back in the case of 5, up in the case of 6), *if the next cue is to be made in the side location*. If the next cue is made somewhere else, the return motion is not made.

Sound and Pronunciation Guide

Schwa—The schwa (the unstressed neutral vowel sound uh (as in *ubout*) is one of the most frequent sounds in our language. It is cued in the side location with a tiny downward movement (about ½ inch). Beginning cuers must be very careful to avoid cueing a word according to its spelling when the schwa is involved. In deciding what sounds you make, remember that unstressed vowels tend to be pronounced *uh*. Keep this sound in mind when deciding how to cue the first and last *a*'s in *banana*, or the first and last vowels in *botanical*. Many short words are unstressed, so that the vowels in them are pronounced *uh*, as in the case of *e* in *the* ball, or *o* in *to*, in the sentence *Ie wahnt tu goe nou*. Other examples are: forest (*fawrust*), children (*childrun*), away (*uwae*), and camera (*kamruh*). The downward movement becomes even smaller when cueing is rapid and the schwa is unstressed in the middle of a word. Note that writing the *h* in Funetik Speling is optional, as in *tHuh*. This is usually done only at the end of a word. It can also be done with *i* and *e*, to make it clear that the other short-vowel sounds are used: *eh*, *ih*. An example would be *tHeh-uh*, to emphasize a southern or British pronunciation of *there*, or *hih-uh*. Once you are at home without the added *h*, drop it, writing *the-u* or *hi-u*, remembering that *e* is pronounced *eh* and *i* is pronounced *ih*.

Prolonged schwa—When the schwa (*uh*) is stressed and therefore prolonged, as in the first syllable of mother (*mutHur*), the downward movement for it (at the side location) is increased from ½ inch to about one inch. Thus, in the example *mutHuh* (southern American or British pronunciation), the downward movement with *mu* will be considerably longer than with the last syllable, *tHuh*. The downward movement is necessary to distinguish words ending in the schwa from those ending in a consonant alone. Examples are:

Pop (*pah p*)   pill (*pi l*)
Papa (*pah puh*)   pillow (*pi luh*)

Plurals—Although plural endings are usually spelled with *s*, they frequently use the *z* sound. They should be cued as they sound: dogs (*daw g z*), cats (*ka t s*), watches (*wah chu z* or *wah chi z*).

Past-tense endings — Some past-tense endings (ed) are pronounced as ending in *t*. Take care to cue according to the sound:

    fished (*fisht*), cued 5 throat, 6 side, 5 side

    smelled (*smeld* or *smelt*)

    learned (*lurnd* or *lurnt*)

The letter *d* is pronounced as *t* at the ends of some words. For example, many Americans pronounce the word *second* as *sekunt*, though the dictionaries specify *secund*. Listen to yourself.

The sounds of ur and r

A distinction should be made between words ending in the vowel sound *ur* and the consonant sound of *r*. The two sounds are much alike, differing primarily in their durations. Thus, the result will vary from person to person and situation to situation. For example, one can pronounce the word *there* as *tHehr*, as it is usually pronounced, or as *tHeh ur*. Southern American dialect may result in *tHeh uh*, or even *tHeh yuh*. Or, if the pronunciation is very southern (*tHeh uh*), it should be cued 2 chin 5 side down.

The word *fur* can be pronounced with the steady, unchanging vowel sound *ur* (*fur,* cued 5 mouth), or it can be pronounced as *fuh r*. It is simplest to choose your usual pronunciation of this word and cue accordingly. Here are some other examples.

Mouth	Side
mower (*moe ur*)	more (*moe r*)
mirror (*mi rur*)	mere (*mi r* or *mee r*)
lower (*loe ur*)	lore (*loe r*)

The sounds of the letter x—There is no separate cue for the letter x. It is cued as it sounds, as *ks*, as *gz*, or as *z*. But, be careful about the preceding vowel. Examples: <u>six</u> (*si k s*), <u>axe</u> (*a k s*), <u>excuse</u> (verb, *i k s k yue z*, noun, *i k s k yue s*), <u>example</u> (*i g za m pu l*), <u>exam</u> (*i g za m*), <u>wax</u> (*wa k s*), <u>fox</u> (*fahks*), <u>exert</u> (*i g zur t*), <u>Xerox</u> (*Zeerahks*).

The sound of qu — Generally, *qu* is pronounced as the equivalent of kw, as in the following: <u>quiet</u> (*k wie u t*), <u>quick</u> (*k wi k*), <u>quit</u> (*kwi t*), <u>quack</u> (*kwa k*).

Words ending in y or ie—There is much debate among beginning cuers about how they pronounce letters such as those at the ends of words such as <u>baby</u>, <u>mommy</u>, <u>Billie</u>, etc. Many insist that they are using the long *ee* sound, but most eventually realize that what they are saying is usually closer to the short i, cued at the throat location. Usually such endings are pronounced with long *ee* only when the last syllable is stressed, or when the vowel sound is lengthened. For example, if one calls: "Bobbie! Come here!" it is very likely that the final sound in the name will be *ee*. However, if one asks: "Where did Bobbie go?" the last sound in the name will likely be the short *i* sound as in *bit*. Reference to the word <u>city</u> (*siti*) may help. The sound of the y will be the same as that of the <u>i</u> in the first syllable. No one is likely to say "*sitee*," because to do so causes one to place an unnatural stress on the last syllable. Normally, when one is speaking rapidly, he/she is more likely to use the short *i* sound at the ends of words and when the sound of <u>i</u> or <u>y</u> is unstressed within words.

Practice in Listening

For beginning cuers, it is frequently difficult to distinguish between similar sounds. Practice listening and comparing the sounds:

s and z	s	z
	hiss	his
	lacy	lazy
	race	raise

w and wh	w	wh
	witch	which
	wail	whale
	wine	whine
	wear	where

Many people substitute *w* for *wh*, as in *wen* for *when*, or *wiet* for *whiet*. This makes the deaf child unable to make the distinctions listed above unless he or she knows the language well enough to do so through context, as hearing children do. Beginning parents with young deaf children may (or may not) wish to make these distinctions easier for the child by pronouncing and cueing the *wh* sound for a year or so.

sh and ch	sh	ch
	sheep	cheep
	mush	much
	dish	ditch

sh and zh	sh	zh
	assure (*u shoor*)	azure (*a zhur* or *a zhoor*)
	action (*ak shun*)	illusion (*i lue zhun*)

dilute (*die luet* or *duh luet*)   delusion (*di lue zhun*)

ng, nj, ngk	ng	nj	ngk
	sing	singe	sink
	swing	sponge	shank
	long	lounge	link

th and tH	th		tH
	thick		this
	thin		that
	thumb .		they
	method		mother

i and e	i		e
	wrist		rest
	did		dead

oo and ue	oo		ue
	should (*shood*)		shoot (*shuet*)
	pull (*pool*)		pool (*puel*)

Pull in CE is written *pool* in Funetik Speling, and FS *puel* shows how pool in CE sounds. When reading FS, you must remember that *oo* is the sound in book and *ue* is the sound in moon.

Listening Suggestions

Most people have difficulty in identifying many of the specific sounds they make. Practice in listening is necessary to determine the exact sounds. The following guide offers suggestions for acceptable pronunciations. If there is doubt about or disagreement about how a word is pronounced, refer to a dictionary for the preferred pronunciation. However, do not cue it that way unless you prefer and plan to use that pronunciation. Remember that in Cued Speech we follow the rule: "Cue it the way *you* say it." Therefore, each person should listen to himself and cue each word the way he is saying it at that time.

ee vs i In rapid speech, short *i* occurs more frequently before *r*: deer (*dir* or *deer*), year (*yir*), hear (*hir*), beer (*bir*).

ee vs i In rapid speech the short *i* sound occurs more often when y is final and unstressed: <u>Mommy</u> (*Mahmi*), <u>army</u> (*ah r mi, lazy* (*lae zi*).

e vs ae In rapid speech short *e* occurs more frequently before r: <u>care</u> (*ke r*), <u>hair</u> (*he r*), <u>tear</u> (te r). Note: the noun <u>tear</u> is pronounced *tir, teer,* or *tiur.*

e vs *a* In rapid speech short *e* occurs more frequently when the spelling is <u>ar</u> or <u>arr</u>: <u>sparrow</u> (*spe roe* or *spa roe*), <u>baron</u> (*be run* or *ba run.* In British and New England speech, the short a is used.

oo vs ue The vowel *oo* is preferable before <u>sh</u>: <u>bush</u> (*boo sh*), <u>push</u> (*poo sh).* Also *oo* occurs more frequently before <u>r</u>: sure (*shoo r).*

oe The diphthong *oe* is cued in the United States as if it were a single vowel, rather than a glide. In England it is cued side-to-throat.

Running Words Together

If you are to cue naturally, as you speak, you must learn to run words together. The young deaf child will understand words run together, just as a hearing child does. This will help him or her in speechreading normal speech. The following examples may make you realize that you run words together more than you realize.

Look at it!	*(loo ka ti t)*	Feel it	*(fee li t)*
Leave it alone.	*(lee vi tuh loe n)*	Stop it!	*(stah pit)*
Give it to her.	*(gi vi tuh hur)*	Keep out!	*(kee pou t)*
One at a time.	*(wu na tuh tie m)*	That's all.	*(tha t sawl)*
Have another.	*(ha vuh nuh tHur)*	Touch it.	*(tu chi t)*
Take it off.	*(tae ki taw f)*	Is it?	*(i zi t?)*

The Timing Movements of Cued Speech

Cued Speech is a time-locked system; that is, the cues must be synchronized with the spoken sounds. Every cue must be accompanied by a hand movement that establishes its time relative to the sound. The movements used include: 1) a movement from one location to another; 2) a change from one handshape to another; 3) a forward movement of no more than one inch in the side location, for syllables containing *ah* or *oe;* 4) a backward movement (in the case above) to the original location, but *only* when the next cue is also in the side location; 5) a downward movement in the side location, for the schwa (*uh*), ½ inch when it is unstressed, and up to one inch when stressed, 6) a return (upward) of the hand to the original location in 5), but *only* if the next cue is in the side location; 7) the *flick,* a small, ¼-inch movement forward and back, required in specific situations; and 8) special movements for pitch indication (p. 171), palatization, and/or aspiration, primarily in foreign languages. Because the first six of the timing movements listed above are probably already familiar to you, and you are not likely to need those listed in 8) at this time, attention will be given in this section primarily to the flick.

Changes in handshape often have to occur during movements 1), 4) and movement 6). In the case of *shee saw,* cued 6 mouth, 3 chin, the change from handshape 6 to handshape 3 while the hand moves form mouth to chin, reaching handshape 3 at the moment the fingers touch the chin. No flick is needed. The same necessity occurs during movements 4) and 6), the returns to the original side location. If one cues pot *(paht),* during the movement back to the original location, the hand must change from handshape 1 to 5. Similarly, in cueing putt *(put),* the handshape must change from 1 to 5 during the return upward. When the cueing is *forward and back,* or *downward and back,* remember that *and back* means *and back, changing to the next handshape on the way, if necessary.*

The flick is used whenever the same cue is repeated two or more times successively, in the same location. This happens at the mouth, chin, throat, and side locations. Consider the word meter *(mee tur),* 5 mouth, 5 mouth. After the syllable *mee* is executed, the hand must move slightly away from its contact with the cheek near the corner of the mouth, and then be replaced just as one says *tur.* Without this little flick, the hand would provide no evidence of the production of a second syllable, and no clue to timing. Practice other examples: sassy *(sa si),* 3 throat, flick 3 throat; pooh pooh *(pue pue),* 1 chin, flick 1 chin. For some of these the second syllable is evident on the mouth; for others it is not. Cued Speech must show both existence and timing.

A similar situation occurs in the side location when a repeated cue is for a consonant not followed immediately by a vowel, as in the word left *(le-f-t),* which must be cued 6 chin, 5 side, flick 5 side. For the final *t,* the hand must be moved forward sharply in a tiny flick, about ¼ inch, and back. Without the flick the CS reader has no way of knowing from the cueing that the *(t)* exists, or when it is made.

To get the feel of the flick in the side location, place handshape 5 in the side location and say and cue *tah,* 5 forward. Now say and cue *t, t, t, t.* Do not make any trace of a vowel with the *t,* but simply flick the tongue to make the stop and explosion of the *t,* and at the same time make a tiny flick of the hand, about ¼ inch, forward and back, each time you say *t.* Unless you do this, the reader of CS will not have any clear indication of when you make the sound unless he can see clearly inside your mouth. Now, experiment with different sequences, in which the rhythm is changed. Cue and say *t t   t*, with some time between the second and third *t*'s. Try *t t t   t t* and other patterns.

Rule: When the same cue appears twice in succession in a specific location, and the second cue is for a consonant that does not immediately precede a vowel, the second consonant must be flicked.

Here are some examples for the side location: lift (*lift*), 6 throat, 5 side, flick 5 side; horse (*hawrs*), 3 chin, 3 side, flick 3 side; leaves (*leevz*), 6 mouth, 2 side, flick 2 side; scarce (*skers*) , 3 side, 2 chin, 3 side, flick 3 side. Without the flicks in the cases above the CS reader will have no way of knowing from the cues that there is a second consonant at the end, or when it occurs, if he suspects its existence. With the flick, he knows a sound is there, and decodes it.

The rule applies also when the first consonant is followed by a vowel cued in the side location: *ah, oe, or uh*. Consider the example tot (*taht*). This is cued 5 side forward (and back to the original location), flick 5 side. Similar examples are mom (*mahm*), cued 5 forward and back, flick 5 side; pop (*pahp*), 1 side forward and back, flick one side. Now, try *pup*, 1 side down and up, 1 flick side. Next, try one in which the handshape changes during the motion, *sup*, cued 3 side down and back (changing to handshape 1), 1 side. No flick is necessary because the handshape changes. If the handshape changes during either motion 6) or motion 4), the appearance of the new handshape at the completion of the motion provides the timing indication, and no flick is needed. Note that in cueing pop (*pahp*), the motion of the hand back to the original location, after *pah,* shows that there will be another cue in the side location. However, from a frontal view it does not make the timing clearly evident, so the flick is required, in accord with the rule.

When 3 consonants occur in succession in the side location, as with hoarse (*hoers*), the last two consonants must be flicked if they are both without vowels. The cueing is 3 side forward and back, to 3 flick side, 3 flick side. Similar is coarse (*koers*), 3 side forward and back (changing the handshape from 5 to 3 during the backward movement), 3 side, flick 3 side. No flick is required for the *r* because of the change from handshape 2 to handshape 3.

The return movements 4) and 6) do indicate that another consonant is to follow, but do not indicate its timing accurately unless a handshape change is made during the movement. If there is no change in handshape, the flick is needed for accurate indication of timing and/or emphasis. However, one can omit the flick to show that the consonant is not exploded. For example, one can cue p̲o̲p̲ (*pahp*) without a flick, to show that the final *p* is not exploded. The flick shows the explosion or completion of the consonant, and is timed with that completion. Another example is m̲o̲m̲ (*mahm*). If the mouth remains closed on the second *m*, the flick is not made. If the *m* is completed (by opening the lips, with or without audible completion of the *m*, the flick is helpful in showing this.

In summary, when pairs of consonants having the same cue (*f* and *t*, *r* and *s*, *v* and *z*, *tH* and *z*) appear together at the ends of syllables, they may require a flick for clear indication of the timing and phonemic content. Practice these: s̲o̲u̲r̲c̲e̲, f̲o̲r̲c̲e̲, h̲o̲r̲s̲e̲ (*hawrs*), f̲i̲e̲r̲c̲e̲ (*fi r s* or *fi ur s*), l̲e̲f̲t̲, l̲o̲f̲t̲, l̲i̲f̲t̲, s̲i̲f̲t̲, r̲i̲f̲t̲, m̲i̲f̲f̲e̲d̲ (*mift*), s̲o̲f̲t̲ (*sawft*), d̲r̲i̲f̲t̲, l̲o̲a̲v̲e̲s̲ (*loevz*), d̲o̲v̲e̲s̲ (*duvz*), c̲l̲o̲t̲h̲e̲s̲ (*kloetHz*).

Examples: mom (*mahm*), 5 side forward and back, flick 5 side; pop (*pahp*), 1 side forward and back, flick 1 side; popped (*pahpt*), 1 side forward and back, flick 1 side, 5 side; harm (*hahrm*), 3 side forward and back, flick 3 side, 5 side; hark (*hahrk*), 3 side forward and back, flick 3 side, 2 side; host (*hoest*), 3 side forward and back, flick 3 side 5 side; doped (*doept*), 1 side forward and back, flick 1 side, 5 side.

After you are accustomed to making the flick in the cases above, you will find other situations in which, though the rule does not require the flick, you can sense that the message and its rhythm will be clearer if you use the flick, as when you are speaking emphatically.[1]

---

[1] In 1978 Cornett became concerned about the difficulty many beginners experienced in synchronizing voice and cues in the side location. In the other locations there tends to be no problem, since beginners are instructed to touch the chin, the corner of the mouth, and the larynx area when cueing in those locations. Thus, they feel the contact as they make the sounds. In the side location there is nothing to establish for them the exact moment at which the cue is made, since it is in position for an appreciable time interval. The tendency is often to make the sound with less-than-accurate synchronization.

Cornett experimented with teaching beginners to use the flick with all consonants not followed by a vowel, and found that this solved the synchronization problem quickly. He recommended this procedure with all beginners, postulating that after the habit of synchronizing voice and cues had been formed, the flick would need to be used only when required or when natural, as in some emphatic or very precise statements. Beginners would be instructed to cue, "That's mine." as follows: 2 throat, flick 5 side, flick 3 side, 5 side, 5 throat, flick 4 side.

Opposition arose from experienced teachers of Cued Speech who doubt that

The vanishing schwa

Unless you are making an effort to speak very deliberately, you will not pronounce, and thus should not cue, a schwa in words such as moment (*moemnt*), 5 side forward and back, 5 side flick, 4 side, 5 side; apple (*apl*) 5 throat, 1 side, 6 side; and able (*aebl*), 5 chin, 5 throat, 4 side, 6 side. But, if you feel that you are pronouncing the schwa, as in *moemunt, moement,* or *apul,* cue the appropriate vowel. Note that a flick is required on the second *m* in *moemnt,* since the schwa movement (as in *moemunt*) is not present in moemnt.

ūh hūh

The expression *ūh hūh,* meaning yes, is one of the most frequently used in American conversation. Yet, neither it nor the vowel sound in it is listed in American dictionaries or lists of English phonemes. When you use this expression, simply cue the vowel at the throat (5 throat, 3 throat). The vowel itself is essentially the same as the French word *un*), cued at the throat, and represented in the International Phonetic Alphabet (IPA) as [œ]. For convenience, we will use the symbol ū writing *ūh-hūh.* The reverse, *hūh-ūh* (meaning no), is cued 3 throat, 5 throat, and *ūh-ūh* (also meaning no), is cued 5 throat, 5 throat. Do not substitute the schwa for this vowel and cue it at the side, thereby admitting that there are things you can't cue.

When he developed Cued Speech, Cornett did not think to put this vowel in the system, since it was not listed as a phoneme of English. Some years later, he noticed the omission and added it, in accord with the principle that one must cue what is said, and must not have to change what is said to fit what one can cue.

The non-vocalic counterparts of the expressions above use the continuants *m* and *n* to replace the vowels. They are *mm-hmm* (yes), *hmm-mm* (no), *mm-mm* (no), *nn-hnn* (yes), *hnn-nn* (no), and nn-

---

the gains in synchronization skills through having beginners "flick" all consonants not followed by a vowel will compensate for possible delays caused in fluency. As a result, Cornett decided to alter his position. He now recommends that beginners practice using the flick consistently for only an hour or so to get the feel of precise synchronization of voice and cues in the side location. Then, if no difficulty with synchronization remains, he recommends using the flick only where it is necessary.

Some self-instructional materials, notably the 1984 videocassette and audiocassette lessons produced at Gallaudet University, include the flick consistently. Most materials do not. In this chapter, the flick is indicated only in situations in which it is necessary.

nn (no). You may feel that enough is enough if you learn to cue the vocalic forms, which are cued at the throat. But, if you want to cue these non-vocalic forms, cue them in the side location, moving the hand forward with each syllable, and following the usual cueing procedures. Keep the lips tightly closed for *mm* and relaxed for *nn*.

"Wahdur"

In conducting workshops on Cued Speech, we occasionally encounter speech pathologists and teachers who have the impression that the *t* in *water* and *thirty* is pronounced as a *d* by many people. The reason for this incorrect impression is that the sound actually made (the flap t, or single-tap trill) feels like a *d* as you make it. The confusion comes from overlooking the fact that *t* is a *stop*, with or without the explosion that usually completes it. The flap t is an unexploded *t*. In other words, the first half of a normal *t* is made, but the air-burst of the normal *t* is omitted.

It will clarify the matter of the flap *t* to consider the words *waiter* and *wader*. These words are alike except that the first contains a flap *t* and the second a *d*. If the flap *t* were equivalent to *d* the two words would sound and feel the same, but they clearly do not.

Cueing of Consecutive Identical Consonants

The cueing of consecutive identical consonants involves some rather complex problems. Cases in which a consonant occurs at the end of a word and again at the beginning of the next word, if cued incorrectly, are much more likely to cause errors by the CS reader than incorrect cueing of a double consonant within a word. If, in speaking, the two identical consonants are actually combined into a single consonant sound, then only the one consonant should be cued. However, some teachers have not given sufficiently careful attention to cases in which this should not be done, and are giving incorrect explanations and instructions for cueing. Several different situations arise, depending on whether the consonant in question is a continuant, a stop, or another type of consonant.

Before you go through the rather complicated and lengthy explanation below, be advised that the techniques involved are much easier to learn through imitation and demonstration than by studying our written explanation. If you know someone who is sufficiently well versed in the "fine points," by all means ask for a demonstration.

A doubled consonant within a single word is usually pronounced as a single consonant, and should be cued that way if it is. Examples are apple (*apul*), little (*litul*), and rabbit (*rabut*). Note that the Funetik Speling shows only single consonants in such cases.

In some words formed by combining two words, and resulting in consecutive identical consonants, the situation is entirely different. Consider the word *missent*. One does not pronounce this word as either *mi-sent* or *mis-ent*. Instead, taking advantage of the fact that *s* is a continuant, one simply maintains it through the interval between the two syllables, saying *mis-ss-sent*. Although the intensity of the *s* does not disappear during the interval between te syllables, its intensity does usually diminish and then rise. One is combining the two consonants into one very long one, but with enough drop in intensity in the middle to approximate two identical consonants. The only appropriate way to cue the articulation accurately is 5 throat, 3 side, 3 chin, 4 side, 1 side. Notice that it is quite natural to maintain handshape 3 while the hand moves from side to chin, accurately portraying the status of the vocal mechanism (maintaining the *s*) during that interval. Keep in mind that in many other cases of the double *s* within a word, the prolongation of the double *s* is optional, if the *s* does not need to be prolonged. A *continuant* is a consonant that can be sustained for a period of time, such as <u>m</u>, <u>n</u>, <u>ng</u>, <u>l</u>, <u>r</u>, <u>f</u>, <u>v</u>, <u>th</u> (as in *three*), *tH* (as in *tHis*), <u>sh</u>, <u>zh</u>, <u>s</u>, <u>z</u>, and <u>h</u>. In cases in which a continuant at the end of a word is followed by the same sound at the beginning of the next, the carry-over of the cue shows that one sustains the continuant during the interval. All these except h can be sustained through the boundary between one word and the next. There are many cases in which continuants are habitually prolonged by carrying them over from one word to the next. The following illustrate some of them: <u>with-these</u> (*witH-tHeez,* if the <u>th</u> in <u>with</u> is voiced), <u>loaf-for-a while</u>, <u>live-very well</u>, <u>foul-language</u>, <u>all-levels</u>, <u>for-Ralph</u>, <u>some-mothers</u>, <u>wash-sheets</u>, etc. In such cases the combinations do not sound right if the two consonants are simply combined into one of short duration. For example, <u>loaf for a while</u> does not sound quite right if pronounced *loe faw-ruh whiel*. Only if the **f** is lengthened and both the cue and the sound are carried over to the next word does it sound right: *loef-faw-ruh-whiel*. The two <u>f</u>-sounds are connected, and the cue at the end of *loef* is carried over to the beginning of *faw*. The cueing is 6 side forward and back, 5 side, 5 chin, 3 side down and up, 4 side-5 throat, 6 side. For example, <u>with these</u> can easily be misread as <u>with ease</u>, if the cue for tH is not carried over. Similarly, <u>some mothers</u> cannot be distinguished from <u>some others</u> unless the cueing shows it by cueing *m* as a continuant.

In the case of <u>with-these</u> (if the voiced **tH** sound is used in <u>with,</u>

as is natural when the next word begins with the voiced **tH,** the cueing must be 6 throat, 2 side-2 mouth, 2 side. The voiced **tH** sound is maintained while handshape 2 is moved from side to mouth, accurately depicting the duration of the continuant. The cueing of *witH eez* would, of course, be 6 throat, 2 side, 5 mouth, 2 side, or 6 throat, 7 side 5 mouth, 2 side, depending on whether one uses the voiced **tH** or the unvoiced **th.** Of course, one can run the two words together, in which case the natural expectation would be *wi theez,* if the <u>th</u> is unvoiced.

If one chooses not to prolong the continuant, cueing both phrases 6 throat, 2 mouth, 2 side, he delivers an ambiguous message, leaving the cue reader to discriminate through context.

In the phrase <u>some mothers</u>, in which the *m* is prolonged to distinguish it from <u>some others</u>, the cueing must be 3 side down, 5 side flick, 5 side down, 2 mouth, 2 side. In the case of <u>all levels</u> what should be done depends on how long one chooses to prolong the l. Since there is no ambiguity if it is not prolonged, the urgency is less. The cueing 5 chin, 6 side, 6 chin, 2 side, 6 side, 2 side would go with prolongation of the l. Without the prolongation, the cueing would be 5 chin, 6 chin, 2 side, 6 side, 2 side. Note that the cueing cannot be faithful to the vocalization, when the *l* is prolonged, except by placing the cue at the side location and then moving it across to the chin location. In this case it is only the prolongation of the *l* that is optional. The cueing is not optional; it must follow the articulation.

Other words formed by combining two words produce situations in which the cueing of a double stop consonant involves introducing a time interval between them. An example would be *note-taker.* If one says and cues the two *t*'s as one, he will have to choose between saying and cueing <u>noe tackur</u> or <u>noet aekur</u>. To understand what must be done, consider that the sound *t* consists of a stop (a period of silence during which the air flow is stopped by the pressure of the tongue against the alveolar ridge, just behind the upper teeth. To cue *noet taekur* correctly one must cue the first part (the stop) of the first *t* and the second part (the explosion) of the second *t,* with an appropriate time interval between. The explosion of the first t and the stop of the second t are omitted in both articulation and cueing.articulation. The cueing must show the interval of time that elapses between the stop of the first *t* and the explosion of the second *t.* Thus, the cueing must be 4 side forward and back, 5 side, 5 chin, 5 throat, 2 mouth. The t-stop that terminates the *oe* vowel must be shown, establishing the time interval between it and the beginning of *taker,* in synchrony with the articulation. This can be done only by establishing the *t* handshape at the side location and maintaining it during the move from side to chin.

The lengthy explanation given above is needed to clarify what is actually happening in connection with the utterances discussed. Teaching cuers to handle the problems does not require so much explanation. Demonstration with a good many examples will usually suffice. Referring to "holding the *t*" and "holding the *s*" while demonstrating the proper cueing will get the idea across. The key, for the learner, is to associate holding the cue with "holding" the consonant. The cuer must learn to feel his/her own articulation in the situations described. Then he/she can cue confidently.

An example incorrectly taught and explained in a set of published lessons now in circulation is that of "I can't take it!" versus "I can take it." The incorrect explanation given in the lessons is that the two *t*'s are combined in both sentences, so that "I can take it," and "I can't take it!" are spoken and cued alike. This is incorrect. They are not spoken alike, and should not be cued alike.

To understand what actually happens, it is necessary to keep in mind that a stop consonant such as *t* consists of a *stop* (a period of time during which air flow is stopped—in this case by the pressure of the tongue against the alveolar ridge)—and an explosion, or air burst, which comes when that pressure is suddenly released by the tongue.

To verify that the two sentences are auditorily different, have someone say them for you (without exploding the *t* in *can't*), and verify that you can distinguish them. Or, better, say *can* and *can't*, then say *can't* without exploding the *t*. You will find that you can both hear and feel the difference between *can* and *can't* when the latter ends in the unexploded *t*, even though you feel you have hardly said *t*. In fact, you have produced only the first part of the *t*, the stop, which is clearly audible. In the sentence "I can't take it!" the first *t* is unexploded, as it usually is in words such as <u>water</u> and <u>better</u>. Moreover, the stop is omitted in the second *t*, since the tongue is already in the stop position for the first *t*, which is simply held tightly in place with air pressure behind it. Thus, what actually happens is that you articulate only the first part (the stop) of the first *t* and the last part (the explosion) of the second *t*. Since there is an appreciable time interval between these two *t* segments, both must be cued, or synchronization with mouth movements and auditory output is impossible. This is consistent with the practice of cueing *t* in words in which it is unexploded, such as <u>waiter</u>. It is also consistent with the practice of cueing *t* at the beginning of a word, even though only the explosion is audible. Practice will quickly habituate the feeling of "holding the stop." The tongue is held loosely in the stop position in *can take* and tightly in *can't take*. In the latter case it stops the flow of air suddenly to terminate the *n* with an audible stop *t*. The air is held against pressure until released to start the word *take*.

In summary, one must not cue "I can't take it!" and "I can take it," the same way. The correct cueing for the former is 5 side, five throat, 2 throat, 4 side, 5 side (not exploding the *t*), 5 chin, 5 throat, 2 throat, 5 side. One cues the first part of the first *t* and the second part of the second *t*, with the appropriate time interval between, during which the stop position of the tongue is maintained. To cue only one *t*, whether at the chin or the side, does not either synchronize with the articulatory process or distinguish between the two sentences. A similar example with the consonant *d* is "I would do that." The cueing is 5 side, 5 throat, 6 throat, 1 side, 1 chin, 2 throat, 5 side.

When the second of two consecutive consonants is cued in the same location as the first, there must be a clear indication of the exact time at which the stop is articulated. Consider "<u>I can top that!</u>" vs "<u>I can't top that!</u>" The stop of *t* in <u>can't</u> and the explosion of *t* in <u>top</u> are separated by a time interval that needs to be clearly shown. Thus, the first *t* must not only be cued, but must be flicked. "I can top that!" is cued 5 side 5 throat, 2 throat 4 side 5 side forward and back, 1 side 2 throat 5 side. "I can't top that." is cued 5 side 5 throat, 2 throat 4 side flick 5 side, 5 side forward (and back), 1 side, 2 throat 5 side.

Cueing of Consonant Clusters

Consonant <u>clusters</u> are groups of consecutive consonants. Consonant <u>blends</u> are consonant clusters in which the vocal mechanism can be in the right position for the second consonant while the first consonant is being produced, so the second can blend with the first. An example is *bl* as in *blend*. The tongue can be against the alveolar ridge (just behind the upper teeth), ready for *l*, while the *b* is produced.

The first consonant of a cluster is cued in the side location, since it does not immediately precede a vowel. In the word *blend*, one must cue the *b* in the side location, closing the lips for *b* and building up air pressure behind them. Then, you must hold the *b* until the hand is in position for *l*, at the chin. The syllable *leh* is articulated just as the index finger touches the chin, and the thumb simultaneously reaches the up position for handshape 6. A tiny flick in the side location as the lips close for *b* will help make the timing better and the whole process more clear. Actually, the flick needs to be nothing more than a jerky stop exactly when the lips close and handshape 4 reaches the side location. In effect, one is holding the stop in place (lips closed) while the hand gets to the chin. Try both *blend* and *please* as examples.

Practice *tree*. If a skilled cuer is available to show you how to cue this word, by all means ask for help. It is much easier to learn this by imitation than from text. But, if help is not available, or if you can already cue and want to check it out, proceed as follows.

First, cue and say *ree,* 3 mouth. Now say and cue the first half of a *t* (the stop) in the side location, holding the air pressure, and the second half (the explosion) at the mouth with *ree*. Thus, you will cue and say *t* silently at the side, then move to the mouth, changing to handshape 3 on the way, and say *tree*. You are cueing the silent t stop in the side location, and the t explosion at the mouth, holding the t pressure while moving your hand. Your hand must change from 5 to 3 as you move your hand. As your fingers touch your cheek next to the mouth, in the 3 handshape, you say *tree*. You cue the *t* at the side, and move quickly to the mouth, where the explosion is heard, as part of the word *tree*. This enables you to say the word as a unit.

Practice the word *tree* several times, remembering to cue the *t* silently and save the explosion for the mouth, so the word can be all together. Then, you can learn to put *s* before *tree*, to prepare for street.

Consider the word *street*, cued 3 side, 5 side, 3 mouth, 5 side. First practice *tree* a few more times. Then practice cueing (3 side, 5 side) and saying *st* without exploding the *t*. Practice *st-, st-, st-,* letting no air escape on the *t*. Do not begin with the hand in the side location, but relaxed elsewhere. Move the hand to the side location as you form handshape 3, and begin the *st-* exactly when your hand arrives. Now, you are ready for *stree*. Execute the first two handshapes at the side location as you say *ssst-*. Then, hold the *t* pressure while the hand moves to the mouth and simultaneously changes to handshape 3 just in time to begin the articulation of *tree* as the fingers touch the cheek near the corner of the mouth. Since the first sound *s* is a continuant, when you first practice this you can execute it more slowly. First, cue and say *sss — sss*. Then cue and say *ssst—*, but do not explode the *t*. Hold the tongue against the alveolar ridge, letting no air escape. Then move the hand to the mouth, changing to handshape 3 on the way, just in time to say *tree* as the fingers touch. Then complete the word by moving the hand to the side location and changing to handshape 5 on the way, just in time to cue the final *t* in the side location as you complete the word. You can practice this word slowly at first, then faster, until you can do it smoothly and confidently.

Your satisfaction after practicing *street* enough that you can do it smoothly and accurately will be enhanced by the knowledge that this is one of the most difficult things to execute in cueing. You should not cue consonant clusters without first practicing them individually.

Practice all the *str* words you can think of, such as *stray, strawberry, straight, monstrous, distraught*. In a high percentage of consonant clusters, the first consonant is either a continuant or a stop, both of which are easy to "stretch" while moving your hand.

Try *smart*. First, say and cue *sssssssssmah*. Again, start with your hand away from the side location, so that you will change it to handshape 3 while moving to the side location. Start articulating *sss* as you stop your hand in the side location. Lengthen the *s* sound to give you time to prepare to cue and say *mah*. Now, practice *ssssmah* several times, then cue the word, *ssssmahrt*, 3 side, 5 side forward, 3 side, 5 side. Finally, shorten the *s* and cue the word briskly.

Now, cue and say *smear*. First, decide whether you say *smir*, like most people, or *smeer*, or *smiur*. Then, lengthening the *s*, say and cue *ssssmi*. Then, practice sssmir, and *sssmeer*. Finally, reduce the *s* to normal length and practice again.

Cueing Spanish Words When English Is Primary

Families that wish to teach some Spanish words or expressions to their deaf children with whom they are using CS in English need only a few additions to the sounds they already use. The same is true of transliterators serving an American deaf child who is taking Spanish.

First, parents and transliterators can cue all the vowels just the way they do in English, except that for *o* they should use the open *o* in the English word *cork (cawrk)*, cued at the chin, instead of the closed *o* in *hope*. Though Spanish speakers use both sounds, they make no distinction between them. Since English speakers tend to diphthongize the closed *o*, it is better for them to use the open *o*. Cueing the vowels as in English will create no problems unless the child goes to a Spanish-speaking country where CS is used. The arrangement of the vowels is different for Spanish, but this will not be a problem in cueing to an English-speaking deaf child.

All the consonants of Spanish can be cued as in English except the strong *r*, spelled *rr* in the middle of a word, or r at the beginning of a word. The strong *r (rr)* is cued with handshape 7. Thus, *perro* (dog) is cued 1 chin, 7 chin; and *pero* (but) is cued 1 chin, 3 chin. The sound of *ñ* can be cued as *ny* in the English word canyon. Thus, *niña* can be cued as 4 mouth, 4 side, 8 side forward. In cueing Spanish words and phrases, English speakers will have to listen very carefully to identify the voiced *tH* sound of the letter *d*. It occurs in unexpected places, such as in the case of *d* between two vowels *(nada)*, pronounced *nahtHah* and cued 4 side forward and back, 2 side forward;

dedo (*detHo*), 1 chin, 2 chin; for *d* after a vowel and before *r*, and *d* in word-final position. Examples of the last two cases occur in the single word Madrid (*MahtHreetH*), cued 5 side forward, 2 side, 3 mouth, 2 side. To keep all these in mind is not easy unless you know a good bit of Spanish. It will not handicap your student much if you just cue *d* always as *d* instead of struggling with the *tH* sound of *d*. You must remember, however, that in Spanish *v* is pronounced and cued the same as *b,* except in Chili, where it has the normal **v** sound.

Cueing Of French Words

In cueing French words and phrases for an English-speaking, cueing deaf child, you can cue the consonant sounds essentially as in English. There are several vowels in French that do not appear in English, and they must be assigned cues. As it happens, they can remain where they are grouped in the normal cueing of French, since they are visually distinct from the English vowels cued the same.

The additions are as follows: The nasal ũ as in *un*, discussed above as used in informal English in ũh-hũh (5 throat,3 throat), is cued at the throat. Also cued at the throat is the acute (closed) *é*, as in *été*, cued 5 throat, 5 throat. A third French vowel cued at the throat is the sound of French *u*, which can be approximated by rounding the lips strongly as for a very closed *u*, and trying to make the sound of *ee*. At the chin are the open *o* as in *corp*s, or in English *cork*, the grave (open) *è* as in *fève*, *cette,* and *sève*, and the French *ou*, which is equivalent to English *oo* in food. At the mouth are two French nasal vowels, *an* as in *pan*, and *on* as in *mon*. At the cheek location, just below the eye level, are the nasal *in* as in *fin* and *faim*, and *eu* as in *peu*. In cueing French, remember that the stress patterns are not nearly as pronounced as in English, so maintain a smooth flow of the syllables without as much variation in pitch or stress as you use in English.

Dance versus Pants

The word *dance* rhymes with *pants*. Both contain an unexploded *t* between the *n* and the *s* The vocal mechanism cannot make an *s* immediately after *n,* without inserting a stop. To cue the *t* in dance is optional. We suggest you go with the spelling. Cue the *t* in pants, but not in dance.

Chapter 30
Potpourri

This chapter contains a group of items that are too short to appear as separate chapters, but which should be available to parents of hearing-impaired children. It also includes "Origins of Cued Speech" in order to clear up some confusion caused by published errors. The topics in this chapter include: 1) The rights of deaf children and their parents, 2) Post-secondary educational opportunities, 3) Origins of Cued Speech, and 4) Useful devices.

1. The Rights of Deaf Children and Their Parents

The federal laws intended to influence education of the handicapped are clear. They specify that in states receiving federal funds for education all handicapped children have the right to a free public education in an environment that is "appropriate" and "least restrictive." Unfortunately, the path from these clear legal provisions to implementation of the intent of the legislation is a long one. The terms *appropriate* and *least restrictive* must be interpreted. Those interpretations leave much room for maneuvering in support of entrenched interests, biases, and inertia.

Some state laws cloud the issues instead of facilitating implementation of the federal laws. The federal laws make no provision for failing to provide the "appropriate environment" because of factors such as cost, local preferences, or "school policy." In practice all these things exert a powerful and even commanding influence on what happens.

As with most laws governing educational practice, there is no penalty and no provisions for overruling misused authority without protest, pressure, and/or "due process." To get what their child needs, some parents have had to go through as many as five levels of hearings, appeals, and court cases to establish their rights. In most cases in which parents have resorted to due process proceedings to get Cued Speech for their child they have won. However, in some cases they have lost at the first, second, and even third levels of due process, but prevailed through appeal at the state level or in federal district court. The further removed the proceedings are from the local school system, the greater is the chance that the parents' petitions will get appropriate attention. Most parents have neither the financial resources nor the courage to oppose a school system to this extent. Most have to depend on persuasion, on proving that their child needs Cued Speech by showing how much it helps the child achieve. This is often difficult because good performance by the child can be attributed to many factors (good teaching, ability of the child, etc.) other than CS.

Most of the parents who have succeeded in getting what their child needs have done so by a combination of "early warning" (notifying school authorities of what they need and expect well ahead of the need), becoming active in PTA and/or school board affairs, becoming acquainted with school personnel and policies, and conducting a persuasive and persistent campaign. Families that start Cued Speech when their deaf child is very young can do this before the child is spending enough time in preschool to make the use of Cued Speech there critical. Speech/audition therapists are often willing to learn and use CS in therapy sessions even if that is its only use in the school.

Federal law requires that appropriate special services must be available to the deaf child, beginning at the age at which school services are first available to other children. The age at which school services become available to hearing children varies from state to state. The age at which a deaf child becomes eligible for federally funded special services varies accordingly.

The situation was aptly described by Gary Nix (1977):

A historical look at the evolution of the educational rights of hearing-impaired individuals furnishes several important insights for the present and future. A list of the lessons hopefully learned includes:

1. Society has traditionally viewed the hearing-impaired individual as mentally impaired due to the hearing impairment. A massive and continuing effort is needed to educate society regarding the capabilities and talents of individuals who are hearing impaired. *We need to focus more on the individual's abilities and less on his disabilities.*

2. Progress has been possible only through the activists of each era. Child advocates have had to struggle to cause necessary changes. It has never been easy to effect change.

3. Parent advocates for hearing-impaired children have been primarily responaible for the establishment of needed services in North America. A coalition effort of parents working on common problems would be especially effective in bringing about needed changes.

4. There is very little that is new regarding a manual approach, an oral approach, a combined or "total" approach, or

placing children in various educational environments ranging from residential to full mainstreaming. All have been tried before and all have failed to provide THE ANSWER to the education of hearing-impaired children. The lesson to be learned is that **one educational option will not best serve the needs of all children.** Examination of the individual child's needs will enable each to be placed in the most appropriate setting.

Nix's four observations are still relevant today. We wish to comment on his four points individually:

1. Hearing-impaired children are often retarded functionally as a result of their hearing impairment. That is, their mental development is *held back* or *retarded* as a result of their deafness if they do not receive the means to overcome its usual educational, psychological, and social effects. Similarly, their mental health and capacities can be impaired by the untreated or improperly treated effects of their deafness. What Nix means is that society has traditionally and mistakenly viewed hearing-impaired individuals as mentally *defective* due to their hearing impairment, without making a distinction between the initial condition and that resulting from neglect. The terms mentally impaired and mentally retarded are loaded terms only because of their misuse. Their literal meanings, however, apply accurately to the effects of deafness on children whose special needs are neglected. Since Nix made this observation, much progress has been made in dispelling the prevalent notion that hearing-impaired individuals are inevitably mentally impaired or retarded, but much remains yet to be done.

2. This observation regarding the difficulties of effecting change is as applicable today as it was in 1977.

3. Several coalitions of the type Nix suggests have been formed since 1977 and have had a substantial effect. Unfortunately, until very recently they have tended to form along lines of division between methodologies. There is some evidence that this problem is gradually being overcome, or at least reduced.

4. Nix's "nothing new" observation omits mention of two new initiatives: Cued Speech and the movement in support of American Sign Language (which had not yet taken hold). Yet, he is correct in his basic assertion: No one educational option will best serve the needs of all hearing-impaired children.

A Brief Look At The Most Relevant Federal Laws

Nix (1977) lists several pieces of legislation enacted during the 1960s that provided for increased services for all handicapped persons, including:

P.L. 88-210 (1963), which authorized the first vocational education act;

P.L. 89-10 (1965), which authorized Title I funds to be paid to school districts for special programs for educationally deprived children;

P.L. 89-36 (1965), which authorized the National Technical Institute for the Deaf;

P.L. 89-258 (1965), which provided for the cultural rights of hearing-impaired people through the Captioned Films for the Deaf program. The laws passed in 1963 and 1965 evidenced growing legislative awareness of the need for better education of the handicapped. This led eventually to the Rehabilitation Acts of 1973 (P.L. 93-112 and P.L. 93-516) and, most important of all, The Education For All Handicapped Children Act (P.L. 94-142) in 1975.

The Americans With Disabilities Act (ADA), 1990, will have far-reaching effects on the employment, accommodations, transportation, and communications of disabled individuals in general, including hearing-impaired people. It is of immediate interest to parents of deaf children because of its provision for interstate and intrastate relay services for deaf people using TDD's. Now deaf youngsters will be able to keep in touch with relatives and friends who do not have TDD's. This will enhance relationships and use of written English for communication. The regulations regarding accessibility and transportation will also have an impact on the ability of deaf youngsters to interact more fully with society in educational, recreational, and social settings, and in the workplace. Interpreters, assistive devices, and other forms of accommodation are required in most situations.

The interest of parents in the provisions of the ADA regarding employment and accessibility will increase greatly as their children begin to look forward to employment. One of the most important aspects of the ADA is that its requirements apply to both public and private sectors, independently of whether or not they are receiving federal funds.

It is to be hoped that the ADA will in the long term have a beneficial effect on both the earnings of deaf people as well as the conditions under which they work.

Economic Effect of Low Language Acquisition

A low level of attainment in language and reading ability tends to handicap deaf adults economically, causing a high percentage of them to enter manual occupations rather than white-collar jobs. A 1959 study conducted by Gallaudet University and the National Association of the Deaf (Crammatte, 1962) showed that 83% of deaf people were in manual occupations. Only 17% had white-collar jobs, whereas 46.8% of hearing people were so employed. Since this study was made, the upsurge of support for the rights of disabled individuals has helped increase the occupational opportunities of deaf people, even those with limited competence in English.

Data from the *Secondary School Graduate Follow-up Program for the Deaf*, which is conducted by the National Technical Institute for the Deaf, shows that there has been a significant improvement in the occupational and economic status of deaf persons generally. Table 1 demonstrates the apparent effect of higher education on occupational status and income of deaf persons.

Table 1

Labor force characteristics of deaf high school graduates
10 years after graduation, by degree earned

Category	High School	Sub-Bachelor	Bachelor
In the labor force	77%	77%	84%
Employed	80%	91%	95%
Unemployed	20%	9%	5%
White collar job	36%	57%	89%
Weekly earnings*	$330	$381	$440

*Adjusted to 1988 dollars using the Consumers Price Index

The tabulation above is from *Employment Attainments of Deaf Adults One and Ten Years After Graduation From High School*, by Gerard G. Walter and Janet MacLeod-Gallinger (1989). Other data in the same study show that deaf people are well below hearing people in terms of both post-secondary education and income, but the situation is strikingly improved in comparison with that of a few decades ago. Improvement in the conditions reflected in the data above should occur through the combined effects of improved education and the ADA.

Public Law 94-142

Since the Constitution reserves authority over education to the states, the federal laws influence education only through *incentives* in the form of federal funds distributed to the states for educational purposes. The federal laws relating to education of the handicapped specify that all states that receive federal funds for educational purposes must comply. Failure to comply may lead to warnings (if the federal authorities become aware of the failure), and can cause federal funds to be cut off. The power behind P.L. 94-142 lay in the fact that it provided for large increases in federal funds to be distributed to the states for educational purposes.

The passage of P.L. 94-142 implied a basic change in the attitude toward handicapped persons. Not until a decade before its passage was an *appropriate* education recognized to be a basic right of the handicapped person. This law required that a free, public, appropriate education be provided all handicapped children, ages 6 to 18, by September 1, 1980. Provision of the same to handicapped children ages 3 to 5 and 18 to 21 is also required in a given state if it provides services of any kind to children in other categories within those age ranges.

In expenditure of federal monies provided by this law, excluding the amount used for its administration, the states must give first priority to handicapped children who are not being served, and then to the most severely handicapped children in each category who are receiving some services, but not all that they need.

To receive the federal funds, each State Educational Authority must set a full educational opportunity goal for its handicapped children aged 0 to 21 years. This must be a comprehensive and long-range plan embracing the numbers of handicapped children in the various categories and age ranges, with deadlines for reaching specific standards.

Most of the funds allotted to the states (75% or more) are passed on to each Local Educational Authority (LEA). It has the responsibility for implementation of the law for each child. The LEA must 1) set up a system for finding and evaluating children who are eligible and not being served, and 2) prepare an *Individualized Educational Program* (IEP) for each child, for each school year. The law specifically spells out the right of the parents to be involved in the preparation of the IEP at each step and to register their acceptance or rejection of it.

The impact of P.L. 94-142 was greatly enhanced by the approval of regulations on Apr. 28, 1977 for Section 504 of the Rehabilitation

Act of 1973. This provides federal funds for education, transportation, and residential care. It also mandates that all public elementary and secondary programs receiving federal funds provide a "free public education to each qualified handicapped person in the recipient's jurisdiction, regardless of the nature or severity of the person's handicap."

The Individualized Educational Program (IEP)

The rest of this section follows more or less closely the material in the article, Parents and Public Law 94-142, by Judith Kidd (1977). in G. Nix, Ed., *The Rights of Hearing-Impaired Children*, Washington, DC: Alexander Graham Bell Association for the Deaf. pp. 275-280. This out-of-print monograph is available in many libraries.

The IEP for each child is developed in a meeting or series of meetings with a representative of the LEA, the parents, the teacher, and the child (if appropriate). The purpose of the IEP is to provide a detailed educational plan and the means of evaluating the child's progress to determine how the IEP should be changed if he/she is not meeting the objectives specified in the IEP. P.L. 94-142 places on the parents the responsibility for making sure that their child's needs are taken fully into account in the development of the IEP, and that the evaluation process is adequate to determine whether goals are met each year. The IEP must be reviewed at least annually, and may be reviewed at any time by request of the parents.

The IEP must include statements of the following:

1. present levels of educational achievement of the child

2. the annual goals for the child, including short-term educational objectives

3. the specific educational services to be furnished to the child, and the extent to which the child will be able to participate in regular classes and programs

4. the projected date for initiation and anticipated duration of such services, and

5. appropriate and objective criteria and evaluation procedures and schedules for determining, on at least an annual basis, whether instructional objectives are being achieved.

The needs of the child must be determined without regard for such factors as the local availability or cost of the services. If the services are essential to the child's appropriate development, they must be furnished.

The Principle of "Least Restrictive" Environment

Section 612, (5), (b) of P.L. 94-142 requires that "to the maximum extent appropriate, handicapped children are educated with children who are not handicapped." It also specifies that "removal of handicapped children from the regular education environment occurs only when the nature or severity of the handicap is such that education in regular classes with the use of supplementary aids and services cannot be achieved satisfactorily."

Judith Kidd (1977) indicates that this *Least Restrictive Environment* provision caused some parents to fear that their child would be "thrown indiscriminately" into classes with regular students, and teachers "to fear that the attention needed by severely handicapped children will disturb the ordinary procedures in the regular classroom." She also says: "Residential school authorities fear that student populations will diminish." All the outcomes of the least restrictive provision cited by Kidd as feared have materialized to some extent. However, only the diminishing of residential school populations has come about on a scale commensurate with the fears.

For some children, placement in a regular class, with all possible support services, would produce a more restrictive environment than placement in a self-contained class of children with similar characteristics, or even placement in a residential school. So, the key is what is appropriate and least restrictive for a specific child.

The problem is that parents and school personnel often have a difficult time deciding what placement and what educational services are appropriate and least restrictive for a given child. Parents seeking more speech therapy or Cued Speech for their child, or seeking mainstreaming with a CS transliterator, do not always have an easy time convincing or persuading school authorities of the need. Refer to "How to Present the Case for Cued Speech" in Chapter 28.

Parents will need to investigate the laws of their own state, and the practice within that state in implementation of the laws, to find out how and to what extent federal law is being carried out there. In many states there are committees or advocacy groups that can be helpful to parents who are having difficulty. Some even provide free legal assistance when it is needed.

What if the Parents Do Not Agree With the Placement Suggested?

First, if parents disagree with the recommended placement, they should ask for a meeting with school staff and a representative of the administration, and preferably also someone representing the school board. Before that, or at least before the meeting comes up, they should do their homework. They should get help from someone qualified to help them, by telephone, correspondence, or personal conferences. If they think their child needs a placement (or services) different from what is recommended by the school system, they should make sure of that fact, to the best of their ability and that of persons advising them. When they feel sure, they should marshall all available evidence supporting their conclusion.

If recent, reliable data on the child's level of achievement is not available, parents should insist that the child be tested to get such data. Parents have a right to this. If the school is unwilling or not qualified to do the testing, insist that the school hire a qualified professional to do the testing. Or, hire an independent evaluator yourself. The LEA must consider the results.

If not satisfied with the IEP written by school staff, insist on changes that will make it acceptable to you. If you are at an impasse after several administrative meetings, write on the IEP a statement that you are not accepting it, and sign that statement. Do not sign at any place where your signature could be construed as approving the IEP, unless you fully approve it.

If you cannot accept the IEP or get the school personnel to change it, weigh the pros and cons of DUE PROCESS procedures. Due process procedures have been built into the law so that differences can be settled, hopefully in good faith. In the Federal Register, p. 56972, this explanation appears: "Invoking due process does not inherently create adversary settings. The goal of the process is better programming for children, with better understanding of all parties—parents, children, educators, and advocates—of their responsibilities, and a forum for continuous review." Would that it always worked out that way! The authors have testified in a good many due process proceedings, from the local level to federal district court. In only one of these cases was there no adversary relationship. However, in several of the cases the adversary relationship was supplanted gradually by a cooperative and even warm relationship. In most situations, a negative adversarial residue remains, no matter how the case is resolved.

Due process procedures assure parents of their right to obtain an independent educational evaluation of their child if they are not satisfied with the LEA evaluation. If the evaluation done by the LEA is thereby found to be inappropriate or inadequate, the independent evaluation can be at LEA expense.

Suppose that disagreement between the parents and the LEA cannot be resolved in a series of administrative hearings (meetings with an LEA representative, school personnel, and parents present). A formal due process hearing is in order unless the parents decide to give up. A due process hearing must be conducted and a decision rendered by an impartial hearing officer who is not an employee of either a state or local educational agency involved in the education of the child. The program placement and services already in effect continue until after the hearing decision is rendered. At that point they are changed (only) if the decision of the hearing officer is in favor of the parents.

What if the Parents Lose the Due Process Hearing?

Unfortunately, the requirement that the hearing officer be unbiased is not automatic assurance that this will always be the case. Or, as is more frequent, the problem may not be bias but a natural assumption that the LEA is more likely to be right than the parents. At any rate, parents often lose the first due process hearing. For this reason, parents must recognize the importance of presenting as good a case as possible at the first hearing. The reason is not only to have a good chance to win the initial hearing. Usually, in an appeal hearing at a higher level, the parties *are not allowed to introduce any new evidence*. The appeal hearing is for review of the case as it was submitted originally. Parents should use all their ammunition at the original hearing. They will need expert witnesses whose testimony will be helpful. Often school staff members will be sympathetic to the interests of the parents, and may even agree with them. But, it is usually very difficult for a school staff member to testify against his/her own employer, though it has been done occasionally.

In summary, parents should strive long and hard to get what is needed for their child without resorting to due process procedures. The best evidence to use in persuading the school system to furnish what is needed is the effect on your child of what you are requesting. If you are asking for use of Cued Speech at school with your child, you can make a good case only if you can show what the child has done and can do with CS. Get suggestions from experts (in the CS service centers) regarding what kinds of data and demonstrations with your child will be most effective. Of course, this is possible only if you have been using Cued Speech consistently and well at home. If your deaf child has a sibling who cues consistently, it may be very effective to get the sibling into a demonstration with the deaf child, or to submit a written statement from the sibling at an *administrative hearing*.

Several sources of advice and guidance are available. The Children's Rights Program of the Alexander Graham Bell Association for the Deaf provides useful materials. It also has volunteer regional CRCs (Children's Rights Coordinators) who are ready to help. The

National Center for Law and Deafness (see Appendix) and advocacy groups for the disabled in the various states are logical sources of advice and assistance.

2. Post-Secondary Educational Opportunities

A large percentage of children who grow up with Cued Speech under good conditions (with supportive parents and a school system committed to providing adequately for hearing-impaired students) are qualified academically to be mainstreamed successfully in a typical college or university. This does not mean that just any college or university will do. There must be a "fit" between the needs of the student, the characteristics of the institution, and the attitudes of the personnel there. Attending an institution that is not right for the individual student is likely to be more detrimental to a hearing-impaired student than to a hearing student.

In speaking of the optimum college environment, we mean the optimum for the individual student in question. Some students function better in a small college, others in a large university. The deaf student and his/her family need to look at all the characteristics a hearing student considers, including: size, requirements, standards, available curriculums, and cost.

Next comes the ability of the institution to meet the special needs of the deaf student. If the student has grown up with Cued Speech and has been mainstreamed throughout high school with a transliterator and a note-taker for each class, these are necessities in college. A possible substitute for a note-taker is a lap-top computer that the deaf student must be able to use without looking at the keyboard. Another necessity is speech therapy by a qualified person willing to learn and use Cued Speech. Beyond these necessities are many desirable institutional characteristics that suit the student's preferences and needs. The availability of an institutional TDD in an easily accessible location is important, unless the student has one of his own (and access to a telephone line on which to use it).

Other institutional characteristics are also important. We will divide them into these categories:

(1) Policies and traditions conducive to adaptation to the needs and characteristics of individual students with special needs. Does the institution accept and traditionally adjust to the needs of students with various kinds of disabilities? Does it furnish special support services as needed?

(2) Has the institution had experience with deaf students, and

does its track record reflect sensitivity to their needs and interests? Is it committed to furnishing an interpreter or transliterator, as needed, plus note-taking services or a lap-top computer?

(3) Is there a sizable group of deaf students on campus capable of maintaining a social and cultural identity?

(4) Is there evidence of interest among the hearing students in learning to communicate with the deaf students? Is there a sign club? Is there a "cue" club?

(5) Does the institution furnish access to a centrally located TDD for deaf students? Does it have an easily accessible telephone with an amplifier?

The above list is illustrative of the types of institutional characteristics that should be considered. It is far from complete.

The Current Situation

The provision of special services to deaf students in colleges and universities is relatively new except for those institutions that have set up specific academic, technological, and occupational programs for deaf students. Gallaudet University has existed as an institution specifically for deaf students for well over a century. It accepts only deaf children in its Kendall Demonstration Elementary School and its Model Secondary School for the Deaf. Its preparatory program provides entry for students whose qualifications place them close enough to the requirements for entry into the freshman class that most of them can qualify for college admission in one year. Gallaudet offers programs leading to baccalaureate degrees in a multiplicity of fields, 17 M.A.-level degrees, including deaf education, and Ph.D. degrees in Administration and Supervision, Clinical Psychology, and Education. It accepts hearing students at the graduate level.

The National Technical Institute for the Deaf (NTID), a federally funded college of the Rochester Institute of Technology (RIT), maintains an orientation program specifically for deaf students through which those academically capable of doing so can go on to a wide variety of regular university courses and degrees at RIT, with various support services. NTID itself also offers three-year technical degree and certificate programs in several areas.

More than 150 other institutes, colleges, and universities maintain specific post-secondary programs for deaf students, with support services. Many of these programs are in occupational areas. Other institutions accept deaf students and provide special support services to enable them to attend the regular courses offered by the institution, without offering special courses or curricula for deaf students. These institutions do not typically have a large contingent of deaf students capable of maintaining a separate social or cultural identity. Some of them do have clubs that exist to enable hearing students to learn to communicate with the deaf students. Many universities train speech therapists and teachers of the deaf. Most offer this only at the graduate level.

The most comprehensive source of information on institutions that accommodate deaf students is *College & Career Programs for Deaf Students*. Another list of institutions that offer special programs and services for deaf students appears in the annual directory (spring) issue of the *American Annals of the Deaf*, available in libraries. For sources and mailing addresses on these items, refer to the Appendix.

For additional and more specific information on opportunities for deaf students in post-secondary education, parents and students can contact the following sources whose addresses appear in the Appendix: The Alexander Graham Bell Association for the Deaf, The National Cued Speech Association, the Cued Speech Team at Gallaudet University, and The National Technical Institute for the Deaf.

3. Origins of Cued Speech
R. Orin Cornett

The question "How in the world did you happen to develop Cued Speech?" is asked me so frequently that I decided to publish the answer. It is a natural question, because most people who meet me know that my academic background is in physics and mathematics, and that most of my professional life before I went to Gallaudet was spent in higher education administration. Indeed, the only thing that made it possible for me to go to Gallaudet was my experience in higher education planning and management; I had neither background nor experience in connection with hearing impairment.

At the time of my awakening to deafness as a problem, I was director of the Division of Educational Organization and Administration, at the United States Office of Education, now the U.S. Department of Education, having been until a few months before head of the Division of Higher Education. One of the tasks my division was expected to perform annually was to make a study of some aspect of the operation of Gallaudet College, now Gallaudet University, and to report on it to the Secretary of Health, Education and Welfare. Of course, I selected the staff members who were to make the study, and read and approved the report when it was ready for submission.

In the spring of 1965, while reading the finished report on

Gallaudet before approving it for submission, I came upon the statement that prelingually deaf persons, as a group, are typically very poor readers. The report indicated that their average reading comprehension (at 15 to 18 years) was approximately that of a typical 8-year-old child with normal hearing, and that the average had been at approximately that level for at least 50 years. I was horrified, for I had supposed deaf people were all bookworms. After all, an adult with normal hearing, if he suffers a severe or profound hearing loss, almost always increases the amount of his reading by several times. In fact, reading is the only major avenue of access to learning that is undamaged by a loss of hearing.

The reading problems of prelingually deaf persons became an obsession with me. I could find no theoretical reason why hearing-impaired persons should not become good readers. At length I concluded that their problem came from not having any reasonable, easy way to acquire a knowledge of spoken language as a base for reading. The normal child knows the spoken language well before he starts to learn to read. Not only is it the language on which reading is based, but it is the language in which everything is taught at school. Without a solid prior knowledge of this language, the typical prelingually deaf child is doomed to slow, laborious learning.

Just at the time I became sure of the cause of the reading problem, the position of Vice President for Long-Range Planning was created at Gallaudet College. Because I thought that institution would be the ideal location for me to work on the reading/deafness problem, I sent word to the president, Dr. Leonard M. Elstad, that I might consider the position. I went to Gallaudet in August 1965, with the private purpose of finding a way to enable deaf children to learn spoken language easily and naturally, as a base for reading. My contract gave me the right to use one-third of my time "for research of my own choosing." That enabled me to work on my personal objective without neglecting my assigned duties in long-range planning.

My starting point was this idea: If all the phonemes of speech looked clearly different from each other on the speaker's mouth, just as they sound different from each other to normal ears, a profoundly deaf child could learn language through vision almost as easily as the normal child learns it from hearing. I say *almost* because there is certainly some advantage in hearing without looking, and some language is certainly learned from listening to records, radio, etc. So, my initial thought was to supplement the visible evidences of speech, using the hand or hands, in such a way as to make all the speech sounds (strictly, all the phonemes) look different from each other, through the combined appearance of mouth and hand(s), preferably only one hand.

I wrote the following, in advance, as the requirements of an acceptable approach, intended to comply with the basic concepts of both the pure oralists and those who stress the importance of "clear communication" during the early years:

1) It must be in accord with the principle that English should be learned as a spoken language and so used (by hearing parents, I meant) in daily communication with the deaf child.

2) It must include the information visible on the mouth as an indispensable component. Any additional information supplied must be unintelligible without the information on the lips.

3) It must make use only of supporting elements capable of synchronization with spoken English at a deliberate pace. Such elements should convey only information that relates directly to the phonemes of English. They should aid in the identification of syllabication and of syllabic emphasis.

4) It must result in increase of the ability of the deaf person to speak understandably and to speechread without special instruction.

5) It must be feasible for a very young, prelinguallly deaf child to learn the system, simply through its use by parents.

6) It must lift the level (accuracy) of communication at least to that of fingerspelling, facilitating rapid learning and communication.

7) It must be effective at classroom distances—up to 20 feet.

At this point in my thinking I faced a critical decision. It was reasonable to suppose that others before me had tried to produce a system for making spoken language clear to deaf persons. In fact, I already knew about Edmond Lyons' "phonetic fingerspelling." Should I go to the literature and find out what others had attempted, and what they had produced, or should I attack the problem *de novo*? I decided that knowing what others had done might limit the scope of my imagination. Also, after I made my attempt, I could easily go to the literature and see if I had merely duplicated what someone else had already done. So, I decided to use my own resources first.

I had a good theoretical background for what I was attempting to do, despite my ignorance about deafness. I had lectured at Harvard University on mathematical theory of transmission of information. My background in research methodology, though not broad, was adequate. Also, my Ph.D. dissertation was in the field of acoustics, and I had done research related to diplacusis (double hearing), having invented a device for measuring it.

My derivation of the Cued Speech system was largely mathematical. The information visible on the mouth during speech identifies sets of sounds that look alike on the mouth, each set containing two to seven members. For example, the highly visible bilabial compression during speech, with the lips coming together, indicates that the consonant being produced is /m/, /b/, or /p/. The mathematical minimum of information required to produce identification of each member of each set is an orthogonal group of sets, each intersecting singly with the original sets. For example, the single-finger cue used in Cued Speech indicates the group /d/-/p/-/zh/. If the lips, through the bilabial compression indicate /m/-/b/-/p/, the intersection with /d/-/p/-/zh/ is /p/. Note: /zh/ is the sound of *s* in *leisure*. As the hand configuration identifies a group of consonants from which a choice is made according to the appearance and movements of the mouth area, including the lips, teeth, and tongue, the location of the hand determines a group of vowels from which a choice is made according to the appearance of the mouth. The miracle, of course, is that the deaf child has no difficulty in learning to determine the intersections simultaneously for both consonants and vowels, without even thinking of the process. He decodes the input in syllables, the natural units of speech, and can learn to do so at a normal speaking rate. From the beginning, though, his perception of what he is receiving is at the level of meaningful words and phrases, without preoccupation with or teaching of the system as such.

If the hand touches the chin, the vowel sound must be from the set *aw, eh,* and *ue* (as in *blue*). Notice that they are clearly different through vision, as I say them. The possible syllables from the combination of the one-finger configuration and the chin location are as follows: /daw/-/paw/-/zhaw/-/deh/-/peh/-/zheh/-/due/-/pue/-/zhue/. All these syllables differ clearly in appearance on the mouth, and thus can be lipread reliably with the aid of the manual cues.

The complete system, for American English, uses eight hand configurations to group the consonant phonemes, and the vowels are in four groups associated with hand locations. As of January 1992, Cued Speech had been adapted to 53 languages and major dialects.

The complexity of my description should not be interpreted as an indication that the system is itself complex or difficult to learn. Typically, it can be learned in English by hearing parents of a deaf child in 10 to 30 hours (half that long in Spanish). Skill and fluency develop only after several months of daily use of the system. Once parents know the basic system, they can use all the language they know, including even dialect and slang.

I often encounter questions about how long it took me to develop the system. A memo in my files dated November 16, 1965, three months after I went to Gallaudet, describes the principles of the system exactly as they are today, but with three vowel locations instead of four. I had already passed the breakthrough in which I conceived the idea of using handshapes to cue groups of consonants, and hand locations to cue groups of vowels, so that both could be done at once. This double two-dimensional matrix arrangement makes it possible for the basic unit of Cued Speech to be the basic speech unit, the consonant-vowel syllable. Thus, it is possible to synchronize the cues with speech at the rate of normal deliberate speech.

It should be kept in mind that the two-dimensional matrix of the cues accompanies a similar two-dimensional matrix provided by the shapes and motions of the lips. The miracle is that a 2-year-old deaf child can easily perceive the intersections of this double two-dimensional matrix and identify the sounds that are being made.

A second memo of the same date, Nov. 16, 1965, discusses the possibilities of producing the cues automatically by electronic means. This was the first glimmering of the idea of the Autocuer, on which I started work in 1969, and am still far from finished.

Another draft (from my files) dated March 1966, and entitled "Cued Speech: A New Aid in the Education of Hearing-Impaired Children" is virtually identical with the first published article on Cued Speech, which appeared 10 months later in the January 1967 issue of the *American Annals of the Deaf* (Cornett, 1967). This article describes the system exactly as it is today (for General American English), but does not include a few later refinements and additions, such as the small downward movement in the side location to accompany the neutral vowel (schwa), the variation of the angle of the hand to show voice pitch in tonal languages, or the slight rolling of the wrist to show palatization or nasality in languages with many palatized consonants or nasal vowels.

As of August 1966, I had made the final changes, and had a system waiting for a deaf child. There was no assurance that a young child could fathom the system, or even perceive the visual teamwork of the hand and the mouth. Likewise, there was no assurance that if the child could learn the system, spoken language could be decoded fast enough through vision to make it a practical system for communication.

In early August 1966, my secretary (Barbara Grimes, now Caldwell) learned that a friend she had known in high school had a 22-month-old child who was profoundly deaf. Ms. Grimes met with the parents of Leah Henegar and explained the traditional oral and manual approaches to deaf education, and then explained Cued Speech. I then met with the parents, and after our discussion (which included the implications of using an untried method), they decided to try it.

I gave the Henegars 10 weekly lessons beginning Sept. 1, 1966. They started using it immediately in the home with their fourth child, Leah, who was, at 24 months, the first Cued Speech child. We now know the mother as Mary Elsie Daisey, executive director of the Cued Speech Center in Raleigh, N.C., and past president of the National Cued Speech Association. Leah's language growth (from almost zero to 143 words during the first six months, and 307 in the next six months, or 450 words in the first year of use) gave us needed evidence of the value of the system and its practicability for use with young hearing-impaired children. From that time on, I was able to proceed with assurance that the system was worthy of use and evaluation.

In late 1966 and early 1967 I taught the system to a totally deaf member of the Gallaudet faculty, Dr. Mervin Garretson, who demonstrated with me later at the first national workshop, in July 1967. He appeared on stage with me to say words and phrases furnished on the spot by the audience of 98 teachers of the deaf. I specified that the words and phrases should in languages other than English. They were pronounced (in an assortment of languages) essentially without error by Mr. Garretson, except for a strong American accent. The accent was unavoidable because I was limited to the cues for the sounds of American English, and because many of the foreign sounds were unfamiliar to both of us.

All the workshop participants learned the system in the five-day workshop and indicated their intent to try the method on returning to their schools. Six months later, 33 confirmed that they had tried the system and were continuing its use. Almost all of the others indicated that they were prohibited from using it. From this modest beginning the use of Cued Speech has grown, slowly but steadily, over the intervening years.

4. Helpful Devices and Techniques

Additions to the list of devices and techniques helpful to deaf people occur frequently. Parents can keep abreast of developments by getting in touch with the appropriate departments at Gallaudet University and NTID or the other organizations listed in the Appendix. Some of the devices and techniques available at present are:

1) state-wide relay systems to enable deaf persons to use a TDD

to communicate with a hearing person who doesn't have one,

    2) appropriately fitted hearing aids,

    3) special hearing aids (extended range, low-frequency cutting, or frequency-transposing hearing aids),

    4) cochlear implants,

    5) lap-top computers (single-electrode, 22-electrode, and the new cochlear implant under testing at Stanford University.

    6) wrist vibrators,

    7) visual door "bells,"

    8) amplified telephones,

    9) induction loops coupled to hearing aids,

    10) the "no" vs. "okay" scheme for use for limited telephone communication between parents and profoundly deaf youngsters,

    11) remote-control modules for various uses,

    12) bed vibrator alarm clocks,

    13) flashing light alarm clocks,

    14) "hearing-ear dogs,"

    15) oversize rear-view mirrors for automobiles,

    16) large mirrors for reading to young deaf children,

    17) TV captioners, 18) telephone textwriters (TT's or TDD's),

    19) smoke alarms,

    (20) baby-cry alarms.

    Most of the above require no explanation. Exceptions may include the following:

    4) The subject of cochlear implants is given detailed attention in Chapter 14, "Auditory Training, Cochlear Implants," and several case histories are included. Parents should make sure to keep up with improvements and benefits attributed to those improvements. In particular, they should be aware of the new cochlear implant developed and Stanford University. Though information on it is limited at present, it may have important potential, and should be kept in mind.

    5) A lap-top computer can be used by a deaf student with a transliterator if he/she can type without looking at the keyboard. This provides a boost to self-sufficiency in comparison with having a notetaker.

    9) If the deaf person's hearing aids have induction coils, adequate noise-free sound without feedback can be obtained from a TV set or record-player without turning the volume low.

    10) The yes-no scheme for telephone communication to home by a deaf youngster who cannot understand speech on the telephone, but who can tell the difference between one syllable and two, that is, "Okay" vs. "No." The deaf youngster must learn to handle the

communication like a game of charades, by asking questions that can be answered "Okay" or "No," and the parent must be able to understand the youngster's speech reasonably well. Here's a sample. Gina is having a great time at a friend's house. She calls home and when there is an answer she asks: "Is that you, Mama?" **Okay.** I'm having so much fun. Can I stay over tonight?" **"No."** "Well, can I stay until twelve? **"No."** "How about eleven? Please, Mama, can I?" **"Okay."** "Oh, thank you a lot. You'll pick me up at eleven?" **"Okay."** "Okay, bye-bye and thanks." The conversation was functional if not elaborate. When this scheme was first used by a teenage deaf girl and her mother in 1969, they used "Yes" and "No-No." Any combination of a one-syllable utterance and a two-syllable utterance could be used, if tested to make sure the deaf child can distinguish between them reliably.

11) Remote-control modules (as from Radio Shack) can be rigged to alert a deaf person to various sounds and occurrences around the house (doorbell, telephone, garage door opening, etc.), though this may require a bit of handy-man activity.

14) An oversize, curved rear-view mirror facilitates communication in the automobile between a cueing parent and a deaf child in the back seat.

16) A large mirror can be a great help in reading (with cues) to a young deaf child. (pp. 119-121)

17) A portable telephone can give a parent freedom to perform various household tasks during telephone conversations.

Appendix

The Appendix consists of two parts. Part I includes: 1) a list of organizations and agencies serving as sources of information, guidance, and support for parents of deaf children, 2) a list of published materials useful to parents needing orientation and information related to their problems, options and roles as parents of hearing-impaired children, and 3) information on publications and materials for parents to use with their hearing-impaired children, or in teaching others.

Part II of the Appendix is devoted to materials and information designed to be helpful to hearing parents in developing accuracy and fluency in cueing, once they have learned the basics through face-to-face instruction and/or videotape, audiotape, and/or written materials. Included are materials on Funetik Speling, consonant and vowel charts for American English, a basic vocabulary of 500 words and short phrases written in Cuescript to make clear how each word is correctly cued for the pronunciation indicated, a practice primer listing 481 sentences typical of those used by parents with young children, and a list of available videotape, audiocassette and written materials designed for supplemental self-instruction following an adequate amount of face-to-face instruction in classes or workshops.

Appendix, PART I
(1) Sources of Information and Assistance

Cued Speech National Center
National Cued Speech Association (NCSA)
P.O. Box 31345
Raleigh, NC 27622
919-828-1218 (V/TT)

Through the Cued Speech National Center, the NCSA responds to requests for information, initial guidance, and referral to more accessible sources of assistance, materials, and support. Members of the National Cued Speech Association receive the publications of the Association, including *On Cue* and the *Cued Speech Journal*.

Gallaudet University Cued Speech Team
Dept. of Audiology, Speech & Language Pathology
800 Florida Ave. NE, Washington, DC 20002-3695
202-652-5330 (V/TT)

The Cued Speech Team provides information, guidance, materials, and services in response to correspondence or telephone requests. They participate widely in workshops and provide on-campus credit and non-credit courses in Cued Speech and Cued Speech transliteration. They maintain a list of Cued Speech contacts, publish the newsletter, *Cued Speech News*, and produce other materials.

NCSA Training, Evaluation and Certification Unit
1616 Parham Rd., Silver Spring, MD 20903, 301-439-5766 (V/TT)
    The TECUnit is responsible to the NCSA for establishing, maintaining and promulgating national standards for the professional field of Cued Speech Transliteration and for Instructors of Cued Speech. Its functions are described on page 402.

R. Orin Cornett, Ph.D.,
Professor Emeritus of Audiology, Gallaudet University
8702 Royal Ridge Lane, Laurel, MD 20708, 301-490-4974 (V/TT)
    Dr. Cornett is available for consultation through correspondence or telephone communication, without charge.

Regional Cued Speech Support Centers

Cued Speech Center
Mary Elsie Daisey, Executive Director
P.O. Box 31345, Raleigh, NC 27622, 919-828-1218 (V/TT)

North Coast Cued Speech Services
Pamela Beck, Director
23970 Hermitage Road, Shaker Heights, OH 44122
216-292-6213 (V/TT)

West Coast Cued Speech Programs
(Affiliate of the NCSA)
Joan Rupert, Executive Director
348 Cernon St., Suite D, Vacaville, CA 95688, 707-448-4060 (V/TT)

Gulf Coast Cued Speech Services
M. Carolyn Jones, Director
332 Audubon Street, New Orleans, LA 70118, 504-861-8913 (V/TT)

Alternatives in Education of the Hearing Impaired
Deanna Jordan, Executive Director
2020 E. Camp McDonald Rd., Mt. Prospect, IL 60056
708-297-4660 (V/TT)

NCSA-Affiliated Regional and Local Associations

These are state and regional Cued Speech associations that may be able to provide support and encouragement, or who sponsor workshops and family Cued Speech programs. Call or write the National Cued Speech Association for current information, including telephone numbers, contact people, and addresses.

Bay Area Cued Speech Association, Northern California
Central Vines Cued Speech Association, Fresno, California
Cued Speech Association of Minnesota, Rochesterm Minnesota
North Carolina Cued Speech Association
Northern Virginia Cued Speech Association
Ohio Cued Speech Association
Tennessee Cued Speech Association
Tidewater Cued Speech Association, Virginia
Wilmington Cued Speech Association, Wilmington, North Carolina

Information on regional and local Cued Speech Associations not yet affiliated with the NCSA can also be secured from the NCSA.

Organizations Not Connected with Cued Speech

Alexander Graham Bell Association for the Deaf
3417 Volta Place, NW, Washington, DC 20007
202-337-5220 (V/TT)
Members receive the journal *Volta Review,* the newsletter *Newsounds*, and *Our Kids Magazine*. Publishes numerous books and monographs. One-year membership is available free to new parents of hearing-impaired children.

American Society for Deaf Children
814 Thayer Ave., Silver Spring MD 20910, 800-842-ASDC (V/TT)

American Speech-Language-Hearing Association
10801 Rockville Pike, Rockville MD 20852, 301-897-5700 (V/TT)
and 800-638-8255. Publishes several professional journals.

BEGINNINGS For Parents of Hearing Impaired Children,
1504 Western Blvd., Raleigh, NC 27606
919-280-9797 (V/TT) Parents call (800)-541-4327
Provides unbiased information, support and materials. Has two

orientation videotapes, plus a manual for parents.

Convention of American Instructors of the Deaf (CAID)
Check with NCSA for current address, telephone, contact person.
Publishes the *American Annals of the Deaf.*

John Tracy Clinic
806 W. Adams Blvd., Los Angeles, CA 90007
Voice: 213-748-5481, TT 213-747-2924
Voice or TDD, (800) 522-4582
Conducts preschool, workshops, correspondence course, other services.

National Association of the Deaf
814 Thayer Ave., Silver Spring, MD 20910
Voice 301-587-1788, TT 301-587-1789
Serves deaf people and parents. Publishes the *Deaf American.*

National Information Center on Deafness
Gallaudet University
800 Florida Avenue, N.W., Washington DC 20002
Voice 202-651-5051, TT 202-651-5052

Self Help for Hard of Hearing People, Inc. (SHHH)
7800 Wisconsin Ave., Bethesda, MD 20814
Voice 301-657-2248, TT 301-657-2249

(2) Materials for Parent Orientation and Guidance

Journal articles, book lists, and other written materials are available through the support centers. The following lists identify exemplary materials and sources.

Books and Monographs

Choices in Deafness: A Parents' Guide. Sue Schwartz, Editor (1989) Rockville MD: Woodbine House. Identified by several parent reviewers as the book most helpful to them in their initial searching for the right way to go.

BEGINNINGS For Parents of Hearing Impaired Children: A Parent Manual. by J. Craig Greene, 1990, 69 pp. address above. Written by a parent, this manual covers feelings of parents, the auditory system, education and te law, recommended readings, an extensive North Carolina and national directory of relevant sources and services, and other matters of interest to parents.

Cued Speech: Another Option. by Scarlett Horning & Marybeth Walworth I1989) 45 pp. SKI*HI Institute, Dept. of Communication Disorders, Utah State University, Logan, Utah 84322-9605.

Deafness in the Family. by David Luterman (1987) 124 pp. Boston: College-Hill Press Little, Brown and Co. For parents and professionals, a sensitive, thorough treatment of how deafness in one member of the family affects all its members.

Families and Their Hearing-Impaired Children (1987), Ed. by Dale Atkins. Monograph issue of *Volta Review* Washington DC: Alexander Graham Bell Association. Issues, problems, and strategies.

Hearing-Impaired Children in the Mainstream (1990), 536 pp. Ed. by Mark Ross Washington DC: Alexander Graham Bell Association. Provides a current, comprehensive and authoritative perspective on integrating the hearing-impaired child into the regular classroom.

Language Development and Language Disorders by Lois Bloom and Margaret Lahey (1978) 689 pp. NY: John Wiley & Sons. This classic text provides a superb program for developing language in language-delayed children. It is designed for professionals. Parents may wish to recommend it to staff working with their children. Barbara Lee, of Baton Rouge, La., has adapted the curriculum for use with hearing-impaired children, with or without Cued Speech. Her curriculum will be available in Sept. 1993. Meanwhile, she will be glad to supply information, materials, and suggestions. Contact via NCSA.

Negotiating the Special Education Maze: A Guide for Parents and Teachers. by Winifred Anderson, Stephen Chitwood, and Deidre Hayden. Second edition (1990), 269 pp. This book guides parents as effective advocates for their child and encourages them to be equal partners in all decisions that affect their child's education.

College & Career Programs For Deaf Students, available from the Center for Assessment and Demographic Studies (CADS) at Gallaudet University. This is the most comprehensive source of information on college programs for deaf students. The 1992 edition contains listings and descriptions of 156 college programs in the United States and Canada that are available for deaf students. Includes listings by geographic regions, and provides information on admissions, costs, enrollment, degrees, and career areas available, etc. Updated periodically. It can be found in most libraries.

Foundations of Spoken Language for Hearing Impaired Children, by Daniel Ling (1989). Washington DC: Alexander Graham Bell Association for the Deaf, Inc. 442 pp. For professionals and parents.

The New Read-Aloud Handbook, by Jim Trelease (1989) NY: Penguin Books. (This book is discussed on pp. 252-253)

The Silent Garden, by Paul Ogden and Suzanne Lipsett (1982) NY: St. Martin's Press. Odgen is profoundly deaf; Lipsett is a writer. Their combined effort faces squarely the dilemmas faced by parents and provides an impartial discussion of advantages and disadvantages of the different education and communication approaches. Includes CS.

Basic Vocabulary and Language Thesaurus for Hearing-Impaired Children, by Daniel Ling and Agnes Ling Phillips (1977) Washington DC: Alexander Graham Bell Association for the Deaf, 1977. Analysis and classification of spontaneous language used by normally hearing children up to 7 years of age.

The Strong-Willed Child, by James Dobson (1988) Wheaton, IL: Tyndale House Publishers.

Dare to Discipline, by James Dobson (1972) Wheaton, IL: Tyndale House Publishers.

Learning to Listen. Pat Vaughn (Ed., 1981) Toronto, Ontario: Voice for Hearing-Impaired Children.

Talk With Your Child, by Harvey S. Weiner (1988): NY Viking Penguin, Inc.

The Preschool Years, by Ellen Galinsky & Judy David (1988) NY: Time Books, a division of Random House, Inc.

Dancing Without Music—Deafness in America by Beryl Lieff Benderly (1980): NY: Anchor Press/Doubleday. "An unbiased author's attempt (largely successful) to 'explain deafness to a hearing world.'"

Raising Your Hearing-Impaired Child: A Guideline for Parents by Shirley Hanawalt McArthur (1982) Washington DC: Alexander Graham Bell Association for the Deaf.

Videotapes

I See What You Say, Cued Speech demonstration videotape, available from the Cued Speech Center, Raleigh, N.C. A 12-minute video that provides an introduction to Cued Speech and its functions, and shows its use in a variety of settings with a range of ages. Refundable deposit for loan, or purchase. Open captions available.

An Introduction to Cued Speech by Barbara Williams-Scott. A 20-minute captioned videotape which explains Cued Speech and demonstrates its use in a public-school situation. Available from the Cued Speech Team at Gallaudet University.

BEGINNINGS for Parents of Hearing Impaired Infants and Toddlers A 30-minute open captioned videotape expands awareness of different communication approaches, including Cued Speech.

BEGINNINGS: Parental Perspectives A 30-minute videotape in which parents discuss their feelings and experience of raising children who are hearing impaired. For address, see list of organizations.

(3) Materials for Parent Use With Deaf Children

In general, parents of hearing-impaired children who grow up with Cued Speech from an early age can use the same materials that are used with young hearing children. Instead of buying everything they expect to use, they will do well to check first at public libraries, which usually have large collections of books and materials for children. Make use of this source for materials that are likely to be used only a few times.

Visit bookstores that have good collections for or for use with young children. Buy the books your child is most likely to treasure and use again and again. For children who start Cued Speech relatively late, you may need guidance regarding materials likely to fit your child's interest level and still be on the appropriate level for language and communication development.

No published list of materials for use with deaf children will remain up to date very long. New materials appear rapidly. Although we list materials here, our suggestion is that parents get **current** information from the support centers listed above. Several of the series are listed with the hope that they will be updated by the publication of additional items in the series. For this reason we do not list individual items in the series.

Cued Speech Manuals, Workbooks, Videotapes and Practice Aids

Cued Speech Instructional Manual by Mary Elsie Daisey (1992), 174 pp. Designed for use in teaching hearing adults and teens, this manual can be used with older deaf children. Available from the Cued Speech Center, Raleigh, N.C.

Discovering Cued Speech: An Eight-Hour Instructional Program and Six-Hour Competency Review by Pamela H. Beck (1985), 107 pp. North Coast Cued Speech Services. For use with learner's workbook and practice audiocassette tape.

Kids Discovering Cued Speech by Pamela H. Beck (1990), 89 pp. North Coast Cued Speech Services. Designed for use by teachers, this can also be used by parents.

Cued Speech Curriculum, Vol. 1, Acquiring Receptive and Expressive Cued Speech, A Method of Instructing Cued Speech to the Hearing Impaired by Karen Koehler-Cesa (1990) 315 pp. For teaching Cued Speech to hearing-impaired children who have a reasonable base of written language. While designed with TC students in mind, this curriculum can be used with other students. An accompanying workbook is also available.

Teaching Cued Speech to Children of All Ages by Barbara Williams-Scott, Cued Speech instructor/materials specialist, Gallaudet University Cued Speech Team (1990) 87 pp. Designed primarily for teaching hearing children, but usable with hearing-impaired children. Provides assorted materials and outlines procedures and ideas. The Cued Speech team also has an extensive list of useful packets and pamphlets.

Home Education Language Development for the Hearing-Impaired (HELD-HI) is a series of videotaped stories narrated in Cued Speech, made available with sets of the books. For ages 3½-7. Limited availability. Check with NCSA: P.O. Box 31345, Raleigh, NC 27622.

The Self-Monitoring Cue Card Format by M. Carolyn Jones (1990) New Orleans: Gulf Coast Cued Speech Services. Uses, in the writers words, "...a written code that includes, and is designed to extend the usefulness of, Cornett's Cued Speech system." It uses four lines to show how language units are spelled, sounded, and cued. The SMCCF is designed for coordinated use by professionals and parents, for teaching. However, it can be used by them for monitoring their own production.

Other Manuals and Work Books

These materials are not designed for use with Cued Speech, but are very well suited to it. Cued Speech simply accelerates the progress.

Books for Use With Children

The suggested books are not necessarily the best available; they should be considered good examples of the type needed in each category. Most of them can be found in local libraries or bookstores, or can be ordered from the publishers

Picture Dictionaries and Word Books

It is important to have several of these for reference. After the child has had a new experience, use pictures to impress it (and the associated vocabulary) on his/her memory. The pictures will have more meaning if they are used to follow up a first-hand experience, and they will facilitate review and repetition. Among the best pictures for this purpose are photographs actually made during a trip or activity, but such photos can be supplemented with pictures in word books or picture dictionaries.

Best First Word Book Ever by Richard Scarry. NY: Random House, Inc. For beginners. "Busy" pictures with much detail for attention.

Storybook Dictionary by Richard Scarry. NY: Random House. For those with more language.

The Cat in the Hat Beginner Book Dictionary by P.D. Eastman. NY: Beginner Books, a division of Random House, Inc.

Golden Picture Dictionary by Lilian Moore. Golden Books, Inc.

The First 1000 Words and Pictures Book, illustrated by Robert Durham (1991) Wishing Well Books, Joshua Morris Publishing, Inc.

My First Word Book, by Angela Wilkes. NY: Darling Kindersley, Inc. Excellent photos of single items collected on large pages.

For Babies and Youngest Preschoolers

Choose cloth or hard board pages with attractive pictures. Aim for a collection of books with simple pictures, one object to a page, for basic vocabulary building. Then advance to illustrated story books.

My First Look at Home (1990) NY: Random House, A Darling Kindersley Book. Excellent photos of individual items, on smaller pages. Series includes other subjects needed for expanding vocabulary: Opposites, Numbers, Seasons, Sizes, and Shapes.

Nursery Rhymes, illus. by Eloise Wilkin(1979) NY: Random House.

Baby's Mother Goose, Illus. by Alice Schlesinger. Grosset & Dunlap

My Picture Book, Platt and Munk (board pages, photographs; ages 2-5)

Things to See, illustrated by Thomas Matthiesen. Platt and Munk (photographs; ages 3-7).

ABC: An Alphabet Book. Platt and Munk.(realistic photographs of familiar objects; ages 3-7),

The Zoo Book, by Robert Allen and Peter Sahula, Platt and Munk (realistic photographs of animals; ages 3-7).

A Child's Garden of Verses, by Robert Louis Stevenson, illustrated by Eloise Wilkin. Golden Press.

Animal Sounds, illustrated by Aurelius Battaglia. Racine, WI: Western Publishing Co. Inc. A Golden Sturdy Book.

My Goodnight Book Pictures by Eloise Wilkin. Racine, WI: Western Publishing Co., Inc. A Golden Sturdy Shape Book.

Counting and ABC's
Numbers—A First Counting Book, by Robert Allen and Mottke Weissman. Platt and Munk.

My Counting Book, (ages 2-5) Platt and Munk.

Bears on Wheels, by Stan and Jan Berenstain, A Bright and Early Book for beginning readers, Random House.

Best Counting Book Ever, by Richard Scarry. Random House.

The True-to-Life ABC Book, Grosset & Dunlap

Big Golden Animal ABC by Garth Williams, Golden Press

The Child's World

Look for books with pictures of familiar situations and experiences to talk about. Many of the Little Golden Books are good for this purpose. Titles available change frequently. Here are a few examples.

Let's Make a Noise, by Amy MacDonald and Maureen Roffey. Simple pictures to encourager children to make the appropriate noises for the animals and items pictured.

Let's Play House by Lois Lenski, Henry Z. Walck, Inc.

A Visit to the Dentist by Bernard J. Garn, Grosset & Dunlap.

Wide Wide Word Series: River, Circus, Farm, Zoo, Town, Supermarket, Illus. by George Fryer. Tokyo: Froebel-kan Co., Ltd. Miami: P.S.I. & Associates, Inc. Sturdy board books, realistic, detailed pictures and printed words to name items familiar to young children.

Story Books

Pick simple stories with good illustrations (simple, uncluttered, not too detailed; preferably with each step of the story illustrated on a separate page). They should be true to life and remind the child of experiences in his own life, even if they are fairy tales. Adjust the length of the story to fit the child's attention span. The following examples are representative:

The Three Bears Many editions available. Make sure all sequences in the story are fully illustrated (all three chairs pictured, etc.).

Little Red Riding Hood, Sleeping Beauty, Cinderella, etc. Fairy tales can be fully appreciated by deaf children after they acquire a good language foundation.

Peter Rabbit, by Beatrix Potter (get edition with simple, attractive pictures that cover all aspects of the story.

Golden Egg Book by Margaret Wise Brown. Golden Press.

Sleepy Book by Charlotte Zolotov, Golden Press.

Are You My Mother? by P. D. Eastman, Random House.

Go Dog Go by P.D. Eastman, Random House.

The Big Honey Hunt by Stanley and Janice Berenstain, Random House.

The Berenstain Bears & Too Much Birthday, by Stanley and Janice Berenstain, First Time Books, NY: Random House

The Berenstain Bears and the Messy Room same series as above.

The Berenstain Bears and Too Much TV same series as above.

Expanding Vocabulary and Language

The Touch Me Book Golden-Capitol Answer Books, Capitol Publishing Co., distributed by Golden Press. (examples of tactile adjectives: soft, smooth, etc.)

What's in Mommy's Pocketbook? (familiar objects), in series above.

Who Lives Here? (animals and their homes, same series as above.

Where's Spot? by Eric Hill (1980) NY: G.P. Putnam Sons. A very good aid for teaching the concept of "Where's ...?"

In & Out; Up & Down, A Sesame Street Small Board Book, illustrated by Michael Smollin, Random House/Children's Television Workshop. Small book provides simple, fun pictures of opposites on facing pages.

There are many other good books that provide comparable vocabulary, such as large and small, light and heavy, hot and cold, etc. Most are suitable for a parent to read or "talk about" before the child can actually read.

My Book about Me, by Dr. Seuss and Roy McKie. NY: Random House (Beginner Books).

For Beginning Readers

The Nose Book by Al Perkins NY: Random House (A Bright and Early Book).

Old Hat, New Hat by Stan and Jan Berenstain, Random House.

Inside Outside, Upside Down by Stan and Jan Berenstain, Random House.

For Advanced Children

The Big Schoolhouse and *What People Do All Day* by Richard Scarry, Golden Press.(for those about 6 years old who have a lot of language; intricate detail in illustrations causes children to study pages, absorbing much written language while doing so).

Mr. Brown Can Moo! Can You? by Dr. Seuss,NY: Random House. "Book of Wonderful Noises," great practice for a child who has a knowledge of sounds; sounds to imitate, both from written form and in spoken form if someone cues the sounds).

Animal Families by Ann Weil. Children's Press, Inc. (expands vocabulary; such words as ram, bull, gosling, gander)

It's Raining Cats and Dogs (1990) NY: Chatham Press. Collection of 38 idioms, each on an illustrated page, with meaning explained.

Book Clubs

A membership in one of these clubs encourages reading and enjoyment of books. One book is sent on approval each month.

Some of the clubs available are: Bright and Early Books, by Grolier Enterprises; Beginner Books by Random House; Children's Choice Book Club; and Children's Book of the Month Club.

Materials for "Work Sessions"

Look for a variety of items to use when "working" with your child. If desired items cannot be found at a bookstore, check with school supply distributors. Some useful items are:

Easy item puzzles—puzzle inlay boards, with individual objects.

Board match-ups—two-piece puzzles on such subjects as "colors and things" and "people and their jobs."

Picture flashcards—Many different ones are available. Aim for realistic pictures or photos of single items for basic vocabulary development. Children with more advanced language can benefit from the following:

Picture-sequence cards—can be grouped in sets to depict actions in sequence; promote logical sequencing of concepts.

Picture lottos—playing boards with pictures to be covered by matching cards; provide experience in noting likenesses and differences.

Photo "feelings" cards—show children and adults expressing emotions.

Puppets—look for hand puppets with movable mouths.

Many materials are available to furnish ideas for language-development and experiential-play activities. A few suggested ones are:

John Tracy Clinic Correspondence Course (one-year program; available free to parents of preschool-age deaf and hard-of-hearing children), 806 West Adams Boulevard, Los Angeles, CA 90007. Updated regularly, this course can be used effectively with CS for appropriate age range.

The Language of Toys: Teaching Communication Skills to Special

Needs Children by Sue Schwartz & Joan E. Heller MIller (eds.). (1988) Rockville MD: Woodbine House.

Wee Sing: Children's Songs and Fingerplays, by P.C. Beal and S.H. Nipp (1983) Los Angeles: Price/Stern, Sloan Publishers, Inc. Presents fun ways to pattern language and concepts.

Playful Parenting, by R.N. Grasselis and P.A. Hegner (1981), NY; Putnam Publishers. Games to help infants and toddlers grow physically, mentally, and emotionally.

I'll Tell You a Story, I'll Sing You a Song. A parents' guide to the fairy tales, fables, songs, and rhymes of childhood. NY: Delacorte Press.

Reading to Your Deaf Child

Be sure that your "work sessions" involve much reading to your child. Refer to pp. 252-253 for detailed suggestions.

Games

These are traditional games for young children with basic language skills. More complex games can be used as language grows.

Candy Land (Players draw cards and move by matching colors and objects; ages 4-5), Milton Bradley

Winnie-The-Pooh (Played with color only, no reading or counting; ages 4-8) Parker Brothers

Chutes and Ladders (Must read numbers; ages 4-10), Milton Bradley

Match and Move Memory Game (Players math cards to game board pictures; ages 5 and up), Milton Bradley.

Animal Families Memory Game (Matching pairs for young non-reading [;auers' ages 3-6), Milton Bradley.

Card games such as "Old Maid," "Animal, Bird and Fish," and "Uno" can be used with young card players. Others are available. As the child progresses, more complex games such as Scrabble can be enjoyed.

Appendix, PART II

Learning to Cue Accurately and Well

This book contain suggestions as to how to go about learning to cue, in the appropriate chapters. In addition, this section of the Appendix includes some basic materials for supplementary use in learning to cue accurately and well. It also lists self-instruction manuals, workbooks, videotape lessons, and audiotape lessons available from various sources. See p. 760 for other materials intended for teaching that can be used for self-instruction under some conditions.

Materials for Self-Instruction

Self-Instruction Manuals

Cued Speech Practice Manuals A and B, Self-Teaching Flashcards, and Cued Speech ABC Fun'n' Learning by Joan Rupert. Available from Hi I Cue Publishers, West Coast Cued Speech Programs. For use after an initial training seminar.

Gaining Cued Speech Proficiency by Walter J. Beaupré. A manual for parents, teachers, and clinicians. Intended for those who have reason to achieve proficiency in Cued Speech, and who already have gained an understanding of the basic system. (Available from the Cued Speech Team at Gallaudet University and the Cued Speech Center.) Beaupré has also produced a *Basic Cued Speech Proficiency Rating* which is used by the Cued Speech Team and the TECUnit for evaluation of proficiency for certification purposes.

Discovering Cued Speech Learner's Workbook by Pamela H. Beck (1988) 34 pp. North Coast Cued Speech Services. For practice.

Videocassette and Audiocassette Lessons

Becoming a Proficient Cuer, by Melanie Metzger and Earl Fleetwood (1992). Metzger/Fleetwood Productions. Order from TECUnit or CS Team. Videotape (108 min.) with workbook. Video lessons plus workbook drills designed to eliminate common cueing errors. For both new and experienced hearing cuers.

Cued Speech Videotape Training Program, by Scarlett Horning and Marybeth Walworth. Two two-hour videotapes comprising 20 lessons designed to teach families how to cue. Available from HOPE Inc., 780 North Research Parkway, Suite 110, Logan, UT 84321.

Video Lessons In Cued Speech For Hearing Persons by R. Orin Cornett (1984). (single two-hour VHS tape, 14 lessons). Designed to be used **only** in combination with the audiocassette *Beginning Lessons In Cued Speech* (1984). Available from the Cued Speech Team at Gallaudet University, with deposit and use fee. This lesson series is designed for self-instruction by persons who have limited access to face-to-face instruction. The audiocassette lessons can be used without the videotape after a reasonable amount of face-to-face instruction.

Video Lessons for Hearing-Impaired People, Series A, by Mary Elsie Daisey (1977). (two six-hour VHS tapes, 21 lessons). Limited availability from NCSA and the Gallaudet CS Team. Note: we do not recommend that deaf parents learn and use Cued Speech with their deaf children. These tapes are for deaf adults who want to learn for their own benefit. Face-to-face instruction is essential in such cases.

The Need For Spelling According to Pronunciation

Written materials for use in learning or practicing Cued Speech need to be in a form that leaves no doubt as to the sounds in each word. This is not to imply that there is only one acceptable pronunciation in each case, but that each cue must be associated with the appropriate sound. If a hearing person is learning through face-to-face instruction, sound videotape lessons, or audiocassette lessons, he/she will presumably know how each word is being pronounced and will be able to cue it accordingly. When one is using written materials, however, the materials should be spelled phonetically (actually, *phonemically*) in order to make the pronunciation clear.

You are doubtless familiar with phonetic spelling as used by writers to indicate colloquial pronunciations or dialects. For example, a British accent may be conveyed by: "Cawn't yew mek it a bit fahstuh, owld mahn?" The practice materials in this book are written in a similar type of phonetic spelling (Funetik Speling) designed especially for Cued Speech. Its purpose is to clarify the pronunciation that is being used at the time. It can be understood almost completely at sight, and requires no special symbols. The following section explains the phonetic spelling system used in this book. It also explains some of the inadequacies of Conventional English spelling (CE).

Funetik Speling
A Simple Phonemic English Spelling System
By R. Orin Cornett

When learning Cued Speech one must know exactly which pronunciation is intended at the moment, so that the appropriate cues can be associated with the respective sounds. Funetik Speling is not designed for other purposes, such as uniform spelling or preparing for transition to conventional spelling. Its one purpose is to make the intended pronunciation clear. Our reasons for not using diacritical markings from dictionaries are as follows: (1) They cannot all be written with a standard typewriter, (2) their limited list of key words used for illustration does not clear up many differences in dialects, and (3) they are not easy to read in continuous phrases. Funetik Speling, in the more than 25 years since it was developed, has proved to be easy to use for deaf and hearing persons alike. If you are deaf or hard of hearing, remember as you read the following pages that Cued Speech will clarify the sounds just as Funetik Speling (FS) does.

The long ē sound is spelled *ee* in Funetik Speling (FS). It is spelled 12 ways in Conventional English spelling (CE). It is spelled differently in each of the following: team (*teem*), deceive (*diseev*), key (*kee*), field (*feeld*), machine (*musheen*), suite (*sweet*), people (*peepul*), amoeba (*umeebu*), equal (*eekwul*), Caesar (*Seezur*). With FS there is no doubt about what sounds are meant in each of these words.

The short ĕ sound is spelled with the letter *e* in FS. In Conventional English spelling (CE) it is spelled 11 ways. Some of them are: any (*eni*), said (*sed*), heifer (*hefur*), friend (*frend*), bury (*beri*).

The short ă sound is spelled Funetikli (that is, in FS) as *a*, just as it usually is in CE. But in CE we have also other spellings of this sound, as in plaid (*plad*).

The long ā sound is spelled at least eight ways in CE, but only one way (*ae*) in FS. Here are seven: ate (*aet*), rain (*raen*), rein (*raen*), gauge (*gaeg*), ray (*rae*), steak (*staek*), obey (*oebae*). Notice that the addition of e to a changes the sound from short a to long ae. This is true in CE, except that in CE the e is not usually next to the a. Examples are: hat, hate (*haet*); rat, rate (*raet*). Note that in FS the e is put next to the a, for clarity: mate (*maet*).

The short ŭ sound, as in but, is spelled five different ways in CE, but always as *u* in FS: cup (*cup*), son (*sun*), does (*duz*), flood (*flud*), couple (*kupul*).

The short i sound (as in bit) is always written as *i* in FS. It is spelled eight ways in CE: if (*if*), been (*bin*), England (*Ingglund*), sieve (*siv*), <u>women</u> (*wimin*), <u>busy</u> (*bizi*), <u>built</u> (*bilt*), <u>body</u> (*bahdi*).

Short o in General American English is pronounced either *ah* or *aw*, as in <u>box</u> (*bahks*), <u>not</u> (*naht*), <u>dog</u> (*dawg* or *dahg*). In FS the *ah* sound is spelled always as *ah*: <u>box</u> (*bahks*), <u>doll</u> (*dahl*), <u>father</u> (*fahtHur*). The British pronunciation of the short o is always like our *aw* sound. Many persons in New England use this pronunciation, as in <u>not</u> (*nawt*), though most Americans pronounce it as *naht*.

The long ō sound is spelled *oe* in FS. The <u>e</u> goes with the <u>o</u> (with a consonant between) in many words in which o has the long sound: <u>note</u> (*noet*), <u>rote</u> (roet). Other CE spellings are <u>beau</u> (boe), <u>sew</u> (*soe*), <u>so</u> (*soe*), <u>road</u> (roed). Notice that adding the letter e to the word *not* causes it to be pronounced *note*. This pattern runs through FS, with the vowels a, e, i, o, and u. In each case, adding e (after a consonant) changes the vowel to its long sound. Consider: <u>bat</u> becomes <u>bate</u> (*baet*) when e is added; <u>met</u> becomes <u>mete</u> (*meet*); <u>bit</u> becomes <u>bite</u> (*biet*); <u>rot</u> becomes <u>rote</u> (*roet*); and <u>run</u> become <u>rune</u> (*ruen*). In FS the two vowels whose combination represents each long vowel sound are always written together for clarity.

The following words illustrate some of the many spellings in CE for the sound for which the spelling *aw* is used in FS: <u>tall</u> (*tawl*), <u>talk</u> (*tawk*), <u>raw</u> (*raw*), <u>for</u> (*fawr*), <u>broad</u> (brawd), <u>fought</u> (*fawt*), <u>Arkansas</u> (*Arkansaw*).

The sound of oo in book and look, represented also by *oo* in FS, occurs in CE in these and other spellings: <u>should</u> (*shood*), <u>put</u> (*poot*), <u>wolf</u> (*woolf*), <u>foot</u> (*foot*).

The sound of long ōō, as in <u>moon</u>, which in FS is represented by *ue*, is spelled in the following ways in CE: <u>soup</u> (*suep*), <u>two</u> (*tue*), <u>suit</u> (*suet*), <u>spoon</u> (*spuen*), <u>glue</u> (*glue*), grew (*grue*). This is another case in which an added e changes a vowel from short to long, as with tub and tube. Note that ue in FS indicates only the long oo sound, not the sound of the word you, or that of <u>ew</u> in <u>few</u> (*fyue*) and <u>ue</u> in <u>cue</u> (*kyue*). This combination is always indicated by including the letter y before ue. The word <u>you</u> is thus written in FS as *yue*.

The sound of <u>er</u> in <u>her</u>, represented always by *ur* in FS, is spelled several ways in CE: <u>her</u> (*hur*), <u>hurt</u> (*hurt*), <u>learn</u> (*lurn*), <u>thirst</u> (*thurst*), <u>courage</u> (*kurij*), <u>myrtle</u> (*murtl*).

In FS there are no silent letters to confuse you, except that h is used in some digraphs. Notice the silent letters in CE that disappear in FS: <u>know</u> (*noe*), <u>gnat</u> (*nat*), <u>pneumonia</u> (*nuemoenyu*), <u>whole</u> (*hoel*), <u>wrist</u> (*rist*), <u>knowledge</u> (*nahlij*), <u>lamb</u> (*lam*). A silent <u>h</u> is occasionally used as a reminder that the vowel before it is short. For example, in FS *u* is always pronounced uh. Where the temptation to pronounce it differently is great, as in the southern pronunciation of the word <u>other</u> (*utHuh*), the spelling *uh* can be used. This use of a silent final <u>h</u> is optional, as it is in mutHuh, though the spelling mutHu is preferable after one becomes accustomed to FS. The same use of silent h can be made in such examples as *eh*, as in the southern and British pronunciations of the word *fair*. this can be written in FS as *feh-uh* for maximum clarity, though *feu* will be understood if the rules of FS are kept in mind. The letter h is also used in the digraphs ch, sh, zh, th, etc. to indicate special sounds. These uses, of course, are not optional.

In FS the spelling ou is used for the sound of <u>ou</u> in *out* and <u>ow</u> in *brow*: <u>bough</u> (*bou*), <u>brow</u> (*brou*), <u>cow</u> (*kou*).

Did you know that in CE there are eight different ways to pronounce <u>ough</u>? Here are seven. Can you name the eighth? <u>bough</u> (*bou*), <u>thought</u> (*thawt*), <u>rough</u> (ruf), <u>cough</u> (*kawf*) <u>though</u> (*tHoe*), <u>through</u> (*thrue*), <u>hiccough</u> (*hikup*),

The long <u>i</u> sound, as in <u>bite</u>, is written *ie (biet)* in FS because it occurs so often where <u>i</u> and <u>e</u> are separated by a consonant in the same word. In FS the two letters are written together so there can be no uncertainty. This sound is spelled 22 different ways in CE! Here are eight of them: <u>height</u> (*hiet*), <u>aisle</u> (*iel*), <u>aye</u> (*ie*), <u>eye</u> (*ie*), <u>tie</u> (*tie*), <u>buy</u> (*bie*), <u>sky</u> (*skie*), <u>lye</u> (*lie*). How many more can you identify?

The diphthong in <u>toy</u> and <u>soil</u> is written as *oi* in FS (*toi, soil*).

Most consonants and consonant digraphs are the same in FS as in CE, except that there is only one sound for each written symbol (letter or digraph) in FS. Two sounds are never used for the same symbol. The letter <u>c</u> is therefore never used, either for the <u>s</u> sound in city or for the <u>k</u> sound in cat. When the letter <u>s</u> in CE represents the sound of <u>z</u>, z must be written in FS, as in <u>his</u> (*hiz*) and <u>rose</u> (*roez*). When the letter <u>c</u> in CE has an <u>s</u> sound, it is replaced in FS by *s*. When it has the sound beginning the word <u>cat</u>, it is spelled as *k* (*kat*). The letter x is not used in FS. Instead, the spelling that represents the proper sound is used: <u>fix</u> (*fiks*), <u>exact</u> (*igzakt*), <u>Xerxes</u> (*Zurkseez*), <u>Xerox</u>, (*zeerahks*). The letter <u>q</u> is also not used in FS.

The following letters in FS all have the same sounds they have in CE: <u>b</u>, <u>d</u> (as in (*bed*), <u>k</u>, <u>p</u> (as in (*keep*), <u>f</u>, <u>t</u> (as in *feet*), <u>h</u>, <u>l</u> (as in *heel*), <u>m</u>, <u>n</u> (as in *meen*), <u>j</u> (*juj*), <u>r</u>, <u>v</u> (*rivur*). Notice that *ur* in *rivur* is a clear vowel sound (like *ur* in *fur*), not quite the same as *uh* plus *r*. Other consonants used the same way in FS as in CE are <u>w</u>, <u>s</u>, <u>t</u> (*west*), <u>y</u> (*yet*), <u>z</u> (*zeeroe* or *ziroe*). Notice that in FS <u>y</u> always has its consonant sound, never the vowel sound it has in CE as in <u>baby</u> (*baebi*) and <u>city</u> (*siti*).

In CE there are a number of consonant digraphs representing

sounds for which we use the same symbols in FS. An example is <u>ch</u>, as in <u>chief</u> (*cheef*). But notice that this sound is also spelled as <u>teo</u> in CE, as in <u>righteous</u> (*riechus*), and other ways, as in <u>mention</u> (*menchun*) and <u>mansion</u> (*manchun*). In FS it is always spelled *ch*.

The sound of <u>sh</u> in <u>ship</u> is spelled as follows in CE and FS: <u>ocean</u> (*oeshun*), <u>machine</u> (*musheen*), <u>special</u> (*speshul*), <u>pshaw</u> (*shaw*), <u>sugar</u> (*shoogur*), <u>nation</u> (*naeshun*), <u>tissue</u> (*tishue*), <u>mission</u> (*mishun*). It is always spelled *sh* in FS.

In CE the digraph <u>th</u> has two sounds, as in <u>that</u> and <u>thin</u>. In FS we use *tH* for the sound in *tHat* and *tHe*, and the normal *th* for the sound in *thin* and *thing*, to show the difference.

One sound spelled several ways in CE is the one for which we use the digraph <u>zh</u> in FS: <u>measure</u> (*mezhur*), <u>garage</u> (*gu-rahzh*), <u>vision</u> (*vizhun*). Of course, garage is also pronounced other ways, such as *garij, gurahj,* and *gur-ahzh.*

The sound of <u>wh</u> in <u>when</u> and <u>why</u> is also written *wh* in FS (*when, whie*), if it is actually pronounced as <u>hw</u>, or as <u>w</u> if pronounced as *w*. When <u>wh</u> has an *h* sound, as in <u>who</u>, it is written in FS as *h.* Thus, in FS <u>who</u> is spelled (*hue*). The word written <u>hue</u> in CE is *hyue* in FS, showing the pronunciation clearly. In the word *hue* the h is palatized, or blended with the glide of *y*. In FS this is shown by inserting *y* after h, so there can be no doubt about the pronunciation.

There are many words in conventional spelling that look as if they should be pronounced similarly, but aren't. Notice how FS clears up each difficulty: <u>bead - dead</u> (*beed - ded*), <u>beard - heard</u> (*beerd - hurd*), <u>bomb - tomb</u> (*bahm - tuem*), <u>bowl - fowl</u> (*boel - foul*), <u>breath - wreath</u> (*breth - reeth*), <u>does - toes</u>, (*duz - toez*), <u>fury - bury</u> (*fyoori - beri*), <u>love - wove</u> (*luv - wuev*), <u>laughter - daughter</u> (*laftur - dawtur*), <u>lose - hose</u>, (*luez - hoez*), <u>your - pour - sour</u> (*yoor - poer - sour*), <u>what - chat</u> (*whut - chat*), <u>were - mere</u> (*wur - mir or meer*).

When the letters ordinarily used in Funetik Speling in combination as digraphs (<u>th</u>, <u>ng</u>, etc.) are intended to carry their separate sounds rather than representing a single phoneme, they should be separated by a hyphen (*nut-hous, sun-glassiz*) to eliminate the possibility of confusion. The table on page 774 can be used for convenient reference to the details of Funetik Speling.

Dr. Carolyn Jones has devised a modification of our Funetik Speling, called *Foeneemik Speling*, which incorporates slight modifications in two of our symbols. The distinctive feature of her system is the use of capitalization to indicate accented syllables, which are indicated in our *Funetik Speling* by use of an apostrophe. See page 760 for information on Dr. Jones' Self-Monitoring Cue Card Format.

Funetik Speling

ae tape (taep)	b bed	(c) never used in FS	d deep	ee see	f fat
g get	h hat	ie fine (fien)	j jug	k keep cat (kat)	l let
m man	n net	oe home (hoem)	p pen	r red	s see
t tap	v vest	w week	y yes	z rose (roez)	ch cheese (cheez)
sh shut	tH tHis	th three	wh when	zh vision (vizhun)	ng sing
a cap	ah father (fahtHur) not (naht)	aw caught (kawt)	e egg	i lit	u up
oo book	oi oil boy (boi)	ou out cow (kou)	ue blue moon (muen)	ur her (hur) sir (sur)	q never used in FS

About Charts and Written Materials

Refer to the charts on the next two pages in order to see the overall design and arrangement of Cued Speech. If while learning Cued Speech you get only a limited amount of practice with others who can cue, you may need to refer to the charts occasionally to check the cueing of a specific sound.

Do not specifically try to memorize the groups of sounds from the charts or any written materials. Instead, use the charts to get the right sound with the right cue. Make the sound or think it, and then say it again as you cue it. Do this enough times that the cue comes automatically to mind when you think the *sound* (not the letter). Whenever you have to refer to the charts to verify a cue, produce the sound aloud or mentally a few times before cueing it as you say it. If you have to think the letter to remember the cue, this extra step will slow you considerably, and may make you take longer to become a fluent cuer.

Some people can learn the cues faster by memorizing the sound groups in the charts. Since cueing requires that you associate sounds with cueing, it is better if no visual images are involved. Let your memory of the association of cues with sounds come from producing them together enough times that the association becomes automatic. If you do use the charts for memorization, think the sound rather than the letters. It will help if you spend some time drilling the sounds and syllables. For example, say over and over while moving your hand, making a tiny flick with each sound, in the side location: *tah-tu-toe, mah-mu-moe, fah-fu foe*. Then use the chin location for: *taw-te-tue, maw-me-mue, faw-fe-fue*. If you will proceed to use all the handshapes in all the locations this way, you should soon become able to think the sounds without visualizing the letters.

<u>CUED SPEECH</u>

American English

CHART I
Cues for Vowel Sounds

	<u>Side</u>	<u>Throat</u>	<u>Chin</u>	<u>Mouth</u>
open	ah (father) (got)	a (that)	aw (dog)	
flattened-relaxed	u (but)	i (is)	e (get)	ee (see)
rounded	oe (home)	oo (book)	ue (blue)	ur (her)

CHART II
Diphthongs

ie (my)   ou (cow)   ae (pay)   oi (boy)

CHART III
Cues for Consonant Sounds

t m f	h s r	d p zh	ng y ch	l sh w	k v tH z	b n wh	g j th

VOWEL CHART

OPEN MOUTH

AH
(FATHER)

A
(CAP)

AW
(SAW)

FLAT MOUTH

U
(UP)

I
(SIT)

E
(EGG)

EE
(SEE)

ROUNDED MOUTH

OE
(HOME)

OO
(BOOK)

UE
(BLUE)

UR
(FUR)

DIPHTHONGS

AE
(MATE)

OI
(OIL)

IE
(LIE)

OU
(NOUN)

Cueing Guidelines

In Chapter 29, "The Fine Points of Cueing," you will find details on most aspects of cueing that you are likely to encounter. In general, listen to yourself carefully to determine exactly how you are pronouncing what you say, and cue it that way. When in doubt, get help from a skilled cuer or refer to the Basic Vocabulary of 500 words (p.783), which is presented in both Funetik Speling and Cuescript so that you can determine the cueing of each word for the pronunciation indicated.

Cuescript

Cuescript is a notation developed by Mary Elsie Daisey for the purpose of indicating in writing the appropriate cueing of a specific pronunciation of a word or phrase. In the list below Cuescript is used to show the cueing of 500 words likely to be used by parents with young children. In each case the pronunciation used is the first listed in standard dictionaries of General American English, such as *The Merriam-Webster Dictionary, Webster's Collegiate Dictionary,* and *The Random House Dictionary*. In most cases these sources are in agreement. Where they are not, we have used the pronunciation we think most prevalent. When in doubt go with the pronunciation given, or that indicated by the spelling.

Many cases in which the dictionaries are in disagreement are those involving an unstressed short vowel, such as short *i* and short *e*. For example, in the word *blanket*, the pronunciation of the short *e* is listed as *uh* in the Merriam-Webster dictionaries and as short *i* in *The Random House Dictionary*. The reason for this disparity is that the sound typically used by most people in such situations is about midway between the two sounds, so one is likely to think of it as either one. Sir James Pitman and some other phoneticists have referred (perhaps humorously) to this sound as the *schwi*, between the schwa (*uh*) and the short *i*. Such cases are marked with an asterisk* in the word list.

In Cuescript combinations of horizontal, vertical, and inclined lines, as shown below, are used to represent the handshapes, and the letters *s, t, c,* and *m* are used to indicate the hand locations. Diphthongs are indicated by joining the member letters with—as follows: *ou, o--u; ae, a--e; oi, o--i;* and *ie, i--e*.

Remember that many important words have different pronunciations when they are stressed or unstressed. An example is *to*. When stressed, this word is pronounced *tue*. Usually it is unstressed, and is pronounced either **tu** as in **tummy** or like **too** as in **took**. This would be the case when saying **to go** or **to do**, or in a compound word such as **today** or **tomorrow**. The cuer must decide which his/her pronunciation is.

HAND-SHAPE SYMBOLS   LOCATIONS

⊑	t m f vowel without a consonant before it	s	side ah, oe, uh
		c	chin aw, eh, ue
		t	throat a, i, oo
—	d p zh	m	mouth ee, ur
=	k v tH z	<	ng y ch
≡	h s r	∟	l wh sh
≣	b n wh	∟	ɣ j th

PRIMARY WORDS

ball   baw l   hi   hi--e

                   ≡ ∟   = ⊑

                   c   s   s   t

good girl   goo d   gur l

                   ∟ — ∟ ∟

                   t   s   m   t

| bathroom | ba th rue m | | hot | ha t |
| | t s c s | | | s s |

| come | ku m | | hurry | hur i |
| | s s | | | m t |

| cookie | koo ki | | kiss | ki s |
| | t t | | | t s |

| Daddy | da di | | milk | mi l k |
| | t t | | | t s s |

| dog | daw g | | Mommy | mah mi |
| | c s | | | s t |

| eat | ee t | | no | noe |
| | m s | | | s |

| get up | ge t u p | | shoe | shue |
| | c s s s | | | c |

| go | goe | | sit down | si t do--u n |
| | s | | | t s s t s |

| good boy | goo d bo--i | | stop | s tah p |
| | t s c t | | | s s s |

SIMPLE PHRASES

While learning Cued Speech, practice a few simple phrases and use them as soon as possible with the hearing-impaired child. It is not necessary (or desirable) to wait to learn the whole system and feel proficient with it before beginning to cue to a deaf person.

Come here.	Ku m hi r.	It's big.	I t s bi g.
Watch me.	Wah ch mee.	It's little.	I t s li t l.
That's good.	THa t s goo d.	Help me.	He l p mee.
I love you	I--e lu v yue.	Please.	P lee z.
Don't touch.	Doe n t tu ch.	Thank you.	Tha ng k yue
Let's go.	Le t s goe.	Push it.	Poo shi t.
Show me.	Shoe mee.	Pull it.	Poo li t.
Hurry up.	Hur i u p.	Pick it up.	Pi ki tu p.
Be careful.	Bee ke r fu l.	I see it.	I--e see i t.

Some vowels have different pronunciations when stressed or unstressed. An example is **to**. When stressed, this word is pronounced **tue**. Usually it is unstressed, and is pronounced either **tu** as in **tummy** or like **too** in **took**. The cuer must choose.

It's time to eat.	I t s ti--e m tu ee t.
	t s s s t s s m s
It's time to go to sleep.	I t s ti--e m tu goe tu s lee p.
	t s s s t s s s s s m s
I like that.	I--e li--e k tHa t.
	s t s t s t s
Give it to me.	Gi vi tu mee.
	t t s m
That's pretty.	THa t s p ri ti.
	t s s s t t
What happened?	Whu t ha pu n d?
	s s t s s s
It's all gone.	I t s aw l gaw n.
	t s s c s c s
What color is it?	Whu t ku lur i zi t?
	s s s m t t s
Good morning.	Goo d maw r ni ng.
	t s c s t s

BASIC VOCABULARY

This 500-word basic vocabulary is written in Conventional English, Funetik Speling, and Cuescript. Cue them the way you think you say them, or as shown.

English	Funetik (Cuescript cues below)	English	Funetik (Cuescript cues below)
a	u or a--e — s c t	and	a n d — t s s
about	u bo--u t — s s t s	animal	a ni mu l — t t s s
afraid	u f ra--e d — s s c t s	another	u nu tHur — s s m
after	a f tur — t s m	any	e ni — c t
airplane	e r p la--e n — c s s c t s	apple	a pu l — t s s
all	aw l — c s	are	ah r — s s
almost	aw l moe s t — c s s s s	arm	ah r m — s s s
also	aw l soe — c s s	as	a z — t s
an	a n — t s	ask	a s k — t s s

asleep   u s lee p
         s s   m   s

be   bee
     m

aunt   a n t
       t s s

bear   be r
       c   s

away   u wa--e
       s   c   t

beautiful   b yue ti fu l
            s   c   t   s s

baby   ba--e bi
       c   t t

baloney   bu loe nee
          s   s   m

back   ba k
       t   s

because   bi kaw z
          t   c   s

bad   ba d
      t   s

bed   be d
      c   s

bag   ba g
      t   s

been   bi n
       t   s

ball   baw l
       c   s

before   bi foe r
         t   s   s

banana   bu na nu
         s   t   s

behind   bi hi--e n d
         t   s   t   s s

bath   ba th
       t   s

being   bee i ng
        m   t s

battery   ba tu ri
          t   s   t

bell   be l
       c   s

below   bi loe
≡ ⌊
t s

belt   be l t
≡ ⌊ ⊟
c s s

better   be tur
≡ ⌊
c m

big   bi g
≡ ⌊
t s

bird   bur d
≡ _
m s

birthday   bur th da--e
≡ ⌊ _ ⊟
m s c t

black   b la k
≡ ⌊ ≡
s t s

blanket*   b la ng ki t
≡ ⌊ < ≡ ⊟
s t s t s

blocks   b lah k s
≡ ⌊ ≡ ≡
s s s s

blue   b lue
≡ ⌊
s c

boat   boe t
≡ ⊟
s s

boots   bue t s
≡ ⊟ ≡
c s s

bounce   bo--u n s
≡ ⊟ ⊟ ≡
s t s s

boy   bo--i
≡ ⊟
c t

bread   b re d
≡ ≡ _
s c s

breakfast   b re k fu s t
≡ ≡ _ ⊟ ≡ ⊟
s c s s s s

broken   b roe ku n
≡ ≡ = ≡
s s s s

broom   b rue m
≡ ≡ ⊟
s c s

brother   b ru tHur
≡ ≡ =
s s m

brown   b ro--u n
≡ ≡ ⊟ ≡
s s t s

brush   b ru sh
≡ ≡ ⌊
s s s

bug   bu g
≡ ⌊
s s

burn   bur n
        m   s

cereal   si ri u l
        t   t   s   s

by or bye   bi--e
        s   t

chair   che r
        c   s

cake   ka--e k
        c   t   s

change   cha--e n j
        c   t   s   s

call   kaw l
        c   s

chest   che s t
        c   s   s

can   ka n
        c   s

chew   chue
        c

candy   ka n di
        t   s   t

children   chi l d ru n
        t   s   s   s   s

car   kah r
        s   s

Christmas   K ri s mu s
        s   t   s   s   s

care   ke r
        c   s

church   chur ch
        m   s

carry   ke ri
        c   t

clap   k la p
        s   t   s

cat   ka t
        t   s

clock   k lah k
        s   s   s

catch   ka ch
        t   s

close   k loe s
(adjective)   s   s   s

close (verb)	k loe z	could	koo d
closet*	k lah zi t	cover	ku vur
clothes	k loe th z	cracker	k ra kur
clothes (alternative)	k loe z	crayon	k ra--e ah n
clown	k lo--u n	cream	k ree m
cold	koe l d	cry	k ri--e
color	ku lur	cup	ku p
comb	koe m	cut	ku t
come	ku m	dance	da n s
cookie	koo ki	day	da--e
cough	kaw f	dark	dah r k

different	di f ru n t
	t s s s s
dinner	di nur
	t m
dish	di sh
	t s
do	due
	c
doctor	dah k tur
	s s m
dog	daw g
	c s
doll	dah l
	s s
don't	doe n t
	s s s
door	doe r
	s s
down	do--u n
	s t s
draw	d raw
	s c

dress	d re s
	s c s
drink	d ri ng k
	s t s s
drum	d ru m
	s s s
dry	d ri--e
	s s t
each	ee ch
	m s
ear	i r
	t s
ear (alternative)	i ur
	t m
eat	ee t
	m s
early	ur li
	m t
egg	e g
	c s
eight	a--e t
	c t s

elephant	e lu fu n t	fight	fi--e t
	c s s s s		s t s
empty	e m ti	find	fi--e n d
	c s t		s t s s
enough	i nu f	finger	fi ng gur
	t s s		t s m
even	ee vu n	finished	fi ni sh t
	m s s		t t s s
eyes	i--e z	fire	fi--e r
	s t s		s t s
face	fa--e s	fire (alternative)	fi--e ur
	c t s		s t m
fall	faw l	first	fur s t
	c s		m s s
fast	fa s t	fish	fi sh
	t s s		t s
father	fah tHur	flag	f la g
	s m		s t s
favorite*	fa--e vu ru t	floor	f loe r
	c t s s s		s s s
feel	fee l	flower	f lo--u r
	m s		s s t m

flush	f lu sh	funny	fu ni
	s s s		s t

follow	fah loe	game	ga--e m
	s s		c t s

food	fue d	get	ge t
	c s		c s

foot	foo t	girl	gur l
	t s		m s

for	faw r	give	gi v
	c s		t s

fork	faw r k	glass	g la s
	c s s		s t s

four	foe r	gloves	g lu v z
	s s		s s s s

friend	f re n d	glue	g lue
	s c s s		s c

from	f ru m	go	goe
	s s s		s

from (alternative)	f rah m	God	Gah d
	s s s		s s

full	foo l	going	goe i ng
	t s		s t s

gone　　　gaw n
└ ≡
c　s

Halloween　Hah lu wee n
(alternative)　≡ └ └ ≡
s　s　m　s

good　　　goo d
└ ─
t　s

hamburger　ha m bur gur
≡ ≡ ≡ └
t　s　m　m

granddaddy　g ra n da di
└ ≡ ≡ ─ ─
s　t　s　t　t

hand　　　ha n d
≡ ≡ ─
t　s　s

grandma　g ra n mah
└ ≡ ≡ └
s　t　s　s

hang　　　ha ng
≡ <
t　s

grass　　g ra s
└ ≡ ≡
s　t　s

hard　　　hah r d
≡ ≡ ─
s　s　s

green　　g ree n
└ ≡ ≡
s　m　s

has　　　ha z
≡ ═
t　s

gum　　　gu m
└ ≡
s　s

hat　　　ha t
≡ └
t　s

had　　　ha d
≡ ─
t　s

have　　　ha v
≡ ═
t　s

hair　　　he r
≡ ≡
c　s

he　　　hee
≡
m

happy　　ha pi
≡ ─
t　t

head　　　he d
≡ ─
c　s

Halloween　Ha lu wee n
≡ └ └ ≡
t　s　m　s

hear　　　hi r
≡ ≡
t　s

hearing aid	hi ri ng a--e d t t s c t s	hop	hah p s s
heat	hee t m s	horse	haw r s c s s
hello	he loe c s	hot	hah t s s
help	he l p c s s	how	ho--u s t
her	hur m	hug	hu g s s
hi	hi--e s t	hungry	hu ng g ri s s s t
high	hi--e s t	hurry	hur i m t
his	hi z t s	hurt	hur t m s
hit	hi t t s	ice	i--e s s t s
hold	hoe l d s s s	if	i f t s
home	hoe m s s	in	i n t s

into	i n tue		ketchup	ke chu p
	t s c			c s s
is	i z		kick	ki k
	t s			t s
it	i t		kitchen	ki chu n
	t s			t s s
itch	i ch		kitty	ki ti
	t s			t t
it's	i t s		knee	nee
	t s s			m
jacket	ja ku t		knife	ni--e f
	t s s			s t s
jello	je loe		knock	nah k
	c s			s s
jelly	je li		lady	la--e di
	c t			c t t
juice	jue s		lamp	la m p
	c s			t s s
jump	ju m p		lap	la p
	t s s			t s
just	ju s t		large	lah r j
	s s s			s s s

laugh	la f · t s	light	li--e t · s t s
last	la s t · t s s	like	li--e k · s t s
late	la--e t · c t s	lion	li--e u n · s t s s
leaf	lee f · m s	lip	li p · t s
leave	lee v · m s	listen	li su n · t s s
leg	le g · c s	little	li tu l · t s s
let	le t · c s	live (verb)	li v · t s
letter	le tur · c s	living room	li vi ng rue m · t t s c s
lick	li k · t s	look	loo k · t s
lid	li d · t s	lost	law s t · c s s
lie	li--e · s t	loud	lo--u d · s t s

love   lu v
    └ ═
    s s

me   mee
    ≡
    m

lunch   lu n ch
    └ ≡ ˂
    s s s

meal   mee l
    ≡ └
    m s

made   ma--e d
    └ └ _
    ≡ ≡
    c t s

meat   mee t
    └ └
    ≡ ≡
    m s

mail   ma--e l
    └ └ └
    ≡ ≡
    c t s

meet   mee t
    └ └
    ≡ ≡
    m s

make   ma--e k
    └ └ ═
    ≡ ≡
    c t s

mess   me s
    └ ≡
    ≡
    c s

man   ma n
    └ ≡
    ≡
    t s

milk   mi l k
    └ └ ═
    ≡
    t s s

many   me ni
    └ ≡
    ≡
    c t

mine   mi--e n
    └ └
    ▬ ≡
    s t s

marbles   mah r bu l z
    └ ≡ ≡ └ ═
    ≡
    s s s s s

mirror   mi rur
    └ ≡
    ≡
    t m

march   mah r ch
    └ ≡ ˂
    ≡
    s s s

mittens   mi tu n z
    └ └ ≡ ═
    ≡ ≡
    t s s s

match   ma ch
    └ ˂
    ≡
    t s

mommy   mah mi
    └ └
    ≡ ≡
    s t

may   ma--e
    └ └
    ≡ ≡
    c t

money   mu ni
    └ ≡
    ≡
    s t

| mop | mah p | name | na--e m |
| | s   s | | c t s |

| more | moe r | nap | na p |
| | s   s | | t   s |

| morning | maw r ni ng | napkin* | na p ki n |
| | c   s   t   s | | t s t s |

| most | moe s t | need | nee d |
| | s   s   s | | m s |

| mother | mu tHur | next | ne k s t |
| | s   m | | c s s s |

| mouth | mo--u th | new | nue |
| | s   t   s | | c |

| move | mue v | nice | ni--e s |
| | c   s | | s   t   s |

| much | mu ch | night | ni--e t |
| | s   s | | s   t   s |

| must | mu s t | nine | ni--e n |
| | s   s   s | | s   t   s |

| my | mi--e | noise | no--i z |
| | s   t | | c   t   s |

| nail | na--e l | nose | noe z |
| | c   t   s | | s   s |

not   nah t
       s   s

now   no--u
       s   t

of   u v
       s   s

off   aw f
       c   s

okay   oe ka--e
       s   c   t

on   aw n
       c   s

one   wu n
       s   s

only   oe n li
       s   s   t

open   oe pu n
       s   s   s

or   aw r
       c   s

orange   aw ri n j
       c   t   s   s

our   o--u r
       s   t   s

out   o--u t
       s   t   s

own   oe n
       s   s

pajamas   pu jah mu z
       s   s   s   s

pants   pa n t s
       t   s   s   s

paper   pa--e pur
       c   t   m

paste   pa--e s t
       c   t   s   s

pat   pa t
       t   s

peach   pee ch
       m   s

peanut butter   pee nu t bu tur
       m   s   s   m

pear   pe r
       c   s

peek   pee k

pink   pi ng k

pen   pe n

pitcher   pi chur

pencil   pe n su l

plate   p la--e t

penny   pe ni

play   p la--e

pick   pi k

please   p lee z

pickle   pi ku l

pocket   pah ku t

picture   pi k chur

pocketbook   pah ku t boo k

pie   pi--e

pour   poe r

piece   pee s

pop   pah p

pillow   pi loe

potatoes   pu ta--e toe z

pin   pi n

porch   poe r ch

potty	pah ti	rain	ra--e n
	s c		c t s
present	p re zu n t	ready	re di
	s c s s s		s t
pretend	p ri te n d	record (noun)	re kur d
	s t c s s		c m s
pretty	p ri ti	record (verb)	ri kaw r d
	s t t		t c s s
pull	poo l	refrigerator	ri f ri jur a--e tur
	t s		t s t m c t m
purple	pur pu l	ribbon	ri bu n
	m s s		t s s
push	poo sh	ride	ri--e d
	t s		s t s
puzzle	pu zu l	right	ri--e t
	s s s		s t s
quick	k wi k	ring	ri ng
	s t s		t s
quiet	k wi--e u t	robe	roe b
	s s t s s		s s
quite	k wi--e t	rock	rah k
	s s t s		s s

roll   roe l

rope   roe p

rough   ru f

rub   ru b

rug   ru g

run   ru n

sad   sa d

said   se d

salt   saw l t

same   sa--e m

sand   sa n d

sandwich   sa n d wi ch

say   sa--e

school   s kue l

scissors   si zur z

scratch   s k ra ch

screen   s k ree n

scrub   s k ru b

see   see

seven   se vu n

shadow   sha doe

shake   sha--e k

sharp	shah r p	sick	si k
	s s s		t s
she	shee	since	si n s
	m		t s s
sheet	shee t	sink	si n k
	m s		t s s
shelf	she l f	sister	si s tur
	c s s		t s m
shirt	shur t	sit	si t
	m s		t s
shoes	shue z	six	si k s
	c s		t s s
shorts	shaw r t s	skip	s ki p
	c s s s		s t s
should	shoo d	skirt	s kur t
	t s		s m s
shoulder	shoe l dur	sky	s ki--e
	s s m		s s t
show	shoe	sleep	s lee p
	s		s m s
shut	shu t	sleeves	s lee v z
	s s		s m s s

slide	s li--e d	soft	saw f t
	s s t s		c s s
slip	s li p	some	su m
	s t s		s s
slow	s loe	son	su n
	s s		s s
small	s maw l	sore	soe r
	s c s		s s
smell	s me l	sorry	sah ri
	s c s		s t
smile	s mi--e l	spank	s pa ng k
	s s t s		s t s s
smoke	s moe k	spoon	s pue n
	s s s		s c s
snake	s na--e k	stand	s ta n d
	s c t s		s t s s
snow	s noe	star	s tah r
	s s		s s s
soap	soe p	stay	s ta--e
	s s		s c t
socks	sah k s	steps	s te p s
	s s s		s c s s

stomach	s tu mu k	teacher	tee chur
	s s s s		m m
stop	s tah p	tears (noun)	ti r z
	s s s		t s s
stove	s toe v	tears (verb)	teh r z
	s s s		c s s
sugar	shoo gur	teeth	tee th
	t m		m s
sun	su n	tell	te l
	s s		c s
sweater	s we tur	telephone	te lu foe n
	s c m		c s s s
swing	s wi ng	television	te lu vi zhu n
	s t s		c s t s s
table	ta--e bu l	ten	te n
	c t s s		c s
take	ta--e k	thank	tha ng k
	c t s		t s s
talk	taw k	thanks	tha ng k s
	c s		t s s s
tape	ta--e p	that	tHa t
	c t s		t s

the	tHuh or tHee		tissue	ti shue
their	tHe r		too, two	tue
them	tHe m		toast	toe s t
there	tHe r		today	tu da--e
three	th ree		toes	toe z
throat	th roe t		toilet	to--i lu t
throw	th roe		tomato	tu ma--e toe
thumb	thu m		tongue	tu ng
tickle	ti ku l		took	too k
tie	ti--e		toothpaste	tue th pa--e s t
tiger	ti--e gur		touch	tu ch

towel	to--u l	upside down	u p si--e d do--u n
	s t s		s s s t s s t s
toy	to--i	us	u s
	c t		s s
tree	t ree	use	yue z
	s m		c s
truck	t ru k	vaccination*	va k su na--e shu n
	s s s		t s s c t s s
tub	tu b	vacuum	va k yoo m
	s s		t s t s
tummy	tu mi		va k yue m
	s t		t s c s
turn	tur n		va k yu m
	m s		t s s s
umbrella	u m b re lu	very	ve ri
	s s s c s		c t
uncle	u ng ku l	voice	vo--i s
	s s s s		c t s
under	u n dur	wagon	wa gu n
	s s m		t s s
up	u p	wait	wa--e t
	s s		c t s

wake	wa--e k		where	whe r
	c t s			c s
walk	waw k		which	whi ch
	c s			t s
wall	waw l		white	whi--e t
	c s			s t s
want	waw n t		who	hue
	c s s			c
was	wu z		whose	hue z
	s s			c s
wash	waw sh		will	wi l
	c s			t s
wash	wah sh		window	wi n doe
	s s			t s s
water	wah tur		wink	wi ng k
	s m			t s s
watch	wah ch		wipe	wi--e p
	s s			s t s
went	we n t		work	wur k
	c s s			m s
wet	we t		would	woo d
	c s			t s

write	ri--e t	yes	ye s
wrong	raw ng	yet	ye t
yawn	yaw n	your	yoo r
year	yi r	you	yue
yell	ye l	zipper	zi pur
yellow	ye loe	zoo	zue

Practice Primer

The 488 short phrases and sentences below are intended to be useful in communication with a young child. These have a twofold purpose: to give parents an idea of what to talk about with their young deaf child and to provide appropriate material for use in practicing cueing phrases and sentences. Spend some time each day cueing part of this material when the child is not present, in order to develop proficiency. Then try to use some of it with your child, when appropriate. Speed and fluency in cueing develop most rapidly if some time is devoted to practice each day, even if the practice periods are short.

What do you want, <u>name</u>?
Tell me what you want.
Do you want candy?
Show me, <u>name</u>.

What's the matter, <u>name</u>?
What is wrong?
Tell me about it.
What happened?

What do you say?
Thank you, Daddy.
Please, may I have it?
No, thank you.

Please don't throw the ball.
Play with the ball outside.
Throw the ball to the dog.
Roll it to him.

Get your sweater.
You must wear your sweater.
It's late. Hurry up.
It's time to go.

Are you sleepy?
Let's go to bed.
It's time to go to sleep.
It's time for a nap.
Go upstairs now.

Hot! Don't touch it!
It is hot.
It will burn you.
Be careful.

Do you need some help?
Okay. I will help you.
Wait a minute.
Let me help you.
Now you do it.

That does not belong to you.
Do not touch it.
That is Mommy's.
Put it back where it belongs.

Come with me.

This is candy.
You may have a piece of candy.
Do you want a cookie, <u>name</u>?
You may have a cookie, too.

Don't cry, ____.
Act like a big girl.
You are acting like a baby.
Behave yourself.

Your sister is having trouble.
Can you help her?
Your brother needs some help.
Will you help him?

Let's go outside.
Wait, ____. Wait.
It's cool outside.
You will need a sweater.

Wait. Hold it!
Your shoes are all dirty.
Wipe your shoes first.
Take off your shoes outside.

My hands are full.
Shut the door for me.
It's cold outside.
Shut the door, please.
Shut it tight.

Pick it up.
Put it down.
Push it.
Pull it.

Wake up. It's time to get up.
Good morning.
Are you ready to get up?
Run to the bathroom.
Hurry and get dressed.

That is music.
Do you hear the music?
Can you hear the pretty music?
It's loud.

Do you want to go outside?

Can you run?
Let's run.
Run after ___.
Run fast!
Let's see who can run fastest.

Now we are ready to go out.
Open the door.
It's cold, isn't it?
Brrr! It's so cold!

Do you want water?
Would you like some water?
Do you want a drink of water?
Here is a drink of water for you.

That's your rocking chair.
Rock in your rocking chair.
Rock your baby to sleep.
Rock a bye, baby.
Rock, rock, rock, rock.
Rockety, rockety, rock.

You're slow (fast).
Find your cap and put it on.
It's muddy outside.
You need your boots.
Get your boots.
Get them.

I can't hear you.
Use your voice.
Lower your voice.
Your voice is too loud (high).

It's time to go to bed.
It's past your bedtime.
You have to go to bed now.
Put on your pajamas.
Brush your teeth.
Brush them very well.
Now rinse your mouth.

Look at those hands!
They're dirty!
Go wash them.
Don't forget to dry your hands.
Let me see your hands.
Sorry, they are still dirty.
Wash again.
Use the soap.
Use hot water.
Now they look much better.

Not now.
In a little while.
After supper.
We will go in an hour.
We will go in half an hour.
WE will go in 15 minutes.
We will go in a few minutes.

It's time to go out and play.
Stay in the yard.
You may take your bike out.
Jane, where is your wagon?
Put your wagon away.

Let's go outside now.
It is cold outside.
Let's put on your coat.
Here's your hat.
Put it on.

Daddy is going bye, bye.
Daddy is going to work.
He will go to work in the car.
Say goodbye to Daddy.

Let me see your baby.
Nice baby.
Isn't she cute?
That's your baby.

Where's your coat?
You need a coat.
Go get your coat.
Let's put on your coat.
Button it.
Button it all the way down.

Don't be selfish.
Take turns.
Let her play with it now.
You have to share your toys.
Share them.
Share them with her.

That's your sister's toy.
Ask her if you can play with it.
That's your brother's.
Leave it alone.

Oh, you fell down. I'm sorry.
Let me see.
Now, be brave. Don't cry.
I'll fix the cut.
This will hurt a little.
There, it's better now.
Do you want a band-aid on it?

Your room is a mess.
Get your dirty socks.
Put them in the hamper.
Hang up your shirt.
Put your shoes in the closet.
Put them side by side.
That looks neat.
Put your clothes in the drawer.
Let's make up your bed.
Make it all smooth.

We can't go until Daddy comes.
We can go when the baby wakes up.
You can't go swimming yet.
You must brush your teeth first.
You have to clean your room.
Make your bed before you go.
You can go after your dinner.

Get on the swing.
Do you want me to push you?
You are going high!
Be careful. Not too high.
Don't swing any higher.

Don't leave it outside.

Here's a new toy.
Wind it up. Make it go.
Not too tight. Don't break it.
Oh! You broke it.
That's too bad. I'm sorry.

What is that?
Open it.
Show it to me.
Don't do that.
You might drop it.
Please don't break it.

We're going to_____.
Do you want to go with me?
Come on, it's time to go.
You don't need a coat.
It's warm outside.
Go out the back door, please.
Shut the door, please.

That's not for you.
I'll take it away.
Let_____play with your____.
Let_____have a turn.
Now give it to_____.

Now put on your socks and shoes.
Now, red socks to match your dress.
Where are your red socks?
Here are your red socks.
First, we'll put on this sock.
Now this sock. Two socks. There.

Now get off the swing.

Go and play with _____.
Don't fight.
Be nice to him.
Share your toys.
Let him play with your cars.

Look up at the sky.
The clouds are black.
It's starting to rain.
It's raining.
Stay on the porch.
Then you won't get wet.

Let's get dressed now.
First we put on your shirt.
Then we put on your aids.
Put them in your ears.
Turn it down. It's too loud.
It's whistling. Turn it down.
Can you hear now?

Let's put on your dress (pants).
Isn't this a pretty dress?
I like this dress.
Do you like your dress?
Stand still. Let me button it.

Now, where are your shoes?
Let's look for them.
Here they are, under the bed.
How many shoes? Yes, two shoes.
Now we have on one shoe.
Now both shoes are on.

Use simple sentences about all articles of clothing.

It's time to comb your hair.
Show me your hair.
Where is the comb?
Let's use a brush first.
Let me put a bow in your hair.
That looks nice.
Look at yourself in the mirror.
You look very nice.

Sit down.
Here is a sandwich for you.
You need some milk.
Give me your glass.
I will pour some milk for you.
There it is. Drink some milk.
Have you finished your sandwich?
Do you want more milk?
Here's some.
Now use your napkin.

Come eat supper.
Do you like spaghetti?
Would you like some more?
Say, no thank you.

Daddy is in the basement.
He's using his saw right now.
I hear it. Can you hear it?
Can you hear Daddy's saw?

It's time to eat.
Are you hungry?
Go get your bib.
Your hands are dirty.
See how dirty they are.
Let's go wash them.
Wash them very well.
Now we are ready to eat lunch.

Do you want a banana?
Or, do you want an apple?
Isn't that good?
Are you finished already?
I have some cookies.
Do you want a cookie?
It tastes good.
Do you want another cookie?
Okay, here it is.
It's a different kind.

You should eat some vegetables.
Try one bite, please.
Use your fork.
Pass me the salad, please.

We have cake for dessert.
It's delicious.
No, we are not having ice cream
We can't have it every day.

Would you like to go watch Daddy?
He will use his hammer next.
And some nails.
Go help Daddy.
Go hand Daddy some nails.

Pick up your toys.
Put them away, where they belong.
They belong in your bedroom.
Put the books in the bookcase.
The toys go on the shelf.

Mother has to work in the kitchen now.
Would you like to help me?
I'm going to make a nice cake.
Get out the pans for me.
This cake will have two layers.
It's like two cakes, one on top of the other.

Here's the flour.
Now we need eggs and milk.
Go to the refrigerator and get three eggs for me.
There, the cake is ready to bake.
I'll put it in the oven.
After it bakes, you can help me make the icing.
We will put icing on the cake to make it pretty.

Would you like a drink?
Turn on the cold water.
When you are finished, put the glass in the sink.
We need to wash all the glasses before supper.

Look on the porch.
Your dog is waiting for you.
He's wagging his tail.
We wants you to play with him.

Look out of the window.
It's starting to rain.
The wind is blowing the trees.
It's making them bend.

We're going to have a storm.
You must play inside today.
You may watch TV now, for a while.
Turn it on.
No, don't watch that program.
Let's find a good show.
Do you want to watch this show?
It's about Lassie.
You always like the Lassie shows.
Move back. Don't sit too close.
Sit over there. Can you see okay?

Now the show is over.
Turn off the television, please.
Did you like the story.
Let's talk about the story.
Did Lassie get hurt?
What part did you like best?
Are you going to play now?
Go get your friend ____.
What are you going to play?
Can you play hide-and-seek?
Let's play tag now.

As your cueing becomes proficient, begin providing a running commentary on each video program. If you have a VCR, consider making recordings of several good programs. When you play them back, you can stop the tape, comment or explain, and go on. This can make it possible for the deaf child to get everything, since he/she can ask you to stop the tape when he/she has a question. Later, the child can operate the pause button when she/he wants to ask a question.

Baseball is fun.
Let's play baseball.
Be careful with the bat.
Don't let it hit your brother.
He's too close.

Move away, ___.
The bat might slip.
I will pitch the ball to you.
Hit the ball with the bat.
Now, catch the ball.

It's time to go in.
Let's go in the house.
Now ____ has to go home.
No, his mother says he can't stay.
He must go home.

Get your puzzles and games.
We will play until bedtime.
Would you rather read a book?
Okay, let's pick a book.
Now, turn the pages carefully.

You're sleepy. You look sleepy.
Let's get ready for bed.

Let's take off your clothes.
Are you ready for a bath?

Go to the bathroom. I will come.

Now you can get in the tub.

I'll turn on the water.
Some hot and some cold.
Oh! The water's too hot.
I'll put in more cold water.
I'll wash your back.
You can't reach it very well.

You can get out of the tub now.
Here's your towel.
Wrap it around you.
First, dry your face.
Then dry all over.
Rub your wet tummy.

Are you sleepy yet?
let's say your prayers now.
Now you're ready to get in bed.
Lie down and cover up.
Now give me a kiss.
Good night. Sleep well.

Wait for me.
I'm a slowpoke.
Don't walk on the grass.
Stay on the sidewalk, please.

We need to buy some bread (etc.).
We also need milk and cereal.
Push the cart for me.
Put the bread in the cart, please.
Don't touch that.
No, we don't need any of that.

Now we must pay for our food.
We have to buy it.
We will give the lady the money.
You carry the small bag.
I'll carry the big bag.
And another little bag too.

Are you hungry?
It's time to eat dinner.
Come to the table.
Let's pray.
Okay, I'll cut your meat.
Do you want gravy on your potatoes?

Be careful. That dish is hot.
Pass the beans to _____.
Don't spill them. The dish is full.
No coffee for you. Just milk.
You may have more milk.
Do your want more?

You ate all your dinner.
Very good.
You cleaned up your plate.
Now you may have some dessert.
We are going to have ice cream.

Let's scrub you all over.
Let's wash your face and neck.
Wash your legs now. Use soap.
Scrub your dirty knees.
No! Don't splash.
You will get me wet.

I will dry your back.
Let's put powder on your back.
Don't waste it. Just a little.
Now get your pajamas.
Let's put them on.
First the tops, then the bottoms.

Let's go for a walk.
Don't cross the street yet.
We have to wait for the light.
The light is red. Wait.
The light is green. We can go.
You are walking too fast.

Let's go to the store.
We have to go shopping.
Where is my purse?
Thank you for getting it.

Put it down.
Don't go away.
Stay here with me.
Get the cereal.
Which kind do you want?
That's okay. Fine.

We are going to ride on the bus.
It's coming. Here it comes.
It will stop for us.
Get on the bus.
Here's a seat for both of us.
Do you want to sit by the window?
You can see better there.
Don't stand up yet.
We're not there yet.
No, not now.
Here we are.
It's time to get off.
Wait for me.

Use your spoon.
Don't eat with your fingers.
Daddy wants the salt.
Give it to him.
Don't do that. You might drop it.
You might break the dish.

Let's read a bedtime story.
You pick out a book.
Bring me the book.
Sit here with me.
Now let me read to you.

With a young child, teach names of foods and utensils found on the table. Then, let the child help you set the table.

References

Advisory Committee on the Education of the Deaf, Homer D. Babbidge, Chairman.(1965, March). *Education of the deaf—A report to the secretary of health, education, and welfare.* Washington, DC: U.S. Dept. of Health, Education and Welfare.

Air, D. & Wood, A. (1985). In Newman, P., Creaghead, N. & Secord, W. *Assessment and remediation of articulatory and phonological disorders.* Columbus, OH: Charles E. Merrill Publishing Company.

Alegría, J., DeJean, K., Capouillez, J., & Leybaert, J. (1990). Role played by the Cued Speech in the identification of written words encountered for the first time by deaf children. *Cued Speech Journal, 4,* 4-9.

Allen, T. (1986). A study of the achievement patterns of hearing-impaired students, 1974-1983. In M. Karchmer & and A. Schildroth (Eds.), *Deaf children in America* (pp,161-206). Boston: Little Brown & Co.

Atkins, D., (Ed.),(1987, Sept.). Families and their hearing-impaired children. *Volta Review, special issue.*

Bell, A. (1892) Testimony before the Royal Commission on the state of the deaf, the blind, and the dumb. In Joseph C. Gordon (Ed.), *Education of deaf children: Evidence of Edward Miner Gallaudet and Alexander Graham Bell.* Washington, DC: Volta Bureau, 262 pp.

Bentley, T. (1984). Bell, Alexander Graham. *Encyclopedia Britannica, 2,* pp. 827-828.

Berendt, H., Krupnik-Goldman, B., & Rupp, K. (1990) *Receptive and expressive language abilities of hearing-impaired children who use Cued Speech.* Master's thesis, Col. State Univ., Fort Collins, CO.

Berger, K. (1972) *Speechreading principles and methods.* Baltimore, Md. National Educational Press, p. 127.

Bornstein, H., Saulnier, K., & Hamilton, L. (1980) Signed English: A first evaluation. *American Annals of the Deaf, 125,* 467-481.

Bragg, B. (1990) Communication & the deaf community: Where do we go from here? In Garretson, M., (Ed.), *Communication issues among deaf people,* A *Deaf American* monograph. Silver Apring, MD: National Association of the Deaf, p.9.

Brill, R. (1978) *Mainstreaming the prelingually deaf child.* Washington, DC: Gallaudet Press. 1978.

Bunger, A. (1952) *Speech reading—Jena Method.* (rev. ed.) The Interstate Co.

Charlier, B. & Paulissen, D. (1986) Speech audiometry and Cued Speech. *Otica, 10,* No. 19.

Clickener, P. (1991, Jan./Feb.) Taking the mystery out of cochlear implants. *SHHH Journal,* pp. 11-14.

Coats, G. Dewey (1930). *American Annals of the Deaf, 75,* 157, 193.

Commission on Education of the Deaf. (1988). *Toward equality, education of the deaf.* Washington, DC: U.S. Goverment Printing Office.

812

Cornett, R.O. (1972) A study of the readability of Cued Speech. *Cued Speech Training and Follow-up Program,* Project report to the United States Office of Education, 45-72. Washington, DC: U.S. Department of Health, Education and Welfare.

Cornett, R. (1990, fall) Must listening be first? *Our Kids Magazine,* 8-9.

Crammatte, A.B. (1962). The adult deaf in professions. *American Annals of the Deaf, 107, 575.*

Fauth, B., and Fauth, W. (1967, February). *A study of the proceedings of the Convention of American Instructors of the Deaf, 1850-1949.* Bulletin no.2. Convention of American Instructors of the Deaf.

Furth, H. G. (1966) *Thinking without language: Psychological implications of deafness.* New York: Free Press.

Geers, A., Moog, J., & Schick, B.(1984). Acquisition of spoken and signed English by profoundly hearing impaired children. *Journal of Speech and Hearing Disorders, 49,* 378-388.

Hage, C., Alegría, J., & Périer, O. (1990). Cued Speech and language acquisition: with specifics related to grammatical gender. Paper presented at the Second International Congress on Cognition, Education, and Deafness, July, 1989. *Cued Speech Journal, 4,* pp. 39-46.

Hudson, A. (1980) *Co-articulation* - (Handouts from a workshop). Baton Rouge, Louisiana State University.

Jaffé, M. (1986) Neurological impairment of speech production, assessment and treatment. In J. Costello, & A. Holland (Eds.) *Handbook of speech and language disorders.*(pp. 166-186). San Diego, CA: College-Hill Press.

Kidd, J. (1977) Parents and public law 94-142. In G. Nix (Ed.), *The rights of deaf children.* (pp. 275-280). Washington, DC: Alexander Graham Bell Association for the Deaf, Inc.

Knight, Jane (1992, March/April). Climbing mountains, and My son at seven ... My rock of Gibraltar, *SHHH Journal, 13,* No. 2, pp. 22-25.

Lane, H. (1976). *The wild boy of Aveyron.* Cambridge: Harvard University Press.

Lasensky, J. (1979). Use of Cued Speech with a deaf-blind child. Unpublished communication with Cornett.

Ling, D. (1976) *Speech and the hearing impaired child: Theory and practice.* Washington, DC: Alexander Graham Bell Association for the Deaf, Inc.

Ling, D. & Ling, A. (1978) *Aural rehabilitation - The foundations of verbal learning in hearing-impaired children.* Washington, DC: Alexander Graham Bell Association for the Deaf, Inc.

Ling, D. (Ed.). (1984) *Early intervention for hearing impaired children: Oral options.* San Diego, CA: College Hill Press. pp. 12-13.

Ling, D. (1985, September). The effects of hearing impairment. *Newsounds,* Alexander Graham Bell Association for the Deaf.

Ling, D. (1990) *Foundations of spoken language for hearing-impaired children.* Washington, DC: Alexander Graham Bell Association for the Deaf, Inc.

Low, G., Newman, P., & Ranston, M. (1985) From P. Newman, N. Creaghead, & W. Secord, *Assessment and remediation of articulatory and phonological disorders.* Columbus, OH: Charles E. Merrill Publishing Co.

Lowell, E. (1959). *Research in speech reading: some relationships to language development and implications for the classroom teacher.* Proceedings of the 39th Convention of American Instructors of the Deaf.

McGinnis, M. (1963) *Aphasic Children.* St. Louis, MO: Alexander Graham Bell Association for the Deaf.

Neef, N., & Iwata, B. (1985) The development of generative lipreeading skills in deaf persons using Cued Speech training. *Analysis and Intervention in Developmental Disabilities, 5,* 289-305.

Newman, P., Creaghead, N., & Secord, W. (1985) *Assessment and Remediation of Articulatory and Phonological Disorders.* Columbus, OH: Charles E. Merrill Publishing Company. p. 296.

Nicholls, G. & Ling, D. (1982, June). Cued Speech and the reception of spoken language. *Journal of Speech and Hearing Research, 25,* pp.262-269.

Nitchie, E.B. (1930) *Lip-reading: Principles and practices.* Rev. by E.H. Nitchie. New York: F. Stokes & Co.

Nix, G. (Ed.) (1977) *The rights of hearing-impaired children.* Washington, DC: Alexander Graham Bell Association for the Deaf.

Périer, O., Charlier, P., Hage, C., & Alegría, J. (1987). Evaluation of the effects of prolonged exposure to Cued Speech practice upon reception of spoken language. In I.G. Taylor (Ed.), *The Education of the Deaf - Current Perspectives, Vol. 1, 1985 International Congress on the Education of the Deaf.* pp.616-628, Beckenham, Kent, UK. Croom Helm, Ltd. *(Reprinted in the Cued Speech Journal, 4, 1990).*

Périer, O., Bochner-Wuidar, A., Everarts, B., & Michiels, J. (1986). The combination of Cued Speech and Signed French to improve spoken language acquisition by young deaf children. *Signs of Life: Proceedings of the second European congress on sign language research, Amsterdam July 14-18, 1985.* Bernard T. Tervoort (Ed.). Reprinted in Cued Speech Journal, 4, 1990.

Peterson, M. (1991) Data on language of profoundly deaf children with oral, signing and Cued Speech backgrounds. Unpublished data supplied by correspondence.

Pickett, J., & McFarland, W. (1985) Auditory implants and tactile aids for the profoundly deaf. *Journal of Speech and Hearing Research, 28.*

Pintner, R., & Patterson, D. (1916). A measure of the language ability of deaf children. *Psychological Review, 23,* 414-436.

Quigley, S. & Paul, P. (1984) *Language and Deafness.* San Diego, CA: College-Hill Press.

Riley, A. (1980, Fall). Normalizing the Deaf Child. *The North American Montessori Teachers' Association Quarterly, 6,* 1, 10-15.(Also reprinted in the May, 1981 issue of *Cued Speech News.*

814

Rosenbek, J., Hansen, R., Baughman, C., & Lemme, M. (1974). Treatment of developmental apraxia of speech: A case study. *Language, Speech, and Hearing Services in Schools, 5,* 13-22.

Shelton, I., & Garves, M. (1985). Use of visual techniques in therapy for developmental apraxia of speech. *Language, Speech, and Hearing Services in Schools, 16,* (2), 129-31.

Sneed, N. (1972).The effects of training in Cued Speech on syllable lipreading scores of normally hearing subjects. *Cued Speech Parent Training and Follow-Up Program,* 38-44. Project report to the U.S. Office of Education. Washington, DC: Department of Health, Education and Welfare. (Annotated in the *Cued Speech Journal, 4,* 1990, p. 96.)

Stokoe, W., Jr. (1971). An outline of the visual communication systems of the American deaf. *Studies in Linguistics, Occasional Paper No.8,* 1960.

Stokoe, W. Jr. (1972). *Semiotics and human sign language.* The Hague. Mouton.

Tade, W. (1991). *Basic articulation, language, learning (B.A.L.L.) program. Texas Journal of Audiology and Speech Pathology, XVII,* No. 1.

Tervoort, B. (1970, September 15). In *Research and Communications Brief,* V No.2, from *Analysis of Communicative Structure Patterns in Deaf Children,* Tervoort (RD-467. 1967).

Turner, A. (1990) Cochlear implants for Cued Speech children. *Cued Speech Center Lines.* Oct.1989/Jan.1990, 10-15.

Vernon, M. (1970) Deaf not dumb. *Listen to the Sounds of Deafness.* Miller, E. & Bentley, E. (Eds.) Silver Spring, Maryland. National Association of the Deaf.

Walter, G., and MacLeod-Gallinger, J. (1989) *Employment attainments of deaf ddults one and ten years after graduation from high school.* Office of Postsecondary Career Studies and Institutional Research, National Technical Institute for the Deaf, by agreement between the Rochester Institute of Technology and the U.S. Office of Education.

Wandel, J. (1989) *Use of internal speech in reading by hearing and hearing-impaired students in oral, total communication and Cued Speech programs.* Unpublished doctoral dissertation, Teachers College, Columbia University, New York, NY. An extended annotation is in the *Cued Speech Journal, 4,* 1990, pp. 1-3.

Wrightstone, J., Aranow, M., and Muskowitz, S. (1963) Developing reading test norms for the deaf child. *American Annals of the Deaf, 108,* 311-316.

Yoss, K., & Darley, F. (1974). Developmental apraxia of speech in children with defective articulation. *Journal of Speech and Hearing Research, 17,* 399-416.

Index of Authors

Abell, Holly, 630
Abell, Janie, 555
Advisory Committee on Education of the Deaf, 6, 386
Air, D., & Wood, A., 667, 811
Alegría, J., DeJean, K., Capouillez, J., & Leybaert, J., 165, 257, 695
Allen, T., 14
Balderson, Linda, 123, 547
Bazureau, Ariane, 600
Beadles-Hay, Ardith, 452, 469
Bell, A., 4, 5, 152, 153, 164, 168, 179
Bell, Cheri, 593
Berendt, H., Krupnick-Goldman, & Rupp, 159, 699
Bornstein, H., Saulnier, K., & Hamilton, L., 153
Bragg, Bernard, 492
Branscome, Amy, 353
Branscome, Courtney, 563-564
Bunger, A., 177
Burton, Toby, 578
Burton, Winifred, 527
Capouillez, J.M., 98
Center for Assessment and Demographic Studies, 14
Cervantes Gómez, Carlos, 580
Charlier, B., 166, 191, 365, 699
Clements, Aine, 279
Clements, Deidre, 558
Clements, Sinead, 575
Clickener, P., 209
Coats, G. Dewey, 19
Commission on Education of the Deaf, 7, 386
Conrad, R., 14
Consacro, Donna, 480
Cornett, Orin, 20, 202, 497, 743, 747
Costello, Malcolm, 445
Cottam, Daniel, 565, 566
Cottam, David, 356
Crosby, Osmond, 641.
Croyere, Guénolé, 579
Daisey, Mary Elsie, 25, 300
Dejean, K., 98
Dennis, Deborah, 347
Diffell, Joy, 597
Diffell, Leah, 286

Diffell, Tom and Lisa, 319
Dolan, Jane Henegar, 277
Dowling, Beth, 202
Efron, Ros, 407
Engelman, Alina, 568
Engelman, Synnove Trier- & Engelman, Ralph, 362
Fasold, Brett, 571
Fasold, Cory, 285
Fasold, Patricia 412
Fellows, Jay, 447
Flanagan, Marianne, 660
Fleetwood, Earl, 287
Fleetwood, Elizabeth, 321
Furth, H., 150
Geers, A., Moog, J., & Schick, B., 15, 150, 812
Gildea, Maria, 452, 487
Goodall, Beth, 284
Goodall, Kathy, 47
Goodall, Robert, 444
Gourhand, Noémi, 590
Griffith, Kimberley Perry, 282
Hage, C., Alegría, J., & Périer, O., 45, 157, 159, 341, 378, 496, 696
Hakim, Penny,   234
Hanumantha, Shilpa, 582
Heffernan, Sr. Caterina, 676
Herbert, Carol, 522
Hightower, Elizabeth, 476
Hightower, Sarah, 624
Hill, Laura, 292
Hudson, A., 673
Huffman, Anne Henegar, 276
Hurowitz, Amy, 626
Hurowitz, Lois, 144, 308
Iwata, B., 191
Jaffé, M., 542
Johndrow, David, 279
Johndrow, Ken, 442
Johndrow, Kimberley, 278
Johndrow, Nancy, 459
Johndrow, Scott, 567
Jones, Rebecca, 510
Jones, Stasie, 588, 608
Jung, Sèbastien, 582
Keblawi, Suhad, 316
Kidd, J., 737

Knight, Jane, 243
Koo, Daniel, 617, 623
Koo, Hue See, 305
Kujala, Gerald,; 445
Lachman, Benjamin, 575
Lachman, MaryAnn, 216
Lasensky-Curtin, J., 546
LeBlanc, Barbara, 667
Lee, Barbara, 303, 657
Lee, Danny, 222, 569
Lee, Lily, 222, 252
Leitner, Amity, 612
Leitner, Jeanie, 560
Lewis, Julie, 577
Lewis, Leah Henegar, 638
Ling, D., 13, 608, 667, 669, 670, 671, 812
Ling D. & Ling-Phillips, A., 667, 812
Lowell, E., 13
Majors, Jeffrey, 628
Maslin, Janeane, 307
Maslin, Mike, 304, 307
McClure, Nora, 160
McDonnel, Anna, 272
McDonnel, Annette, 550
McGinnis, M., 543
McGlone, Malinda, 274
McGlone, Kent, 444
Metzger, Melanie, 684
Neef, N., & Iwata, B., 191, 701
Nemeth, Christy, 40
Nemeth, Mary, 271, 457
Nicholls, G., & Ling, D., 497, 694
Nitchie, E.B., 177
Nix, G., 732, 733
Périer, O., 508, 528, 702
Perry, Jacquelyn, 318
Peterson, M., 697
Pickett, J., 210
Pintner, R., 14
Poore, Michael, 573
Poore, Teri, 220, 471, 513
Quave, Helen, 691
Quigley, S., & Paul, P., 152
Riley, A., 544
Rimer, Diane, 410

Rimer, Esther, 566-7
Robers, Betsy, 280
Robers, Gina, 591
Robers, Trisha, 281
Robers, William, 107, 221, 453
Roffé, Sarina, 414, 417, 558
Roffé, Simon, 395, 595
Rosenbek, Hanson, Baughman, & Lemme, 543
Ross, Mark, 386
Sánchez Mompeán, Antonia, 275
Sánchez Mompeán, Josefa, 589
Scher, Steven, 295, 602, 604
Schwartz, S., 49, 74
Sharp, Eleanor and David, 310
Shelton, I., & Garves, M., 543
Sokolnicki, Margie, 672
Spinetta, Nicole, 418
Spinetta, Isabelle, 594
Stitzinger, Kim, 295
Stokoe, W., 150
Swadley, Charles, 424
Swadley, Paul, 610
Tade, W., 542
Tervoort, B., 13
Tolleson, Connie, 514
Truett, Freda, 310
Tullier, Tate, 585
Turner, Allison, 211
Vernon, M., 13
Walter, G., & McLeod-Gallinger, J., 735
Wandel, Jean, 256, 258, 694
Weiss, Joseph & Judith, 231
Weiss, Louis, 581
Wellman, Bruce, 293
White, Deborah, 429
White, Mathew, 613
Williams-Scott, Barbara, 662
Wixey, Rachel, 586
Wrightstone, J., Aranow, M., & Muskowitz, S., 14
Yoss, K., & Darley, F., 543
Ziebell, Colin, 580
Ziebell, Jennifer, 290, 312

Index of Subjects

affective development, 39
aphasia, 541
apraxia, 541
ASL/English bilingualism, 493
 rationale for, 493
 position of NCSA on, 491
 model for achieving in CS programs, 505
 model for achieving in TC programs, 500
auditory conceptualization, 59
auditory training, 193
 advantages of CS for, 196
 auditory/visual model for, 204
cerebral palsy, 539
child, deaf
 helping young child adjust to hearing aids, 336
 starting with deaf child, 51
 starting with a very young child, 329
 starting with an older child, 297
cochlear implants, 209
college opportunities for deaf students, 741-743
communication
 effects of inadequate, 4, 40
 with deaf peers, through CS, 107
 with hearing peers, 34, 36, 409
 within the family, 30, 40
context, 69
Cued Speech
 description of, 19, 21
 methods of learning, 52
 origins of, 743
 organizations, 751-753
 research on, 693
cueing, fine points of, 713-730
deaf, definition for this book, 1
deaf children
 major problems of, 17
 manners, 122
 observations of, 563-640
 typical performance of, 13
deaf-blindness, 545
devices, useful, 748
discipline, 40
dyslexia, 543
faith, place of in the education of a deaf child, 74
father and child, 45, 441-447
language, 143
 aberrations and "gaps," 83
 abstract language, 154
 evaluation in deaf children, 151
 growth record, 92
 idioms, 155
 function words, 158

research on, 159
mainstreaming, 386
    aural/oral children, 397
    Cued Speech children, 400
    requirements for success, 386
    role of parents in, 403
    role of transliterator in, 392
    signing children, 397
    support services needed, 389
materials for parent orientation and guidance, 754-757
materials for use by parents in improving cueing, 766-810
materials for use by parents with their children, 757-766
memory problems, 540
mental development of child, 49
methods debate, 19
methods, implication of, 5
mother and child, 43
non-specific learning disability, 546
parents, overwhelming responsibility of, 431
    typical experiences of, 9
peers, role of, 289
    observations of, 292-295
reading, 245
    advanced reading skills, 255
    CS provides base for, 8
    claims of CS advocates regarding, 8
    correlated with language knowledge, 7
    deficiencies in reading skills of deaf, 7
    how deaf child learns to read, 247
    how hearing child learns to read, 246
    reading comprehension of CS children, 8
    reading to your child, 119-121
    reading comprehension of deaf children, 14
rights of deaf children and their parents, 731-741
siblings
    role of, 263
    major problems of, 267
    observations of, 272-287
    value of support of, 269
sign language, 491
    definition of American Sign Language, 492
    need of deaf child for, 493
speech production, 163-176
    expressive efforts, 80
    not easy for deaf child, 172
speechreading, 177
    ability of deaf people, 182
    effects of CS on, 190
support, sources of for parents, 751
time, 431
    ideas for saving, 439
    problems and management of, 435-440
transliteration, 394
Usher's Syndrome/retinitis pigmentosa, 537, **545**